Lovely, Lively Lyrics

Selected Studies in Biblical Hebrew Verse

SIL International®
Publications in Translation and Textlinguistics
5

Publications in Translation and Textlinguistics is a peer-reviewed series published by SIL International®. The series is a venue for works concerned with all aspects of translation and textlinguistics, including translation theory, exegesis, pragmatics, and discourse analysis. While most volumes are authored by members of SIL, suitable works by others will also form part of the series.

Series Editors
Mike Cahill

Volume Editor
Mary Huttar

Production Staff
Bonnie Brown, Managing Editor
Karoline Fisher, Compositor
Lois Gourley, Composition Supervisor
Barbara Alber, Cover Design

Lovely, Lively Lyrics
Selected Studies in Biblical Hebrew Verse

Ernst R. Wendland

With a Foreword by Dr. Brenda H. Boerger

SIL International®
Dallas, Texas

© 2013 by SIL International®
Library of Congress Catalog No: 2013934329
ISBN: 978-1-55671-327-9
ISSN: 1550-588X

Printed in the United States of America

All rights reserved.

No part of this publication may be reproduced, stored in a retrieval system, or transmitted in any form or by any means—electronic, mechanical, photocopy, recording, or otherwise—without the express permission of SIL International®. However, short passages, generally understood to be within the limits of fair use, may be quoted without permission.

Copies of this and other publications of SIL International® may be obtained from:

SIL International Publications
7500 W. Camp Wisdom Road
Dallas, TX 75236-5629

Voice: 972-708-7404
Fax: 972-708-7363
publications_intl@sil.org
www.ethnologue.com/bookstore.asp

For all seekers of wisdom and of him who is Wisdom personified!

וְהַחָכְמָה מֵאַיִן תִּמָּצֵא
וְאֵי זֶה מְקוֹם בִּינָה:
הֵן אֱמֶת חָפַצְתָּ בַטֻּחוֹת
וּבְסָתֻם חָכְמָה תוֹדִיעֵנִי:
יִרְאַת יְהוָה רֵאשִׁית דָּעַת
חָכְמָה וּמוּסָר אֱוִילִים בָּזוּ:
וְרָאִיתִי אָנִי שֶׁיֵּשׁ יִתְרוֹן לַחָכְמָה מִן־הַסִּכְלוּת
כִּיתְרוֹן הָאוֹר מִן־הַחֹשֶׁךְ:
אֱמֹר לַחָכְמָה אֲחֹתִי אָתְּ
וּמֹדָע לַבִּינָה תִקְרָא:
מִי יִתֶּנְךָ כְּאָח לִי
יוֹנֵק שְׁדֵי אִמִּי

But where can wisdom be found?
Where does understanding dwell? (Job 28:12)

Surely you desire truth in the inner parts;
you teach me wisdom in the inmost place. (Ps. 51:8)

The fear of the Lord is the beginning of knowledge,
but fools despise wisdom and discipline. (Prov. 1:7)

I saw that wisdom is better than folly,
just as light is better than darkness. (Eccl. 2:13)

Say to wisdom, "You are my sister,"
and call understanding your kinsman. (Prov. 7:4)

If only you were to me like a brother,
who was nursed at my mother's breasts! (SoS 8:1)[1]

---

[1] According to the symbolic interpretation of Rabbi Abravanel (16th C.), the 'lover' in the Song of Songs is King Solomon and the 'beloved' (speaking in this passage) is divinely given 'wisdom' (cf. Marvin Pope, Song of Songs, Anchor Bible 7C, Garden City, NY: Doubleday, 1977, 110–111).

"Solomon" by Gustave Doré

Doré Bible Illustrations • Free to Copy
www.creationism.org/images/

2Ch 1:11 And God said to Solomon, Because this was in thine heart, and thou hast not asked riches, wealth, or honour, nor the life of thine enemies, ... Wisdom and knowledge *is* granted unto thee....

Contents

Foreword xiii
Acknowledgements xvii
Abbreviations xix
Preface xxi
1 Job's Wisdom and its Communication in Chewa. 1
   Introduction: Where can wisdom be found? (Job 28:12, 20) 1
   1.1 Job 28 and its compositional cotext 3
   1.2 Tectonic wisdom in the organization of Job 28. 4
   1.3 Job 28: The fulcrum of the book 9
   1.4 A sapiential ode to spiritual wisdom. 12
   1.5 Formatting the poetic-rhetorical structure of Job 28 17
   1.6 The wisdom of Job 28 in today's Chewa setting 20
   1.7 Conclusion: The rhetorical function of poetic form. 23
2 The Lyric Heart of the Psalm at the Center of the Psalter. 29
   Introduction: Introit 'into the sanctuary of God' (Psalm 73:17) . 29
   2.1 Text typology 31
   2.2 Intertextuality 34
   2.3 Theological message. 37
      2.3.1 Destiny 38
      2.3.2 Sanctuary 41
      2.3.3 Purity of heart in proximity to God. 43
   2.4 Text function 45
   2.5 Application: Poetic analysis of Psalm 73. 50
      2.5.1 On structural and thematic importance. 50
      2.5.2 Overview of the structural framework 51
      2.5.3 A dynamic contemporary Psalm 73. 60
      2.5.4 Evaluation 71
   2.6 Implications 72
3 From Hebrew Acrostic to a Tonga Praise Poem:
   Proverbs 31:10–31 77
   Introduction: Praising the beauty of a 'worthy wife' 77
   3.1 'Worthy wife': A biblical Hebrew perspective 78
   3.2 Structural organization of the eulogy. 79
   3.3 Stylistic features of the eulogy 84
      3.3.1 Phonological 85
      3.3.2 Syntactic 86
      3.3.3 Lexical-semantic 87

        3.3.4 Discourse mode 89
   3.4 Rhetorical dynamics of the poem..................... 90
        3.4.1 Frames of reference......................... 90
        3.4.2 Genre...................................... 91
        3.4.3 Rhetorical exigency......................... 92
        3.4.4 Rhetorical purpose 93
        3.4.5 Implied audience........................... 95
   3.5 The eulogy in relation to Proverbs as a whole 96
   3.6 A 'worthy wife' from a Zambian perspective 100
        3.6.1 A Tonga-Hebrew sociocultural commentary:
            Proverbs 31:10–31 101
        3.6.2 Strategy for dealing with diversity in translation ...108
   3.7 Towards a greater measure of oratorical equivalence.....110
        3.7.1 A *ciyabilo* poem (Salimo Hachibamba)............114
        3.7.2 A *kweema* poem (Perdita Chenjela) 115
        3.7.3 Conclusion: Narrowing the aesthic-rhetorical divide ..116
4 Lyric Ideology: The Complaint of Psalm 137 119
   Introduction: Ideology...................................119
   4.1 How does ideology relate to Bible translation?..........119
   4.2 The complex communicative framework of Psalm 137... 122
        4.2.1 The text of Psalm 137—
            a reflection of its contextual setting 122
        4.2.2 The context of Psalm 137—
            its possible influence on the text................ 127
   4.3 Ideological factors in contemporary translation 133
        4.3.1 Translation technique 133
        4.3.2 Translation technique – applied to English 137
        4.3.3 Translation technique – applied to Chewa........ 138
        4.3.4 Paratextual supplementation...................141
   4.4 The translation *brief*: Balancing ideologies............145
5 Lyric Wisdom and Rhetoric in Proverbs 26:1–12 151
   Introduction: Text and impact............................151
   5.1 Answering a fool 151
   5.2 The rhetoric of wisdom in Proverbs 153
        5.2.1 Wisdom (and folly) in sapiential literature of the
            Hebrew Bible...............................153
        5.2.2 The malleable rhetoric of proverbs 157
   5.3 What is a proverb? 160
        5.3.1 Form—a sharpened style.....................161
        5.3.2 Function—incisive paraenesis..................167
   5.4 The sapiential rhetoric of Proverbs 26:1–12 169
        5.4.1 Extrinsic and intrinsic features 169
        5.4.2 A structural-thematic outline 170
        5.4.3 Hermeneutical approaches to a *crux interpretum*....172

Contents

5.5 The rhetoric of folly versus wisdom 174
5.6 Sharpening the lyric rhetoric against folly in English 175
5.7 Sharpening the lyric rhetoric against folly in Chewa 177
    5.7.1 Your audience: For whom are you translating
         and why? 178
    5.7.2 Chewa proverbial structure and style 179
    5.7.3 A rhetorical rendition—poetic functional
         equivalence 183
5.8 Conclusion: Wisdom of rhetoric in Bible translation 185

6 Love Lyrics in the Song of Songs 189
   Introduction: Form and meaning 189
   6.1 Two outstanding stylistic features 189
   6.2 Imagery 192
   6.3 Recursion 198
      6.3.1 Intertextual recursion 201
      6.3.2 Intratextual recursion 206
   6.4 A pair of structural-stylistic peaks in the Song 222
   6.5 Style and structure in the Song's message 230
      6.5.1 Figurative language 230
      6.5.2 Symbolic language 231
   6.6 Evidence for significant theological import 232
      6.6.1 Superfluity 232
      6.6.2 Pastoral poetry 233
      6.6.3 Explicitness 233
      6.6.4 Composition 234
   6.7 Translating the Song in a *LiFE*-like manner 239
      6.7.1 Above all, lyrically! 239
      6.7.2 The poetic muse: The computer-assisted
          translation (CAT) 241

7 Preparing an Oratorical Translation of Qoheleth 265
   Introduction: Culture in an oral-aural society 265
   7.1 The setting 267
      7.1.1 Original setting of communication 268
      7.1.2 Current setting of communication 272
      7.1.3 Interposed setting of communication 273
   7.2 The Song: How 'strong' (or sweetly sounding) is it? 275
      7.2.1 Genre and purpose 276
      7.2.2 Structural and stylistic analysis 281
      7.2.3 Aspects of stylistic (poetic) form 291
      7.2.4 Types of poetic function 295
      7.2.5 The message—what is the sense of Qoheleth's
          closing song? 297
   7.3 Synthesis: The pressing task of the translator 300
      7.3.1 Target audience 302

  7.3.2 Towards a lyric lament in a Bantu language 304
  7.3.3 Conceptual and cultural incongruities in
    the paratext 312
 7.4 Conclusion: Qoheleth on the cultural factor 320
8 How Lovely the Lyric? 325
 Introduction: Frame of reference for testing a translation 325
 8.1 The text and its meaning 329
  8.1.1 Structure and style. 330
  8.1.2 Sense and significance. 331
 8.2 Testing for artistic quality in translation 333
  8.2.1 The versions tested 334
  8.2.2 Sample questions for hearers and readers 336
  8.2.3 Results 338
 8.3 A textual frame of reference for interpretation. 346
 8.4 Enhancing the value of a Bible translation 351
 8.5 Conclusion: Cooperation, accountability, and quality. ... 353
9 Lyricizing the Poetry of Scripture 355
 9.1 Oral Artistic Approaches 355
Appendix A Preparing a Poetic Analysis and Translation of Psalm 24:
  A Guided Self-study 365
 Recognizing and reproducing the glories of a psalm 365
 A.1 Read 365
 A.2 Variants 367
 A.3 Context. 368
 A.4 Genre 369
 A.5 Linguistics 371
 A.6 Disjunction. 372
 A.7 Repetition. 373
 A.8 Po-rhetoric 373
 A.9 Discourse 376
 A.10 Outline 377
 A.11 Translate. 377
 A.12 Test 380
Appendix B Preparing a *LiFE* Translation 385
 B.1 Motivation for a literary (oratorical) translation 385
 B.2 The oral-aural factor and an oratorical version 388
 B.3 Method for discovering 'lovely lyrics' in the vernacular .. 392
 B.4 Organizing a literary translation project. 393
 B.5 Some implications of a literary (oratorical) approach 400
References 405
Index 425

Foreword

In *Lovely, Lively Lyrics* Wendland serves up a banquet for our enjoyment. Imagine your favorite holiday meal, complete with beverages, appetizer, soup and salad, a full main course, then ending with coffee and dessert—or imagine whatever constitutes a feast in your home or work culture. In the Melanesian context, where I worked, a feast is comprised of raw fruits and vegetables, rice, yams, taro and other root crops. But the two essentials are leaf-wrapped packets of pork baked in a stone oven and a 'pudding' made of grated root crops baked with coconut cream. My mouth waters. Such feasts not only take significant time for the hosts to prepare, but also for the guests to digest. And one can become so full that quiet meditation is needed afterward. The same can be said for the banquet prepared for us in this volume.

Let me whet your appetite. One of Wendland's primary concerns is that translators seem to miss the literary aspects of the source language (SL) in their translations. He says elsewhere in this book,

> As in the case of all good literature, so also with the various biblical documents, the literary...form of the text *is an integral, indispensable part of* the meaning...
>
> *Form* (genre) *conveys significant meaning,* comprising pragmatic impact and appeal as well as rhetorical credibility and persuasiveness.

But it is inadequate to merely recognize and appreciate the literary genius of the Hebrew source text; translators should also incorporate equivalent and parallel literary features into the target language (TL). Two more quotes from the book demonstrate his point:

> Yet what do we observe when we peruse virtually all available translations today, whether in a language of wider communication (LWC) or some major lingua franca? Usually it is only a pale or largely indistinct reflection of the original, completely unworthy of being called even a 'mediocre', let alone a 'satisfactory', literary equivalent. In other words, most versions simply try to express the text's basic [lexical – BHB][1]

---

[1] A parallel example from the New Testament occurred recently in the Sunday School class I attend, showing that failure to translate genres appropriately leads to zero or wrong meaning. We were reading 2 Corinthians 11 and 12, and a native speaker of English with a good education could not confidently assert that Paul was being sarcastic, for there were

content, displaying little cognizance of or concern for its poetic appeal and rhetorical persuasiveness in Hebrew.

But is it right (*ethical!*) to do nothing at all—to simply allow the text to stand bare and unmarked—not formally, ideally audibly, distinguished in the TL? In my opinion, this would be not only the path of least resistance, but it would also constitute a certain degree of dereliction of duty.

There are scholars, teachers, and preachers who tell us what to do, but not how to do it. There are others who tell us how to do it, but fail to show us what that might look like. In all of the items on the menu in *Lovely, Lively Lyrics*, Wendland not only tells us what should be done and how to do it, but he also demonstrates for us that it can be done and shows us how to do it by providing cross-cultural examples, such as the following passage from Song of Songs. In chapter six he explains the rhetorical impact of the underlined portions of the English back translation. But even without knowing Chichewa or reading his explanation, one can look at the target language text and identify similar line lengths for the lines, alliteration in every line, and rhyme or assonance at the line endings. Surely such a composition was planned and edited; it was not someone's first draft.

Chikondi chimenechi palibe madzi a chigumula	**A love like this,** there are no flood waters
angathe kuchizimitsa kapena kuchikokolola, ai!	**able** to **put it out** or **sweep it away,** not at all!
Ngakhale munthu atapereka chuma chonse,	**Even if** a person were to give all his wealth,
kufunitsitsa kugula chikondi choterechi,	trying his best to purchase **love of this sort,**
iyeyu adzangonyozeka nazo zyolizyoli!	he'd be **fully embarrassed** in the effort—**for shame!**

Wendland shows that this literary passage in Chichewa is not just a fluke by providing multiple, extended examples of his point, his procedures, and his products. And he doesn't just choose short and relatively easy passages, but bites off huge hunks of meat and sticks with us while we swallow and digest what he is saying. The banquet he serves is comprised of the following courses:

---

too few clues in the translation to make it clear exactly what Paul's point was. Instead, that person could only exhibit confusion about why Paul was talking that way and why he was repeating himself.

- chapter one's discussion of Job 28 and the rhetorical function of poetic form

- chapter two's structural-stylistic, text-contextual study of Psalm 73

- chapter three's acrostic from Proverbs 31 with regard to oratorical equivalence

- chapter four's use of Psalm 137 to illustrate how to include all stakeholders in the translation goals and philosophy

- chapter five's focus on audience, illustrated by Proverbs 26

- chapter six's incisive discussion of the form and meaning of the Song of Songs

- chapter seven's tackling of the oral-aural style of Qoheleth 12 and how to effectively translate it

- chapter eight's using Psalm 134 for an examination of testing procedures for translations

- chapter nine's concluding remarks enfolding the whole

My cravings as a linguist, translator, poet, and ethno-arts supporter were all satisfied by the buffet Wendland sets before us. He compares the grammatical structures of Hebrew with those of various vernaculars while at the same time suggesting ways to translate them which are accurate, clear, natural, and dynamic using target language poetic devices and cultural forms. This is literature translating literature, and as such it is much more gratifying to hear or to read.

Wendland's chapters are beautifully presented and nutritionally rich dishes. In the past I have incorporated his insights when translating the Psalms into both Natqgu and English, using material from his book *Analyzing the Psalms* (2002a). The present text is even more detailed in its presentation of Hebrew structures and poetic devices, making application to the corresponding rhetorical devices in one's target language fairly straight forward, assuming these have been identified and their functions described.

Each chapter is self-contained and it is not necessary to read the entire book at one time or to read it sequentially to be fed by it. Rather, one can view the whole as a smorgasbord, with many selections available, depending on one's appetite. Experienced or novice, the reader hungry to move deeper into literary translation will surely relish this book. I certainly do.

Bon appétit!
Brenda H. Boerger, SIL International Linguistics
Dallas, Texas, USA
Spring 2010

Acknowledgements

I am most grateful to Dr. Brenda H. Boerger, SIL International Linguistics, for taking the time from her schedule to write a *Foreword* for this monograph. She also suggested many helpful editorial and stylistic improvements to an earlier draft and contributed a number of her own poetic translations of many of the Hebrew texts that I examine in this book. Dr. Boerger helped complete a New Testament and Psalms in Natqgu, a language of the Solomon Islands and taught at the Graduate Institute for Applied Linguistics (Dallas, TX) during 2008-2009. She has also taught at the University of Texas at Arlington and the University of North Texas in an adjunct faculty role. Dr. Boerger has recently published a highly creative literary translation in English that duplicates the diversity of the various genres of the Psalter and which provides helpful study notes for each text, entitled *POET Psalms* (*Poetic Oracle English Translation*, Dallas: GIAL, 2009). Indeed, the diverse psalm renditions to be found in *POET* are excellent instances of what I mean by 'lovely lively' lyric translation.

In addition, I wish to thank all my colleagues in the United Bible Societies, Wycliffe Bible Translators, the Nida Institute, and other translation organizations for listening to and critically commenting on various sections of this work as it has developed over the years in various conferences, workshops, and journal publications. Furthermore, I express my deep appreciation to the many biblical scholars whom I either cite or refer to in this study, as well as those with whom I have had the privilege to interact over the years while working on my twofold topic of text analysis and translation. They have helped me to better understand the literary character of the lyric writings of the Hebrew Bible as they were composed and enscripted for their original audiences in such a rhetorically powerful and moving manner. I also sincerely thank all of my national translation colleagues whose help has proved indispensable as we confronted together the challenge of how best to communicate these dynamic lyric texts in a corresponding way in vernacular translation via various media today. A special word of thanks is due Mary Huttar for her careful and most helpful editing of this volume and to the publication department of SIL International for preparing the text to see the light of print.

Finally, though in most cases I use my own translations of the original Hebrew text, I do on occasion cite one or another English version, in particular, the *New International Version* (NIV) © 1984 by the New York

Bible Society. I use all of these translations within the normal guidelines by prior permission, for which I am grateful. I also express my gratitude for permission to reproduce the frontispiece illustration by Gustave Doré, courtesy of www.creationism.org (Paul Abramson, Editor; paul@zzz.com).

Abbreviations

ANE	Ancient Near East
BCOT	Baker Commentary on the Old Testament
BL	*Buku Lopatulika* ('Sacred Book')
BY	*Buku Loyera* ('Holy Book')
CAT	computer-assisted translation
CEV	*Contemporary English Version*
DC	deuterocanonical books
ESV	*English Standard Version*
FOTL	Forms of the Old Testament Literature
GNT	*Good News Translation*
GW	*God's Word*
JSOT	*Journal for the Study of the Old Testament*
LiFE	literary functional equivalence
LWC	language of wider communication
LXX	Septuagint
MT	Masoretic Text
NAB	*New American Bible*
NEB	*New English Bible*
NET	*New English Translation*
NICOT	New International Commentary on the Old Testament
NIV	*New International Version*
NJB	*New Jerusalem Bible*
NRSV	*New Revised Standard Version*
NT	New Testament
OT	Old Testament
OTE	*Old Testament Essays*
OTSSA	Old Testament Society of Southern Africa
POET	*Poetic Oracle English Translation*
PV	Poetic *(ndakatulo)* Version
REB	*Revised English Bible*
RSV	*Revised Standard Version*
SL	source language
SoS	Song of Solomon/ Song of Songs
ST	source text
TEV	*Today's English Version*

TL	target language
UBS	United Bible Societies
YHWH	Yahweh
ZAW	*Zeitschrift für die Alttestamentliche Wissenschaft*

Preface

This monograph is the third in a series of volumes that seeks to apply a 'literary functional equivalence' (*LiFE*) approach in a practical, procedure-documented manner to the text analysis and translation of various biblical books.[1] The first volume focused on the New Testament epistles (*Finding and translating the oral-aural elements in written language*, Edwin Mellen Press, 2008) and the second on the Hebrew prophets (*Prophetic rhetoric: Case studies in text analysis and translation*, Xulon Press, 2009 [expanded in a revised edition, SIL International, forthcoming]). The present study now examines a selection of some biblical texts that are more difficult to understand as well as to convey meaningfully in another language-culture, namely, the lyric literature of the Hebrew Scriptures.

How were the various 'lovely lively lyric' texts chosen for this volume, since a selection from a rather large corpus had to be made? Samples for detailed analysis and translation have been taken from all five of the so-called 'poetic' (lyric) books of Scripture (Job, Psalms, Proverbs, Ecclesiastes, and Song of Songs), which of course include a wide range of genres. In particular, I wanted to include portions from some of the passages which are the most challenging to interpret, namely, those of a *sapiential* nature, and given that, readers will encounter a diversity of texts that convey biblical 'wisdom' to a greater or lesser extent, in one literary form or another, and in a more or less explicit degree. These lyric passages are not only 'lovely' in terms of their *literary artistry*, but they are also 'lively' with regard to their *rhetorical power*, as well, in that the form of the text shapes and enhances its religious content in order to effectively convey the author's intended communicative aims. I have spent most time on two biblical books that are rather controversial in terms of their hermeneutics, Ecclesiastes (Qoheleth) and Song of Songs (Solomon), and hence are not always given the attention that they deserve either in exegetical or translation studies.

The presuppositions that orient and guide the different analyses of this monograph remain essentially the same as the two volumes mentioned above, namely, that:

---

[1] An updated explanation and application of this methodology may be found in *LiFE-style translating: A workbook for Bible translators* (2nd ed., SIL International, 2011). This approach is also exemplified in a practical way with reference to Psalm 24 in Appendix A of this volume.

1. The linguistic *forms* of a literary text convey important *pragmatic* (interpersonal, contextualized), and at times also *semantic*, meaning.

2. The fundamental literary/oratorical (artistic-rhetorical) character of the Scriptures is assumed—in short, vital *information* coupled with *intention*, *attitude*, and *emotion* that have been textually embedded for the purpose of motivating *persuasion* and *acceptance*.

3. The literary/oratorical resources of any contemporary 'target language' (TL) can *match* those that are manifested in the biblical text when accessed and applied according to the cognitive-inferential principles of *relevance* and a context-sensitive *functional equivalence* methodology.

4. The text of Scripture is ideally suited—in fact, most often specifically composed—for *public oral proclamation* to a listening audience.

5. Many stylistic and structural features of the original text are not readily apparent, or fully appreciated, when that text is studied or read *silently* to oneself.

6. One creative way to bridge the communication gap between principles 1–2 and 3 is via an *oral-rhetorical* methodology applied first to the source language (SL) text analytically and then synthetically with regard to a TL rendition by means of an *informed-intuitive* compositional approach (carried out by competent translators and their support team).

7. Any vernacular version of this nature must first be carefully *explained* to, then clearly *understood* and *approved* by the target constituency that commissions the translation to be done, whether a full Testament, a Bible, or a Scripture portion.

So what are the purpose and expected benefits of this type of 'oral-rhetorical' structural-stylistic text analysis of the original biblical documents? Such a careful, comprehensive literary study, as exemplified in subsequent chapters with respect to a selection from among the lyric-sapiential corpus, aims to achieve the several goals listed below. Thus, it better enables the analyst to discern:

- instances of rhythmic diction and other distinctive phonological features of the Hebrew text—the primary aspects of dynamic elocutionary utterance;

- various text breaks and structural transitions, both major and minor—plus greater and lesser pause points to indicate compositional boundaries;

- the crucial points of rhetorical emphasis and attractive artistry in the original document;

- a book's principal themes and hortatory motifs made manifest through its extensive and varied patterns of lexical recursion;

- the chief stylistic features that render the text more beautiful as well as memorable / memorizable; and

- abundant evidence that the biblical text is semantically and pragmatically 'richer' than many biblical scholars realize, incorporating additional aspects of meaning (in the fullest sense) that need to be conveyed—whether textually or paratextually, via translation or commentary—in order for a greater degree of communicative correspondence to be attained.

In support of the preceding assumptions and aims, I present a number of analytical case studies of eight works from the lyric corpus of the Hebrew Scriptures, in the following chapter order: Job 28, Psalm 73, Proverbs 31, Psalm 137, Proverbs 26, Song of Songs, Ecclesiastes 12, and Psalm 24 (in Appendix A: a practical exercise in analysis and translation). Various facets of an oral-rhetorical, literary-structural method of analysis are explained and illustrated during the course of these studies, each of which has a somewhat different focus and emphasis in accordance with the form, content, and communicative aim of the poetic book being considered (e.g., the disputational book of Job, which includes a lyric praise poem at its core).

To conclude each chapter, a number of pertinent implications for and applications to the practice of Scripture translation are pointed out, with examples from English (by Brenda Boerger) and Chewa, a SE Bantu language. Appendix B presents an overview of the 'literary functional equivalence (*LiFE*)' method of translating. The set of texts included here (most of unknown or uncertain authorship) come from biblical books that are not so frequently considered by scholars, teachers, and preachers, while translators may tend to neglect them due to their perceived difficulty.

Therefore, it is hoped that a closer look from the perspective of a more dynamic, oral-aural oriented, literary method of investigation might encourage a greater awareness of, and attention devoted to these emotively powerful passages, which, it will be shown, are just as important and relevant for God's people today as they were in the ancient past.

As was the case with the companion volumes on the epistles and the prophets, the primary target readership of this monograph also includes, in particular, the following groups—namely, to serve as a principal *resource* and *enrichment* text for:

- theological and pastoral students as well as those in biblical (OT/NT) studies, ideally having completed at least one year of biblical Hebrew;

- students in translation studies, especially Bible translation, again with one or more years of Hebrew language training;

- undergraduate and graduate teachers, trainers, and consultants who are involved in instruction and/or research with regard to the preceding studies as well as in the various areas of Bible translation;

- cross-cultural communicators of any field, especially those who are working with non-traditional methods and modes of representing the orality-based texts of Scripture in an equally dynamic manner to contemporary audiences.

In several chapters, especially those based on earlier studies, I have used a transliteration of some or all of the Hebrew text; this follows the simplified format that is used in handbooks and monographs published by the United Bible Societies (e.g., Zogbo and Wendland 2000:xiv).

The author would be grateful for any and all comments regarding this publication; he may be reached via email either at wendland@zamnet.zm or erwendland@hotmail.com.

Ernst R.Wendland
Centre for Bible Interpretation and Translation—University of Stellenbosch, RSA
Easter – 2010

1

Job's Wisdom and its Communication in Chewa

Introduction: Where can wisdom be found? (Job 28:12, 20)

Job 28 is a panoramic wisdom poem that ostensibly comes from the mouth of the book's main protagonist, who otherwise seems on the virtual brink of despondency. It is a surprising speech within its immediate textual setting since it expresses a comparatively optimistic ray of hope in the midst of a discourse that is otherwise rather dark with despair. The chapter is also noteworthy from a literary, compositional perspective. It will be shown that this familiar text selection (*pericope*) has been masterfully constructed, both intrinsically in terms of itself and also extrinsically in relation to the organization of the *theodicy* of Job as a whole.[1] After a descriptive survey of some of its most prominent tectonic features, I present a brief study of its associated thematic relevance as an outstanding biblical instance of Ancient Near-Eastern (ANE) sapiential literature. This leads finally to a consideration of how such a subtly didactic text might be contextualized in the (chi)-Chewa[2] language-culture for a select, contemporary audience. The aim is to better communicate certain crucial aspects of its stylistic form, theological content, and rhetorical function in a relevant way.

The relative structural, thematic, and rhetorical importance of Job 28 is sometimes overlooked because of its medial placement within the book—buried deep within the vigorous back-and-forth disputation of the main protagonist and his 'friends'.[3] However, this well-formed wisdom pericope is a crucial constituent of the text as it has come down to us, both *intrinsically* with respect to its own value in terms of form and content and also *extrinsically* in relation to the overall discourse arrangement and theological message of this theodicy in defense of God's justice, which is at the same time a poetic homily on human frailty and

---

[1] A 'theodicy' is a religious text (an apologetic disputation) that defends the ways of God, especially his justice, in the face of all the evils and calamities that occur in this world.

[2] Chewa is a dialect of Nyanja [nya] spoken in Malawi, Botswana, Mozambique, Swaziland, Zambia, and Zimbabwe. Total number of speakers: 8,659,700 (*Lewis* 2009:151).

[3] The 'disputation', or controversy speech, resembles a dialogue, but is more formally constructed. It consists of "a series of speeches set against one another in a debate format (e.g., Job 3–41). The disputation draws the reader into the complexities of a wisdom problem" (Garrett 1993:31).

fickleness in contrast to divine forcefulness and fidelity.[4] In a subtle but effective way, this elaborately constructed but seemingly misplaced poem anticipates YHWH's climactic rejoinder of personal reproof in Job 38–39. Its distinctively contemplative style highlights the poet's sublime message by revealing the divine Source of true wisdom and ethics for all people. This stands in graphic contrast to everything that has been uttered thus far by Job and his irritating 'comforters', an intense debate that pits Job's persistent claims of personal righteousness against his friends' aggressive calls for humble repentance before God.

The first goal of the present study then is to reveal certain prominent aspects of the discourse structure and rhetorical dynamics of Job 28, along with the communicative implications of these stylistic features with regard to the book as a whole in its canonical form. Certainly there is more 'wisdom' that is manifested in the original composition of this Hebrew pericope than I can adequately reveal or evaluate within the confines of this essay. On the other hand, a great deal of wisdom, too, is exhibited in the scholarly debates that rage with reference to this pericope, which I will unfortunately not be able to discuss. This is because the scope of my investigation is not limited to the source language document, but it extends also to a contemporary setting and various efforts to produce a dynamic oral and written vernacular representation of the text. The African target constituency includes individuals who, though living in a very different sociological and religious setting, often experience life in a way that parallels the sufferings of Job.

My second objective focuses upon the dynamic wisdom tradition of the Chewa people and the current challenge of conveying Job 28 relevantly (appropriately, acceptably, and affectively—that is, with corresponding emotive impact) within the conceptual framework that is evoked by their typical south-eastern Bantu language and African culture. To that end, several experimental proposals are made and illustrated by a sample translation in support of my efforts to stimulate creative thinking about communicating the wisdom of the Word more 'wisely' in the idiom of today. This is by means of a functional equivalence rendition that would have particular 'relevance' (in a pragmatic sense) for specifically targeted receptor groups and in specially formatted publications.

---

[4] The importance of the legal metaphor in the structural development of the argument of Job as a whole is discussed by Norman Habel (1985:54–57; cf. Steinmann 1996:89–90). The issue of 'frailty' versus 'fidelity' in this book (e.g., Job ↔ YHWH, Job's wife and his friends ↔ Job, or the divine covenantal principles of justice in relation to humanity and the universe at large) appears to be rather obvious, yet it is a subject that is not often discussed by commentators.

1.1 Job 28 and its compositional cotext

At first reading, this chapter sounds radically out of place. Job begins his final complaint to his three colleagues in chapter 26, a bitter discourse that is explicitly resumed in 27:1 and again in 29:1 ("And Job again took up his dispute [מָשָׁל] and said..."); this speech is formally concluded at 31:40 ("The words of Job have come to an end").[5] There is a sharp break then in both content and tone as one moves, unannounced, from chapter 27 to 28—that is, from an agitated diatribe against the wicked of Job's world (27:7–23), in contrast to his own unrecognized righteousness (27:2–6), to a calm, reflective meditation on man's search for divine wisdom (ch. 28).[6] The shift back to a personal lament at the onset of chapter 29 is just as pronounced, for here Job presents a nostalgic review of his former blessed and acclaimed state. This poem highlights the close fellowship that he enjoyed with YHWH (vv. 2–6) and, on the other hand, the great honor and renown that he was accorded 'like a king' in his society (v. 25). It is possible that ch. 28 could be viewed as an anticipatory citation given in illustration of the wise verbal counsel that Job was accustomed to enrich his fellow citizens with (e.g., 29:21–25), but in the light of the book's overall organization, there is a more likely explanation.

From a rhetorical-structural perspective, this "wisdom poem" (Murphy 1981:34) is realized as the virtual midpoint of the entire book. It thus acts as a dramatic, functionally significant pause within the acrimonious alternating debate between Job and his three friends, providing an indirect but objective, didactic response to the inadequacy of the previously offered solutions to the issue of divine justice as it pertains to the pitiful experience of this suffering man of God.[7] This distinctive medial text

---

[5] In Habel's view (1985:30), "Job's first *mashal* (27:1–12) serves as a closure for his dispute with the friends...Job's second *mashal* is a formal testimony before an assumed court. The hero's testimony relates his past achievements (ch. 29), laments his present condition (ch. 30), and culminates in an oath of purity (ch. 31)."

[6] The fact that the poem begins with *kiy* in Hebrew does not necessarily indicate a discourse continuation and is certainly no firm evidence that the text originally stood in some other setting. There are a significant number of places where this introductory particle leads off a distinctly new portion of a text (e.g., Isa. 2:6, 15:1) and/or may best be rendered as an intensive assertive, e.g., 'surely, indeed' (e.g., Gen. 18:20; cf. footnote at 28:1 in the New English Translation [NET], 1996, p. 866; Habel 1985:389). Hartley suggests that "[p]ossibly the *kiy* works in conjunction with the *waw* of v. 2. The former introduces things accessible, the latter things inaccessible [to human beings]" (1988:373, material in brackets added).

[7] "It seems as if in this hymn the poet of the composition as a whole here draws his own conclusions from the futile efforts of Job and his friends to convince each other" (Van Selms 1985:102). "It judges the efforts of the comforters to teach Job wisdom as a failure" (Hartley 1988:384; cf. Habel 1985:38). From a compositional perspective, v. 28 in relation to ch. 28 as a whole functions in a way that anticipates and is analogous to the later answer of YHWH. The closing divine discourse (38:1–41:34) represents "a major divergence from

serves both to set in relief Job's varied summation of his pathetic situation—his last defense, as it were, before God and man (chs. 29–31)—and also to set the stage for the anticlimax of Elihu's rather presumptuous and verbose attempts to show all the previous speakers where they have gone wrong. Though not succeeding as an 'arbiter' between Job and God (31:35, 32:12), Elihu at least points the discourse in the right direction as the book moves towards a final 'answer' to the great moral dilemma and judicial problems it poses (32:12–14, 33:12, 36:22–33, 37:1–24).

In chapter 28 then the author-poet provides a deep thematic reflection upon the drama's current state of affairs: human beings, despite all their other impressive achievements, simply cannot attain the 'one thing needful' in this life—namely, true 'wisdom' (חָכְמָה) with regard to the deity and his doings or dealings in the world. Rather, such a perceptive 'understanding' (בִּינָה) is a matter of divine revelation, and it is realized only in the context of a dynamic interpersonal relationship—'the fear of the LORD' (יִרְאַת אֲדֹנָי, 28:28). In a significant way, this concluding 'editorial' comment also gives a subtle preview of the climactic resolution to the controversy, which is later delivered in a highly rhetorical fashion by YHWH himself (chs. 38:2–41:34).

The elaborate literary patterning that is manifested in chapter 28 would itself seem to suggest that it is a focal point in the larger development of this sapiential discourse in defense of divine sovereignty and justice in relation to a just man's struggle to maintain his personal integrity and faith.[8] We turn now to an overview of the structural organization of this magnificent lyric piece: first in relation to its internal arrangement, and second with respect to its positioning within the texture of the book as a whole.

1.2 Tectonic wisdom in the organization of Job 28

The outline below is a rough general summary of the careful, instructive manner in which this poetic pericope has been patterned. The structure itself serves to highlight the poem's basic thematic contrast and features an alternating arrangement that may be divided into three distinct sections, as shown on the following diagram of the strophic structure of Job 28:[9]

---

the basic structure, which should obviously be interpreted as a literary device designed to stress the exceptional importance of this speech in the book" (Hoffman 1991:410). The LORD's climactic response to Job is not a structural 'divergence', however; it is rather the debate-ending culmination that the book has been building up to all along—one that ultimately silences also the Satan (1:6–2:10).

[8] The latter part of this thematic summary follows Steinmann 1996:89.

[9] This is a revised analysis of an unpublished discourse analysis of the book of Job, and chapter 28 in particular, that I originally presented in 1984; it was subsequently referred to

1.2 Tectonic wisdom in the organization of Job 28

A (1-6)   men seek out and mine precious stones deep in the ground[10]
B (7-8)   the way to this wealth is not clearly visible or accessible
A' (9-11) men seek out and mine precious stones deep in the ground
===
B' (12-14)   the way to 'wisdom' is not readily known
A" (15-19) men cannot purchase wisdom for any wealth of this world[11]
B" (20-22)   the way to 'wisdom' is not readily known
===
B''' (23-24)   God alone knows the way to wisdom
A''' (25-27) God mined and modeled wisdom in the events of Creation
B''' (28)   God clearly reveals the way of wisdom to men

The breaks between the three constituent portions (stanzas) of this thematically coherent discourse unit (ode) are clearly defined both by sudden shifts in subject and grammatical form, and also by means of the internal cohesion of the respective segments (to be discussed later).[12] The topical shifts between these different 'strophes' of the unfolding sequence form a zigzag pattern which may be viewed as a structural metaphor that corresponds to the ceaseless human search for precious stones and also for 'wisdom', that is, A—'[non]*acquisition*' (economics) and B—'[non]*cognizance*' (epistemology).[13]

---

in Reyburn 1992:497.

[10] I am using the term 'men' in a generic sense and for ease of reference to designate all human beings—young and old, male and female, black and white.

[11] There are some rather important intertextual allusions here and elsewhere in the poem. In the section vv. 15–19, for example, we note some correspondence with passages in the Proverbs that compare wisdom to items of human value (e.g., Prov. 3:13–15, 16:16). "Here, however, the poet reverses the traditional imagery. One *cannot* buy wisdom for all the precious metals and jewels in the world" (Newsom 1996:531, italics added). As Culler astutely notes: "Poems are energized by past poems" (1997:76)—and, we may add, by any significant verbal echo or resonant chord.

[12] Habel provides a useful chart of the 'motif development' of ch. 28 in terms of three primary concepts: 'place' (or 'source'), 'way' (or 'access'), and 'discovery' (or 'acquisition') (1985:394–395). His proposals overlap in several respects with my structural diagram of the chapter.

[13] Two key terms from the sapiential semantic field are used—the first, *hokmah* 'wisdom', is more general (its precise meaning being determined according to the specific cotext), and the second, *binah* 'discernment', referring both to a potential intellectual capacity for understanding as well as the actual "knowledge produced by such discernment" (Newsom 1996:531). "Understanding designates…an attitude which serves wisdom interests.…[It] makes wisdom an achievable goal" (Berry 1995:126). These words are crucial to the text not only semantically, but also structurally as well—that is, with respect to the poem as a whole (occurring in the boundary verses 12, 20, and 28) as well as each of the three passages in which they occur (i.e., in first and last position in vv. 12 and 20; at the end of the last two cola in v. 28). The pairing of these key terms for wisdom and discernment "is common in sapiential texts (Prov. 1:2; 4:5, 7; 9:10; 16:16)" (Habel 1985:397).

This mode of circumscribing, or 'ringed' (A-B-A'...) textual development is quite unexpectedly and climactically broken off at (B''') with the revelation of the One who is 'wisdom' personified and its only genuine source and norm. This is 'God' (אֱלֹהִים), who is mentioned only once in the entire poem—that is, in emphatic, unconnected initial position at the beginning of the final stanza (v. 23), a sub-unit that ends in a further peak which is highlighted by an *inclusio* with the mention of 'Lord' (אֲדֹנָי) (v. 28).

A closer examination of the enclosing structural organization of this chapter reveals an even more intricate arrangement of patterned elements within the individual strophic segments that comprise the three progressively developed stanzas (vv. 1–11, 12–22, 23–28) as displayed below on the chart of lexical-semantic patterning in Job 28.[14] The first two stanzas (I–II) are analogous in terms of their number of poetic lines (11 each, for a total of 22, a structurally significant figure in Hebrew acrostic compositions) and also in word count (82/81 respectively); the third stanza (III) is just over half the size, 6 lines and 44 words.

Theme of the sapiential ode of Job 28: **WHERE CAN WISDOM BE FOUND?**

I. ==
[A] *Introduces the analogical theme of mankind's disciplined, determined search for wealth*
    a. (1)   a 'place' where men search for 'gold' (זָהָב) and 'silver' (כֶּסֶף)
        b. (2)   'from the earth' ore is taken
            c. (3)   men mine 'to every [far-away] recess' in darkness
            c' (4)   men mine 'far from' where people live and move
        b' (5)   'from the earth' food is taken
    a' (6)   a 'place' where men search for 'gold' (זָהָב) and 'sapphire' (סַפִּיר)

---

[14] For a partially corresponding, yet still significantly different proposal for the textual organization of Job 28, see Clark 1982. Steinmann presents a convincing argument for a structure "based on the author's repeated use of fourfold groupings" (1996:91–92; cf. the original proposal in Andersen 1976:19–22), which refines our understanding of the internal arrangement of the book's subsections. Another, still different and very detailed discourse analysis based on lexical repetition may be found in van der Lugt (1995:314–324, 521–529).

The elaborate structural patterning of this chapter confuses many modern critics, who typically resort to all sorts of hypothetical proposals to reconfigure the text to suit their personal opinion of what the author *should* have written. Murphy, for example, suggests that "There is reason...to think that several verses in vv. 1–11 pertain to God's work (vv. 3, 9–11, appropriate after v. 24), or fit in with the inaccessibility of wisdom (vv. 7–8, appropriate after v. 21)" (1981:37). Worse is his conclusion that "The claim that v. 28 lies outside the thrust of the poem is true..." (Murphy 1981:37). Thus the thematic and rhetorical climax of the poem, the point to which the entire discourse is building up, would seem to be superfluous (cf. also van der Lugt 1995:324).

1.2 Tectonic wisdom in the organization of Job 28

[B] *Reinforces the motifs of 'remoteness' and 'difficulty' in the search for wealth* [cf. A, c-c']
    a. (7a)   generic: a 'bird-of-prey' (עַיִט)
        b. (7b)   specific: a 'falcon' (אַיָּה)
  a' (8a)   generic: 'sons of pride' (בְנֵי־שָׁחַץ)
        b' (8b)   specific: a 'lion' (שָׁחַל)

[A'] *Reiterates the topics of A in a poetically heightened manner to focus on human success!*
    a. (9a --- 10a --- 11a ---) man's strenuous search for treasure in the earth
    b. (--- 9b --- 10b --- 11b) man's great success in bringing hidden things to light

II. ===
[B'] *In contrast to wealth, man cannot seek and find wisdom*
    a. (12) 'where…wisdom?' – 'where…understanding?'
        b. (13) her [wisdom's] 'value' cannot be 'known';
            she cannot be 'found' on the 'earth of living beings'
            c. (14) *Tehom* and *Yam* say, 'She is not in/with me!'

[A''] *Wisdom is more valuable than wealth and cannot be bought by any man*
    (15–19) This is strongly cohesive, recursive strophe whose integrity is established by the repetitions of the negative (as in B') and various synonyms for 'gold'. There are several interesting poetic variants: two synonyms for gold are found in the middle (17), but none in the next verse where 'wisdom' is again explicitly mentioned (18). In (19) the two verbs appear in reversed order from their previous occurrence: 'it [nothing] can compare with her [wisdom]' (17); 'she [wisdom] cannot be bought' (16)

[B''] *Reiterates the topics of B' to emphasize man's difficulty in finding wisdom*
    a' (20) 'where…wisdom?' – 'where…understanding?' [almost an exact repetition of v. 12]
        b' (21) she is 'hidden/concealed' from every 'living being', even in the 'heavens'!
            c' (22) *Abaddon* and Death say, '…we have only heard a rumor of her!'

III. ===
[C] *Divine resolution to the mystery about how to find and exemplify wisdom*
    a. (23) God (אֱלֹהִים) 'understands' wisdom's way and 'her place' of dwelling [cf. vv. 12, 20]
        b. (24) he 'sees' everything on 'earth' and in the 'heavens' [cf. vv. 13, 21]
            c. (25) creation (wind and waters) demonstrates his wisdom [cf. 38:8–11]
            c' (26) creation (rain and thunder) demonstrates
                his wisdom [cf. 38:24–28]
        b' (27) he 'saw'—appraised + confirmed + tested her [wisdom]
    a' (28) [God] reveals the [way] of wisdom to mankind—'Look!' →
        'the fear of/faith in the Lord (אֲדֹנָי)' – that is what *wisdom* is all about (+)
        'to avoid all evil' – that reveals true *understanding* (-) [cf. vv. 12, 20, 23]

The final verse of this masterful ode, itself a tribute to its own sublime topic, couples with its parallel in v. 23 to answer the text's key thematic query: "where can wisdom be found?" (vv.12, 20).[15] This traditional instruction also forms an *inclusio* of sorts with the first verse of the book, which refers to Job's righteous 'fear' of God (1:1; cf. 38:4, 42:3).[16] The negativity of stanza II, in contrast to the positive optimism of I, is overcome as the path to divine knowledge is revealed during the course of climactic stanza III. In other words, stanzas I and II are subtly reflected off each another in order to prepare for the discourse peak in stanza III. Thus the central teaching of the book of Job, that fundamental presupposition upon which all other of its didactic principles are based, is set forth here in chapter 28 at the structural midpoint of the entire text (see section 1.3). Just as YHWH's wisdom is displayed in his perfectly righteous dealings with a sinful humanity (cf. 37:23, contra 27:2), so man's wisdom is demonstrated in his faithful obedience to the Lord. God's irreproachable justice stems from his omnipotent sovereignty over the universe, which was most clearly manifested at the time of creation—and then ever since in the mighty wonders of nature (vv. 25–26, as already noted, foreshadow YHWH's discourse in chs. 38–41; cf. also Elihu's pensive observations in ch. 37).

These divine judicial principles are not open to debate on the basis of human ideals, standards, and judgments of right or wrong; that was where Job and his fellow debaters made their fundamental mistake. God's justice is simply, but also significantly, an immutable, if at times, inscrutable, fact of life—one that does not fluctuate according to one's condition or circumstances in this world as Job had concluded in his state of misery (27:2; cf. 42:2–3).[17] In short, the 'fear of the Lord' is a concrete moral philosophy that

---

[15] The unexpected, disjunctive prosaic opening of v. 28 calls attention to the significance of its content and establishes an additional connection with the book's initial verse. Furthermore, "v. 28 does provide an interpretive conclusion to the poem by means of a voice that distinguishes itself from the voice of the poem and so sets up a[n interpretive] dialogue with it" (Newsom 1996:533, added material in brackets). The initial margin of this divine quotation may be fit into its poetic cotext by being analyzed as an *anacrusis* (i.e., an overlap of information from the preceding poetic line; cf. Ps. 1:1, 4; Prov. 4:4; Hartley 1988:383).

[16] "In the opening tale Job was certified by Yahweh as possessing what the 'Hymn to Wisdom' presents in 28:28 as the divine definition of wisdom" (Good 1990:292). The distinct character of the personified Wisdom being referred to in this chapter may be hinted at by the presence of the definite article on *hokmah* in vv. 12 and 20 (a possible allusion to Prov. 8:1, 9:1 where the noun is anarthrous).

[17] "The Book of Job questions magical formulas by which good behavior controls God's responses or all suffering can be traced back to some previous sin. If God is transcendent, God cannot be confined to human explanations—not even those of justice" (Melchert 1998:90). However, the fact is that YHWH has also graciously made himself personally immanent to his people by providing them with at least some explanations for life's experiences and, more important, a theological and moral framework for making sense of reality

naturally leads to a right-minded worldview and a righteous lifestyle. It is embodied in a penitent person's understanding and obedient response to the privilege of being allowed to enter into a unique fellowship of faith with his/her almighty Creator and sovereign Lord,[18] an intimate personal relationship that is established, maintained, and ultimately evaluated by the incontrovertible, but trustworthy righteousness of God himself (cf. 40:2, 8; 42:6–8; cf. Alden 1993:39).

> The fear of the Lord is more like an attitude or posture, a standing expectantly on tiptoes in the presence of the holy. Such a stance is a "knowing" (that God is near or present) and, at the same time, an emotional response to that knowing. This cognition (knowing) is inseparable from the emotion (awe) because of God. (Melchert 1998:38)

Since God is a mystery and his ways inexplicable, explanation is not what he expects of his people, nor should they expect it from him. Rather, 'wisdom' is manifested by one's reverent submission ('fear') in all of life's diverse circumstances, for "we live in this world more by trust than by knowledge" (ibid., 91, original emphasis).

1.3 Job 28: The fulcrum of the book

I am certainly not alone in calling attention to the central significance of chapter 28 within the complete book of Job. Many commentators give a general impression of its tectonic and rhetorical importance as part of the text's overall discourse development, but few do this in any degree of detail or precision. Others note the distinctiveness of this wisdom poem, but not its thematic salience or its dynamic structural function, viewing it along the lines of a mere restful interlude (e.g., Andersen 1976:53; Eaton 1985:19), a preliminary point of closure to the disputation thus far, or a passing transitional comment (Habel 1985:38–39, 391–395; Hartley 1988:373). In fact, as already noted, a number of more pessimistic scholars have come to the conclusion that this chapter was

---

and the human condition, no matter how seemingly pointless and confusing.

[18] In commenting on the expression 'fear of God' in Job 15:4, Berry observes that "the phrase means 'sincere Yahwistic faith,' not unlike our usage of the term *belief*. It often carries the connotation of mystical commitment" (1995:124). Writing from the perspective of a detailed comparison of the theological concept in Deuteronomy and the Psalter, Miller suggests that "[t]he songs of praise and the 'new' song of the psalms express the fear of the Lord that is the first commandment of all....Israel's praise as set forth in the Psalter was its most visible expression of obedience to the First Commandment" (1999:16). For a new study of the importance of the notion, 'fear of the Lord,' within the book of Proverbs as a whole, we look forward to Prof H. Bosman's, "The rhetoric of reverence—the 'fear of the Lord' (*yir'at yhwh*) in the book of Proverbs" (forthcoming).

perhaps misplaced or added later as some sort of a corrective afterthought to the book, either by the original author or some later redactor.[19]

The following summary-outline strongly supports the thesis that chapter 28 is authentically original and extremely well-placed within the larger composition. It is situated at the core of a chiastic, or progressively centered, structural arrangement that points to YHWH as the principal protagonist on the dramatic stage of both the narrative action and also the dialogic exchanges, as shown on the diagram of the symmetrical structural organization of Job:[20]

CONCENTRIC STRUCTURAL OUTLINE OF THE BOOK OF JOB

A. **Prologue**: Job is severely tested with suffering and loss (1:1–2:13)
    a. *introduction*: Job is living an upright, God-fearing life (1:1)
        b. *his children*: 7 sons and 3 daughters (1:2)
            c. *his flocks*: 7000 sheep, 3000 camels, 500 yoked oxen, 500 donkeys (1:3)
                d. *celebration*: family feasts—with intercession (1:4–5)
                    e. *Job's affliction by God*: terrible losses, instigated by the Satan (1:6–2:10)
                        f. *three friends:* Eliphaz, Bildad, and Zophar come to console Job (2:11)
                            g. *no words:* silence [7 days/7 nights] in view of Job's suffering (2:12–13)
B. **Job's debate-opening speech**: he curses the day of his birth
    a. *key terms*: birth, womb, offspring, counting months, day, night, light, darkness, dawn, Leviathan, clouds, freedom, captivity, life, death, awakening, etc.[21]
    b. *complaint*: my life is a mistake—a dark tragedy—and God is the cause
C. **An interactive cycle of speeches**: a varied iteration of the two arguments (4:1–27:23)
    a. *Job's focus*: I am righteous/innocent and am suffering unjustly
    b. *friends' focus*: Job, you have sinned and must repent in order to be restored
→D. **Ode to divine Wisdom**: [outlined above] (28:1–28)
    a. YHWH alone knows 'wisdom'—why life/the world is the way it is

---

[19] A representative listing of some of these works is found in van der Lugt 1995:521, who considers ch. 28 to be "Job's opening speech within the third cycle" (1995:520).

[20] This diagram, though conceived in my initial work on Job (1984), has been refined with reference to Dorsey (1999:170; Dorsey refers also to Cooper 1982). See also Habel's chiastic arrangement of the book from the perspective of the preeminent 'legal metaphor' (1985:54). In this last framework, ch. 28 does not have a distinct place within the whole.

[21] Dorsey comments: "Every verse in Job's curse has at least one verbal echo in God's speech, and most verses have multiple echoes. It would appear that Yahweh is responding almost entirely to Job's initial outcry in ch. 3, virtually ignoring the intervening debate" (1999:171). Their whole disputation had missed the point: God's ways of 'wisdom' and 'righteousness' in this world do not correspond to mankind's, either qualitatively or quantitatively.

1.3 Job 28: The fulcrum of the book

        b. to become 'wise', man must 'fear' God, trusting his just judgment
    C' Job's final summary speech and Elihu's rejoinder: more reiteration (29:1–37:24)
        a. *Job's focus*: I am righteous/innocent and am suffering unjustly
        b. *Elihu's focus*: Job, you have sinned and must repent in order to be restored
B' God's debate-closing speech: Job's birth and life are under God's sovereign rule (38:1-42:6)
    a. *key terms*: birth, womb, offspring, counting months, day, night, light, darkness, dawn, Leviathan, clouds, freedom, captivity, life, death, awakening, etc. (cf. B-a)
    b. *correction*: there are no mistakes in a world that God has created and justly controls
A' Epilogue: Job's suffering and loss are graciously reversed, with interest! (42:7-17)
    g' *too many words*: Job's friends spoke unjustly—sacrifice 7 bulls /7 rams (42:7-8)
    f' *three friends*: Eliphaz, Bildad, and Zophar appeal to Job for prayer (42:9)
    e' *Job's affliction by God*: he is doubly restored; the Satan has disappeared (42:10)
    d' *celebration*: feasts for family and friends—with consolation (42:11)
    c' *his flocks*: 14000 sheep, 6000 camels, 1000 yoked oxen, 1000 donkeys (42:12)
    b' *his children*: 7 sons and 3 daughters—the latter more beautiful than before (42:13-15)
    a' *conclusion*: Job lives a long and fruitful life [the blessing of fearing-God?] (42:16-17)

The intricately constructed, surrounding narrative frame (A + A') presents a captivating riches to rags (and back) account that rhetorically serves both to engage any potential audience and to situate the interactive speeches (C + C') and the book's powerfully didactic theodicy (B + D + B') within a turbulent personal life history.[22] The sapiential-theological moral of this drama is quite straightforward, albeit rather unconventional in relation to current beliefs of that time: man has no right either to blame God for his misfortune in life or to congratulate himself for any personal success and prosperity. Neither can one assess the quality of the spiritual relationship that others have with the Lord based on their outward appearance or present circumstances.

In sickness and health, weal or woe, the lives of YHWH's 'servants' (like the man Job—עַבְדִּי אִיּוֹב, e.g., 1:8, 42:8) are in his merciful hands, and therefore they fully commit themselves to a God-fearing, trusting existence in a world where so often it seems that Deity is ignored, despised, or just plain misunderstood. They do so confidently trusting that their 'Lord'

---

[22] Steinmann presents a good summary of how "[t]he prologue serves as a guide through the winding and twisting paths of chs. iii–xlii" (1996:95).

(אֲדֹנָי) will work things out aright, whether they happen to know it or not, according to his sovereign will, but also in keeping with his gracious purpose for each one of them. If the dramatic lesson of Job's life teaches anything at all, it is simply this—that God does have a just, salvific plan for the universe, and yet it is also personalized so that all of his faithful people have their individual roles to play within it. This is a vibrant ongoing *creative* activity where, even in the most intense suffering and pain, the believer can demonstrate the sort of piety ('fear of the Lord') and morality (remain 'turned away from evil') that constitute godly wisdom (cf. v. 28). This is because:

> [W]isdom cannot be found by mining…Similarly, wisdom is not a commodity that can be possessed. Even God's relation to wisdom is described in ways that challenge notions of wisdom as some objectified thing. Wisdom is perceived and known fully only in the act of creation itself. What the poet describes is rather like what an artisan experiences….God's acts [cf. vv. 25–27] are cosmos-creating acts, and God perceives and establishes wisdom in the midst of that activity. The human actions of true piety—fearing God and turning from evil—those too are acts of creation…of moral creation. … One cannot possess wisdom; one can only embody it [in one's life-style]. (Newsom 1996:533, added material in brackets)

1.4 A sapiential ode to spiritual wisdom

The preceding intrinsic and extrinsic text analyses of Job 28 in relation to the pericope itself and the book as a whole have clearly suggested its structural and thematic importance. Thus this chapter is formally foregrounded in terms of both its distinctive style and its placement as a means of highlighting the text's essential content—namely, a sapiential ode in celebration of 'wisdom' in this world and its divine Source of supply. An 'ode' may be defined as "a lyric poem of some length, usually of a serious or meditative nature and having an elevated style and formal stanzaic structure" (Soukhanov 1996:1253). In the classical Greco-Roman tradition, such a poetic composition was often associated with music and dance in a public performance of some sort (Preminger and Brogan 1993:855). All of these features, even the musical aspect, could well have applied to the discourse of chapter 28 at one stage or another of its history of compositional development and usage. Although the three 'stanzas' of this wisdom poem are not regular in terms of meter, syllabic length, or lineation, they are clearly distinct from each other and quite intricately fashioned so as to qualify under this designation of literary genre. That should be clear to anyone who studies the original design of the Hebrew text.

1.4 A sapiential ode to spiritual wisdom

Sharp controversy continues to rage, however, with regard to the actual contextual (extralinguistic) setting of the book of Job, that is, who wrote it, to whom, when, where, and why. Eaton summarizes the diverse options fairly well (1985:65):

> Opinions have varied from a Jewish belief in Moses' authorship to the view of critics who, supposing Plato's influence, look to Hellenistic times. If we confine ourselves more realistically to the mature achievements in Hebrew language and thought, we could still range from the tenth to the early fifth centuries BC.

Since I can shed no new or convincing light on any of the main possibilities or alternatives, I will leave these issues aside and concentrate on the concrete text in its ANE literary environment. Here too, one cannot be dogmatic about one's opinion, but a few general comments may be helpful to situate the text and its message within the artistic wisdom conventions and according to which it was originally composed.

There is little doubt that this poetic ode contains "genre elements [that] are almost all drawn from [Israelite] wisdom teaching" (Murphy 1981:37),[23] in particular, the thematic motifs that refer to God's creative control of nature (e.g., vv. 25–26) as well as the incomparability and inaccessibility of divine *hokmah* ('wisdom', cf. Prov. 8:22–31). The didactic question and answer format of the poem's structure, established by the interrogative refrain of verses 12 and 20, is then resolved by the appropriate reply of the final stanza, its first and last verses in particular (vv. 23, 28).[24] Though not an emic genre within the Hebrew literary tradition, this piece may be regarded as "an adaptation of the [tripartite] poetic hymnic form for the purpose of showcasing one or more motifs basic to wisdom teaching" (Giese 1995:262). Its style and structure as a reflective hymn surely lends itself to an *oral* proclamatory performance whether by recitation, chanting, or singing—a compositional feature that has considerable relevance for our contemporary attempts to reproduce its dynamic form, content, and function through various modes of translation and textual transposition to the non-print media (see section 1.6).[25]

---

[23] In this respect, chapter 28 follows the stylistic pattern of the book as a whole in which "the poet adapts a rich variety of materials including complaints, hymns, axioms, taunts, and sarcastic pleas...to capture and heighten the theological conflicts developed within the book" (Habel 1985:42–43).

[24] "Westermann [1981] classifies [chapter 28] as a pure wisdom poem which is the expansion of an ancient riddle encapsulated in vs. 20 and 23" (Habel 1985:392). Such a speculative proposal cannot of course be proved, but it does serve to establish the ancient sapiential roots of this poem. The refrain of vv. 12 and 20 serves to introduce major sections of the poem, thus performing the discourse demarcating function termed *anaphora*.

[25] From a broader perspective, Eaton observes that "the form of *Job* is ideally suited to

So far our discussion of this pericope has treated its nature and purpose in positive terms, but there is an alternative perspective that has been growing in acceptance in recent years. Put in the form of a question, the issue is this: does chapter 28, a hymnic ode to divine 'wisdom', represent the thematic ideal or its antithesis—that is, some sort of parody or mockery of the 'traditional' wisdom philosophy of Israel? Following the earlier arguments of Budde, Dhorm, and others, van der Lugt (who regards Job as the speaker of ch. 28, together with 27) puts the latter case as follows:

> The repeated questions *m'yn...w'yzh* in vv. 12 and 20 characterize the poem as a *litany-like lament* rather than as a hymn....The concluding refrain (v. 28) does not really give the composition a twist. When it is maintained in this line that, as far as man is concerned, the fear of the LORD *(sic)* is 'wisdom' and shunning evil yields 'understanding', we have to take into account that these words have a hidden meaning. At first sight we are dealing with a resigned declaration of piety by Job. In the context of our book as a whole, however, v. 28 has a negative ring to it....[T]he poem indirectly accuses God of withholding Job *(sic)* a satisfactory answer to the question why he has to suffer... (1995:522, 523, 524; original italics)

In a similar vein Norman Habel comments:

> But is this the final solution of Job or the poet? Hardly! For clearly, 'fear/piety' (*yir'a*) has not provided Job with the wisdom to understand the crisis he faced. ... For Job to return (in v. 28) to the traditional 'fear of the Lord' would therefore mean returning to a posture of pious unquestioning submission which the friends had advocated all along and which he had repudiated time and again....But clearly 'shunning evil' neither protected Job from being afflicted by God nor gave him any discernment to understand that affliction....The poet thereby emphasizes once again that the traditional orthodox answer...is not acceptable to Job. (1985:392–393)

I cannot enter fully into this debate, one that naturally hangs on the credibility of the 'hidden meaning' seen by van der Lugt, or how one construes Job's state of mind at this point in the development of the book's argument, or indeed, one's interpretation of 'the poet's personal reflection on the debate thus far' (Habel 1985:392). Suffice it to say, a systematic structural study of the book as a whole would suggest that the traditional positive assessment of chapter 28 seems to offer a more satisfying resolution to the hermeneutical crux of this theodicy as it relates to the life story of Job.[26] The concentric arrangement of the complete discourse, if

---

dramatic recitation or presentation...We can likewise imagine that *Job* also was declaimed from memory with the relishing of every syllable, evoking fascination with the suspense and resolution of its drama" (1985:39, 41).

[26] The traditional wisdom perspective on Job 28:28 is supported by the later texts of Jewish sapiential literature. In Sirach, for example, it appears that wisdom "[s]*ophia* even seems

1.4 A sapiential ode to spiritual wisdom

granted, would surely indicate that the process of interpretation must follow a similar pattern—not merely a linear progression of thought, but with the external framework of God's speech and the narrative outcome (B' and A' on the structural diagram above) providing the hermeneutical key to the whole.[27]

Thus YHWH's closing, un-'answer'-able (38:3, 40:2) verdict concerning Job's situation (chs. 38–41), followed by the total rehabilitation of his servant in the subsequent narrative coda, clearly shows that neither Job's righteousness nor his suffering was really at issue after all.[28] It is the sovereign will of the Creator and Ruler of life that determines both—and everything else that goes on in the universe, even allowing the evil machinations of the Satan. True wisdom is to fearfully (trustfully) accept this state of affairs (40:4–5; 42:2–6), a universal, unfathomable dominion that is, nevertheless, always motivated by divine justice operating in grace (40:8). According to human standards, Job was ethically upright (1:1, 8, 22; 2:3, 10); this was true despite his external situation, which was the basis for the erroneous conclusions on the part of his comforters and Job himself. The terrible trials and suffering that he experienced had nothing at all to do with his standing in God's eyes, as shown by his blessed restoration at the end[29] —and his vital ministry of intercessory mediation on behalf of his erstwhile detractors (42:8–9).[30]

---

synonymous with 'the fear of the Lord'" and that "[c]learly, the link between the fear of the Lord, the covenant, *Sophia*, and the specifically Israelite Torah, the ten commandments, has been forged much more tightly than in Proverbs" (Melchert 1998:154–156).

[27] In addition to the strong correspondence between Job's opening lament (ch. 3) and God's closing response (chs. 38–41), we may also note as another example of concentric hermeneutics the critical rhetorical function of the book's narrative prologue and complementary epilogue. The former introduces that essential dramatic irony that accompanies the entire progress of the plot—namely, that Job is in fact righteous and is not being punished by YHWH for any grievous sins. The epilogue, on the other hand, reveals that Job's arguments were right in contrast to those of his friends (42:7). This was not always true in terms of content, intent, or tone (e.g., 40:1–4), but due to Job's forthright honesty and righteous heart-attitude over against a God whom he personally *knew*, in contrast to the remote, manipulatable deity that the others seemed to acknowledge as mechanistically controlling the events of this world.

[28] The speeches of YHWH in Job 38ff. illustrate *presentational* argumentation, which features a paralleled series of inductive, descriptive examples, facts, and comparisons (vs. *discursive*, causal discourse; Gitay 2009:50).

[29] The message of Job thus involves paradox as well as irony. Based on appearances, he seemed to be utterly cursed by God; in reality, he was standing upright before God (42:7–9), as the audience knows full well from the beginning (chs. 1–2). The source and nature of genuine wisdom too is paradoxical. It is a quality that cannot be discovered by looking at things from a strictly human perspective, produced from human resources, or experienced by using human means. On the other hand, within the framework of God's ordered creation and his established standards of judgment, wisdom is potentially everywhere, being manifested by all those who worship him and seek to serve him in righteousness (28:28; cf. Newsom 1996:534).

[30] We note that Job's acting as a mediator before the Lord on behalf of his friends (42:7–10)

During the course of the book's argument, Job and his friends go round and round two standard wisdom themes of the day as they seemed to apply to his tragic circumstances. These were the doctrine concerning the 'two ways' (one righteous, the other wicked) and the related principle of receiving a just 'retribution' in this life, i.e., righteousness always leading to blessing, but sinfulness inevitably to punishment.[31] The increasingly acrimonious, back-and-forth repartee produces no real winners in the dispute (chs. 3–27, with Job's summation in 29–31). Elihu then pretentiously reviews the preceding arguments and their unproductive outcome (32–37), thus unwittingly preparing the way for the LORD to put an end to it all by placing not only this debate but also all world history and philosophy into a divine perspective. This is the doctrine of 'natural' or 'cosmic' wisdom, which shifts the focus completely away from conventional interpretations (justice versus iniquity), the position of Job's friends, and Job's own personal self-evaluation ('I know I am innocent!'). Only one way is right, and just—God's way (28:23–24)—and it is possible to 'find' (or rather, experience) it. This is because YHWH himself has given explicit directions (28:28), having already shown the way through his creative action (28:25–27; chs. 38–41). That is all the wisdom man ever needs to know—which in a biblical sense means, to put into everyday practice.[32]

Therefore, the moral of this engaging poetic drama about the relation between wise thinking and righteous living (or speaking) does not simply consist in the 'all's well that ends well' final summary (42:12–17). Rather, the variable theological meaning and personal significance of this powerful literary discourse (i.e., wisdom) is derived from the slow process of hearing it move back and forth through to completion, of carefully apprehending the artistry of the text and involving oneself in all the intense emotion and sharp rhetoric of its shifting sequence of eloquent speakers. Then one must inevitably apply that message to one's own variegated experiences in life, ideally coming to the same 'fearful' conclusion as did Job (42:1–6). To humbly live in faith ('fear of the Lord') and to avoid

---

is anticipated in the narrative prologue where he is described as performing the same action for his family (1:5). Such intertextual allusion, foreshadowing, and interweaving is a prominent feature of the book as a whole—take, for example, the seemingly simple word 'place' *maqowm*, which reappears periodically in the poem of ch. 28 and at sixteen other points in the book. In the wisdom cosmology of ch. 28 this word "focuses on the primordially assigned 'home' of all things in the cosmic order, including wisdom herself" (Habel 1985:49). 'Way' (28:23), on the other hand, refers to wisdom's characteristic mode of operation or manifestation (ibid., 57).

[31] The 'Satanic corollary' to this second principle is that people trust in God and/or obey him simply because they profit from it in this life (i.e., *do ut des*) (cf. Steinmann 1996:97).

[32] Van der Lugt observes: "in the Hebrew world of thought there was not an absolute contradiction between the more or less philosophical conception of wisdom (28:1–27) and the practical interpretation of it (v. 28)" (1995:525).

folly ('evil') gives one the peace of having an implicit knowledge that transcends all understanding, no matter how chaotic or unanswerable the earthly circumstances may seem to be (28:28; cf. Phil 4:7).

1.5 Formatting the poetic-rhetorical structure of Job 28

The discourse structure of many poetic texts in the Bible presents us with an issue that is rather controversial, not only among commentators (where differences of opinion might be expected), but also among the various translated versions that have been published. One might think that there would be more consistency in the case of Scripture texts that are more widely distributed, and where editorial decisions are quite open to scrutiny and debate. On the contrary, the following comparative chart on Job 28 summarizes the disparate situation that we have with respect to text segmentation and arrangement in a selection of major English translations (x marks a paragraph break within the printed format).[33]

Verses:	1	2	3	4	5	6	7	8	9	10	11	12	13	14	15	16	17	18	19	20	21	22	23	24	25	26	27	28	Total
GNT:					x				x											**X**		x						x	5
GW:		X			x				x											x			x						5
CEV:									x																				1
NRSV:				x	x				x											x			x						5
NJB:												x											x						2
REB:												x											x						2
NIV:												x								x									2
NET:												x								x									2
Total:		1		1	3				6			2								5		1	4					1	

As shown by the X's, the paragraph sequence of these versions differs considerably. These published proposals may be compared with the textual organization that is displayed on the preceding chart, one that includes three major divisions (stanzas) and seven minor ones (strophes): I:1, 7, 9; II:12, 15, 20; III:23. What is one to make of all this diversity? Which format is most reasonable/defensible ('wise'), and where do problems occur?

Obviously, different criteria are being used in this discourse demarcating operation. There are several broad areas of agreement that correspond

---

[33] These English versions are as follows: GNT = Good News Translation, GW = God's Word, CEV = Contemporary English Version, NRSV = New Revised Standard Version, NJB = New Jerusalem Bible, REB = Revised English Bible, NIV = New International Version, NET = New English Translation. The large boldfaced X's indicate problem areas that are briefly discussed below.

with my tripartite structure for the chapter, i.e., with six versions making a segmental break at v. 12 and five at v. 20. Ideally, sectional headings, or titles, might be employed to differentiate the larger stanzas from the strophes (see the example of Job 28 below); otherwise, it is more difficult for readers to discern the difference in relative importance between these two discourse units. If lectors misread the text (e.g., by means of inappropriate pauses and intonational patterns), then it is likely that it will be mis-*heard* by the audience as well, thus opening the door to various kinds of conceptual confusion. A comparative check such as this also reveals certain inconsistencies (e.g., GNT's break *after* the refrain in v. 13 but *at* the refrain in v. 20) along with those structural divisions that cannot really be supported (e.g., GW's break at v. 5).[34] In these and many other subtle ways (e.g., indentation, use of different types styles and sizes, the amount of white space allocation), the format of the discourse serves an essential function to guide both the reading and also one's interpretation of the biblical text.

The following chart is a more radical display of chapter 28 (using the NIV text), one that aims to reveal some of the intricate patterns and parallels that it contains as part of the implicit tectonic 'meaning' (including semantic significance) that the discourse organization itself conveys. Naturally, some initial instruction may be required in an introductory comment or footnote to guide the reader through the communicative details of this sort of format. More or less of these compositional features may be included, depending on the literary sophistication and experience of the readership concerned. In any case, a relatively novel layout such as this needs to be thoroughly tested on readers and revised as necessary, e.g., at points where any interpretive errors or difficulties recur for a significant number of participants during the evaluation process.

Job 28 WHERE IS TRUE WISDOM TO BE FOUND?

Man's successful search for wealth

1	There is a mine for silver
	and a place where gold is refined.
2	Iron is taken from the earth,
	and copper is smelted from ore.
3	Man puts an end to the darkness;
	he searches the farthest recesses

---

[34] These two incongruities are highlighted by the boldfaced Xs on the preceding chart.

1.5 Formatting the poetic-rhetorical structure of Job 28

	for ore in the blackest darkness.
4	Far from where people dwell he cuts a shaft,
	in places forgotten by the foot of man,
	far from men he dangles and sways.
5	The earth, from which food comes,
	is transformed below as by fire.
6	Sapphires come from its rocks,
	and its dust contains nuggets of gold.

7   No bird of prey knows that hidden path,
                                       no falcon's eye has seen it.
8   Proud beasts do not set foot on it,
                                       and no lion prowls there

9   Man's hand assaults the flinty rock
           and lays bare the roots of the mountains.
10 He tunnels through the rock;
           his eyes see all its treasures.
11 He dams up the sources of the rivers
           and brings hidden things to light.

Man's unsuccessful search for wisdom

12 **But where can wisdom be found?**
     Where does understanding dwell?
13   Man does not comprehend its worth;
                  it cannot be found in the land of the living.
14   The deep says, 'It is not in me';
                      the sea says, 'It is not with me.'

15   It cannot be bought with the finest *gold*,
                              nor can its price be weighed in silver.
16   It cannot be bought with the *gold* of Ophir,
                              with precious onyx or sapphires.
17   Neither *gold* nor crystal can compare with it,
                              nor can it be had for jewels of *gold*.
18   Coral and jasper are not worthy of mention;
                              the price of wisdom is beyond rubies.
19   The topaz of Cush cannot compare with it;
                              it cannot be bought with pure *gold*.

20	Where then does wisdom come from?
	Where does understanding dwell?
21	It is hidden from the eyes of every living thing,
	concealed even from the birds of the air.
22	Destruction and Death say,
	'Only a rumor has reached our ears.'

God—He is the only source of wisdom

23	God understands the way to it
	and he alone knows where it dwells,
24	for he views the ends of the earth
	and sees everything under the heavens.
25	When he established the force of the wind
	and measured out the waters,
26	when he made a decree for the rain
	and a path for the thunderstorm,
27	then he looked at wisdom and appraised it;
	he confirmed it and tested it.
28	And he said to man,
	'The fear of the Lord—that is wisdom,
	and to shun evil is understanding.'

1.6 The wisdom of Job 28 in today's Chewa setting

Both the ancient biblical and corresponding Bantu cultures have an extensive wisdom tradition of written and oral literature (orature). The latter continues to be very influential in many segments of contemporary secular and religious society—in public discourse (e.g., political speeches, sermons), the arts (e.g., various publications, paintings, crafts, radio broadcasting, video and television productions), as well as in closed or secret usage (e.g., traditional initiation rites for the youth). Among the Chewa people, for example, such words of wisdom (whether more artistic in nature—*miyambi*, or didactic—*miyambo*) are judged to a great extent by their style of composition and manner of articulation.[35] This is true in relation to both the larger structure of a given text (i.e., 'genre' along with its typical macro-features of construction) and the characteristic artistic features on the micro-level of organization. Such a verbal style, we must remember, is still recognized and evaluated principally on the basis of its heard oral-aural qualities rather than in terms of the visible or printed word. The good public speaker is

---

[35] For a recent, integrated survey of Chewa indigenous art forms, including the wisdom tradition, see Chimombo 1988:ch. 3.

1.6 The wisdom of Job 28 in today's Chewa setting

therefore regarded much more highly than his/her literary counterpart. This is a factor that must be carefully considered by Bible translators, who must take into account the fact that far more of their target audience will actually listen to the text of Scripture than those who will (or can) read it for themselves.

There are many options available to translators today with regard to the version that they seek to prepare (a specific, designated communicative aim is always essential!), ranging on a broad continuum of possibilities from a relatively more strict formal correspondence technique to one that is more flexible in terms of functional equivalence. The pragmatic criterion of 'relevance' in relation to a specific target audience is a major factor for consideration in this decision making process (Gutt 1992:25). That is to say, the actual intelligibility of the translated text needs to be thoroughly assessed in comparison with the various communicative effects or cognitive and emotive benefits that are derived from it.[36] I need not rehearse what I have written on this subject (e.g., Wendland 2002b and 2003a), but will simply focus on a particular option that I have been promoting in recent years, namely, a version that aspires to being a vernacular 'literary equivalent' of the original Hebrew/Greek text, whatever the genre. In the present case, the issue is this: can we find an ode-like correspondent to Job 28 in the Chewa language?[37]

In contrast to West Africa, there is no indigenous tradition of epic or heroic poetry among the Chewa people or their recognized artistes and sages. Poetic discourse is popular, but it is restricted mainly to musical compositions and communal songs that are sung when working (e.g., in the fields, on a hunt, or doing domestic duties) and when attending social occasions such as funerals, weddings, dances, initiation ceremonies, religious rites (e.g., to appeal to the ancestors for rain), or telling folktales (*nthano*). Royal praise (panegyric) poetry, sung or chanted by experts, is also common in some areas for lauding the past or present attributes of the paramount chief and other revered dignitaries.

---

[36] No matter what the translation type that is agreed upon for the version at hand, there is also a further need, that is, for a generous supplementation of explanatory notes to make the reader 'wise' as to the contextual background, nature, and purpose of Job 28: for example, with respect to all the technical terms and allusions that are included in this masterful ode, the major intertextual citations and echoes, the threefold stanzaic discourse structure of this chapter, and its key position in the arrangement of Job as a whole. There is also the crucial cultural factor that will require some elaboration—the conceptual "gap [that exists] between contemporary worldviews and those of the ancient audience of the author" (Habel 1985:24), e.g., the deep-seated ANE religious connotations of the 'deep', 'sea', 'death', and 'decay' in vv. 14 and 22. On the other hand, there are a number of important cultural similarities or analogies too that need to be pointed out, e.g., about mining practices (in Zambia, it is copper) and man's closeness to nature (vv. 7–8).

[37] An ode is lengthy lyric poem, written in praise of some person, object, or quality and often suitable to be sung. This would certainly fit the poetic discourse of Job 28.

In addition, there exists a very personal form of spoken or sung lyric poetry (*ndakatulo*) that is composed for various, usually quite emotional, occasions by masters and novices alike (e.g., to woo a lover, to lament a loss, to proclaim a victory, or to taunt an enemy). I have found this to be a very productive model to emulate in the effort to render certain appropriate biblical passages in a rhetorically heightened manner that corresponds more with the communicative function(s) of the original text (cf. Wendland 1993:ch. 3). This genre may be variably blended then with a 'sapiential' style (*miyambi*) when translating the didactic poetry of the Hebrew Scriptures, such as we have in Proverbs and Qoheleth.[38] In general, when dealing with the argumentative discourse of Job, translators would want to give their text a more proverbial flavor; in the specific case of the ode of chapter 28, however, a more lyrical tone and meditative mode should probably be preferred (except for verse 28).

The following is a poetic (*ndakatulo*) rendition of the third and concluding stanza of the Job 28 wisdom pericope. This would be an especially appropriate place for a distinctive, 'skillful' manner of composition to be manifested,[39] that is, as a means of drawing verbal attention to the significance of the text at this apical point of the poem, which itself needs to be clearly distinguished stylistically from its co-text. It has been formulated with a specifically 'oratorical' presentation in mind—a piece that can be orally declaimed or even sung to the accompaniment of a musically complementary melody. The text has also been formatted accordingly on the page (e.g., in measured poetic lines) so that it can be easily read—hence hopefully also understood—aloud, as emphasized in the earlier discussion of this important aspect of translation. The Chewa version is paralleled with a back-translation into English, one that is relatively literal so as to draw attention to some of its outstanding stylistic features.

Mulungu ndiye yekha amadziwa,	God is the one who knows,
kudziwa njira yopitira kumeneko,	knows the way of going there,
kumene kumapezeka nzeru imene.	to where wisdom itself may be found.
Paja amayang'ana soo! mpakana	As is known, he looks long and hard, SOO! right up
kumathero a dziko lonse lapansi,	to the ends of the whole land down here,
kuona zonse zakunsi kwa thambo.	to see everything that is below the sky.

---

[38] I deal with the major structural and stylistic similarities and differences between Chewa and Hebrew proverbs in chapter 5: 'How to answer a fool...'

[39] In Hebrew thinking, a 'skilled' manner of construction could well be regarded as a manifestation of 'wisdom' (*hokmah*), for that is the very term chosen to describe the expert talents of Bezalel and Aholiab with reference to their creative endeavors to beautify the Tabernacle (Exod. 31:3) with 'artistic designs' (*machashaboth*, v. 4).

Iyetu popatsa mphepo mphamvu	Surely he in giving power to the wind
ndi kuyesa kuchuluka kwa mvula,	and in measuring out the amount of rain,
poika lamulo loti madziwo agwe	in setting a command for those waters to fall down
ndikukonza njira yoyenda mphezi,	and in preparing a path for the lightning to travel,
pamenepo ndiye adapeza nzeruyo	then is when he found that wisdom
ndi kufufuzafufuza wake mtengo,	and carefully investigated the worth of it,
inde, n' kuvomereza phindu lake.	yes, and to assert its value.
Tsono Mulungu anthu onse awauza,	So now God all people he tells them,
'Kuopa Chauta ndiyo nzeru ndithu,	'Fearing Chauta the Creator is really wisdom,
kuchotsa zoipa m'moyo, apo ndipo!'	removing evils from life, that's where it's at!'

The main artistic attributes of *ndakatulo* lyric poetry are clearly evident from this short trial selection, for example, balanced lineation, use of a vivid ideophone (*soo!*), the introduction of various interlineal transitional devices, divergences from prosaic syntactic word order, enjambment, additional emphasizers and intensifiers, a distinctive divine name, alliteration, reiteration, and contemporary idiomatic language (including the final rhythmic *apo ndipo!*). This is not to claim that such a dynamically rendered version is suitable for all audiences and every occasion. But if composed for the use of an active, community-involved youth group, for example, this sort of text would certainly help the intense debates of the original Hebrew to come alive for this current generation of Chewa-speaking wisdom-seekers. In a superficial, live-for-today world that offers so many competing options, opinions, and answers concerning the adjudication of right and wrong, the practice of exploitation versus genuine empowerment, the manifestation of wasteful superfluity in contrast to large-scale suffering and human deprivation, or the equitable and sustainable management of this earth's resources, people of all walks of life need to consider more seriously the basic principles of personal relationship that are advocated in the Scriptures, all of which are founded on a healthy 'fear of the LORD'.

1.7 Conclusion: The rhetorical function of poetic form

Does 'wisdom', like proverbial 'beauty', lie merely in the ears of the hearer? Certainly it depends to a large extent on the particular text and tradition in which it has been recorded and according to whose standards it is being analyzed and assessed. As we have seen, both the original Hebrew and the ancient Bantu literary (and oral) conventions place a high value on the sharp pen (or tongue) of the rhetor, or orator. 'Wise' discourse is widely recognized, highly valued, eagerly pursued, and frequently memorized, for it performs an essential multiple function in society—to instruct, inspire, and implore all members of the community with regard to the fundamental beliefs, precepts, and mores of the past. The aim is also to carry out this didactic task in an impressive, memorable way so that these traditions, both religious and secular, will not be downplayed or forgotten. There are, indeed, some major stylistic and conceptual differences: for biblical Israel, YHWH (יְהוָה) was the central focus of their sapiential lore, whether directly or indirectly (e.g., oblique reference, ideological orientation); for the Chewa people, on the other hand, it is their ancestors who are similarly regarded as having the principal influence and impact, for good or evil, on the lives and destiny of the living. Thus biblical 'proverbs', for example, are very religious, often overtly theological in character, whereas the Chewa corpus is much more socially-oriented and influenced by ethnically specific relationships, customs, and values.

In my earlier study of Job (1984), I took special note of the rhetorical function of the stylistic device of *inclusio* and A-B-A' ring structures, which of course embrace the more intricate chiasmus or concentric arrangement (*palistrophe*). Amidst the multitude of lexical recursions to be found throughout the text, including chapter 28 as we have seen, there are many particular instances of paired patterns of inclusion that serve several major compositional aims:

- to delineate the discourse into discernable (hearable!) segments of varying sizes having both syntagmatic and paradigmatic links with their respective co-texts, the whole being harmoniously related to its various constituent parts;

- to give the main message a perceptible thematic unity and continuity, with its forward progression and development being continually reinforced by the recycling of a cluster of key motifs;

- and to highlight certain corresponding or contrastive aspects of these interrelated topics by means of their careful positioning at crucial nodes within the overall discourse framework.

In one sense then, the ode of Job represents the central B constituent of the book's overall structural organization—not simply a transition from A to A' or a peaceful pause in the verbal action, but a key semantic and pragmatic element that provides a vital hermeneutical perspective on

1.7 Conclusion: The rhetorical function of poetic form

everything that comes before and after in the text, including the climactic speeches of YHWH at the end.[40]

How does the technique of verbal inclusion contribute towards a more effective communication of the Joban theodicy and homily? On one level of meaning, this topically diverse and formally flexible, but rhetorically very focused, A-B-A' pattern acts as a symbolic representation of the typical life of most 'righteous' folk, whether in terms of their social and material fortunes or their spiritual and religious fervor. Normally, neither the physical nor the psychological quality of everyday experience is uniformly 'level' for the duration of the believer's presence on earth, but it generally consists of a continual succession of peaks, troughs, and plateaus of sometimes tedious regularity. While this is true for any individual of every age, the philosophical difference for some is religious in nature and import. The faithful community of 'God-fearers' has the verbal assurance that YHWH directs and controls the final outcome—the last act of their personal drama of existence (e.g., 42:16–17)—no matter what may precede or follow it in human history. Furthermore, with reference to Job's life, this A-B-A' arrangement acts as a structural metaphor for the emotional vacillations in his tortured thoughts and words, as he agonized not only over his present wretched condition, but also, more importantly, with respect to his ambiguous and (to his mind) inexplicable personal relationship with God.[41]

On a more subtle stylistic plane of meaning then, one might interpret an A-B-A' inclusion as being a formal reflection of the author's artful cyclical treatment of his main theme. No simple, clear-cut or decisive answers are forthcoming in the vigorous, often heated, rounds of argumentation that lead up to the book's medial peak in chapter 28—nor thereafter, in Job's recapitulation and Elihu's elaboration of the theological and moral issues involved in his case. Rather, there is a varied shifting back and forth from one position, pole, and perspective to another (with Job speaking in lone opposition to the lot) as the relevant issues are poetically and rhetorically examined and commented on from many different angles. One argument is introduced, debated, dropped, picked up again (not necessarily by the

---

[40] The inclusive/chiastic aspects that constitute the structure of Job 28 have already been pointed out. This central chapter, like the book as a whole, also builds up to a peak of thematic salience at its close: 28:28—an instance of discourse level 'end-stress'.

[41] It is interesting to note that *the Satan* metaphorically refers to this same concept of 'inclusion' (or is it 'exclusion'?) by accusing the LORD of 'hedging' Job in from all evil in life (1:9–11), and even Job's life itself from death (2:4–5). Although YHWH does lift this hedge, as it were, to allow the Satan to put Job to some hard testing, God puts it back into place again by bringing the debate to a conclusion and by restoring Job's life to an even greater level of joy and blessedness.

same speaker), interrupted, modified, developed some more—and so on throughout the disputation sequence (a manifest diversity that is reflected also in the host of commentators on this book throughout the ages).

The discourse proceeds in this manner of overlapping structures and semantic enclosures right up until the final, decisive answer of YHWH, which is so simple, in contrast to all the proceeding polemic, that it sounds almost banal. From the primordial time of the world's creation, God has concretely demonstrated 'wisdom' and correspondingly established what is right in his eyes, and this is all that matters in any personal or corporate epistemology.[42] In other words, God's wisdom underlies, defines, and sustains righteousness as opposed to wickedness in the universe (not just the realm of human experience—cf. the Satan and his diabolical ilk).[43] And since all people, the good as well as the evil from a divine viewpoint, can be assured of perfect, immutable justice, there is no need (indeed it is futile) to debate the issue either in general terms or with respect to specific cases, like Job's. A true servant learns in trust to follow the path of wisdom as charted in the word of Wisdom by humbly accepting her/his unique situation in life, knowing that this is always made right in the prevailing context of a personal relationship with the Creator.[44] The fitting response then to any controversy or crisis, condition or circumstance that one happens to be in is a faith-filled, faithful 'fear of the LORD'. One's beginning (A) and ending (A¹) are in the hands of Yahweh, the Almighty himself (cf. 29:5, 'with me' שַׁדַּי עִמָּדִי)—so why should one worry about what's in between (B)?

---

[42] Thus, wisdom is not only "the pivotal principle of [God's] creation" (Habel 1985:400; cf. Prov. 8:22ff.), it is also the constitutive principle of morality as YHWH has established it in the world—according to his own definition of the concept (e.g., 28:28; cf. Prov. 2:1–22; 9:10). Furthermore, according to Sirach, "Torah is to be followed because it is wise: 'If you desire wisdom, keep the commandments' (1:26). Thus Torah is a means to wisdom!" (Melchert 1998:156). From the perspective of natural theology, one could say that "Israel's doctrine of creation is crucial to its wisdom. Genesis 1:1 stands behind all biblical wisdom literature" (Garrett 1993:53).

On the other hand, mankind's first sin (Gen. 3:6) was a blatant perversion of divinely intended fear-of-the-Lord 'wisdom' in the personal desire for a hedonistic Qoheleth-like substitute. Yahweh's punishment of such a vain pursuit (Gen. 3:17–19) thus echoes ironically in the disappointed Philosopher's varied laments (e.g., Eccl. 2:1, 5, 8, 10–11, 16, 17–20; cf. ch. 7, section 7.2.5).

[43] "[God] is not bound in his administration of the cosmos by a moral law according to which the wicked are necessarily afflicted and the righteous inevitably blessed....God is above any such law and the design of the cosmos reveals this higher order of God's ways" (Habel 1985:56–57).

[44] Job expresses his personal faith in a righteous, saving God on several significant occasions in the book, e.g., 1:21, 13:15–19, 14:13–17, 16:19–21, 19:25–27, 23:3–7, 42:2–6.

1.7 Conclusion: The rhetorical function of poetic form

Such a distinctive passage as Job 28 with regard to its form, content, purpose, and discourse placement clearly warrants some correspondingly 'wise' techniques of reproducing the text in any vernacular translation. This means that whenever possible translators will utilize the full artistic and rhetorical resources of the target language to formulate a suitably persuasive poetic style coupled with an appropriate genre adaptation from the local oral tradition. Only such a carefully domesticated composition will be relevant enough to capture the interest and attention of audiences who urgently need to hear the same divine message that Job did—and just as forcefully worded or emotively expressed.[45]

A mother-tongue dramatic stage production of the narrative frame, with the included speeches of the disputation suitably condensed, would be very effective in south-central Africa, for example, where the vital theme of causation in the events of life is just as important an issue.[46] In this localized, anthropocentric world, however, a transcendent 'God' has nothing to do with it: extraordinary blessing is viewed as being a result of manipulative magic, while undue suffering or misfortune is attributed to the human practice of sorcery and witchcraft. Job teaches African (and all other) audiences that, on the contrary, the Creator is superintending his creation globally (despite man's worst efforts to pollute and destroy his environment!). Furthermore, the immanent Lord is intimately involved with the minute everyday affairs of his subjects and vitally concerned about their future ultimate welfare. Indeed, he has already made ample provision for that through his Messiah-Son. What he wants now from all humanity is the appropriate righteous respect (fear), a perceptive awareness of how to avoid evil (understanding), and an uncompromising faith-life like Job's that goes with it (wisdom)!

---

[45] "The prevailing view among most, though not all, *literary translators* is that a translation should reproduce in the TL reader [or hearer] the same emotional and psychological [including aaesthic] reaction produced in the original SL reader [or hearer]....Most *translators* [as opposed to theorists] judge the success of a translation largely on the degree to which it 'doesn't read [or sound] like a translation.'...(W)ho other than scholars would want to read [or hear] prose [or poetry] that bears the heavy imprint of foreign grammar, idiom, or syntax?" (Landers 2001:49–50; the italics and words in brackets have been added). These pointed comments come from a professional translator of literature (Portuguese into English), as distinct—significantly—from those of us who mainly/merely theorize about the subject.

[46] Eaton provides a short summary of the prevalence of dramatic productions in the ancient Near East, including a general "appreciation of recited poetry" (1985:40). For a sample of their African counterparts, see Wendland 2004a.

2

The Lyric Heart of the Psalm at the Center of the Psalter

Introduction: Introit 'into the sanctuary of God' (Psalm 73:17)

The purpose of this literary-structural and topically-oriented study of Psalm 73 is to demonstrate how a careful text analysis, carried out internally in relation to the work's discourse development and externally with respect to its canonical setting, gives one a better understanding of its vital message in terms of sense and significance. This provides an entrance, as it were, into 'the divine sanctuary' (v. 17) of meaning of the original poem. A broad *inter*textual perspective is given by an overview of several important matters concerning the mixed genre of Psalm 73, some prominent cross-psalmic resonances, and its crucial position at the compositional centre of the Psalter. An initial contextual orientation of this nature facilitates a more informed examination of some of the psalm's chief *intra*textual properties.

To begin with, several important thematic and rhetorical features are investigated. First, I survey the usage of several key terms that convey a special theological import both in relation to each other and the discourse as a whole. This lays the foundation for a consideration of the principal religious functions of Psalm 73, as revealed by an overview of its chief pragmatic properties (speech acts) and rhetorical dynamics (argument structure) in relation to the text's essential religious content. The central issue which motivates this poetic instance of intense interpersonal communication involving the psalmist (representing his people) and the LORD God concerns the apparent lack of divine justice in view of the prosperity, arrogance, oppression, and impiety which characterize the wicked majority of this world. The psalmist's transforming sanctuary experience leads to a resolution of this apparent contradiction through a revision of the conventional notion of 'purity of heart'. The relative 'goodness' of one's situation can be properly evaluated only when one compares the terrible final destiny of the wicked in contrast to the glory of God's ever-present nearness to his children.

Anyone who reads through Psalm 73 will be struck by the dramatic turning point that occurs in verse 17 when, in the midst of all his mental anguish (v. 16), physical affliction (v. 14), and doubts concerning the justice of God (v. 13), the psalmist reports that he 'enters into the sanctuary [-ies] of God'.[1] The importance of this passage is reflected in the psalm's overall structural arrangement and stylistic artistry (see section 2.5.5), and such a conclusion is reinforced by a complementary investigation of some of the psalm's central theological concepts and communicational objectives. An examination of the semantic interrelationships that progressively link the key terms 'goodness' (טוֹב–1, 28), 'to the pure of heart' (לְבָרֵי לֵבָב–1; cf. 13), 'sanctuaries of God' (מִקְדְּשֵׁי־אֵל–17), 'their destiny' (אַחֲרִיתָם–17), 'glory' (כָּבוֹד–24), and the 'nearness of God' (קִרֲבַת אֱלֹהִים–28) reveals a deeper level of religious meaning than what first appears on the textual surface. This underlying significance is enhanced by means of a pragmatic-rhetorical approach that similarly encompasses the entire discourse—now as a highly emotive 'speech-event', or dialogue, involving the psalmist and his enemies, on the one hand, with him (as a representative of 'Israel', v. 1) and his God on the other. Further support for the relative prominence of Psalm 73, 'a high point in the Psalter' (Goldingay 2007:419), and its highly personal, yet also fundamentally communal, message is gained by viewing it from a wider perspective as an entrance into the sacred Psalter as a whole. This carefully positioned 'wisdom poem' (its primary genre) forms a critical part of the total architectonic design of the canonical book of books that we call the 'Psalms'. A careful survey of the communicative dynamics of this inspiring verbal 'sanctuary' will convince one of the special relevance of Psalm 73 also for the contemporary people of God, especially those who either individually or corporately may be even now experiencing a faith-attack similar to the one that this psalm so eloquently dramatizes. My study concludes with a consideration of several important issues that pertain to the dynamic translation of this moving psalm in other language-cultures (2.5.3).

---

[1] Unless noted otherwise all English translations are my own semi-literal renderings of the Hebrew. Only some of the text-critical issues (cf. Goldingay 2007:397-399) that pertain to the central exposition and argument of this chapter will be considered, and even then, the discussion will necessarily be selective and incomplete. Most commentators take the intensive plural noun מִקְדְּשֵׁי־אֵל to be a figurative (metonymic) reference to the Jerusalem Temple (Bratcher and Reyburn 1991:640, including its precincts, Ross 1978:169). While this may be a valid proposal on the textual surface, the overall structure of the psalm suggests a different, theologically richer, possibility.

2.1 Text typology

An entrance into this investigation of Psalm 73 is provided by the discourse perspective offered in form-criticism, which examines individual psalms in terms of their generic qualities in relation to others having a similar textual organization, religious function, and possible original setting of use (*Sitz im Leben*) (on 'form/genre criticism', see Westermann 1980, Wendland 1994b). In the absence of concrete contextual information (not even a heading other than 'to/for/of Asaph'), it is not possible to say anything substantial about the initial situation of necessity or need that gave rise to Psalm 73, so we focus our attention on the nature of the text itself. What can its general character tell us about the probable purpose for which it was composed and which typifies its use even today?

There is a certain amount of disagreement about the typological classification of Psalm 73. McCann summarizes the position as follows (McCann 1996:986; cf. McCann 1987:247; Tate 1990:231; Goldingay 2007:400):

> Because of the apparently instructional intent, many scholars classify it as a wisdom psalm. But others consider it a song of thanksgiving, a lament/complaint, a song of trust, or a royal psalm.

Indeed, a case could be made for each one of these genre categories on the basis of one or more verses from text itself, e.g., thanksgiving/hymn: v. 28; lament/prayer: vv. 13–14; trust: vv. 23–26; royal: vv. 18–20 (e.g., Allen 1982:113, 118; Ross 1978:168–169). Certainly a composite, didactic-liturgical (cultic) 'psalm' (מִזְמוֹר v. 1) of this nature would be appropriate for its central position in the final arrangement of the Psalter. However, an examination of the text in its totality would suggest a number of reasons for regarding Psalm 73 to be primarily (though not purely) an instance of the *wisdom* macro-genre of didactic poetic literature:

> (a) It conveys a strong impression of being an instructional *theodicy*, that is, a discourse intended to explain, justify, defend, or confess the at times inscrutable ways of God in this world. A *torah*-text of this nature applies in particular to the people of 'the Sovereign LORD' (אֲדֹנָי יְהוִה—v. 28) as they confront life's trials in conflict with the overt hostility, or in contrast to the outstanding prosperity and well-being, of the wicked (along the lines of Job; cf. Bratcher and Reyburn 1991:632; Luyten 1979:73–80). In this regard, we also note the lack of any explicit plea or petition, which would be characteristic of a *lament* psalm (cf. 25b), or an initial word of exaltation or extolation, which is typical of a *thanksgiving* psalm (e.g., Pss. 30, 34).

(b) Following from (a), there is a prominent, text-spanning *antithesis* drawn between the wicked, who in their state of well-being have no thought or care for God (e.g., vv. 3–12), and the righteous who continually seek to serve him (e.g., vv. 1, 13). This contrast extends even up to the point of final divine judgment, when the tables will be turned and just retribution meted out (vv. 27–28).

(c) Several other important *themes* often (but not exclusively) found in the wisdom literature appear also in Psalm 73, e.g., 'jealousy' (קִנֵּא) over the 'peace/prosperity of the 'wicked" (שְׁלוֹם רְשָׁעִים) (v. 3); the 'violence' (חָמָס) of the wicked (v. 6) applied against the righteous (vv. 7–8); the limitation of human knowledge in relation to God's operation and works in the world (vv. 16, 22); and the swift and total ruin that will one day befall evildoers (vv. 18–20) (Luyten 1979:71–73).

(d) There is a comparatively large number of explicit *transitional markers* within the text of this 'great nevertheless' psalm (Bratcher and Reyburn 1991:632), including contrastives (cf. b; e.g., וַאֲנִי 'but I' [2, 22, 28; cf. 14], common in *Qoheleth*) and intensives (e.g., אַךְ 'surely/indeed!' [1, 13, 18, 19], and הִנֵּה 'just look/consider this!' [12, 27]), as well as temporal (e.g., עַד 'until' [17], כִּי 'when' [21]), and logical connectives (e.g., כִּי 'for' [3, 4, 27], לָכֵן 'therefore' [6, 10], אִם 'if' [15]).

(e) There is also an important corpus of key wisdom-related *vocabulary* scattered throughout the text, for example: 'heart' (לֵבָב–1, 13, 21, 26); 'know' and 'knowledge' (יָדַע–11, 16, 22); 'understand' (בִּין–17); 'senseless' (בַּעַר–22); 'counsel' (עֵצָה–24); 'guide' (נחה–24); and 'recount' (ספר–28) (cf. Ross 1978:167–168; Luyten 1979:67).

(f) Several other favorite sapiential stylistic devices appear in Psalm 73, such as micro-chiastic structures (e.g., vv. 1, 3, 5, 8–9, 23–24, and indeed, the psalm as a whole); rare and abstract terms, including feminine plural forms (cf. Luyten 1979:66–67); the 'topicalizing' demonstrative construction, e.g., 'these' (אֵלֶּה, v. 12), 'this' (זֹאת, v. 16); an aphoristic opening (v. 1, like a 'testimony psalm'; Goldingay 2007:401);[2] and passages employed as a thematic summary of the whole prayer, e.g., vv. 12, 27–28.

---

[2] As Goldingay observes: "[I]t begins with its conclusion, with a 'yes' introducing the affirmation the suppliant is now able to make in the light of the process the psalm will recount.... [T]he thing I want to leave with you is just this: the goodness of God" (2007:401).

2.1 Text typology

(g) Perhaps the most significant piece of evidence to support a classification of this psalm in the category of 'wisdom literature' is the obvious intertextual connection with its pristine counterpart at the start of the Psalter. In effect, Psalm 73 could be construed as a practical poetic 'commentary' on Psalm 1—a lyric but experience-tempered *midrash* on the validity of faith in Yahweh that relates the clear-cut, idealized precepts of the *torah*-way to the uncertainties and exigencies of real life and more active opposition from the ungodly. Some thus view it as being an experience-tempered commentary on the idealistic precepts set forth in Psalm 1 (Gitay 1996:237; Brueggemann and Miller 1996:46–47), and Psalm 2 as well (cf. Goldingay 2007:418–419).

One cannot claim that any one or two of the preceding features in isolation is enough to justify the classification of Psalm 73 unambiguously as a wisdom psalm. But taken together, they do represent a significant body of evidence for making such a generic conclusion. But what is it that the psalmist wants to teach and why did he adopt this particular form of poetic expression? This question will be the focus of our attention in section 2.3, where the theological content of this lyric composition is more fully explored.

Its didactic character notwithstanding, Psalm 73 must still be classified among the familiar exponents of religious 'prayer' (תְּפִלָּה, e.g., 17:1; contra Whybray 1996:65) and 'praise' (תְּהִלָּה, e.g., 145:1) in the Hebrew Scriptures, as the affinity of its verses to many others in the Psalter would indicate, especially verses 23–26. What better way (than lament) to express the serious, soul-threatening feelings that the psalmist had experienced (vv. 2–14, 21–22)—or to laud (via thanksgiving) the spiritual 'repose/well-being' (שָׁלוֹם, v. 3) that he was now enjoying in the virtual presence of God (vv. 23, 28)? Furthermore, although the psalmist speaks only in the first person throughout, it is clear that he views himself as part of a large worshipping *community* of faith, not merely as an isolated member of God's faithful family (i.e., 'children', v. 15). Thus his words are uttered as a personal representative of a closely-knit fellowship and as a follower of the sacred liturgical tradition of David, Israel's ideal king and 'torah keeper' (Brueggemann and Miller 1996:48). His particular 'recounting of all the deeds of *YHWH*' (v. 28) may therefore be appropriated by the group as a whole and applied to their common religious experience.[3] This joint perspective is suggested once more by the placement of Psalm 73 in the Psalter, for it heads a 'book' collection (III) that is dominated by such texts of communal expression (e.g., Pss. 74–76). This

---

[3] I do not see the need for classifying Psalm 73 as *either* communal *or* individual in nature since it could well serve in both settings. An argument for the former is found in Allen 1982:116–118; for the latter in Ross 1978:163.

point of composition brings us to the second type of background information that helps one to lay an adequate foundation for correctly understanding and interpreting the pivotal nature of Psalm 73, namely, the canonical collocation of this artful literary and liturgical 'sanctuary'.

2.2 Intertextuality

A relatively new way of looking at specific psalms is with respect to key counterparts to which they may be related intertextually in terms of form, content, structure, and function within the Psalter as a whole in its final redaction. This 'canon (composition) critical' approach appears to be increasing in importance among scholars and cannot be ignored in any analysis of a given individual psalm that aspires to present a fuller treatment of the subject (cf. Wilson 1985; Childs 1979; Brueggeman 1991:63–64; and especially McCann 1993). Most biblical scholars have come to the reasonable conclusion that the Book of Psalms is not a haphazard or random collection of prayer-song texts, even outside the bounds of its obvious internal 'books' (i.e., I: 1–41, II: 42–72, III: 73–89, IV: 90–106, V: 107–150) and other major sectional groupings (e.g., 'Davidic' 51–72, 'Korahite' 42–49, 'Asaphite' 73–83, 'Elohistic' 42–83, 'Pilgrimage' 120–134). Not only are adjacent psalms often closely related to one another either in form (e.g., 42–43), content (e.g., 111–112), and/or function (e.g., 1–2), but the entire Psalter gives evidence of an even larger, more comprehensive architectural design, one that incorporates and provides an overarching framework as well as a point of reference and interpretation for the others. This theologically-oriented macrostructure cannot be discussed in detail here (for an overview, see the essays in McCann, ed., 1993), but the following observations will suggest how Psalm 73 fits into the flow of the whole.

Upon reading the first verse, it seems as if Psalm 73 will carry on with the optimistic note that Book II ends with, from both an individual and also a communal perspective (cf. 71:19–24, 72:18–19). Subsequent verses quickly dispel this notion, however, but the connection with Books I and II remains as we appear to be entering another of the laments which predominate in these sections, especially one of those that calls Yahweh's covenant loyalty into question by complaining about the overt prosperity of the psalmist's enemies and their persecution of the righteous (e.g., 10, 17, 28, 37, 55, 56, 64, 69, 71). There is a particularly strong thematic and functional (i.e., didactic) linkage between 73 and Psalms 37 and 49, except that the latter are more optimistic in tone overall and view the situation of evildoers from a controlling divine perspective right from the

2.2 Intertextuality

beginning of the discourse. The dramatic *contrast* between verses 1 and 2 (i.e., shifting from a positive, communal vista to an introverted, individual viewpoint) calls attention to a major new beginning and a predominant focus upon the 'wicked' (רְשָׁעִים), v. 3. For an experienced Psalms reader/hearer this mention is likely to ring a bell of recollection, namely, back to the onset of the Psalter and the clear-cut wisdom poem found there. This association is reinforced by the antithetical ending that concludes both psalms (made concrete in the verb 'perish' אבד). A partial thematic correspondence continues in Psalm 2, which has long been regarded as being a deliberate companion piece to Psalm 1 in serving to set the general keynote of the entire Psalter. Here then we have a strong religious-liturgical poetic tradition that is firmly founded upon the covenantal *torah* ('instruction') of the King Yahweh יהוה אֲדֹנָי (Ps. 1, his 'knowledge'—73:11, 16–17), which proclaims his just judgment and victorious rule on behalf of his people (Ps. 2, cf. 73:18–20, 27).[4]

Several recent commentators have proposed that there is an even larger pattern of structural organization evident within the book of Psalms—an underlying intertextual bridge that extends from one end to the other—with the key points of support being found at the beginning, middle, and conclusion, namely, Psalms 1–2, 73, and 150:

> Psalm 73 is a sort of summary of what the reader of the Psalter would have learned after beginning with Psalms 1 and 2 and moving through the prayers of Psalms 3–72; that is, happiness or goodness has to do not with material prosperity and success but rather with the assurance of God's presence... (McCann 1993:143)

> ...Psalm 73 is pivotal. The psalm begins a new phase of the book of Psalms. It does so by reiterating the theological assumption of Psalm 1....[vv. 2–13], however, immediately issues a protest against that confident affirmation...[vv. 23–26] stand in sharp contrast to verses 2–14. They are a decisive response to the misgivings voiced in the laments and complaints [i.e., which predominate in Pss. 1–72]...Verses 23–26 move toward the trustful affirmation voiced in Israel's hymns and songs of thanksgiving [i.e., which predominate in the Psalter's second half].(Brueggeman 1995:206, 209)

> Ps. 73:1 sounds like an echo of Psalm 1. Thus the second half of the Psalter...begins as does the first half, with an affirmation of God's faithfulness to the obedient....Thus the two genres of lament and

---

[4] A key positional match occurs in the term 'refuge' (מַחְסֶה) which is found at the end of each psalm, 2:12 and 73:28. "Psalm 73 thus draws together the two 'conclusions' of the introductory Psalms 1 and 2: the perishing of the wicked and the good and blessing that come to those who take refuge in the Lord" (Brueggemann and Miller 1996:53; cf. Goldingay 2007:418–419).

> complaint, and praise and thanks are essential voices in the move from Psalm 1 through Psalms 72–73 to Psalm 150....In terms of the dramatic function of the whole, we are permitted to see the Psalms as a dramatic struggle from obedience (Psalm 1) through dismay (Psalm 73 after 72) to praise (Psalm 150). (Brueggeman 1993:40–41)

This holistic and integrative conception of the Psalter is a helpful way of viewing both its overall canon-compositional arrangement and its theological development. Indeed, the centrally placed Psalm 73 in and of itself presents "a powerful paradigm for Israel's often-enacted journey from obedience [Ps. 1] through trouble to praise [Ps. 150]" and a lyric-liturgical drama-in-miniature of "the crisis and resolution of God's *chesed*" as it is worked out in relation to his people (Brueggemann 1991:79–81).

The pivotal nature of Psalm 73 is also highlighted by additional links that it manifests with the onset as well as the close of Book II and more specifically with the subsequent psalms of Book III. In this regard it may be noted that Books II and III conclude with distinctly 'royal' (kingship) psalms, the former (72—Solomon) strongly optimistic in tone, the latter (89—David) being correspondingly pessimistic in outlook (cf. McCann 1993:660). The thematic relationship between Psalms 72, 73, and 89 may be summarized as follows (Brueggemann and Miller 1996:50, 52):

> ...Ps. 73.1 'begins the Psalter again'. Psalm 72, the final Psalm of Book II, is 'for Solomon'. This Psalm is constructed to place together royal attentiveness to 'justice and righteousness'....Psalm 89 reflects a judgment, if we are to accept the premise of 73.1 [sic, = 73.28], in which the king did not 'stay near' God and so experienced the disastrous consequence of God's departed ḥesed.

As far as their respective beginnings are concerned, we find that in each case the two Books lead off with individual laments (Pss. 42–43, 73) which are followed by topically very similar communal cries of a people who feel unjustly abandoned by their God (Pss. 44, 74). The connections between Psalms 73 and 74 are particularly striking, e.g., in the parallel terms 'violence' (73:6/74:20), 'sanctuary/-ies' (73:17/74:7), 'ruins/deceptions' (73:18/74:3), and 'right hand' (73:23/74:11) (McCann 1993:96). Then within Book III as a whole, there is evidence of an alternating psalmic pattern that reveals a greater measure of hope for the future of Zion, an optimism that is based on the everlasting covenantal attributes of Yahweh—his mercy, faithfulness, and righteousness (Ps. 89:1–37). This bright vision is dimmed, however, by the great disillusionment that resulted from an honest evaluation of Israel's current socio-economic and political situation along with that of her king (or in post-exilic times, the lack of one), a position so eloquently expressed at the very close of this corpus (Ps. 89:38–51). The Asaphite collection (Pss. 73–83) in particular deals generally with the LORD's mighty deeds of deliverance performed during the history of his chosen people, a fact which is either applauded or appealed to in the nation's present adverse circumstances (cf. Ps. 50:15). The lone Asaphite psalm of Book II (50) anticipates the larger group of Book III by calling the people to account for their failure to keep their part of the covenantal obligations that bound them to Yahweh, their saving God (cf. vv. 4–7, 16ff., 23). Within the perceptible 'ascending' (lament → praise) development of the Psalter, this set of psalms is later replied to in a mighty affirmation of his divine kingship in the so-called 'enthronement psalms' of Book IV (Pss. 93, 95–99, with 94 being a lingering reminder of the Asaphite group).

As the preceding short survey would suggest, the Psalter is without doubt a deliberately and carefully shaped corpus of religious-cultic prayer, poetry, and song, which displays a functionally motivated design intended to foreground its primary religious motifs and edificational purposes. Psalm 73 plays a pivotal role in the overall pattern. Such a conclusion pertaining to the body as a whole is clearly supported by a consideration of the tightly knit thematic interrelationships that bind together its various parts, in particular, a corpus of crucially placed (i.e., with respect to the psalm's overall discourse structure) and semantically vital theological terms. These formally familiar, but situationally reinterpreted expressions serve both to distinguish and to internally demarcate the implicitly didactic text of this highly significant, centrally positioned, instructional psalm.

2.3 Theological message

Our survey of the generic form and intertextual features of Psalm 73 has brought us into initial contact also with some of the main elements of its principal religious content. This allows us to embark more confidently upon an overview of the psalm's central theological significance, both as an instance of emotively intense personal prayer and also as a communal expression of the trust and hope of God's people as a whole as it has been articulated throughout the ages (read 'Israel' for 'I' in v. 26; cf. v. 1) and throughout the Psalter. This semantic survey will prepare the way for an exploration of certain key aspects of the pragmatic (functional) organization of Psalm 73 as communicated in its original biblical setting and also in terms of the lives of the present-day 'pure-hearted' 'children' of the LORD.

The recognized generic complexity of Psalm 73 (cf. section 2.1) would tend to lead analysts to a similar conclusion regarding its distinctive message and purpose. In his study of this psalm, McCann calls it "a microcosm of OT theology." In his opinion, this is because "it represents attempts both to legitimate structure and to embrace pain".[5] Granted the possible presence of such an abstract conception of the inner tension that dominates Psalm 73, one nevertheless finds this viewpoint rather too narrow in itself to qualify the work as a theological 'microcosm'. There must be something more. What is 'more' in this case may be summarized with respect to a quartet of primary concepts—destiny, sanctuary, purity, and proximity—which together set the prevailing tone for the wise poet-psalmist's instruction concerning some of the salient notions of basic *torah* theology.

2.3.1 Destiny

A fuller dimension of overall compositional meaning in Psalm 73 is revealed by a simple surface reading of the text in the light of the complete Psalter. One discovers the semantic scope of this poem to be quite inclusive as it touches upon themes that range across the broad spectrum of familiar Hebrew theological and didactic polarities: goodness and evil, justice and injustice, humility and arrogance, deeds and words, prosperity and poverty, understanding and ignorance, health and sickness, blessing and punishment, life and death, soul and body, God in relation to man, and the divine immanence versus his transcendence. But the harmonizing perspective that seems to bring all these diverse topics and treatments into a unified whole is that embodied in a term which, despite its occurrence in the thematically and structurally crucial verse 17, often gets overlooked in all the scholarly discussion and debate—namely, 'their end/destiny' אַחֲרִיתָם; (on this complex poetic term, see Tate 1990:229). So what sort of fate or future is the psalmist talking about and to whom is he ascribing it? What does 'the sanctuary of God' have to do with this? And how does this relate to God's 'goodness' and the 'heart-purity' of his people on the one hand, as opposed to 'the prosperity of the wicked' on the other (vv. 1, 3)?

---

[5] McCann 1987:253. To explain: "On the one hand, the psalmist legitimates structure by professing his loyalty to the community and its institutions and by upholding the traditional definition of purity of heart....At the same time, however, the psalmist's experience impels him toward the embrace of pain....Thus the psalmist rejects the traditional understanding of the consequences of maintaining purity of heart; that is, he challenges any 'common theology' which would suggest that suffering is a sign of punishment or separation from God" (ibid., 252–253).

2.3 Theological message

To begin with, the expression '*their* destiny' (v. 17) evokes an immediate, though implicit, contrast to '*our* destiny', namely, that which will be experienced by the people of God—'*those* who are pure in heart' (v. 1) and are called his 'children' (v. 15). Thus while the overt perspective of Psalm 73 is clearly autobiographical, its important communal dimension is unmistakably implied. A further vital connection with the psalm's beginning is forged by the hermeneutical key that v. 17 provides as a framework for understanding the initially all-embracing—and, as in Psalm 1, rather overly optimistic or contra-experiential—proposition which asserts that God is 'good to Israel/the upright'. How does this assumption jibe with the tough and trying sort of lives that most believers lead? The answer, as this sage and sensible poet appears to be putting it, lies in 'the afterwards' (אַחֲרִית), not in the earthly present as most religious folks, then and now, seem to expect or anticipate—often on the basis of an overly pragmatic, worldwide *do ut des* religious philosophy.[6] Indeed, a longing for the latter is sure to disappoint not a few of God's faithful, as the psalmist himself laments when he compares his present hostile environment and seemingly unjust circumstances to those that he sees the 'wicked' enjoy (vv. 2–12 [Part I of the discourse]; cf. also the structurally interlocking flashbacks or anaphoric references found in vv. 15–16 [within the Transition of vv. 13–17] and 21–22 [in Part II, vv. 18–28]).

But is it a legitimate hermeneutical procedure to apply the semantic reference inherent in 'their (our) destiny' past the bounds of human earthly existence, that is, beyond the grave? In other words, does this expression, when coupled with the enthusiastic claims of later verses such as 24 and 26, represent a genuine "breakthrough in understanding" since "as is well known, the Old Testament has no clearly developed conception of life after death except as a shadowy existence in Scheol, the common home of all" (Rice 1984:84)?[7] All *a priori* assumptions regarding Old Testament the-

---

[6] The traditional 'truth' that God more or less 'gives to the giver' in return for his/her acts of piety and devotion, and its correlate that God will sooner or later punish the wicked or impious, is an overt or covert expectation in all of the world religions that I have encountered. This includes the system of African indigenous beliefs, cf. the Chewa proverbs, *kupatsa ndi kuika* 'to give [to someone else, including God] is to lay up in store [i.e., for the day when the former recipient will pay you back]', and *choipa chitsata mwini* 'evil follows its owner [i.e., doer]'.

[7] Among the eminent commentators who conclude that Ps. 73 has absolutely no reference or allusion to life after physical death are Snaith (1950:89n) as well as Gunkel and Schmidt, who resort to emendation to eliminate any notion of the life beyond (James 1965:210). A number of scholars prefer to hedge on this issue, e.g., Westermann: "All that is said is that the psalmist's fellowship with God cannot be destroyed even by death. Such certainty does not need any particular concept of a life beyond" (1989:142). But would such an abstract explanation have satisfied the concrete Hebrew thinker and devotee of *YHWH*?

ology aside, a straightforward reading of this psalm in its entirety would lead one to answer the preceding questions in the affirmative. Although it cannot be claimed that this particular hybrid wisdom poem in and of itself teaches a *bodily* resurrection, it is clear that as far as the psalmist himself is concerned, death did not end one's existence or the possibility at least of some form of intimate fellowship with God. Indeed, he does more than "push the boundaries of the usual Israelite conception of life and death" (McCann 1996:970; cf. the *midrash* on Psalms – Goldingay 2007:414); instead, these boundaries are definitely traversed and the immortality of a believer's soul is assumed (cf. also Pss. 16:9-11; 49:15; 71:20). This is shown not only by the explicit wording of the text (if accepted on its face value), but also by the structural patterning that is displayed by Part II of the psalm (strophes = vv. 18-20, 21-22, 23-26, 27-28). Thus the notion of a divinely guided and concluded destiny is poetically, but also patently, supported in the psalm's thematic peak of vv. 23-26, for example:

(a) by the double emphasis that is placed upon the related concepts of personal inseparability (the reiterated 'with you' עִמָּךְ —vv. 23, 25; cf. 28) and temporal continuity ('always' תָּמִיד —v. 23 + 'forever' לְעוֹלָם —v. 26);

(b) by the lexical linkage that is established between 'their afterward' (אַחֲרִיתָם) and 'after' (אַחַר) in vv. 17 and 24 respectively, the latter incorporating the important theological term 'glory' (כָּבוֹד), here with obvious reference to some significant manner of prolonged divine communion with the godly (for a narrative dramatization of the connection between the LORD's 'glory' and being in his 'presence', see Exod. 33:12-23);

(c) by the verb 'take/receive' (לקח, v. 24) which is used also in the accounts of the assumption to heaven/God of Enoch and Elijah (Gen. 5:24; 2 Kgs. 2:1, 3, 5, 9-10), as well as in the topically and functionally similar parallel passage of Psalm 49:15—a strong intertextual allusion that would not be lost on the pious singers and hearers of this psalm;[8]

(d) by the complete spatial, and in this context perhaps also temporal, contrast between being 'in heaven' and 'on earth' (v. 25);

---

[8] Rowley observes "that if 23ff. refer only to this life, then the poet has an odd way of expressing it, for he speaks of God receiving him, rather than giving him some material blessing. He first declares he enjoys fellowship with God now, and then he says God will receive him; so it must be of future fellowship that he speaks" (Smith 1974:182, paraphrasing Rowley 1956:173).

2.3 Theological message

(e) by two familiar poetic metaphors that depict the notion of divinely established 'permanence', namely, 'rock' (צוּר) and 'heritage' (חֵלֶק) (v. 26);

(f) by a complementary, non-material—perhaps even mystical ('spiritual')—interpretation of the crucial preceding predication in v. 17: 'until I entered into the [very] sanctuary of God' (עַד־אָבוֹא אֶל־מִקְדְּשֵׁי־אֵל), which constitutes the effectual means whereby the resultant revelatory insight regarding the bipolar 'destiny' of humanity is realized; and

g) stylistically, perhaps, by "the longest line in the psalm thus far" (i.e., v. 26; Goldingay 2007:415) that appears to voice the psalmist's trust in God beyond life—'forever' (לְעוֹלָם).

2.3.2 Sanctuary

Given such an eschatological perspective of the 'destiny' of the psalmist (and those in his fellowship), how then is one to construe the subsequent, obviously important, but somewhat enigmatic foundational expression: '**into** the sanctuaries of God' (אֶל־מִקְדְּשֵׁי־אֵל—note the wordplay plus a plural of amplification, v. 17)? Is this a reference to God's visible 'house' of sacrifice and worship? Indeed, such a construal cannot be excluded (cf. Bratcher and Reyburn 1991:640; McCann 1996:969; van Gemeren 1991:480), but the denotation of the unusual plural form here, particularly in conjunction with 'destiny', need not be limited to some specific physical location on earth. Whether or not the psalm is post-exilic in date of origin, there was plenty of reason to doubt the current popular, almost superstitious and magical notion of the Jerusalem Temple (and site) along with its associated hyper-religious and ritualized cultus (v. 13)—its aura of 'numinous efficacy'—even in the pre-exilic age, especially any time after the division of the Davidic Kingdom. It is the prophetic, perhaps iconoclastic, conclusion of our psalmist that YHWH cannot be confined to some temple made with human hands (see 1 Kgs. 8:27; Isa. 66:1–2; Jer. 7:2–15; Mic. 3:11; cf. Acts 7:48–50; 17:24). Neither can he be genuinely communed with by means of mere external reverential activities (v. 13). Rather, such spiritually regenerative, reformational, or restorative contact takes place anywhere, whether in heaven or on earth (v. 25). It occurs whenever the penitent believer (vv. 21–22), the person who is 'pure in heart' and life (vv. 1, 13), recognizes the corporate nature of his/her faith (v. 15) and comes into reverent, prayerful fellowship with his-her/their God (vv. 15–17).⁹ That is when God is near and functions as one's ever-present 'refuge' (מַחְסֶה)—or 'rock' (צוּר) and everlasting 'inheritance' (חֵלֶק, vv. 28, 26).

This divine, transformative event may be intratextually likened to that of waking up from a bad dream (vv. 20, 21–22).¹⁰ It makes it possible for the perceptive participant to look at life in a new way (v. 17), in particular, to gain a true perspective on one's 'destiny' and how this affects the here and now with regard to one's central value system (the psalmist's former, self-centered point of view is expressed in vv. 3–14, 21–22). It enables every one—and all of 'God's children' (v. 15)—both to persevere in and at the same time also to transcend their current unfavorable, even inimical, external circumstances, when the very goodness of God may be questioned (vv. 11, 13, 21).¹¹ The dialectic framework proposed by Walter Brueggemann (1980) is helpful here: The psalmist's initial setting of psychological *orientation* in a comfortable conventional religiosity (v. 1) was shaken into one of theological *disorientation* due to an attack of personal pride (vv. 3–12), self-pity (v. 13), and some form of hard faith-testing (v. 14). After a period of honest soul-searching in the presence of God, however, a stroke of divine intervention (i.e., a *deliverance* [an element not included by Brueggemann]) led him to an entirely new assessment of his situation—a *reorientation*, one that was considerably more consecrated in nature, theological in focus, and communal in outlook (vv. 15–17). From then on, his whole point of view was changed, and as a result of this basic paradigm shift, he was reoriented in his relationship to the wicked (vv. 18–20, 27), to himself (vv. 21–22), and to his saving, Sovereign LORD (vv. 23–26, 28).

---

⁹ Westermann comments on this 'sanctuary experience' (Tate 1990:238): "...the pilgrimage to the sanctuary is to be understood as a turning to God...of a sufferer [we might add, also a sinner] who implores God to turn back to him" (1989:139). The fact that this is a 'wisdom' psalm and related to those of the *torah* sub-group would lend support to the interpretation that 'sanctuaries' may also be a figurative reference to the 'Law of the LORD'—the source of all true 'understanding' (v. 16), 'discernment' (v. 17), and 'counsel' (v. 24; cf. Pss. 33:11; 48:9–14). If so, then yet another thematic and canonical linkage with Ps. 1 is established (Ps. 1:1–2).

¹⁰ It is possible that that poet here modifies the conventional psalmic notion of God's 'waking' or 'arising' from sleep to act on behalf of his persecuted people to include a reference to his own revelational experience, a movement from a 'dreamy' ignorance about the LORD's providence and purpose to a clear-eyed 'perception' of what life and the future are really all about (v. 17).

¹¹ The theodicean argument underlying Ps. 73 complements the established wisdom precept of Ps. 1 which pronounces ultimate blessing for the righteous and condemnation for the ungodly (cf. Gitay 1996:232).

2.3 Theological message

As a poetic spokesman for 'Israel' (v. 1), the psalmist suggests that this is a sanctifying process that must be undergone by everyone who sincerely wishes to be 'near God' in a spiritual sense (v. 28). The distinct novelty of the term 'sanctuaries' (מִקְדְּשֵׁי) suggests this deeper level of meaning, a hermeneutical intimation which is subtly reinforced by the psalm's overall discourse organization, for example, in the pointed reversals that appear in Part II to contrast with those of Part I, such as: who is situated on 'slippery ground'—vv. 18–20/2–3; who enjoys 'peace/prosperity'—vv. 23–26/4–5; the attitude of one's 'heart'—vv. 21–22/6–7; the quality of one's 'speech'—vv. 15, 28/8–9; and the nature of one's relationship to 'the Sovereign LORD'—vv. 27–28/10–12. Thus by engaging in the religious dialogue and rhetorical dynamics of Psalm 73, a believer also enters "the sphere of God's holiness, the holy mysteries of God" (Buber 1983:113)—truly a life-changing, life-sustaining experience![12]

2.3.3 Purity of heart in proximity to God

Although a consideration of these two interrelated concepts, 'purity' and 'heart', has been anticipated in the preceding discussion, they are of such importance to a proper understanding of Psalm 73 in terms of both form and function that it would be well to examine the pair again in specific relation to one another. "[I]n Ps. 73 'the heart determines'" (Goldingay 2007:418, citing Buber 1983). The occurrence of the phrase 'pure [ones] of heart' (לְבָרֵי לֵבָב) in the generalized thematic maxim of 73.1 immediately suggests its significance to the psalmist's overall message. The expression refers to a person's internal heart attitude in relation to YHWH, as distinct from his (her) external behavior, which will necessarily reflect or reproduce that quality of purity or holiness with respect to both speech and action. This resultant behavioral component is suggested by the possible reading 'upright' (יָשָׁר) in line A of the bicolon as well as by intertextual resonance, as already noted, with Psalm 1 (v. 1 = outer, v. 2 = inner manifestation), but also with the important parallel passage of Psalm 24:4, where a 'pure heart' is coupled with 'clean hands', an image which is reproduced in Psalm 73:13. The problem initially facing the psalmist was that his concept of purity and its expected consequences for his life did not seem to coincide with God's agenda. Why did those who were impure and unrighteous in thought, word, and deed appear to enjoy

---

[12] Thus translators and commentators who demote or degrade *miqdeshe* to refer to something like 'sanctuaries of the gods' *(New Jerusalem Bible)*, i.e., the 'ruins of pagan sanctuaries' (NJB footnote), probably do not realize what they are missing (cf. the unrealistic, convoluted argument for such an interpretation in Birkeland 1955:100ff.).

total 'peace' (שָׁלוֹם) in all of its worldly aspects (v. 3) while those who 'kept [themselves] clean/pure' (Piel זכה, v. 13) were continually 'stricken' and 'chastised' (v. 14)?

The psalmist's predicament is contrastively summarized in terms of 'heart' language by means of the hyperbolic imagery of verse 7 (whatever this difficult verse means; cf. Bratcher and Reyburn 1991:635–636, Tate 1990:228, van Gemeren 1991:478) and the bitter flashback of verse 21 (note his 'sour heart'!). Thus it is not surprising that he—along with many other 'jealous' saints (cf. v. 3)—nearly comes to a faith-frustrated conclusion as a result of his inward focused assessment of the situation: "Surely in vain I have kept my heart pure!" (v. 13, at the onset of the transitional and transforming 'sanctuary' episode in his life, vv. 13–18). From this pit of spiritual pessimism the psalmist is suddenly, almost miraculously (considering his position in vv. 13–14), resurrected, as it were, in 'God's sanctuary' to look at life anew. His divinely inspired vision of the present and future begins with a 'clear perception' (בִּין) of the ultimate fate of 'the wicked' (רְשָׁעִים, vv. 17–20, the pronominal referent for 'their' being implied from vv. 3 and 12). But the climax of his confession of complete confidence certainly comes in verse 26 where the poet reports that his 'human' (characterized by 'flesh', שְׁאֵר) 'heart' has been changed into a 'heart' (a double occurrence of לֵבָב) which now, and 'forever' (לְעוֹלָם), manifests the very 'strength' (lit 'rock', צוּר) of God.

But what was it that the psalmist now perceived that he did not know in his former 'senseless' (בַּעַר), 'beastly' (בְּהֵמוֹת) state of mind (v. 22)? It was simply, but most significantly, the unfailing attendance of God, who was indeed there at all times to 'guide' (נחה) him with the wise 'counsel' (עֵצָה) of his written word (i.e., the *torah*—v .24, the latter being intimated also by the close intertextual parallels of Pss. 16:7–8, 32:8, and 48:14). It is important to observe how the poet has stylistically provided his hearers with a verbal image of his theological point here. The contrastive double occurrence of 'heart' (v. 26) is surrounded, as it were, by various pointed references to the vital divine immanence: three instances of 'with you' (עִמָּךְ) coupled with 'you [will] take me' (תִּקָּחֵנִי) in the preceding verses, and afterwards, the antithetical notion 'those far from you' (רְחֵקֶיךָ, v. 27) followed by the central thematic phrase 'nearness of God to me' in v. 26. All in all, Psalm 73 gives us an impressive example of rhetorical form (primarily lexical recursion plus discourse placement) utilized in the service of theological content. By the time we have reached the end of the carefully mapped literary journey that extends from v. 1 to v. 28, we have not only come to understand, but we have also empathetically experienced a conversion of the 'heart' and an 'entrance' into the 'holy environs/ = proximate presence' of 'the LORD Almighty' (אֲדֹנָי יְהוִה, v. 28).

McCann makes the following pertinent observation with regard to the thematic progression of Psalm 73:

> [O]ne can conclude that purity of heart was traditionally defined as the proper ritual observance and ethical behavior that the psalmist has maintained.... By the end of the psalm, however, he has forged a new understanding of the consequences of maintaining purity of heart.... [he] rejects the traditional notion of maintaining purity of heart (vv. 1, 28 as opposed to vv. 4–12), suggesting that the 'pure in heart' or 'Israel' are those who continue to obey, serve, and praise God even while stricken and troubled. (1987:250–252)

The preceding close reading of the psalm would lead one to qualify the preceding statement somewhat: The psalmist was not rejecting ritual observance and ethical behavior per se, nor was he automatically equating the quality of being pure in heart with serving God in the midst of suffering. Rather, he appears to be teaching us that purity of heart involves a dynamic inner relationship with the covenant LORD, one of intimate proximity based upon an implicit trust in God's power to preserve and protect his child both in this life and beyond the grave. This is where genuine, saving faith begins, and it may be subsequently manifested either by remaining faithful in times of trouble or by performing deeds of devoted ritual observance and thankful worship in accordance with the traditional norms of religiosity. In other words, the psalmist was by no means condemning the precepts of the *torah* regarding the worship of Yahweh; instead, he puts all such rites in their proper, secondary place as far as defining true religion goes. Worship practices, when rightly conceived and conducted, can serve to enhance one's perception of the divine presence, but they can never establish such fellowship nor duplicate its essential spiritual 'goodness'.

2.4 Text function

Can a prayer, whether a lament, petition, thanksgiving, or hymn, also have a rhetorical, or persuasive, purpose? Believers brought up in a Western tradition of worship do not normally think of prayers as functioning in this capacity, for the principal aim, they feel, is not to try to persuade God about anything, but simply to inform him of their needs and problems, or to praise him for his many blessings. Thus prayer is not a dialogue, but basically a monologue, with the thoughts and words flowing only in one direction—heavenwards. But such a perspective is rather too passive if the biblical teachings and accounts concerning the power of petitionary prayer are to be taken seriously. We cannot develop this point here but can merely suggest that the Scriptures appear to present us with a much more *dynamic*, interactive notion of the nature and intention of prayer. In the first place, this spiritual speech activity is viewed as being more of a *dialogue*—as a conversation having both a 'virtual' partner (i.e., always present if not overtly represented in the text) and also a potentially 'vocal' one. This is certainly the case with regard to the various prayer-discourses that comprise the Psalter. The very fact that God is periodically cited or designated as actually speaking during the psalmist's act of praying would support this assumption (e.g., Pss. 2:5–6; 50:5, 7–15, 16ff. [another Asaphite composition]; 60:6–8; 68:22–23; 75:2–5; 81:6–16; 82:2–7).[13]

If petitionary prayer then is viewed as involving a dialogue with the Deity, it must necessarily include *persuasion* as one of its basic goals. The pray-er argues, as it were, his case before Yahweh and believes that if his words are effective and in keeping with the LORD's will and plan (e.g., Ps. 81:13–14), his heartfelt appeal will most certainly be granted (Ps. 34:6, 15, 17; cf. Matt. 21:22; Rom. 8:26–27; 2 Cor. 1:11; Jas. 5:16; 1 Pet. 3:12). The persuasive forcefulness of biblical supplication is manifested on two distinct levels of discourse, internal and external. The *internal* dimension is developed with variable intensity and emotion as the prayer proceeds, and the central petition—which in the case of Psalm 73 is replaced with a debate concerning the nature of God's goodness—is rhetorically introduced, presented, supported, and concluded (cf. Abraham's intercessory plea on behalf of Sodom, Gen. 19; the lament psalms, e.g., 27, 38–39, 44, 80). The *external*, more implicit, aspect of persuasive prayer becomes evident when one considers its intended effect(s) upon those who may be either hearing it spoken (recited/sung) on their behalf, or those who read such an entreaty meditatively or devotionally for themselves. That the psalm-prayers were composed with this eventuality and secondary purpose in mind is indicated by passages such as Pss. 22:22–23, 25; 33:1–3; 66:3–4, and the many other types of 'call to worship' that are found in the Psalter.

Psalm 73 closes with an emphatic reference to this confessional function of praying to the Sovereign LORD for the added benefit of all who may be listening, whether the holy congregation of God's children (v. 15), or the surrounding masses of their enemies (v. 10): "(I will be someone who is continually) telling (about) all your (wonderful) works!" (v. 23c). Indeed, such a public testimony may be effected by the very words of this psalm, which on the whole puts great emphasis upon the power of speech, both bad and good. This criterion concerning the quality of spoken discourse further supports our division of the text into two principal portions. The

---

[13] In his survey of the strategy of 'dialogic discourse' in the Psalter, Levine notes that "...quoting another's word...is one of the stylistic hallmarks of the biblical Psalms" (1990:268).

2.4 Text function

boastful 'mouth' metaphors of verses 8–9, impious threats of the wicked (v. 11), and frustrated exclamation of the psalmist himself (vv. 13–14) in Part I are effectively countered in Part II by the psalmist's inner speech of penitent self-recognition at the text's turning point (v. 15), his climactic profession of faith (vv. 23–26), and by his concluding vow of conviction, namely, to fill his mouth with praise for the LORD (v. 23).

An analysis of the major speech acts of Psalm 73 reveals that these too are closely related to the generic nature of this text as an instance of didactic wisdom literature. The textual surface abounds in speech acts of the *evaluative* variety, which function to assess or judge the quality of another person's behavior (here, paradoxically, that of God as well as the godless) in terms of just—unjust, good—bad, right—wrong, beneficial—harmful, etc. In poetry of course this is not done overtly through verbs that express opinionated illocutions such as: approve, estimate, deem, criticize, rate, consider, conclude, etc. Rather, the preferred mode is that of indirection as exemplified in the use of life-related, including figurative, description, as we see for example in vv. 4–12 and 18–22. *Expressive* acts, which verbalize the feelings or attitudes of the speaker, and *representatives*, which provide information or set forth some state of affairs, are also evident, e.g., vv. 13–14 for the former, and vv. 1, 27 for the latter. Naturally, there is a great deal of mixing and overlapping in the use of such categories, for example, in v. 26 where certain aspects of evaluation, expression, and representation may all be identified. But an analysis in terms of this sort of pragmatic framework gives us at least a rough idea of the operation of the biblical text as verbal *action* having diverse communicative intentions, that is, as distinct from being regarded simply as a vehicle for conveying pure theological or religious content. Selected distinctive speech acts are also made to stand out more clearly in relation to the rest, such as the text final instance of a *declarative* act (v. 28c), in which the speaker firmly commits him/herself to some future course of action, e.g., to promise, vow, pledge, agree, guarantee, assure.

The primarily evaluative nature of this psalm's textual surface, however, masks a deeper, more fundamental purpose with regard to its overall 'text act', that is, the predominant, overarching illocutionary force of the psalm's complete inventory of speech instances (Hatim and Mason 1990:78). Here is where the didactic quality of the discourse is manifested, as characterized by the speech-text act of *direction*, which seeks to influence (change, modify, reinforce, curtail) the behavior (thoughts, words, actions) of the text's addressees, e.g., via verbs that convey illocutions such as: instruct, order, request, dare, appeal, pray, etc. Thus a wisdom psalm's typical depiction of the contrasting characters and fates of the righteous as opposed to the wicked is not presented merely as a point of information or comment. Instead, the strong antithesis is meant to function more fundamentally to communicate an implicit rebuke coupled with warning, that is, either to cease or avoid such behavior, as well as an exhortation to the faithful to remain fully committed to the covenantally established ways of Lord Yahweh as expressed in his revealed *torah*.[14]

This ethical implication, one which is set forth so clearly in the blessings and indirect curses of Psalm 1, is just as strongly reiterated here in Psalm 73, though in the form of an argument 'contextualized' by the psalmist's life, in which varied opposition to the divine plan—its reality, relevance, and rightness (vv. 2–14)—is expressed from both within and without the fellowship, that is, by the psalmist and his (as well as God's) opponents. By vicariously 'working through' the representative debate of the text along with its underlying principles of direction and instruction, all those who read or hear it are themselves encouraged to 'enter the (divine) sanctuary' in order to receive enlightenment (v. 17), critical reproof (vv. 21–22), support (v. 23), guidance (v. 24), and hope for the future (v. 25–26), despite all earthly troubles and trials that may persist in the present (vv. 2–14). We thus hear the former disheartened reflections of a bitter believer being completely reformed by the power of a divinely motivated argument that persuasively strikes home within his receptive heart (v. 26).

Development of the pragmatic structure of Psalm 73 is heightened and enhanced by the dramatic dialogic interaction that takes place either explicitly or implicitly within the text. There are four main participants (groups) involved as the psalmist 'stages' the semi-narrative, poetic account of his near fall from favor/fellowship with the LORD and his people. The dialectic tension concerned may be summarized as follows, with the various characters serving to represent different theological positions on the religious continuum moving from wrong to right (within the interpretive framework provided by a theodicy-type text of the Hebrew wisdom tradition):

A   B

[the enemies <=== the oppressed/psalmist\appellant ===> God/LORD + his 'children']
outright rebellion/apostasy--a questioning of the norms--the standard of torah truth--fidelity

---

[14] The paraenetic (hortatory) dimension of the rhetoric of Ps. 73 thus includes the components of both 'exhortation' (προτροπην) and 'dissuasion' (αποτροπην). In classical Greco-Roman rhetorical terms, the discourse is overtly 'epideictic' in nature (i.e., manifesting either praise or blame in relation to an established value system, namely, the covenantal *torah*). However, the deeper communicative purpose of the text is decidedly 'deliberative' (i.e., aimed at encouraging or discouraging the audience to adopt an attitude, along with the appropriate behavior, that is characterized by 'purity of heart' and which reflects the essential 'goodness' of Yahweh, v. 1) (cf. Gitay 1991:7).

2.4 Text function

Thus there is a fairly distinct demarcation of emphasis in Psalm 73 as we observe a special focus upon A-type interaction in first half of the text and on the B-type in Part II. In terms of its overall ideological argument structure, this poetic composition takes the form of a counter-argument.[15] It is one that is both clearly marked by means of various logical transitionals and also heavily biased in favor of traditional psalmic ideology (though not as obviously as in Ps 1). The dual, negative-positive organization of the discourse may be displayed in outline form:

Thesis (1): ***God is good [+ righteous] in relation to the pure in heart***

    Counter-Proposal (2–3): *why then do evildoers prosper--is God truly just?*

Part I   **Substantiation** (4–12): *examples of the proud ways of the wicked*

    Conclusion (13–14): *it does not pay to remain pure in heart; God is not fair!*

    Counter-Proposal (15–17): *a recognition of the justice of YHWH comes only in the light of a right understanding of the internally focused covenantal principles of his torah*

Part II   **Substantiation** (18–26): *the present life is not always what it seems to be; there will be justice in a future destiny of divine reward and retribution*

    Conclusion (27–28): *goodness [+righteousness] is realized through nearness to God, both subjectively (now) and objectively (then)*

The psalm's initial twofold thesis is thus progressively and poetically specified as the discourse unfolds and the author comes to a new, transforming realization of what God's goodness really means. It has basically nothing to do either with one's external worship practices or with one's external, material circumstances in the world, as the psalmist had first assumed. Rather, it concerns the true spiritual condition of a person's 'heart' (its 'uprightness' and 'purity'—v. 1) in terms of its relative proximity to Yahweh—an existential situation that has profound implications for one's ultimate destiny, indeed, even in the after-life!

---

[15] Hatim and Mason propose a tripartite 'text typology' consisting of 'exposition', 'instruction', and 'argumentation'. Argumentation involves 'the evaluation of relations between and among concepts through the extraction of similarities, contrasts, and transformations', and this may take the form of either a 'through' (unopposed) or a 'counter' structural development (1990:154, 159). Counter-arguments in turn may be either implicit ('balanced') or explicit ('lopsided') in nature—that is, covertly or overtly signaled in terms of contrast and/or concession (Hatim and Mason 1997:213). I have modified the definition of these terms somewhat.

2.5 Application: Poetic analysis of Psalm 73

2.5.1 On structural and thematic importance

As has already been noted, Psalm 73 is a key biblical composition in several respects. First of all, it occurs at the virtual midpoint of the Psalter at the beginning of Book III—after 'the prayers of David, son of Jesse, have ended' (72:20). Here at this crucial juncture it may be viewed as serving as a general, and yet at the same time a highly personal, summary of psalmic theology as it has been previously presented in the development from Psalms 1 through 72. It furthermore points forward in the direction of Psalm 150 within the overall functional progression from prayers which emphasize lament and complaint to songs that major on thanksgiving and acclamation.[16] Putting it in another way, Psalm 73 presents a more experience-oriented, true-to-life reflection upon the idealized wisdom (*torah*) principles enunciated by Psalm 1, while in its call to 'declare all the deeds' of YHWH (73:28), it anticipates the worshipful paean of praise that constitutes Psalm 150 and concludes the Psalter.

We have also noted that the generically mixed didactic prayer-poem of Psalm 73 is also "a microcosm of OT theology" (McCann 1987:248) because it touches upon a wide range of familiar sapiential polarities, such as goodness and evil, justice and injustice, wisdom and folly, prosperity and persecution, blessing and punishment, life and death. In the working out of his central theodicy the psalmist demonstrates from his own representative experience that the existential relationship between 'God's goodness' and a person's 'purity of heart' (v. 1) is much more complex than the simple cause-effect linkage that traditional, natural-materialistic religious philosophy has propounded through the ages. Rather, it has to do with one's conscious affirmation of the ultimate, universal justice of God, on the one hand (vv. 17–20, 27), and one's recognition of the constant strengthening presence of YHWH on the other (vv. 23–26, 28).

---

[16] For a useful overview of the many intertextual connections that give structure and sense to the Psalter as a whole, see McCann (1993); with specific reference to Ps. 73, see Tate (1990). For example, Ps. 73 resonates markedly with Ps. 1 in its antithetical conclusion (for example, with a significant recurrence of the key verb 'destroy' *'bd*; 1:6/73.27) and also with Ps. 150 with respect to the prominent thematic topic-noun 'sanctuary,' based on the root *qdsh* (73:17/150:1). It should be pointed out that this 'compositional' perspective on the Psalter is not without its critics. Some scholars would claim, for example, that such an approach is selective in its use of the textual evidence and hence simply reflects an organization externally imposed by the analyst. While recognizing the value of such criticism, I feel that it is still outweighed by the presence of so many concrete linkages between and among individual psalms that do indicate some type of larger editorial arrangement within the collection as a whole.

2.5 Application: Poetic analysis of Psalm 73

The purpose of this discourse-oriented survey is to suggest how a careful text analysis of Psalm 73 as a whole can give one an even fuller, and in certain respects also a clearer, understanding of its vital theological message with a view towards communicating the same in another language. We begin with a consideration of the structural organization of the psalm and an overview of its overlapping macro-organization, which is broadly delineated by introductory transitional terms. This basic compositional framework is then shown to be supported by a number of key stylistic features on the micro-level of structure, both synonymous and antithetical. The results of these interactive text studies are then applied to several area-specific problems that pertain to the contemporary transmission of Psalm 73 via Bible translation. Here I briefly touch upon four areas of special concern: the 'poetic' nature of the larger discourse organization, the text's significant oral-aural dimension, formatting it more meaningfully on the printed page, and finally, producing a fuller contextualization of the psalm's central message within the sociocultural setting of south-central Africa.

2.5.2 Overview of the structural framework

The framework of discourse has reference to the particular manner in which a given literary text has been constructed so as to manifest an integrated set of artistically desirable compositional characteristics, such as unity in diversity (interrelated parts comprising a unified whole), balance / proportion, progression / development, cohesion / coherence, differentiation (foreground / background), rhythm / phonation, and various degrees of emphasis—coupled with associated pragmatic features like impact, appeal, appropriateness, relevance, and purpose.[17] An author utilizes such organizational features in order to highlight and as well as to interrelate the key aspects of his theology or ethical admonition. I will consider the poetic construction of Psalm 73 first in terms of its larger text structure (the macro-level of discourse), and then in relation to its style or texture (the micro-level).

---

[17] A poorly or unskillfully constructed discourse will of course display these qualities in lesser measure or perhaps not at all. An evaluation of this nature is usually made on the basis of some form of comparative *stylistic* analysis and/or a descriptive exposition of a large corpus of related texts such as we have represented in the Psalter. Several recent studies have again reaffirmed the validity of compositional analyses of larger discourse units in Hebrew poetic literature, for example: "Although the question can be rightfully asked whether textual structures only exist in the brain of the researcher, a number of contributions to this volume... make it far more likely that they do not" (de Waard 1996:242). For a survey of such functional discourse arrangements in the Bible as a whole, see Wendland (2004b).

2.5.2.1 Structure

Although it has been claimed that "there is general agreement on the structure of the psalm" (Ross 1978:163), "no less than thirty-seven literary patterns have been proposed for Psalm 73" (Tate 1990:232).[18] However, the broad compositional contour of Psalm 73 appears to have been overtly marked by the psalmist himself by means of precise patterns of lexical *recursion* (both exact and synonymous repetition), as is usual in Hebrew poetic discourse.[19] Of special note in this text (and in keeping with its principal character as an instance of the wisdom genre) are several carefully placed sets of function words which perform the structural role (termed *anaphora*) of serving to initiate the *beginnings* of major poetic sections. The first set is comprised of four occurrences of the initial exclamatory particle '*ak* 'truly, surely' which operate sequentially to divide the text into its three primary *functional* constituents, as shown below:

Part I— **lament** over the prosperity and oppression of the wicked (vv.1–12)
    Transition—a *turning point* of internal debate and spiritual perception
        (vv.13–15/15–17)
Part II—**profession** of confidence in the LORD's protection and provision (vv.18–28)

The validity of this segmentation of the text is supported by a second structural marker, *wa'ani* 'and I'—the emphatic pronoun here being considered a function word due to its optional grammatical character and its structural operation within the discourse. In Parts I and the Transition, *wa'ani* occurs in the bicolon immediately following the one initiated by '*ak* (vv. 2, 14—*wa'ehi* in the latter). It is not surprising that the psalm's thematically focal portion, Part II, manifests a variation of this pattern, namely, a double articulation of '*ak* (vv. 18–19) coupled with a twofold repetition of *wa'ani*, not in the very next verse as before, but on both sides of the compositional boundary (vv. 22–23) of the next major poetic unit (vv. 23–26), which is the obvious theological climax of this psalm as a whole. Further structural marking and interlocking is manifested in Part II by the fact that *wa'ani* is preceded by the conjunction *kî* 'for, when, indeed' at the onset of the strophe comprising vv. 21–22 and yet again at the beginning of the psalm's concluding strophe (vv. 27–28).

---

[18] For a survey of some of this structural diversity, see Allen 1982:93–118.
[19] For a discussion of this issue in relation to Old Testament prophetic texts, see Wendland 1995b: ch. 2; the same methodology was applied in the present discourse analysis of Ps. 73 (cf. Wendland 1998:132–134).

2.5 Application: Poetic analysis of Psalm 73

Superimposed upon and complementing the tripartite division of Psalm 73 as described above is a binary *topical* segmentation of the discourse into two nearly equal halves:

A. Focus on earthly circumstances surrounding the psalmist and the 'wicked' (vv. 1–14)
B. Focus on God as the just arbiter between the psalmist and his adversaries (vv. 15–28)

According to this scheme, the first half of the text (which poses a theological *problem*) contains eighty-six 'words' in Hebrew (that is, two lexical items joined by *maqqeph* count as one), and eighty-five are found in the second half (which proposes a theological *solution*). The onset of the distinctive central point of initial religious perception (v. 15) features the psalm's sole occurrence of another function word, the hypothetical (contrary-to-fact) particle *'im* 'if', which is reinforced by a subsequent emphatic *hinneh* 'behold!' This exclamation appears earlier in the climactic utterance that closes Part I (v. 12) and it is reiterated once again at the start of the psalm's final strophic unit (v. 27; thus *hinneh* too occurs in every instance on a structural boundary). Two other important function words that help to announce the beginning (aperture) of section internal strophes (that is, distinct poetic units composed of two or more bicola) are: *kiy* asseverative 'surely' (4, 27) or temporal 'when' (21); and *lakhen* 'therefore' (6, 10). The only putative strophe in the entire psalm that is not explicitly marked by such an initial transitional term (thus rendering the border in this case debatable) is the segment covering verses 8–9.

Several other instances of structurally significant recursion, which serve both to cement the major compositional boundaries and also to highlight the thematic development of Psalm 73, are listed below:[20]

(a) The focal proposition that 'God is good' encloses the entire psalm (vv. 1, 28; *inclusio*). The traditional religious precept of v. 1 is really the thematic *conclusion* of the entire psalm (the initial positioning of this key element is duplicated elsewhere in the Psalter, for example: Pss. 23, 27, 30).

(b) The declarative verb 'recount/narrate' (*s-ph-r*) appearing in vv. 15 and 28 forms an *inclusio* for the psalm's second, spiritually optimistic and proclamatory half.

---

[20] For a definition and illustration of the different structural terms employed here and in the preceding discussion, see again Wendland 1995b: ch. 2.

(c) Topical correspondence at the respective *endings* of distinct compositional units *(epiphora)* is displayed in pointed references to the earthly prosperity of the 'wicked' (vv. 3, 12).

(d) The notion of purity of heart opens Part I as well as the Transition portion of the psalm (vv. 1, 13; structural *anaphora*). The prominent thematic and emotive term 'heart' *lebab* occurs also in v. 21, and it is further highlighted by means of a connotatively contrastive double iteration in v. 26 at the climactic close of the strophe that constitutes the discourse peak (vv. 23–26).

(e) The antithetical ideas of divine retribution for the wicked and blessing for the righteous (namely, being in proximity to God) is found both at the end of the Transition and also the text as a whole (vv. 17, 27–28, structural *epiphora*).

(f) The repetition of a strophe-final 'forever' (*'olam*) heightens the dramatic contrast in perspectives which characterizes the psalmist's outlook (introspective and temporally limited versus divinely centered and unbounded) at the respective endings of Parts I and II (vv. 12, 26; *epiphora*).

(g) Mention of some form of the divine name occurs at or near many of the psalm's major discourse borders, namely, vv. 1, 11, 17, 20, 26, and 28, with a double occurrence appearing to mark the close of Parts I and II: 'God' + 'Most High' (*'el...'elyon*, v. 11); 'God' + 'Sovereign LORD' (*'elohim...'adonay-YHWH*, v. 28).

Applying these and other structural markers (communicative clues) to the discourse as a whole, we find that Psalm 73 gives evidence of a general inverted ('ring' or palistrophic) plan of structural arrangement, one that alters in participant viewpoint and also in primary topic as one section moves to another:[21]

---

[21] Van Gemeren appears to misread or overlook the key structural signals of this psalm and proposes an introversion that has as its core vv. 18–20, which is designated as an "affirmation of God's justice" (1991:476). How this section alone "accounts for the shift (vv. 21–28)" in the discourse development from a decidedly negative to a positive direction, that is, in isolation from v. 17, is difficult to see. Equally problematic is the structural correspondence that is posited between vv. 13–17 ('personal reaction') and 21–22 ('evaluation of the psalmist's reaction'). Similarly, Allen would include v. 4 within the psalm's opening unit (1982:102), thus disregarding the prominent shift in subject from 'I' to 'they' (vv. 3–4) as well as the bounding *inclusio* formed by parallel references to the carefree state of the wicked in vv. 4–5 and 12. Brueggemann and Miller suggest that "Psalm 73 divides into four unequal thematic units," namely, vv. 1, 2–16, 17, and 18–28 (1996:46). However, this structural proposal smoothes over the psalm's clearly defined medial bridge (vv. 13–17) and misses

2.5 Application: Poetic analysis of Psalm 73

A (1): Initial *perspective*—God's 'goodness' to the psalmist / the 'upright' + 'pure in heart'

    B (2–3): The *problem* of the psalmist is enunciated—'I' focus (positive to negative progression)

        C (4–12): The *prosperity* of the wicked is described—'they' focus

            D (13–14): The psalmist's *complaint* is summarized—'I' focus

turning point >> = = = = = = = = = = = = = = == = = = = <<

            D' (15–17): The psalmist's *penitence* is begun—'I' focus

        C' (18–20): The *downfall* of the wicked is described—'you' (Lord) focus

    B' (21–26): The *solution* for the psalmist is proclaimed—'I' + 'with you'! (negative to positive progression)

A' (27–28): Final perspective—what 'goodness' is for the psalmist (the upright + pure), namely, to be 'near to God'!

Each of the major compositional segments concludes with a structural peak point: I = v. 12 (connotatively negative), *transition* = v. 17 (positive), II = v. 26 (positive), and of course the complete text with the antithetical thematic proclamation of vv. 27–28 (negative-positive, = contrastive *end stress*). There is also a mixed pattern of correspondence and contrast manifested with regard to rhythmic and verbal 'mass' since the number of poetic 'lines' (bicola) per section exhibits the following correspondence: A+B = 3 lines, C = 9 lines, D = 2 lines; D' = 3 lines, C' = 9 lines, B'+A' = 2 lines.[22] In an approximate manner then, the reverted discourse organization of Psalm 73 embodies a structural metaphor that reflects the circumstantial inversion which typifies the change in the psalmist's outlook on life and his future 'destiny' (*'acharitam*) as a result of a spiritually transforming 'entrance into the sanctuary of God' (v. 17, the crucial turning point of the text).

2.5.2.2 Style

By 'style' I am referring to those linguistic features in both the macro- as well as the microstructure of discourse organization which either individually or in total serve to distinguish a particular text (or a related corpus of texts). Style may be further defined and described from an individual or a collective perspective, that is, in terms of the set of verbal characteristics, or optional literary choices,

---

the prominent formal and thematic distinctions that appear in Part II, namely, vv. 18–20, 21–22, 23–26, and 27–28.

[22] On this point, see McCann (1996:968).

which differentiate a single author's compositions or those of a group of authors writing within the framework of a particular genre. Thus the Psalter as a whole manifests a number of prominent stylistic qualities which, taken together, help to typify the poetic technique of the collection as a whole—such as: balanced, usually binary lineation (parallelism) and broader strophic structuring; condensation (for example, verb 'gapping' and deletion of the so-called 'prose particles'); topically religious vocabulary of prayer/praise that focuses upon the attributes, activities, and personal attentiveness God/YHWH; a preference for emotively charged direct speech; an abundance of imagery and figurative language relating to worship, especially the three related complexes of simile-metaphor, metonymy-synecdoche, and personification-anthropomorphism; periodic emphatic utterances (for example, exclamations, rhetorical questions, the use of sarcasm); plus much phonaesthetic, auditory appeal (for example, rhythm, alliteration, paronomasia).[23]

Psalm 73 naturally exhibits many instances of all of these features. It is not necessary, however, to cite specific examples here, except for those prominent clusters where a combination of poetic devices occurs (convergence), presumably in order to perform a particular structural, topical, or pragmatic function within the text. A selection of these compositionally significant devices is listed by way of summary below, roughly in diachronic order:

(a) A potential double wordplay opens the discourse, poetically interlocks its covenantally linked participants, and proverbially announces the text's general theme,[24] that is, colon A: *leyisra'el 'elohim* (MT) 'to Israel God' ([is] good) and/or *leyashar 'el* (possible emendation) 'to [the] upright God' ([is] good);[25] colon B: *lebare lebab* 'to the pure ones of heart' (manifesting sound similarity + a chiasmus, with the emended reading).

---

[23] For a fuller description and exemplification of these features in relation to psalmic discourse, see Wendland 2002a: chs. 3–5.

[24] Allen follows Perdue in discerning a proverbial form of speech in v. 1 (1982:114).

[25] The potential ambiguity of word division with respect to *leyisra'el* may well be deliberate. The proposed emendation "retains the consonantal text, improves the meter, and offers a good parallelism between 'upright' and 'pure in heart'" (Tate 1990:228; cf. Westermann 1989:134). However, the fact remains that "there is absolutely no textual evidence for the suggested reading" (Tate 1990:228). Nevertheless, several modern translations do follow this proposal, for example, [N]RSV, NEB, NAB, and it is supported in Tov 1992:361. Could the two readings be an instance of poetically intentional 'semantic density', that is, a case where two or more complementary meanings fit the cotext and may in fact be intended to reinforce each another? Luyten observes that the emendation would also produce a reading more characteristic of wisdom literature, namely, "Surely El is good *to the upright*" (Luyten 1979:65).

2.5 Application: Poetic analysis of Psalm 73

(b) Additional functionally significant phonological highlighting distinguishes the last and peak strophe of Part I. First, a strong alliterative sequence of /m/ sounds calls attention to the 'abundance' (*male'*) which seems to characterize the life-style of the wicked (v. 10). Next, a snatch of direct speech featuring a double rhetorical question has these enemies of both 'God Most High' (*'el...'elyon*) and the righteous indict themselves with their own words (v. 11). Finally, to round out this portion of the discourse, a dramatic double deictic *hinneh 'elleh* 'look at these [fellows]!' foregrounds the alliterative referent-group, who have been the principal subject of this entire section: *resha'im weshalwe* 'evildoers and easy livers' (vv. 3, 12).

(c) The transitional bridge portion (vv. 13–17) begins with a sudden, emphatic shift back to the perspective of the now bitter and frustrated psalmist (compare vv. 2–3, Part I): *'ak-riq* 'surely in vain' (v. 13a). This dramatic contrast in tone with v. 1a is followed by additional figurative depictions of his initial, unhappy situation (vv. 13b–14; compare 21–22 of Part II), which markedly contrasts with the prosperous state of his supercilious adversaries. The impious arrogance of the latter is foregrounded by a series of graphic images—all vividly based on the human anatomy (vv. 4–9). The text-spanning, tension-building key term 'my heart' (*lebabi*, 6x) gives an internal perspective on the serious nature of the psalmist's problem (v. 13) and the only possibility for its resolution (v. 26). We notice that the reiterated imagery of slip-sliding into ruin, first in relation to the psalmist and then his enemies, forms part of the introduction to both Parts I and II (vv. 2, 18; structural *anaphora*). This vivid metaphor acts to concretize the religious reality of the poem by portraying "the argumentative matter in terms that are conceived by our senses" (Gitay 1996:239).

(d) The central turning point of Psalm 73 (v. 15) is spotlighted by another segment of direct discourse and a juxtaposed pair of locutionary verbs: *'-m-r* 'say' + *s-ph-r* 'speak.' The poet quotes himself, as it were, in order to stress this utterance and his fresh recognition of the fellowship of the faithful in sharp contrast to both his former sarcastic thoughts (vv. 13–14) as well as the insolent words of the wicked (v. 11).

(e) The Transition ends with the psalmist's holy 'entrance' into a new world, as it were (v. 17), which is marked by an appropriate concentration of stylistic features. First, there is poetic *enjambment* as his pessimistic conclusion at the close of v. 16 is unexpectedly reversed by the immediately following revelation of spiritual reorientation. This totally 'converted' point of view is underscored by means of a phonological chiasmus featuring /'/ consonance, namely: *'abo' 'el...'el 'abina* 'I entered into...God I understood.' The momentous middle term *miqdeshe* 'sanctuaries' (an augmentative plural) is no doubt emphasized by its contrasting intitial sound. Thus the LORD's holy presence is declared to be central to the psalmist's poetic inspiration as well as his renewed vision of the future.

(f) This psalm, like certain others of the lament genre (for example, 22, 30), gives evidence of an autobiographical, seminarrative mode of discourse development: initial setting (v. 1) → problem/ complication (2–3) → development (4–9) → crisis (10–12) → emotive climax (13–14) → turning point (15–17) → dramatic peak (18–20) → flashback (21–22) → resolution/denouement (23–26) → conclusion (27–28). In addition to the temporal 'flashback' to the setting of internal crisis, this plot includes a typical reversal of fortunes with regard to the psalmist and his adversaries (see the imagery in vv. 1–3//18–20).

(g) The psalm's faith-confessional core (vv. 23–26) is embellished by several rhetorical devices. It is introduced by a pair of connotatively contrastive usages of the same lexical item, that is, the thematically focal expression *'immak* 'with-you' (having negative to positive overtones) on the opening boundary (the close overlap between vv. 22 and 23 being an instance of structural *anadiplosis*), and *lebabi* 'my heart' (again, negative to positive) near the close of the strophic unit (v. 26). This logical *inclusio* is reinforced by one of lexical synonymy in *tamid* 'always' (v. 23a) and *le'olam* 'forever' (v. 26b), which confidently point to the psalmist's blessed present and future with YHWH. In between, we have the verbal sense-sound alikes *tancheni* 'you guide me' and *tiqqacheni* 'you take me' in v. 24, plus a locative antithesis ('in the heavens'/'on the earth') enclosed within an affirmative rhetorical question in v. 25. The latter thus provides an effective reply of humble confidence that counters the brash antagonistic query of the wicked in v. 11).[26]

---

[26] It is important to recognize the series of semantic reversals that distinguishes the final

2.5 Application: Poetic analysis of Psalm 73

(h) The antithetical strophe of closure (cf. Ps 1.6) features a reiteration of the thematic spatial opposition involving separation and destruction, which is the fate of the 'unfaithful' (v. 27), versus proximity and fellowship for every religious 'refugee' in relation to his/her God (v. 28). Such nearness and fellowship is the gracious benefit that belongs to all who enter the LORD's 'sanctuary' (v. 17). In effect, v. 27 summarizes what was said about the damning destiny of the ungodly in vv. 18–20, while v. 28 does the same for the ever-present blessing that is confidently ascribed to the faithful in vv. 23–26.

(i) The prominent cluster of divine appellations in v. 28 appears intended both to accent the psalmist's main message and also to mark with emotive end-stress the closure of this heart-felt and heart-filled prayer: 'God,' 'Lord,' YHWH, and 'my refuge' (*machsi*, the latter *epiphorically* echoing its referential counterpart—*chelqi* 'my inheritance'—at the close of the preceding strophe, v. 26). Thus among 'all the [mighty] works' of God that will be made manifest to the nations, especially the wicked in the world, are those which are carried out quietly within the deep psychological and spiritual recesses of the individual soul, but revealed in a strong public confession of faith and life (that is, vv. 23, 28 in contrast to vv. 13, 15).

Thus, literary structure and style harmoniously merge, to delineate and to accentuate the psalmist's message and also to attract as well as captivate each and every listener. The audience is thereby encouraged to identify with these fervently uttered words, especially the pray-er's ultimate emotive expression of his reliance upon an ever-present Sovereign LORD (v. 28).

2.5.3 A dynamic contemporary Psalm 73

My concluding remarks are devoted to an important, but not always fully addressed need, namely, that of conveying the structure, sense, and significance of the Psalter in general and Psalm 73 in particular to a contemporary audience. How does a careful structural and stylistic study of a passage of Scripture serve to facilitate not only the process

---

third of the psalm (vv. 18–26). This is effected by lexical reiteration and wordplay whereby the psalmist's new vision is clearly reflected in his lyric vocabulary, for example, the real ruler of 'heaven' and 'earth' (vv. 9/25). For a detailed listing of these parallels, see Allen (1982:104, although he extends his 'ground' too far, that is, to include v. 20).

of analysis but also the text's meaningful transmission today? Certainly a great deal of assistance is available in the form of the many and varied translations, commentaries, scholarly articles, study Bibles, and student guides that one can access, at least in the major languages of the world. But considerably more can and must be done, especially in view of the changing communication dynamics of the modern era and media age, now that we have embarked upon an uncertain and unstable new millennium. We may highlight the importance of such respondent-oriented concerns by briefly considering their challenge in relation to the following four special areas of application.

2.5.3.1 A lyric rendition

The rhetorical force of Psalm 73 is obviously enhanced by the typical poetic form in which it is expressed. There is no doubt that the special emotive impact and aaesthic appeal of Asaph's opening morose reflections on the prosperity and pride of the wicked, which dramatically contrast with his subsequent revelation of their destiny in contrast to his own, would be greatly diminished had he penned his thoughts in ordinary prose. But that is how most readers and hearers of the text in translation are exposed to his message today. It is true that a number of the features of Hebrew poetry can survive the shock of translation, for example, the balanced lines in parallel pairs, the vivid figures of speech (at least those whose sense is not changed during the transfer operation), and the emphatic snatches of direct speech. Much, however, is inevitably lost in a literalistic rendering, particularly if little or no attempt is made to heighten the quality of discourse in the target language (TL) in some corresponding way. That is to say, while it may not be possible or appropriate to render the text as pure poetry in the translation, at least some effort should be devoted to the task of finding a functionally equivalent manner and mode of discourse (suitable as an instance of 'oratory'), especially to convey the power and connotative overtones of the many expressive, imperative, and evocative speech acts that are present in the original text.[27]

The following excerpt is just a small sample of what might be done to convey a larger proportion of the full intended meaning of the Psalm 73 in all its diversity, including some of the prominent emotive, aesthetic, and other non-referential aspects of significance. The form approximates that which is characteristic of the *ndakatulo* lyric genre of oral (now also written) poetry in Chewa, a Bantu language spoken widely in Malawi and

---

[27] For a pioneering, and still extremely helpful, presentation of the subject of 'poetic' translation in relation to the Psalter, see Smalley (1974).

2.5 Application: Poetic analysis of Psalm 73

Zambia. It is hoped that the more dynamic speech style that is typical of this genre, for example, featuring the use of ideophones, exclamations, word order shifts, and multiple deictic 'pointing,' might serve to compensate for some of the rhetorical power that is lost in transfer due to the non-equivalence of linguistic and literary forms between Hebrew and Chewa.[28] Only a portion of the *ndakatulo* version of Psalm 73 is reproduced below, namely, its theological peak found in verses 23–26 (a relatively literal English back-translation follows the Chewa text).[29]

[23] *Koma chonsecho inu nthawi zonse ndili nanube.*
 But everything considered, you—at all times I am with you.
 Dzanja langa GWI! muligwiradi kuti ndisagwe.
 My hand TIGHTLY! you firmly grab it lest I fall.
[24] *Malangizo anu andiwongolera munjira yolungamo;*
 Your counsel leads me straight along the righteous path;
 Pomaliza pake mudzandilandira kuulemerero wanuwo.
 in the end you will receive me into your glory.
[25] *Nanga ine kopanda inu kumwamba ndidzakhala ndi yani ine?*
 As for me—without you in heaven whom will I remain with?
 Ndidzafunafunanji pansi pano? Palibiretu m'pang'ono pomwe!
 What will I search for down here below? Nothing at all, not in the least!
 Inu nokha Chauta mulipo—ndinu mumandithangata.
 You alone O God are present—you are the one who supports me.
[26] *Ha! Ngakhale ine thupi ndi moyo zingoti LEFU!*
 Ha! Although for me body and soul become completely TIRED!
 Mphambe Mulungu ndiye amandilimbitsa mtima ndithu!
 The Almighty God is the one who strengthens my heart indeed!
 Adzandisandutsa wolowa-dzina kwao mpaka MUYAYAYA!
 He will transform me into an heir at his place FOREVER!

---

[28] Hatim and Mason define 'compensation' as "a set of translation procedures aimed at making up for the loss of relevant features of meaning in the source text by reproducing the overall effect in the target language" (1997:214). De Waard comments on the importance of such a procedure in carrying out a "functional equivalence type of translation": "...most rhetorical features are language specific, making any kind of formal correspondence between languages impossible. Therefore, not the rhetorical features as such have to be rendered, but their function" (1996:242). For a more detailed text-comparative analysis of the similarities and differences between the Hebrew and Chewa (*ndakatulo*) poetic styles, with an extensive application to Ps. 22, see Wendland (1993).

[29] This translation is the product of a joint compositional endeavor on the part of two of my former seminary students, Patrick Magombo and Daison Phiri (both Malawi nationals), and myself. It was prepared as part of an exegetical-translational exercise during a course on the Psalms.

Naturally the Chewa text features some formal differences from the literal Hebrew in order to maintain an overall *functional* fidelity in relation to the original message. For example, word order variations for focus and emphasis (23a, 25a: foregrounding the intimate 'you'/'I' bonding that is such an important part of this psalm's thematic resolution); ideophones and exclamations (23b, 26a: accenting the vital emotive aspect of the psalmist's new perspective on life); local figures and imagery (26b–c: highlighting the close parental ties that characterize the psalmist's relationship with his God, e.g., 'heir'—'the one entering [the] name'); the use of assonance (23b), alliteration (25b), and rhyme (23–25: rendering the text in more memorable rhythmic terms); rhetorical questions (25a–b: emphasizing the LORD's constant presence and protection in life); a traditional Chewa praise name (*Mphambe* 'Storm-Ruler', 26b: evoking the connotative context of prayerful petition).

The purpose of incorporating these stylistic devices is not verbal artistry for its own sake. Rather, the individual features are selected in keeping with the *ndakatulo* genre to contribute en masse towards a faithful reproduction of the essential content, intent, and impact of this stirring Hebrew religious poem by means of a natural Chewa lyrical equivalent. Although considerable attention is devoted to the target language and its cultural context in such an exercise of literary recreation, the basic communicational core of the original message must always remain clearly in view to ensure that the theological inventory, functional orientation, and structural framework of the biblical text is preserved along with the general impact and appeal that is generated by the poetic format.

2.5.3.2 *The oral-aural dimension*

Poetry of course is meant to be heard, and this crucial factor of *orality* invites a consideration of the use of multi-media techniques in the transmission of biblical poetry, in particular the medium of sound, for example, audio cassettes (modern) and oral recital (a traditional mode of expression).[30] In

---

[30] Visual presentations (for example, video cassettes) occasion much greater problems of media 'transposition' because so much non-textual information usually needs to be added in order to make a given production artistically complete and aesthetically acceptable to the normal audience. Thus the danger of 'transculturation' becomes almost impossible to avoid. This might not be an issue where some sort of religious application is envisaged; such local contextualization may even be highly desirable in order to increase the product's situational relevance, message impact, and connotative appeal. But where Bible translation is concerned, a misrepresentation or skewing of the original setting must be avoided whenever possible in order to preserve a valid hermeneutical 'horizon' of sociocultural and religious reference.

many parts of the world, the relatively low level of active or functional literacy denies direct access to the Scriptures to all who cannot read the printed word. Most members of the public must therefore encounter the biblical text by hearing it, oftentimes a verbal record that is transmitted in flawed form due to the inexperience or incompetence of the reader. In such situations, it is an effective, perhaps necessary, evangelistic and/or translational strategy to offer receptors a professionally prepared *audio* version of the intended message, especially one that adopts an indigenous genre typically used for texts of an important nature. Such an oralized version may be enhanced by the addition of an appropriate local idiom of *music*—in the form of a prelude, interlude(s), and/or coda to the poem; as a background to the text as it is being recited or chanted; or as an accompanying melody to make solo or choral singing possible.

Translations intended for any of these non-liturgical settings (i.e., not for use in public worship) may have to assume a more flexible form and format (see 2.5.3.3), but if the basic content and intent of the psalm remains close enough to the original, then there is really no difficulty in calling them 'translations'. Indeed, oral-aural versions of this type may duplicate the communicative dynamics of the biblical text much more closely than any printed (and either unreadable or poorly read) version can do under the circumstances that pertain for the majority of the target audience. Carefully composed audio texts (possibly prepared also for broadcast on the radio) may thus serve to initiate a new 'oral tradition' among the people, one that celebrates and perpetuates the key teachings and texts of Scripture—the Word of God as it is meant to be *heard*. In this connection, it should be pointed out that every Bible translation ought to be both readable and hearable, that is, a rendering that is relatively easy to enunciate and also sounds good to the ears of the audience. Thus even a more form-oriented version intended for liturgical use can—and should—be composed in a manner that pays close attention to the phonology of the text, so that it becomes a literary (oratorical) translation in at least this important dimension.

2.5.3.3 The printed format

The main problem with a printed literary composition, especially where poetry is involved, is the presence of the less-than-friendly format in which the piece is displayed on the page. Conventional publishing procedures are not often decided upon with the best interests of communication in mind. The result is a text that may be very economical in terms of its cost per page, but rather inefficient as a means of message transmission.

For example, a typical Scripture text from the Psalms is normally printed in two tightly placed vertical columns, a practice that results in lines that are divided at points which are structurally and/or semantically inappropriate; hyphens break up many of the line-final words; paragraph divisions do not reflect a natural strophic organization of the discourse; and there is loss of many of the patterns formed by the varied repetition that is characteristic of poetry. Such a format makes it difficult if not impossible to read the text with an appropriate intonation and rhythm pattern that reflects the meaning structure of the original, and a poem that is not articulated accurately will often be heard incorrectly and certainly not with the phonological dynamics that the author intended to complement his message.

The following text is a reproduction of the *New International Version*, reformatted in a way that presents a clearer display of the major structural parallels and contrasts of the Hebrew text. This page design is also intended to enhance readability and hence also comprehension, both for the reader and, via a more 'informed' lector, also the hearers of Psalm 73:[31]

[1]   Surely God is good to Israel,
           to those who are pure in heart.

[2]   But as for me, my feet had almost slipped.
                   I had almost lost my foothold.
[3]   For I envied the arrogant
                   when I saw the prosperity of the wicked.

[4]   They have no struggles;
                           their bodies are healthy and strong.
[5]   They are free from the burdens common to man;
                           they are not plagued by human ills.
[6]   Therefore pride is their necklace;
                           they clothe themselves with violence.
[7]   From their callous hearts comes iniquity;

---

[31] For a study of the importance of graphic design in relation to Bible translation, see Louw and Wendland (1993). I realize that I am entering a rather controversial area within the domain of 'Scripture presentation', for there is always the danger of the translator or publisher imposing a wrong or misleading structural arrangement upon a given text, psalmic or otherwise. Clearly, this is a procedure that requires some careful joint thinking (analysis) and planning, along with a large measure of agreement before it can actually be applied. However, if the discourse structure of the original text conveys a certain aspect of its intended meaning (as I believe that it does), then it would be good if this could be somehow transmitted in the closest, functionally equivalent way for the benefit of all Bible users today.

2.5 Application: Poetic analysis of Psalm 73

[8]   the evil conceits of their minds know no limits.
                                    They scoff, and speak with malice;
                                    in their arrogance they threaten oppression.
[9]   Their mouths lay claim to heaven,
                                    and their tongues take possession of the earth.
[10]   Therefore their people turn to them
                                    and drink up waters in abundance.
[11]   They say, "How can God know?
                                    Does the Most High have knowledge?"

[12]   This is what the wicked are like--
                                  always carefree, they increase in wealth.

[13] Surely in vain have I kept my heart pure;
        vainly I've washed my hands in innocence.
[14] All day long I have been plagued;
        I have been punished every morning.

[15] If I had said, "I will speak thus,"
        I would have betrayed your children.
[16] When I tried to understand all this,
        it was oppressive to me
[17] **till I entered the sanctuary of God;**
        then I understood their final destiny.

[18]   Surely you place them on slippery ground;
                                  you cast them down to ruin.
[19]   How suddenly are they destroyed,
                                  completely swept away by terrors!
[20]   As a dream when one awakes,
                                  so when you arise, O Lord,
                                  you will despise them as fantasies.

[21] When my heart was grieved
        and my spirit embittered,
[22] I was senseless and ignorant;
        I was a brute beast before you.

[23] Yet I am always with you;
        you hold me by my right hand.

[24]	You guide me with your counsel,
	and afterward you will take me into glory.
[25]	Who have I in heaven but you?
	And earth has nothing I desire besides you.
[26]	My flesh and blood may fail,
	but God is the strength of my heart
	and my portion forever.

[27]	Those who are far from you will perish;
	you destroy all who are unfaithful to you.
[28]	But as for me, it is good to be near God.

I have made the Sovereign LORD my refuge;
I will tell of all your deeds.

Such a novel, single-column printed format (however, manifesting a normal type size here) first needs to be carefully explained to readers of course so that they realize the significance, for example, of the various levels of indentation, the internal poetic paragraphs (strophes) in relation to the form and function of the psalm as a whole, and other special features, like the matched blocks of indentation, the isolated verse numbers, and the distinct typefaces (for example, the **bold** for the psalm's dramatic 'turning point' and *italics* for its theological 'peak', as above). After the required introduction, however, it may be expected that speakers, reciters, chanters, or singers will be able to enunciate the text more meaningfully in terms of textual segmentation, internal connection, thematic projection, and rhetorical patterning.

Brenda Boerger has prepared an English version of Psalm 73 which preserves many of the poetic and discourse features discussed above (with *italics* here being used for emphasis). This may give English readers a glimpse of the dynamic impact of the original Hebrew text, which corresponds in many lyric respects to that of the Chewa rendering.

Psalm 73
WHEN THINGS LOOK BLEAK
by Asaph
a wisdom psalm
rime couée
Tune: "Ye Righteous in the Lord, Rejoice" (8.8.6.8.8.6. Annetta)

[1] *"God's good to Israel, be sure;*
   To those whose hearts have been kept pure."

2.5 Application: Poetic analysis of Psalm 73

[2]   But me? My faith was gone.
      By then I'd slipped, begun to doubt,
[3]   Becoming jealous of the proud,
      Who profit in their wrong.
[4]   Their bodies now have no constraints.[32]
      Those healthy wicked ones get gains.
[5]   But burdens we abide
      Don't fall on them when troubles strike.
[6]   They flaunt their violence as they like.
      They strut about in pride.

[7]   With calloused hearts' iniquities,
      Their minds transgress with wicked schemes.
[8]   They speak derision cruel,[33]
      And make oppressive threats in pride.
[9]   Each makes the claim, *"All earth is mine,"*
      Thinks heaven's his to rule!

[10] Now Yahweh's own wander astray,
      Would swallow what the wicked say,
[11] *"Do you think Most High sees?*
      I doubt that God will ever know."
[12] Look what the wicked ever show –
      Their wealth gives them great ease.

[13] *"I'm sure my goodness is in vain.*
      Why should I struggle so, and strain,
      Avoid the taint of sin,
      And keep my heart both clean and pure,
[14] *Since, as for me, I now endure*
      The pain of punishment?"

[15] If I'd aped what the wicked say,
      Behold, your own would be betrayed.
[16] For when I sought the whys,
      The difficulty met was hard.
[17] 'Til sanctuaried where you are,
      I grasped their soon demise.

---

[32] 73:4 'Constraints' is used only here and in Isaiah 58:6. The root means 'ropes' and is used metaphorically.

[33] 73:8 'Derision' translates a verb which means 'to mock', and which only occurs here in the OT.

[18] I'm sure they're on a shaky place,
　　　Where one slip leads to ruin, disgrace.
[19] They're swept away by fear,
　　　Destroyed when safety sure breaks up.
[20] Like fading dreams as one wakes up,
　　　You make them disappear.

[21] Sharp bitterness in my heart dwelt.
　　　Resentment made it all your fault.
[22] And me? I was a beast,
　　　Behaving like a boorish brute.
[23] Yet where I was, there you were too.
　　　My safety never ceased.

[24] Your wise advice is now my guide;
　　　With you in glory I'll reside.
[25] Lord, you are all I need.
　　　Is there another heavenly hope?
　　　Is there another earthly help?
　　　No, only you indeed.

[26] My heart may think all things look bleak,
　　　My body may be tired and weak,
　　　But you're my Savior sure,
　　　A shelter strong to guard my heart.
　　　So when things start to fall apart
　　　Forever I'm secure.

[27] Those far from you will perish all.
　　　Rejecting you, they'll surely fall.
[28] For me, it's good near you.
　　　For You, God, Yahweh Adonai,
　　　You are my refuge and delight.
　　　I'll tell all that you do.

2.5.3.4 A contextualized annotation

Another vital dimension of the biblical text that needs to be considered is its situational *context* in relation to the particular sociocultural environment in which it is being communicated today. This concern centers on all of the culturally-related information that pertains to the original setting in

2.5 Application: Poetic analysis of Psalm 73

which the various books of Scripture were composed and transmitted in the initial instance, as nearly as this may be determined on the basis of reliable scholarly research. Such background material would have as its aim the elucidation of important facts, figures, and other 'paratextual' features which are necessary for the interpretation of the text itself, for example, details of a historical, political, social, economic, geographical, biological, military, artistic, and religious nature. Comparative notes relating to the cultural context of the target group, especially local customs and literary usage, should be included to assist in the hermeneutical process, especially in cases where a clash, incongruence, or non-equivalence with regard to form or function is involved. Various additional readers' helps such as illustrations, cross-references, glossary entries, sectional headings, diagrams, maps and charts could also be added, depending on their expressed desires and level of literary competence. Once again, it would be important to provide some preparatory training to lay people so that they learn how to utilize these aids to their best advantage—and how to most effectively pass on such knowledge to an unseeing audience. Eventually, given the time, resources (both human and financial), and sufficient demand, a full-sized (or a scaled down) study Bible might be produced, incorporating all or a selection of the material just mentioned.

What does Psalm 73 *sound* like in a setting typical of Bantu south-central Africa, for example? What are some of the points that are likely to be misunderstood and misinterpreted by a majority due to conceptual interference from their own cultural background, namely, their world view (presuppositions, beliefs, values, goals, etc.) and way-of-life (social institutions guiding and governing all forms of individual and communal behavior)? What are the principal conceptual features that would need special attention if a local contextualization of this prayer-poem were undertaken, especially in view of the likelihood of a clash due to the ancient indigenous ideology of religion? The following is a representative selection of a few of the issues that would need to be addressed in such an enrichment exercise, whatever form the text supplementation eventually takes. These are stated as hypothetical questions that are intended to anticipate similar queries that ordinary average churchgoers might conceivably ask of a discussion leader (pastor, catechist, priest, etc.), were they given the opportunity, after hearing this psalm articulated in the vernacular (and via a relatively literal translation):

(a) Why is God 'good' only to the man named Israel (v. 1)—of what relevance then are these words to us?

(b) What kind of a person is someone who is 'pure in heart' (v. 1; in Chewa this may suggest a sinless 'saint')?

(c) Why did the speaker's 'foot slip' so that he almost fell down (v. 2)—and what is so bad about falling to the ground anyway? We all do it from time to time.

(d) What type of magical substance ('medicine') or sorcery did the psalmist's enemies apply against him to cause him all the mentioned troubles and to get rich (apparently) at his expense (vv. 3–5)?

(e) What does 'pride' have to do with 'violence' and 'oppression' (vv. 6–8)? Such characteristics are not so directly associated in a Bantu social setting.

(f) What sort of powerful sorcery are these wicked folk putting into practice that they control even the communal water supply, including the rain (namely, the 'rain-binders' apparently alluded to in v. 10)?

(g) Why do the wicked insult God so impudently—do they not know that they are thereby calling a terrible curse down upon themselves by uttering such impious words (v. 11)?

(h) Why did the pray-er not go to a diviner or medicine-man to find out who was doing these evil things to him, how to protect himself, and how he might also punish them in retaliation (vv. 13–14)?

(i) Whose 'children' are being referred to in v. 15, and how exactly was the speaker in danger of 'betraying' them?

(j) Why does the psalmist simply want to understand all the problems that are happening to him (much too cognitive a process, v. 16)? Why does he not get out and *do* something about it (compare g)?

(k) Which type of church, or sanctuary did the suppliant 'enter' (v. 17)? It sounds like a place where African traditional religion is practiced because it resulted in a divinatory or revelatory sort of mystical experience.

(l) How can a 'slippery slope' (= mud?) bring these powerful enemies to 'ruin' or 'destruction' (v. 18, cf. v. 2)? What will cause them to be so terrified (v. 19)?

2.5 Application: Poetic analysis of Psalm 73

(m) Do not the ancestral spirits bring 'dreams'; why does the psalmist say that Jesus (that is, the 'Lord'!) causes these bad dreams (v. 20)?

(n) Why do the psalmist's moods shift back and forth so quickly, and why does he insult himself by calling himself an 'animal' in front of God, his Creator (vv. 21–22)?

(o) In what sense can a person be or come 'close' to his/her Creator-God (vv. 23–26)? According to traditional belief, such an approachment is possible only metaphorically and through the effective mediation of the ancestors.

(p) Only sorcerers and witches deliberately 'destroy' others—why does the text attribute such action to God (v. 27)? Is the notion of a just punishment for their wickedness implicitly apparent in the text?

(q) Is the psalmist a public preacher? Why else would he take upon himself the duty of telling others about the 'works of God' (v. 28)?

(r) Does the psalm as a whole convey the notion of *theodicy*, at least implicitly? Has the crucial issue of the goodness or rightness (justice) of God been clearly communicated?

As the preceding sample would indicate, it is a translation-related task of some urgency to provide the culturally conditioned biblical background necessary to help text consumers correctly understand and effectively apply to their life-situation the belief-system, connotative background, and rhetorical dynamics of the passage of Scripture that they happen to be reading.

2.5.4 Evaluation

Number 73, the vital psalm at the heart of the Psalter, must not remain buried in the midst of this great worship collection (or 'hymnbook'). Indeed, as I have attempted to show in the present structural-stylistic, text-contextual study, this energetic Asaphic composition has a great deal to offer biblical scholars and ordinary Bible readers alike. The psalm speaks in terms of its placement in the Psalter as well as its content—that is, with respect to our understanding of the overall construction and theology of the Psalter as a whole, and also on a more intimate level in terms of our recognition of the close spiritual relationship that we have to a very personal God, the Sovereign LORD [our] refuge (v. 28). It is therefore very much worth the effort to communicate this vital theological and functional significance more effectively through varied, perhaps somewhat novel, translation techniques today, applied not only to Psalm 73, but also to the entire corpus contained in this consummate 'songbook of the saints.' Surely that would be a most excellent way to carry out the text's final injunction to 'proclaim [in word and deed] all the [wonderful] works' of YHWH (v. 28).

The Chewa *ndakatulo* lyric poem selection in 2.5.3.1 is an example of a more or less complete genre-for-genre translation. Many of those who must evaluate this rendition on the basis of the English back-translation may be inclined to judge it negatively—as pushing the original too far stylistically in the direction of an alien discourse type. It might also sound at times as though the Chewa version has been verbally over-emotivized and is therefore not very fitting as an equivalent for a poetic plea to the Lord. It may be that this is a manner of addressing God that we are not comfortable with, based on our own prayer experience and worship traditions. But, on the other hand, it is not up to us as outsiders to make the final decision to criticize or condemn the vernacular version in response to our personal preferences. The ultimate assessment for or against—and why either way—ought to be given by the 'owners' of the language in keeping with the original *Skopos* statement that was drawn up for this text in its envisaged setting of primary use. Perhaps it is intended to be set to music as a contemporary song to the Lord; thus, instead of 'I will tell of all your deeds' (v. 28c), it may be adapted to 'I will sing of all your deeds!'

A final consideration to keep in mind: when evaluating the potential acceptability of a given translation in terms of its communicative relevance coupled with comparative degree of functional equivalence, one must do this first in relation to the *discourse as a whole*, not its individual bits and pieces of structure and style. Once this process has been completed by means of a thorough process of systematic audience testing (along with some pre-education regarding the various options available), then those features that are determined by the majority to be inappropriate, misleading, or in error can be eliminated, revised, or corrected as necessary.

2.6 Implications

As we are about to leave the 'sanctuary' of this centrally-placed poetic prayer text, it may be worthwhile to remind ourselves of a few items of possibly personal significance that result from our study. The analytical methodology presented above is not really all that important in and of itself, but only insofar as it contributes to a better understanding of the text under consideration. A discourse-oriented, thematic-rhetorical, text-context based approach was applied in order to provide a somewhat broader perspective on the stylistic and topical dimensions of the poem in its entirety. But any analysis of Scripture, no matter how detailed in a

2.6 Implications

technical sense, is only partial at best. There is always another relevant semantic vista to be viewed, some new nugget of divine truth to be mined for practical application to one's spiritual (inner) and religious (outer) life. Thus a careful 'entrance' into the sanctuary of a poem's formal manner of construction is able to provide readers with an essential area of (re-)orientation or a new vantage point that better prepares them (preacher, teacher, evangelist, commentator, theologian, liturgical specialist) to arrive at a coherent and meaningful interpretation of the theological message of the whole. That message is not monolithic, of course, but as reader-response criticism has instructed us, every responsible receptor will adapt and apply the basic author-intended core of biblical significance to his/her own life setting and personal experience.

What then is one perception of the vital spiritual truth to be appropriated from Psalm 73? I sum up my own impression in terms of the following three interrelated points:

(a) First of all, we return to the psychological 'turning point' of the psalm in v. 17 and the importance of its positioning within the whole. The dramatic impact and theological significance of this sanctuary experience (perhaps similar in a way to that undergone by Martin Luther) cannot be fully appreciated without pairing it up with the psalmist's deeply pessimistic spiritual state as expressed in Part I of the text (vv. 1–14). Here is yet another powerful articulation of the age-old issue of *theodicy*—justifying the (at times) inscrutable ways of God in this world to his faithful, but currently frustrated, people. Just how can they venture to claim that God is 'good' (v.1) or by implication 'just' (v. 17) when all around they see the manifest 'well-being of the wicked' (v. 3)? Why remain 'pure in heart' (v. 13) if varied 'punishment' is the only apparent result (v. 14)? This is a pressing query that most believers eventually face at one time or another in the present life. It thus draws the serious listener inevitably into the tense theological dynamics of the psalm as one compares, perhaps even relives, one's own experience along with that of the psalmist and asks, "Why me, Lord—why now—why this? Where is your justice here?"

(b) The complex compositional midpoint of the discourse serves to shift its thematic and emotive direction and sets the psalmist (as well as every empathetic receptor) on a productive, divinely-guided course away from his/her own feelings of self-pity. This drastic shift begins almost imperceptibly with the speaker's quiet realization that he does not stand alone on the earthly stage on which the vicissitudes of life play out. He (we) thus bears an inalienable responsibility to fellow members of the household of God (v. 15). What effect would his (our) words of denial or acts of apostasy have upon them? Reason things through as he might, the poet/pray-er cannot arrive at a satisfactory solution according to a purely human or secular way of thinking (v. 16). The only—and ultimate—solution lies in the holy presence and gracious provision of a just and merciful God (v. 17), who bears the psalmist and his people up with promises of a future, but certain, retribution for the wicked (vv. 18–20) and restoration for the righteous (vv. 23–26). This 'final destiny' (v. 17), whether good or bad, is immutable and integrally bound up with the eternal purposes of the almighty 'Sovereign-LORD' (v. 28). His salvation is not necessarily effected within the limited temporal span of this lifetime, and it is certainly not a deliverance upon demand (as many contemporary Christians would claim). But the psalmist's point—one of them at least—is to encourage the faithful and to admonish the unrighteous that this 'rewarding' event, whether good or bad, may be experienced psychologically and spiritually even now, on this side of the grave (vv. 23–26).

(c) Therefore, our future is bright, no matter how bleak the present situation may look because the LORD is with us to lend his sure support in the face of all opposition, no matter how much or how little this may be (vv. 26–27). But this is not an individual or even a corporate human affair; we must not overlook the vital issue of *divine* fellowship (immanence). In a world that is being increasingly characterized by growing alienation and interpersonal relationships of an ever more unstable and transient nature, it gives believers comfort to know that they always have someone at their side who is ready, willing, and able to provide the resources that they need to meet and overcome the many crises and problems of life—no matter when, what, or where. The Yahweh of Holy Scripture is not irrelevant to or inappropriate for our sophisticated, modern, technological age, which has now expanded into a new millennium. But we must note well where the emphasis lies (v. 28): it is not so much *my* nearness to God (NIV) that makes the difference, but *his* movement nearer to me in the dark hours of difficulty or despair—his grabbing me by the hand (v. 23) and eventually taking me along into a certain, future 'glory' (v. 24). It is this assurance of the Rock's constant presence, provision, and protection that gives us hope in this life and enables us to 'rise above' our potentially depressing contemporary circumstances (v. 25). Indeed, his strength is most clearly manifested in the witness of all those whom he empowers in situations of hard testing (v. 28; cf. 2 Cor. 1:11, 3:5, 4:10–11, 11:30–31, 12:9–10).

This then, according to Psalm 73, is the optimistic response of faith of all who 'take refuge' in the LORD (v. 26), those who are 'pure in heart' (vv. 1, 28). It concerns a destiny that may not be explainable in worldly terms or in harmony with human plans, but it is 'upright' and 'good' (v. 1) nevertheless—in fact, the best prospect possible. Such an encouraging

2.6 Implications

message is not one that believers will want to keep to themselves. On the contrary, O LORD, we greatly desire 'to tell about all of your [gracious] deeds' (v. 28) and to testify concerning your goodness to all 'your children' (v. 15), even as we continue to learn about and personally experience these wondrous works in their great diversity day after day, being surely and safely 'guided by your counsel' (v. 24).

3

From Hebrew Acrostic to a Tonga Praise Poem: Proverbs 31:10–31

Introduction: Praising the beauty of a 'worthy wife'[1]

An *encomium* of praise to a most excellent woman and wife draws the book of Proverbs to a close (31:10–31) on a memorable high note that communicates on several levels of meaning. I begin with a selective overview of the salient stylistic features of this stirring eulogy (regarding structure, artistry, and rhetoric) as these relate to the poem's apparent literary function and theological message.[2] This partial analysis of the original text lays the foundation for considering certain key aspects of its re-expression in the language and culture of the Tonga people of Zambia. Several important translation problems in this regard are first discussed and some possible solutions tentatively offered. This includes a survey of a number of the main conceptual correspondences and barriers that sensitive present-day Tonga speakers notice when they hear this text in their language. How 'worthy'—or beautiful—is the image of the vibrant and vigorous 'wife' that is evoked for them—from the perspective of today's men and women, traditional as well as modern?

What then constitutes a wise and worthy re-presentation of such a crucial passage in the Tonga language? I cannot consider all of the relevant issues but will focus my attention on the search for a possible functional

---

[1] This chapter is the revised edition of a paper first presented at the 49th Congress of the Old Testament Society of South Africa, University of South Africa, 13–15 September 2006 (theme: *Wisdom and Gender: Constructing each other wisely in reading the Old Testament*). Note that the Tonga of Zambia need to be distinguished from a people of the same name who speak a Polynesian language and live on a group of islands in the SW Pacific.

[2] I have not considered the putative compositional setting of this pericope (cf. Lawrence 2009:339). It could well be a later addition to form an epilogue to Proverbs, possibly intended as a bracketing structure *(inclusio)* for the book as a whole (Hunter 2006:75). But whether an early or later composition "the interpretation of the text is not affected" (Garrett 1993:247).

equivalent for the dominant Hebrew acrostic format that distinguishes this personal hymn of praise, and arguably encodes a deeper stratum of symbolic significance and emotive resonance. To this end, a poetic Tonga rendition of the paean's climactic final strophe (vv. 28–31) is presented as an illustration in the form of two distinct song genres for comparative purposes, that is, in relation to the dynamic Hebrew original text.

3.1 'Worthy wife': A biblical Hebrew perspective

Ode to a 'worthy (noble, valiant, excellent) wife' (אֵשֶׁת־חַיִל)— what a seemingly strange subject to present as the final, obviously foregrounded message of the book of Proverbs.[3] The *positive* activities of women, normally in the singular 'wife, woman' (אִשָּׁה), are not prominent in the book as a whole,[4] so to find them featured here at the end is rather unexpected. My study suggests, however, that this 'heroic' poetic portrait of an exemplary woman/wife is most appropriate as a conclusion to this assorted collection of sapiential sayings that give concrete expression to what it means to lead a life of 'wisdom' (חָכְמָה), which 'faithfully' (withחֶסֶד!) reflects the fear of the LORD (יִרְאַת יְהוָה)— e.g., 1:7, 1:29, 2:5, 3:7, 8:13, 9:10, 10:27, 14:26, 15:16, 16:6, 19:23, 22:4, 23:17, 24:21, 31:26, 30).

But what does this focal concept of a 'worthy wife' mean to people who read and hear it from the Scriptures today—does it have any particular relevance for them? Naturally, the image and associations that this notion evokes will vary greatly, according to the particular sociocultural context in which it is used.[5] In the present study, I will not be able to examine this important issue in any great detail, but

---

[3] An 'ode' may be defined as "a lyric poem...typically addressed to some person or thing and usually characterized by lofty feeling, elaborate form, and dignified style" (Neufeldt 1988:938; cf. section 1.4). The literary genre of this passage will be discussed more fully below in section 3.4.2.

[4] אִשָּׁה occurs some twenty-four times in Proverbs, usually with a negative connotation or in unfavorable circumstances, e.g., 2:16, 6:24, 9:13, 19:13, 21:9.

[5] For example, from a Western female (gender-based) perspective, any use of Prov. 31:10–31 as a "model for modern Jewish women...is damaging, to say the least, because of its sheer unsustainability....A gender-critical lens provides the reader with the sense that something is wrong with this poem, that its expectations are too high, that its values are rooted in outdated gender roles, and that a modern reader should not accept it too willingly" (Lawrence 2009:344). The preceding opinion might be shared by a minority of urban, educated Tonga women in Zambia (Africa), but certainly not the majority of wives, for whom a traditional way of life, as reflected in the poem, is still a major source of domestic stability and security.

I do wish to explore it from a rather distinct point of view, namely, that of a group of middle-aged Zambian adults, especially those representing the Tonga-speaking and related peoples. How does the poem of Proverbs 31:10–31 strike average respondents in terms of a possible application to their mindset and lifestyle? To what extent do they grasp the poet's message and its relevance for changing some traditional negative attitudes towards women in this dynamic African society?

These are some of the concerns that will be taken up in the second part of this chapter (section 3.6). In this connection, the matter of meaningful communication must also be considered, for how can people properly understand and appreciate an ancient poetic text which comes to them via translation from an alien cultural environment? Here I will briefly discuss some of the main difficulties that arise in this connection along with some possible solutions for coping with these conceptual disparities. In part three then (3.7), attention will be focused on what is undoubtedly the greatest translation challenge, that is, how to deal with the original alphabetical acrostic format. To illustrate the poetic potential in Tonga, two lyric renderings of the proverbial eulogy's concluding strophe (vv. 28–31) are offered as possible functional equivalents. But to begin with, we must study this proverbial descriptive poem on its own terms and in view of its assumed setting of composition. Therefore, in section 3.2 a structural, stylistic, and rhetorical overview of Proverbs 31:10–31 is delineated with reference to the Hebrew text's Ancient Near Eastern (ANE) situational setting.

3.2 Structural organization of the eulogy

The structure of this ode to a godly wife (and wisdom) is dominated by its perfect acrostic format; the initial consonant of the first word of each verse begins with a different letter of the Hebrew alphabet—from א to ת, a sequence of twenty-two letters and corresponding bicola in all.[6] There also seems to be a rather clear division of the poem into a thematic Introduction, a lengthy Body of topical development, and a marked Conclusion that brings this eulogistic epilogue to a final peak of emotive

---

[6] The twenty-first line of the Hebrew text (v. 30) begins with שֶׁקֶר 'deceitful'—there was no distinction between the letters שׁ *(shin)* and שׂ *(sin)* at the time that Proverbs was composed, even granting a rather lengthy period for the collection and editorial process to take place.

and semantic significance. A short description and explanation of this basic segmentation of the poetic discourse follows:

Introduction (31:10-12)
The central theme of a 'most worthy wife/woman' (אֵשֶׁת־חַיִל), whom we might designate as the 'heroine' of this text (to be further substantiated below), is announced at the very onset of the discourse (v. 10a). This notion is developed by means of a twofold general statement of support that manifests a positive-negative pattern in each case. First, we have a personal perspective—from the 'heart' (לֵב)— of the one who counts most, namely, 'her husband' (בַעְלָהּ –v. 11). This opinion is then reinforced by the poet's own authoritative testimony of the woman's great worth to her man, as stated in both qualitative and quantitative terms: 'goodness...*all* the days of her life' (טוֹב ... כֹּל יְמֵי חַיֶּיהָ –v. 12). The *kôl* of summation brings the Introduction to a close which anticipates her 'virtuous' specifics that follow.

Body (31:13-27)
In this relatively long medial portion, the discourse organization becomes considerably more complex to highlight its superlative subject. The unit as a whole may be analyzed as consisting of two complementary thematic segments, both of which emphasize the heroine's diverse outstanding (praiseworthy) activities—first, with regard to (A) *production* (vv. 13-19), then (B) in terms of *provision* (vv. 20-27). A pair of formally distinct internal structures, which overlap in the center (v. 20), delineate these two interrelated thematic subsections.

The opening section (A, vv. 13-19) features a linear, semi-narrative, gently intensified progression that outlines the various productive domestic and commercial activities of this most wonderful of women. The specific weaving work described at the end in v. 19, however, appears to be displaced from a more logical position after the introduction to that topic at the beginning of the unit in v. 13. Perhaps this is a way of signaling the closing boundary of the first section. In any case, a reiterated trio of catchwords lends additional cohesion to this segment: the lady's 'palms'

3.2 Structural organization of the eulogy

(כַּפֶּיהָ) engaged in fruitful labor (vv. 13/16)—her vigorous 'trading' (סוֹחֵר), or commercial ventures, strengthening the household (vv. 14/17–18a)—with her daily duties extending virtually from one 'night' (לַיְלָה) to the next (vv. 15/18b, the latter marking a minor peak of intensity within the text).

The seemingly misplaced verse 19 of section A is seen to perform a structural function as we transition to section B of the poem's Body (vv. 20–27). A clear chiastic lexical arrangement joins vv. 19–20 together to form a compositional 'seam', despite the fact that their respective contents are quite different (cf. Waltke 2005:527):[7]

> **A** 'her hands' (יָדֶיהָ) 'she extends' (שִׁלְּחָה) to the distaff – v. 19
>   **B** 'her palms' (כַּפֶּיהָ) grab the spindle
> ==
>   **B'** 'her palm' (כַּפָּהּ) she spreads out to the poor – v. 20
> **A'** 'her hands' (יָדֶיהָ) 'she extends' (שִׁלְּחָה) to the needy

Thus "the hands that grasp to produce open wide to provide" (Van Leeuwen 1997:262)—with others at all times being the focus of this woman's undivided attention and efforts.

Verse 20 then acts as the start of a new discourse unit (B) that extends through v. 27 and underscores the worthy woman's various acts of provision in the community at large. There is an apparent *intensification* in subject matter here (similar to that which accompanies the A-B parallelism of poetic lines) as our heroine's personal characteristics and wider contributions to the society (especially in vv. 25–27) are exemplified in a series of images that roughly (imperfectly) pattern in a chiastic fashion as follows (cf. Waltke 2005:528):

---

[7] Verse 21 (ל-initial) begins the second half of the Hebrew alphabet, letters 12–22.

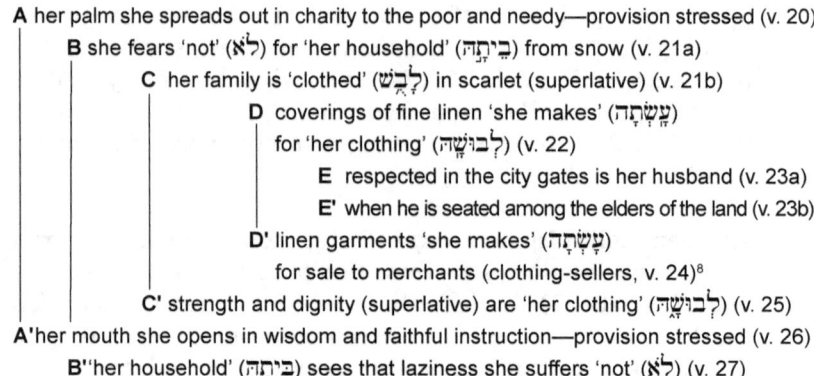

    A her palm she spreads out in charity to the poor and needy—provision stressed (v. 20)
       B she fears 'not' (לֹא) for 'her household' (בֵּיתָהּ) from snow (v. 21a)
         C her family is 'clothed' (לָבֻשׁ) in scarlet (superlative) (v. 21b)
           D coverings of fine linen 'she makes' (עָשְׂתָה)
             for 'her clothing' (לְבוּשָׁהּ) (v. 22)
               E respected in the city gates is her husband (v. 23a)
               E' when he is seated among the elders of the land (v. 23b)
           D' linen garments 'she makes' (עָשְׂתָה)
             for sale to merchants (clothing-sellers, v. 24)[8]
         C' strength and dignity (superlative) are 'her clothing' (לְבוּשָׁהּ) (v. 25)
A' her mouth she opens in wisdom and faithful instruction—provision stressed (v. 26)
    B' 'her household' (בֵּיתָהּ) sees that laziness she suffers 'not' (לֹא) (v. 27)

The validity of this structural pattern is certainly debatable, but it does appear to foreground several noteworthy features of section B—in particular, the central core that unexpectedly shifts the focus of attention from the worthy wife to 'her husband'. There is probably a subtle implication suggested by this arrangement of content that it is in fact *her* excellent character and industry which has contributed a great deal to what *he* is in society. The structural twist at the end, from B'-A' to A'-B' might also be thematically significant, for the shift draws attention to v. 26 and the assertion that our heroine is distinguished by typical 'elder'-like discourse, as characterized by a pair of crucial sapiential concepts, 'wisdom' (חָכְמָה) and 'faithful instruction' (תּוֹרַת־חֶסֶד). Indeed, these are the qualities that epitomize the godly understanding that Proverbs promotes (cf. 1:2, 1:8, 3:3, 3:19, 5:13, 13:14, 24:3, 28:26), and all the implicit and overt 'instruction' of this God-fearing woman was in turn wholly informed by the divine principles expounded in this book.

If we exclude the only verse in the Body that refers to someone other than the 'worthy wife' (the structurally central v. 23), we find that there is an essential quantitative lexical parity between sections A and B—that is, forty-six versus forty-seven word units. On the other hand, it is also important to observe a major syntactic feature that distinguishes these two sections: each verse of A, except for the transitional v. 19, displays a consistent verb-initial sequence, while this is not the case in section B, where each verse begins with some constituent other than the verb. In v. 28 there is a return to

---

[8] Literally, 'Canaanites' (כְּנַעֲנִי)—the name of the people came to designate (metonymy) the activity that characterized them in ANE times, that is, as merchants and traders.

3.2 Structural organization of the eulogy

the syntactic pattern of A, that is, a (perfective) verb-initial verse, now accompanied by a major shift in subject (to 'her children' בָּנֶיהָ), which thus marks the onset of the poem's conclusion.

Conclusion (31:28–31)
Three key terms link the poem's Conclusion with its Introduction by way of a prominent mirrored *inclusio*: 'wife' (אִשָּׁה, vv. 10/30); 'worthy' (חַיִל, vv. 10/29); 'her husband' (בַּעְלָהּ, vv. 11/28). 'Praise' is the keynote of this closing section, and the focus shifts from what the worthy wife does for her family and community to the acclaim which they accord her in return (e.g., 'she is praised' תִתְהַלָּל – v. 30b). There is a progressive widening of social scope and emotive intensity as this segment moves from 'her children' (v. 28a), to 'her husband' (v. 28b), to the entire community of Israel (v. 31), including the leaders and most honored who sit in the council of elders 'at the city gates' (בַּשְּׁעָרִים)—where she may also be seated beside 'her husband', v. 23; cf. v. 26). The climax of this encomium comes as its female subject, the most excellent lady who exemplifies the essence of Covenantal character (v. 26), is pointedly conjoined with the topic of book of Proverbs as a whole: 'the woman/ wife who fears YHWH, she [= indeed!] is to be praised!' (אִשָּׁה יִרְאַת־יְהוָה הִיא תִתְהַלָּל –v. 30b; thus a unifying semantic linkage is forged with the book's beginning in 1:7).[9]

We see how the foundational acrostic format that delineates this poem as a whole is itself artistically demarcated by other distinctive structural as well as semantic patterns.[10] The essence of this encomium could be condensed within the scope of its Introduction (vv. 10–12) plus the Conclusion (vv. 28–31). The motivation, or rationale, of the latter is fully expressed in the former (v. 12). The Body then constitutes a poetic expansion that celebrates its personal subject— the 'worthy wife'—and urges the audience to identify emotively with the poet's rhetorical purpose and application, namely, to 'praise' this wonderful woman (along with all those like her) and the godly 'wisdom' she personifies. Garrett has

---

[9] Lawrence summarizes the descriptive lexical choices that "are reminiscent of masculinity in the Bible. Furthermore, "the woman is praised for characteristics that are highlighted throughout [Hebrew] wisdom literature" (2009:341–343; cf. the discussion of 'heroic poetry' in 3.4.2).

[10] This praise poem also manifests certain intertextual links with the poems of personified wisdom in the first section of the book. For example, both Lady Wisdom and the virtuous woman are more valuable than precious jewels (31:10 > 8:11; cf. also: 31:10 > 3:15; 31:26 > 1:20-33, 8:1-11; 31:28 > 3:18, 8:34; 31:30 > 8:17).

suggested that the entire poem is structured as an intricate chiasmus, as shown below (1993:248—I have modified the wording of his parallel panels):

A: The high value of a 'worthy' wife—asserted (v.10)
  B: The husband is greatly benefited by such a wife (vv.11–12)
    C: This wife works very hard to manage her household—the details (vv.13–19)
      D: his wife gives generously to the poor in society (v.20)
        E: This wife fears no material adversity (v.21a)
          F: Her children are 'clothed' in the finest dress (v.21b)
            G: This wife 'makes' woven coverings and clothing (v.22)
              →H: *This wife brings public prestige and position to her husband!* (v.23)
            G' This wife 'makes' woven products, supplying them to merchants (v.24)
          F': This wife is 'clothed' in the best moral character (v.25a)
        E': This wife fears no moral adversity (v.25b)
      D': This wife teaches wisely in her community (v.26)
    C' This wife works very hard to manage her household—a summary (v.27)
  B': The husband and children praise such a wife (vv.28–29)
A': The high value of a 'YHWH-fearing' wife—reaffirmed (vv.30–31)

Garrett rightly concludes, "Either one of these [the acrostic or the chiastic structure] is sufficient evidence of the poet's skill; the integration of the two is astounding" (1993:248).

These internal units and their intricate arrangements in relation to each other function to give the eulogy a thematically well-developed poetic shape as well as periodic stress points that accent certain key junctures of the author's sapiential argument in favor of divine 'wisdom' and a devoted 'wife' (or are they metaphorically one and the same?). The manner in which these varied and seemingly flexible subsections are created within such a rigid structure as the acrostic further demonstrates the superb artistic skill and keen theological insight of the author.

3.3 Stylistic features of the eulogy

In this section I call attention to a selection of the varied stylistic features that not only establish the poetic quality of this text but, more importantly, also perform a distinctive discourse function as structural and/or thematic 'markers'.[11] Again, it is interesting to observe how many creative literary

---

[11] There are many more, functionally significant literary features that we might have drawn attention to, but space does not allow for it; for more details, consult especially the commentaries by Garrett (1993) and Waltke (2005), plus the extensive study notes in the New English Translation (NET).

3.3 Stylistic features of the eulogy

features the poet was able to incorporate within the apparently rigid shape of an acrostic macro-form.

3.3.1 Phonological

Any type of poetry must emphasize the *oral-aural* features of discourse, for the text, certainly in Scripture, is preeminently meant to be proclaimed (sung, prayed) aloud. So it is not surprising that this ode exhibits the full repertory of Hebrew phonological poetic devices, such as: a relatively balanced lineation throughout,[12] regularized line length (3–4 lexical units) creating a typical word-accent rhythm, plus the special features of alliteration, assonance, and even some wordplay. Below then we list several prominent instances of artistically deployed phonology—sound being used to create formal cohesions and also in service of certain aspects of the poem's meaning:[13]

- Alliteration in /b/ near the beginning of the ode highlights the 'trust' (בָּטַח) that the 'heart of her husband' (לֵב בַּעְלָהּ) has 'in her' (בָּהּ), that is, his noble wife (v. 11a).[14]

- Assonance in /a/ and alliteration with /p/ associate the first pair of words in v. 20 as well as v. 26—thus reinforcing the thematic linkage between these two key verses, which occur in parallel positions within the chiastic structures noted above: כַּפָּהּ פָּרְשָׂה — פִּיהָ פָּתְחָה.

- Alliteration in /l/ marks the final poetic colon of the Body (v. 27b), an effect that is heightened by the mirrored order of sounds in the final two words: לֹא תֹאכֵל '(laziness) she does not eat (i.e., tolerate)!'

- There is a possible interlingual wordplay that distinguishes the onset of v. 27 as well—i.e., the initial verbal צוֹפִיָּה ('she [is] watching over') which

---

[12] Each of the poem's twenty-two verses is a standard bicolon, except v.15, which has three lines. The second and third are similar to Prov. 27:27b-c, so the final line of the tricolon is "suspicious" to some commentators (e.g., Murphy 1998:244), i.e., possibly "an editorial expansion" (Van Leeuwen 1997:261). There is not much textual support, however, for any excision (the LXX, for example, includes the last, a nominal, line).

[13] As Nielsen notes "[P]oetry and sound are closely associated… In Hebrew, the rhythm of the text is created by the use of stressed syllables, whereas unstressed syllables are not counted…. 'Hebrew poetry is marked by a delicate balance between regularity and variation'…" (2009:294, citing D. Petersen and K. Richards).

[14] It is extraordinary in Scripture for anyone or anything to be 'trusted' other than YHWH/God—"One can successfully place confidence only in Yahweh…" (Gerstenberger, cited in Waltke 2005:521).

clearly resembles the Greek noun for 'wisdom' (σοφία), obviously a most significant correspondence in the present context (see Waltke 2005:513 and Murphy 1998:244 for the argumentation regarding this point).

- Echoes of 'praise' for the worthy wife ring out in the poem's Conclusion (vv. 28b, 31b), an effect that is intensified by the reiterated verbs' phonic proximity to the familiar psalmic appeal 'praise Yah!': הַלְלוּ יָהּ – וִיהַלְלוּהָ + וַיְהַלְלָהּ (cf. the earlier reference to 'trust in her' in v. 11a).

3.3.2 Syntactic

The important requirement of an acrostic poem of course is to position a word beginning with the right letter in its proper sequence at the front of the verse—and to do so naturally, so that the text does not sound strange or disjointed, despite the relative lack of conjunctions or other transitional expressions. It is quite impressive to observe how well the poet has managed this in Proverbs 31:10–31 so as to give the whole piece a sense of cohesive progression along with a definite compositional shape (*Introduction—Body—Conclusion*), including periodic thematic peak passages (e.g., vv. 23, 26, 29; cf. the structural analysis above).

This feature of strategic syntactic placement is prominently manifested at the very start of the poem as the central personage and theme is immediately announced via object-fronting: (אֵשֶׁת־חַיִל –v.10a). The mirrored chiastic text structures displayed above are a larger instance of this literary facility. Similarly, the contrastive opening grammatical structures of successive verses in the two sections of the ode's Body have already been noted, namely, A = verb-initial, B = non verb-initial.

In v. 28 we find an example of such positioning on a smaller scale, though it is significant here as an initial boundary marker (i.e., of the Conclusion) as well as an indication of a shift in focus from the heroine's activities and qualities to her family's acclaim of the same: the initial verb '*they* rise up' (קָמוּ) in line A calls immediate attention to the fact that something important is about to take place—namely, 'they call her blessed' (וַיְאַשְּׁרוּהָ)—while the first word of line B is a nominal absolute that focuses the discourse spotlight more sharply on 'her husband' (בַּעְלָהּ). An elaborate double chiasm appears to function as an extra device to foreground the pair of verses that describe the praiseworthy character of this distinguished lady (vv. 25–26; cf. Waltke 2005:532):

v. 25: A: nominal clause + B: *verbal* clause

3.3 Stylistic features of the eulogy

v. 26: A: *verbal* clause + B: nominal clause
v. 26: A: 'her mouth' (m) – *'wisdom'* (f) // B: *'instruction'* (f) – 'her tongue' (m)

Finally, the poem's last two words reflect back upon the high esteem that this worthy wife *shares* with her husband in the community in v. 23 (which is also the core of the chiastic structure that hypothetically spans the discourse): 'at the gates, her makings/doings/works' (בַּשְׁעָרִים מַעֲשֶׂיהָ); cf. 'she makes' (עָשְׂתָה –v.22), 'at the gates' (בַּשְׁעָרִים –v.23), 'she makes' (עָשְׂתָה –v.24).[15]

3.3.3 Lexical-semantic

In this section we simply mention and exemplify four chief facets of the verbal inventory employed in the eulogy to distinguish the outstanding nature of the special object of its admiration, a most wonderful wife: concrete imagery, figurative language, lexical choice, and local repetition.

- Concrete imagery: An interwoven series of diverse, ANE life-related images reveals the multifaceted talents and capabilities of the heroine: a valuable trade (weaving, vv. 13, 19), domestic management and provision (14–15, 21–22, 27a), commercial activities (16, 18, 24), industry (17, 27b), charity (20), social skills (25–26). Like Wisdom in contrast to Folly, she thereby brings her husband 'good/prosperity' (טוֹב), not 'evil/poverty' (רָע); the implied antithesis to a contentious, rapacious wife/woman runs throughout the text (vv. 12, 30a; cf. 9:13, 21:19, 25:24, 27:15).

- Figurative language: The imagery just noted is punctuated by a sequence of similes, metaphors, and especially metonymies that similarly accent the lady's diverse skills and aptitudes, thus supporting and elaborating on the opening assertion that 'her worth [is] far more than jewels (פְּנִינִים—rubies, corals?)' (31:10—note the analogy to Wisdom, 3:13–15). Reiterated references to 'her hand' (יָדֶיהָ) or 'her palms' (כַּפֶּיהָ) (e.g., v. 13) and related body parts, for example, lend cohesion to the poem, while at the same time underscoring the heroine's productive labors as she takes up one vital activity after another (vv. 13, 17, 19, 20, 31). Correspondingly, her remarkable

---

[15] In fact, every word of v. 31 reiterates one that occurs elsewhere in the poem—a fitting summary indeed.

intellectual aptitudes are stressed through metonymies of speech involving 'her mouth' (פִּיהָ) and 'her tongue' (לְשׁוֹנָהּ) (v.26).

- Lexical choice: Here it is important to observe a stylistic feature that normally lies beneath the surface of any translation. On several occasions extraordinary, largely male-oriented terms are applied to the wife's activities or attributes, thus lending an element of hyperbole and a heroic tone to her ongoing description—beginning with the poem's second word: (חַיִל), i.e., 'valiant, vigorous, vibrant, brave, bold', even 'prosperous' (e.g., Gen. 47:6, Exod. 18:21, Josh. 1:14, Judg. 3:29, Ruth 2:1, Ps. 18:32, Isa. 5:22). This dynamic woman brings her husband 'plunder, booty' (שָׁלָל—i.e., gain. profit, v. 11); she is like unto wide-ranging, profit-producing 'merchant ships' (אֳנִיּוֹת סוֹחֵר, v. 14); like a wild animal hunting at night (implied?) she provides 'prey' (טֶרֶף) for her family (i.e., needed food, v. 15); 'she girds her loins with strength' (חָגְרָה בְעוֹז מָתְנֶיהָ), i.e., she energetically tackles every task (v. 17); like a military officer she 'sends forth, commissions' (שִׁלְּחָה) her hands to do their daily duties (v. 19); she trades her wares on the open market, like all the other 'merchants' ('Canaanites' כְּנַעֲנִי –v. 24). Also highly significant as far as word selection is concerned is the paired set of terms used in vv. 25–26 to describe the woman's exceptional character and manner of discourse: 'strength and majesty/dignity' (עֹז־וְהָדָר) coupled with 'wisdom and loyal teaching' (חָכְמָה וְתוֹרַת־חֶסֶד). Such language is usually reserved for royalty and the leaders of Israel, so there is no doubt that she (and every woman like her) is to be included!

- Local repetition: Many instances of structurally significant recursion within the eulogy have already been pointed out, along with several figurative examples, e.g., 'hand' and the reiterated call to 'praise' the wise and wonderful wife in the poem's Conclusion (vv. 29–31). Three additional instances of crucial repetition should be mentioned: first, there is the 'clothing' metaphor, which not only distinguishes the heroine's honorable character (בּוּשָׁהּ –v. 25), but also by implication her husband's as well, for he is virtually surrounded by her 'clothing' industry (vv. 21–22/23/24). "Just as clothes immediately indicate something of the nature and circumstances of the person, so do [the] virtues" attributed to his wife in vv. 25–26 (*NET*, p.1107). Accordingly, a woman who 'fears' (יִרְאַת) the LORD will 'never fear' (לֹא־תִירָא) for her family (vv. 30, 21)! More surprisingly, the characteristic of 'valor' (חַיִל) is first said to be exceedingly rare among women (v. 10)—nevertheless, even though 'many women' in

3.3 Stylistic features of the eulogy

the world could possibly be found displaying it (v. 29a),[16] the female object of this ode would still 'surpass them all' (v. 29b).

3.3.4 Discourse mode

In this section we mention a few remaining stylistic features of somewhat larger scope that distinguish the panegyric poem of Proverbs 31:1–31. These perform an obvious rhetorical, personal persuasive function within the text (cf. section 3.4) since, as in the case of repetition and phonological accentuation, they appeal more or less to a present listening audience. Each of the following four devices also involves a noticeable shift in expectancy with regard to either the current development of the discourse or its prevailing manner of verbal expression.

- Rhetorical question: This attention-grabbing technique (v. 10a) opens the ode and helps set the tone for the eulogy to follow. The implied answer to the rhetorical question 'Who can find…?!' (מִי יִמְצָא) is *not*: 'Nobody (can find such a wonderful woman)!'—but rather: 'How valuable she is (when found)!' (cf. v. 10b). The further implication is that 'her husband' must surely take this to heart and act accordingly towards her (vv. 11–12).

- Imperative predication: This unexpected utterance mode at the end of the poem (v. 31) balances out the rhetorical question (RQ) at the beginning of the poem. We have meanwhile been lulled into a certain rhythm with the thick description that characterizes the overall discourse. All of a sudden, the audience is called to attention and stirred into making some tangible response, at least in their minds and with their voices: 'Give her…!' (תְּנוּ־לָהּ) and then 'let them praise her…!' (וִיהַלְלוּהָ).

- Direct speech: A single snatch of direct discourse is incorporated into this poetic hymn of praise, again, at a key point within the text, namely, as part of its concluding strophe (v. 29). The heroine's husband—who owes so much to her (perhaps even his very status and role within the community, cf. vv. 12, 23)—is moved to exclaim in her very presence: '…as for you, you surpass all [women]!' (וְאַתְּ עָלִית עַל־כֻּלָּנָה).[17]

---

[16] The term used to designate 'women' here—lit. 'daughters' (בָּנוֹת)—is not really chauvinistic or deprecating (e.g., J. P. Lange, cited in Waltke 2005:534); rather, in this poetic setting, it is probably a heroic or epic reference that further highlights the one who surpasses them all.

[17] Note too the amplifying alliteration here formed by the reiterated guttural and

- Hyperbolic discourse: As noted above, a touch of hyperbole resonates throughout the eulogy, thus contributing to its heroic tone and implication. This worthy woman seems larger than life—indeed, she would put many men to shame with her varied activities and personal achievements, both at home and within the society at large (e.g., vv. 14, 16, 21, 24–25). Verse 18 exemplifies the richness of expression that such discourse inspires: 'She perceives (lit. 'tastes' טָעֲמָה) that her merchandise (i.e., its profit) is good—her lamp is not extinguished during the night'. She probably does 'burn the midnight oil', literally, in order to get things done, but in this context a figurative sense is also apparent, i.e., the 'lamp/light' (נֵרָהּ) of her prosperity does not grow dim or go out.

3.4 Rhetorical dynamics of the poem

Up to this point in our study we have focused upon the artistic form of the acrostic poem that spans Proverbs 31:10–31 and to some extent also the literary function of certain stylistic features within that poetic structure. We must now widen the scope of consideration to briefly, and somewhat speculatively, comment on the ostensive *communicative purpose* of the discourse within its textual as well as extratextual setting.

3.4.1 Frames of reference

The following diagram is a summary of the principal 'frames of reference' (Wilt 2003:55–56) that specify the contextual dynamics of this climactic poem to a worthy wife; five levels of inclusion may be posited:

1. **Contemporary**: Tonga living in present-day Zambia
    2. **Original**: the ANE setting of Proverbs and the religious philosophy of the author/redactor
        3. **Literary**: *father* ('Solomon') instructing his son (1:1, 8; 2:1, etc.)
            4. **Incorporated**: *mother* (of King 'Lemuel') instructing her son (31:1–31)
                5. **Incorporated'**: an acrostic poem (31:10–31)

The first level applies only to a *translation* and dissemination of the original Hebrew text, which will be dealt with in section 3.7 below. Level 2 constitutes the communicative setting of the book of Proverbs as a whole and

---

dental consonants.

3.4 Rhetorical dynamics of the poem

the presumed aims of its author(s) and subsequent editor(s). An adequate consideration of this topic lies well beyond the scope of our study, and we can only state our general concurrence with the conclusion of Murphy (1981:52–53; cf. 6–9; confirmed more recently by Waltke 2005:58–63):

> Whatever may be the ultimate origins of the sayings and instructions (family, tribe, etc), the collections in this book are attributed by title to 'wise men' and kings (Solomon, Lemuel, perhaps Agur; cf. the mention of Hezekiah in 25:1). It is reasonable to conclude, therefore, that in this form they derive from the school associated with the royal court.

The 'literary' level (3), which features a number of distinct 'incorporations' throughout the book, in particular, its conclusion (31:10–31; level 5) will be the focus of our attention.

3.4.2 Genre

Any investigation of the communicative function of a literary work—or from a related perspective, its chief rhetorical aims—must at some point take up the issue of *genre*, how the discourse was generally intended to operate in its primary setting of use. The elaborate lyric of Proverbs 31:10–31 is rather complex in this regard, for it may be seen to function in several mutually complementary ways, some of which have already been mentioned— namely, 'ode' and 'eulogy' (a text that formally praises a person's character and achievements). The acrostic structure plus the poem's very inclusion within the corpus of Proverbs would certainly commend it more broadly as an instance of sapiential or didactic wisdom literature. Its resemblance in certain salient respects to Psalms 111 and 112 (twin acrostic psalms with reference to God and man respectively) would allow one to classify the ode also as an example of liturgical praise,[18] or more specifically as a 'heroic hymn', with similarities to the song of Deborah (Judg. 5; cf. Waltke 2005:516–517; Wolters 1988; Lawrence 2009:342). *Heroic* poetry typically lauds the daring exploits, usually military, and the extraordinary character of the central personage in elevated descriptive and hyperbolic language, and such a categorization would seem to apply very well to what we have in chapter 31.

---

[18] Ross gives a handy summary of the main correspondences with Ps. 111 (e.g., 'fear of the LORD', 111:10) and comments: "Usually a hymn is written to God, but here apparently it was written to the wife of noble character" (1991:1006). And we observe in this connection also the patent links with Ps. 112, which details the various blessings that come to 'the man who fears the LORD' (v. 1). Thus Prov. 31:10–31 makes a strong case for the fact that such blessings also accrue to the God-fearing woman/wife!

But why would such a hymn be found in Proverbs, situated at its very close as an apparent epilogue—and why would it be written in honor of a woman, rather than the king or one of Israel's most eminent wise men? This issue, too, has generated all sorts of scholarly speculation, which we will not go into here (cf. Waltke 2005:518–520). Suffice it to say that the presence of this particular ode at the end of the book is a surprise that must have some important rhetorical motivation; thus it does not appear here as a literary accident or as a result of the clumsy work of some final editor of the collection. We might begin by taking seriously this composite text on its own terms, that is, as it presents itself on the overt 'literary' level of discourse (level 3 in the diagram above). Obviously, the acrostic structure sets the portion covering vv. 10–31 off on its own as a distinct literary unit—but is it completely independent, having no connections with any preceding text? That never happens in verbal art, oral or written, secular or religious; the very fact of juxtaposition automatically relates one pericope conceptually to another (and often many more) that has preceded it within the larger whole. This brings us to the opening portion of ch. 31, vv. 1–9, and the question of the ostensive *rhetorical exigency*, or setting: *Who* is speaking to *whom* under what situational *circumstances*?

3.4.3 Rhetorical exigency

What is the ostensive life-setting of the worthy-wife ode? The chapter begins with a *superscription*, or heading: 'The words of King Lemuel—an oracle that his mother taught him': (דִּבְרֵי לְמוּאֵל מֶלֶךְ מַשָּׂא אֲשֶׁר־יִסְּרַתּוּ אִמּוֹ).[19] Thus, according to the text, the king is simply serving as a mouthpiece for his mother! The fact of her royal authorship is underscored by the three vocatives referring to her 'son' (the Aramaic form בַּר), found in the opening verse (2) along with a direct mention of his name in v. 4 (לְמוֹאֵל). This speech is noteworthy for several other reasons, over and above its forthright didactic content. It is the only time that a 'king' is addressed in the entire book, a feature which was normal in the wisdom literature of other ANE traditions. Furthermore, it is the only time we have a woman represented as actually giving *beneficial* advice (cf. 1:8b), other than that of the female personification of 'wisdom' (חָכְמָה), e.g., 8:1 (cf. the enticing words of the prostitute in 7:14–20). So at the onset of this chapter, the discourse is carefully distinguished, perhaps implicitly suggesting to the audience (or readership) that the book of Proverbs is proceeding to some

---

[19] Through a slight emendation of the MT, the text reads: "The words of Lemuel, King of Massa, which..." (Murphy 1998:239). This reading does not affect my interpretation of the passage.

3.4 Rhetorical dynamics of the poem

point of content culmination—thus a text to take notice of and to reflect very seriously upon.

But the next issue to consider is one of scope: where does the queen mother's address to her son conclude? Many commentators find the terminus in v. 9, with a completely new and separate discourse beginning at the acrostic poem of v. 10. But there is no other formal indication of such a break in the Hebrew text, which reads as if the royal lady-cum-sage simply carries on, now with a much more highly embellished as well as a contrastive close to her motherly instructions (i.e., from 'watch out for'—v. 3, to 'watch for'—v. 10). Furthermore, as Kitchen notes (1977:100-101, cited in Waltke 2004:28):

> The subject matter of verses 10-31...is wholly consistent with the reputed origin of the work...both being feminine....Conversely, if verses 10-31 be excluded from Lemuel, then (i) the resulting first 'work' of only 9 verses becomes ludicrously brief, and (ii) the supposed second 'work' of vv. 10-31 becomes an isolated poem with no title and falls outside the instructional literary genre altogether. It would then be an anomalously foreign body in the Proverbs.

There is also an explicit interlocking device that ties the two texts, vv. 1-9 and 10-31, together—namely, the very act of speaking. Both King Lemuel and the most excellent wife are said to 'open the mouth' (פָּתְחָה פִּיהָ) in a positively proactive way in society—he, at the urging of his mother, to uphold the rights of the downtrodden (vv. 8-9), and she to dispense wise, covenant-supportive discourse (v. 26). Similarly, he is enjoined to demonstrate, while she already manifests, a heart for 'the poor and the needy' (עָנִי וְאֶבְיוֹן – vv. 9b, 20ab). From a larger compositional perspective, the final female-oriented pericope of ch. 31 as a whole neatly balances out the book's initial section by way of correspondence (didactic discourse) as well as contrast (the king (Solomon) speaks in chs. 1-9).

3.4.4 Rhetorical purpose

So taking the biblical text at face value then and hence assuming a strong 'motherly' focus and didactic orientation throughout ch. 31, what is the rhetorical point and purpose of this ode to the noble wife? What did the original author of this poem and/or the final editor of the book of Proverbs want to teach any potential audience through such an artistically composed discourse? Of course, one must again remain on the tenuous level of speculation here, but that has not prevented commentators from advancing a number of complementary theories, a representative summary of which follows, with my own suggestion beginning the list:

- The *acrostic* poetic form suggests at the outset that its portrait of the female in the foreground is idealized to a greater or lesser extent. She is not to be construed as the 'average' lady of that day in Israelite society. Rather, she is in many respects exceptional—everything that a woman of that day and age could (and *should?*) be in relation to her husband and family, the wider community, and above all, her God—YHWH (v. 30b is a passage at the poem's peak).

- "The poem captures all the themes of wisdom that have been presented in the book and arranges them in this portrait of the ideal woman....The heroic mode [of poetry]...allows the sage to make all the lessons of wisdom in the book concrete and practical, [and] it provides a polemic against the culture that saw women as merely decorative..." (*NET* 1106).

- "[V] 23 actually establishes the central message of the poem: this woman is the kind of a wife a man needs in order to be successful in life....[T]he original intended audience was not young women ('this is what kind of wife you should be') but young men ('this is what kind of wife you should get')" (Garrett 1993:248).

- "[T]his valiant wife has been canonized as a role model for all Israel for all time. Wise daughters aspire to be like her, wise men seek to marry her (v. 10), and all wise people aim to incarnate the wisdom she embodies, each in his [her] own sphere of activity" (Waltke 2005:520).

- "The poem describes the ideal wife from the husband's vantage point [though supposedly composed by a woman]; these were qualities a man should look for in his beloved (see Canticles as offering a complementary point of view). On the other hand, the poem also holds out an ideal which Israelite society held up for the woman herself" (Murphy 1981:82). Perhaps she is to be viewed as the composite portrait of perfect womanhood in Israel—indeed, "an illustration of what happens to the man who marries Woman Wisdom" (Clifford 1998:68).

3.4 Rhetorical dynamics of the poem 95

- As admirably exemplified in the concluding acrostic ode, "the gender slant in Proverbs is a matter of audience orientation rather than ideological bias. Proverbs directs the reader away from the prostitute and toward the good wife because its implied reader is a young man" (Garrett 1993:248–249).

- The closest Jewish equivalent to ANE heroic poetry shifted the emphasis from military to moral heroism and that is evident in Proverbs 31:10–31: "Heroism of the battlefield is transposed in this case...to a woman's *vita activa* in home and community" (Wolters 1988:457).

- "The Wisdom of God is here expressed in the creativity, responsibility and artistry of managing a home, providing for the needs of others, and taking a stand on the side of the poor" (Atkinson 1996:169). At this point a pertinent question would be: to what degree did this exceptional woman and wife range further out into the wider community to exert a more significant intellectual and moral influence in the society at large—and, to what extent was she (as a vehicle for the author) encouraging other women to do the same?

Virtually all commentators assume that the author of this ode was a male and, due to the evident perfection of its composition, perhaps even Solomon himself. What difference would it make to the rhetorical dynamics of this eulogy, whether then or now, if it had actually been composed as stated in the original instance by the mother of King Lemuel (31:1)? Could a woman not learn to imitate the courtly, and in this case also heroic, style of poetic expression? Obviously, there are several clear lyric precedents in the canon of Hebrew religious literature (e.g., Judg. 5, 1 Sam. 2:1–10; cf. Luke 1:46–55).

3.4.5 Implied audience

Finally, we also need to say a word about the *audience* point of view on this closing piece, for the effect of rhetoric cannot be evaluated from an authorial perspective alone. This matter too raises some interesting, but unanswerable questions. How controversial would this female-oriented ode have been in its original setting, for example, with regard to the assertion of v. 26? Would Hebrew hearers (readers) regard this poem as evincing a standard or a novel point of view, and would men and women differ on this issue? Is there an element of irony involved in the eulogy's development—who among a typical audience would expect a woman, any wife, in Israel to perform so well and to be so prominently acclaimed in society? True, there is an emphasis on the status of her husband 'at the city gate' (v. 23, cf. the earlier structural analysis), but he is completely enveloped in the admirable exploits of his wife,[20] a fact which he himself recognizes (v. 29)! Could this possibly be a subtle protest against chauvinistic attitudes and associated customs that restricted the activities of women, thus greatly limiting their potential, not only in social and intellectual circles, but also in the religious sphere (v. 30)?

But questions such as these, inscrutable as they are based on our present knowledge, may best be transferred from the realm of exegesis to that of contemporary application. What is the relative impact and appeal of this heroic hymn in praise of a wonderful woman—and by extension women in general—in the hermeneutical setting of the Tonga people of Zambia, where a discourse of this strength and stature is very much needed in a society that has traditionally been oppressively patriarchal in character? Such current issues will be explored more fully in section 3.6. In any case, whatever the audience in whichever language, there is one effect that should be common to all, as in the original setting of performance: this is the force of the final imperative of v. 31. Here at the poem's climax, *no matter who* you might be, you are called upon to render to this woman in word and deed the public commendation she is due—and to wonder, perhaps, whether there are not others like her in your own society and culture who deserve the same. Paraphrasing the words of C. S. Lewis, "If we do not admire what is praiseworthy and act accordingly with regard to that which is so deserving of our praise, we shall be stupid, insensible, and great losers" (cited in Waltke 2005:536).

3.5 The eulogy in relation to Proverbs as a whole

The heading of chapter 31 (v. 1) announces what appears to be the seventh (a significant number?) distinct 'collection' within the canonical book of Proverbs (with similar headings or collection markers occurring

---

[20] "The husband is hardly present in vv. 10–31, and he is only a foil for the description of the wife" (Murphy 1998:249). Perhaps that is being a bit too hard on him: the structural positions in which the husband appears in the poem, i.e., at the beginning, the middle, and the end, would surely suggest that his thematic role is rather more significant, though obviously downplayed to that of his wife. "The language used to describe the wife ascribes to her physical, emotional, and intellectual strength, while the male is a bystander, an observer of her abilities. His most important task in the poem is to praise his wife, to point out and honor the extent to which she is remarkable" (Lawrence 2009:343).

3.5 The eulogy in relation to Proverbs as a whole

at 1:1, 10:1, 22:17, 24:23, 25:1, and 30:1; Waltke 2004:9).[21] The eulogy (function) and epilogue (form) of vv. 10–31 then constitutes the concluding climax of the entire book—the proverbial 'capstone' that reflects the key educational themes and moral requirements of the entire literary edifice, including its central defining worldview notion regarding 'the fear of the LORD' (v. 30). This last expression (יִרְאַת־יְהֹוָה) is apparently meant to be a communicative clue that conceptually links up listeners (readers) with the book's beginning (1:7) and the critical attribute of 'wisdom' (חָכְמָה), which is a quality that the 'worthy wife' displays in all her everyday dealings (31:26).

Thus, from a larger thematic perspective, it is arguable that the twofold formal and semantic nature of ch. 31, in which a wise woman (vv. 10–31) is contrasted with a potentially foolish man (vv. 2–9, i.e., King Lemuel, if he disregards the advice of his mother) is meant to correspond to and reinforce by recursion the antithetical character of 'Dame Wisdom' and 'Dame Folly' in the first major structural unit of Proverbs (chs. 1–9, e.g., 9:1–12 versus 9:13–18).[22] These verbal and topical similarities and the *inclusio* which they patently forge thus bring the book of Proverbs to an aesthetically satisfying close from a structural or literary-compositional point of view.

But is there not more here in terms of meaning and functional significance? Are we to view the 'woman/wife' of this poem as an exceptional true-to-life character (such as Ruth),[23] as some idealized paragon of female virtues, or indeed, as a symbolical personification of the divinely-or-

---

[21] The text of Proverbs as a whole is quite symmetrical, consisting of the following primary units: I—A Prologue, 'the proverbs of Solomon' (1:1–7); B Paired contrastive exhortations to receive Wisdom and reject Folly (1:8–9:18); II—A First collection of Solomon's proverbs (10:1–22:16); B Two appendices of wise 'sayings' (22:17–24:34); III—A Second collection of Solomon's proverbs, by King Hezekiah (25:1–29:27); B Two appendices of wise 'sayings' (30:1–31:31). As for the final unit, in the LXX 31:10–31 is separated from 31:1–9 by chs. 25–29, thus suggesting an independent origin. However, the two passages are combined in the MT, which is our primary point of reference. The absence of any transitional linkage between vv.9 and 10 suggests that the two texts were meant to be read and interpreted together as a motherly didactic and panegyric 'oracle' (31:1).

[22] "[T]he conjunction of the two descriptions [in ch. 9] implies that the immoral woman is the personification of folly" (Berry 1995:133). In another respect 31:10–31 serves to redress the apparent 'imbalance' in the treatment of women within the book of Proverbs—here so overwhelmingly positive in contrast to what has been up to this point a largely negative (though not entirely, e.g., 12:4a, 18:22, 19:14) portrait of unfaithful women and prostitutes (2:16–19, 5:3–6, 6:24–29) as well as nagging, belligerent wives (12:4b, 19:13, 21:9, 25:24; cf. Alden 1983:219).

[23] Ruth too was praised in the town of Bethlehem as being a 'worthy woman' (אֵשֶׁת חַיִל – Ruth 3:11; cf. 4:11, 15). It may also be intertextually significant that the book of Ruth follows Proverbs, hence ch. 31:10–31, in the Hebrew Bible (MT).

dained Wisdom ethos that motivates and orientates the entire content of Proverbs? This question has exercised the minds of scholars over the centuries, and we certainly cannot decisively settle this admittedly important exegetical issue. In fact, we wonder whether it really needs to be resolved at all, for does such an effort not in effect diminish the full hermeneutical potential of the text? In other words, it seems more likely that we are dealing with a problem of interpretation that is not a matter of 'either-or', but rather 'both-and'. Thus instead of categorical conclusions such as:

> ...Prov. 31:10–31 is a hymn to Lady Wisdom, written in the heroic mode (Ross 1991:1006)

> ...the valiant wife belongs to the historical, not the allegorical realm (Waltke 2005:518)

I would prefer a more nuanced, accommodative approach that allows for a, b, c…and 'all of the above'. A passage so artfully constructed as Proverbs 31:10–31 would seem, like Wisdom herself (e.g., 3:13–14), to invite a correspondingly manifold mode of construal and cognitive enrichment—one that sees *semantic density* instead of uncompromising options.[24]

Just as there presumably would have been different audiences hearing this verbal portrait of the wonderful woman being lauded in this passage, so we must take into account the possibility of different *levels of interpretation*. A literate sage or scribe in the royal court might immediately view the concluding ode in the light of Proverbs as a whole and thus be inclined to adopt a broader, more sophisticated understanding of the text—as the book's final masterful portrayal of Wisdom and all she stands for in the home, in the surrounding society, as well as in the individual's (male or female) 'fear'-full relationship with Yahweh. Ordinary, down-to-earth listeners would probably interpret the text more literally and locally, hence also practically. For them, this lady would be the supreme example of the

---

[24] A similar hermeneutical phenomenon occurs also on the microlevel of discourse investigation. A salient case in point is the interpretation of the vital, nuclear expression 'fearing YHWH' in v. 30: "יִרְאַת of the MT can be interpreted as a feminine adjective…modifying 'woman'; thus, 'the woman who fears the Lord', although [this is not] the normal vocalization… It is also possible to understand the consonantal text as…[a] construct of the noun meaning 'fear'. Then this could be seen as apposition to 'woman'; thus 'the woman, the fear of the Lord, she is to be praised'. But it is also possible to construe 'fear of the Lord' as the object of the verb; thus, 'the woman, she is to glory in (i.e., find praise in) the fear of the Lord' " (Murphy 1998:244). For its part, the LXX has, "…but the fear of the Lord let her praise." Does one reading contradict another? Not in any significant sense—so might the original author possibly have intended more than one sense to apply here? We cannot put it past him (her!).

3.5 The eulogy in relation to Proverbs as a whole

Yahweh-revering wisdom principles that have been proverbially enunciated throughout the book—someone who puts God and family first, before self. Furthermore, as suggested earlier, she might be viewed as 'the ideal' in two senses—for a young woman to seek to emulate, and for a young man (the principal implied audience) to seek to engage as his wife (while strictly avoiding the antithesis—Lady Folly in the person of a prostitute!). However, such ideals must not be allowed to dissipate and die after marriage,[25] and so this eulogy could also serve as a reminder for a wife and her husband to keep striving to realize, in particular, its evocative vision of mutual admiration, encouragement, and support for one another within the home (vv. 11–12, 23, 28–29). On the other hand, the ode's heroic expressions of manly energy and enterprise may also carry an underlying polemical tone: "...the praise of women here is designed to alter errant male perceptions of women" (Van Leeuwen 1997:264), no matter what deviant or deprecating forms these might assume within a given culture.

I might best summarize my blended (concrete-abstract), more open-ended understanding of the message of Proverb's eulogistic epilogue in the words of two scholars who have stated the case from a Hebrew (in contrast to a Hellenistic) perspective better than I could:

> In chapter 31 Wisdom is a faithful wife and a skilled mistress of her household, finally settled with her own. This ingenious symbolic framework of the book of Proverbs presents a consistent picture of Wisdom. She is not some lofty, remote ideal for those initiated into her mysteries, but a practical, ever-present, faithful guide and lifelong companion for all who choose her ways. Her origins are with God (8:22–30) and her teaching wins blessings from God (8:35). But her home is in this world. This is the way Wisdom herself wanted it. (Murphy 1998:250)

> So most likely what we have in this beautiful poem is not only the idealized picture of the wife whose noble character fills out the blessed life to which 'the fear of the LORD' leads. What we also have is a demonstration of what the life of Wisdom herself would look like, were she to manage the home. Wisdom is no esoteric concept which floats in some mystical realm, out of touch with the ordinary world. (Atkinson 1996:168)[26]

Nothing in ancient literature quite equals this remarkable attestation to the individual qualities and capabilities of a pious, God-fearing woman of

---

[25] "The poem is traditionally recited by Jewish men to their wives on Sabbath evening before the Kiddush (the sanctification of the Sabbath over wine)" (Berlin and Brettler 2004:1497; cf. Ross 1991:1126).

[26] Waltke (2005:518) provides a partial listing of the many correspondences between the

that age (Ehlke 1992:313). From an ANE social setting, value system, and prevailing opinion regarding a wise lady and most excellent wife, we turn now for reflective comparison to a modern African point of view, one that is still heavily influenced by traditional customs and mores. This is set forth to illustrate the need for such a careful comparative study before attempting to *meaningfully* communicate a poem like Proverbs 31:10–31 via translation to a contemporary audience living in a much different place, age, sociocultural context, and religious environment.

3.6 A 'worthy wife' from a Zambian perspective

How do modern-day Zambians regard and respond to the poetic portrait of this heroine of Proverbs 31? How wonderful or ideal does she sound when viewed from the standpoint of a Bantu worldview and sociocultural setting?[27] Of course there are many answers possible, and so the range of consideration must be narrowed considerably in order to fit within the scope of this essay. I will therefore focus my attention upon a selection of the elicited (oral and written) reactions of two distinct audiences: a diverse group of urbanized, second-year theology (seminary) students, and the more homogenous viewpoint of mainly female villagers living in a traditional Tonga rural setting of Zambia.[28] In 3.6.1 I present a verse-by-verse comparison that reveals some of the salient disparities presented by this passage to an average listener/reader. This is followed in 3.6.2 by a few brief suggestions as to how to deal with the main lexical and conceptual discrepancies. Section 3.7 will then be devoted to a more detailed attempt to provide a greater measure of *literary* equivalence in relation to the original text, namely, by means of a poetic re-creation in Tonga.

---

character of the noble wife in 31:10–31 and the sapiential values of Wisdom in the preceding passages of Proverbs.

[27] No Tonga woman, in any setting, could aspire to the accomplishments of the wonderful lady described in the Proverbs passage, who is at once a manufacturer, importer, manager, realtor, farmer, seamstress, upholsterer, merchant—and above all, an excellent mother and overseer of the home!

[28] Specifically, these groups are: (1) a class of sixteen male Lusaka Lutheran Seminary students (who were asked to consult their wives before writing an essay on the subject), and (2) research carried out by the Media Officer of the Bible Society of Zambia, Ms. Perdita Chenjela in June, 2006 among several remote rural villages in the Gwembe Valley Tonga-land of Zambia's Southern Province. The cattle-herding, largely subsistence agricultural Tonga people who live in this region are matrilineal, but patrilocal (i.e., they practice the custom of *lobola* 'bride-wealth' to establish a marriage of two clans) and manifest a lower percentage of Christianity coupled with a greater incidence of polygamy than that which is found in other areas of Butonga, e.g., on the plateau of the Zambezi River Escarpment.

3.6 A 'worthy wife' from a Zambian perspective

3.6.1 A Tonga-Hebrew sociocultural commentary: Proverbs 31:10–31

We present here a sample of the significant divergence in perspectives that exists between an ancient Hebrew and a traditional Bantu worldview, value system, and way of life as manifested in a recent informal survey of public opinion:

v.10: Tonga wealth is not reckoned in jewelry or even cash, but in the number of cattle that a man owns. 'Rubies' are unknown, but emeralds are, and thus could act as a functional equivalent in translation. An 'excellent wife', in turn, is one who is able to bear [many] children, discipline them, cook, wash, clean, dress modestly, till the land, respect and care for her husband and in-laws (especially his parents), offer good advice to her husband—and, keep quiet when men are talking.

v.11: Men 'have confidence in' women who live up to traditional social and cultural expectations, especially in the ability to keep family secrets and produce (female) offspring. Thus the value of a woman is measured by the number of children she has and how well she cares for them. Childlessness, which is normally considered to be the woman's fault, is grounds either for divorce (and the full repayment of *lobola* 'bride wealth'), or an occasion for a man to marry another wife (though the 'senior' wife is still respected on the homestead).

v.12: A good Tonga woman is a hard worker—she makes life 'easy' for her husband. In addition to labor, she also provides him with children, thus increasing his productivity and status in the community. 'All the days'—a marriage arrangement is initially undertaken as a life-long relationship, but her failures may occasion periodic beatings, divorce, or polygamy. A suspicious or jealous wife may even be dangerous when she resorts to the use of powerful 'love' potions (*muzyondo*), hidden body charms, and 'medicine' (for secretly putting into food or drink) in order to maintain the affections and favors of her husband. 'Without the use of such magic,' said one commentator, 'there could be no lasting marriage.'

v.13: Sheep are known in Tonga-land (but not common in the Gwembe Valley), however, the technology of 'wool' preparation is not widespread (though wool products are available in urban shops). 'Cotton' might be a good functional substitute for the unknown 'flax' in this verse. Sewing is familiar to women, but weaving is not.

v.14: Great 'ships' are not known among the Tonga, not even those who live on the shores of Lake Kariba where the biggest boats seen are the *kapenta* fishing trawlers that operate at night. Women bring food only from the family garden nearby; only the men would normally travel away from home for this purpose. Perhaps the closest Zambia-related equivalent would be the large freight 'lorries' that keep the country supplied with various consumer goods from South Africa, whether for commercial sale or personal use.

v.15: This verse is very true among the Tonga people too, and a women is expected to leave her husband sleeping in bed in the morning while she begins her daily chores. The last line, which mentions the woman having 'servant girls', is not the norm however. This would be the case only among the very wealthy ladies who live in urban areas. In rural areas of Butonga there is no such thing as 'servants', not even for the chief. Where polygamy is common, there are usually plenty of hands available for all the household and farming chores to be done. A man will normally have many children one way or another—either through his first wife or, if necessary, by marrying a second wife (or more). Many men think that the hiring of a servant or two to help around the house would only serve to make his wife and children lazy!

It should be noted that men do not regard women's domestic duties like cooking and washing as 'work' per se; this is just what women are expected to do. In any case, in rural areas, a woman's first job is not to prepare food, as this verse implies, but rather to go draw water for cooking and to heat for her husband's morning bath (or the rough equivalent of one). Among poorer families, there might not be enough food (e.g., maize meal) available to prepare a breakfast—the 'fast' would continue until later in the morning after some work in the fields had already been done.

v.16: Among the rural Tonga people, land (e.g., a 'field') is not bought and sold, but is rather inherited (*kukona*)—by men—from relatives or distributed by the chief. Even in towns women do not normally own property (except for her clothes!) or operate large businesses on their own. In the case of small shops or stalls that they may open near the home, the proceeds are usually given to their husbands. Furthermore, a woman may actually be included among the 'possessions' of her husband. Accordingly, female children are desirable because they add to the wealth of the clan both actual (work-related) and potential (in the form of *lobola* from a future husband's family). In recent times, more government legislation is being enacted and NGOs organized to document and protect the civil

3.6 A 'worthy wife' from a Zambian perspective

rights of women in society. However, it will take time for these changes to affect the majority. According to custom, women are prevented from owning land so that if their husband dies and the widow remarries, the land will not be transferred to a clan other than that of the deceased. If possible, when a man dies, a form of the levirate is practiced whereby the wife is 'cleansed' (*kusalazya*—traditionally by means of a sexual rite) and then 'inherited' (*kulya zina* 'to eat the name') by his brother or another close relative.

v.17: This description of the ideal woman sounds familiar, an extension of the first two lines of v. 15. Women are not generally regarded, even by men, as 'the weaker sex'—no doubt because of all the hard work they perform both at home (e.g., hauling water) and in the fields. It is occasionally reported in urban (not rural) areas that a certain well-built woman has physically beaten up her husband during a domestic dispute.

v.18: Women are not 'traders', but some may be small-scale sellers of personal garden produce. In fact, women are not considered (by men) to be good at any type of business venture or trade; if one lady happens to succeed, sorcery (*bulozi*) or the use of magical charms (*musamu*) is suspected. Wives are supposed to be 'cared for' by their husbands, which is rather ironic when one considers the respective amounts of actual work done for the family by each sex. Another irony is that the relative value of women and their abilities or achievements are determined by the men of society. A final note on this verse: lamps do not burn at night for that would be wasteful; the nighttime is either for sleep or for serving one's husband!

v.19: The skills of spinning thread and weaving cloth are generally unknown (cf. v. 13), and thus the terms 'distaff' and 'spindle' are unavailable in the Tonga language. Perhaps 'needles' for knitting or sewing could be used as the closest cultural correspondents, but obviously these are rather far off the mark in terms of form, if not function as well.

v.20: Able-bodied beggars are non-existent in Tonga society—only people who happen to be physically or mentally impaired with no relatives to care for them are seen begging. The term 'beggar' is actually applied to lazy folks who depend on others for their support in life. For their part, 'the poor' will always depend on their own kinship for help in time of need. Thus, those who may arrive on one's doorstep needing food are normally visitors or travelers, whether relatives or strangers, passing through. And whenever possible, hospitality is always offered, for as the proverb puts it: *icakulya taciceyi* 'food is never too little', meaning that a meal should never be denied to any person who needs it, no matter how little there may be in the house. Another saying goes: *mweenzu ulangwa abula* 'a visitor/stranger is viewed on [his/her] stomach'—meaning, one must make sure that a visitor is well fed, i.e., is properly cared for. Women are known for their kindness and generosity; those who manifest the opposite characteristics are not well liked and may even be divorced. One proverb says, *imukaintu tezele kuba simujika toko toko,* literally translated: 'a woman should not be a stingy cook'. This means a woman should always have an open hand where the giving of food is concerned, whether to her own family or to others.

v.21: It never 'snows' in the warm Zambezi Valley of Zambia, and even up north on the plateau country a 'winter' (July) frost is rare. Warm clothes are needed none the less, for it does get 'cold', relatively speaking, especially during the winter nights (5C), or on cloudy and windy days at that time of year (10C). Men, however, are the providers of clothes for a family because they control its financial resources. They generally prefer to purchase according to cost, not the quality of the clothing, certainly not for children. A man who loves and values his wife might buy her a special dress from time to time, but not necessarily one that is 'scarlet' in color, which would be associated with prostitutes (*bavuule*).

v.22: As noted in v. 21, a man normally does all the purchasing of clothing and other household items (including the bedding) for the family. If he buys a new dress for his wife, it will be for a special reason—for something that she has done to please him, and he wants to show his appreciation, e.g., after a good harvest or the birth of a girl child. A rural wife usually does not have the money to purchase clothing on her own or for herself; in fact, before self, she would be expected to provide for her children.

v.23: Generally speaking, a rural woman is recognized in the community due to the outstanding deeds, possessions, or character of her husband; socially, she is not an independent entity nor can she do anything without the explicit permission of her husband. Of course, this perception has changed in towns where many women are well-to-do business persons, civic leaders, and even members of government. Traditional men become insecure if their wives outshine them in any respect (when she might be idiomatically termed *mukaintu mulombwana* 'a woman-man'!), and this can lead to quarrels in the home or the jealous suspicion that she is showing off to attract other men.

3.6 A 'worthy wife' from a Zambian perspective   105

On the other hand, women are expected to be the moral leaders and role models of Tonga society, as the proverb goes, *bulemu bwamunzi mmukaintu* meaning, 'the honor of a village is [the] woman'. Women are expected to be morally pure and upright in all their behavior, whereas men are regarded as being weak in this regard. Therefore, in cases of adultery, women are suspected and judged much more severely than men, who often escape scot-free, or on payment of a fine (levied by fellow males!).

There is no 'city gate' in a Tonga setting, but the equivalent of a 'town council' in most villages is the *gowelo* 'elders meeting place'. This is where men and mature boys meet to socialize, play games, or discuss judicial 'cases' (*milandu*) that need to be decided. Women are not present unless the case at hand involves them, either as the accused or a witness. There is no special honor in being a member of the *gowelo* since all males may participate there simply by virtue of their gender. Youths, however, come there primarily to learn from their elders but they are not expected to contribute anything weighty or wise. Those men without children, too, have not accrued enough respect or authority to speak very much when serious matters are being discussed.

v.24: The comments applied at v. 18 are also relevant here since a similar situation is being described. Business women in the community, certainly a rural one, are not admired for their success and prosperity. On the contrary, they intimidate the men around them and may be accused, at least privately, of practicing witchcraft. Clothing merchants are well known (except for the item 'sashes' mentioned in line B), but this is the job of men because they must travel from house to house in the community. A woman who did that would be accused of soliciting for prostitution.

v.25: Compared with the generosity, industry, keen business acumen, and economic success that is attributed to the ideal Hebrew lady of Proverbs, a model Tonga woman is respected (if not really honored) for the following qualities (a compendium of local responses): being properly initiated according to the ancient rites, observing traditional customs regarding female demeanor and domestic responsibilities, being faithful and respectful to her husband, working hard at home and in the family field, being friendly and hospitable towards all, not getting involved in public disputes, not being too talkative, a complainer, or a gossip, not revealing her husband's failures or weaknesses even in private to fellow women, not being greedy or even eating in public, not being a drunkard (a 'beer-lover'), and not wearing suggestive clothing (e.g., short dresses) or being a flirt. A wife's dignity is manifested in the way she walks, talks, gets on with other people, and in the respect that comes from the kind of children she raises (*maulu amufu azibilwa kumwana* 'the legs of the deceased are recognized in her offspring'). A woman is the primary person who brings up and educates both girls and boys—the latter before puberty, after which they go off to sit at the village *gowelo*.

A woman will not worry about whether she can 'laugh at the days ahead' because her future does not extend much further than the morrow. In any case, all future planning and decision-making in the family will be done by her husband. If they have a good relationship, he may consult with her over important issues, but many times a man will not even inform his wife about where he is going, what he is going to do or when. He alone is responsible for managing the family resources and for making sure that they will survive for the coming year.

v.26: It is only counsel that comes from a mature woman who has achieved something in life which can be regarded as worth listening to at all. Most young and middle-aged husbands consider any advice from women to be quite useless, perhaps even confusing or dangerous. *Simumvwa twabakaintu yaamukola lyookolwa* 'the person who listens to women suffers from famine at harvest time'. This opinion may differ among some elderly men who have learned to value advice from their faithful wives.

Among the Tonga, one of the traditionally-taught roles of a wife is to advise her husband (normally, only when called upon), but most men will think twice before they take it seriously. Even among more educated urban men, very few would listen to the suggestions of their wives because tradition and society have implanted within their thinking that no woman can offer sound and reliable advice to a man. Women can only instruct and counsel themselves or children. A man, on the other hand, is thought to be capable of and expected to offer guidance and direction to a woman without any question. This pattern changes as men grow older—a result of experience teaching them that women (mothers, grannies, aunts, and wives) have probably played a major role in their lives and decision-making over the years.

v.27: This verse is quite true to Tonga traditional values: women *are* regarded as being the managers of their household and are responsible for the family's success in life. *Bwami bwa ciluli mbwaanda* 'the wealth of the roof are the walls'—i.e., it is the wife in the home who generates prosperity

3.6 A 'worthy wife' from a Zambian perspective

for the entire household. If domestic problems develop, however, she will be blamed, even if her husband is the real cause (e.g., by his drunkenness or gambling away their resources). She must then take the proverbial 'fall' for him lest he be publicly shamed. Thus 'idleness' is a social 'sin' among the Tonga too—but this will not be expressed with reference to foreign 'bread', but rather to local *nshima* 'hard-cooked maize-meal porridge', the traditional Bantu staff of life.

v.28: A man would not publicly praise his wife for anything lest he be regarded as being weak and overly subservient to or dominated by her in the home. A 'strong', respectable man is not expected to overtly express such emotions. On the other hand, children may openly praise their mothers, for example, when they have sewed or patched up their clothes, prepared them nice meals, or protected them from their rivals. In fact, the proverb reminds them that *lukolo lwanyoko talulubwa* 'the breast of your mother must not be forgotten!'

v.29: In this case it sounds as if the man is directly lauding his wife personally, but this would be done in private. This is a more likely scenario than that suggested in v. 28, but still it would not be a very common occurrence. In general, women are not really appreciated by their husbands for all that they do, and they are often mistreated both publicly and at home. However, as one respondent stated her plight, 'she would rather be married and suffer than to endure the shame of remaining single in her parents' home'.

v.30: Many proverbs teach one to avoid judging from outward appearances, e.g., *mwanaakoo ndaba ndisubilila balitala* 'the daughter of our neighbor looks beautiful from across the river'. This advice was normally followed much more in the past when parents would arrange the marriages of their children. Nowadays, however, modern young men consider physical beauty and charm to be more important in a potential wife. Traditionally, a woman would not be known for her God-fearing piety, but since the advent of Christianity, many men would prefer such a woman as a wife since she would be more likely to care well for his children and manage the home. If the husband is a member of some church, then she would normally have to adopt the same. Note that the expression 'fear the Lord' in the old Bible is usually understood to be afraid of God. But in the new Tonga translation this has been rendered *uulemeka Mwami* 'who respects the Lord'.

v.31: A woman may be publicly praised for her deeds by fellow women, but not by men other than her husband, for this would arouse jealousy and perhaps suspicions in his mind. No concrete 'reward' for such excellent performance of duty can be expected, however, for women were created to serve others, so the belief goes. And such service is all too frequently rendered out of fear—the fear of getting beaten, of being ignored and neglected for another woman, or worse, of being divorced by her fickle husband. The vast difference between the overall social situation and consequent personal outlook of the confident, well-to-do woman of Proverbs 31 and the typical Tonga wife is almost too great to comprehend. This poetic text may thus serve an important purpose in providing some needed godly instruction and hence also an authoritative biblical alternative that can help change the unacceptable present status quo of many women today—not only in Africa, but the world over. Among the Tonga, *ng'anda n'ciluli calungu* 'the house is [like] a roof [made] of pumpkin leaves'—i.e., the family is very fragile. This implicitly didactic portrait of Proverbs may help to lend some stability to marriages whose partners take seriously the crucial characteristics of 'fearing the LORD' and respecting their spouses (vv. 28–30).

The various conceptual contrasts and incongruities which we have noted naturally lead to a number of significant problems or challenges during any audience-oriented act of interlingual, intercultural communication. Space prevents me from discussing all these here, but several general suggestions for dealing with them in a Bible translation are given in section 3.6.2.

3.6.2 Strategy for dealing with diversity in translation

Why does such a linguistic and conceptual bridge need to be built from the source text to the target audience? That question can be best answered by another: what happens if we don't—that is, do not appropriately contextualize the biblical text for a particular group of receptors? Further informal testing among theological students and rural parishioners has shown that a more or less laissez-faire, literalistic translation policy results in many aspects of these passages eliciting no (zero) meaning, the wrong sense, or an inaccessible (too difficult) text for the majority (e.g., with regard to the conceptual problems listed in 3.6.1). The case cannot be argued here (see Wendland 1998: ch. 5), but from a positive perspective we are concerned about preserving a significant level of cognitive as well as emotive (including aesthic) equivalence or parity

3.6 A 'worthy wife' from a Zambian perspective

in terms of the overall quality and value of the current communication event. The paean of Proverbs 31 was meant to sound like one, in another language as well, and hence also to be understood in a manner that both respects and resembles, as nearly as possible, the communicative goals of the original text. The excellence and important of the original eulogy has already been demonstrated; now, what can/should we do about it in a given TL—in this case, Chitonga?

There are three principal ways of handling this problem of verbal and cognitive disparity during translation—or stating the position more positively, of dealing with the artistic and rhetorical challenge that a passage like Proverbs 31 presents us within another language, literary tradition, and sociocultural setting. These options are summarized here:

- Textual—Potential conceptual difficulties are handled linguistically, that is, by means of various 'verbal engineering' techniques within the translation itself. This would involve a more 'domesticated', target language oriented rendition, one that seeks to express the essential meaning in the most natural and appropriate TL language forms. For example, use of the cultural substitute 'cotton' *(kootoni)* in place of the unknown 'flax' (פִּשְׁתִּים) in v. 13a or 'village men's meeting place' *(gobelo)* for the 'city gate' (שְׁעָרִים) of v. 23a. On the other hand, in the case of the key personage, the 'worthy' wife/woman (חַיִל—v. 10a), a more general expression has to be used, i.e., 'a woman who is good' *(mukaintu uuli kabotu)*. Her excellence then has to be filled in conceptually, as it were, by means of the following specific descriptions of her character and abilities.

- Paratextual—The strategy of using a more meaning-based, target-focused translation may be accompanied by various types of supplementary aid to enrich the cognitive environment of the target group with regard to the particulars of the original text and its cultural context. These would include such standard features as well-worded section headings, cross-references to an illuminating passage of Scripture, illustrations that can evoke a thousand words, glossary entries that provide dictionary-like definitions of key terms, and of course explanatory or descriptive footnotes, which tend to be the most relevant and helpful for those who know how to use them. Such notes would be essential to elucidate the nature of the original 'rubies' (פְּנִינִים) in v. 10b, for example, or the 'merchant ships' (אֳנִיּוֹת) of 14a.

- Extratextual—The different paratextual tools just mentioned will probably not be sufficient to cue TL readers and hearers in to the full sense and significance of certain aspects of the biblical text, especially where a number of closely related concepts are involved. The deep religious dimensions of the expression 'the fear of the LORD' (יִרְאַת־יְהוָה), for example, cannot be handled within the scope of a single footnote. A separate, more sustained and developed treatment is needed, such as that which may be supplied in some type of accompanying commentary, study guide, instructional book, magazine or journal article, or even an audio tape (CD) that has been prepared to explain the chief aspects of Jewish religion as set forth in the Mosaic Law. Other types of illustrated study material may be used to provide an exposition of the different aspects of knowledge that are needed to more fully comprehend the Scriptures as rendered in a given translation, for example, with regard to important geographical, literary, historical, social, and cultural matters. There is an obvious need to clarify for a specific audience or readership the great significance of this entire closing pericope of the book of Proverbs (31:10–31). People must be able to feel the impact and import of this foregrounded model of womanhood in Israel and the fact that women, too, had the God-given ability and right to 'speak with wisdom and faithful instruction' (בְחָכְמָה וְתוֹרַת־חֶסֶד) in the land (v. 26).

These three ways of enhancing and augmenting the communicative capacity of the biblical text in translation are ideally employed together within the framework of an integrated, grass-roots educational program that is put into effect by the wider community of believers, working in harmony through the local Bible Society or some other cooperative translation agency. In the final section (3.7) of this chapter, we will consider one of the most difficult and challenging aspects of the present Hebrew poem to deal with satisfactorily in any translation, namely, its alphabetic acrostic form. Due to the problems that translators experience in understanding and appreciating this prominent literary feature on its own terms, the acrostic form is generally simply ignored, frequently without even a footnote to record the slightest trace of its presence in the original. Consequently, its substantial semantic implication and associated religious connotations are completely lost in translated versions, both in minority vernaculars and major world languages.

3.7 Towards a greater measure of oratorical equivalence

In Hebrew, the form of an alphabetic acrostic (A-B-C...) poem functions to convey the connotative notions of completeness, perfection, unity, the

3.7 Towards a greater measure of oratorical equivalence

ultimate in quality! This elaborate structure is no doubt intended to be a verbal reflection of the text's principal content—whether theological, e.g., the 'law' (word) of God in Ps. 119, or moral, e.g., the most excellent woman of Proverbs 31. Perhaps an acrostic sequence was also a handy way of organizing the poem's main ideas and rendering them in more memorable fashion as an oral learning and performing device. The aspect of *orality* is a crucial consideration, for the artistic and rhetorical impact of such a format would be greatly reduced were it to be relegated solely to the visual medium of script or print. Indeed, it is likely that an oral performer (lector) would have audibly accented the pronunciation of the first word of each verse in Proverbs 31. This would be to heighten the impact of the sequence of initial Hebrew letters as s/he progressed through the poem and moved towards its conclusion, which in this case, as noted above, also marks a culmination in terms of meaning. It is clear then that any translation of such a piece must take this vital sonic facet of the original composition into serious consideration—even if it is ultimately determined by the translation team that they can do very little about it in their rendition.

But is it right (*ethical!*) to do nothing at all—to simply allow the text to stand bare and unmarked—not formally, ideally audibly, distinguished in the TL?[29] In my opinion, this would be not only the path of least resistance, but it would also constitute a certain degree of dereliction of duty. At the very minimum (which is the policy of most versions, even in the major languages), the presence of the acrostic format ought to be noted in a footnote and its ostensible communicative significance pointed out there in appreciable detail. This may be coupled then with a representation of the Hebrew letters as they occur to demarcate the individual verses—ideally, right alongside the text itself either adjacent to or replacing the verse numbers.

A competent and creative translation team might proceed from there to accomplish something considerably more significant in terms of communicative equivalence. That would be to distinguish this passage by means of

---

[29] Vail (2005:66–67) has made a valiant attempt at a poetic acrostic equivalent in English. The following is an excerpt covering our select portion of the closing verses 28–31:
"Very blessed you are," her children say.
Worthy is she of her husband's praise.
Excellent women abound,
But none better than you are found.
Youth's charm will mislead while its beauty fades,
Yet a God-fearing woman will always be praised.
Zealously having done well, she deserves respect.
Public praise for her work is what she should get.

a more-or-less poetic rendering, perhaps making use of a TL genre that is stylistically appropriate, or at least compatible with, the content of the biblical source. Such a version would also be intended to serve as an oral-aural equivalent—that is, a poem which is specifically designed for public *performance*, as the original undoubtedly was. In this case, we are dealing not so much with a 'literary' version (though some such genre might be used as a model), but with a distinctly 'oratorical' text, one that is composed with the factor of sound always in mind (or ringing in one's ear).

An *oratorical* version thus aims for an appreciable phonological impact and appeal—that is, for both an effective *oral* articulation (i.e., a rhythmic enunciation, recitation, chanting, or singing) of the text and also an equally powerful *aural* reception and appreciation on the part of a listening audience (cf. Wendland 1993:223–228). In this connection, one must also note the importance of *formatting* the text on the printed page in such a way that it is more legible and easy to read—or better, to overtly enunciate in a more or less dramatic fashion. Such a procedure would involve techniques such as the use of individual lineation for distinct 'utterance units', an unjustified right-hand margin, additional white space and indentation to distinguish breaks in the text or special structural formations (parallelism, chiasmus, terrace patterns), plus various type styles or features (e.g., italics, underlining, boldface) to highlight particular key terms, repetitions, and thematically prominent lines.

In addition to her work on Psalms, Boerger[30] has been interested in biblical acrostics in general. Her translation of 'The Wise Wife' provided here has a number of merits:

- All poetic lines are part of the acrostic.
- Some verses have been stretched across more than one letter to achieve all twenty-six for English in place of the twenty-two letters of the Hebrew alphabet.
- There is rhyme with attention to meter, in that long and shorter lines alternate.
- Some specifics have been made generic for use with English speakers today.
- The two chiastic patterns are highlighted with italics and bolding.

---

[30] An earlier rendering of this acrostic was revised by Brenda Boerger for insertion here, after having read the full analytical discussion in chapter 3.

The Wise Wife

10-12 **Her Partner**
A good wife is the crown of her husband,
A treasure, who's worth much indeed.
Because he can ultimately trust in her for
Bringing in what they might need.
Continuously she is a blessing,
Contented to cause him well-being.

13-19 **Her Enterprise**
Dedicating her hours to working,
Dealing in fabrics and wool,
Each day then she sails out to market,
Enters her portals with gunnels packed full.

First light finds her cooking and baking
Fragrance of cakes and of bread;
Giving tasks for helpers' undertaking,
Granting food to do what she's said.

Her hands are always creative,
Her mind would advance in her field.
Investing in a plan, she pursues it,
Intending it bring a good yield.

Joyfully she juggles her work load,
Just reveling in her great might.
Keenly she's content with her profits;
Keeps her light burning all night.

Lovingly, she takes up her sewing—
Late night spinnings in wools and in flax,
Meaning her *hand*'s always busy
Making sure *family* won't lack.

20-27 **Her Character**
Now she's **open** with strangers, like *family*;
Needy and poor get a *hand*.
Our lady's **own** don't feel winter's coldness
Outer **clothing** that cold can withstand.

Purples, and woolens, and **linens**
Provide her with her own gowns
Quite respected there is her **husband**
Quickly called when **elders** sit down.

Reams of **linens** she's woven for selling,
Rich belts for the stores far and near.
Strength and dignity act as her **clothing**;
She smiles, *"Our future's secure."*

True wisdom comes when her mouth is **open**;
True kindness is what others hear.
Unfailingly she undertakes for her **own**,
Unceasingly all day and all year.

28-31 **Her Praiseworthiness**
Voices of her children will bless her,
Validating her husband's acclaim,
*"Wife, the most wonderful one in the world,
Way beyond what others could claim."*

Exceeding charm's exceedingly deceitful;
Excessive beauty's excessively vain.
Yet the woman who reverences Yahweh,
Yes, she's the one on whom praises rain.
Zeal for her work brings her a reward—
Zestful praise from all in accord.

Boerger's version works quite well for English, but what then can be done in Tonga to reproduce more of the poetic flavor of the Hebrew paean of Proverbs 31—as well as its function of calling audible attention to the exceptional qualities of the person being praised? A formal-correspondence rendering, as found in the old Bible (1953), cannot serve this purpose. In fact, the text is so literal and lackluster that an inattentive reader or listener might not even realize at many points that a woman is being featured because the passage is not foregrounded in any way, due to the lack of gender-marking on Tonga pronouns, which leaves the reference ambiguous and dependent upon the cotext. A modern meaning-based translation (1997) presents the pericope in a more natural mode of expression, but is still quite deficient in terms of its relative poetic and rhetorical equivalence in relation to the Hebrew. In order to suggest some possibilities for redressing this imbalance in overall communicative effect, the two lyric versions given below were composed to re-present the eulogy's final climactic strophe (vv. 28–31). Two radically different genres were selected to illustrate the potential for providing at least some compensation for the loss of the multifunctional acrostic format of the original.

3.7.1 A *ciyabilo* poem (Salimo Hachibamba)

A *ciyabilo* poem is usually sung to the accompaniment of a traditional Tonga drum, either a *ngoma*, *namalwa*, or *ndandala*, which is beaten by two sticks. As shown below, this oral style features a two-line utterance format (like Hebrew) along with a repeated refrain, many rhetorical questions, exclamatory utterances, verbal condensation and ellipsis, plus the periodic reiteration of certain key concepts.

v. 28 *Nguni cileleko ku bana bakwe?*
    Who is a blessing to her children?
    Nakulumbwa ku mulumi wakwe, nguni?
    The one praised by her husband, who is it?
v. 29 *Mulumi uleema: Batalivulili bakaintu balemeka.* [REFRAIN verse]
    [Her] husband adores [her]: My, but there are so many honorable women around.
    Wangu, pe, ulabainda mbobabelele!
    But mine, no, she surpasses them all—no comparison!
v. 30 *Zilisakatizyo tee nducengo? – Bubota, tee bulamana?*
    Ornaments, are they not deceit? – Beauty, does it not finish?
    Mukaintu nakulemeka Leza – atalumbaizigilwi nzi, basaama?
    A woman who honors God – why should she not be praised, my friends?
v. 31 *Amumulumbule kweelana anzyacita!*
    Reward her in accordance with what she does!
    Mukaintu ooyo alemekwe agobelo lyamunzi!
    This woman must be honored at the men's club of the village!

3.7.2 A *kweema* poem (Perdita Chenjela)

The *kweema* manner of poetic declamation illustrated in this section is much more expansive or redundantly expressed than the preceding *ciyabilo*. It would thus be classified as a looser type of paraphrase that treats each major concept of the original from several perspectives, including local figures of speech, before moving on to the next. This genre is more commonly (though not exclusively) composed among women (representing, perhaps, the perspective of King Lemuel's mother, cf. 31:1), whereas the *ciyabilo* is traditionally preferred by men (the viewpoint of King Lemuel, or possibly even King Solomon, cf. 1:1).[31]

A Blessed Woman (Proverbs 31:28–31)	***Imukaintu Ulelekedwe***
Here is a woman blessed—	*Ngoyu imukaintu ulelekedwe*
All the people hold her in high esteem.	*Ibantu boonse balamusumpula*
Who would not give her way to pass?	*Sena nguuni utamusiili inzila ikuuti ainde*
Who? When she's so dignified, my!	*Nguuni? Nkambo ulalemekwa ma!*
When she walks in the village,	*Na ikuuti wainda mumunzi*
Even the chickens stop scratching—	*Inkuku azyalo zilalekaa ikuyanga*
To let the honorable woman pass.	*Ikuti imukaintu ulemekedwe ainde*
They give her the respect she deserves.	*Zimupa bulema bumwelede*
Clothed in honor,	*Ibulemu mbwaasamide*
Everything about her is just so good.	*Walo mbwabede mbubotu buyo.*
As for dressing...	*Pele ikusama...*
So beautiful is her dressing,	*Ikusama kwakwe nkubotu*
Pleasing to all who see her.	*Kulabotya ikulanga*
Her comrades wish to be like her.	*Benzinyina inga nkwebela nainda*
As for speaking...	*Nkabela ikwambaula...*
All her words are pleasant.	*Imajwi akwe oonse alakoma*
The bad [words] gulp! she swallows [them].	*Mabi alo! ulamena.*
She only speaks words of dignity,	*Wambaula buyo majwi abulemu*
For what she speaks promotes unity.	*Nkambo ncaamba nca lukamantano*
As for her steps...	*Pele intaamu zyakwe...*
Just see how she moves,	*Kolanga mbwaenda*
Even a chameleon cannot match [her].	*Nalutambwe inga watyompwa*
So swiftly and surely,	*Inga alyatwa alasalwa*
Her legs always carry her to worthy duties.	*Maulu amutola kumilimo mibotu buyo.*

---

[31] The *kweema* genre can also be used when mourning for the dead. At a Tonga funeral house, very early in the morning, women will begin to cry one by one, and then men join in with their *ziyabilo* (plural). It is a way of venerating the dead; people praise the deceased, at the same time worshiping God and the ancestors.

This woman…	Ooyu imukaintu…
Fending for her children is her joy.	Ikubelekela bana bakwe kulamukonda
Her prayer is this:	Ikukomba kwakwe nkwakuti
"My family must have [enough] food!"	"Imukwasi wangu ube acakulya!"
Who would ever starve on her doorstep?	Peele nguni uyofwa njala amulyango akwe
Nobody! Listen friends!	Taku! Nobanyina!
Hunger is held slavery there!	Inzala ilyangidwe mubuzike kooko
Her family is blessed indeed!	Imukwasyi ulamuleleka kapati!
Her children say, "O blessed one!"	Ibana bakwe balati, Kolelekwa
"Matchless she is!" sings her husband.	Ngolike buyo! imusankwa ulaimba ikumulumba
"So blessed I am!" boasts her husband.	Ndililelekedwe kwiindilila! ulalipunda
"I'm the only one with a wife like her!"	Ndili ndelike ni nindila mukaintu uli boobu!
Her beauty is not only outward,	Ikubota kwakwe takuli buyo kwaatala
That's the truth!	Ncobeni!
But always emerges from her good heart.	Peele buzwa mumoyo wakwe lyoonse
Diminishing the blemishes on her face,	Ibubotu bwinda mabala ali kumeso akwee
Righteousness alone comes from her life.	Ziluleme buyo nzo zizwa mu buumi bwakwa
May this woman always be lauded,	Ooyu imukaintu alumbaizigwe,
For her life's work is to honor the Lord God.	Nkambo buumi nkulemeka Mwami Leza
That is a genuine life!	Mbo buumi bwa ncobeni!
Everything she does is praiseworthy,	Ziciito zyakwe zilisumpukidwe
Her deeds honor her in the whole village.	Zilamupa bulemu mumunzi oonse.
Oh! Is this not what it means to be honored?	Ii! Sena teelelwi ikulemekwa?

3.7.3 Conclusion: Narrowing the aesthic-rhetorical divide

Is the semantic content of any passage of Scripture not its most important feature by far? If that element can be conveyed in understandable terms, if not laudable ones, in the vernacular, why should the translators worry? Have they not done their best? In short, I would answer no—not with respect to the *full communicative potential* (intention/implication) of the original text and its connotative as well as denotative significance. Thus, having carefully read, studied, and admired a passage like Proverbs 31:10–31 in the original language, translators should not be satisfied with an 'incomplete' on their assignment and obligation regarding the overall quality of communication—that is, of re-presenting, at least to a perceptible degree, a minimum of the emotive impact and aesthic effect of the biblical message in their mother tongue. The beautiful manner of expression and powerful rhetoric of this impressive eulogy to a female role model of Scripture (as well as her symbolical representation of the principle of God-

3.7 Towards a greater measure of oratorical equivalence

fearing wisdom) is an integral part of its intended meaning and for that reason also a necessary responsibility to assume when translating the poem in a given TL. This pericope stands as the emotive climax of the entire book of Proverbs, certainly in its final edited canonical form. Therefore, it must accordingly be given the attention it deserves in any contemporary re-creation, no matter what the language and culture concerned.

Yet what do we observe when we peruse virtually all available translations today, whether in a language of wider communication (LWC) or some major lingua franca? Usually it is only a pale, largely indistinct reflection of the original, quite unworthy of being called even a mediocre, let alone a satisfactory, literary equivalent. In other words, most versions simply try to express the text's basic content, displaying little cognizance of or concern for its poetic appeal and rhetorical persuasiveness in Hebrew.[32] Now it may well be true that most Bible translation teams operating in the world today are unprepared, perhaps ill-equipped to deal with this interpersonal (pragmatic) dimension of interlingual communication. But that does not excuse them from acknowledging this fact and then attempting to do something more substantial about it in the vernacular version at hand.

But what can be done? The first step is recognition—realizing that there is this facet of the biblical text that is present and probably completely unaccounted for in their current translation. To begin with, it is up to the translation consultant or adviser responsible to make translators aware of this urgent need (if they have not noted it already during their prior exegetical study). Perhaps a local oral poet or *griot* can then be engaged to join the team in order to help them express the text in a more appropriately poetic fashion. Or maybe this local language expert or wordsmith can be privately engaged to compose a crucial passage of this nature independently, making use of his/her own artistic intuition and gift for lyric expression. This version can be subsequently edited and revised, where necessary, in order to render it more exegetically accurate. There are many compositional and procedural options along these lines that are available to project organizers who are willing and encouraged to explore them—not all at once or intermittently, of course, but as a regular established practice, ready to be implemented when the occasion arises in the Scriptures.

---

[32] The only acknowledgement of the special character of the original is often a mere unenlightening footnote along the following lines (from a recent edition of the NIV): "Verses 10–31 are an acrostic, each verse beginning with a successive letter of the Hebrew alphabet." Now how helpful is that to most readers—and would such minimal information even be available to the hearers of this passage?

In any case, all serious translators must take the time and make the effort to do some serious local *research* into the literary/oral resources of their language in order to discover and record what resources are actually available for use in their work. In this particular case, a similar poetic genre (or style of discourse) is required, one that may be used, either as is or in some adapted form, to verbalize the lovely, yet also compelling portrait that is present in the original Hebrew text. Their degree of failure in this respect means a corresponding loss of communicative value in the translation, one that unfortunately diminishes and mars this magnificent image of divine Wisdom personified—or at least modeled—and made concretely memorable in the lyric life-story of a faithful woman of God.

Instead, let this rather be said, by way of analogy, about many more current and future translations of the Scriptures in Africa—from the point of view (hearing!) of each individual audience: וְאַתְּ עָלִית עַל־כֻּלָּנָה 'now you surpass them all!' (v. 29b). Similarly, may the words of such a rendition not only accurately express 'the wisdom and faithful instruction' (חָכְמָה וְתוֹרַת־חֶסֶד) of the original (v.26), but also verbalize this vision in a most praiseworthy way, thus generating widespread public acclamation and approval 'in the city gates' throughout the land (בַּשְּׁעָרִים – v. 31b).

4

Lyric Ideology: The Complaint of Psalm 137

Introduction: Ideology

The primary investigation of this chapter relates the topic of ideological text production more specifically to the practice of Bible translation within a particular social and cultural setting, namely, that of south-central Africa. This case study is necessarily quite selective in nature and focused upon the text of Psalm 137 both in the original Hebrew and also, via translation, in the English and Chewa[1] languages.

The *ideology* of any human language is shaped by the total culture of the people who speak it, while that of a given text is also influenced by the communicative goals of its author in relation to an envisaged readership within a given context of reception and use. Similarly, the ideology of a certain translation is motivated by both the explicit and unstated objectives of those who commission and oversee it. This includes the particular translation method that they adopt to accomplish their aims in relation to their primary target audience and sociocultural milieu. The purpose of this study is to call attention to some of these significant ideological factors and to suggest how important a coordinated communal approach is to the achievement of a translation committee's chosen set of goals. Various aspects of this subject and the salient issues involved are illustrated primarily with reference to the communication of Psalm 137 in Chewa. Brenda Boerger has provided her own English translation to serve in parallel to the Chewa lyric rendition.

4.1 How does ideology relate to Bible translation?

According to one popular (American) English dictionary, 'ideology' may be defined as "the body of ideas on which a particular political, economic, or social system is based" (*Webster's...Dictionary* 1988:670). I wish to

---

[1] The Chewa portion of this study was originally prepared with reference to the theme of the OTSSA annual conference: *Ideological text production: Text, interpretation and reception of poetic texts* (Johannesburg University, Sept. 2004).

refine this definition in three respects: three important qualifiers (among others) may be added to the 'political, economic, or social' above—namely, *cultural, religious,* and *translational.* An intrinsically systematic, but not always explicitly stated, 'body of ideas' forms the basis for any given culture, religion, or indeed, approach to the theory and practice of Bible translation. This influential, all-encompassing cognitive environment, or worldview, affects the composition as well as the transmission and reception of any verbal composition, especially in cases where two or more language-cultures confront each other. I will elaborate on this notion by considering certain characteristics of the text, context, and transmission of Psalm 137 in relation to its communication today among the Chewa people of Malawi and Zambia.

Biblical scholars and critics have long studied the various ideological facets involved in producing the original documents of the Hebrew and Greek Scriptures, with regard to the following:

- supposed authorship (including the selection and incorporation of presumed oral precursors),
- successive stages of redactional reconstruction,
- the collection of related works (such as the Pentateuch or the Pauline corpus),
- the process of canonization,
- the production and transmission of 'large scale' translations (e.g., the Septuagint or Vulgate), and
- the ongoing creation of critical editions of the biblical text.

Naturally, a great deal of guesswork and hypothesis formation takes place as various theories are proposed, tested, criticized, and refined or replaced by newer theories and models (e.g., from source > tradition-historical > form > redaction > social-scientific > canonical > rhetorical to orality 'schools of criticism'). In recent years, similar receptor-oriented studies have been carried out cross-culturally with respect to the current interpretation and application of the diverse texts of Scripture, resulting in another set of 'schools' and methodologies, each reflecting a somewhat different perspective on the hermeneutical and communicative process (e.g., narrative, reader-response, post-structuralist, deconstructionist, new-historical, post-colonial, and feminist criticism).[2] Each of these academic approaches, whether focused on the source or the target text and

---

[2] To help students and nonspecialists sort them all out, it is common to find various collections of these critical schools surveyed and explained in popular anthologies, such as McKenzie and Haynes (1993) or Barton (1998).

4.1 How does ideology relate to Bible translation? 121

setting, inevitably superimposes (or even imposes) its own ideological framework on the activity of interpretation. Therefore, it is advisable that a compatible combination of methods be applied, with one technique being used to complement and correct another.

Within the past several decades the assortment of contemporary, often contrastive and competing, *translation ideologies* has also come under closer scrutiny and debate (cf. Munday 2001, Naudé and van der Merwe 2002, and Wilt 2003). The old 'literal' versus 'free' dichotomy no longer suffices as a general characterization of the translation task, and most scholars recognize that there is a broad continuum of possibilities in terms of both theory and practice. Part of the difficulty then of initiating a Bible translation today is making the right choices from among various options available within the situation concerned. In section 4.3.3 I will discuss some of the techniques for conveying the controversial verses of Psalm 137 in Chewa. Each technique is the product of a different ideological, some would say 'theological', approach to the intercultural transmission (or re-presentation) of biblical discourse, coupled with a distinct set of local communicative objectives and translation resources.

There is one further crucial ideology that impinges on the translation of Scripture, and this is the *cultural* factor, which affects both the interpretation of the source language (SL) text as well as the rendering of the target language (TL). The ideology of culture embraces various facets of perception and conception that comprise a people's worldview—their core religious and philosophical beliefs. These include assumptions about reality, life, death and the hereafter; their entire 'world' of experience; along with their values, ideals, hopes, fears, goals, and the diversity of attitudes that shape everyday living and interaction with their environment. It is encouraging to see recent efforts to analyze biblical texts, the Psalter in particular, using a combined holistic, literary (poetic) and sociological emphasis that has provided credible hypotheses about the ideology underlying the discourse in its original setting (e.g., Botha 2001, 2002).[3]

Similar studies are needed which investigate the wider context of *reception* (or 'consumption') of these same texts as they occur in translation.[4]

---

[3] In the Abstract of his second article, Botha states that "it is not possible to understand the text as an instrument of communication if the social context is not taken into consideration. [Therefore] the psalm [must be] analyzed on a poetic and a social-critical plane" (2002:320). He later concludes: "In the light of a growing awareness of the importance of the social values of honor and shame in the ancient world, a re-evaluation of the psalms as ideological rather than cultic documents is called for" (ibid., 332).

[4] Perhaps in the context of this chapter, 'reception' is not really the most appropriate term to designate the activity whereby people interpret and respond to verbal texts. Indeed, they are not passive 'receptors' in the communication event but *actively* make their own distinct, conceptual contribution to the varied degrees of success or failure of the transaction as a whole. Thus individual readers (or hearers) are independent 'processors' who have many interrelated formal, semantic, and pragmatic choices and decisions to make during inter-

What effect do significant situational factors such as a different language, literature (orature), society, geography, time, and place have upon the textual understanding and contextual application of contemporary audiences? In section 4.3, I give special attention to the collective influence of what we might term an 'indigenous ideology', incorporating the traditional cultural and religious belief system in operation during the interpretation of Psalm 137 in Chewa by lay readers and hearers.[5]

4.2 The complex communicative framework of Psalm 137

Before looking at translations into Chewa, though, it is important to examine the source text its cultural context. Therefore, in this section I survey a selection of the salient features[6] that pertain to the poetic composition of Psalm 137 and its relation to its co-textual and putative circumstantial setting in an effort to uncover the author's basic ideological motives. The Hebrew original is first displayed below alongside a relatively literal English translation. The text has been formatted according to two levels of indentation in order to indicate its apparent structural design, while the major repeated terms are highlighted in the English through the use of conventional typographical devices.

4.2.1 The text of Psalm 137—a reflection of its contextual setting

¹ By the rivers of **Babylon**,	עַל נַהֲרוֹת ׀ בָּבֶל ¹	A
there we sat and wept,	שָׁם יָשַׁבְנוּ גַּם־בָּכִינוּ	
when we **remembered** Zion	בְּזָכְרֵנוּ אֶת־צִיּוֹן׃	
2 On the poplars in that place	עַל־עֲרָבִים בְּתוֹכָהּ ²	
we hung up our lyres.	תָּלִינוּ כִּנֹּרוֹתֵינוּ׃	
³ For there they demanded of us,	כִּי שָׁם שְׁאֵלוּנוּ ³	
our captors did, words of a *song*,	שׁוֹבֵינוּ דִּבְרֵי־שִׁיר	
and our mockers,[7] [called for] joy,	וְתוֹלָלֵינוּ שִׂמְחָה	
"*Sing* us one of the *songs* of *Zion*!"	שִׁירוּ לָנוּ מִשִּׁיר צִיּוֹן׃	
⁴ But how shall we *sing* the **LORD's** *song*	אֵיךְ נָשִׁיר אֶת־שִׁיר־יְהוָה ⁴	
on foreign soil?	עַל אַדְמַת נֵכָר׃	
⁵ *If* I forget you, O *Jerusalem*,	אִם־אֶשְׁכָּחֵךְ יְרוּשָׁלָ͏ִם ⁵	B

---

pretation. In this way text 'processing' complements text 'production', and the latter must always be analyzed or evaluated in relation to the former.

[5] The present study is a followup to a much more detailed and lengthy field experiment with regard to the poetic translation of Ps. 23 in Chewa, as reported in Wendland 2004b.

[6] For a much more thorough exegetical study, the commentary by Goldingay (2008) is recommended.

[7] On the translation 'mockers' for the hapax legomenon תוֹלָלֵינוּ, see Goldingay (2008:599).

4.2 The complex communicative framework of Psalm 137

let my right hand forget...!⁸ ⁶ Let my tongue stick to my palate, *if* I do not **remember** you,⁹ *if* I do not raise *Jerusalem* above the peak of my highest joy!	תִּשְׁכַּח יְמִינִי׃ ⁶ תִּדְבַּק־לְשׁוֹנִי ׀ לְחִכִּי אִם־לֹא אֶזְכְּרֵכִי אִם־לֹא אַעֲלֶה אֶת־יְרוּשָׁלִַם עַל רֹאשׁ שִׂמְחָתִי׃
⁷ **Remember**, O LORD, against the Edomites the day of *Jerusalem*, those who said, "Expose, expose [it] down to its very foundation!" ⁸ O Dame *Babylon*, about to be devastated! *Good for* anyone who repays *you* for the deeds you have done to *us*! ⁹ *Good for* anyone who seizes and dashes your children against the rocks!	⁷ זְכֹר יְהוָה ׀ לִבְנֵי אֱדוֹם אֵת יוֹם יְרוּשָׁלִָם הָאֹמְרִים עָרוּ ׀ עָרוּ עַד הַיְסוֹד בָּהּ׃ ⁸ בַּת־בָּבֶל הַשְּׁדוּדָה אַשְׁרֵי שֶׁיְשַׁלֶּם־לָךְ אֶת־גְּמוּלֵךְ שֶׁגָּמַלְתְּ לָנוּ׃ ⁹ אַשְׁרֵי ׀ שֶׁיֹּאחֵז וְנִפֵּץ אֶת־עֹלָלַיִךְ אֶל־הַסָּלַע׃	A'

James Kugel, for one, is not very impressed with the poetic style of this psalm:

> Psalm 137 [is] one of the "prosiest" psalms in the Bible....[E]ven the relatively short or normal-sized lines...lack the niceties of Part A and Part B, the connectedness amid disjunction, that is the heart of biblical prosody. We *can* pause in the middle, so we do, but the spring, the fulcrum of the poetic line is not there. (1999:235-236)

On the contrary, I would suggest that this psalm is quite poetically constructed—perhaps not according to classical psalmic norms for the genre, but arguably close enough. In fact it exhibits a number of prominent stylistic devices that shape the text into an extremely tight poetic composition. In the interest of space, I will merely list some of these features, and not discuss them in detail:

- A relatively regular, rhythmic lineation appears throughout (supported syntactically), with somewhat longer lines possibly calling attention to a special aspect of form and/or content, e.g., the complaint of 4a and a key point of the oath regarding 'Jerusalem' in 6c.[10]

---

[8] This is a truncated self-imprecation with the object of the verb 'forget' (put out of mind) implicit, as in Ps. 132:3-5 (Goldingay ibid., 606).

[9] The final suffix on 'I remember you' (אֶזְכְּרֵכִי) is an unusual Aramaic-like form (cf. Ps. 103:3-5), perhaps used here to create a striking rhymed paronomasia with the preceding line-end 'my palate' (לְחִכִּי) (Goldingay ibid., 606).

[10] Strophe B is the most problematic in terms of lineation. In favor of my proposal is the overall 'pressure of symmetry' (two extra long lines would distort the pattern as a whole) and an alternating, thematically significant lexical pattern that overlaps with strophe A': 'Jerusalem' (5a) – 'remember' (6b) – 'Jerusalem' (6c) // 'remember' (7a) – 'Jerusalem' (7b).

- A general concentric discourse arrangement organizes the text as a whole, specifically, an A—B—A' 'ring' construction. Strophe A features a setting-oriented conceptual inclusio, i.e., 'by the rivers of Babylon' (1a) and 'on foreign soil' (4b). The two communally expressed A strophes (vv. 1–4 + 7–9) manifest a focus upon 'Babylon' while the central, individualistic B strophe (vv. 5–6) features the central theme of 'remembering (not forgetting) Jerusalem'. There is a temporal progression: A—past → B—present → A'—future. Several structural similarities serve to relate the separated A strophes: parallel constructions in vv. 1a and 2a correspond to a different parallel pair in vv. 8b and 9a; minor wordplays are found within each unit: (A) תְּלִינוּ and תּוֹלָלֵינוּ ('we hung', 'those tormenting us') in vv. 2b and 3c – (A') יְרוּשָׁלִַם and שֶׁיְשַׁלֶּם ('Jerusalem', 'who repays') in vv. 7b and 8b; in vv. 3 and 7 disparaging direct quotations of Israel's enemies (featuring plural imperatives) are highlighted as patent judicial evidence against them.

- Intra-strophic cohesion is constructed by reiterated terms and by a number of parallel syntactic constructions. Strophe A also demonstrates strong morphological and phonological connectivity created by the reiterated first person plural references (וּ + נ),[11] while the inner B strophe manifests a first person singular sequence (י + א).

- The middle B strophe, with its sudden shift to the first person singular, is posited as being the psalm's *thematic* peak, as distinct from the *emotive* peak that comes at the end in v. 9. This nuclear segment is comprised of a dramatic response to the rhetorical question that ends strophe A.[12] The entire B unit is chiastically structured by means of a twofold self-malediction (*condition:* 'if I forget...'/5a + *curse:* 'let my right hand forget...'/5b ↔ *curse:* 'let my tongue...' /6a + *condition:* 'if I do not remember...'/6bcd). This oath climaxes in the second half with the double condition featuring the key term 'Jerusalem' at its core. Thirteen poetic lines precede the middle boundary between the two vows of B; another thirteen follow it.

---

[11] "[The] ninefold repetition of the ending –*nû* ('we,' 'our') ... carries a ring of pathos, as in Isa 53:4–6" (Allen 1983:241).

[12] Commentators and translations alike are divided over the issue of where to place v. 4—at the end of strophe A or the beginning of B. I prefer the former arrangement because of the cohesive nature of vv. 1–4 and 5–6 respectively and since I feel that v. 4, which leads off with the exclamation אֵיךְ 'Oh, how...', functions more effectively in rhetorical terms as the climax of A, rather than as an emphatic opener to B.

4.2 The complex communicative framework of Psalm 137

- The linkage of 'Jerusalem' with 'joy' (6cd) suggests a greater symbolic import for this capital city, namely, as an implicit metonymic reference to Yahweh himself (*place* for the *person* associated with it). Thus the 'song of the LORD' that leads off strophe B is in effect a song *to/in praise of* Yahweh, and the subsequent oath involves a promise never to 'forget' the LORD (5a, 6b), but always to consider God as the people's greatest cause for rejoicing, hence worship. This interpretation is suggested by the very close semantic connection that YHWH has with 'joy' (שׂמחה) not only here, but also elsewhere in the Psalter, e.g., 16:11, 21:6, 68:4, and especially 43:4, 97:11. The LORD is mentioned explicitly then at the onset of strophe A' (v. 7).

- Ironic interlocking creates a conceptual bond between strophes A and A': the captors mockingly call for 'songs of joy' and 'songs of Zion' (cf. Pss. 46, 48, 76, 84) from the captives (3cd). What they get in return is a shocking imprecation in vv. 8–9 (sarcastically disguised in the form of a blessing)! The present and recalled sorrow of the (former ?) exiles links up with the wished for sorrow that should be experienced by a severely punished Babylon. Strophe B verbalizes the devout loyalty of every true follower of the Lord, who will ever 'remember Jerusalem'—in contrast to the deceptive treachery of the 'Edomites' (v.7), who did not remember their ethnic kin in the day of battle with a foreign enemy and who must therefore be punitively 'remembered' by Yahweh (cf. Jer. 51:49–51, Lam. 1:7, Obad. 10–14).

- A fervent appeal to 'remember' or 'call to mind' (זכר) is the main thematic concept of this psalm, one that recurs in each strophe (also via its antonym '[not] forget' – 'may it forget' in the central core, B) and thus colors the entire text.[13] However, somewhat different semantic nuances in each cotext complement each other to enlarge the intended frame of reference along the following lines: (1c) a literal 'remembrance' of 'Zion', the nation's capital city and worship center, is being referred to; (5a) Israel must 'never forget', that is, disown, disparage, or dishonor their ethnic and spiritual heritage, as symbolized by 'Jerusalem'; (6b) the faithful continue to 'remember' in the sense of reverence 'Jerusalem' and to worship its one and only

---

[13] "'Be mindful' implies not just an accidental remembering but a deliberate focusing of attention and thought, a focused mindfulness on the part of a community gathered for recollection" (Goldingay 2008:603). "This psalm is often recited on the 9th day of Av, the day that commemorates the destruction of the Temple..." (from a note in *The Jewish Study Bible (Tanakh)*, Jewish Publication Society, Oxford: Oxford University Press, 2004:1435).

God, Yahweh; (7a) the LORD is called upon to 'remember' 'Edom' (and also 'Babylon') in righteous judgment by punishing these ungodly nations as they deserve.

- In terms of its genre, on the whole Psalm 137 probably fits best into the broad category of a 'communal lament' (cf. Gerstenberger 2001:394; Mays 1994:422), that is, in keeping with its outer strophes, A and A' (the singular references of B thus being interpreted as representative expressions). But the discourse has been artfully modified from the typical lament pattern to incorporate a panegyric promissory theme (vv. 5–6, mindful of a 'song of Zion', cf. v.3b), along with prominent imprecatory (vv. 7–9), and commemorative elements (a psalm of 'remembrance' in the heading). Such an incorporation of other genres was probably effected in order to enhance the psalm's major communicative purpose, probably liturgical, during its initial setting of use as well as its subsequent corporate reiteration. This compositional hybrid thus stands as a vivid verbal memorial both of the appalling events being recalled and also of the people's steadfast, even stubborn, God-based hope for their future.[14]

Are there ideological implications that we can draw from the structure and style of Psalm 137, given its lyrical creativity and liturgical context? Admittedly, any imputation of motive to such a distant artistic impulse is hypothetical, but I would suggest that the high compositional quality of this rhetorically motivated prayer indicates that the destruction of Jerusalem and the horrible exilic experience had not extinguished the poetic muse among the religious faithful of Israel. The same forthright appeal and confessional purpose is present here as in pre-exilic psalms, namely, to reaffirm in passionate song, whether collectively or as individuals, a potent pledge of religious allegiance and personal commitment, as it were, to Yahweh.

The people may have been bowed by the recent devastating events of history and politics, but they, perhaps only a resilient minority, were certainly not broken. Their trust in the God, whom they still regarded as sovereignly controlling a larger destiny for the nation, had suffered some

---

[14] A much more complete, or standard, example of a communal lament would be Ps. 22, which consists of the following characteristic compositional elements (cf. Gerstenberger 1988:12): invocation (22:1a), complaint (22:1–2), profession of innocence/fidelity (22:8–9), affirmation of confidence (22:3–5), plea for help (22:19–21), assurance of a divine response (22:24), vow or pledge (22:25), expressions of praise (22:3), anticipated thanksgiving for deliverance (22:22–24). The element of 'imprecation', missing in Ps. 22 is made prominent here in 137, while the 'vow' is strengthened to a self-directed oath.

4.2 The complex communicative framework of Psalm 137

damage, but it was not completely deflated, let alone dead. The utter shame of their defeat and exile (vv. 1–4) only drove them to renewed zeal for the honor and glory of Yahweh, which they were prepared to defend at all costs (vv. 5–6) against their bitterest of enemies (vv. 7–9). Accordingly, this artistic composition and the vigorous polemical force it conveys may be intended as a poetic 'statement,' a public profession of faith with regard to this supreme theological fact: Israel's hope remained firmly fixed upon the physically ruined 'foundation' of 'Zion' (v. 8), more precisely, in what the sacred place 'there' (v. 1) symbolized—the eternal presence and support of Yahweh, their covenant-keeping Savior and Lord. This produced within these spiritual loyalists a tough, enduring 'joy' (v. 6) that could not be repressed, poetically or otherwise, due to an unfavorable environment (e.g., v. 3).

4.2.2 The context of Psalm 137—its possible influence on the text

This is no doubt the most situationally marked, setting-specific psalm of the Psalter. Though the author may still have been in the vicinity of 'the rivers of Babylon' (v. 1) when he composed this complaint to the Lord, it is more likely that he was among the first groups of exiles who eagerly returned to Jerusalem only to be dismayed by the devastation there, including the site of their beloved Temple.[15] What sort of a religious ideology did he and like-minded singers now espouse? Was it one of disillusionment and despair as they gazed upon the ruins and rubble of what had formerly been their central house of worship—indeed, the place where their forefathers could regularly commune and communicate with Yahweh? Did a bitter pessimism and skepticism, perhaps bordering on agnosticism, sour their thinking as they reflected upon the humiliation of what had happened and why? Had the LORD actually deserted his covenant people? Was their supreme Deity in fact weaker than and subservient to the pagan gods of the Babylonians? These were issues of vital religious, social and political concern which affected the very identity of Israel as

---

[15] Allen concludes: "The early years of return from exile, either before the rebuilding of the temple (537–516/5 B.C. or of the city walls (537–445 B.C.) were evidently the period in which the psalm was composed" (1983:238). In any case, the psychological effects of the destruction of 'Zion' and its national significance would be much the same whether the psalmist and his audience were actually back in the vicinity of Jerusalem's ruins (as the initial sequence of suffix tenses and the repeated locative particle שָׁם 'there' would indicate)—or not. It is impossible to say, however, how many Jews would agree with the religious ideology and sentiments expressed in this psalm. Probably a majority of the former exiles who had actually returned would be included—but not so many of those who had for whatever personal reasons remained behind 'in a foreign land' (v. 4).

the people of the one God—their Lord, Yahweh. Despite the depressing external circumstances, as reflected in the first three verses, the author of Psalm 137 gives an ardently optimistic reply. His song strongly reaffirms the nation's traditional beliefs, values, and ideals—their Scripture-based ideology—with respect to 'Zion' and all that this holy place symbolized.

Israel's musical tradition, as anthologized in the Psalter, seems to indicate that Psalm 137 may be viewed as functioning like an ideological and theological 'pep song', written and sung to encourage fellow Israelites not to forget their history, their culture, their religion, or their vision for the nation's future. This construal derives not only from a consideration of the psalm's presumed extratextual circumstances, but it is indirectly supported by its canonical placement within the Psalter and relationship to the multiple liturgical genres combined in its composition. It begins (vv. 1–4) in a manner that befits the general pattern of a 'communal lament' which appeals to Yahweh to come to the aid of his beleaguered people in their great distress (e.g., Pss. 12, 44, 74, 89–137 would be the last of this type). The psalmist immediately captures his audience's attention with the plaintive narrative anecdote that any listener could identify with. As already noted, however, the typical poetic structure of such a corporate complaint is then modified by the author through the incorporation of two familiar sub-genres, as a means of more directly and dramatically addressing Israel's current social and religious crisis.

The war with Babylon had been lost, the nation destroyed, and many of her leading citizens dispersed. The main threat then was not a military one from some pagan adversary; rather it was a serious internal, psychological challenge: how would people adjust to the current adverse status quo? Was accommodation and settlement in a foreign land the best option or at least a path of lesser resistance? There was no doubt that those who returned to Palestine with Persian permission would have no שלם 'peace' at all; rather, they could expect to face some very tough times and much hard testing. After the recent tragedies that had occurred to provoke this state of affairs, how many people would be prepared to again risk everything by starting all over? How many, whether those still in exile in Babylon or those who had returned to Jerusalem, would be inclined to agree with the pessimistic outlook expressed in the rhetorical question that ends the first strophe? There is no way that they could happily 'sing the songs of Yahweh' (v. 4), of thanksgiving and praise to him, under such disheartening circumstances.[16] The irony is that the poet begins just

---

[16] For the devout Jew, being separated from Zion/Yahweh and his dwelling place (the Temple) in exile was like being in hell *(Sheol)*; it was simply not possible to 'praise the LORD' there (Pss. 30:9, 88:10–12). Furthermore, as Allen points out: "By the location of the psalm

4.2 The complex communicative framework of Psalm 137

such a song in the very next line, and this more positive, forcefully defiant viewpoint occupies and characterizes the remainder of this psalm.

Thus the psalmist's determined response (vv. 5–6) to the demeaning taunts of all enemies of Zion and her God, Yahweh, is a double vow to 'remember Jerusalem'—the city and site of the Temple as she once was and what, with divine blessing, she could one day become again. In this context, the concrete act of *remembrance* (זכר) is equivalent to overt displays of fidelity, worship, reverence, total devotion, and service—not to a place, but to the praiseworthy person thereby symbolized, the covenant Lord of Israel. Any hint of 'forgetting'—of compromise, accommodation, 'foreignization', or outright apostasy—was completely out of the question. A first person, self-malediction seals this representative oath—to be reaffirmed by every advocate who utters it (a symbolic, 'performative' speech-act). This was in effect a bold act of defiance pronounced against all persecutors of God's people (Yahwistic ideology in action!) as well as a confession that they would remain faithful to their cultural traditions and true to the beliefs and rites of their ancestral religion.

Psalm 137 reflects a number of Jerusalem-oriented paraenetic prophecies, especially in Isaiah (e.g., 2:2–5, 62). Within Psalm 137, its symmetrical core functions as a mini 'song of Zion', and as such is the last in the corpus of some thirteen Zion songs that appear periodically throughout the Psalter from Book 2 to Book Five, (e.g., 46, 48, 76, 84, 87, 122, 126, 129, 132–135). Several of the preceding Zion salvation songs seem to point forward intertextually to 137:

- 126: Yahweh brought back the captives (or: restored the fortunes) of Zion (v.1), and as a result their tongues were filled with songs of gladness (v.2—the term 'gladness' is emphasized throughout; cf. 137:3, 6).

- 129: Yahweh is fervently petitioned to punish 'all who hate Zion' by dealing with them (vv. 5–8) in like manner as they ferociously terrorized the people of God (vv. 1–4).

- 132: This psalm lauds the surpassing theological significance of 'Zion' as the 'dwelling place' of Yahweh and his anointed king, as epitomized in the promised Messiah (vv. 11–18); the 'gladness' of

---

immediately after two psalms which celebrate Yahweh's gift of the land to the covenant nation, the reversal here expressed is conveyed in even more poignant tones than when the psalm is read in isolation" (1983:241).

God's honored saints (v. 16) will contrast with the 'shame' of their enemies (v.18).

Indeed, how could any faithful Israelite ever 'forget' such an exalted place or so great a God? This seems to be a basic motivation for the trio of psalms that some commentators, such as Allen (1983:239), view as being a 'supplement' to the 'song of ascents corpus'—specifically Psalms 135, 136, and 137, which variously highlight the total loyalty-to-Yahweh theme that is so prominent in Psalms 120–134. To be sure, the initial pathos of the lament in 137 stands in sharp contrast to the buoyant faith expressed in passages such as these (NIV):

> Praise the LORD, all you servants of the LORD
> who minister by night in the house of the LORD. (134:1)
>
> Praise be to the LORD from Zion, to him who dwells in Jerusalem.
> Praise the LORD! (135:21)
>
> ...to the One who remembered us in our low estate *[His love endures forever.]*
> and freed us from our enemies... *[His love endures forever.]* (136:23–24)[17]

Nevertheless, that same faith, albeit tested to the limit in the destruction of Jerusalem and the exile to Babylon, remained steadfast and thus required a suitable poetic vehicle for both personal and communal expression. Psalm 137 in all its succinct starkness well serves this ideological purpose for those Jews whose religious determination and devotion to Jerusalem matches that of the psalmists—past and present (cf. Neh. 1:3-4; 2:3-5). 'Zion', even in total ruins, stood as a testimony to their firm trust in an almighty God who would, one day, most surely administer justice and transform their present shame into permanent honor!

The psalm's imprecatory conclusion (vv. 7–9), sarcastically clothed in the form of a double beatitude, is intended to stir the minds of the faithful and to stimulate hearts of the willing to action. However, this response was not to be manifested in rebellion against their foreign masters, for Yahweh would deal with them; in fact, he had already 'remembered' to do so (with judicial implications). Both Edom and Babylon were to be 'repaid' with destruction (v. 8),[18] politically if not physically—the former for their treachery, the latter for their merciless slaughter of God's people

---

[17] Ps. 137 may be viewed as a historically updated postscript to the majestic litany of Ps. 136, the 'Great Hallel' of the Jewish liturgy.

[18] Indeed, most fittingly 'to be destroyed' *(shedûdâ)* (v. 8a) from God, the almighty 'Destroyer' *(shadday,* cf. Isa. 13:6) (Goldingay 2008:609).

4.2 The complex communicative framework of Psalm 137

and their impious sacking of his holy place (cf. Jer. 51:35, 49-50, 56), making it a clear case of *lex talionis*—the LORD punishing in like manner the pagan nations whom he had used as instruments of chastisement upon his rebellious people. The faith of Israel was severely tested but finally vindicated during the course of these tumultuous events.

The author of the Psalm must have had in mind the covenantal principles of Deuteronomy, given his conservative theological perspective (e.g., 28:20, 25, 37, 64-66; 29:24-28; 30:1-7; cf. also Lev. 26). Such thinking was also an important part of the prophetic message uttered in condemnation of Israel's own chronic wickedness and appalling apostasy (e.g., Isa. 13:16; 14:22; Jer. 49:17; 50:6-7; 51:5, 24). How then could such a distinctive ideology of righteous retribution be dramatically and poetically expressed? The ritualized *imprecation* was the standard genre available for precisely such a purpose in this Ancient Near Eastern literary and cultural setting, and here the literary form is further heightened emotively as a climactic touch by stating it as a (mock) blessing.[19]

If readers today are tempted to recoil with distaste or disgust at the sentiments expressed in a passage like 137:9,[20] they must not forget their current historical distance and alien perspective—that they are strangers to this dynamic literary and religious tradition. Furthermore, they should note the fact that such imprecatory language always features conventionalized hyperbolic sayings that cannot be interpreted literally; rather, the literary style is highly figurative and operates functionally in a very specific manner. The psalmist is here pleading with God to uphold his honor and that of his covenant people by exercising penal justice in vengeance upon the wicked. He does so by utilizing the most vivid, emotively cathartic, and spiritually healing terms that are available in his precative vocabulary and the religious corpus from which it springs.[21]

While the personified proper names here (Edom, Babylon) refer to the Edomites and Babylonians from the specific time referenced in Psalm 137, they also symbolize all enemies of Yahweh and his righteous saints (Jerusalem). Such

---

[19] For a good summary of OT imprecations and their significance in the Psalms, see Van Gemeren 1991:830-832.

[20] In another reversal of spiritual and national fortunes, Christ laments the coming fate of Jerusalem, citing the 'dashing' of children as one outcome of the people's rejection of their Messiah (Luke 19:44). See also 2 Kgs. 8:12, Isa. 13:16, Hos. 13:16, and Nah. 3:10, which all speak of infants being dashed to death in times of war.

[21] "Although it is not explicit, we may assume that the psalmist's submission of anger to God obviates the need for actual revenge upon the enemy" (McCann 1996:1229). That is one way to hermeneutically resolve potentially conflicting biblical ideologies and the challenge of holding "in tension the requirement of love and the hatred of evil" (Van Gemeren 1991:831).

symbolic execrations function first of all as condensed oracles of divine judgment which pronounce the Lord's verdict on iniquity, in that just as fervently as God loves the faithful, so zealously does he abhor evil and chasten the wicked (cf. Jer. 49:7-22; 50:1-51:58). Second, these imprecations also allow the oppressed to verbally release in a liturgically acceptable manner for that time and place some of the pent up mental anguish, as well as rage and hatred, that they feel towards their former and present tormentors. How could Israel's history be turned around and Zion restored to prominence? Only by returning to their religious roots in repentance and by remembering to faithfully observe the clear stipulations of the Mosaic covenant. The attitude that inspires such a return to righteousness is poetically expressed in the Davidic psalms that follow 137 in the Psalter (e.g., 138:2;[22] 139:17-18, 23; 140:12-13, 141:2-5, 143:5-8, 144:2), which include repeated appeals to punish the unrighteous (e.g., 138:7, 139:19-22, 140:8-11, 141:5-7, 143:12).

Thus Psalm 137 acts as a structurally and thematically *transitional* segment of psalmody in the sense that it sharply (in terms of style) and incisively (in terms of content) reminds the people of God where they have come from in their spiritual journey, even as it sets the tone for what is yet to come. It does this in a way that leaves their traumatic past behind (vv. 1-4) and sets the course of believers confidently towards a joyous outcome for Zion (vv. 5-9; cf. Pss. 145-150). The crucial transformative activity that will make such blessing possible is *remembering*: the people must always *remember* (worship) 'Jerusalem' (= Yahweh), and he will in turn *remember* (deliver/vindicate) them. A single-minded zeal for the glory of the Lord and wholehearted service to him in whatever circumstances one happens to be—that's what the timeless message of this lyric lament continues to promote beneath the surface of its contextually specific, and at times shocking, details.[23]

In summary, I might depict the hybrid communicative quality of Psalm 137 as follows. The piece is a masterful liturgical composition in which a revitalized theological ideology concerning 'Zion' is fashioned with great feeling into a novel, composite textual form to carry out a distinctive

---

[22] The placement of Ps. 138 right after 137 sounds rather ironic in the reference to 'bowing down to [God's] holy temple' (v. 2). The overall spirit of the psalm, however, does coincide with the sentiments expressed in 137:5-6, which are also based upon Yahweh's love and faithfulness.

[23] Several contemporary applications: "[Ps. 137] can quicken our awareness of the anomaly involved in singing the Lord's song in an alien culture without any sense of the contradiction between our words and our world" (Mays 1994:424). In this psalm, "the stark claims of the holy God override all our conventional humanness" (Brueggemann 1984:76). "Whatever the desires in the hearts of people who say the psalm, their words leave it to God to decide of that character [i.e., mercy vs. judgment] God gives expression to" (Goldingay 2008:614).

religious and prophetic purpose. It is a text that profoundly reflects its Jewish cultural setting and the grievous historical situation in which it arose, even as it defiantly generates an encouraging prospect for the future of God's people:

Surface literary form	*Underlying religious function*
1. Communal lament (1–4)	Summons to remembrance
2. Individual oath (5–6)	Profession of trust and loyalty
3. Beatitude > Curse (7–9)	Polemical judgment oracle

4.3 Ideological factors in contemporary translation

The influence of ideology on the hermeneutical process certainly does not end with the original text of Scripture. It is a critical factor that also needs to be carefully considered when that same passage is translated into another language and its unique cultural environment. In this section I will survey two general areas of concern in which ideological issues come to the fore, namely, with regard to translation technique and accompanying paratextual supplementation. Here we find all too often that certain pertinent, at times contentious, problems are not even recognized, let alone honestly and openly discussed or debated so that they might be resolved by all the parties involved. Alternatively, important and relevant issues may be ignored, downplayed, or simply decided by the fiat of a few, with serious adverse consequences for the overall progress of the translation project. What sort of ideologies are engaged in the practical work of Bible translation, and how may they be evaluated, prioritized, and balanced out in relation to each other within the organizational framework of the whole enterprise?

4.3.1 Translation technique

During the past several decades, the theory and practice of translation in general has been introduced to a variety of field-specific philosophies or ideologies. In this respect, the discipline has been opened up primarily by secular theorists and professional practitioners. The old literal versus idiomatic dichotomy appears to have been done away with, at least on the surface of the debate, and the gap between these two virtual poles of possibility has been filled with a number of perspectives, along with their proposed methodologies (cf. Wendland 2002b:180–183). Thus a recent introduction to what is now known as 'translation studies' includes a diversity of approaches distinguished by terms such as: 'functionalist', 'communicative', [assessing] 'equivalence' – 'similarity' – 'relevance' – or 'rewriting', 'descriptive', 'textual', 'pragmatic', 'semiotic', 'discourse'-oriented, 'norm'-based, 'manipulative', 'post-colonial', 'cultural', 'feminist', and 'integrated' (Munday 2001:passim).

Some of the ideologies that drive these theories are more social in nature, where the emphasis is upon the range of communicative options that exist in relation to different target audiences, while others are more politically motivated, thus advocating the rights of particular minority or disadvantaged communities. In essence, however, it is debatable whether we have moved all that far from the basic distinction that was drawn in the classic description of Friedrich Schleiermacher:

> Either the translator leaves the writer alone as much as possible and moves the reader toward the writer, or he [sic] leaves the reader alone as much as possible and moves the writer toward the reader.[24]

In practice, any sort of ideology will inevitably have to develop a translation technique that positions itself *somewhere between* the two options of 'alienating' as opposed to 'naturalizing' the TL text, to use Schleiermacher's terms (more commonly expressed by Venuti and others as the strategies of 'foreignizing' and 'domesticating', respectively (Munday 2001:146–148)). As far as secular translation situations are concerned, the principal factors that determine which of these two methods to follow (and how far) are these: (a) the personal objective(s) of the translator (e.g., having a particular cause to promote) and (b) the preferences or requirements of his/her intended readership. Consideration for the target audience has become the central focus of the so-called *Skopos* school of translation:

> The Skopos rule thus reads as follows: translate/interpret/speak/write in a way that enables your text/translation to function in the situation in which it is used and with the people who want to use it and precisely in the way they want it to function.[25]

Certain prominent aspects of this functional approach have also become important in the work of translating the Scriptures, as will be pointed out in sections 4.3.2 and 4.3.3.

---

[24] From Schleiermacher's 1813 treatise on translation, *Über die verschiedenen Methoden des Übersetzens*, cited in Munday 2001:28. Ellington comments insightfully on this principle: "Any attempt by translators to take the reader all the way to the writer is doomed to frustrate and alienate the average reader. Yet any endeavor to take the writer all the way to the reader risks trivializing the message and creating disinterest" (2003:315).

[25] Hans Vermeer, translated and cited in Nord 1997:29.

4.3 Ideological factors in contemporary translation

A reception-oriented methodology in Bible translation was popularized by Eugene Nida's theory of 'dynamic equivalence', which aimed to "present the message [of the biblical text] in such a way that people can feel its relevance (the expressive element in communication) and can then respond to it in action (the imperative function)".[26] This target-centered tactic, arising from what has been termed a 'theological and proselytizing' impulse,[27] emphasizes the production of a translation that is 'meaningful' and 'natural' in keeping with TL stylistic norms. The appearance of many works by Nida and like-minded translation scholars has sparked an ideological debate that continues to the present day.[28] Since others have documented the varied contours of this controversy (e.g., Mojola 2002:1–10), along with related issues (such as the use of gender-sensitive language), I will not attempt to duplicate their efforts. It is enough to point out the fact that nowadays the influence of an underlying ideology is generally accepted, whether or not it has been explicitly stated by the translators of a given version (e.g., in a preface of some sort). For example, the following states a pertinent portion of the translation philosophy of the relatively new *English Standard Version* (ESV):[29]

> The ESV is an 'essentially literal' translation that seeks as far as possible to capture the precise wording of the original text and the personal style of each Bible writer....Thus it seeks to be transparent to the original text, letting the reader see as directly as possible the structure and meaning of the original. In contrast to the ESV, some Bible versions have followed a 'thought-for-thought' rather than a 'word-for-word' translation philosophy, emphasizing 'dynamic equivalence' rather than the 'essentially literal' meaning of the original. A 'thought-for-thought' translation is of necessity more inclined to reflect the interpretive opinions of the translator and the influences of contemporary culture. Every translation is at many points a trade-off between literal precision and readability, between 'formal equivalence' in expression and 'functional

---

[26] Nida and Taber 1969:24. 'Dynamic equivalence' is defined as the "quality of a translation in which the message of the original text has been so transported into the receptor language that the RESPONSE of the RECEPTOR is essentially that of the original receptors" (ibid., 202).

[27] Edwin Genztler, cited in Munday 2001:43.

[28] Two recent books are representative of the different perspectives that become apparent in this debate: "The contributors to this volume, though not in lockstep, are generally united in their support of the translation theory of functional equivalence in its basic contours" (Scorgie, Strauss, and Voth 2003:24) –versus– "Even dynamic equivalent translations claim faithfulness to the original as their goal. But in fact only an essentially literal translation that claims fidelity to the language of the original achieves a consistently credible degree of faithfulness" (Ryken 2002:227–228).

[29] Cited from pp. vii–viii of the Preface; the ESV (2001) is published by Crossway Bibles, a division of Good News Publishers (Wheaton IL, USA), which is in fact also the publisher of Ryken 2002.

equivalence' in communication, and the ESV is no exception. Within this framework we have sought to be 'as literal as possible' while maintaining clarity of expression and literary excellence.

Such position statements are clearly ideologically motivated[30] and worded (with a certain measure of hyperbole) so as to appeal to the widest possible readership within a particular religious constituency, in this case, 'conservative evangelical'. Thus the preface is deliberately phrased to contrast with the position underlying the translation method of dynamic equivalence, which is implicitly characterized in a rather negative light as being 'more inclined to reflect the interpretive opinions of the translator and the influences of contemporary culture'. The problem of course is how to assess the accuracy, or indeed the relevance, of these claims (and all the major versions do make them) when such a well-formulated theory of translation is actually put into practice. The following, for example, is how Psalm 137:7 is rendered and displayed in the ESV:

> Remember, O LORD, against the
>   Edomites
>   the day of Jerusalem,
> how they said, "Lay it bare, lay it bare,
>   down to its foundations!"

One might ask how 'directly…the structure and meaning of the original' is reflected in this rendition—when compared, for another example, with that of the *Good News Translation*:

> Remember, LORD, what the Edomites did
>   the day Jerusalem was captured.
> Remember how they kept saying,
>   "Tear it down to the ground!"

Virtually all the native speakers of English I surveyed preferred the second with respect to both structure and meaning. So what does that prove? Not a great deal, except to support the more general translation principle that both an ideology (when stated) and its methodology (when applied) manifest themselves more along a sliding scale of preference and choice rather than as fixed policies and procedures that can be put into practice in a uniform, non-subjective, non-controversial manner. This is

---

[30] For a brief but incisive critique of this translation philosophy, see Crisp 2004.

4.3 Ideological factors in contemporary translation

true whether we are concerned with a translation of the Bible or any other instance of literature. What then can help guide translators in their impossible task, that is, to make the right decisions? The answer is personal and audience-oriented; it must always incorporate an accurate impression of those for whom the version at hand is intended. It is their 'ideology' regarding the Word of God and how they wish to use the text that needs to be given the utmost consideration.

4.3.2 Translation technique – applied to English

A poetic English version of Psalm 137 is found in Boerger's *POET Psalms* (2009), which contains her translation philosophy and goals as part of its preface. I fully cite her version below, including its footnotes, to illustrate what she thought important to include to help native speakers of English (who may be quite biblically illiterate) understand the complexities of this psalm.[31] She also includes footnotes regarding how Hebrew features are captured poetically in the *POET* rendition. Boerger composes this poem in iambic pentameter, the most natural meter of English and that used to compose sonnets; this contributes to its formulaic quality.

Note that she groups v. 4 with vv. 5–6 in order to achieve balanced octaves. While it breaks stanzas in a different place than was discussed above, the word 'but' which starts v. 4 may also function as a discourse level break. To tie these two verses together, *POET* adds 'Each vowed' at the beginning of v. 5, facilitating the transition from first person plural to singular.

Psalm 137[32]
WE SAT BY STREAMS IN BABYLON TO CRY:
IN REMEMBRANCE
(A historical psalm of retribution in heroic octave variations)[33]

1   We sat by streams in Babylon to cry.
      In sorrow heads were drooping down to weep,
      Remembering Zion which had been destroyed.
2   Along the rivers, stood some trees nearby.

---

[31] The importance of footnote content is relevant to section 4.3.4, where paratextual aids are discussed.

[32] Ps. 137. In 587 BC Babylon destroyed Jerusalem, assisted by Edom, Israel's relatives, leading to Israel's exile and captivity.

[33] 137 subtitle. The lines are all iambic pentameter, but each stanza has a different rhyme scheme and none are those prescribed for heroic octaves: abba-abba, abab-abab, or ababab-cc.

	And in the spreading branches of those trees
	We set aside for good our harps of joy.
3	*"Say, serenade us,"* our enslavers hissed.
	"So chant a Zion cadence, we insist." [34]

4	But we could not profane God's liturgy,
	Performing it in our captivity!
5	Each vowed, *"If I forget Jerusalem,*
	I'll ask my hands to forfeit all their skill—
	Can't pluck a lyre or strum a string again.
6	*If my great joy's not still Jerusalem,*
	Call me a liar. Tongue and lips be still
	And never cant another note again." [35]

7	When Babylon all Salem[36] ripped apart,
	The Edomites said, *"Strip her! Strip her bare!*
	And leave just the foundations lying there."
	So Yahweh Lord, remember Edom's part.

8–9	And Babylon, destruction is your due.
	May our avenger be blest in his wrath
	And bash your babes[37] on rocks until their death.
	He's blest who pays back all that's owed to you!

4.3.3 Translation technique – applied to Chewa

The same necessity of considering the audience, their attitude toward the Word of God, and the intended use of the Scriptures also applies to the Chewa translation of Psalm 137—perhaps more so, since here we

---

[34] 137:3 Verse 3 is filled with the hissing of [s], [sh], and [ts] sounds in Hebrew, showing the mocking of the captors. *POET* uses [s], [ch], [st], [ts] and [z] and compresses four lines into two lines for this effect in English.

[35] 137:5–6 Verses 5–6 have a wordplay, which increases the formality of the self-directed oath. In it, Hebrew uses 'forget' twice in verse 5, which *POET* renders 'forget/forfeit'. *POET* adds three further wordplays: can't/cant, lyre/liar, and two meanings of 'still', making the two halves of the oath sound parallel and ritualistic.

[36] 137:7 Salem is the short form of Jerusalem, and is used here to maintain the iambic pentameter beat.

[37] 137:8–9 The sarcastic blessing in vv. 8–9 is a type of ritualized curse practiced in the Ancient Near East. So, while talk of killing infants makes modern readers cringe, it was part of the formulaic language of such curses and a reality of the times. See 2 Kgs. 8:12, Isa. 13:16, Hos. 13:16, Nah. 3:10, and Luke 19:44. See also Rev. 18:6, which talks about the judgment of Babylon. *POET* combines vv. 8 and 9 to make relationships clearer.

4.3 Ideological factors in contemporary translation

are dealing with a much larger non-literate constituency and one that also evinces a relatively low general level of biblical literacy. It will be constructive to compare three translations into Chewa. The first text is taken from the 1923 translation *Buku Lopatulika* ('Sacred Book', **BL**); the second is the 1998 'popular language' version *Buku Loyera* ('Holy Book', **BY**); the third text is an experimental poetic (*ndakatulo*) version (**PV**), prepared for a young people's Bible study group. Verse seven from each of these translations in turn is given below and formatted as published. The latter two were guided by a distinct communicative goal in relation to a particular target audience.

Yehova, kumbukilani ana a Edo-mu	Yehova, remember the children of Ed-om
Tsiku la Yerusalemu;	On the day of Jerusalem;
Amene adati, Gamulani, gamula-ni,	Who said, Break down, break do-wn,
Kufikira maziko ace.	Reaching its foundation. (**BL**)

Kumbukirani, Inu Chauta,	Remember, O Creator-God
zimene adachita Aedomu	the things the Edomite people did
pa tsiku lija la kuwonongeka kwa Yerusalemu,	on that day of the destruction of Jerusalem,
muja ankati,	how they were saying,
"Mgwetseni pansi, mgwetseni pansi,	"Pull her down, pull her down,
mpaka pa maziko ake."	right down to her foundation." (**BY**)

Kumbukirani, inu Chauta, mulipsiretu	Remember, O Creator-God, you must take vengeance
zonse zachiwembu ankachita aEdomu	for all the acts of treachery that the Edomites did
pamene adani adagonjetsa Yerusalemu.	when enemies destroyed Jerusalem.
Paja patsikulo aEdomu ankafuula m'*fuu!*	You know on that day the Edomites shouted LOUDLY!
n'kumati, Chipasuleni chimzinda *mwaa!*	saying, Tear that awful city down DISPERSE-IT!
Chigwedi pansi *psiti!* m'maziko ake omwe.	Let it fall to the ground COMPLETELY! down to its very foundation. (**PV**)

The first version (BL) was prepared as an initial translation of the Bible in the Chewa language for the general Protestant church-going public. It was produced primarily by missionaries who did not fully control the linguistic, stylistic, and rhetorical resources of the vernacular.[38] This project was undoubtedly founded upon the theological premise that the only 'accurate', 'faithful', and 'reliable' translation of the Word of God is a more or less literal reproduction of the original text, in this case Hebrew and/or concordant English versions such as the KJV. Such a rationale may be ideologically defensible, but in practical terms it all too often turns out to be a disaster, for the BL sample above is nearly unintelligible, even when read by educated respondents within its verbal cotext.

In contrast to the BL, the ideology of the more domesticated 'popular language' BY version was more ecumenical in its outlook and designed to reach people who had difficulty in really understanding *Chibaibulo*, the ritualized ecclesiastical dialect that had developed under the influence of the BL in churches and schools. The BY version, composed and edited completely by mother-tongue speakers, was inspired and guided by Nida's principle of dynamic equivalence, though this was adapted and contextualized in various ways (Wendland 1998:67–113).[39] The third, experimental poetic text (PV) was developed with a much more specific target audience in mind—namely, young people who desired a more vibrant verbal rendering of the Scriptures to use both as a comparative Bible study tool and also as the basis for popular musical and dramatic presentations of the Scriptures. It was prompted by the desire to communicate the Word in a fresh, thought-provoking style—having both aesthetic appeal and rhetorical impact. To that end, the PV has the following features: balanced rhythmic lineation, syntactic condensation, word order variations, dramatic diction, some end rhyme, alliteration, and the Bantu poetic device par excellence—ideophones shown in italics/capitals. (For further details, see Wendland 1998:20–37, 185–189.) It thus aims to serve a youthful constituency which appreciates a text that speaks more energetically and pointedly in the context of their particular life-related questions and concerns about contemporary moral as well as spiritual issues.

---

[38] Furthermore, as Masenya rightly observes: "Usually Western ideologies have comfortably found a foothold in the African vernacular Bible translations because many missionaries had a share in the translation..." (2001:284). How much of a 'foothold' this has turned out to be is an issue for African theologians and translation specialists to determine.

[39] It should be pointed out that the BY was drafted primarily with reference to various English translations and commentaries. Exegetical advice based on the original text (Hebrew or Greek) was furnished in the main by expatriate reviewers. Thus this translation program faced the conceptual and ideological barrier of reliance upon an 'intervening' English base text. An extensive set of review procedures was put in place to counteract this dependency, but Masenya's point is well taken: "Wouldn't it have been better if the [Chewa] translators were in a position to draw the meaning directly from the Hebrew and Greek texts without having first to request the assistance of a foreign medium of communication?" (ibid., 288).

4.3.4 Paratextual supplementation

The cognitive conditioning created by one's sociocultural framework has already been noted as a crucial ideological factor that has not always been given due consideration in the practice of Bible translation around the world. One or the other side of the cultural divide that separates the source and target settings may be thoroughly investigated, but it is rare to find both fully accommodated, at least not by means of a close form-functional comparative study (cf. Wendland 1991). The communicative 'interference' caused by linguistic and conceptual differences between the SL and TL was briefly illustrated in 4.3.3 with reference to verse seven of Psalm 137. Thus a literalistic version such as the BL is difficult for most lay people and even many pastors to read and understand at first because the language of the translation is both unnatural and not clearly phrased in terms of natural TL lexical and semantic categories. For example, the expressions 'the children of Edom'...'said', 'the day of Jerusalem', and 'reaching its foundation', reinforce one other to compound the difficulty of comprehension within the scope of this single verse (7).

Linguistic and stylistic obstacles can often be dealt with by competent translators within the text of the translation itself, as shown in the BY version's naturalizing transformation. Cultural or situational clashes, incongruities, and lacunae however, are not so easy to handle, especially when important theological overtones are activated or worldview assumptions are denied. Many times such difficulties are occasioned by a lack of sufficient background information that pertains to the overall setting of the biblical book at hand or its specific contents. A number of these barriers confront Chewa text consumers, listeners in particular, during their interpretation of Psalm 137. For example, they would have the following questions about particular verses (in parentheses), and in fact, these same questions would appropriately be asked by any meaning-oriented translation team:

- What is the significance of 'Babylon' and 'Zion' and their actual and symbolic relationship to each other (1)?
- Why would 'remembering' Zion cause people to 'weep' (1)?
- Why would the singers of this psalm ('we') want to hang their traditional stringed instruments *(apangwe)* upon willow trees that grow by the river *(misondodzi)* (2)? It sounds like some strange magical rite.
- Why would 'tormentors' request to listen to 'songs of Zion' (3)? Who are these 'captors' anyway?

- How do the 'songs of Creator-God' *(Chauta)* (4) relate to the 'songs of Zion' just mentioned—are they the same or different?
- How can a person possibly 'forget' the city where he came from (5)?
- Why would the speaker wish to curse his own 'right hand', or indeed, his 'tongue'—what would be the point or purpose of that (5-6)?
- What could cause the poet not to 'rejoice over' his home town and native country (6)?
- What crime exactly did the 'Edomites' commit—was it only a matter of invoking evil upon 'Jerusalem', or was there more malice involved (7)?
- From a traditional Chewa perspective, a valid curse requires that God 'see' (punishment implied) what the offender has done, not simply to 'remember' it (7).
- Why does the poet praise someone who 'takes revenge' against another (8)?
- Again, how can a 'blessing' be pronounced upon those who blatantly 'smash infants upon a rock' (9)? Such persons should rather be condemned and punished as befits wicked 'witches' in society!

Obviously, there is great potential for misunderstanding here—a confusion that grows incrementally as the psalm progresses from one verse to the next. The reason is twofold: first there may be a lack of information about the ANE cultural milieu and the various beliefs and customs that are a part of this foreign environment. More difficult to cope with are the clashes in perspectives and values that occur at the basic world view level, where a much greater amount of education and explanation are called for.[40]

The paramount instance of such perplexity, not surprisingly, is found in the seemingly mysterious, twisted curse of v. 9, where 'infants' (traditionally regarded in most African societies as being pure and sinless) are the specified objects of appalling punitive action. That is indeed a cause for concern—a certain disquiet that is felt in relation to the anonymous psalmist who composed these dreadful words that border on taboo. Consequently, this particular passage will not often be uttered in the usual public places of worship among Chewa Christians. The apparent vengeful

---

[40] In any system of supplemental annotation, whether for a study Bible or an ordinary version, "Africa and matters related thereto, including those in her diaspora, should be shown to be an integral part of the Biblical drama as well—not just in a negative sense but positively too" (Gosnell Yorke, cited in Masenya 2001:294). In this compositional effort, the editors of these notes need to be actively encouraged, perhaps even guided at first, along the path of such 'Africa-conscious' (Masenya 2001:294) awareness and application; the crucial 'contextualizing' process cannot be simply taken for granted or left to chance.

4.3 Ideological factors in contemporary translation

ideology underlying these words is just too alien and sacrilegious either to voice aloud or even to listen to.⁴¹ On account of that final line then, many people discount the psalm as having much spiritual value. Thus any communal use of Psalm 137, whether as a liturgical reading, a sermon text selection, or a congregational hymn, is normally abbreviated to its first four verses, often too in a manner that misses much of the point of the piece as a whole. This is a great pity for, as we have seen, the prayer's great communicative power and spiritual implications come to the fore only after the cognitive and emotive stage has been contrastively set by its initial narrative vignette.

So what can be done about such serious conceptual gaps, disparities, contrasts, and conundrums, especially in cases where fundamental religious principles and biblical ideals are concerned? In recent years most Bible translation agencies have been strongly promoting the use of various paratextual 'conditioning' devices in order to provide more adequate background for understanding particular terms, passages, and complete books. Some of the tools commonly used nowadays in this text-supportive elucidative role are sectional headings and introductions, illustrations, intertextual cross-references, glossary entries, and above all, through the liberal use of culturally-sensitive and appropriate explanatory footnotes. But here the influence of ideology again enters the picture to complicate the hermeneutical undertaking. Expository and descriptive notes, for example, cannot simply be imported wholesale from Western sources. To give an exaggerated instance—a comment on Ps. 137:9 that seeks to point out how recent military and political events in the Middle East are occurring in direct fulfillment of such biblical prophecies regarding 'Babylon'. This sort of hermeneutical perspective is not only highly tenuous, hence debatable, but it is also largely irrelevant to many audiences in the non-Western world. Far more important then would be annotation that interacts with the prevailing ideology of the local culture and religious environment. With respect to 137:9, for example, it might be helpful to supply an explanation about the hyperbolic and symbolic character of ritualized 'curses' in the ANE as compared with those commonly uttered in central Africa, having a different surface form, but perhaps a similar maledictory function.⁴²

---

⁴¹ Thus in the poetic rendition (PV), the psalm is softened as follows (v. 9): *Indedi, odala iwo odzalanga aBabulo bbu! – mpaka kumenyadi ndi ana ao omwe!* 'Yes indeed, fortunate [are] those [who] will punish the Babylonians SMACK!—to the extent of thrashing their kids as well!'

⁴² In fact, in some indigenous (non-Western originated) churches of Africa, imprecatory psalms and passages are not problematic at all, but rather are welcomed as expressions of communal appeal for protection and defense from enemies of all kinds, seen and unseen.

The Bible translator must act as a resourceful 'mediator' between disparate cultural ideologies, and when firmly-held, often conflicting religious beliefs and traditions enter the mix, this task of negotiation becomes very complicated indeed. At least it does for those who are genuinely interested in communicating the biblical text, as opposed to merely re-stating it via the closest lexical correspondents. Thus the perceptive and experienced translator's role approximates that of an ancient foreign exchange *trader* (not necessarily a 'traitor'!), someone whose job it was to maintain a relatively similar balance in recognized values when working with two rather different commodities, e.g., gold as distinct from silver, bronze, precious stones, or African cowrie shells. The general standard and ideal was gold, so the trader's problem would be how to appraise, calculate, and apportion other forms of exchange representing different local values so as to arrive at a mutual agreement with regard to parity in terms of a particular transaction. A similar process occurs in Bible translating, which moves from the 'gold standard' of a supreme, determinative original text into a host of other linguistic currencies, each having different semantic, connotative, and sociosemiotic values in its own unique situational setting. The challenge then for translators is how to remain ideologically (that is, culturally, socially, religiously, ecclesiastically, theologically, and academically) 'neutral' (as impartial as feasible) while attempting to convert one text into another in view of a specific target audience.[43] Obviously, the use of paratextual tools will assist in this educative operation, but before such an implementation is carried out, there is another, more fundamental decision that must be made, as surveyed in section 4.4.

In Nigeria for example, "[p]eople are aware that enemies will use spiritual means such as curses to cause harm to them, and traditional religion gives people charms and recitations to counteract these. When people came to believe in Christ, these means of protection became forbidden, but they discovered the imprecatory psalms and came to use them in this way" (Goldingay 2008:611; cf. Adamo 2001).

[43] In addition to 'neutrality', the criterion of 'fidelity' is also important. However, in contrast to former claims about the relative quality of one translation or another, current thinking recognizes that complete faithfulness to the total communicative significance of the original is completely impossible. Rather, translators must carefully choose which aspects of the SL document they will endeavor to be more or less 'faithful' to—that is, in the sense of reproducing that particular feature, whether pertaining to form, content, or function, in the TL text. The issue of fidelity, now 'loyalty', pertains not only 'to what', but it also concerns 'to whom'—with a bias towards either the original author and his intended audience or to text interpreters and consumers today.

4.4 The translation *brief:* Balancing ideologies

In this closing section I suggest a possible twofold solution to the dilemma posed in this chapter, namely, a how-to-reconcile, compromise, integrate, or counterbalance, conflicting ideologies and differing communicative intentions during the activity of Bible translation—those deriving from the SL text/context and the ones related to the TL text/context. The proposal that I outline here is neither novel nor fully developed; furthermore, it needs to be combined with other key factors that are integrally involved in the organization, management, and production of a successful Bible translation project (cf. Wendland 2002b:180–185). In short, any resolution of the matter must pay close attention to the rather complex, unpredictable human component of this undertaking. Thus every progressive translation development program must, of necessity, incorporate a practical interactive strategy that both begins and ends with *people*—that is, with a significant measure of individual as well as local community involvement. All participants must in turn see themselves as comprising a diverse but unified team whose members are engaged in a collaborative venture that operates on the foundation of a comprehensive, mutually agreed-upon job commission, or prospectus (more technically termed a translation *brief*).[44]

Project planners now recognize that it is not enough simply to identify and define a potential target audience when preparing a new or revised Bible translation (i.e., 'for whom' it is intended). One must go on to specify the *purpose* (*Skopos*) which this particular version is expected to perform ('why') in one or more *settings* of religious communication ('where') along with the *means* for accomplishing these specified objectives ('how'), either within or alongside the text. Questions of this nature have to be systematically researched, thoroughly discussed in meetings with project sponsors and the representatives of various prospective audience groups, and finally precisely summarized in the formal written commission, which outlines the nature of the translation enterprise in its various aspects, including factors such as the following:

- amount of Scripture to be translated (e.g., a complete Bible +/– DCs, NT, individual book/text)

---

[44] The importance of producing a comprehensive project commission was brought to the fore by the *Skopos* (purpose) school of functional translation theorists. Christiane Nord, for example, says that "[t]he ideal brief provides explicit or implicit information about the intended target-text function(s), the target-text addressee(s), the medium over which it will be transmitted, the prospective place and time and, if necessary, motive of production or reception of the text" (1997:137; cf. Munday 2001:82–83; Wendland 2002b:183–185).

- audience and/or readership envisaged (the speech community at large or a specific subgroup)
- primary function and intended use of the translation (e.g., a liturgical or pulpit Bible, one designed for personal reading and meditation, study groups, an evangelism or outreach tool, to celebrate a popular religious festival or national holiday)
- initial medium of transmission (e.g., a print, audio, video, electronic, or combined format)
- type and style of translation (e.g., modified literal, limited idiomatic, eclectic, 'Islamized')
- major translation principles and operating procedures to guide the work
- qualifications and job descriptions for all participants: translators, reviewers, consultants, etc.
- structure of the translation team and manner of project management
- method(s) of evaluating the translation and stipulated means of quality control
- project time frame set out according to projected stages of completion
- details about the program's available resources and community support structure (with signed commitments)

The list adds up to an almost intimidating amount of information that needs to be gathered and communally agreed upon, but experience has shown that the more relevant material that can be incorporated into the guiding brief, the better the project will run along its anticipated course of development and actually accomplish the goals that it has set for itself. The success of such a multifaceted, long-term venture naturally also depends very heavily on the quality of both the translators and also the management team (or administrative committee) that has been representatively selected to oversee and supervise the program of production on behalf of the whole target language community, its main supporters in particular.

Obviously, a substantial amount of precise, issue-specific audience sampling will have to be carried out in preparation for drawing up such a project commission. This is when the various local ideological matters of importance must be identified and investigated in order to estimate how much they might impinge upon the goals that have been set for the project or the general nature of the translation itself. These would range from theological concerns expressed by any of the participating church or parachurch bodies to controversial sociological topics (e.g., the AIDS crisis, the negative influence of Western materialism) and domestic cultural considerations (e.g., traditional religious beliefs and customary practices) that may need to be addressed by means of extratextual annotation.

4.4 The translation brief: Balancing ideologies

It is imperative, therefore, that these exploratory questions be accompanied by an appreciable amount of setting-specific education relating to the Bible and its translation. The aim of such an introductory course of instruction would be to provide a sufficient frame of reference for the organizational decisions that need to be made and also to clarify for respondents the different translation options that are available to them (cf. Wilt 2003:43–58). All too often questionnaires are conducted without contextualizing them with the necessary cognitive conditioning. As a result, people are left to respond in ignorance, or from a limited perspective, or on the basis of long-held biases and prejudices (e.g., with respect to a particular Christian denomination and its assumed beliefs, a particular mode of translating the Scriptures, or the alleged theological 'dangers' of extratextual supplements). The need for enlightening the wider community about the Bible and its proper 'reading' (or 'hearing')—that is, how to interpret the text on the basis of knowledge (hence 'power') rather than mere localized intuition—is too important a matter to be left either to chance or to existing ecclesiastical institutions. A specific, pedagogically-sound program of educating teachers and learners alike concerning the biblical text (or translation) in relation to its ANE context on the one hand and the target sociocultural setting on the other is a matter of the highest priority. Faulty beliefs and ideas can thereby be corrected and a more informed ideological foundation established to encourage and enhance the entire hermeneutical process, including the proposal of lay-suggested revisions to the current vernacular version(s).[45]

Audience-engagement efforts are not a one-time affair; rather they must be exercised for the duration of a Bible translation venture—and beyond. Consumer-oriented opinion surveys, for example, cannot be discontinued after the management brief has been finalized at the start of a project. The testing should be adapted as needed and carried on while the work progresses, as long as translation drafts are being prepared and circulated for critical assessment by specialists, scholars, and potential ordinary readers as well. This is the only way to ensure that any outstanding or as yet unrecognized ideological (theological, cultural, ecclesiastical, etc.) issues can be identified, debated, and eventually resolved either within the translated text itself or without, through pointed notes aimed at clarification and/or expansion (e.g., to allow for the expression of valid

---

[45] An example or model of such a grass-roots educationally-empowering organization is The Institute for the Study of the Bible in South Africa, which aims "to establish an interface between biblical studies and ordinary readers of the Bible in the church and the community that will facilitate social transformation" (West 1995:219; cf. 219–238). My point here is that such agencies not only contribute to "our understanding of the Bible and what God is doing in [country X]" (West 1995:219), but they also provide a much-needed people's perspective on the very rendering of that Word in their language. It is a point of view that is too easily overlooked in the rush to produce a modern translation for the general public.

differences of opinion). The matters causing disagreement will have to be frankly and freely discussed, and then firmly negotiated in order to reach a suitable degree of consensus or some compromise solution—perhaps not the preferred option, but one that is at least agreeable to all active translation agencies and partners. I have found that no conflict in ideology is irresolvable if the negotiators are flexible and work together towards the common goal, always being fully committed to the success of their larger venture, which is to make available an accurate and acceptable translation of God's Word in their common mother tongue.

A similar process, with specified situational variations, needs to be carried out in the case of translations that are prepared for transmission via other, non-print media. In these cases even more options are usually available; for example, concerning the tone and timbre of a speaker's voice, or the visual background to accompany a given narrative scenario, or the type of musical 'bridge' music to choose, or which background sound effects to include. This often requires difficult choices, and these in turn must be made with care so as not to deny or distort the original biblical text and context on the one hand, or to disturb subtle connotative associations and emotive values that pertain to the TL setting on the other. Such media transpositions and/or adaptations can be effectively created only if the production team and their associates are experienced vernacular communicators with a clear vision of the purpose of their production within the local religious environment. They should also have a transparent set of translation guidelines to work from as well as a competent committee in place to monitor, manage, and mediate their work, especially when disagreements arise over substantial matters. Fundamental ideological matters that might need to be confronted in the case of these modern productions include the following:

- the theological question concerning whether or not non-print editions of Scripture 'count' (are they valid, credible, authoritative, etc.?) as the recognized Word of God and, more practically, can they be marketed as such;

- the communicational question of how a production team can manage or control the process of domesticating, and inevitably also 'interpreting', the dialogues when scripting the character speech exchanges for a dramatized audio cassette (or radio) 'retelling' of a certain narrative of Scripture, especially with respect to some of the key characters, such as Adam, Noah, Mary, Jesus, Paul, or

4.4 The translation brief: Balancing ideologies

even Satan, each of which needs to be cast with a connotatively appropriate voice;

- the cultural question of what type of local contextualization to introduce when preparing the visual background and other imagery for a video presentation, which often comes under pressure to be 'indigenized' according to prevailing market pressures or resident church expectations, desires, and demands, as well as models that have already been successful in the community.

The diverse ideologies involved in Scripture translation and its transmission confront practitioners with a significant compositional variable that is as crucial for success as it is complicated to organize and manage in a satisfactory manner. This factor can affect anything, from the most detailed point of biblical exegesis to the most intricate aspect of a people's indigenous belief system. One thing is certain: ideology, whether ancient or modern, can neither be 'innocently' ignored nor resolved by individuals working in isolation. It requires the entire Christian community's acute awareness of the various potentially divisive issues among them, which must then motivate them to active participation in a cooperative and creative search for the most relevant, context-sensitive solutions. This is, in fact, the time-honored, traditional Bantu way: *Malonda akoma ndi kugulana* 'Business is better when you buy from one another!'

5

Lyric Wisdom and Rhetoric in Proverbs 26:1–12

Introduction: Text and impact

There is a twofold challenge connected with the hermeneutics of the wisdom literature in Scripture. The first is to correctly interpret any given text and genre within its specific Ancient Near Eastern literary, religious, and sociocultural context. The second is to convey the impact of such sapiential discourse to a contemporary audience in their local environment. In this chapter, I discuss some crucial aspects of this complex enterprise from a translation perspective. After an initial overview of rhetoric in relation to proverbial literature, I examine its particular manifestation in the lyric structure and style of Proverbs 26:1–12, with a focus on the paradoxical pair of verses 4–5. There is more textual organization and communicative significance here than meets the ear of the hearer in terms of form, content, and emotive intent. This added rhetorical dimension greatly increases the difficulty of re-presenting such passages adequately (appropriately, as well as acceptably) within a different linguistic, literary (oral), and social setting. Several critical issues of relevance will be discussed and illustrated with reference to a creative translation of this passage into the language and lyrical poetic tradition of the Chewa people living in Malawi, Zambia, and Mozambique—with a sample from English as well.

5.1 Answering a fool

Do not answer a fool according to his folly, or you will be like him yourself.

Answer a fool according to his folly, or he will be wise in his own eyes. (Prov. 26:4–5, NIV)

Samva-mnzake ndi tsiru 'Un-advisable [lit. 'He does not listen to his friend'] is a fool' (Chewa proverb)[1]

---

[1] I could not find a Chewa proverb that corresponds to these two Hebrew verses. My collected examples from the local corpus that deal with speech and folly stress the fault of not listening to parents, elders, and/or advisers. In Chewa proverbial lore, the 'fool' is typically referred to by one of his foolish characteristics, e.g., *Nzeru-n'za-yekha anamanga nyumba yo-*

So are we to answer the fool then or not—yes, no, perhaps—or does it not matter at all? Before we can begin to answer this question, we must first decide whether or not the pair of verses found in Proverbs 26:4–5 presents us with a conundrum, a contradiction, or worse (some sort of a scribal gloss). Assuming the best—that the text is, or was, meaningful as it stands and intentionally composed—we need to determine who a 'fool' actually is in the biblical sense, and what it means to 'answer' him (or not to do so). This necessarily invites a comparison with the literary and religious opposite of this character type, namely, the 'wise' person. We must then proceed to posit an explanation for the rhetorically motivated juxtaposition of these two passages and how they relate in turn to their wider textual context of chapter 26:1–12. Finally, it behooves us to put forward a credible suggestion regarding how all this detail about 'fools' and 'folly' pertains to the message about 'knowledge' and 'wisdom' in the book of Proverbs as a whole (cf. 1:7, 9:10–13).

Proverbs are a distinct and recognizable type of oral and/or written discourse in virtually every literary tradition that includes them. We must therefore apply the proper analytical and translational techniques to this important genre of literature or we will end up sounding rather foolish in the target language. This is a vast and complex topic, one that has been well treated by many wise men of God. I can just scratch the surface in relation to this single pericope and with special reference to the various options for translating the text at hand into a Bantu language (Chewa) and its associated oral tradition, as manifested in a traditional south-central African sociocultural setting and a contemporary religious environment.

After a survey of the notion of rhetoric in relation to sapiential literature, I will examine the focal passage in more detail from a literary compositional perspective, with regard to both its structural (macro-) and also its stylistic (micro-textual) organization. We might call this a study of the *poetic rhetoric of wisdom*. I turn next to the challenge of meaningfully communicating this thematically related collection of proverbs in another language and culture through a context-sensitive translation. Again there are several possibilities available, depending on the nature of the target audience, their religious environment, the relative skill of the translators, and the purpose designated for the version under consideration. I conclude with a few comments in support of a more dynamic, functionally-oriented lyric rendition of Proverbs 26:1–12, with samples from Chewa and English (Brenda Boerger). The specific target audience envisioned is that of a younger generation who are eagerly seeking persuasive and

---

panda khomo 'Know-it-all built a house without a door,' or *Safunsa anadya phula* 'Never-ask ate bee's wax (instead of the honey).'

powerful advice from the Scriptures concerning life's greatest, most urgent issues and questions. Here then we are dealing with the *wisdom of rhetoric*, that is, biblical sagacity—sapientially and artistically expressed in a contemporary Bible translation.

5.2 The rhetoric of wisdom in Proverbs

The proverb genre is the mainstay of wisdom literature ('orature') in societies around the world. It illustrates in a most succinct, incisive, and salient manner a focused application of rhetorical discourse principles to the composition of gnomic verbal art—in short, 'the rhetoric of wisdom'. In this section I present a brief overview of the Hebrew semantic concept of 'wisdom' and its antithesis, 'folly', along with an analysis of the artful application of rhetoric as it relates to the literary category of 'proverbs' in the biblical book known by that name.

5.2.1 Wisdom (and folly) in sapiential literature of the Hebrew Bible

An adequate discussion of the topic of 'wisdom' and its associated Hebrew terminology would require at least a full chapter in and of itself (see, for example, the many entries under this topic in Van Gemeren 1997b:750–751; cf. Hunter 2006:ch. 1). The important thing to recognize here is that for the ancient Israelite, 'wisdom' (חָכְמָה—e.g., 1:7) was not simply one key concept among many, but as Williams puts it, a comprehensive "way of looking at the world" (1987:263) because the entire created universe was seen to be "indwelt with Wisdom" (Van Leeuwen 1993:257). This divinely ordered, covenantally oriented worldview or philosophical stance was manifested in an appropriate lifestyle and an associated set of positive character traits as set out in Proverbs: diligence (10:4), patience (14:29), humility (11:2), prudence (8:5), generosity (19:17), and honesty (12:19).

Wisdom was in effect an all-embracing ethical and epistemological perspective on life, a flexible model that revolved around a varied application of the preeminent principle of divinely ordained retributive justice in the world (cf. Hunter 2006: ch. 2). From this viewpoint, good or evil human behavior inevitably results in prosperity or punishment, respectively, whether sooner or later in life—or thereafter (according to eschatological prophetic passages and apocalyptic literature, e.g., Dan. 12:2–3). Such wisdom was no blind impersonal or mystical force, but was believed to be measured and administered justly according to the primary tenets of *torah*-governed personal piety. The latter is summed up in the central principle concerning 'the fear of the LORD', which also serves as "the fundamental point of orientation for the entire book" of Proverbs and arguably the Hebrew Bible as a whole (Van Leeuwen 1993:258; e.g., Prov. 1:7, 3:1–7, 6:20–23, 9:10, 10:2, 31:30 [a complete discourse *inclusio*]; cf. Deut. 4:5–10; 6; Job. 28:28; Ps. 33:8; Jer. 5:24; Eccl. 12:13).[2] This Yahwistic faith-life stance constituted "the religious orientation of wisdom" in Israel (Nel 2000:313) and synopsized "the whole Israelite theory of knowledge" (von Rad, cited in Melchert 1998:37).[3] It provided the theological and moral foundation upon which both a conservative and also a later reactionary tradition of interpretation was based—the former (e.g., Proverbs) to optimistically propound in detail, the latter (e.g., Qoheleth) to more pessimistically protest against.

> This tension focuses around two important questions: Does retribution really work? (i.e., do the wise/righteous prosper while the foolish/wicked perish?); and, Is it really possible for human understanding to discover the orderly purpose of God in the universe? (Van Gemeren 1997a:1281).

The fundamental assumptions and guiding principles of the traditional Hebrew doctrine of wisdom (which would give an unequivocal 'yes' answer to both questions above) is the chief focus of interest in the present study of Proverbs. This viewpoint was influenced to some degree also by Old Testament narrative 'creation theology' and therefore stressed careful observation, experience, and reflection with respect to a natural and social world that was believed to operate according to the perfect plan and creative purpose of God (Van Gemeren 1997a:1278–1279). Such wisdom, which could be expected to 'bless' or benefit one in life (Prov. 3:13–18), was acquired intellectually and augmented through diligent personal

---

[2] "Much of the book reverberates with the ethical demands of Torah... In addition, Proverbs contains emphasis on social injustices forbidden in Law and condemned by the eighth-century prophets" (Berry 1995:124).

[3] Melchert stresses the wide semantic scope that is encompassed by the biblical notion of 'fear' in relation to YHWH. "[M]ost often it means simply knowledge of and obedience to God.... This cognition (knowing) is inseparable from the emotion (awe) because of God" (1998:38). The Hebrew term is therefore much broader than the corresponding English word or that in most other languages, a point that has significant translational implications. He suggests that Prov. 1:7, which is repeated (with variations) more often than any other didactic passage in the book, shows that in Israelite thought "wisdom itself is grounded in *loyalty* to God" and "that all human knowledge is grounded in *commitment* to God" (ibid., 36–37, emphasis added).

study, perceptive discernment, and the obedient practice of righteousness in all of one's interpersonal relationships (1:1–6, 2:7–11).[4]

These beliefs, especially the interrelated doctrines of divine 'retribution' and 'the two opposite ways' (cf. Berry 1995:722), paid special attention to the potential power of words, including the proper appreciation and 'wise' secular as well as religious use of language, either for just/beneficial or wicked/harmful purposes (10:13, 15:1–2, 18:21). Thus discipline, tact, and self control needed to be manifested also in one's formal and informal use of public speech as part of an overall orderly lifestyle for both individuals and society as a whole (17:27). It was not only the ethical content (the *what*) of these wisdom utterances that was important, but their form or expression (the *how*) as well as their context and timing (the *when*) were also matters of interest and concern (cf. Prov. 12:18, 25:11, 29:20; cf. Jas. 3:5). Thus the collected sayings of recognized sages were thought to provide a timeless repository of theologically motivated wisdom as an essential resource to guide the thoughts and actions—the entire way of life—of all those who would honor and please the LORD, indeed, providing the means to discern God's salutary will in a wicked world.

In such a devout and disciplined community "even fools who keep silent are considered wise" (17:28a, NRSV; cf. 10:19).[5] This passage exemplifies the strongly contrastive approach that typifies the conventional Hebrew exercise of sapiential instruction. Two basic, black-or-white choices of lifestyle thus continually confront every individual and society, two personal orientations that are sharply antithetical in respect to the deliberative-epideictic rhetoric of *logos* (verbal expression), *ethos* (personal attitude), and *praxis* (behavioral application). Paradoxically, however, their didactic point is the same—namely, to teach about wisdom (what is just and true) through juxtaposition with that which is deemed to be 'folly' (what is socially, morally, and spiritually wrong).

So it is then that the proverbial 'fool' (especially the rhyming synonyms אֱוִיל or כְּסִיל) also comes into prominence in Proverbs, and various uncomplimentary portraits (as in 26:1–12) or shorter vignettes (e.g., 23:9) abound in the book, from beginning (1:7b) to end (29:20). Foolish persons, in contrast to the wise (or indeed, Lady Wisdom herself, 9:1–6 as opposed to 13–18), are characterized by their wicked words (10:18) as well as by their typically impervious, impious, and iniquitous behavior (14:8–9). "Folly is practical atheism" (Berry 1995:125, citing

---

[4] For an excellent survey of the relationship between 'wisdom' and 'righteousness' in the wisdom literature of Scripture, including its cosmic and social-ethical implications, see Nel 2000.

[5] In all human societies, "[l]anguage and silence are inextricably linked" (Melchert 1998:42), but the significance of each mode of communication is often regarded and used differently. "In an oral culture, when language is sound, it interrupts silence" (Melchert 1998:42), which is itself meaningful. In the Hebrew wisdom tradition verbal tact and restraint were valued more highly than silence per se (e.g., Prov. 29:20).

Von Rad), and "the fool is regarded as the equivalent of the sinner" (Melchert 1998:20). Moreover, such people are not regarded as 'fools' because of some innate mental defect or deficiency,[6] but rather due to their defiant choice (Ps. 14:1), as the result of a deliberate act of their self-centered will, to live contrary to God's given norms, thus serving only their own selfish appetites (Prov. 13:19, 14:16, 15:20–21).[7] In their overweening, all-consuming pride they tend to injure and often destroy not only themselves, but also the innocent with whom they come into contact (13:20, 18:6–7, 20:3, 27:3). Fools perversely despise YHWH (10:23, 12:15, 28:25–26) and in consequence are severely punished, as they fully deserve (14:24, 18:6). To sum up: "Wisdom...affirms a divine cosmic order and represents folly as disorder" (Williams 1987:265). Accordingly,

> [f]or the most part...the [Hebrew] sages are careful to provide a *moral* foundation for wisdom. In this context wisdom becomes synonymous with righteousness, while folly is not simply ignorance, but wickedness. (Van Gemeren 1997a:1281)

> Ultimately [then] Proverbs is a book of faith (1:7), insisting on the reality of God's justice and righteousness, even when experience seems to contradict it... (Van Leeuwen 1997:25)

A closing observation may be offered to connect the preceding discussion with the major literary-rhetorical concern of the current investigation. Divinely ordered proverbial 'wisdom' in a *semantic* sense would seem to be inseparable from a pronounced sapiential manner of verbal formulation in a *stylistic* sense, as well as some significant rhetorical function in a *pragmatic* sense. In other words, the distinctive literary shape of the typically critical 'observation', in contrast to that of the stylistically less dynamic hortatory admonition or maxim (see 5.3.1), constitutes an essential aspect of its overall religious meaning or communicative significance, as determined by a functional analysis of the text in a particular context of usage. The very form of expression renders such discerning instructive sayings authoritative in terms of their larger communicative intention and emotive effect.

Thus proverbs, whether sacred or secular, both individually and in creative combination, are designed to evoke or promote an astute perspective on human life and discourse. They should therefore be formulated

---

[6] In this light, a rendering like 'dullard' (Tanakh) appears to be somewhat off the mark.

[7] "The root of [the fool's] trouble is spiritual, not mental....At bottom, what he is rejecting is the fear of the Lord (1:29)" (Kidner 1964:40). (For a detailed comparative characterization of 'fools' in relation to the 'wise' in Proverbs, see Westermann 1995:46–47, 50–56.)

5.2 The rhetoric of wisdom in Proverbs

accordingly, that is, 'wisely' worded—featuring shrewdly selected vocabulary items that are skillfully conjoined in order to create a striking mental picture, aural impact, and aesthic appeal. Their manifold meaning is thus molded into a memorable form so as to be more easily recalled and applied in the appropriate social situation, where an ethical or religious decision needs either to be made or to be reinforced in keeping with the revealed will (word) of the LORD. Given the complex compositional and communicative nature of proverbs, it follows that they must also be analyzed and evaluated in a correspondingly comprehensive manner, including that which is offered by the text-linguistic, literary rhetorical approach chosen for this study.[8]

5.2.2 The malleable rhetoric of proverbs

In what sense may the rhetorical character of most proverbs be considered 'malleable'? As suggested above, this is due in part to the concentrated, interactive nature of the various stylistic features that appear juxtaposed both diachronically (in ordered sequence) and synchronically (simultaneously within the same speech segment) in the typical proverbial instance. Such a consequential poetic compaction is effected especially by the multifaceted (but often unrecognized) phonological patterning of the texts (cf. 5.3.1; also McCreesh 1991: *passim*)—in which *sound* not only complements, but also constitutes significant *sense*. A single proverb thus exhibits the smallest example of an independent genre of literature (orature), for it can be a semantically complete discourse unity condensed within the scope of a simple bicolon. It normally manifests a diverse assortment of poetic devices that have been artfully, often innovatively, combined and crafted so as to render its lexical content in a highly appealing, persuasive, and potent manner.

Due to their discrete and compressed nature, coupled with a highly metaphoric manner of expression, proverbs tend to be general and not very audience-specific. They usually "do not express qualifications or exceptions to their rules" (Van Leeuwen 1993:261). Therefore, a certain saying may be applied to fit within a variable range of sociocultural settings and interpersonal situations, such that its particular communicative significance (impact, appeal, appropriateness) is derived in large measure from its textual (if literary) or extratextual (if oral) context. The latter applies to proverbial usage in Chewa; the former to the corpus- of proverbs that appear in Hebrew wisdom literature. This is true also for the selection

---

[8] For a helpful outline of an analytical methodology to be applied to Proverbs, see Salisbury 1994:437–439 and Schneider 1992:108–109.

of passages dealing with 'wisdom' and 'folly' in the book of Proverbs, particularly, the pericope on 'fools' found in ch. 26:1–12. A given proverb in this collection must therefore be interpreted both semantically and pragmatically in the light of the structure and style of the discourse as a whole and also with reference to topically similar texts in this or any of the other wisdom books.

The rhetorical dimension of a given literary text or book, including those recorded in the canon of Scripture, may be examined and evaluated in terms of either form or function, with the understanding that these two aspects of a text are completely interactive and closely interdependent. In other words, the general sociocultural function of a particular discourse, whether oral or written, will determine its macro-form (genre), which in turn consists of an organic system of interrelated micro-forms. The latter are chosen and combined within a specific composition to effect the realization of the text's communicative significance in relation to its intended audience and the social setting of message reception. We might use the following logical progression to summarize the rhetorical process from the perspective of its interpersonal persuasive dynamics:

ISSUE → INTENTION → MOTIVATION → *APPEAL*

These four sequentially related cognitive elements, which are present in any persuasive, affectively toned, rhetorically shaped utterance or text, may be briefly defined as follows:

- *Issue* = a negative or positive opinion or position held concerning a particular action, state, condition, volition, attitude, idea, etc. that is controversial or debatable with respect to the principal ethical-thematic polarity of righteousness/wisdom versus wickedness/folly.

- *Intention* = what a particular verbal text seeks to accomplish in terms of communicative speech acts, or illocutionary functions or force with regard to the issue, topic, failure, or fault under consideration.

- *Motivation* = the reason(s) adduced, which in proverbs are often implicit or indirect, in support of an appeal that stems from the point at issue, that is, either to accept the argumentation and act according to whatever is wise/right or to reject it and persist in whatever is foolish/wrong.

- *Appeal* = an explicit exhortation, whether literal or figurative, that vividly verbalizes the principal discourse intention in the

5.2 The rhetoric of wisdom in Proverbs

sociolinguistic context at hand, either by prohibition or prescription, possibly along with other, subordinate pragmatic aims.

In Proverbs, the principal issue of concern is to instruct the young in particular how to avoid wicked, 'foolish' behavior and consequent punitive retribution by behaving 'wisely' in God's eyes (note the occurrence of 'son' in every major section of the book, e.g., 1:8; 10:1; 24:21; 27:11; 31:2; cf. 1:4; 30:17). The quality of one's character is thus evaluated in accordance with traditional torah piety, hence by this same sapiential code also to avoid thinking, speaking, and acting like a fool. The primary discourse 'intention' is therefore to persuade the target audience to accept the perspective, opinion, and advice that are being offered in the proverbs and sayings that have been selected for inclusion as typical samples of the entire range of life-related options.[9] Various types of direct and indirect pragmatic 'appeal' are expressed by means of the textual assortment that is cited in great stylistic diversity. This includes a number of 'defamiliarized' sayings that occasionally appear to surprise the reader or listener "by highlighting the unpredictability of human experience, the limitations of human knowledge, and the [mysterious] freedom and inscrutability of God" (McKenzie 1996:37).[10] A good example of such 'subversive' proverbs is the pair that we will be looking at more closely later, Prov. 26:4–5.

However, these injunctions and admonitions, whether conventional or novel in terms of the received sapiential tradition, all fall under the same broad paradigmatic category of (un)desirable ethical and religious behavior. They are all 'religious' because YHWH is viewed as being the ultimate lawgiver, judge, and agent of reward or punishment.[11] Similarly, a range

---

[9] Longer topically related sections, such as we have in Prov. 26:1–12, are the exception in Proverbs, where the usually disjointed style seems to call attention to the selective, representational nature of the various didactic warnings and encouragements that have been included in this book.

[10] The rhetorical strategy defamiliarization is of course undone as proverbs that have become part of the accepted tradition of wisdom, whether oral or written, are made more familiar through repeated usage and ongoing instruction. Nevertheless, their relative density of stylistic expression coupled with their juxtaposition within a larger literary context (including the entire Hebrew canon) renders both the individual as well as combined passages of Proverbs capable of further levels and degrees of signification, hence also of increased didactic and reflective import. This ongoing hermeneutical process continues as these ancient proverbs are now applied to present-day situations that further augment their semantic potential and enhance their moral and theological relevance.

[11] Y. Gitay points out that in the dialogues of Scripture "[t]he biblical discourse provides numerous examples of argumentative speeches, based on dialectical [as distinct from analytical] reasoning that might reflect conflicts of thoughts between God and human beings. In other words, there is a need to argue and justify the position rather than to take it as inference or a matter of God's authority" (2009:45).

Such dialectical reasoning may, in turn, present an argument by means of "presentation-of compelling 'motivations' is simultaneously offered to illustrate the vicissitudes and vagaries of life in a world where fools abound and the pathway of folly is indeed broad. But there is a single central impulse (namely, 'the fear of the LORD'), which is in keeping with the unified nature of the rhetorical intention regarding the principal appeal for 'wisdom' in its manifold facets of everyday manifestation. Thus, the many individual instances of proverbial advice may be viewed collectively as embodying a synecdochal (part-whole) representation of the entire gamut of human experience, considered from an ANE Hebrew perspective on God's people living in a wicked world.

5.3 What is a proverb?

The relative complexity of the proverb genre in Scripture is revealed by the diversity of descriptions that have been used in the ongoing attempt to define this familiar literary category.[12] Difficulties begin with its Hebrew designation 'proverb' (מָשָׁל), for this word may refer to a wide range of what in many other traditions of verbal art are distinguished as distinct discourse types, from a single evocative term (a 'byword' calling attention to a notorious object lesson, e.g., Job. 17:6; Ps. 44:15, Jer. 24:9) to a much more lengthy discourse, such as a 'parable' (Ezek. 17:2–24), a victory 'ode' (Num. 21:27–30), or a prophetic 'oracle' (Num. 24:15–19). My concern here is not so much with definition, however, but with the effort to explain with reference to a particular passage (Prov. 26:1–12) how Biblical 'proverbs' operate individually and in synchronic-diachronic combination to convey the main message of the biblical text, both in the original Hebrew as well as when translated as an idiomatic, oratorical Chewa text. For these purposes, the four definitions below serve as an adequate preliminary orientation to the subsequent discussion:

> The proverb/saying is usually a two-line composition, characterized by literary parallelism, that normally forms a world unto itself... [and] urges a course of action, either implicitly or explicitly. (Murphy 1998:xxii)

---

al discourse (parallels/comparisons), which differs from the discursive (causal) discourse" (e.g., Isa. 1:2–3 as opposed to Mic. 1:2–6). In presentational argument "[o]ne verse is presented after the other, tending to work on the readers'/listeners' minds through parallels. The series of parallels expands the meaning" (ibid., 50). In the rhetoric of Proverbs, however, it would seem that the parallelistic (presentational) and causal (discursive) types of argument are combined in order to more emphatically dramatize the case or point at hand.

[12] This difficulty of definition seems to be common to most languages, as noted even in classical studies of the proverb in world literature (e.g., Taylor 1931).

5.3 What is a proverb?

> [T]he genuine proverb is 'a short, pregnant sentence or phrase whose meaning is applicable in many situations, with imagery or striking verbal forms to assist memory.... It has shortness, sense and salt'. (R. B. Y. Scott, cited by Schneider 1992:131)

> A proverb is a short, generally known sentence of the folk which contains wisdom, truth, morals and traditional views in a metaphorical, fixed and memorizable form and which is handed down from generation to generation. (Mieder 1993:5)

> The Biblical Hebrew literary proverb is a self-contained, often elliptical sentence in the form of a bicolon, comprising at least one topic and one comment, which normally express some kind of similarity, contrast, or consequence. It is pedagogically and rhetorically motivated, having...vivid imagery [and/]or a striking and memorable form. This is achieved by the complex interplay between its several poetic features (such as sound patterns, rhythm, parallelism, repetition, and paronomasia). (Salisbury 1994:439)

I further describe certain prominent artistic aspects of proverbial form by considering some (but certainly not all) of the main possibilities of Hebrew gnomic expression in terms of a set of distinctive stylistic features. I then summarize their manifold rhetorical significance with reference to a variable inventory of common communicative functions. The major premise and purpose of this study accords well with that of Schneider who has proposed that "[w]isdom forms and wisdom insights are demonstrably sharp, and [therefore] they need sharpening in translation" (1992:3, material in brackets added).[13]

5.3.1 Form—a sharpened style

We find two basic types of two-lined proverbial utterance in the book of Proverbs: *observations* and *admonitions,* both of which enjoin expected and expedient (God-pleasing) ethical and/or religious character and behavior. Observations are typically 'sharper' in style, that is, more vivid (e.g., figurative) in formal construction and often paradoxical, enigmatic, or even cryptic (darkly proverbial) in terms of their manifest sense. They are usually expressed in synonymous, comparative, or antithetical form as condensed, elliptical topic-comment sayings in the 3rd person.[14]

---

[13] This notion of 'sharpening' in relation to biblical proverbs may originally derive from Kugel who noted some years back that "one characteristic most often associated with Hebrew proverbs is the quality of 'sharpness'" (1981:11).

[14] Observations may be more, or less, overtly didactic—that is, with or without "an *ex-*

Admonitions tend to be more direct and straightforward in both form and function; they are realized either as a 2nd person prescription or prohibition along with a supporting explanatory, motive (purpose), or result clause.[15] In either case the characteristic parallelism encourages a comparative reading and a differential interpretation of the two cola, which normally involve at least one shared point of focus (involving similarity, contrast, alternation, gradation, or consequence). Both kinds of proverb are present in Prov. 26:1–12, in fact, all of the bicola of this passage are observations, except for the admonitions found in the middle (vv. 4–5) and again at the end of the discourse (v. 12).

Six stylistic features characterize biblical Hebrew proverbs, especially the more linguistically dynamic observations. These same devices also appear in other poetic texts, hence they do not necessarily constitute a "special linguistic code" for Proverbs (Schneider 1992:54), but their concentrated, mutually reinforcing application in Proverbs, including the pericope of 26:1–12, is distinctive and semantically productive in both denotative and connotative terms. The rhetorical aim of such stylistic diversity is to develop thematic significance and didactic relevance. This is accomplished by the poetic tendency, often heightened in proverbial literature, to leave conceptual 'gaps' in any given text, thereby requiring readers or listeners to fill in the blanks according to the written or situational setting. We thus have a rich corpus of passages that regularly allows for several levels of interpretation and implicature, depending on the textual and sociocultural context in which a given proverb is situated and those intertextual resonances that its specific vocabulary evokes. This adds complexity when combined with the periodic instances of ambiguity and enigma, irony and sarcasm, or hyperbole and humor, also found in Proverbs. The six compositional devices of special interest are briefly described below along with illustrative examples from Prov. 26:1–12. These are literally rendered and at times emended from the MT reading as noted.

- *binary parallelism* – Hebrew proverbs feature phonological, morphological, lexical, and syntactic repetition and patterning in a dual arrangement of paired poetic lines (bicola). The norm is for there to be a progressive development whereby the B line builds on and specifies, focuses, elaborates, intensifies, emphasizes, explains,

---

plicit moral evaluation" (Garrett 1993:29). Prov. 26:1 would be an example of the former; 26:3 of the latter.

[15] Williams terms these two types "sentence proverbs" and "instruction proverbs", respectively (1987:270).

5.3 What is a proverb?

and/or contrasts with the A line to produce a heightened whole. In the pericope under consideration, each observational bicola contains a first line which presents the dominant imagery, and a second which compares this in some pertinent and pungent way to the 'fool', for example:

כַּשֶּׁלֶג ׀ בַּקַּיִץ וְכַמָּטָר בַּקָּצִיר   Like the snow in the summer and like the rain in the harvest;
כֵּן לֹא־נָאוֶה לִכְסִיל כָּבוֹד׃   so [also] not fitting for a fool [is] honor. (v. 1)

The arresting juxtaposition of this text's two main terms at the very end is certainly no accident (cf. also the ל-כ [*l-kh*] alliterative pairing that further links this antithetical word pair). Rather, it is characteristic of the careful way that proverbial passages are constructed so as to simultaneously reflect on the levels of sound, syntactic structure, and lexical selection the primary tenets, attitudes, and emphases of the sapiential tradition. In this case, the binary nature of proverbial discourse is revealed already in the four terms of the first (A) colon, which may in turn be divided neatly into two at the medial *waw*— two 'unnatural' images of nature run amok, as visualized by the conventional word pair 'snow' and 'rain'. The jarring character of the various parings here is further stressed by the explicit negative expression '*not*-fitting' (לֹא־נָאוֶה).

- *stark conciseness* – The normal compaction of form and condensation of meaning that one expects in Hebrew poetry is frequently intensified in proverbs through such devices as, ellipsis (gapping), use of nominals (deverbalized), interclausal asyndeton, verbless utterances, and the avoidance of 'prose particles' (especially the sign of the direct object, definite article, relative pronoun, as well as most prepositions and conjunctions). This results in a formally and semantically dense discourse, as revealed by any standard translation of the following compact proverbial couplet [implicit elements are in brackets]:

מְקַצֶּה רַגְלַיִם חָמָס שֹׁתֶה   [Like] cutting off feet, [or] drinking down violence;
שֹׁלֵחַ דְּבָרִים בְּיַד־כְּסִיל׃   [is] one sending words by [the] hand of a fool. (v. 6)

The nucleus of this dynamic, but rather opaque, proverb is formed by the juxtaposition of three action-depicting Hebrew participles (P) and their respective objects (O), appearing in a chiastically arranged syntactic chain (P-O, O-P, P-O), perhaps to suggest the feckless, unpredictable, and unstable actions of a 'fool'. Surely, any urgent message is undone if his (or her?) 'hands' get hold of it.[16]

- *phonological patterning* – As McCreesh has convincingly demonstrated, this is a prominent and pervasive feature of most proverbs. Thus rhythm, rhyme, assonance, consonance, paronomasia, and sonic symmetry serve not only to decorate and distinguish the discourse, but also to foreground sound-selected key concepts, to aid memorization of the text, and hence to facilitate its further transmission.[17] Note how the beating rhythm of verse three provides an oral-aural image of its content:

שׁוֹט לַסּוּס מֶתֶג לַחֲמוֹר   A whip for the horse, a bridle for the donkey;
וְשֵׁבֶט לְגֵו כְּסִילִים׃   and a rod for [the] back of fools. (v. 3)

A climactic effect is created by this combination of images in a verbless progression that ends with 'fools', the entire pericope's only plural form of this term, which in this case also falls outside the bicolon's main rhythmic pattern of two-word units. The overall impression is heightened further by a cohesive consonantal sound pattern (with an emphasis upon the ל) that basically follows the same sequence in each colon, thus reflecting a coordination between the imagery of both lines. This device also phonologically links several of the key terms, e.g., 'whip' and 'rod' (for more details concerning the elaborate sound patterning of this verse, see McCreesh 1991:117–118).

- *distinctive diction* – Proverbs feature a corpus of standard Hebrew paremiological terms, word pairs, and highly specific items of vocabulary chosen to leave a lasting mental impression that is frequently incongruous, contrastive, and/or shocking in nature. Certain key words and semantically related sets may be employed to give coherence to a larger section of discourse, for example, כְּסִיל 'fool'

---

[16] We note here also the highly symbolical nature of wisdom language in which "[t]he parts of the body are used metaphorically" and "almost anything physical takes on an extended meaning" (Murphy and Huwiler 1999:10). In this case, the reference to 'feet' and 'hands' suggests how fools cripple themselves intellectually, emotionally, as well as socially by their inappropriate and often destructive behavior.

[17] "The semantics of the text saturate the sounds of the words with certain implications, which in turn reinforce a total pattern of meaning or meaning-tone" (Williams 1987:276). This convergence of sound, syntax, and sense is particularly intense in proverbial discourse and thus also equally provocative in terms of stimulating additional levels of cognitive, including symbolical, and emotive significance in relation to the extra-textual setting of use.

5.3 What is a proverb?

in Prov. 26:1–12 or עָצֵל 'sluggard' in vv. 13–16. Such characteristic lexical usage may be coupled with variations in word order that deviate from usual prose patterns in order to create sound patterns and rhythms that suit the overall psychological mood and semantic pressure points of the particular proverb at hand (e.g., the utterance-final 'honor' כָּבוֹד in 26:1, duplicated in v. 8). This technical, often allusive terminology would have been quite familiar to those who lived within the tradition, but it can be enigmatic or even opaque for today's audience of hearers, readers, and interpreters; for example:

חוֹחַ עָלָה בְיַד־שִׁכּוֹר A thorn(bush) goes up in(to) [the] hand of a drunkard,
וּמָשָׁל בְּפִי כְסִילִים: [so] also a proverb in [the] mouth of fools. (v. 9)

Drunkards and fools tend to troop (or droop) together, often as one and the same person, which may be the critical implication of this passage. In any case, the meaning of the several concrete lexical items of the first line is not entirely clear: does the (foolish) drunkard here hurt only himself or others too? (See the commentaries for many different possibilities.)[18] One thing is certain—that is, 'wise speech' (מָשָׁל), including the word of the LORD, has no business in the mouths of fools, whether as subject or object, i.e., whether spontaneously generated or only transmitted secondhand (like colloquial or specialized idioms coming from the mouth of a language learner).

- *complex antithesis* – Antithesis is ubiquitous in Proverbs, for the ideal character (i.e., qualities of the wise/righteous person) is often graphically examined or emphasized by images of the opposite (folly/evil), such as we have throughout 26:1–12. The effect of such a contrast or incongruity may be heightened by a chiastic ordering of linguistic elements, either within a line or between lines, e.g., 'for a fool honor' at the end of v. 1 (see above) reverses the preceding pattern of parallel constituents: 'like the snow in the summer' and 'like the rain at the harvest'. The impact of an antithetical passage usually involves a subtle combination of features of correspondence and contrast, which may be mixed with certain elements of enigma and ambiguity, encouraging further thought and reflection. We observe this in v. 12, which manifests the greatest amount of explicit

---

[18] Dr. Boerger suggests this as the possible point of similarity: both entities are oblivious to the presence of the 'sharp' thing in their immediate vicinity. A drunk cannot feel the sharpness of the thornbush that he happens to grab on to, and a fool cannot perceive the wisdom of the proverb that he is uttering.

contrast in the entire pericope—thus also effecting a considerable degree of textual end-stress:

רָאִיתָ אִישׁ חָכָם בְּעֵינָיו [When/if] you see a man [who is] wise in his [own] eyes,
תִּקְוָה לִכְסִיל מִמֶּנּוּ: [there is more] hope for a fool than for him.

A chiastic reversal in the order of the key antithetical terms חָכָם 'wisdom' and כְּסִיל 'fool' from that of verse 5 highlights the correspondence between these two verses, thereby suggesting a hermeneutical clue to the interpretation of this paradoxical pair, vv. 4–5, discussed in section 5.4.3.

- *graphic imagery* – Proverbial texts feature situationally concrete images, pregnant allusions, and vivid figures, especially metaphor and metonymy, often provocatively juxtaposed with one another and imbued with symbolic import. In many instances, a given proverb evokes a dramatic interpersonal scenario or a natural scene that may be readily visualized by a 'contextualized' audience (i.e., people who are familiar with an ANE cultural setting, religious background, and ecological environment).[19] A traditional Jewish milieu illumines the following familiar proverb with much greater emotive and connotative significance:

כְּכֶלֶב שָׁב עַל־קֵאוֹ As a dog returning to its vomit,
כְּסִיל שׁוֹנֶה בְאִוַּלְתּוֹ: [so also is] a fool repeating his folly. (v. 11)

The incorrigible fool, therefore, is not only someone who cannot learn from his mistakes, like a dumb dog, but his unrighteous behavior also renders him ritually unclean, to be rigorously excluded from all contact, like the despised creature that he is here compared with. "To refer to another human as a dog is to insult the other as among the lowest in the social [and religious] scale" (Ryken et al. 1998:214). One must remember, however, that his sad state and status is no accident, for the 'fool' in a biblical sense is someone who has deliberately determined his fate by deciding to align himself against the stipulated moral and spiritual principles of YHWH. By choosing to repudiate the supreme authority and relevance of God in the world (e.g., by asserting 'there is no God!' אֵין אֱלֹהִים Ps. 14:1; cf. 49:13, 92:5–6), fools automatically render themselves unfit for worship and unworthy of any sort of personal or group fellowship. Nature-based experience thus reinforces

---

[19] In William's view, "metaphoric play is the most important element of Wisdom poetics," for it creates indeterminacies or gaps that the listener must resolve or fill in, thus stimulating a productive search for the "seeker of wisdom" (1987:275–276).

5.3 What is a proverb? 167

the lessons that divine law reiterates about unenlightened human nature (cf. Prov. 13:19-20).

There are other important stylistic devices to be found in Proverbs, for example, the unexpected opening rhetorical question of 26:12 (also common are personification, merismus, enjambment, and phrasal disjunction). However, the several categories described above are sufficient perhaps to illustrate the manifold way in which they all are efficiently and artistically integrated with one another to effect a specific set of communicative purposes. This includes a highlighting of the impact and appeal of their poetically pointed, culturally conditioned moral and religious messages.

5.3.2 Function—incisive paraenesis

The lyric, audience-engaging rhetoric of Proverbs naturally implicates an overall *didactic* (informative + instructive + imperative) function that may be factored into a number of more specific communicative aims, which vary according to the immediate and sectional cotext. As illustrated above, this stylistically sharpened style is manifested by a range of poetic-proverbial forms, all designed to effect a correspondingly 'piercing' paraenetic purpose, especially in the case of the more colorful and pithy 'observations'. This formal framework usually includes an elaborate phonological structure that achieves several important discourse objectives, such as: establishing audible cohesion within the same and between different cola; foregrounding certain key words and related concepts, whether synonymous or antithetical; and delimiting or demarcating cola and bicola boundaries (cf. McCreesh 1991: ch. 2; Salisbury 1994:440).

As they convey their typically jarring, at times enigmatic overt content, many proverbs are obviously meant to attract—often also to shock or puzzle—their audience (clearly more so than silent readers). They therefore activate the critical cognitive and emotive capacities of listeners with respect to a variety of promoted and prohibited human behaviors. At the same time, certain sayings may stimulate a hermeneutical search for some deeper, symbolical meaning (e.g., concerning the feminine qualities of Wisdom personified in Proverbs 9, or with reference to the dynamic healing, helpful, or hurtful power of the spoken word, as depicted in a number of proverbs in Proverbs 25).

In addition to the general *didactic* function pertaining to people's thinking, speaking, and especially acting in life, we normally find expressed by the surface literary forms of a given biblical proverb a variable combination of other types, such as the *affective* (emotive), *aesthetic* (artistic), *mnemonic* (memorial), and *ritual* (relational) functions. The description of such general communicative purposes may be sharpened in precision though the use of speech act methodology, in particular, a determination of the implied illocutionary force of utterances (cf. Briggs 2008:89–90), e.g., proverbs that rebuke, warn, advise, admonish, praise, encourage, approve, condemn, validate, or vindicate (and so forth, depending on the available inventory of such discourse intentions within the lexicon of a particular language). There is thus an intentional, illocutionary, and/or functional priority established in relation to a given proverb or proverbial cluster that varies according to the current audience, which would of course differ in its sociocultural constitution and religious interests or needs over the ages from one place to another. However, one fact seems fairly certain: these "aphorisms were written not in order to motivate the foolish, wicked, and lazy to change their ways but to motivate the virtuous" (Clifford 1998:54)—namely, to emulate the positive personages among the various antithetically paired character types that people the Proverbs.

While the actual response or opinion of the original and subsequent receptor groups with regard to the book of Proverbs cannot be ascertained, an assessment of the pragmatic effect of these texts was formally or informally recorded by the rabbis, followed then also by early Christian writers and commentators (see Garrett 2008:568–569). However, such an evaluation is not a particular concern of the current study. Given the ongoing significance and timeless relevance of these sapiential sayings, my interest centers upon their overall communicative value within the framework of a present-day southeastern African setting. This contemporary interpersonal scenario features a major Bantu language (and *lingua franca*) of the region (i.e., Chewa), a specifically youthful social constituency, and a long-standing tradition of verbal art forms in which proverbs and other forms of oral rhetoric continue to hold a prominent place.

The crucial question then for current communicators is this: what do these diverse proverbial speech acts actually 'say' to people today? And how effective then is such instruction in terms of indigenous models or standards of structure and style? This issue poses a serious challenge to all Bible translators: how can they best render a given proverbial text in the vernacular so that it retains its overall gnomic flavor or connotation as well as its principal pragmatic purpose? The maintenance of these or equivalent artistic and affective qualities is essential in order to equip modern readers and hearers to reflect on and apply these ancient scriptural truths anew within rather different social settings, having a very localized sort of interpersonal dynamics. In the following survey, then, I focus on the stylistic features and rhetorical functions of the passage in Proverbs 26:1–12.

5.4 The sapiential rhetoric of Proverbs 26:1–12

In this pericope we find a special emphasis on the semantic aspect of interpretation because all of the individual proverbs that comprise the text are linked by the common general topic of 'foolishness'. Thus each of the proverbs of this mini-corpus deals in some penetrating way with the typical causes and consequences of folly in the biblical sense. One proverb therefore needs to be examined and evaluated in the light of another.[20] Taken together, this set strongly warns the listener or reader to refrain from initiating or participating in any sort of imprudent or inexpedient activity, as specified by the sapiential tradition. On the other hand, the antithetical pole of interpersonal behavior—that which characterizes the spiritually 'wise' in God's eyes—is implicitly propounded and thus also promoted throughout the sequence.[21]

5.4.1 Extrinsic and intrinsic features

This combination of twelve proverbs in ch. 26 is quite clearly delineated both extrinsically in relation to its surrounding cotext and intrinsically by means of several strong elements of cohesion. As indicated by prominent metalingual headings at 25:1 and 30:1, chapter 26:1–12 forms an integral portion of the larger proverb collection that is attributed to 'the men of Hezekiah, king of Judah' (as distinct from the subsequent 'sayings of Agur'). The loosely related assortment of proverbs found in ch. 25 comes to an end in v. 28 with a rebuke of any person who lacks 'self control'.[22] This leads to the grouping that focuses on 'fool(s)' (כְּסִיל), a term which is explicitly mentioned in the singular or plural in every verse except two, where s/he is clearly implied—namely, as the foolish author of 'an undeserved curse'.

As noted earlier, a different topical mini-set begins in 26:16, one that foregrounds the inaction of the lazy 'sluggard' (עָצֵל, vv. 13–16). There

---

[20] "Far from providing absolute guidelines for every circumstance, proverbs require that we master a repertoire of sayings from which we can choose wisely, fittingly" (Van Leeuwen 1993:265), that is, according to the life setting and social situation that happens to apply.

[21] "On a deeper level, the passage uses the problem of interaction with fools to teach about the need to properly [i.e., wisely] 'read' other people, situations, and even oneself (v. 12). In doing so, it also teaches about the nature of proverbs and their use (vv. 7, 9)" (Van Leeuwen 1997:223; the word in brackets has been added). A proverb loses all its validity if its speaker has no credibility, i.e., if he has not first applied its words to himself and been found 'not guilty' of its instruction or warning, etc.

[22] Garrett begins this pericope in 25:28, apparently the basis of an *inclusio* found in the expressions 'a man without control in his spirit' (v.28) and 'a man wise in his own eyes' (26:12) (1993:211).

is also a lexical correspondence, a parallel unit-end marking device (epiphora), which indicates that verses 12 and 16 are section-final passages of closure ('wise...in his own eyes' חָכָם...בְּעֵינָיו). In addition, the tectonic organization of the pericope covering 26:1-12 as a whole, including a final peak of thematic salience, further establishes its structural viability as a coherent and cohesive segment of poetic discourse. We could call it a 'proverbial poem'. The hermeneutical implication is that the text must be perceived and interpreted, hence also translated, as a unit, not merely as a string of wise sayings.

5.4.2 A structural-thematic outline

Based on a semantic and structural analysis of the pericope of 26:1-12, I would propose the following as an appropriate thematic title for this section: *On folly and fittingness, honor and pride*. There is no doubt about the key term 'folly', for this concept is featured throughout the discourse as various representative facets of the behavior of a 'fool' (כְּסִיל) are put on display. The modifier 'fitting' (נָאוֶה), more specifically its negative converse, is introduced in the non-figurative 'observational' portion of the proverb in v. 1 (colon B). This is coupled with 'honor' (כָּבוֹד), a quality completely unbefitting a fool (cf. v. 8b). The unexpected notion of 'pride' (i.e., self-ascribed honor) is reserved for the climactic last line, being evoked by means of a lexical reversal that is attached to the book's central term, 'wisdom' (חָכָם)—'a man [who seems] wise in his own eyes'. Thus this section presents us with a partial 'hermeneutics of wisdom' as viewed from the perspective of its opposite, that is, with a negative focus upon the fool. More importantly, however, this practical ethical philosophy is promoted and reinforced by the divine standard established in the entire book of Proverbs, the corpus of wisdom literature more generally, and ultimately by the former Hebrew Scriptures as a whole.

A symmetrical arrangement of four structural subsections organizes the preceding thematic summary within this pericope according to the alternating pattern: A – B – A' – B'. Perhaps this manner of organization was chosen (whether consciously or intuitively) to reflect the ever changing life situations that one finds oneself in, where wisdom frequently comes into conflict with folly in respect to one's personal moral and religious behavior.

A (1–3): This opening segment features a threefold set of naturalistic paired images, each having various negative connotations in application to a 'fool'. All three proverbs are of the 'observational' (3rd person perspective)

5.4 The sapiential rhetoric of Proverbs 26:1–12

kind and manifest very similar syntactic constructions which link them together also on the implicit linguistic level.

> **B** (4–5): This pair of 'admonitional' (2nd person perspective) proverbs displays extensive anaphora (parallel lexical openings), except that the first is negative (4), while the second is stated in the positive (5). The apparent contradiction in advice that these two proverbs advance will be considered further below.

A' (6-11): Another set of observational proverbs seems to link up with and extend the sequence begun in segment A. The former is explicitly associated with the latter by the repeated motif 'honor for the fool' (vv. 1b, 8b). An alternating pattern of topical motifs is evident in the B-cola: thus 6b, 8b, and 10b talk about giving the fool more responsibility (honor) than he deserves or is capable of handling, while 7b and 9b reiterate the fact that folly may be manifested also by those who seemingly have the 'right' words to say (cf. 4a and 5a).[23] A minor chiastic arrangement formed by a selection of A-colon elements lends some cohesion to this subsection: 6a and 10a portray violent action; 7a, 8a, and 9a exemplify futile action. Verse 11 then seems to act like sort of a general proverbial summary of the hopeless, pitiful state of all those who in effect categorizes themselves by such behavior: a fool simply cannot escape his folly.

> **B'** (12): The repeated '*wise* in his own eyes' connects this with its parallel B, thus forming an *exclusio* around the longest sub-section A'. The dramatic rhetorical question of 12a automatically involves the reader/hearer personally in the rhetorical argument of this section. The rather surprising insertion of this query suggests that it may offer the hermeneutical key to the whole. In any case, verse 12b exhibits climactic end-stress since it also introduces an ironic little surprise, one that reveals the relevance of this section (B') in keeping with the overall ethical theme of Proverbs. Thus, as it turns out ('in the eyes of YHWH', implied, cf. Deut. 4:25), there actually is someone worse off than a fool—namely, the person who is unduly proud, whether in relation to other people or God himself. Pride makes it impossible for one to perceive his/her foolish behavior. It also blocks off all 'fear of the LORD' from within him (1:7); accordingly, there is no 'hope' for such an individual either in life or in death.

---

[23] "[The] knowledge of proverbs does not automatically make one wise" (Van Leeuwen 1997:224). The same caveat applies to all scholars, including the present author, who presume to write or teach about proverbs!

What the back-and-forth (observational ↔ admonitional) discourse structure of 26:1–12 appears to highlight then is the need for clear moral and spiritual *discernment*—how to do or say what is apt and appropriate in one's current cultural setting and social situation. People, who due to their pride cannot perceive and assess the realities of self or life properly ('fools'+!), have no 'honor' in the eyes of God or man. On the other hand, those who have learned to discriminate things rightly and to act accordingly, that is, righteously and with integrity according to YHWH's relational *torah* precepts, are indeed honorable (Prov. 10:9, 28:6; cf. Deut. 4:5–6). Not every set of circumstances is the same, or even similar enough to permit rote or routine behavior. On the contrary, in most cases the 'wise' must carefully consider the entire context of speech and setting, including the pertinent interpersonal dynamics—both implicit and explicit, verbal and non-verbal—in order to make an apt decision in the light of the LORD's covenantal principles for a holy and just society. On one occasion, solution A needs to be applied (e.g., v. 4); at another time, solution B may be more suitable (e.g., v. 5). How one is to determine *which* and *when* requires divinely directed perception, coupled with a strong personal determination to live according to this decision.

5.4.3 Hermeneutical approaches to a *crux interpretum*

אַל־תַּעַן כְּסִיל כְּאִוַּלְתּוֹ   Do not answer a fool according to his folly,
פֶּן־תִּשְׁוֶה־לּוֹ גַם־אָתָּה: lest you be like him you yourself.
עֲנֵה כְסִיל כְּאִוַּלְתּוֹ   Answer a fool according to his folly,
פֶּן־יִהְיֶה חָכָם בְּעֵינָיו: lest he become wise in his [own] eyes.

In his helpful study of the various cohesive, as well as disjunctive, devices that interrelate Hebrew 'proverbial pairs', Hildebrandt refers to 26:4–5 as being "perhaps the most frequently cited" instance of this linkage due to its many contrary elements (1988:209–210). A careful examination reveals that these two verses really do not contradict each other. Instead, they must be interpreted together, with one passage complementing the other to provide a subtle insight as to how 'wise' folk are to interact with 'fools'. Indeed, the pair offers an implicit warning to the wise concerning the sort of attitude that might unwittingly transform them into fools.

A number of exegetical explanations have been given in the search for a way to hermeneutically 'solve' this apparent antilogy. Among them are the following plausible attempts (there are of course others that might be suggested):

a. The rabbis recognized the potential problem in interpretation that these verses pose, and so they proposed a completely different contextual

5.4 The sapiential rhetoric of Proverbs 26:1–12

setting for each proverb. Thus v. 4 was applied to 'answers' in the secular sphere of human interaction, whereas v. 5 was seen to refer to controversies of a more significant, religious nature—where the 'fool' must by all means receive a fitting critical rejoinder. In other words, "in negligible issues one should just ignore the stupid person; but in issues that matter, he must be dealt with lest credence be given to what he says" (Ross 1991:1088).

b. Some have turned to a possible linguistic explanation, which appeals also to many Bible translators: does the paradox of vv. 4–5 perhaps turn on different senses attached to the marker of similitude— כְּ (plus a certain amount of implicit information), i.e., 'like his folly' = in a foolish manner (4) versus as befits his folly (5)? Thus the preposition alters in meaning according to the advice being given in the particular setting of use. In v. 4 we hear: 'don't speak in a foolish manner, lest you show yourself to be like a fool'; in v. 5: 'speak in a way that is appropriate when addressing a fool, to show him up for what he is'.[24] "Then the advice would be always to answer fools as befits their folly [but] without stooping to their level" (Loader 2001:243).

c. Another linguistic insight points out the fact that there is a sudden shift in pronominal person in v. 5b, that is from 2nd person to 3rd person singular "thus revealing the interpretational key to understanding the pragmatic relationship between the two contrary sentences" (Hildebrandt 1988:211). That is to say, in v. 4 the speaker is concerned about his own self respect in public discourse: don't engage in fruitless debates with fools. In v. 5, on the other hand, a person has the welfare of the fool in mind: silence him with a sharp answer, one based on the wisdom tradition, in order to keep him from becoming arrogant—'wise in his own eyes'.[25] As v. 12 clearly indicates, nothing is worse than that.

d. Some view these patently paired sayings from a more general perspective. The apparent contradiction draws attention to the ever-present ambiguities of life and the difficulty of avoiding 'foolish' speech and/or behavior on the part of others. The first proverb appears to give the socially expected advice, a warning that would apply to most confrontational situations where fools are concerned. The second proverb then suggests a strategy for the exceptional cases, namely, those times when

---

[24] This would appear to be the hermeneutical position that has been adopted by the GNT in its rendering of vv. 4–5: "If you answer a silly question, you are just as silly as the one who asked it. Give a silly answer to a silly question, and the one who asked it will realize that he's not as clever as he thinks."

[25] I will use the masculine gender for rendering the 3rd person singular pronoun; somehow that sounds more appropriate with reference to cases of blind folly in religion and life.

leaving a fool unanswered would do more damage than exposing his folly. So it is that "[w]isdom is a matter of fittingness and timing. But here, no clues are given for making the right decision" (Van Leeuwen 1997:224; cf. Loader 2001:243). This seems to be the translation technique that was adopted by the new Chewa popular language version—that is, to explicitly indicate the possibility of variable settings by the transitional expression *Koma mwina* 'but perhaps/sometimes' (suggesting an alternative) at the beginning of v. 5.

One thing is clear concerning this crux: any proposed hermeneutical solution to the seeming paradox of vv. 4–5 must take the entire cotext into consideration, in particular, the segment's extension or parallel at the close of the discourse in v. 12.[26] As noted earlier, there are several prominent connections between these two passages, namely, the obvious overlapping repetition ('wise in his own eyes') as well as a correspondence in general proverbial type (both are 'admonitions'). Such verbal cues seem to call for the verses to be construed together, that is, with reference to each other regarding the issue of religious (ethical + theological) 'fittingness' from YHWH's inscripturated point of view. In short, folly is bad, but there is still hope, at least for some fools (the penitent?—e.g., Prov. 28:13). Arrogant conceit, on the other hand, is hopeless for it cuts a person off from all rehabilitating, sight-restoring alternatives (cf. Prov. 8:13), including any sort of a potentially redeeming or transforming divine intervention. The 'wise-eyes' of the proud can clearly perceive only themselves.

5.5 The rhetoric of folly versus wisdom

This study has suggested that both the use as well as the interpretation of Proverbs is not always as straightforward as it may seem on the surface of any given text, considered in syntagmatic and paradigmatic isolation from semantically and/or co-textually related passages. With so much discourse about folly, what does 26:1–12 have to say about biblical wisdom and the 'wise' person who actively puts its principles into practice? It may at first seem a simple matter to avoid foolish words or actions and to behave circumspectly at all times. But anyone who has seriously tried to accomplish this spiritual discipline soon discovers that it's not so easy after all. In fact, oftentimes it is just as complicated and difficult as the attempt to propose a clearcut or ironclad interpretation of the provocative proverbial pair of verses 4–5. But then again, should the 'single solution'

---

[26] This co-text would include, of course, other semantically related proverbs in the book (e.g., 8:13, 11:2, 16:18, 29:23 in connection with 26:12). Furthermore, from a wider perspective "Proverbs must be interpreted in the context of the whole biblical canon" (Garrett 1993:55).

be the chief goal of our hermeneutical efforts in every case? Perhaps the primary meaning lies, at least in part, along the winding path that leads towards its destination. As Van Leeuwen aptly reminds us:

> Rather than forcing us to erase or 'harmonize' the ambiguities and 'contradictions', biblical wisdom invites us to ponder the nuances and complexities of life; it invites us to become wise (1993:266).

In this connection, we might also wish to rethink our facile application of v. 12 as well: all the talk about fools could easily lull us into thinking that this verse has nothing at all to say to the present reader(s). But have we never, if only on occasion, felt at least a little bit 'wise in our own eyes' in the light of some personal victory or achievement, perhaps after enlightening an eager, appreciative audience with the proverbial pearls of our scholarly wisdom? The shocking B-line conclusion then becomes rather uncomfortable—could there really be 'more hope for the fool than for me'?

Of course, in Proverbs, read holistically as it always must be (i.e., with a sense of the whole and all of its parts), the solution is not far away from any given context. Indeed, this was announced at the very beginning of the book. To act wisely, we must strive to 'fear YHWH' and 'flee evil' (1:7, 3:7), that is, to give full 'honor' (glory) to him in everything we think, say, or do. Putting the focus there, and on the divine source of true wisdom—the word of the LORD (2:1–8; cf. Job 28; Ps. 119:105)—instead of worrying about playing the fool, is undoubtedly a more positive and productive policy to adopt as we confront the diverse, frequently ambiguous situations and decisions of life. These would include the various hermeneutical challenges to be found in the Scriptures themselves, especially those encountered in Bible translation, where to render the original text wrongly or inappropriately is tantamount to putting 'a proverb in the mouth of a fool'! (26:7b, 9b).

5.6 Sharpening the lyric rhetoric against folly in English

In the passage below, Boerger provides an English rendering for our consideration, this time one that she prepared as a special complement to this chapter. Rather than trying to duplicate every feature of the Hebrew, she uses three main principles to compose this passage: (1) each couplet should be rhymed AA; (2) each verse should sound like a proverb to native speakers of English; and (3) in each couplet, the (a) line should have ten syllables and the (b) line eight, with the hope that this would add force to the punchline. There are two kinds of exceptions to (1). First, often consonance or assonance is used in place of perfect rhyme; and second, an ABAB rhyme scheme occurs in the quatrain of verses 4–5. Others will have to be the judge of principle (2), and some slight variation was allowed in (3).

So what compromises were made by following these three principles? While exact repetition was maintained in 1b and 8b, yet verses 7a and 9b, which are identical in Hebrew, were allowed to take shape in relation to the partner lines of their respective couplets, masking the exact repetition. The Hebrew has eleven repetitions of 'fool,' while Boerger's English version uses the word only seven or eight times. This is probably legitimate in that English speakers have been said to tolerate less exact repetition than that found in the Hebrew text, and her adjustments help convey the full moral semantics of 'fool.'

I would also point out several devices, in addition to rhyme, which Boerger uses effectively to heighten impact and help accomplish her second goal. There are a number of instances of alliteration, such as that in verse one with *r-r* and *s-s* in line a, followed by an echo of 'r's in the b line. See also 2b and 3b. Note further the sound correspondences in verses 4–5. The sounds of 'stoop' and 'level' in 4a are echoed by 5a's 'stupid' and 'evil,' while three lines repeat the same sounds in 4b 'likewise', 5a 'whys' and 5b 'wise.'

Proverbs 26:1-12—Don't Tolerate Fools

1 Like rain when reaping or summer with snow—
  Is it right to honor error? No!
2 Like fluttering swallow or darting bird
  A curse with no cause cannot hurt.
3 Like whip on a horse, or rope on a mule—
  A belt on the back of a fool!

4 Don't stoop to a fool's level in replies,
  Lest you likewise land in the same boat.
5 But show the stupid his evils and whys,
  Lest he think he's so wise and boast.

6 Cut off one's own feet, drunk violence seek,
  Send news by one prone to misdeeds.
7 A fool spouting proverbs is just the same
  As dangling limp legs of the lame.

8   Like tying a stone in a sling to throw—
    Is it right to honor error? No!
9   A thorn in his hand, a drunk doesn't care;
    A fool spouts proverbs unaware.
10 To shoot whatever a hunter sees move—
    To hire any vagrant or fool.
11 Like dogs go back to their vomit, you see,
    Fools keep on acting foolishly.

12 Just think, how fares the one so wise he boasts?
    Just think, for fools there's far more hope.

5.7 Sharpening the lyric rhetoric against folly in Chewa

Translation is a complex communication task made considerably more difficult due to the fact that two (or more) distinct and variously divergent language-culture settings are involved in this interactive process. Just as in the use of proverbs, especially when 'fools' may somehow be involved, so also careful discrimination between overt and covert causes or effects (means or results) is necessary. One must first determine precisely the time, place, occasion, personnel, and audience concerned. Thus an initial analysis of the total communicative setting is needed for a translation team to decide the most appropriate strategy to be applied during the activity of message formulation and text transmission. In this section, I will present a brief discussion of this subject with reference to Proverbs 26:1–12. I have borrowed the descriptive keynote of the translation technique I propose from Theo Schneider, who observes that:

> [T]he elevated style of biblical aphorisms tends to get lost or blunted in translation... Wisdom sayings are all too often paraphrased in translation instead of being re-crafted and *sharpened. Traduttore traditore* indeed! (1992:124, original italics)

The aim then of a version that intends to achieve an appreciable amount of 'functional equivalence' in literary rhetorical terms (Wendland 2003a) is to resharpen the biblical text when expressing it idiomatically in a given target language. In other words, one seeks to reproduce the 'wisdom' (in other words, 'craft' or 'skill,' i.e., חָכְמָה, Schneider 1992:125) of the original in a contemporary sapiential style of vernacular speech—even in singable (lyric) form. Several key aspects of this challenging process are surveyed below in relation to our focal passage.

5.7.1 Your audience: For whom are you translating and why?

There are many translation possibilities in terms of text and cotext nowadays. The United Bible Societies no longer promote and encourage a single recommended option—namely, the 'dynamic' or 'functional' equivalent, 'common' or 'popular' language rendition. Rather a wide range of contextually determined 'frames of reference' are crucial in helping a planning committee to decide upon the version that will be 'right' for them, that is, the envisaged rendition for the primary target audience (cf. Wilt 2003:ch. 1). One needs to ask, "Who is the intended audience and what are their expressed wishes, interests, resources, limitations, and needs?" These answers will, or should, determine the stylistic nature of the translation, whether more literal, more idiomatic, 'literary' (poetic), or a compromise, middle-of-the-road version. The pre-project research done to determine the right style for the translation needs to be more in depth, rather than merely routine or informal, since such research is essential in the effort to have the type of translation conform more closely to the target constituency in mind. This means that the potential text consumers themselves must be integrally involved in planning and implementing the production of any version that is specifically meant for their use and edification.[27]

As far as Africa and the book of Proverbs are concerned, one must keep in mind the fact that:

> The various types of African sapiential lore are also best understood against the background of changing world views, sociocultural attitudes, customs and beliefs. They are equally caught up in the historical flux of cultural dynamics. (Schneider 1992:46)

This would indicate that in the case of such a specialized literary corpus, some intensive setting-specific research in the same generic field is also required. Thus the use, purpose, and significance of proverbs within a given speech community may well alter and adjust over the years. As in all areas of social change, what was deemed appropriate by the ancestors and elders in their time will probably not be viewed in exactly the same way today. The appropriation and application of proverbs does not take place in a sociocultural or temporal vacuum. The traditional meanings and conventional usages, even the more exotic and esoteric ones, change

---

[27] This does not mean, though, that the expatriate translation facilitator neglects educating the community with regard to the translation options and their relative strengths or weaknesses, as s/he sees them. Many communities are unaware that literary translations are permissable since this has not been modelled in any of the standard translations in western languages.

5.7 Sharpening the lyric rhetoric against folly in Chewa 179

with the passage of years, like their social situations. But proverbs are flexible—their 'standard' interpretation can be modified in keeping with the occasion and also to accommodate to the current interpersonal milieu or modernized cultural background, like a chameleon (given verbally competent, communication-committed speakers and hearers).

What then constitutes this local environment and interactive setting into which we propose re-creating the wisdom of Proverbs, the pericope of 26:1–12 in particular? In section 5.7.2 I overview only the oral-literary component of this situational context, with specific reference to artistic 'wisdom' discourse.[28] Within the confines of this chapter, it is not possible to present many relevant details concerning the linguistic and cultural dimensions of the Chewa worldview and way of life.[29] The following discussion gives just a hint of what stands today as a rich oral heritage and more recently a developing written tradition.

5.7.2 Chewa proverbial structure and style

There is some dispute concerning the exact term that should be used to designate a 'proverb' in Chewa. I cannot get into the various linguistic arguments here, but will simply summarize what appears to have happened during the course of linguistic change, especially in recent years due to the influence of English. The term *mwambi* (pl. *miyambi*) originally referred generically to all types of narrative, whether long or short, factive or fictive; it would thus include the category of proverbs (Chimombo 1988:5–7). Other words such as *chisimo*, *nthanthi*, and *mwambo* were alternatively used to designate proverbs, maxims, and all sorts of clever sayings. Nowadays, however, these latter terms seem to have lost out, and most grammars, dictionaries, and anthologies much prefer *mwambi*, restricting its reference to the reduced literary form generally known as a 'proverb' in its particular form and distinctive usage (e.g., Kafantenganji 1986:111).

In terms of purpose or social function, perhaps it is best to allow actual users to describe the various possibilities in their own words (translated from an original Chewa published text, with certain key terms included in parentheses):

---

[28] The essential oral-aural character, or 'orality,' of the book of Proverbs needs to be remembered during any analysis and assessment of its literary quality. As Berry suggests: "Perhaps the proverbs function as literary compositions designed for rather than arising from oral performance" (1995:134, original emphasis). This would certainly correspond with the use of most Bible translations, which tend to be publicly heard much more often than silently read.

[29] I have dealt in part with some of these aspects in Wendland 1990a and 1992. Readers may consult the references cited there for other cultural and religious studies of the Chewa people, some 10 million of whom live in the adjacent east-central African countries Malawi, Zambia, and Mozambique.

[People] had sayings (*nthanthi*) and proverbs (*miyambi*) of all types that contained various teachings (*ziphunzitso*). Some proverbs would be spoken at court cases (*milandu*) in a figurative manner (*mophiphiritsa*) but having clues (*zolozera*) so that people would recognize [them] when uttered. Others would instruct about people's behavior, about the unmarried state, about family life, about illnesses, about death, and things like that. Many teachings were linked up with (*zinakolekedwa*) proverbs. Even though they did not know how to write and read, they would remember these things when conversing according to the topic at hand. (Kumakanga 1949:iii)

Among the various things that embellish (*zimakometsa*) and enlarge (*kukulitsa*) the Chichewa language are proverbs (*miyambi*). There are proverbs of all kinds. Some are spoken at court cases, while others instructed about one's heart-attitude (*chikhalidwe cha mtima*), and still others were spoken at various times. But all these proverbs, no matter how different, have their [specific] meanings (*matanthauzo ake*). (Nankwenya 1974:139)

The preceding citations would suggest that there is a clear parallel with biblical proverbs in the strong emphasis upon the broad didactic function of proverbs as they relate to proper moral and social behavior, along with the corresponding rhetorical usage in public judicial and disputative settings.[30]

Several of the major stylistic features noted earlier as being characteristic of Hebrew proverbs (at least those found in the book so named) are common also in Chewa *miyambi*, which generally consist of a single utterance that ranges between two and ten words (the average being three to four).[31] They do not manifest the binary parallelism of the Hebrew, but many examples are clearly twofold in construction and may actually be

---

[30] In his survey of 'African proverbs', Westermann rightly observes that "the proverbs appear to be a component of collective life, without which community would be unthinkable....Without an awareness of their function and the setting in which they were employed, proverbs cannot be properly understood" (1995:141–142). In a literary work and tradition such as pertained in ancient Israel, the enveloping intertextual setting and usage becomes equally, if not more, important to local interpretation. After noting that African proverbial traditions include both "indicative and imperative sayings," Westermann points out the "significant difference...that in Africa, proverbs quite frequently appear in the context of jurisprudence [e.g., at the court of the paramount chief], whereas in Israel (as is the custom throughout the Near East) jurisprudence had its own language" (ibid., 144, 147).

[31] I have been interested in Chewa proverbs and proverbial lore ever since my early days of language study some 40 years ago. I have several larger collections of Chewa proverbs at my disposal, but the descriptions offered in this section are more or less intuitive observations and not based upon a thorough statistical study such as that of Schneider (1992) with regard to the Tsonga.

articulated as two-part utterances (see discussion below). Chewa proverbs do not display as much overt antithesis as their Hebrew counterparts, but the sapiential emphasis on conciseness, various sound plays, graphic imagery, and distinctive diction (but reflecting rather different sociocultural and ecological semantic domains) is very prominent. Special distinctive features of the African *miyambi* are ideophones (phonologically distinct, dramatic verbal predications), neologisms (often as distinctive designative names), and idiomatic language that may be either ancient or colloquial in origin.

While I have not discovered many traditional Chewa proverbs that can be simply substituted on a one-for-one basis with biblical proverbs, there are a few. For example, *chikomekome cha mkuyu, mkati muli nyerere* 'the fig may look good on the outside, but inside it's full of ants' for Proverbs 16:25, 'There is a way that seems right to a man, but in the end it leads to death' (NIV). But a more feasible translation goal is rather to render the biblical text in such a way that on the whole it sounds magisterial as well as sapiential in nature from an oral vernacular perspective. This would be not only didactic and authoritative, but also having a certain rhetorical impact and appeal that will attract and impress listeners, encouraging them to take seriously what is being said.

It is not really very difficult to mimic a traditional proverbial style, at least not in Chewa. For example, this is how v. 11 might sound: *Monga galu **abwerera masanzi** ake, momwemo chitsiru **amabwezera zopusa** zake* 'As a dog keeps returning to its vomit, so a fool keeps repeating his foolishness' (note the sound play that links two of the analogical pairs of key terms [in bold]). The word 'fool' then is translated as *chitsiru* (i.e., the pejorative prefix and concord marker *chi-* plus the noun *tsiru* 'mad person'), referring to an obstinate, obnoxious character who consciously acts contrary to social norms and community values. In this case, a more idiomatic Chewa equivalent would be the derisive epithet *wogodomala*, which refers more forcefully to the same sort of person—'stupid'. As for the fellow who is worse off than the lout in God's eyes (v. 12), an ideal functional match is the compound folkloristic appellation *Nzeru-n'zayekha* 'Wisdom is his alone', i.e., Mr. Know-it-all![32]

---

32 These last two proposals raise the issue of *humor* in the Proverbs—exactly how humorous was the Hebrew text when such topics as 'fools' and their antics came up for criticism and reproach? I have not seen any scholarly discussion of this matter. Certainly the connotation of a word like כְּסִיל must have been decidedly negative—but how amusing, laughable, or even ludicrous? The Chewa terms cited, including *chitsiru*, do sound rather funny, as does the English 'fool(s)' in many of these passages, especially

When one considers the content and style of Proverbs as a whole, one encounters two major aspects of non-equivalence in comparison with the typical proverbs of the Chewa tradition. Hebrew proverbs of course are more overtly 'religious' and focus on biblical morality, with a special emphasis upon 'wisdom' and 'righteousness' in contrast to their opposites, 'folly' and 'wickedness', with respect to a person's thoughts, words, and actions. Another major difference is that 'God' (or the 'LORD') is periodically referred to by name within the biblical corpus (e.g., 10:3, 25:2), something which happens only rarely in Chewa vernacular sayings. Furthermore, the latter put more of a stress on interpersonal behavior and social etiquette within the corporate community—not so much on one's talk and very little on cognition, except for such universal negative attitudes or humors as pride, jealousy, lust, and anger.

Then, in addition to these formal differences, we might note one more significant compositional variation that appears quite clearly in a corpus such as we find in 26:1–12, especially the 'observations' of verses 6–10 (v. 11 is more straightforward again in terms of its imagery). This concerns the riddle-like quality of these proverbs due to the indirect, ambiguous, enigmatic, or imperceptible relationship between the metaphoric colon in line A (the image) and the application to a 'fool' in line B (the topic). Verse 9, for example, could be easily cast as a 'riddle' *(chirapi)* in Chewa, i.e., verbal *stimulus:* 'a thorn stuck in a drunkard's hand' → standard response: 'a proverb in a fool's mouth'.[33] As was mentioned earlier, many Chewa proverbs readily divide into two sections, namely, a longer opening assertion and an optional, shorter response that 'fills out' the second half or conclusion. But the two portions of a proverb are always closely connected both semantically and syntactically, e.g., *choipa chitsata chiani—mwini wake* 'evil follows what?—its very owner' (cf. Prov. 17:13). In any case, it is not too difficult to duplicate certain key aspects of a proverbial style in translation, e.g., *monga miyendo ya munthu wopunduka, momwemo miyambi m'kamwa mwa chitsiru* 'just like the legs of a lame person, so [are] proverbs in the mouth of a fool'. The explanatory ground of the comparison, e.g., *yopanda nchito* 'without any work' (completely useless),

---

when coming in a sequence such as we have in Prov. 26:1–12.

[33] Kugel comments: "The sense of this verse is: you may hear fools citing words of wisdom, but they have gotten them without understanding their real meaning, by chance, like a burr that sticks into the hand of a groping drunkard. The proverbist's image is, however, significant; he associates *mashal* (a proverb, or perhaps more generally, a parallelistic line) with something sharp. A similar image appears in Ecclesiastes 12:11" (1981:11).

5.7 Sharpening the lyric rhetoric against folly in Chewa

may or may not be included, depending on the anticipated hermeneutical skills of the audience.[34]

5.7.3 A rhetorical rendition—poetic functional equivalence

> The task of proverb translators is to establish the closest functional correspondence between the sapiential discourse of Israel and the wisdom code of modern receptors. 'Wisdom into wisdom' constitutes the practical, communication-oriented goal for a contemporary rendering of sentences from the Book of Proverbs. (Schneider 1992:17)

This brings up the issue of how idiomatic or 'proverbial' a team may/can be when translating the Proverbs into their mother tongue. Some suggestions were offered in the preceding section as to how a translation could be stylistically sharpened in Chewa in order to help it sound more 'salty', sagacious, or gnomic in nature, e.g., through the use of nuanced condensation, a more parallelistic format, colorful vocabulary, and figurative language. But the ambitious goal of putting 'wisdom into wisdom' discourse would certainly take the translation task a step further in the process of carefully domesticating the biblical text within a specific vernacular language. How valid or realistic is such a communicative objective?

It must be stated at the outset that this is only one of many possibilities along a hypothetical continuum of translation types. The choice is not a matter of either-or as was often suggested in the past—that is, a formal correspondence (literal) versus a functional equivalence (idiomatic) version. If well done (a very important qualification!), one translation may be just as good as another, depending on the setting concerned. The cognitive-emotive-volitional criterion of relevance or communicative congruence (i.e., textual efficiency in relation to conceptual effectiveness) has been introduced in recent years both to qualify and to specify our options more precisely in relation to all of the pertinent frames of reference that may apply in the case of a given project. Thus there are many variables based on the target setting that need to be taken into consideration as a

---

[34] To make this proverb sound more traditional or authentic in Chewa, some dynamic, graphic, and/or humorous figure, hyperbole, or irony would need to be added, for example: *panjinga* 'on a bicycle'—i.e., referring to the sphere of operation in which a lame person's legs are useless, to correspond with 'the mouth of a fool'. From a translation point of view, however, this would of course be an unwarranted anachronism. This example serves to illustrate the difficulty that one has when trying to 'proverbialize' ancient biblical sapiential sayings in a contemporary, living language.

certain translation program *brief* (job commission) and *Skopos* (purpose statement) are being considered and agreed upon. These may include the scope of the proposed version (e.g., full Bible, testament, book, selection), the appropriate sociolinguistic register to be approximated (e.g., formal vs. colloquial), the time frame available, the skill or competence of the translators, the opportunities available for their further training, the composition and particular wishes or needs of the envisioned user group, and others (see Appendix B).

But let us say, for the sake of illustration, that a more dynamic literary-poetic version has been chosen to be used in a youth ministry as a dramatic or even a musically adapted rendition of a topically-related compilation of biblical proverbs. In a language like Chewa, where a recognized vernacular verbal style contributes to such a heightened dimension of communication, we find a suitable indigenous candidate worth testing, namely, the *ndakatulo* genre of lyric composition. Translating in this style would create a 'sharper' alternative than a version that only made use of selected sapiential features, because it would superimpose a poetic upon a proverbial style and tone and thereby create more impact, appeal, and memorability.[35] Ideally, such a literary version would also be 'oratorical' in nature—that is, more amenable to an oral proclamation, for example, via a public recitation, a dramatic production, an audio/video cassette rendition, a musical composition, or even a radio broadcast.

It is not necessary to describe the stylistic features of such lyric poetry here (see Wendland 2002b), for these characteristics should be perceptible enough in the following example. (This is offered for the purpose of illustration only—i.e., it is not a published text.). I precede my poeticized proverbial rendering of Proverbs 26:4–5 with a citation of these same verses from the literal *Buku Lopatulika* ('Sacred Book') translation; in both cases, a relatively literal back translation into English is provided to facilitate an informal comparison.

Buku Lopatulika

Usayankhe citsiru monga mwa utsiru wace,	Do not answer a fool in like manner as his folly,
Kuti ungafanane naco iwe wekha.	Lest you be similar to him yourself.
Yankha citsiru monga mwa utsiru wace,	Answer a fool in like manner as his folly,

---

[35] Landers calls attention to the importance of tone when translating literary works: "By tone I mean the overall feeling conveyed by an utterance, a passage, or an entire work, including both conscious and unconscious resonance. Tone is more than just style.... Tone can comprise humor, irony, sincerity, earnestness, naïveté, or virtually any sentiment" (2001:68)—including the pithy, pungent, provocative character of proverbial lore.

Kuti asadziyese wanzeru.	So that he does not consider himself wise.

Wendland

Kodi n'kwabwino kuyankha chitsiru?	Say, is it expedient to answer a fool?
Iyai kapena inde—yankho lili pawiri.	No or yes—the answer is twofold.
Chitsiru usamachiyanka	Do not answer a fool
potsata *ucitsiru wakewo,*	by **following** his own folly,
kuwopa kuti nawenso	fearing that you yourself
ungafanefane nachotu;	might readily resemble him;
ichi sichingakome konse.	that would be not be good at all.
Komanso mwina mwake,	However at certain times,
uzichiyankha chitsiru inde,	you must answer a fool, yes indeed,
potsutsa *wake uchitsirutu,*	by **rebuking** that folly of his,
kuwopa kuti icho nachonso	fearing that he for his part
chingamadziyese chanzeru!	might consider himself wise!

The many differences between these two versions are plain to see—and hear, if the texts are spoken aloud. Note the rhythm, alliteration, redundancy, and dynamism of the second text, especially the prominent play on words for the two key verbs (in boldface). However, this is not a matter of one text being automatically better or worse than another, certainly not in the context of this short illustration. The critical evaluation of quality and relevance can be carried out only in relation to a specific target group and communicative purpose, according to specific criteria of assessment, and on the basis of a thorough testing or audience sampling procedure. For example, would the Chewa community find that the longer lyric text is too long to match well with their mental picture of proverbs? Or perhaps that text might be more amenable to an adaptation of this passage to a repetitive musical setting or perhaps a rhythmic chanting mode. A few concluding thoughts on the importance of this lyric-rhetorical approach will bring this chapter to a close.

5.8 Conclusion: Wisdom of rhetoric in Bible translation

Like a lame man's legs that stand—oh so weakly,
sounds a proverbial line in the lisp of a literalist.

(Prov. 26:7, adapted from the original Hebrew)

דַּלְיוּ שֹׁקַיִם מִפִּסֵּחַ וּמָשָׁל בְּפִי כְסִילִים׃

While I grant the fact that a deliberately literal rendering of the Scriptures, Proverbs included, may well have its place within the religious setting of some Christian communities, I am not prepared to accept just any brand of literalism. Thus a mechanical, word-for-word rote manner of verbal reproduction only rarely communicates effectively in any respect, and even then quite by accident. The norm is for such a version to fail completely since it all too often sets forth a vernacular text that is misleading, erroneous, opaque, awkward, nonsensical, or totally meaningless. Instead of a physical lameness in the legs, as imaged in the proverb above, we have a text that is verbally 'lame'—unable to move or operate at all on its own. It is the product of a literal application of the concept of translation—primarily through a superficial transference of linguistic forms from the SL to the TL—as opposed to a studied re-creation of the essential content and intent of the former into the latter.[36]

However, a stylistically shaped and polished formal correspondence rendering might be very appropriate for certain audiences—that is, if the TL text has also been sharpened in selected ways to highlight and accentuate its gnomic nature and purpose. This is no doubt best carried out by verbal experts using a vernacular translation technique that mimics the key features and functions of a proverbial style in the original document. These would include in particular the lexical and syntactic compactness of the biblical text (e.g., use of participles, infinitives, nominal clauses, parataxis, juxtaposition, etc.), its parallel phrasing, vivid diction, including local imagery, and above all, plenty of sound play and patterned sonic sequencing (e.g., rhythm, alliteration, paronomasia). Clearly, this type of a literal-literary version calls for highly skilled and experienced translator-artists; the typical heavy-worded theologian simply will not be able to cope with such a challenging artistic assignment. The aim is to re-create (i.e., after the model of the original) proverbial discourse that the intended audience not only learns *from* (content) but also *through* (form).

On the other hand, it must be noted that many modern meaning-based translations also fail to do justice to the Proverbs and sapiential discourse in general by clumsily applying conventional restructuring techniques such as disambiguation, coupled with frequent syntactic transformation

---

[36] "Poetry cannot be translated; it can only be recreated in the new language" (Clement Wood, cited in Landers 2001:97). This principle could of course be applied to any literary genre. And where such artistic 'creation' is needed, not just any wordsmith will do; the gifts of a translator must be equal to the magnitude and difficulty of his/her assigned task.

5.8 Conclusion: Wisdom of rhetoric in Bible translation

or semantic generalization in the over-zealous defense of semantic clarity and readability. To be sure, the resultant text turns out to be very understandable—almost too easy at times. In addition, all too often certain crucial aspects of a distinctive proverbial nature get washed out in the simplification process—not only the seasoned, memorable style, but also the power of a proverb to stimulate further reflection, deeper meditation, a search for some solution, or a new perspective on things. For example, this is GNT's rendering of v. 10: "An employer who hires any fool that comes along is only hurting everyone concerned." The rendering of the *God's Word* version is even worse in this respect: "[Like] many people who destroy everything, so is one who hires fools or drifters." What is the problem here? The Hebrew imagery of a dangerous, misfiring bowman is completely excised, and nothing with a corresponding rhetorical purpose or impact is inserted to replace or compensate for it. Furthermore, the proverbial 'sound' of the original text has been almost fully muted and we are left with a rather flat, indeed a very limp, verbal style that reflects nothing of the vigorous forcefulness of the Scripture source.[37]

This leads to a related, practical observation: the title that most translators give to the book of Proverbs is the same as that which designates the proverbial genre in their own language and oral or literary tradition, e.g., *miyambi* in Chewa. This must surely lead all listeners or readers to come to a certain conclusion, one that incorporates a reasonable expectation—namely, that the text at hand will *sound* sufficiently proverbial in specific relevant respects. This would apply on first perception to the formal style of the discourse, but such an evaluation would inevitably be extended also to its sapiential content and implications, for these two always go hand in hand. Accordingly, there must be at least something concrete within the composition to esthetically reward and thus also further stimulate and enrich this crucial rhetorical expectation and hermeneutical stance. The specific features used to achieve this would naturally vary with the target group concerned.[38] Any translation committee and production team that

---

[37] Theo Schneider gives many excellent examples of this sort of 'de-proverbialization' along with many keen suggestions for stylistic improvement in ch. 8 of his monograph (1992).

[38] A professional translator of secular literature (Portuguese to English) states this principle in familiar terms (to most Bible translators) as follows: "...all facets of the work, ideally, are reproduced in such a manner as to create in the TL reader the same emotional and psychological effect experienced by the *original* SL reader" (Landers 2001:27). One needs to add here that the translated text in and of itself will probably not be sufficient to provide a given target audience, no matter how current and educated, with enough of a frame of reference to contextualize and understand such a culturally specific text as Proverbs. The hermeneutical background and perspective will therefore have to be expanded in certain respects, e.g., by means of appropriate descriptive and explanatory footnotes, in order to allow the process of

either ignores or downplays this essential principle of 'thick' communication may be justly likened to those who have put 'a proverb in the mouth of a fool' (vv. 7b, 9b)—and a similar negative reaction or emotive result with regard to their version may be awaited (vv. 7a, 9a). A more serious judgment would be that by thus showing little or no regard for their intended audience, these proverb-users consider themselves 'wise in their own eyes' (v. 12a).

Finally, let us engage in some provocative sapiential semantics also with respect to the opening thematic question of this chapter. In doing so, this query might be recontextualized, transformed into its opposite, and rephrased to read, "How, in fact, is one to rightly 'answer' the 'wisdom' of the Scriptures in a contemporary translation?" The answer I propose is that just as there is no single tactic available for 'answering a fool' (vv. 4-5), but only a variable range of possibilities, depending on the setting and purpose—so also it is in the case of Bible translation. Here we are not dealing with religious fools and their unwitting associates, but with the opposite—genuinely 'wise' folk who eagerly desire to increase their spiritual understanding through a focused study of the Scriptures for a particular purpose (cf. Acts 17:11). So let us resolve to speak—perhaps even to sing—to them in an appropriately nuanced manner by means of a relevant, communication-oriented and setting-sensitive rendering of the Word of God. This is a strategy featuring the 'wisdom of rhetoric' that should apply in greater or lesser measure to all contemporary versions of Scripture, no matter what their place on the stylistic continuum of translation technique (cf. Col. 4:6).

---

interpretation to continue in a communicatively efficient and effective manner.

6

Love Lyrics in the Song of Songs

"To many, Song of Songs remains hopelessly inaccessible."
(Schwab 2008:738)

Introduction: Form and meaning

What is the Song of Songs (SoS) all about and what characterizes its singing? It is my contention in this chapter that one can answer the first half of the question only after properly analyzing the second. Accordingly, the Song's two chief and interrelated stylistic features, *analogical imagery* and *verbal recursion*, are described and illustrated as a means of determining the main contours of its overall structural organization. This leads in turn to a partial explication of the symbolic nature of its fundamentally theological message—one that is firmly grounded in the divinely ordained love between a man and a woman, established at creation in the garden. This symbolic nature also reaches beyond that as a text conceived within a theologically constituted and constrained context (the canon of Scripture), to reflect upon the ineffable affection of the LORD for his people—past, present, and future. This study employs a discourse-oriented, literary-structural methodology that is applicable to the other poetic texts of Scripture as well as to efforts to reproduce the beauty and impact of this Song in other languages via a lyric approach to translation.[1]

6.1 Two outstanding stylistic features

> Where has your lover gone, most beautiful of women?
> Which way did your lover turn, that we may look for him with you?
> My lover has gone down to his garden, to the beds of spices,
>   to browse in the gardens and to gather lilies. (Song of Songs 6:1–2, NIV)

---

[1] With reference to the title and contents of this chapter, the following observation is germane: "When we compare the lyrics in Song of Songs with some of the psalms [e.g., Pss. 24, 73, 134, 137], we see that all lyrics are not the same. They differ according to their content, emotional tone, and social context" (Weems 1997:367). The literature of Scripture is indeed diverse and for that reason all the more instructive and relevant for dealing with the variety of life's experiences and human relationships from a religious perspective.

There are a number of reasons why 'the Song of Songs which is Solomon's' (1:1) is one of the least known and read books of the Bible. First of all, it is in the form of Hebrew poetry, not a very popular choice nowadays. Second, it appears ostensibly as a love song, indeed, a very emotional one, involving a man and a woman—hence hardly the source for some deep theological thought or spiritual insight. And finally, it is very difficult to understand: what sense is one to make of the suddenly shifting speakers as illustrated in 6:1–2 (and just who are they anyway?); or, of all the graphic but obscure language and imagery (e.g., gardens, spices, and lilies); or of the apparent lack of an overall compositional structure to give one some direction towards comprehending this text? These and other hermeneutical difficulties have frustrated general readers as well as commentators throughout the ages, though many have made valiant attempts to come to grips with the manner in which this Song was written and with what it means. The problem is, as Saadia, an early Jewish commentator remarked, that the book's interpretation is like a lock for which the key has been lost (cited in Pope 1977:17). However, my study suggests that, in fact, there may not be a single key to the locked interpretation of the SoS or, for that matter, just a single preferred interpretation.

Today of course we no longer have access to the original poet so that he might inform us as to the identity of the 'lover' and to clarify who the speakers are or what exactly they are saying. This is a major problem, not only here, but in many other places throughout the Song. So, instead of strolling through a neatly cultivated garden of interpretation, we must chart our path through what at first seems to be a veritable verbal jungle—a complex concentration and combination of poetic symbolism and other literary devices. And since the biblical author is not clearly identified, though it could really be Solomon, we have to adopt a rather indirect procedure for probing his communicative intention, by a careful examination of the Hebrew text within its supposed Ancient Near Eastern context. Thus, we must seek through various literary-structural analytical procedures to uncover the Song's style and method of organization, so that we can in turn discover its intended message and purpose. In other words, an explication of literary form will hopefully lead us to a better understanding of the text's meaning, and this will result in a greater appreciation for its special significance as a richly lyric Word of the Lord to his covenant people, especially those who are bound, or about to be, by the covenant of marriage. This vital interpersonal message must in turn also be communicated in a correspondingly dynamic manner via translation to readers—but ideally to *hearers*—in their language.

6.1 Two outstanding stylistic features

The present chapter[2] is but a partial introduction to a most weighty subject, namely, the verbalization of what is assumed to be a *divine perspective on human love* and male-female relationships within marriage. I will not deal directly with such important background topics as theories regarding authorship, the date and place of writing, the setting and circumstances of composition, or even matters of a text-critical nature.[3] Thus, my study charts merely one possible course through the verbal garden of this fascinating, multifaceted, deeply figurative composition. I will discuss three primary and closely interrelated aspects of the Song: a pair of key stylistic features, which helps us to establish an overall *structural outline* that leads naturally to a brief consideration of the book's *essential message*. It is hoped that this overview will help to stimulate readers and listeners alike to make their own way more confidently, not only through the poetic text itself, but also with reference to the vast array of literature that has been written about the Song, ranging in size and scope from succinct overviews (e.g., Brenner 1989) to the massive tome of Marvin Pope (1977).

The pair of poetic techniques that are especially important in the Song of Solomon and have been selected for study, are supported by the insights of four prominent literary critics of the Bible: Robert Alter (1985), Harold Fisch (1988), Francis Landy (1987), and Leland Ryken (1992). They are *poetic imagery* (primarily simile/metaphor) and *linguistic recursion* (phonological, syntactic, and lexical). The first is probably the most captivating and immediately distinctive. Who can fail to wonder at the beauty and complexity of the various sets of sense-provoking images that sequence, overlap, and often merge with one another—from the 'kisses' of the opening lines to the 'spices' at the end?[4] However, the second device, verbal recursion, is probably even more important since it not only encompasses the former (along with other stylistic characteristics, formal, e.g., terseness, as well as semantic, e.g., hyperbole), but also plays a major role in the thematic expression, the structural arrangement, and the rhetorical dynamics of the Song as a whole. Lexical reiteration is typically embedded within Hebrew poetic parallelism, but in this text it is manifested not only

---

[2] This is a revised and updated version of Wendland 1995a.

[3] For a helpful discussion of these and related issues, consult the major critical commentaries, such as Fox 1985, Garrett 1993 and Longman 2001. I might simply note here that "[t]he Hebrew text (MT) of the Song of Songs is without major problems [and] is strongly supported by the versions" (Longman 2001:19).

[4] For an overview of the figurative language of the SoS and its ANE background, see Keel 1994:25–29; more detailed explanations with reference to specific passages are found throughout this commentary. However, while well documented and argued, Keel's interpretations are frequently unsatisfying because they give preference to the SoS's literary relationship with its secular or pagan religious setting rather than the book's canonical context.

syntagmatically in the typically paired lines, but also paradigmatically in strategic positions throughout the text. Thus, imagery in combination with recursion contributes to the Song's 'golden style,' which Ryken calls "the most purely poetic thing in the Bible" (1992:276). It is sensuous, pictorial, passionate, pastoral, and symbolic: "...a poetry full of emotional and imagistic fireworks...in keeping with the subject matter of the book" (ibid., 276–277).

Imagery and recursion, which are also manifested prominently in other types of Hebrew verse, will be described below in a non-technical way and illustrated by selected examples. The various passages cited will also suggest how these devices function on a local as well as on a global level within the complete discourse, a subject that will be summarized in a consideration of the Song's manifold message in section 6.5.

6.2 Imagery

"Certainly, the Song is a riot of images; it has a greater abundance and confusion of similes and metaphors than any other book in the Hebrew Scriptures" (Fisch 1988:90). The imagery in the Song of Solomon is of two kinds: figurative and non-figurative (or literal). It is based on the central areas of ancient life in Israel: the royal court, family affairs, nature, the physical environment, and military matters. The appeal is primarily to the sense of sight, but this is often accompanied by sensory evocation of a tactile, olfactory, auditory, gustatory, and spatial quality (e.g., 8:1–3). Figurative imagery consists most commonly of metaphor and its more overt cousin, simile.[5] Both are figures of comparison, but a *metaphor* is direct (hence usually more forceful), whereas a *simile* is always marked by some explicit term of comparison, such as 'like' or 'as'.[6] The difference is illustrated in the two examples below (given in literal translation) with the figure indicated by boldface and the marker by italics:

---

[5] "[W]hat is characteristic of Hebrew poetry is the choice and number of similes and metaphors that help to give the poetry its special style.... It is often fruitful to look for links between metaphors. They can therefore also function as referential markers that point us to other texts where the same or similar metaphors are used. These intertexts can then act as keys to interpreting the text in question" (Nielsen 2009:298–299; see section 6.3.1).

[6] The nature and function of living (as opposed to 'dead') metaphor is well summarized by Longman (2001:13, my added comments in brackets): "Metaphor catches our attention by the disparity between the two objects [being compared] and the daring suggestion of similarity [or even equivalence/correspondence]. Readers [or hearers] must ponder and reflect on the point [or possible points] of the similarity and, by so doing, explore multiple levels of meaning and experience the emotional overtones of the metaphor."

6.2 Imagery

> I [am] a **crocus** of the Sharon,
> a **lily** of the valleys. (2:1)
> *Like* a **lily** among the thorns,
> so [is] my darling among the maidens. (2:2)

In the first passage the woman ('I' – the topic of the figure) likens herself to two wild flowers of Palestine (the image, here doubled). The comparison is direct, so this is a metaphor. But what is the basis, or ground, of the resemblance? This frequently presents a problem for all such analogical figures in the Song, namely, the matter of specifying in what way the topic is like the image, which in sum total constitutes "a curious mixture of pastoral, urban, and regal allusions" (Alter 1985:186) to both an age and an environment that is no longer familiar to most readers. In this instance, the intended sense is not too difficult to perceive: the woman coyly describes herself as being as common or plain looking as an ordinary wildflower out in the field. To which her lover responds demurringly with a corresponding figure, this time, a simile. If she is homely, he says, then she is still outstanding among all other women in the world, who are as ugly as 'thorns' in comparison.

We are so far removed from the original setting of the poem that this conceptual linkage is in many cases no longer obvious, as it undoubtedly was to the first listeners of the Song.[7] Sometimes the ground of comparison may be at least partially indicated in the immediate co-text of the figure. Other passages of Scripture in which the image occurs may also help to clarify the reference. Scholars and commentators who have studied the biblical and ANE background of a particular text, corpus, time period, or location (e.g., Keel 1994) can sometimes assist in the process of interpretation. But all too often even the experts do not agree among themselves, or they are far too speculative in view of the available evidence, thus leaving one to make one's own decision. In this connection, we note the jarring incongruity of some of the combinations of images, or the seemingly strange rationale that joins certain images with their topics. We see both problems illustrated in the following passage: how, we might ask, could a woman's navel be compared to a 'goblet of wine', or her waist to a 'sheaf of wheat'?

---

[7] A foreign phonology might also be involved, for example in SoS 1:3, which states literally 'Your name is an oil poured out'. "This is a somewhat surprising expression unless one is familiar with Hebrew, where the word 'name' *(shêm)* resembles the word 'oil' *(shemen)*, creating a wordplay that links the two. Thus, listening to the beloved's name is similar to the pleasure of being anointed with fragrant oil" (Nielsen 2009:295).

> Your *navel* [is] a round goblet, never lacking fine wine;
> Your *waist* [is] a heap of wheat, encircled by lilies. (7:2)

In fact, a rendering somewhat closer to the literal Hebrew might even sound like an insult to any sensitive lady nowadays, that is, 'navel' (שֹׁר) = umbilical cord (Prov. 3:8; Ezek. 16:4); 'waist' (בֶּטֶן) = belly, womb (Job 3:10–11; Ps. 139:13). Although the precise ground of comparison between these two extended images and their topics is no longer clear to us, the general sense in the present context is more obvious: these are euphemistic ways of referring to a woman's sexual organs—a veritable 'garden' of pleasures (6:2) whose produce never ceases either to intoxicate (wine) or to sustain (wheat) the male species. As for the 'lilies' (שׁוֹשַׁנִּים), they appear to be added, as elsewhere (for example, 6:2-3), simply as a way of highlighting the intimate sexual relationship that is being referred to. Certainly there is no insult intended in the original; in fact, quite the opposite. Unfortunately, most contemporary readers, in English at least, are probably completely unaware of the desired sense and significance.

The unique thing about the usage of imagery in the Song of Solomon, whether *conventional*, *intensive*, or *innovative* in nature (the difference being almost impossible to determine in the absence of a sufficient corpus of comparative data), is the *diversity* as well as the *density* with which it occurs. Isolated figures are the great exception, and most metaphors and especially similes are found in concentrated clusters—one after the other as a person reads or hears the poem (that is, diachronically), but one on top of another as a given description takes shape in the listener's mind (that is, synchronically). The images therefore tend to merge with one another to create a total impression and to evoke a particular atmosphere or mood. This sort of figurative flexibility and creativity is manifested especially in the distinctive physical portraits that describe the 'beloved' (4:1-7, 11-15; 6:4-9; 7:1-8) and her 'lover' (5:10-16). The latter is exceptional for this type of poetry, since the norm is for the man lavishly to praise his woman. Here he is portrayed by her in terms that evoke the splendid image of some golden temple statue:

The Ideal Man

A	B
His arms are rounded gold,	set with jewels
His body is ivory work,	encrusted with sapphires
His legs are alabaster columns,	set upon bases of gold
His appearance is like Lebanon,	choice as the cedars

(5:14–15, New Revised Standard Version [NRSV])

6.2 Imagery

We observe that each initial half-line (A) is expanded in the second half (B) by further description. It should be noted that strict synonymous parallelism such as we find in the Psalms is relatively rare in the Song. Robert Alter characterizes the 'additive' variety that we usually have here as involving a "prepositional or adverbial modifier of the first verse [that is, (A)]" (1985:187). When compounded, as it often is, this procedure produces a "flamboyant elaboration of the metaphor [or simile], in which the metaphoric image takes over the foreground" (ibid., 200–201), thus drawing attention to the poetic process of figuration itself in relation to its object. However, a more basic semantic intent may also be operative over the parallels, that is, to express a *consequential* (cause-effect) complementation of some kind in addition to the topical attribution illustrated above, for example:

> Perhaps **reason**:
> Let him kiss me with [the] kisses of his mouth,
> *for* your lovemaking [is] better than wine (1:2).

> Or **purpose**:
> I went down to [the] grove of nut tree[s]
> *in order to* look at the shoots of the valley,
> *in order to* look at the bud[s] of the vine[s],
> (to see whether) the pomegranates bloomed (6:11).

> Or **condition**:
> *If* you do not know yourself, [most] beautiful among women,
> [*then*] follow for yourself the tracks of the sheep...(1:8).

This fundamental cause-effect sequence, expressed both figuratively and non-figuratively in such a diversity of ways, serves to reinforce the Song's central theme, namely, the many different faces of love (or human affection and its manifestation).

Frequently, as is typical of biblical parallelism, the (B) portion of a couplet incorporates an intensified reiteration or re-expression of the image introduced in (A), for example:

> Just look at you, my beautiful one, my darling;
> Just look at you, my beautiful one,
>   *Your eyes* [are like] *doves!* (1:15).

In the preceding passage, as in most instances, the intensification is effected by some manner of specification, that is, the woman's external 'beauty' is concentrated in her 'eyes' [which are gentle, shining, and/or prominent = the probable compound ground of comparison]. A re-expression in the (B) colon normally presents some additional information, as we see in the next example:

> Catch for us the foxes,—the *little* foxes,
> that ruin the vineyards, yes, our *vineyards* [in] *bloom*! (2:15).

One half-line overlaps with another in the form of incremental repetition to develop progressively the prevailing imagery and also to heighten it. At times the amorous scene being set is almost narrative-like in nature (cf. Alter 1985:187–188; Fisch 1988:85):

> Hark! [Listen, it's] my lover!
> Look! Here he comes—
> > leaping over the mountains,
> > bounding over the hills!
> My lover is like a gazelle,
> > or a young buck [among] the stags.
> Look! Here [now] he stands behind our wall,
> > gazing through the windows,
> > peering through the lattices (2:8–9).

At several points in the book, the figures seem almost to fade away—perhaps for dramatic contrast—and an actual mini-narrative is recorded, apparently as part of a dream recollection by the beloved (3:1–4; 5:2–7). On other occasions, notably in the personal portraits referred to above, an extended description is presented, that is, by means of a spatial, rather than a temporal, development. For example, in chapter 7:1–6 where we begin at the woman's 'beautiful feet' and move up from there to the 'legs', the 'navel', the 'waist', the 'two breasts', the 'neck', the 'eyes', the 'nose', and finally we reach, 'on top of [her] head', the 'flowing locks', which are fittingly described further as being a luxurious 'deep purple' in color. At this point we are confronted with a little surprise, when as a climax to this exquisite poem in praise of the woman's attractiveness, the lover and singer suddenly introduces himself with the disabling admission that he finds himself like:

> ...a king held captive *by the tresses* (that is, of hair) (7:6).

6.2 Imagery

Thus, this greatest of songs does not consist of pure descriptive characterization, as may at first seem to be the case. Instead, it features all sorts of unexpected twists and surprises that captivate the close reader and careful listener alike, even as the woman's lovely locks (and looks overall) completely captured the heart of her lover.

As already suggested, there are certain places in the Song where the concentration of figurative language is somewhat reduced. This does not mean that there is no more imagery—only that it is mainly of a non-figurative nature, for example, in the first dream report:

> Let me get up now and move about the city,
>   through the streets and through the squares;
> Let me search around for the one whom my heart loves!
>   I searched for him, but I did not find him (3:2).

In fact, this entire dream (if that is what it is meant to be) may be construed as an enlarged image—an imaginative depiction, either of the woman's great longing to be with her man, of a disappointment due to a planned meeting that did not materialize, or of some problem which had led to tension, perhaps even a sudden estrangement, in their relationship. Thus the poetic text segment (strophe) in 3:1-4 is to be interpreted on the whole as a generic image, the individual details of which function together to relate a single moving experience. A similar comment could be made about the non-figurative expressions that occur in the Song's various descriptive and panegyric (praise) poems. In such cases, however, the literal is so intertwined with the figurative that the two types of speech merge to form a composite, conceptually enhanced picture of a particular event, emotion, circumstance, and/or setting. For example:

> Dark [am] I, but lovely, O Daughters of Jerusalem,
>   like the tents of Kedar, like the tent curtains of Solomon.
> Do not stare at me because I am dark,
>   because the sun has tanned me.
> The sons of my mother were angry with me;
>   they made me care for the vineyards—
>   my own vineyard I could not care for! (1:5-6).

Whether or not the woman's soliloquy had any basis in physical or historical fact is not the issue, for this set piece (1:5-7)—the apparent literal statements as well as the figures of speech—has a higher literary purpose in keeping with the lyric genre of which it is a part. The aim here, in contrast to the book's opening words of exultation (1:2-4), is to express the maiden's modesty as she likens herself (more specifically, her physical features, that is, 'vineyard') to her companions (rivals?) and as she confesses her assumed unworthiness in comparison with her beau, who of course responds with just the opposite sentiments (1:8-11; cf. 2:1-2). Such graphic contrasts and hyperboles are typical of love language and pastoral poetry the world over. The nature of this complex sort of imagery and the intricate poetic form in which it is set reinforce one another to suggest a deeper, symbolic level of meaning for the Song as a whole, one that will be considered more fully during a discussion of its communicative function in section 6.5.

6.3 Recursion

"The only substantive grounds for considering the Song to be a unity is the density of repetition within it" (Landy 1983:36). This conclusion may be stated more positively: there is so much reiteration—both formal and semantic, of sound, sense, and syntax—in the Song of Solomon on all levels of discourse organization and throughout the text that there can be little doubt that the entire book is the product of a single author-artist. It would take a full-length study to explore this subject adequately; I can but scratch the surface with a few observations as to how such recursion, whether exact or synonymous, serves to structure both the text as a whole and also its constituent parts. Since, as was pointed out above, figurative imagery is so pervasive in the Song, it may come as no surprise to learn that some key aspects of this language perform a demarcative purpose by means of their placement on the principal borders of discourse organization, whether to begin a section (strophe, stanza; i.e., *aperture*) or to conclude one (*closure*).

Many commentators have despaired of discovering a larger principle of arrangement in the Song. The following pessimistic, postmodern-like statement is typical:

> The Song does not follow any definite plan. It is a collection of songs united only by their common theme of love...it is useless to look for any marked progression of thought or action from one [poem] to the next...[Rather, the text offers] a choice according to circumstance or audience. ('Introduction to the Song of Songs' in the annotated *Jerusalem Bible*, p. 1029)

Similarly, the introduction in the Catholic study edition of the *Good News Translation* (GNT) assumes an amorphous organization: "This book

6.3 Recursion

is not easily outlined, and various schemes can be used" (p. 562).[8] But the question is: are all such 'schemes' of equal value? Do they all 'mean' the same thing in the end? Can each one be equally defended or substantiated? The fact is, however, that structure does make a difference, for "...the general stance we adopt profoundly influences the way we interpret individual verses and words within the book...behind each of these different ways of dividing the text there lie decisions as to how we are to understand it" (Davidson 1986:99, 102).

In a careful and generally illuminating study of "centripetal and centrifugal structures in biblical poetry," Daniel Grossberg concludes that the Song of Solomon in particular exhibits "a structural character nearer to the centrifugal extreme of the continuum with strong balancing centripetal features" (1989:56). A *centrifugal* type of structure is one that is characterized by "the loose connection of heterogeneous parts, the lack of strong terminal closure, and the accumulation of new and unusual metaphors" (ibid., 6). *Centripetal* texts, on the other hand, "display an ordered and goal-directed movement and completeness...a unified whole marked by formal figures of closure, for example, refrains and strong final close" (6–7). According to Grossberg's analysis, the Song's organization is "antiteleological" in nature, one that "is essentially open and loose" and teeming "with phonological, lexical, syntactic and imagistic associations—inextricably bound with no logical order" (57, 70–71). As was noted above, however, though the imagery of the Song is extremely diverse, it is all unified under a common subject—and generically typical (that is, lyric pastoral), which would make it less disjunctive in tone (61) than it may at first appear, or sound.

It will also be demonstrated below that, while the book may not manifest a prominent teleological movement in the manner of a prose narrative text, there is clearly a unified, cumulative progression of thought that does come to a peak near the end of the work. The primary mode of arrangement, as is typical with lyric poetry, is largely taxonomic or paradigmatic, rather than syntagmatic, but the consequent organization is still tightly integrated by the progressive exchange of speakers (though the boundaries of where individual speeches begin and end may be debated) and as clearly demarcated as any so-called centripetal text. In fact, of the "partial catalogue of centripetal and centrifugal features" outlined by Grossberg (ibid., 8–12), the Song gives clear evidence of all

---

[8] The fact that "[n]o two scholars agree on where every section begins and ends" (Schwab 2008:748) does not vitiate or detract from one's efforts to discern the macro- and microstructure of SoS. Schwab summarizes the diversity that is apparent in seven scholarly proposals, including his own (ibid., 747).

those attributed to a centripetal arrangement, except his numbers 9 (a *linear* plot development) and 11 (manifesting an objectively demonstrable *historicity*). To be sure, the text does display a palpable "poetic tension" (ibid., 57), but this does not seem to be the product of conflicting internal centripetal and centrifugal stylistic forces. It appears rather to be the result of a certain tension that arises due to the two principal levels of thematic meaning according to which the work may be construed, that is, the literal *human* (physical) versus the symbolic *divine* (spiritual) planes. And even this seemingly contrastive pairing can be shown to be complementary, as discussed in section 6.4.

To be sure, a "loose collection or concatenation of poems" (Snaith 1993:7) cannot be expected to exhibit much overall structural organization. But is that what we are dealing with in the case of the Song? How then can one analyze such a text? One answer is: to determine the literary structure of a book like the Song, we must turn to an examination of the text's primary genre (Longman 2001:21)[9] and content (Bullock 1979:237). But the genre proposed by most scholars, 'love poetry' (see section 6.3.1.1) is ill-defined, and content on its own is not sufficient, especially in the case of a book like the Song of Solomon, for there is but a single central topic throughout, namely, female-male love, and the text plays many artistic variations on this dominant theme. If content is assumed to include the characters, or participants, of the poem, as well as the context, that is, their situational setting, then we do have a criterion of some value because a shift in either one or both of these features would normally designate a structural boundary of some kind. But there must be something more concrete to use as a cue, some formal marker(s) that provide a less arbitrary way of segmenting the composition, or which operate in the absence of any substantial modification of content. Here in the Song, as in virtually every other biblical text, whether written essentially as poetry or prose, I have found patterned recursion to be such a diagnostic criterion that illuminates the discourse structure, at least in its broad outline.

While I certainly cannot claim that my method offers the perfect (all-explanatory, fully defensible) key, I would like to show how selective recursion can give us a significant insight into the organization of this enigmatic book. On this basis then, I will propose a structural framework that organizes the entire text in a meaningful way, and does it in keeping with the central message that is being conveyed. Certain lapses and indeterminacies

---

[9] "Proper genre identification unlocks the proper interpretation of the book" (Longman 2001:21). However, Longman is forced to admit that "the individual poems are of uncertain and often even doubtful connection with one another....this psalter is not clearly delineated" (ibid., 43).

6.3 Recursion

remain, of course, and these will no doubt provoke further developments, revisions, and corrections of what is presented below. In order to limit the scope of this study, my discussion of recursion will be more or less restricted to issues of a larger compositional ('stanzaic') nature. After an overview of some of the primary types of repetition and related criteria that are useful in discourse demarcation, a summary outline of the Song's organization will be given. A discussion of the major implications of both of the work's outstanding stylistic features, namely, imagery and recursion, will then follow—before some concluding consideration is given to translating the Song into another language and cultural setting.

6.3.1 Intertextual recursion

The Song of Solomon does not present us with a style or structure that is *sui generis*, for like the other forms of ancient Hebrew literature, it was not created in a literary vacuum. Rather, it was subject to important, though largely ill-defined influences of both a biblical and an extrabiblical nature.

6.3.1.1 Extrabiblical intertextuality

Detailed comparative studies such as those of Fox (1985), Long (2008), Longman (2001), and Murphy (1990), for example, have pointed out a number of the striking similarities in form and content that exist between the Song and certain genres of Babylonian and Egyptian poetry. Carr (1982) provides a handy summary of "the love poetry genre in the Old Testament and the ancient Near East," which he regards as being a subspecies of "wisdom literature" (1982:491). He lists such common features as: an ordered arrangement involving the alternation of female and male speeches in a two-to-one ratio (surprising, perhaps, for a male-oriented society); "some sort of progressive movement from one place to another" (ibid., 493); the prevailing "search" (seek/find) motif (ibid., 494); the frequent use of euphemism and double entendre; specific vocabulary items (from semantic domains such as: kinship terms, plants, animals, birds, perfumes, jewelry, commerce, geography, and places); and so-called *topoi*, or preferred topics (e.g., the uniqueness of the loved one, love sickness, playful teasing, obstacles to love, lovemaking in a sylvan hideaway, and the appeal of "voices"; cf. Murphy 1981:102). The apparent presence of several speaking parts (e.g., 'lover,' 'beloved,' 'friends') suggests some type of lyric drama as an organizing framework for the Song. In fact, "…the presence of speakers, dialogue, and audiences gives the book an unmistakable dramatic quality" (Weems 1997:372; cf.

Delitzsch 1984:9).[10] However, other commentators see a number of major problems with such an approach to the SoS; for example, the absence of convincing extratextual evidence; the lack of a real narrative plot with a narrative voice or a definite progression of events having an obvious conflict, climax, and resolution; no division into acts or scenes; the nonexistence of precise speech assignments; and no stage directions (Carr 1984:33–34; cf. Longman 2001:39–43)

In addition to the basic similarities to alien amatory literature, it is important to draw attention to several crucial differences in content, form, and style, which considered together have a bearing on the most important characteristic of all—*function*. Thus, on the whole the SoS is essentially didactic and not intended for entertainment, as in Egyptian love songs, for example.[11] Furthermore, in the Song there is no reference or even a solid allusion to the cultic fertility rituals involving a mythological "sacred marriage" of the gods or some sort of an "enthronement festival" which served as a background to much of the Near Eastern love poetry (Carr 1982:491; 1984:49; Kinlaw 1991:1205). In addition, Carr notes the absence in the Song of other typical elements such as an explicit mention of the deity, the personification of nature, scenes of drunkenness and seduction, or the presence of a "love triangle" (1984:39–40). A very obvious formal difference is that, whereas the foreign "love poems are relatively short" (Carr 1982:491), the Song is clearly a carefully unified and integrated piece of much longer duration. Moreover, the comparative richness in its treatment of the common theme of human love and the surpassing nature of its literary artistry is apparent to even the casual reader. In short then, I would conclude along with Harold Fisch that "…the Song really stands out as unique. It touches heights and depths that are unknown in love poetry of the ancient Middle East, indeed in love poetry of any time" (1988:85). All this would indeed suggest a unique or at least a thematically enriched message and purpose as well (to be discussed in sections 6.5 and 6.6).

---

[10] "Audiences (and readers) are expected to be able to perceive within the poem's 'progression' all the ambiguities, uncertainties, tensions, shortcomings, and suspense of love itself. In other words, drama and contents come together in the Song of Songs to create a poem intent on gripping its audience" (Weems 1997:372).

[11] Thus in the SoS there is an oblique "intention to teach [for example, the 'friends' or members of 'the chorus'], by example and admonition, the nature of love and its appropriate behavior" (Longman 2001:54). The 'implied audience' was probably young adults—those about to get married (betrothed) as well as newlyweds, but ultimately including married partners of any age, all of whom are encouraged (by pattern rather than precept) to live, and to love, in the light of the principles of Yahweh, as recorded in the sacred texts of the Law and the Prophets.

6.3 Recursion

Studies of such broader literary parallels are complemented by those that delineate some of the different kinds of poetry which one or more passages of the Song appear to manifest. These so-called 'genres' may be rather general and inclusive in nature, for example, "love poetry" (an anthology, Longman 2001:48; Carr 1984:37–41) or "pastoral poetry" (Ryken 1992:274–275). Alternatively, certain subtypes are posited, usually with reference to a specific passage, such as the "descriptive song," or *wasf*, a feature-by-feature lyric portrait of the physical charms of the loved one (Landy 1983:75–76, 85–86; Brenner 1989:43–44), the *epithalamium*, or "wedding song" (Ryken ibid., 273), a song of invitation, longing, or admiration, the boast or a tease (Murphy 1981:101–102; Ryken ibid., 283–287; Longman 2001:49). Particularly interesting is the genre (or is it rather a more all-embracing literary style?) that Fisch terms a "dream vision" (1988:99). This manner of poetic composition bears a definite resemblance to the stream-of-consciousness technique of narrative prose (cf. Kinlaw 1991:1211; Ryken ibid., 278; see also section 7.2.3 with reference to Ecclesiastes). Viewing the Song in this latter light helps to explain some of its ambiguity and indeterminacy with regard to both form and content. Perhaps, as Fisch suggests, we ought to construe the entire book from such a perspective (1988:98, 89):

> ...the only way to account for the amazing richness of the poem's imagery and also for the effect of this imaginative overspill is to see it composed in the manner of a dream...in formal terms the poem seems to be a jumble of different lyrics and snatches of story...[or] rather the shifting iridescent movement of a dream where stories merge into one another and identities change and combine.

Whether or not the Song is all a big, beautiful dream (including a few nightmarish lapses, e.g., 3:1–3), the purpose of this study is to show that its overall structure may have a little more shape than it is usually given credit for. Furthermore, this overarching, organizational framework is one that is concrete enough to remain in place once the analyst awakens the next day.

6.3.1.2 Biblical intertextuality

From a general sort of imitative recursion which emanates from extrabiblical sources, we turn to that which stems from within the Hebrew canon itself. In this respect, an intertextual comparative study reveals many allusions, as well as a number of formally distinct parallels, though apparently no actual quotations. Carr, for example, observes a number of general similarities to Psalm 45, which is also a lyric that celebrates the love between a man and a woman (1984:3). But he goes on to point out a number of significant differences (ibid., 30–31), in particular with respect to the Song's vocabulary, which does not reproduce any of the important cultic or theological terms that are found in the Psalm (ibid., 28–29). Brenner is of the opinion that Hosea 1–3 and the Song of Solomon are "genetically and stylistically" related: "Both seem to have originated in a common tradition of Hebrew love poetry, of which the Song of Solomon is the most extensive remnant" (1989:80); Weems (1997:369) focuses on Hosea 2. Fisch (1988:87) cites several noteworthy instances of the "seek and [not] find" motif in the Scriptures (that is, Hos. 2:7; Deut. 4:29), and he also sees a resemblance in the triadic relationship between God (the groom), his people (the bride), and the land of Israel as reflected in Isaiah 62 (ibid., 92–94).[12]

Another prominent correspondence lies in the Song's extensive 'garden' (and related, for example, 'fountain/spring', 'trees', 'fruit', 'wall') imagery and the description of the Garden of Eden in Genesis 2–3 and in many other OT passages (cf. Carr ibid., 56; Landy 1987:312–313, 318; Brenner 1989:83–84; Sailhamer 1994:360). Thus Kinlaw remarks: "In a sense there is...an Edenic quality to much of the Song of Songs, almost as if it were a commentary on Genesis 2:18–25" (1991:1207). This metaphorical garden is in turn linked up with some of the familiar associations of fertility figuratively attributed to 'Lebanon' (for example, 1 Kgs. 10:17, 21; Pss. 72:16, 104:16; Hos. 14:5–7; cf. Landy 1983:90–92, 102–103).

A number of commentators have noted the similarities between the Song of Solomon and other instances of the so-called 'wisdom' texts with which it is grouped in the Hebrew canon (that is, the corpus of Writings or *Kithuvim*) and even more closely in English Bibles. Thus genre "links the poetry of the Song of Solomon with biblical Wisdom literature, with which Hebrew poetry is generically associated" (Brenner 1989:79). Alter concludes that the Song's "continuous celebration of passion and its pleasures makes this the most consistently secular of all biblical texts—even more so than Proverbs, which...also stresses the fear of the Lord..." (1985:185). But as Davidson aptly observes, "The distinction that we tend to make between the sacred and the secular, the religious and the non-religious, would have been quite meaningless to the wise men in Israel" (1986:99). Murphy

---

[12] Longman gives a good overview of the divine-human relationship as portrayed in Scripture through the metaphor of marriage (2001:67–69). He comes to this conclusion: although one should not "read a theological meaning onto the surface of the [Song]....[when] read within the context of the canon, the Song has a clear and obvious relevance to the divine-human relationship. After all, throughout the Bible God's relationship to humankind is likened to a marriage" (ibid., 67).

6.3 Recursion

also sees a link with Proverbs in that the Song of Songs may be viewed as "an expansion of the wonder perceived in Prov. 30:19, the way of a man with a maiden, and expressed also in Prov. 5:18-19" (1981:104). Indeed, the proverbial search for 'Lady Wisdom' could be easily metaphorized to depict a marriage relationship (e.g., Prov. 4:5–9; cf. 3:13–17). Put somewhat differently we could say that "the book is an object lesson, an extended proverb or parable (*mashal*) illustrating the rich wonders of human love, itself a gift of God's love" (LaSor, Hubbard, and Bush 1982:610).[13] Fee and Stuart, some of the strongest proponents of the proverbial connection of the Song, call it an example of "lyric wisdom" which presents the listener with some "godly choices" (1993:226, 230):

> This is similar to what we have already said about interpreting Proverbs—they are true as suggestions and generalizations rather than precise statements of universal fact. One of the closest parallels in Scripture to the Song is Proverbs 1–9. There one finds poems about the attractiveness of wisdom and the counter-attractiveness of folly, in a manner that suggests lyrically, rather than propositionally, what our right choices ought to be.

The style of Proverbs is clearly reflected in passages such as SoS 8:7 (NRSV):

> Many waters cannot quench love,
>   neither can floods drown it.
> If one offered for love all the wealth of his house,
>   it would be utterly scorned.

Of course, the implicit manner of instruction in the Song differs greatly from the overt precepts of Proverbs, but given that "[w]isdom is the application of God's will to the nitty-gritty of life,...[b]y describing a love that is intense, exclusive, and faithful in spite of obstacles, the Song indirectly but passionately reveals God's will for that special relationship between a man and a woman" (Longman 2001:49), as constituted and covenanted in marriage.

Surprisingly perhaps, Landy (1987) observes a correlation with yet another book traditionally attributed to Solomon: "...to Ecclesiastes' thesis that everything is illusory the Song answers with one possible antithesis. Like Ecclesiastes it is a work of comparison, though one that results not in

---

[13] Schwab also highlights the possible *didactic* function of SoS: "In order to break the hold of Baalism on the people, a very different interpretation of sexuality had to be asserted and taught and embraced. ... Song of Songs seems to be a sampling of a Yahwistic understanding of human sexuality, seen against the backdrop of the polytheistic fertility cult" (2008:745).

confusion but in cumulative affirmation" (318).¹⁴ More specifically, Archer finds "a considerable similarity in vocabulary and syntax between the Song of Solomon and Ecclesiastes" (1964:489). Such connections with Israel's wider wisdom tradition lend further support to the suggestion that the theme of the Song involves considerably more than meets the eye, and that one will profit much by delving more deeply into its structure and message.

6.3.2 Intratextual recursion

The Song of Songs is a veritable sonic and sensual maze of verbal recursion. The discourse is permeated with the reiterated imagery of love, a vital stylistic feature which develops as well as reinforces the central theme. This superfluity of form and content, I would argue, also gives the work a certain thematic (symbolic) import that rises above the ordinary referential level of the text—in effect moving it from the purely human to the divine sphere of thematic significance. The repetition is both syntagmatic and paradigmatic in nature. In other words, it is clearly evident sequentially as the discourse dialogue poetically unfolds. It is also manifested less obviously as the various topics and motifs keep recurring, often at significant junctures within the text, thus building incremental mounds of meaning that resonate with one another in ever widening circles of sense, sentiment, and relevance.

To some extent, the repetitive quality of the Song was exemplified during the earlier survey of its manifold imagery in section 6.2. That discussion will be supplemented here with a few additional passages which illustrate its diversity and artistry on the microstructure of discourse. The main purpose of this section then will be to demonstrate the operation of recursion on the macrostructural level where it functions as a primary literary

---

[14] In contrast to Ecclesiastes, however, "Song of Songs introduces the reader to the non-public world of ancient Israel" (Weems 1997:363). Furthermore, and perhaps more significantly by way of contrast with Ecclesiastes, in the SoS the female voice leads and predominates throughout the book. "In fact, the protagonist's voice in Song of Songs is the only unmediated female voice in all of Scripture," and this point of view is reinforced by the text's "strong female imagery" (ibid., 364). The juxtaposition of these two books in the Hebrew Scriptures (MT as well as the LXX) may even lead one to this conclusion: "As meditations of a woman's heart, Song of Songs might have been viewed as the feminine counterpart to...Ecclesiastes" (ibid., 364), that is, as a passionate personalized reflection on traditional religious 'wisdom' and conventional attitudes towards life's most intimate relationships and experiences.

Longman makes the following noteworthy observations about the canonical placement of the Song: "While in the English canon it follows Ecclesiastes, in the Hebrew it precedes it. In the latter, as a result, we have the interesting and surely intentional order of Proverbs, Ruth, and the Song. Proverbs, it will be remembered, concludes with the poem concerning the virtuous woman (31:10–31). Ruth and the Song, then, both present virtuous and assertive women for our contemplation" (2001:2).

6.3 Recursion

compositional device to segment, unify, and shape the Song as a literarily complete, esthetically satisfying, and communicatively purposeful whole.

6.3.2.1 Microstructural recursion

The composition of biblical Hebrew verse is characterized by the coupling of paired (sometimes triadic or isolated) lines (cola) which normally bear a close semantic and frequently also an overt formal relationship with one another, based on some type of linguistic correspondence. Synonymy is often thought of in this regard, and such similarity in content does characterize a large percentage of the bicola of a lyric work like the Psalter. But in the Song of Songs, as was already mentioned, the so-called *additive* type of parallelism predominates, particularly in its attributive and consequential varieties (Wendland 2002a:77–97). Thus an overlapping *lexical* pattern that is typical of the Song unfolds in many of the strophic segments of which it is composed. Such an incremental terracing of meaning constituents serves to highlight the totality and/or the mutuality of love in the descriptive portions of the text, for example:

> My beloved is to me a bag of myrrh
> > that lies between my breasts.
> My beloved is to me a cluster of henna blossoms
> > in the vineyards of En-gedi.
> Ah, you are beautiful, my love;
> > Ah, you are beautiful; your eyes are doves.
> > > Ah, you are beautiful, my beloved, truly lovely. (1:13–16, NRSV)

In the several narrative-like passages, on the other hand, this stylistic technique functions to accent the inexorable progression in the events being reported, that is, within the stanza/scene being depicted. These events may be portrayed as 'real' (from the character's point of view) or imaginary (that is, in a dream-like vision), for example:

> Upon my bed at night
> I sought him whom my soul loves;
> I sought him, but found him not;
> I called him, but he gave no answer.
> I will rise now and go about the city,
> > in the streets and in the squares;
> I will seek him whom my soul loves.
> I sought him, but found him not.
> The sentinels found me… (3:1–3a, NRSV)

The thematic significance of such measured repetition is pointed out by Fisch, who comments that it "suggests the unremittingness of the search, a longing ever increasing, an intensity of devotion seeking but never quite finding its embodiment in language" (1988:85). Such highly patterned lexical reiteration exists over and above the more common—but no less significant—instances of non-structured reduplication involving important roots and complete words, which produce points of intense local emphasis. In this way the Song's principal topic is announced at its very beginning:

> Indeed, your lovemaking (lit., 'loves') is better than wine...
> No wonder the maidens [all] love you...
> We will laud your lovemaking more than wine.
> How right they [all] are to love you! (1:2–4).

In the complex cases of recursion that texture and embellish the Song, syntax too is pressed into poetic service. Reiterated grammatical frames, both with and without lexical correspondence, permeate the discourse to underscore implicitly, as it were, the more overt message being lyrically conveyed. This feature is most obvious in the several praise-portraits (*wasfs*) that describe the object of the singer's desire, for example:

> Your hair [is] like a flock of the goats
>   which flows down from Mount Gilead.
> Your teeth [are] like a flock of the shearlings
>   which comes up from the washing. (4:1b–2a)

Frequently, too, we find reversed syntactic patterns or chiastic constructions which focus upon some key aspect of a poetic portrayal, for example:

> Show me *your appearance*—let me hear **your voice**,
>   for **your voice** [is] sweet—and *your appearance* [is] lovely! (2:14)

This technique of foregrounding, (highlighting certain features or aspects of a whole) can be quite impressive when such crossed constructions are combined (that is, the reversed lexical-grammatical structure is repeated), as we see in the following passage:

6.3 Recursion

A There [may be] sixty **queens** and eighty **concubines**,
    B and *virgins* [may be] without number—
        C [but] **one of a kind [is] she**,
            D *my dove,*
            D' *my perfect one,*
        C' **one of a kind [is] she**...
    B' They saw her, the *young maidens* [did], and they pronounced her fortunate,
A' the **queens** [did], and the **concubines**, they praised her (6:8–9).

Thus one chiasmus embraces another to throw the grammatical spotlight, as it were, upon the 'perfect dove' of the lover's dreams—who most certainly is worthy of 'praise'. This would be an instance of 'end stress,' where the final instance within a diachronic progression of elements receives special emphasis and is often stylistically marked accordingly.

The least obvious form of recursion, even to those who read Hebrew (unless they happen to speak or hear the text aloud, which is how the text is meant to be presented), is that of a *phonological* nature. Yet this too is an important stylistic feature of the Song of Solomon and one that not only enhances its lyric quality but also exhibits more fully its love-encased theme. A number of commentators have called attention to the ubiquitous *alliteration* that distinguishes the Song (and Hebrew parallelism in general; cf. Landy 1987:307). According to Landy (1983:96):

> Alliteration interlaces the extreme articulation of images characteristic of the *wasf* with an abstract musical sensuality, generating similes, a play of colors, voices, fusions and divisions. There is an active coherence, an implicit syntax, subtending the discrete images...[one that] couples and merges the distinct images, perceiving deeper inter-connections...

The very title to the Song (1:1) suggests the crucial compositional role that alliteration is about to play (and probably indicates that the title itself is not some later addition):

שִׁיר הַשִּׁירִים אֲשֶׁר לִשְׁלֹמֹה
shîr hashîrîm asher lishlômôh

The /sh/ (שׁ) sound is immediately picked up at the onset of the first strophe with the woman's passionate wish: יִשָּׁקֵנִי מִנְּשִׁיקוֹת 'Oh that he would kiss me with kisses...!'—and then a little later as she likens his very 'name' (שְׁמֶךָ) to a sweet-smelling 'savor' (שֶׁמֶן). This /sh/ sound, the occurrence of which is exaggerated in the Song due to the apocopation of the common relative pronoun (that is, אֲשֶׁר > -שֶׁ), reappears to mark the onset of the second strophe as the beloved laments her 'darkness' (שְׁחוֹרָה 1:5). She explains this as follows (1:6):

שֶׁאֲנִי שְׁחַרְחֹרֶת שֶׁשֱּׁזָפַתְנִי הַשָּׁמֶשׁ
"...because I am dark—the sun darkened me!"

Here we may also have an instance of sound symbolism as the phonological environment reflects, as it were, the presence of the 'sun' (שֶׁמֶשׁ). In any case, the demonstrative function of alliteration in the Song cannot be doubted, for /שׁ/ again features in the (perhaps figurative?) designations of the three major participants, that is, 'Solomon' (שְׁלֹמֹה), the 'Shulamite' (שׁוּלַמִּית; cf. 7:1—with additional /m/ alliteration), and the recurrent chorus comprised of the daughters of 'Jerusalem' (יְרוּשָׁלָםִ; for example, 1:5).

A repetition of personal pronouns also highlights the sound of the speaker, the addressee (or referent), or both participants in a given poetic speech event. This also serves to accentuate the close interpersonal interaction between them, for example:

> Oh that one could make you like a brother to me,
>   [like] he who nursed the breasts of my mother!
> [Then] should I find you in public,
> I could kiss you,
> and [people] they would not despise me.
> I would lead you, [yes] I would bring you
>   to the house of my mother [who] taught me.
> I would give you to drink of spiced wine,
>   from the nectar of my pomegranates. (8:1–2)

Such morphophonemic reiteration is a prominent aspect also of the various plays on sound that are made throughout the Song, in its pervasive *paronomasia*, or punning. By means of this device, certain key terms are made to complement each other in semantic as well as in auditory terms: for example, 'from Lebanon' (4:8, מִלְּבָנוֹן) and 'you have stirred up my heart' (4:9, לִבַּבְתִּנִי—the preceding word ends in /m/); the 'garden' (גַּן) and its 'fountain' (גַּל) in 4:12; or 'two breasts' (שְׁנֵי שָׁדַיִךְ) and the 'love-lilies' (שׁוֹשַׁנִּים) of 4:5. One of the most significant puns in the book (should it prove to be one) is the cluster of male-female antelope images that are used in the woman's reiterated adjuration (for example, 2:7): 'I charge you...by [the] gazelles (צְבָאוֹת) or by [the] does of the field (אַיְלוֹת הַשָּׂדֶה) ...'—which sound suspiciously like the important theological appellations, the LORD

6.3 Recursion

[יְהוָה] 'of Hosts' (צְבָאוֹת) and 'God Almighty' (אֵל שַׁדַּי), respectively. Could God possibly play more of a role in the underlying symbolic meaning of this Song than many have been willing to acknowledge (cf. the possible reference to 'Yah[weh]' in 8:6, that is, שַׁלְהֶבֶתְיָה 'flame of Yah')?

In any case, these skillfully integrated phonological features contribute to the overall resonant *musical* score of the Song.[15] It is truly a symphony in (Hebrew) verse—one in which the sound complements the sense as well as the imagery of the words to evoke a synesthetic whole. Francis Landy states the case more poetically (1987:306):

> The poem has an enchanting quality, whatever the precise meaning of the words, that derives in part from its musical quality, its function as voice; and in part from its imaginative play with the beauty of the world, corresponding to our own reverie on the sensations with which it continually surrounds us.

6.3.2.2 Macrostructural recursion

Macrostructural recursion, which takes the form of either exact repetition or a less precise synonymous or contrastive reiteration, is essentially an extension of the principle of lineal parallelism. This difference is that instead of the coupled lines (or cola) being found in juxtaposition, they appear at some distance removed—'displaced parallelism,' as it were. In many instances this sort of restatement—always in the dramatic form of direct discourse—does not occur arbitrarily. Rather, it is carefully positioned as an indicator of some point of special significance, either an initial or final text boundary or a place of increased importance, with regard to either content (that is, *peak*) or emotion (that is, *climax*). Such recursion serves to give shape to the text as a whole and also to its constituent segments (pericopes) on various levels of structural organization. As we shall see, the imagery that is so prominent throughout the Song also plays an important role in this compositional function because the various diagnostic parallels always manifest a certain conspicuous figurative notion.

As was already noted, for many commentators the overall structure of the Song of Solomon remains one of its enigmatic mysteries. Despite his massive study Pope, for example, is forced to confess that with regard to what he terms the "charming confusion in the Canticles [he] has not been convinced by any of the efforts to demonstrate or restore order or logical sequence and progression" (1977:54). A female perspective does not seem

---

[15] This potential musical dimension of the Song is one that may be developed more fully in certain settings of translation (see section 6.7).

to help, for Weems too concludes that "it is difficult to discern any straightforward rationale or logic to the book's structure" (1997:366). Thus, the Song is commonly regarded to be nothing more than an anthology or collection of smaller love songs that are bound together primarily by theme, emotion, subject matter, and an assortment of catchwords (for example, Snaith 1993:6; Brenner 1989:39; Falk 1990:108–109). Accordingly, Falk posits "thirty-one poems" (1988:525) including two within a single verse, that is, SoS 8:5a and 8:5b. Such an extreme disjunctive approach does not do justice to the text itself, however, for as Carr observes (1993:291):

> ...the composition as we now have it reveals a very careful arrangement of these [that is, not necessarily Falk's] units in a way that certainly forbids seeing it as a haphazard collection and almost certainly precludes mere editorial arranging of some previously selected poems.

But what sort of a structure do we have from "the hand of [this] master craftsman" (Carr 1993:291)? Here again we are unfortunately confronted with quite a broad spectrum of interpretation, much of it conflicting in nature. Murphy finds a sequence of thirty "genres which succeed each other" to comprise a complete "love song" (1981:100–101). However, the lack of any structural differentiation in this proposal does not help us much. Some, following Delitzsch, see a dramatic linear progression, consisting of from four to six major segments, for example, "The Courtship (1:2–3:5)... The Wedding (3:6–5:1)...The Maturation of the Marriage (5:2–8:4)...The Conclusion (8:5–7)...The Epilogue (8:8–14)" (Deere 1985:1010–1011). Bullock accounts for the lack of a prominent story line by viewing "the Song as an ancient lyrical ballad, the narrative of which was known to the original audience but has now been lost" (1979:238). Certainly there is not enough actual narrative present within the text to support a credible diachronic framework, let alone a plot reconstruction. Other scholars have looked for a concentric or chiastic method of organization, perhaps because it is so perspicuous elsewhere in the Hebrew Scriptures, in prose as well as poetry (cf. Welch 1981:chs. 4–5). Thus Carr postulates that the Song "is constructed in chiastic form with the individual units arranged symmetrically around a central pivot" (1984:46), as shown below (from Carr 1993:291):

I. Anticipation (1:2–2:7)
II. Found, and Lost–and Found (2:8–3:5)
III. Consummation (3:6–5:1)
IV. Lost–and Found (5:2–8:4)
V. Affirmation (8:5–14)

6.3 Recursion

However, this structure is partially vitiated by his subsequent "detailed outline of the book," which is basically sequential in its formation (Carr 1993:292–293). Most other proposals for some sort of introverted arrangement (for example, Shea 1980) are "marred by arbitrariness and an attempt to force the units to fit the [desired] schema" (Grossberg 1989:69; cf. Landy 1983:40). A more credible structural outline is found in the following scheme (adapted from R.L. Alden, as reproduced in Garrett 1993:376), which indicates how the entire book may be viewed on the basis of *key terms* that, taken together and in conjunction with each other, lend an essential cohesion and coherence to the whole as a compositional unity:

```
A  1:1–4a 'take me away'
  B  1:4b friends speak
    C  1:5–7 'my own vineyard'
      D  1:8–14 'breasts', 'silver', 'we will make'
        E  1:15–22 'house'
          F  2:3–7 'his left arm', 'daughters of Jerusalem...so desires', 'apple', 'love'
            G  2:8–13 'fragrance', 'come my darling', 'blossoming'
              H  2:14–15 'vineyards', 'show me'
                I  2:16–17 'my lover is mine'
                  Ja  3:1–5 'the watchman found me'
                  Jb  3:6–11 description of the carriage, 'gold', 'Lebanon',
                              'daughters of Jerusalem'
                  Jc  4:1–7 description of the girl, 'your eyes...hair...teeth'
                    K  4:8–15 'myrrh', 'spice', 'honey', 'honeycomb', 'wine', 'milk'
                      L  4:16 **'into his garden'**
                      L'  5:1a **'into my garden'**
                    K'  5:1bc 'myrrh', 'spice', 'honey', 'honeycomb', 'wine', 'milk'
                  J'a  5:2–9 'the watchman found me'
                  J'b  5:10–6:1 'gold', 'Lebanon', 'daughters of Jerusalem'
                  J'c  6:4–11 description of the girl, 'your eyes...hair...teeth'
                I'  6:2–3 'my lover is mine'
              H'  6:13–7:9a [10a] 'vines', 'wine', 'that we may gaze on you'
            G'  7:9b–13 [10b–14] 'fragrance', 'come my darling', 'blossom'
          F'  8:1–5 'his left arm', 'daughters of Jerusalem...so desires', 'apple', 'love'
        E'  8:6–7 'house'
      D'  8:8–9 'breasts', 'silver', 'we will build'
    C'  8:10–12 'my own vineyard'
  B'  8:13 'friends'
A'  8:14 'come away'
```

Since the center of a chiastic structure is normally a point of thematic significance, the preceding arrangement would suggest that this occurs within the metaphoric conjugal 'garden' at the time of sexual union between a man ('the lover') and his bride ('the beloved'): L-L' (4:16–5:1a).

The literary format that I am about to propose also includes *linear* as well as *concentric* elements, for as was suggested in the earlier discussion of imagery, both syntagmatic as well as paradigmatic forces are at work in the formation of this multifarious lyric poem. In addition to repetition, which is the principal structuring device, several other poetic features play into the analysis by their *convergence* at key points in the demarcation of the discourse. In other words, a significant reiteration of lexical form at the beginning (aperture) or the ending (closure) of a discrete poetic unit (that is, strophe < stanza < song) will generally be supported by a *concentration* of other literary operators, which either constitute the recursion or co-occur with it, such as: metaphor/simile, metonymy, hyperbole, euphemism, exclamation/verbal intensification, dramatization (direct discourse), condensation, phrasal expansion, intertextual citation/allusion, colorful diction (including archaisms and neologisms), syntactic perturbation (word order variation), grammatical shifting (enallage; for example, tense, person), along with the usual alterations in cast (participants/characters), setting (time, place), perspective (speaker), or circumstance (emotive tone or psychological attitude). Any combination of such devices may function this way, especially if they recur, and all of them at one time or another are utilized in the Song for marking a boundary. The more of them that happen to converge at a particular point in the text along with some form of verbal recursion, the more confirmation we have that the border or peak posited there is genuine. (For an overview and application of this methodology to Psalm 22, see Wendland 1993:ch. 5.)

On the basis of a detailed literary-structural analysis of שִׁיר הַשִּׁירִים, I view the book as being composed of eight distinct 'songs' (the largest internal compositional units)—eight perhaps itself symbolic of great plenty or even blessed superfluity (cf. *sh-m-n* 'be fat'; Bullinger 1967:196). These songs vary in size and complexity, but they all highlight the same general theme of abundance, intensity, purity, fidelity, and exclusiveness that marks the loving relationship between the man and woman who alternate as speakers (or singers). Thus the central subject is progressively explored from different perspectives and with diverse attitudes as the essential material is recycled from one song to the next. This may be regarded as the lyric equivalent of the 'overlay' mode of composition that investigators have found to characterize certain traditions of oral narrative performance (Grimes 1972; Wendland 1975).

6.3 Recursion

This iterative, paradigmatic development of the Song's main message does not remain static, however. Rather, there is a perceptible progression in emotive intensity, sensual evocation, and semantic elaboration as the cyclical pattern turns into an increasingly resonant or cumulative spiral of overall thematic significance. In addition, there is a complementary "circularity" in construction (Landy 1983:44) which adds a further aesthic dimension to the work. Thus the Song is subtly divided into two, with each half of four lyric cycles concluding with a pointed emotive climax of feelings (that is, 4:16–5:1 and 8:14, as verbalized by both the beloved and her lover), even as the whole text builds up to a thematic peak in an expression of hortatory content, that is, the "homily on wisdom" in 8:6–7 (Weems 1997:373).[16] There is a recursion of topics, motifs, and sequences on both sides of the divide, as it were, with the concentration being particularly heavy in the first and last chapters (which leads some to posit a chiastic or introverted format for the book, see below). The internal boundaries of a given song's constituent units (strophes) are not always clearly defined, a feature that may, as Landy suggests, be a deliberate indication of the "composite speech" or the "common personality" of the two lovers (1987:305); is it necessary to add also the possibility of a covert reference to their intimate physical and psychological union? In any case, the complete discourse evinces a tightly constructed hierarchical organization as the strophes combine to form the eight constitutive songs (or stanzas) of the Song of Solomon in its full poetic complexity.

One of the most diagnostic among the verbal artist's inventory of recursive structuring devices is the *inclusio*, or 'sandwich' (head-tail) construction, which demarcates a given discourse segment/section, large or small, through a reduplication of formal and/or semantic material at its initial and end points. The book as a whole, for example, is circumscribed by the following *inclusio*—an urgent appeal by the beloved to her lover to flee away into amorous seclusion:

> Take me away with you—let us hurry!...(1:4)
> Come away, my love!... (8:14).

In the immediate co-text of each of these passages there are also some lexically equivalent references to 'the king/Solomon' (1:4; 8:11–12) and

---

[16] Weems is of the opinion that "[u]nder no circumstances can one argue that the book closes on a note of resolution or conclusion" (1997:373). But such an assumption appears to be based upon a "Western reading" (1997:373) and ignores the possibility that the meaning and ultimate significance this wisdom discourse is not necessarily found in a surface reading of the text and the sequence of songs of the two lovers. Rather, the point and purpose of the book is undoubtedly revealed in the proverbial assertions concerning the strength and resilience of genuine, God-like 'love' in 8:6–7. A similar hermeneutical key to the composition as a whole is found near the end of the related Solomonic book of Ecclesiastes, i.e., in 12:13–14.

to several important images of sexual enjoyment, that is, 'wine/scent/ perfume' (1:2–4) and 'vineyard/fruit/ spices' (8:11–14). This technique of strophic bounding is typically supported in poetically structured texts by several complementary, but less frequently recognized, compositional cues such as: *anaphora* (where corresponding unit-beginnings resonate), *epiphora* (where the respective endings are parallel), and *anadiplosis* (a tail-head 'overlapping' construction) (Wendland 1993:142; 2004b:126–127).

It turns out in my analysis that epiphora is found to be especially prominent as a demarcative device in the Song of Solomon. Its operation is realized primarily through the recurrence of various types of unit-ending *refrain*, of which seven are especially important in delineating the eight (4 + 4) songs (thematic cycles) as well as the entire, the great Song. A table listing these in terms of their basic motifs (involving both vocabulary and imagery) is given here, along with an indication of where the refrains converge, most frequently in triads, either at or near the close of the designated passage. At each of these epiphoric junctures, a major boundary of *closure* is posited, that is, the conclusion of one of the macro-Song's eight constitutive songs (the brackets indicate a refrain that seems to be implied, but is not overtly expressed in the text):

Song	Verses	Refrain markers	Description of the set of seven epiphoric refrains
1.	1:2–2:7	A, B, C, E, G	A = left/right arm embrace
2.	2:8–2:17	B, D, E	B = gazelle/doe/stag imagery
3.	3:1–3:5	B, C, F, G	C = do [not] arouse/waken love[17]
4.	3:6–5:1	C, [D], E, F	D = I am my lover's/my lover is mine
5.	5:2–6:3	D, E, F	E = garden and related (fruit) motifs
6.	6:4–7:10	D, E, F	F = movement imagery (coming/going)
7.	7:11–8:4	A, C, [E], G	G = daughters of Jerusalem
8.	8:5–8:14	B, E, F	

As indicated in the table, the first song is apparently concluded in the most concrete terms, with five of the seven refrainal motif markers converging in the vicinity of 2:7. This is shown in more detail below:

A.	His left arm…and his right arm embraces me.	Song	2:6
B.	…by the gazelles and by the does of the field…		2:7a
C.	…do not arouse and do not awaken love…		2:7b

---

[17] Sailhamer feels that this particular refrain is the single most important one in the SoS, for it serves to "mark the progress and larger structural movement given to the poem by the author" (1994:360). In fact, all of the refrains listed above operate together in concert to perform these, and other rhetorical functions.

6.3 Recursion

E.	...apple tree...trees...fruit...raisins...apples...	2:3, 5
G.	Daughters of Jerusalem, I adjure you...	2:7a

We may also observe here that motif (B) is reiterated (with some variation) in verse 9, while another motif, (F), appears at the onset of the second song: 'Look! here he comes...' (2:8a). One might then ask how we know that a break separating the two songs occurs between 7 and 8, and not after 8? Here, as elsewhere, a careful sifting and evaluation of the textual evidence is necessary; one cannot rely solely on the markers of recursion. In this case, a comparison with other co-texts (that is, 3:5, 8:4) indicates that motif (C) manifests a greater diagnostic capacity than any of the others since it occurs at the end of each of the four songs in which it is found. Furthermore, its final manifestation is immediately preceding the apical hortatory strophe of the entire book, namely, 8:5–7. Similar intratextual comparison indicates that a relative *scale of structural potency* could be established for all seven markers, proceeding from the strongest, most diagnostic to the least as follows: [C > B > A > D > E > F > G]. Thus (G): 'daughters of Jerusalem' is least indicative, relatively speaking, because it occurs in other positions in the text—usually as a signal of closure as well (for example, 3:11, 5:8, 5:16), indeed at least once also at a unit's aperture (1:5).

With regard to the border between the first two songs in chapter 2, we also observe in verse 8 a number of other features that characteristically appear at the start (aperture) of a new poetic unit. For example, a shift in speaker and seemingly setting as well, an explicit reference to the 'lover' (דּוֹדִי) and the exclamatory, demonstrative nature of the initial utterance—that is, with 'voice' (קוֹל = hark!), 'look!' (הִנֵּה), and 'this' (זֶה = right here!). Thus, it is quite clear that a new song (or cycle) begins at this point. None of these poetic devices would be reliable enough on its own as a marker of aperture (or closure), but taken together, they have a disjunctive effect that is rather substantial as compositional markers at a relatively high level of discourse organization. Coupled then with the corresponding indicators of closure on the other side of the boundary, so to speak, we have conclusive evidence for a compositional break.

A similar process of close *comparative analysis* plus reasoning from the perspective of the complete text is carried out when subdividing a given song into its constituent (sub-) strophes and stanzas (if an intermediate level of segmentation seems warranted). A shift in speakers is probably the most diagnostic, that is, where the male and female voices are explicitly differentiated, for example by means of their respective pronominal forms (M/F):

Tell me (M) ... where do you (M) pasture [your] flock? ... (1:7)
If you (F) do not know, most beautiful among women, follow (F) ... (1:8)

A strophic boundary is thus placed between verses 7 and 8. Other devices are also strongly demarcative, the *inclusio* in particular, for example:

> My lover spoke and he said to me,
> "Arise, my darling, my beautiful one, and come along! 2:10
> "Arise, come along my darling, my beautiful one—yes, come along!" 2:13

This clearly differentiated 'bounding' construction sets off verses 10–13 as a distinct strophe within the second song. Most internal borders are quite apparent, being signaled by two or more of the markers mentioned earlier.

In some cases, however, there may be a debate as to whether or not a break should occur, or exactly where it should be placed in the text. In such instances, the various markers have to be evaluated in relation to one another and a decision made in favor of where the greatest structural evidence lies. At 4:12, for example, the GNT begins a new strophic unit whereas the NIV and NRSV do not. In support of the latter is the surrounding textual arrangement, that is, the *wasf* poem of 4:1–7 (note the *inclusio*: 'How beautiful you are, my darling!' in 1, 7), which would seem to be better balanced by a subsequent strophe/stanza of corresponding size (note another *inclusio* involving the 'Lebanon' motif in 4:8,15). In favor of the GNT's decision, however, are several, equally compelling signals of a medial boundary, namely, an *inclusio* formed by 'Lebanon' (4:8, 11), and one that introduces the prominent 'garden' motif (4:12, where 'garden' is foregrounded, and in 15 'gardens'). A concentration of the preposition 'from' (*m[in]* -מִ) lends cohesion to the segment spanning verses 8–11, while the preposition 'with' (עִם) does the same for the strophe of 4:12–15. In addition, the exclamation and vocative 'my bride' probably indicates a (sub-) strophic break at v. 10. Note the chiastic pattern:

> 'my bride' (8) : 'my sister, my bride' (9) :: 'my sister, my bride' (10) : [my] 'bride' (11)

This double *inclusio* thus delineates a pair of parallel poetic segments, 4:8–9 and 10–11 (cf. 4:12–5:1—that is, *anaphora*) within the strophe that spans 4:8–11.

Space does not permit a further elaboration (and justification) of the internal composition of each of the eight songs, but a tentative structural description of the entire Song in terms of its major 'songs' and included strophes is outlined by way of summary in the following table.

6.3 Recursion

Section	Reference to Section plus Strophes	Section Title
Title	1:1	**Solomon's song of songs**
Song 1	1:2–2:7	**A mutual admiration society**
	1:2–4a, 4b–4c, 5–7, 8–10, 11, 12–14,	
	15, 16–17	
	2:1, 2, 3–4, 5–6, 7	
Song 2	2:8–17	**Comings and goings**
	2:8–9, 10–13, 14–15, 16–17	
Song 3	3:1–5	**Lost and found**
	3:1–4, 5	
Song 4	3:6–5:1	**A beautiful movement to the**
	3:6–10, 11	**garden of love**
	4:1–7, 8–9, 10–11, 12–15, 16	
	5:1a–b, 1c	
Song 5	5:2–6:3	**Portrait of a lover, lost**
	5:2–5, 6–7, 8, 9, 10–16	
	6:1, 2–3	
Song 6	6:4–7:10	**How beautiful, the beloved!**
	6:4–7, 8–9, 10, 11–12, 13a, 13b	
	7:1–5, 6–9a, 9b–10	
Song 7	7:11–8:4	**Movement towards the mar-**
	7:11–13	**riage home**
	8:1–3, 4	
Song 8	8:5–14	**A message of love and**
	8:5a, 5b–7, 8–9, 10, 11–12, 13, 14	**retrospect**

Turning once more to the book's larger structure, we observe the apparent imbalance in the length of the various cycles, for example, the short third song (3:1–5) compared to the relatively long fourth one (3:6–5:1). While such a mode of composition might offend a modern poetic sensitivity with regard to balance and symmetry in the different stanzas of a song, it can on the other hand be said to contribute some formal diversity to the whole. This complements the overall variations-on-a-theme message, namely, the beauty of an all-embracing, multifaceted loving relationship. We observe furthermore a similar, unusually short stanza in the book's second half, that is, the corresponding third segment in the sequence, song 7 (7:11–8:4). So there is in fact symmetry; it just happens to be of a somewhat different nature than what would be expected in a Western musical or poetic tradition.

There is also a larger compositional question concerning whether or not the so-called wedding song of 3:6–11 ought to be treated as an independent section. Certainly it seems to record a voice distinct from any other previously heard in the text—the implied poet perhaps? Carr is of the opinion that "these six verses pose one of the most difficult questions in the interpretation of the Song" and he goes on to ask, "How does this unit fit with the rest of the book?" (1984:106). Being the competent commentator that he is, Carr answers his own query as he points out the similarities between the lavish extravagance of Solomon's carriage (which is the real focus of attention, rather than Solomon himself) and the great beauty of the beloved who is appropriately praised in the subsequent poems of chapter 4. Such correspondences include: the appeal to a lovely vision, 'behold!' (3:6–7; 4:1); a sweet smell, 'myrrh' and 'frankincense' (3:6; 4:6, 14); reference to the majestic quality of 'Lebanon' (3:9; 4:11, 15); and the striking contrast between the arid 'wilderness' (3:6) and the Edenic 'garden' (4:12–15). This skilled manner of structural patterning thus verbally foregrounds the lover's 'beautiful dove' (4:1) as one who surpasses all the 'daughters of Jerusalem'—even 'Zion' (3:10–11). She is therefore a 'bride' (4:8–12) who is most worthy of his utmost attention. The masterful organization, here as elsewhere, also demonstrates how carefully all of the poetic bits and pieces, the individual imagaic segments and sections, of the Song are interwoven and made to cohere meaningfully, despite their superficial stylistic diversity.

Finally, it is worth pointing out the chiastic structure for the Song as a whole posited by Dorsey (1999:212). As noted earlier, most extended introverted arrangements fail the test of credibility, the foundation of which is exact or synonymous lexical reiteration. In this respect, however, Dorsey is more careful and his proposal can, for the most part, be defended on formal grounds. I have summarized this discourse-level chiasmus below:[18]

---

[18] The lexical and topical evidence for this manner of organizing the discourse is given in Dorsey 1999:212. Dorsey proposes quite a few other chiastic and linear structures which serve to demarcate and lend cohesion to the various internal units of the SoS. Some of these are quite convincing while others are less so. In any case, they need to be examined and evaluated with greater care than I have space for here. However, I do strongly support Dorsey's general conclusion and the end of his study (1999:213): "[T]he final author intensively reshaped the material of the Song from beginning to end. The sophistication and homogeneity of the Song's surface structure design strongly suggests a unified poem that was composed by a single author. The author's structuring designs reinforce and enhance the Song's main themes. The most prominent of these themes is the idea of the reciprocity, or mutuality, of the lovers' love."

6.3 Recursion

A Opening words of mutual love and desire (1:2–2:7)
   B The young man's invitation to the young woman to join him in the countryside (2:8–17)
      C The young woman's nighttime search for the young man (3:1–5)
         D **Their wedding day** (3:6–5:1, framed by the poet's words)
      C' The young woman's nighttime search for the young man, and their speeches of admiration and longing (5:2–7:10)
   B' The young woman's invitation to join her in the countryside (7:11–8:4)
A' Closing words of mutual love and desire (8:5–14)

It is interesting to observe the general correspondence in Dorsey's major text boundaries with those that I have posited above. The principal disagreement lies in the lengthy section C', which I have divided into two 'songs' (5:2–6:3, and 6:4–7:10) on the basis of the concluding 'refrains' found in 6:2–3. These two verses also reveal that the woman's nighttime search for the young man appears to have ended at that point, thus calling Dorsey's categorization of C' into question (the designation "and their speeches of admiration and longing" could be assigned to just about any portion of the SoS). Furthermore, Dorsey's middle pericope of D ("their wedding day") seems to be overly long and diffuse for such a macro-chiastic structure (3:6–5:1). On the contrary, the midpoint of the book rather appears at the very conclusion of that unit, in 4:16–5:1, where the marriage of the man and the woman is arguably consummated "in his/my garden."

Peter Leithart has called attention to the chiastic patterning that Davidson (2003) noted between the first and last Songs (i.e., 1 and 8) of the SoS:[19]

> Richard Davidson's structural analysis of the Song is particularly helpful in showing the coherence of the last section of the Song, often viewed as a collection of disconnected fragments. 8:5–14 matches 1:2–2:7 in that both are arranged in seven speeches, alternating between female and male voices. More strikingly, Davidson shows, very persuasively, that these two sections form a chiastically arranged inclusion around the entire poem, as follows:

---

[19] Posted by Peter J. Leithart on Thursday, March 4, 2010 at 5:00 am – http://www.leithart.com/category/bible-ot-song-of-songs/; cf. 6.3.2.2.

A 1:2–7: key words: Solomon, 'my own vineyard,' keeper (*natar*), companions, haste
  B 2:8–11: key word: silver
    C 1:12–14: key phrase: 'my breasts'
      D 1:15–17: key phrase: building, with 'planks of cedar
        E 2:1–5 key words: love (*'ahavah*, house, love (*dod*, 3x),
          F 2:6–7: key phrases: double refrain: 'left hand under head....';
            'I charge you…
          F' 8:3–4: key phrases: double refrain: 'left hand under head....';
            'I charge you…
        E' 8:5–7: key words: love (*'ahavah*, house, love (*dod*), apple tree
      D' 8:8–9: key phrase: building, with 'beams of cedar
    C' 8:10: key phrase: 'my breasts'
  B' 8:11: key word: silver
A' 8:12–14: key words: Solomon, 'my own vineyard,' keepers (*natar*),companions, haste….

Davidson links 3:1–5 with 5:2–8, both scenes where the bride seeks her lover, and he shows that these are arranged in a panel construction. The D sections are 3:6–11 and 5:9–6:3, again arranged in panels. The two *wasfs* in 4:1–6 and 6:3–12 match as well, and are arranged in parallel, as are the sections 4:8–15 and 6:13–7:9. At the center he places 4:16–5:1, both of which end with references to garden, spices, and eating.

6.4 A pair of structural-stylistic peaks in the Song

I will conclude my structural overview of the Song of Solomon, which is based upon the mutual interaction of recursion and imagery, with a brief description of the two high points of the discourse, namely, its middle climax and final peak at the ends of the two halves of the SoS.[20]

As shown on the table of songs and strophes above, four major song-poems lead up to the highly evocative (and structurally important) medial position at the end of chapter 4 (including 5:1). The fourth song (3:6–5:1) is distinctive in terms of its length and because it ends with a praise poem by the male 'lover' that constitutes his most sustained and impassioned

---

[20] As was noted earlier, there is an emotive climax of sorts also at the end of the Song in 8:14 as the lovers seemingly plan a getaway to celebrate their love, but this is largely evocative and hence anticipatory in nature. The audience is invited to let their imaginations run free to envision for themselves how this proposed rendezvous will differ, perhaps even surpass, those that have already been lyrically depicted throughout the book.

6.4 A pair of structural-stylistic peaks in the Song

discourse (4:1–15). The two verses 4:16 and 5:1 then are situated at the physical midpoint of the entire book with four thematic cycles (songs) on either side. This central position was also highlighted by the extended lexical chiasmus that was presented in section 6.3.2.2. Furthermore, according to a line-count these two verses "form the exact middle of the Hebrew text, with 111 lines (60 verses, plus the title, 1:1) from 1:2 to 4:15, and 111 lines (55 verses) from 5:2 to 8:14" (Carr 1984:127). The beatific vision of the 'garden' (4:12–15) —Eden revisited—is echoed in verse 16 by the woman, as she for the first time invites him, figuratively but obviously, to come consummate their love, the expression of which has been building up to a crescendo throughout the Song:

> Let my lover come into his garden,
> and let him taste its choicest fruit! (4:16b)

There is a dramatic pause—the climax occurs, literally and otherwise. Then the man responds, essentially repeating her words—what more could he say?

> I have come into my garden, my sister bride! (5:1a).

He proceeds to elaborate upon her reference to 'fruit' in a series of images that relate to 'eating' and 'drinking' (5:1b)—all euphemistically evocative, perhaps even erotic, with reference to sexual fulfillment and pleasure. A final closure to this particular song and the first half of the book is appropriately enunciated by the chorus, as they celebrate and encourage the couple's pleasure with a rousing (rhythmic, rhyming, and reiterative) exclamation to enjoy their festal 'meal' (5:1c):

> אִכְלוּ רֵעִים Go ahead and eat, friends!
> שְׁתוּ וְשִׁכְרוּ דּוֹדִים Drink your fill, you lovers!

The heightened artistry here in terms of (Hebrew) poetic technique (featuring sonic similarity) is further indication that a culminating juncture in the Song has been reached. From this climactic point of *emotion*, which is greatly obscured by the traditional chapter division, a new set of four lyric cycles starts out (note the assonantal overlap (*anadiplosis*) in the repeated [-î] 'me/my' sounds). This half of the book begins contrastively with another disturbing 'dream report/vision' (5:2–7; cf. 3:1–4, both of which conclude [*epiphora*] with a solemn appeal to 'the daughters of Jerusalem', 3:5, 5:8).

Then after three formally and semantically reiterative songs, which some see as "the consolidation and confirmation of what has been pledged" in 4:16–5:1 (Carr 1984:127), the *thematic* peak of the book is reached in the complex strophe that leads off the fourth and final song of the second set, 8:5–7b. Many commentators observe with regard to this poem something to the effect that "in all literature there are few passages on the power of love compared to this unit" (Kinlaw 1991:1241). This structurally distinct lyric (8:5b–7) is arguably the primary instance of the poet's literary expression of love. The Hebrew text of this artistically beautiful and rhetorically powerful passage reads as follows:

תַּחַת הַתַּפּוּחַ עוֹרַרְתִּיךָ
שָׁמָּה חִבְּלַתְךָ אִמֶּךָ
שָׁמָּה חִבְּלָה יְלָדַתְךָ׃
שִׂימֵנִי כַחוֹתָם עַל־לִבֶּךָ
כַּחוֹתָם עַל־זְרוֹעֶךָ
כִּי־עַזָּה כַמָּוֶת אַהֲבָה
קָשָׁה כִשְׁאוֹל קִנְאָה
רְשָׁפֶיהָ רִשְׁפֵּי
אֵשׁ שַׁלְהֶבֶתְיָה׃
מַיִם רַבִּים לֹא יוּכְלוּ לְכַבּוֹת אֶת־הָאַהֲבָה
וּנְהָרוֹת לֹא יִשְׁטְפוּהָ
אִם־יִתֵּן אִישׁ אֶת־כָּל־הוֹן בֵּיתוֹ בָּאַהֲבָה
בּוֹז יָבוּזוּ לוֹ׃

Before one can properly evaluate a given passage or its translation, one must first apply a critical eye closely to its original text. Beginning with the task of textual demarcation, we note that the onset of this pericope is delineated first of all by the formulaic *closure* of 8:3–4 (RSV):

> [3] O that his left hand were under my head,
>   and that his right hand embraced me!
> [4] I adjure you, O daughters of Jerusalem,
>   that you stir not up nor awaken love
>   until it please.

This distinct structural border is followed by an equally strong marker of *aperture* (commencement) in 8:5a, namely, the rhetorical question that duplicates 3:6a of structural segment 4 of the Song (an iterative compositional device termed *anaphora*; see also 6:10a).

> [5] Who is that [fem.] coming up from the wilderness,

6.4 A pair of structural-stylistic peaks in the Song 225

> leaning upon her beloved?

This question serves to fix the spotlight of attention (the oral-aural microphone, as it were) upon the participant next referred to, in this case, the female speaker. She begins with a figurative, allusive, and rather enigmatic description of her intimate relationship with her lover (8:5b; note the intratextuality, e.g., the 'wake-up' call which reverses the choral prohibition of 2:7/3:5):

> *Under the apple tree* I awakened (or aroused) you.
> *There* your mother was in travail with you,
> there she who bore you was in travail.

In the Ancient Near East, the topics of love and sexuality were often expressed figuratively using the imagery of fruit and fruit trees (cf. 2:3; 'apple'—but more likely, the apricot). Here, the female speaker picturesquely compares the birth and growth of love that she produced in her man to his mother giving birth to him. *Assonance* in the vowel-sound /a/ reinforces the point that it is the woman who is the main actor in this event (the object 'you' [ךָ–] is masculine singular).

The preceding notice leads in verse 6 to a highly personal appeal for intimate proximity—not only physically, but the imagery would suggest socially as well, that is, in their communally and religiously sanctioned ('sealed') marriage vows (a development of the metaphor of 1:13). The cylinder-seal (or signet ring) symbolized personal identity and possession along with connotations of preciousness and authority. The closeness of this amorous relationship is further reinforced by the metonymic figures of the 'heart' and the 'arm' (or 'wrist'), to which such seals would always be most closely attached.

> ⁶ Set me as a seal upon your heart,
> as a seal upon your arm;
> **for** love is strong as death,
> jealousy is cruel as the grave.
> Its flashes are flashes of fire,
> a most vehement flame.

The consequential 'for' (כִּי, more idiomatically: 'for sure!') in the middle of verse 6 announces what sounds like a clear shift in the speaking voice—from the woman to the poet (implied author) as he proverbially expresses the point of the Song, which goes like this (a very literal English translation):

For strong	like (the) death	[is]	love,	
unyielding	like Sheol	[is]	passion,	
its blazes the blazes of fire	[like]	—	the flame of **Yah**[weh]!	

A host of Hebrew literary devices converge here to mark this passage as a high point (arguably the supreme peak) of the entire passionate discourse, which is also distinguished by means of a shift in genre, for the strong overtones of wisdom literature are obvious. Observe these poetic features, for example: strict *parallelism* (the first two lines); syntactic *placement* (the utterance-final key terms, 'love' and 'passion'); *imagery* (simile and metaphor); *symbolism* (death and fire); *paradox* (the compelling power of death [destructive] in contrast to love [creative]); *condensation* (especially the final line, where the fiery close is concentrated by an implicit marker of comparison); an ascending *rhythmic pattern* $(3+3+4)$ with variation (the extraordinary last word, or is it a half-line?); more *assonance* in [a] (to tie the text in to v. 5b); *alliteration* (the repeated [*sh*] of lines 2–3) with possible *onomatopoeia* (imaging the hissing of a fire); and finally, a possible cryptic mention of the divine name (-*yah*) in ultimate, climactic position (שַׁלְהֶבֶתְיָה).

In verse 6 then we have the fullest, most sustained attempt to describe (or better, evoke) the supreme subject of the Song, namely, paired male-female love (note the definite article of abstraction in v. 7). It is indeed a most irrepressible, irresistible, unquenchable force. Furthermore, the clipped and suffixed reference to 'Yahweh,' while it could be a mere idiomatic substitute for the superlative (i.e., the 'hottest/brightest/purest' flame),[21] in this structural position (cf. the equally unique 'your name' in balance as a possible *inclusio* at 1:3) and in conjunction with so much stylistic embellishment, definitely seems to signify something more. Thus the final term *shalhebet-yah* 'the flame of God' could well stand as the apex of the credo and of the Song.[22] Yahweh is the Source not only of love in all its power and passion, but also of the marriage relationship in which affection is most completely and intimately experienced. In these verses (6–7) the Song again strongly alludes to humanity's pre-fall condition in the Garden of Eden, keying

---

[21] Harold Fisch makes an appropriate comment on the import of this passage: "Love for the Shulamite and the *dôd* is not a lighthearted game, but a consuming fire ... by the time we reach the intensity of כִּי־עַזָּה כַמָּוֶת אַהֲבָה 'for love is as strong as death,' we have left the charm of the pastoral far behind" (1988:81).

[22] Landy concludes: "שַׁלְהֶבֶתְיָה 'the flame of God' is the apex of the credo and of the Song" (1983:129).

6.4 A pair of structural-stylistic peaks in the Song

off the man's exultant lyric declaration of Genesis 2:23.[23] Yahweh would surely seem to be present in this context (cf. the NJB, GW, and ASV), for fire is employed as a symbol of God's purifying presence throughout the Bible—here too then as the inexhaustible spark of a shared life of total devotion.

The subdued presence of the LORD in the single theophanic flash of a flame here towards the end of the Song contrasts also in implicit intertextuality with the contemporary love poetry of other cultures (e.g., *Mowt* 'death' and *Reshep* 'flames' in Ugaritic cultic texts).[24] Such pagan poems made frequent mention of some local deity, often in conjunction with immoral, allegedly worshipful sexual activities. The clear divergence in the case of the Song would thus seem to be indicative of a radically different nature, purpose, and message.

There's still more of course: the poet does not finish in 8:6 but goes on in grand panegyric fashion to figuratively suggest the practical significance of '[this] love' (הָאַהֲבָה), with still more accentuating assonance in verse 7:

> [7] Many waters cannot quench love,
>> neither can floods drown it.
> If a man offered for love
>> all the wealth of his house,
>>> it would be utterly scorned.

---

[23] Richard Davidson supports this interpretation and draws attention to its typological significance (1989:18–19; cf. Delitzsch 1984:147): "If this interpretation is correct, then true human love is explicitly described as originating in God as 'a spark off the original flame.' To put it another way, human love at its best, as described in the Song, points beyond itself to the Lord of love. In the final analysis, therefore, the allegorical interpretation of the Song may be correct in its conclusion that the Song shows God's love for man, but incorrect in the way in which the conclusion is reached. The love relationship between Solomon and the Shulamite is not a worthless 'husk,' to be stripped away allegorically to find the Song's kernel or the 'true' meaning—the love between God and his people. Rather, the love relationship between husband and wife, described in the Song, has independent meaning and value of its own that is affirmed and extolled. At the same time this human love is given even greater significance as it typologically points beyond itself to the divine Lover in the Song's climax (8:6). Rather than an allegorical understanding (with its fanciful, externally-and-arbitrarily-imposed meaning that is alien to the plain and literal sense), the Song itself calls for a typological approach, which remains faithful to, and even enhances, the literal sense of the Song by recognizing what the text indicates—that human love typifies the divine."

[24] "[I]n the ancient Near East, death is personified as a god of great power. In Ugaritic mythology that god's name is Mot ('Death'), whose power is such that he at least temporarily defeats and swallows Baal, who represents fertility, the power of life. Here the woman boldly asserts that his love is stronger than death. It is, in other words, irresistible, resolute, and unshakable. ... [T]he term flame translates the word reshep, which is related to the Ugaritic god of plague, Resep, thus rendering even more likely that the earlier references to Death and Sheol are personifications" (Longman 2001:210, 212).

From a mighty fire to a cosmic flood, a divinely motivated affection simply cannot be quenched. The allusions here need not be primarily mythological, for the psalmists had already dealt polemically with that issue through poetic 'defamiliarization' (citing a supposedly sacred alternative only to deny or downplay it) when proclaiming the almighty Lordship and mercy of Yahweh in caring for his people (e.g., Pss.18:6–16; 32:6; 93; cf., Exod.15:1–10). The imagery of water is especially relevant here due to the preceding references to the fiery passion of love. The extra-long cola of verse 7a and 7c mimic both the amplitude of the content and the rhythmic movement of the language, each concluding with the key word—'love' (אַהֲבָה).

This magnificent poetic depiction is rounded out in a more conventional wisdom fashion by means of a contrastive, probably ironic, reference to the proverbial 'fool' who misunderstands and hence by implication also misuses personal affection. No price can purchase love. Such a misguided materialistic attitude deserves only 'utter scorn' (an intensified *boz yabuzu loh* בּוֹז יָבוּזוּ לוֹ) from the society at large for polluting a godly gift (like the adulterer, who is severely punished for his desecration of love; cf. Prov. 6:30–35). The strophe-final pronoun *loh* 'to him' forms a homophonous (same-sounding) link with the preceding double occurrence of the negative *lo'* לֹא 'not/no'. No self-seeking idiot can either buy or bar legitimate love!²⁵

I close this section by citing James Kugel's rendition of this supreme lyric of the SoS, taken from his selection of "the great poems of the Bible" (1999:274, added indentation, italics, and boldface):

> Make me a locket on your heart, a signet on your arm.
> > For **love** is as strong as *death*, and as harsh as *Sheol*.
> > > Its flames burn like fire, **a holy burning**.
> > *Deep waters* can't put **love** out, and *rivers* will not drown it.
> If a man gave all his family's wealth for **love**, would anybody blame him?

The preceding analysis has suggested that a careful study of the structure and style of a literary text, whether of prose or poetry, is an essential part of analyzing its meaning. As we have seen, the style of the Song of Songs, its imagery and recursion in particular, is closely bound up with a delineation of the book's larger organization in terms of a demarcation of the principal compositional units, a description of how these segments

---

[25] Fisch ironically comments on the relationship of the poetic style in this preeminent strophe to its subject (1988:85): "…if a poet offered for love all the wealth of the poetic catalogue as the tribute to a supreme and triumphant beauty, that too would be scorned."

6.4 A pair of structural-stylistic peaks in the Song

are unified and made to cohere with one another, and a specification, or projection, of where thematically crucial peak points occur within the discourse as a whole. The textual framework of the Song thus gives one an overall impression of formal and semantic unity despite certain ambiguities with regard to the speaking voice(s), the "dream symbolism" that often characterizes its "language and imagery" (Fisch 1988:89), and even the slight ruptures alluded to in the several snatches of semi-narrative plot (that is, 3:1–2; 5:2–7). The work's "intricate web of cross-references" (Landy 1983:315), which has been carefully woven into a multi-layered poetic texture, overcomes what on the surface might appear to be "a compositional structure marked by predominant, fragmenting features which tend toward a prevailing emphasis on the parts" (Grossberg 1989:83). On the contrary, the major discourse units of the Song of Solomon—the eight included songs and their strophic constituents—all wonderfully complement one another to enhance the unity that is embodied in its very theme: one man and one woman coming together, not only in the physical 'garden' of love (4:16b–5:1a), but also in the joint social and moral establishment of a permanent, loving marriage relationship, a union 'sealed' in the presence of God (8:5b–7).

A well-formed, 'lovely and lively' poetic text, especially within the canonical collection that constitutes the Scriptures, does not exist as an ornament on its own or for itself—that is, art for art's sake. Rather, its *total literary inventory* of structural and stylistic resources is utilized for the purpose of rhetorical effect as well as communicative effectiveness, both general and specific. In other words, the artistry of form is employed to augment the emotive impact of the work as well as its persuasive appeal, and these experiential, hortatory dynamics in turn serve a further cognitive, thematic function. This is to enhance and enrich the transmission of the poet's message in all of its intricacy and complexity as it relates to particular theological issues as well as to a host of associated connotative dimensions of a religious, ethical, and yes, also a purely secular, interpersonal nature. Certainly, the attitude-action of love significantly concerns all of these, and more. It is up to each and every listener—or better, wife-husband couple—to allow the dynamic recursive imagery and message of the Song to fully engage their psyche, hence also to deepen their mutual affection and consequent behavior towards one another.

The preceding analysis, though tentative and incomplete (as it must be when dealing with the medium of poetry and a composition as semantically rich as the Song), offers readers at least one path, perhaps one that has not been followed before, through the thick forest of reiteration and figurative language which constitutes the exquisite lyric form and content of the SoS. But what does all this symbolism signify? My study continues with several observations on the multiple levels of meaning according to which this 'Song of/to/for Solomon' legitimately may be read, felt, and applied by all mutually committed, biblically informed, and spiritually enlightened 'lovers' today—that is, an engaged (or married) male-female couple, as the text implies.

6.5 Style and structure in the Song's message

So what is the overall meaning of the Song's abundant and recurrent imagery? That is a question which has excited as well as exercised Bible students and commentators for centuries, beginning apparently soon after the work was initially composed and circulated (sung). The text, as already indicated, is certainly no patchwork product, a quilt stitched together, whether roughly or skillfully, of an assorted lot of little love poems. Pre-existent poetic pieces may well have been utilized by the author, to be sure—either in whole or in part, by allusion or direct citation. But whatever was thus borrowed has been completely restructured to create a veritable "isomorphic equivalent" of its complex but unified subject (de Waard and Nida 1986:64-66)—the manifold, all-encompassing, completely devoted nature of genuine loving affection. At any rate, whatever individual messages there were have also been *re-signified* to communicate a whole that is not only more than, but in this biblical instance, also quite different from the sum of its parts. The result of this new, perhaps unique, compositional process is a masterful artistic discourse and, I wish to suggest, an evocative work that conveys significant theological implications as well.

6.5.1 Figurative language

The SoS conveys a message that is distinct from what it appears to say on the surface of the verbal text. When the woman says, for example, 'I [am] a rose (crocus [?]) of Sharon' (2:2), she does not mean that she is actually a plant instead of a person. Rather, she indicates that in her opinion (whether real or feigned) she is as plain and ordinary as a common flower of the field. That much is obvious: 'rose' is a semiotic image, or *signifier*, while the topic, or *signified*, of the figure (a metaphor) is 'I', meaning the woman herself. What is not nearly so apparent, however, is the extent to which such figurative language permeates the Song. How much of the text can be taken literally, and what must be construed as analogizing, imagistic speech? When the lover refers to 'winter' in 2:11, is he speaking about a specific time of the Palestinian climatic year that is now over—or is it a certain 'season' of hardship and adversity? Is there

6.5 Style and structure in the Song's message

perhaps some mythological allusion here, or is 'winter' simply a term that is characteristically used in pastoral poetry? Thus the problem in interpreting the Song of Solomon is not only what is figurative, and what is not, but also—if figurative usage is likely—what does it mean and how is it connected meaningfully with its immediate and wider context? We are back to the larger discourse and its significance as a whole. That brings up the issue of symbolism and its bearing, if any, on the text.

6.5.2 Symbolic language

In the case of symbolic language, as the French Structuralists have suggested, both the form (*signifier*, whether literal or figurative) and the content (*signified*) function together as a composite unit, that is, as a distinct signifier on its own. The text thus communicates its message on a higher plane of meaning, namely, with a new signified, embodying a theme that may well be *denotative* in import, but one which is always markedly *connotative* (expressive, affective, and evocative) in its ultimate impact (cf. Neusner 1993:109). Now, real symbols are normally perceived only by those in the know, that is, people who are familiar with the symbolism involved or at least the hermeneutical process of interpreting such usage in the particular language and culture concerned. However, as in the realm of figurative speech, so here too the question of degree (or depth) arises: just how much symbolism is there in the discourse? For the allegorist, just about every concrete reference, whether nominal or verbal, can be imbued with a superimposed, as it were, symbolic (or allegorical) meaning. The excesses of this long-practiced hermeneutical method need not be documented here (cf. Carr 1984:21–23; Garrett 1993:353–358). The same goes for the distinct, but related, cultic (liturgical, dramatistic) approach, which in the case of Scripture introduces all sorts of pagan mythological notions into the interpretation (Davidson 1986:97–98; Longman 2001:44–46).

But what does that leave us with—a literal love song (or a collection of them) intended only to enliven the ardor or to laud the attraction between a man and a woman? Certainly an attentive and reflective (re)reading of the text within its canonical context, the Hebrew wisdom literature in particular, may well convince one that there is something more here. A purely naturalistic reading (Carr ibid., 34), which in many instances ventures off into blatantly sexual and erotic (even *baalistic!*) speculation,[26] leaves much to be desired as far as understanding this particular composition is concerned. Currently the most popular approach views Song of Songs as little more than the ancient equivalent of a top twenty

---

[26] Such irrelevant interpretation is typical, too, of 'psychological' approaches where "once again we encounter a type of allegory, in this case the allegory of one's psyche, rather than an exposition of the text" (Longman 2001:47).

pop tune (or even all twenty of them rolled into one). Surely this scriptural Song is a good deal more than "an anthology of profane love lyrics loosely—if often meaningfully—strung together" (Brenner 1989:75).

6.6 Evidence for significant theological import

It is not possible here to elaborate upon all the controversial issues regarding possible theological overtones in the SoS (cf. the various commentaries cited in the following sections). I merely want to suggest (along with several other, notably literary, observers) that the text of Song of Songs in its canonical location (adjacent to Ecclesiastes) does seem to indicate that it conveys rather more than meets the eye—or, in the original event—the ear. The significance of the Song as a whole thus goes beyond human sexual, or even married relational, love, important and worthy though these topics may be in their own right. The book's consummate style and structure impart to it certain divine implications (as has already been pointed out in the earlier discussion of intertextually related imagery) like that of the garden and associated biblical motifs. What is the evidence for such deeper (or higher) theological import?

6.6.1 Superfluity

For one thing, the very superfluity and saturation of figuration would intimate that there is something more to the message, that is, over and above the celebration of a man's and a woman's love. A number of recent commentators have drawn attention to this prominent feature of the Song—its "richness of imagery" and "hyperbolic" style (Ryken 1992:276-277); its consequent "flooding" of the senses (Brenner 1989:42); or "synesthesia" (Landy 1987:310); its "flaunted figuration" (Alter 1985:196); and a progressively developed "allegorical imperative" (Fisch 1988:80). Furthermore, this imagery is not left as static embellishment; rather, it is cohesively integrated and dynamically augmented in terms of both meaning and feeling through reiteration (plus or minus variation) and re-signified by juxtaposition with new collocations of figures. Robert Alter describes the result of this distinctive nature of the Song as follows: "[W]hat makes the Song of Songs unique among the poetic texts of the Bible is that, quite often, imagery is given such full and free play that the lines of semantic subordination blur, and it becomes a little uncertain what is illustration [that is, the 'image/vehicle'] and what is referent [that is, 'topic/tenor']" (1985:193). In short, we have a textual milieu

6.6 Evidence for significant theological import

that is pregnant with meaning, hence also a literary environment that encourages more than one level of interpretation.

6.6.2 Pastoral poetry

However, it is also true that as an instance of the macro-genre of love lyrics coupled with *pastoral* (nature-oriented) poetry (Ryken 1992:274-275), the Song's imagery is to a considerable degree conventionalized.[27] The various combinations and complexes may well be novel, but the figures themselves are largely familiar and characteristic of other love lyrics of the ancient Near East (Carr 1984:37-42)—a cross-cultural "storehouse of poetic motifs" (Ryken ibid., 275).[28] In this case then, as Alter notes with reference to the Psalms: "[T]he advantage of working with such conventional figures is that our attention tends to be guided through the metaphoric *vehicle* (that is, 'image') to the *tenor* (that is, 'topic') for which the vehicle was introduced" (1985:190). Thus meaning is not open-ended, but is generalized according to its principal subject and the poetic genre itself. The "pastoral [in turn] is a ready-made vehicle—an accepted language for love poetry" (Ryken 1992:275). However, the overall meaning is also particularized to a considerable degree by the sacred canon within which it is set, specifically by the many intertextual allusions that its imagery is both based upon and also gives rise to. As Fisch observes, "The Song of Solomon [is] linked by so many other parts of the Old Testament Scripture where the 'theological' sense is not in doubt" (Fisch 1988:96).

6.6.3 Explicitness

Another quality to note in addition to the excess of imagery, is its overt explicitness: "[I]n the Song of Songs the process of figuration is frequently 'foregrounded'...[which] calls attention to [the poet's] exploitation of similitude, to the artifice of metaphorical representation"

---

[27] Such macro-genres naturally manifest a number of subordinate literary forms, such as: the admiration song *(wasf)* (e.g., 5:10-16), song of yearning (e.g., 8:1-2), arrival song (e.g., 2:8), boasting song (6:8-9), invitation song (e.g., 8:14, which concludes the SoS)—but no prayer for success in love, no doubt because "orthodox Israelites were unwilling to risk any degradation of their covenant relationship whereby God might be reduced to the level of a love charm. Yahweh is not Aphrodite" (Garrett 1993:371; Murphy 1981:101).

[28] Among such conventional motifs to be found in ANE love poetry are the following: lovesickness (SoS 5:8), the open/shut door (5:5-6), the gazelle/stag (2:9), the kiss (8:1), the name (1:3), breasts (1:12), an authority figure (e.g., watchmen, 5:7), sister/brother (4:9-12), the garden and/or vineyard (4:16), trees (1:15-17), theft of one's heart (4:9), obstacles (8:7), horses/chariots (3:7), precious metals to describe bodily features (5:14-15) (Garrett 1993:371-374; Murphy 1981:102).

(Alter 1985:193). This making explicit the operation of comparison in the textual surface structure is accomplished by and large through the device of simile, as opposed to metaphor in which the comparative marker is missing. Not only is the normal preposition *kiy* 'like, as' used, but the Song is exceptional in employing the patently comparative verbal root *d-m-h* 'be like/comparable to/resemble' five times, including at the beginning (1:9) and the very end of the composition (8:14). Such a style tends to 'defamiliarize' the poetic technique itself by laying it bare on the surface, as it were, thus calling subtle attention to the need for semantic *comparison* in the process of interpretation—for seeking a deeper level of encoded content. Therefore, the particular sort of 'love' that is foregrounded throughout the Song would seem to involve something more than the accentuation of a fundamental human quality, no matter how praiseworthy a topic on its own.

6.6.4 Composition

As was pointed out in the outlined structural overview of the SoS (section 6.3.2.2), imagery and recursion also play an important compositional role in the discourse, especially in the reiterated set of *refrains* which function to demarcate the text into eight larger segments (strophic poems or songs). This particular poetic arrangement is also of hermeneutical significance for the work's central message. The formulaic motifs that bring each of the constituent songs to a point of *closure* also serve to highlight the theme in a more abstract sense, that is, to reify the purely secular to the level of the divine.

This is especially true in the case of the central *emotive* climax (4:16–5:1) where the idyllic 'garden' imagery comes to the fore—Eden restored! (Gen. 2:21–24) and again at the onset of the eighth song, at the *conceptual*, perhaps also *rhetorical* peak of the work, where the preeminence and permanence of love is stated in textually authoritative proverbial language (8:6b–7). These latter words in particular lift the Song as a whole out of the realm of specific, male-female affection, and place it into an interpretive mode which encourages the attachment of an additional plane of significance. Not just any construal will do, however, for the carefully integrated and orchestrated poetics of this discourse definitely seem to push us in the direction of the steadfast love of God—the eternal 'flame of Yah(weh)' (שַׁלְהֶבֶתְיָה). The object of the LORD's ardent devotion might possibly be the land of Israel (the source of so much of the work's imagery; cf. Fisch 1988:92; Landy 1987:314), but it is more likely that the blessed beneficiaries are human—namely, YHWH's beloved chosen people who live in loving fellowship

6.6 Evidence for significant theological import

with him from age to age (cf. Fisch 93–94; Kinlaw 1991:1208).[29] Thus "Israel's holy life is metaphorized through the poetry of love and beloved, Lover and Israel" (Neusner 1993:3), and this latter, holy congregation is not limited to any given ethnic group, cultural setting, or historical period.[30]

Of course this theological sense is not overtly stated in the Song of Songs; it is rather generously implicated by its evocative poetic style and structure. The Song in its totality of form and content thus acts as a symbol, or signifier, of another—not necessarily a more important, but certainly a distinct—sense.[31] It is the theological which appears to be signified by the discourse as a whole in the manner of a typology, though the characters or voices of the work are not

---

[29] Some conservative commentators on the Song (e.g., Christopher Mitchell) are reluctant to admit that the Song plays off pagan mythology, poetry, and iconography. But the evidence provided by other commentators (such as Keel) is overwhelming: the Song does make use of standard ANE love lyrics and alludes with some frequency to pagan myths. But all these techniques and allusions push against paganism. Where the myths place a goddess, the Song places a human beloved which, as Jewish and Christian commentators have always said, is the people of God, Israel and the church. Does Yahweh have a consort? Yes, but she's a human consort, the covenanted bride Israel. (posted by Peter J. Leithart on Tuesday, February 23, 2010 at 9:11 am -- http://www.leithart.com/category/bible-ot-song-of-songs/).

[30] Sailhamer argues that "the Song of Songs is intended as a portrait of the promised Messiah's love for divine wisdom. The Messiah is here pictured by Solomon, and 'wisdom' is personified by the young and beautiful beloved....There is general recognition today that the time of the formation of the OT canon coincided with a significant surge in the hope of the imminent return of the messianic king. This book was included in the canon...because it was intended as a picture of the Messiah" (1994:360–361).

[31] According to the cognitive theory of mental spaces (interrelated conceptual complexes), what is going on here may be described (in a very simplified manner) as follows (cf. Stockwell 2002:97–98; Fauconnier and Turner 2006:301–315): In operation is a "conceptual blending" process, which is a "cross-space mapping" activity that brings together the ideational counterparts of two distinct "mental spaces," each of which has its own larger cognitive frame of reference ("schema"). In the case at hand, there is a "base space" that is constituted by the surface relationship and imagery connected with the two lovers in the SoS. Being guided by the interpretive framework of Scripture and the principle of contextual "relevance" (Gutt 1992), readers or hearers of the text are likely to "project" another "hypothetical space" upon the original base space, namely, the relationship between Yahweh and his covenant people. Accordingly, selected common features between these two spaces, the base and the hypothetical, are conceptually linked and integrated within a "generic space," e.g., two very distinct personal parties/entities are intimately associated in an exclusive, life-long, loving relationship. From this generic space a new "emergent structure" is mentally generated, one that is not the same as the base or the hypothetical space, but which combines analogical elements from both to form a "blended space." This stimulates a new way of thinking about the significance of the conjoined common constituents within the current (religious) setting of communication and any relevant background knowledge. Within the hermeneutical context of canon, this would most likely be a religious scenario in which biblically literate "believers" conceptualize the male lover ("Solomon") as being analogous to God (the transcendent Lord of creation) and the female beloved (the "Shulamite") to the covenant people of God, with the primary focus of attention being on the immanent, totally devoted and mutually committed nature of the relationship between them.

necessarily historical personages, for example, Solomon and the Shulamite (cf. 3:11; 6:13). Through the ever-varied recursion of a primary corpus of distinctly pastoral as well as royal imagery and terminology the Song makes its point—yet without overt reference to its principal symbolic agent, the LORD. The eminent Jewish scholar, Jacob Neusner, states the case this way (1993:112):

> How is the form just described pertinent to our inquiry into the use of language for the representation of symbols, so that, within the cited form in particular, I can adduce evidence that words are utilized solely (*I would not limit the sense so drastically—E.W.*) to portray symbols? Two considerations pertain. First is the matter of repetition, integral to the execution of the form just now introduced. Second, and concomitantly, there is the consideration of a restricted vocabulary, which signals the utilization of a restricted, privileged code.

What other subject than divine love would be worthy of (yet still fail to be captured by) such an artistic abundance of superbly crafted lyric expression? The uniqueness of the Song's literary style is thus an imperfect reflection, but a 'dim image' (1 Cor. 13:12, GNT), of the incomparably unique topic—that involving the one and only sacred Source—which it seeks to express. In such an impossible effort a certain amount of frustration is inevitable, a theological point that Harold Fisch puts in apt poetic terms (1988:101):

> [U]ltimately we reach the point where poetic language fails. "To whom then will you compare me, that I should be like him?—says the Holy One" (Isa. 40:25). If the Bible points to poetic imagery as in a way the only path of knowledge, it also points just as surely to the limits of art, the impotence of poetry.

It is this ineffable or transcendent sense of the Song, this "theology... [of] sentiment and emotion" (Neusner 1993:123), which was apparently perceived by the ancient commentators (including early Christian theologians) and was no doubt the reason for its inclusion in the Hebrew Scriptures, though not without debate, as is well known. At any rate, the apparent conclusion of this controversy in Jewish circles was eloquently summarized by Rabbi Aqiba early in the second century C.E.:

> ...all ages are not worth the day on which the Song of Songs was given to Israel: for all the Writings are holy, but the Song is the Holiest of Holies. (The Mishnah, *Yadayyim* 3:5, cited in Snaith 1993:3)

6.6 Evidence for significant theological import

Indeed, there is no other lyric song of love extant in all of ancient Hebrew literature; it is *sui generis*. Therefore, one could argue, along with Gordis (cf. Snaith 1993:4), that the optimistic, enthusiastic Song was canonized with its uniquely expressed theological meaning preeminently in mind (most notably, Hosea chs. 1–3) and pointedly juxtaposed (in many manuscripts) with its apparent opposite, the most pessimistic, apathetic passages of the Scriptures, Ecclesiastes—also attributed of course to Solomon, the son of King David. Richard Beaton makes some pertinent comments to this point in relation to the history of the Song's interpretation (2008:769):

> The overwhelming tendency of both Jewish and Christian communities has been to read the Song either symbolically or allegorically. Apart from a few disparate voices, it was not until the development of the historical-critical method that there was a noticeable shift concerning how the text was read....Rejection of a minority or aberrant reading is one thing, but to dismiss many centuries of a particular method may not be entirely appropriate. Further, if the Song was received into the canon based on a symbolic/allegorical reading, it seems legitimate to ask whether this does not itself provide a hermeneutical key for interpreting the book. It is perhaps the poetic nature of the Song that allows for a meaning beyond the literal....It may also be that it expresses in poetic form what it means to love the Lord your God with all your heart, soul and might.

Thus literary genre, poetic style, canonical location, and hermeneutical history conjoin to provide a significant interpretive frame of reference that must guide contemporary exegetes in their efforts.[32] In this connection, another dimension of the intertextual factor already referred to becomes relevant, namely, the canonical collection into which the SoS was placed and within which it has resonated hermeneutically from a theological as well as an ethical perspective. The SoS is situated in the

---

[32] There is also the *intertextual* factor to add to the literary argument for exploring further semantic-thematic significance in a composition such as the Song: "What characterizes both metaphor and simile is that they connect two contexts that are normally unconnected. The result is a statement that demands that the audience actively sort through the potential meanings of the expressions in order to decide which of them are relevant....[In poetry] the frequency of metaphors gives rise to the need to compare several different intertexts to throw light on a particular text....The many literary devices available to poets thus serve to emphasize that when we speak of the ultimate questions of existence—be it the relationship between two people as we know from love poetry or between God and humanity as we know it from the Bible [combined in the SoS?]—the poet must choose a language that does not define the beloved to such a degree that limits are set on further insights" (Nielsen 2009:298–299).

third major division of the Hebrew Bible *(Tanakh)* known as the Writings *(Kitubim),* in close proximity to other recognized instances of "wisdom literature": the Psalms, Proverbs, Job, and Ecclesiastes. This frame of immediate textual reference would certainly help define the range of legitimate interpretation regarding theSoS in such a way that would harmonize with the other books in the Hebrew corpus. A nonliteralistic, symbolic understanding would therefore be encouraged—if not the majority opinion involving God and his covenant people, then a reading that is strongly promoted by the book of Proverbs, where divine Wisdom is personified as a female being (e.g., Prov. 1:20–33, 8:1–36, 9:1–12). She then would represent the prominent "beloved" personage in the SoS, while her lover (Solomon?) would signify any godly person who seeks to follow a blessed, God-fearing path in life (cf. 1:7, 9:10, 31:30). This interpretation was advanced by the sixteenth C. Jewish theologian and commentator Don Isaac Abravanel (Longman 2001:27). A similar process of reinterpretive, perhaps even polemically motivated, theologizing (as in SoS 8:6b–7a) took place in cases where ancient pagan mythological allusions occur in passages that demonstrate the absolute supremacy of YHWH (for example, Psalms 29, 74, 87, 89; Habakkuk 3).[33]

It is interesting to note that this additional, superimposed dimension of meaning is often sensed and described by literary critics (for example, Landy, Alter, and Fisch), but not so readily by contemporary biblical theologians. Does this perhaps suggest that a commentator must actually 'be' one (that is, a poet, or at least a person with poetic sensibilities) in order to 'know' one (that is, a poem in all of its semantic richness, emotive power, and theological implications)?[34] I do not deny the fact that the Song is—maybe even in the first instance—a superb love poem, an artfully composed amatory lyric that eulogizes the passionate and complete

---

[33] With regard to the potential polemical force of the SoS, Garrett observes (1993:378–379): "A neglected point in the study of Song of Songs is that it is not only the similarities but also the differences between the Song and ancient Egyptian, Canaanite and Mesopotamian texts that bring out its meaning....It never implies that the sexuality of the couple has any cultic or religious significance or that their joining promotes the mythical powers of fertility in the renewal of nature....It has no ritual powers....Sexuality falls into its greatest perversion and excess when it is mythologized and given cosmic significance."

[34] Longman is a Bible scholar commentator who insightfully sees these connections: "The allegorical approach was not wrong in insisting that we read the Song as relevant to our relationship to God.... More than any other human relationship [ideal] marriage reflects the [intended] divine-human relationship....We may have only one spouse and only one God. Accordingly, these are the only two relationships where jealousy can be a positive emotion [cf. 8:6]....[F]rom the Song we learn about the emotional intensity, intimacy, and exclusivity of our relationship with the [Creator] God of the universe" (2001:70, material in brackets added).

commitment of a woman to a man (in the original Hebrew setting, a wife to her husband) and vice-versa. The argument is, however, that this singular work—the actual text being supported by both its linguistic cotext and also its situational context—conveys a message that is notably more, and that "no one can read the Song of Songs without seeing the poetry as analogy for the love he or she holds most dear" (Neusner 1993:4).

6.7 Translating the Song in a *LiFE*-like manner[35]

6.7.1 Above all, lyrically!

In this section I offer a few thoughts on some of the practical implications for translating the SoS. I have already suggested that, questions of historicity and authorship aside (not that these are unimportant), there is a certain hermeneutical continuum that may be applied with reference to most contemporary interpretations of this wonderful lyric passage. This cline extends from the most literal construal of its sense on one pole, yielding a naturalistic secular approach, to a totally symbolic conception on the other, that is, the allegorical point of view. As has been indicated, my own preference is for an overlap in the middle, surrounding the point where the primarily, surface level of signification begins to incorporate a second, an underlying dimension to the message. In other words, the Song is viewed as a lyric court-pastoral form having a conventionalized meaning, that is, idealized human sexual love, that allows, perhaps even urges, also a typological sense which implicates or connotes a strong theological component—YHWH's *chesed* for his people, Israel.

From this hermeneutical standpoint, the *naturalistic* method on the one hand, especially one with an erotic bent, overinterprets the figurative element of the discourse and thus ignores or undervalues the factor of literary genre in relation to its sacred, canonical co-text. The *allegorical* approach, on the other hand, overinterprets the symbolic component of the text and by thus spiritualizing every aspect of the message also undervalues the influence of the poetic genre, but not in relation to its original overt secular context. The proper position, in balance, would seem to be somewhere in between, as shown by the Song's own literary style and structure. What then are some of the implications of such an interpretation on one's translation of the Hebrew text into a contemporary language and sociocultural setting? I will first offer a few thoughts in general on translating the SoS and then present a more detailed case study of how

---

[35] *LiFE* stands for the method of 'literary functional equivalence' as described and illustrated in Wendland 2004b and 2011; see also Appendix B.

a computer-aided approach might assist translators in approaching their task, with special reference to the key text of 8:5–7b. How might a greater measure of *literary* 'functional equivalence' (cf. de Waard and Nida 1986:36ff.; Wendland 2004b:31–97) in the process of communication be achieved in these two respects for both the enlightenment and the enjoyment of an audience/readership today?

With regard to the organizational structure of Song of Solomon, translators should try to render the repetitive elements of this discourse more or less concordantly (to the extent possible, in keeping with TL naturalness) so that the reiteration of the formulaic refrains in particular, might also serve a boundary-marking function in their translation. Of course, this would have to be supplemented by the language-specific means of signaling junctures and borders in the target language, for example, through the use of transitional terms and expressions, word order variations, emphatic particles, specially marked syntactic constructions, rhetorical questions, and so forth. However, one would generally not attempt to smooth over the abrupt textual transitions (e.g., 5:2; 6:11) or to clarify the genuinely ambiguous speaker exchanges (e.g., 1:4, 16) or situational references (for example, 6:12, 13b) where these occur, especially if such a style of discourse would be characteristic of certain dream accounts or even panegyric poetry in the receptor culture and literary tradition. In addition, any passages that have been 'marked' in a literary (artistic-rhetorical) manner in the Hebrew text (i.e., to indicate a thematic 'peak' and/or a hortatory/emotive 'climax') should also be signaled by appropriate means in the translation (e.g., 8:5b–7, see section 6.7.2.1).

The intra-text delineation strategies discussed above can be further complemented by means of certain standard extra-textual *formatting* procedures that draw attention to where major and minor breaks in the discourse occur. These would include, for example, new paragraph indentation, additional interlineal space, changes in typeface (for example, to mark the major refrains), section headings—or in the case of SoS, clearly indicated designations for the identification and shift of speakers (cf. Louw and Wendland 1993: ch. 4). The aim is to provide readers and listeners alike with a text that not only sounds poetic and natural in relation to the Song's lyric subject and communicative purpose, but one that also guides them both visually and audibly through the forest of symbolism of which it is composed.

Solomon's sonorous and symbolic Song definitely needs to be given more attention and effort than it is usually afforded in most translation programs. We are dealing here with a work that stands supreme as one of the highest exponents of its genre in world literature. Why should it not

6.7 Translating the Song in a LiFE-like manner 241

also sound that way—as much as possible—when rendered in the various languages of the world? A great deal of the poem's significance lies in the literary beauty, expressive force, and evocative power of its language in the original Hebrew. Why should much, if not most of this aesthic and emotive element be missing in a given translation? And what about the central message of the Song? Can any topic be more relevant than 'love' today, in any society, when the word is in danger of losing its conceptual and connotative meaning in an age where just about any kind of affection may be so designated, and where the nature of male-female/wife-husband relationships is undergoing a fundamental change? The same could be said of many current religious circles where the amazing character of a holy God's loving-kindness toward a sinful humanity is not adequately comprehended nor fully appreciated by its recipients due to their abysmal ignorance of the nature of the Lord of inspired Scripture. Surely these wise Solomonic words need to be indelibly 'sealed upon our hearts'—as well as on our contemporary attitudes, communication, and behavior:

> Love is as overpowering as death.
> Devotion is as unyielding as the grave.
> Love's flames are flames of fire, flames that come from the LORD.
>
> SoS 8:6 God's Word, cf. Jerusalem Bible

6.7.2 The poetic muse: The computer-assisted translation (CAT)[36]

In dealing with the Song's manifold imagery, our challenge as Bible translators is how to give the target audience at least some idea of the overall significance and emotive impact of the many diverse, but related, figures of the text without overly explicating it, hence destroying its essential poetic nature. A certain amount of literary and cultural contextualization in terms of an appropriate indigenous genre of love (or lyric) poetry will undoubtedly be necessary in order to preserve the dynamic impact, aesthic character, and even the musical dimension of the original. But one cannot go as far in this regard as would contradict the biblical situational context or cause the loss of important intertextual resonances (such as vines/vineyards, cedars, sheep/goats, Lebanon, Mount Carmel). The translator would thus want to look for indigenous conventional figures which have lost their immediate semantic reference and which convey rather an idealized impression of ardor and affection in the target language (cf. Wendland 1987:ch.

---

[36] This section presents the revised version of a paper that was first read at the International Conference on Translating with Computer-Assisted Technology: Changes in Research, Teaching, Evaluation, and Practice – University of Rome 'La Sapienza' (April 14–16, 2004).

5). Furthermore, there should be an effort to avoid a naturalistic, *overly* sexual explication, a rendering that might well turn out to sound pornographic, hence completely unacceptable to those for whom the translation is intended (for example, to replace the fruit-tasting imagery of 4:16 with terms referring too overtly to sexual intercourse).

As a broad working policy then it would perhaps be best to begin by adopting a relatively literal approach throughout and to explicate (for example, by means of paraphrase, qualifiers, or cultural substitutes) only those figures that refer to love in more general terms or those that would turn out to be misleading and misunderstood in the language of translation. Expository footnotes are always possible of course, but even when they happen to be consulted, they tend to be disruptive of the communication process, especially where poetry and other highly emotive-affective works are concerned. Such explanations should be reserved for clarifying the biblical sociocultural setting in terms of the receptor environment and not relied upon as a crutch that aims to compensate prosaically for losses to the dynamic style and rhetoric of the poetic text itself. The following are some more detailed procedures for producing a more lyric rendition of the original Hebrew through the use of computer-aided technology.

6.7.2.1 Select an appropriate target language (TL) genre

Unless a translation team has the benefit of a skilled performing poet in their midst, the process of composing a lyric version of a biblical text will probably be something similar to the following procedure. The first task is to select an appropriate TL genre to use as a translation model. This may have to be adapted in some way to render it suitable for use in the Scriptures, especially if a public worship setting is envisaged. Often a mixed vernacular 'oral-written' style is most effective for a printed text that will usually be presented in spoken form. This is what we tried to achieve in Chewa.[37]

The general lyric genre known as *ndakatulo* appears to be the most fitting and is flexible enough to represent the diverse forms of biblical poetry, including the panegyric, petitionary, sapiential, and prophetic

---

[37] By 'we' I am referring to myself along with a succession of seminary class members that I have been privileged to interact with during a periodic Psalms exegetical course. The closing portion of this time of joint study and research is always devoted to an effort to compose selected psalm texts in the vernacular, employing a musical-choral form if possible. My students normally speak a variety of east-central Bantu languages in addition to English, and most are also able to refer to the original text of Scripture in Hebrew or Greek.

6.7 Translating the Song in a LiFE-like manner

(judicial, homiletical, eschatological) subtypes. Chewa *ndakatulo* poems are characterized by ten crucial stylistic features (Wendland 1993:ch. 3):

- balanced rhythmic lineation (with variation for special effect; there is no 'meter')
- vivid imagery (especially similes and metaphors)
- graphic verbal ideophones (including sound symbolism)
- phonesthetic appeal (alliteration, assonance, selective rhyme, paronomasia)
- syntactic transposition (front- or back-shift—that is, away from a normal S-V-O clause constituent order)
- special referential specification (featuring compound deictics)
- formal and semantic condensation (e.g., ellipsis) or expansion (e.g., reiteration)
- lexical intensification (including synonymy, affixes, and exclamations)
- dialogic dramatization (the prominence of direct speech)
- discourse architecture (text patterning by means of parallelism, inversions, reduplication, and contrastive juxtaposition)

However, it is not simply a matter of matching up feature for feature, or even genre for genre, in a mechanical sort of way, when translating any piece of excellent literature. There are two other important factors to consider, namely, the communicative function(s) and also the *expressed emotions* as well as personal *attitudes* of the original text in relation to any TL genre or sub-genre that is selected to represent it. In other words, how is a particular TL poetic genre, including its associated stylistic devices, normally used in comparison with a given biblical text and with regard to such non-referential aspects of meaning?[38]

In the case at hand, some extensive text-based research has revealed that the *ndakatulo* genre rather closely corresponds with the pastoral-personal love poetry of the Song of Song in terms of several prominent communicative goals (Wendland 1993:ch.4), in particular, the *imperative, expressive, relational,* and *artistic* motivations. Similar speech acts are also performed, such as, to complain, praise, encourage, rebuke, inspire, comfort, or warn someone. This makes a successful poetic trans-formation quite likely—if a

---

[38] Weems rightly calls attention to the important emotive dimension of the SoS, which must accordingly play a corresponding role in any translation: The "[l]yrical poems...function in Song of Songs as the discourse of interior life and the rhetoric of heartfelt emotions.... To see Song of Songs merely as a collection of love poems...is to fail to appreciate the deep and complicated emotions expressed in the book...the poetry of personal sentiment" (1997:366).

skillful translator (or stylist) is available for the task, especially one with a clear inclination towards popular poetic expression in his or her mother tongue.

With a capable translator or translation team in place then, the next step is to fashion a 'base text' that may be subsequently poeticized through the progressive application of various stylistic features that are typical of the genre chosen to serve as a translation model. A question that applies in many translation settings, including Chewa, requires another key choice: is it possible to adapt the text of an existing version for the model, or is it necessary in the interest of expediency to prepare a completely new translation?

In the case of Song of Solomon one must evaluate what is already available to see if that will serve as a textual foundation to start from. Such an assessment exercise is carried out in limited fashion below with reference to the crucial core passage of 8:6b. Selection A comes from the old (1923) Chewa missionary version and B from the more recent (1997) idiomatic popular language version. Relatively literal English back translations are given after each selection:

A. **Pakuti** cikondi cilimba ngati imfa;
    Njiru imangouma ngati manda:
    Kung'anima kwace ndi kung'anima kwa **moto**,
    Ngati **mphenzi** ya Yehova.

> Because love is strong like death;
> Envy becomes hard like a grave:
> Its flashing is the flashing of fire,
> Like lightning of Jehovah.

B. Paja chikondi nchamphamvu ngati imfa,
    nsanje njaliwuma ngati manda.
    Chikondi chimachita kuti **lawilawi** ngati **malawi** a moto,
    ndipo nchotentha koopsa.

> As you know, love is powerful like death,
> jealousy is stubborn like a grave.
> Love often goes flash-flash! Like flames of fire,
> and it is terribly hot.

It would be very difficult to adapt anything on the basis of text A due to its literal unnaturalness, as indicated in the words bolded for this illustration.

6.7 Translating the Song in a LiFE-like manner

For example, its use of the prosaic conjunction *pakuti* 'because'; a term with a strongly negative connotation, *njiru* 'envy'; syntactically linking the 'flashing' (*kung'anima*) of 'lightning' (*mphenzi*) also with ordinary 'fire' (*moto*); and the difficult to understand descriptive expression 'its flashing is the flashing of fire'. Text B is considerably more intelligible and natural in style—but it does not have a distinctively poetic sound. For instance, it does not feature a prevailing rhythmic flow, and there are no striking phonological effects—except for the combination of *lawilawi* 'flashing brightly' (an ideophone) and *malawi* 'flames,' bolded in the text.

So how does one appropriately 'lyricize' and contextualize the imagery of this passage so that it conveys the poetic and semantic essence of the original without going too far—that is, without explicitly denying the biblical setting from which this poem sprung? One possible solution in such instances is the use of indigenous conventional figures which, due to their familiarity, have lost their immediate semantic (sexual?) reference and consequently convey instead an idealized impression of ardor and affection. Another option is to incorporate compact qualifiers that point listeners in the direction of a likely interpretation. We see examples of both solutions in the poetic text C; the preceding standard versions (A and B), neither of which was used as a base, may now be compared with the independently composed poetic rendition, once again with some of the relevant features bolded for discussion purposes, but not in the proposed text.

C. *Kunena inetu, **ch**ikondi si**ch**itha mpaka imfa;*
    *ch**ayaka psi! monga moto uwala wa **Ch**auta!*
    *Ch**angu **ch**anga n'**ch**ouma gwa! ngati manda.*

> Well as for me, [my] love does not end until death;[39]
> it's on fire, ashes! like the shining flame of the Creator![40]
> My zeal is rock-hard! just like the graveyard.

Other characteristic Chewa literary-stylistic features in text C include alliteration, assonance, rhyme, rhythm, intensive (self-) reference, descriptive ideophones, elaboration ('rock-hard' = resolute 'zeal'),

---

[39] In Chewa, it is not natural to say that love is as 'strong' as death; rather, true love 'persists' until death.

[40] In Chewa the fire of love is described as 'shining' like fire in order to eliminate the grounds of this simile that do not fit in the context, e.g., a destructive blaze or a fire for warming/cooking/lighting/etc.

and balanced lineation, lineation with 16, 14, and 11 syllables per line respectively.

6.7.2.2 Computer-prompted and perfected poetry

What was done then to compose passage C poetically—in other words, how was it possible to 'prompt the poetic muse' here? More specifically, how did the computer facilitate this process of literary creation? Thinking back on my experience when composing not only this passage, but many others as well (a reflective translation protocol), nine procedures came to mind, as summarized and exemplified below. Thus, a word-processing program and other computerized tools may assist the poet-translator as follows:[41]

1. The ease of composition on a computer, compared to longhand writing, stimulates the *smooth flow of ideas*—that is, compositional fluency, with a minimum of delay or interruption between the mind and a page of print; similarly, all sorts of corrections and revisions (alterations, deletions, additions) can be swiftly carried out without having to rewrite an entire line, stanza, or page.[42]

2. Words, phrases, and even entire lines can be quickly modified and moved, that is, shifted around within a document in order to create or improve the *oral-aural sound dimension* of the draft—that is, in

---

[41] I should also mention here some excellent electronic text-processing tools and translation helps such as *Paratext* (currently, version 7) and *Translator's Workplace* (5.0), which are most helpful when carrying out the tasks of source-text exegesis and target-text revision. However, in this section I am focusing on computer-aided techniques that are applied during the later *compositional* process, (i.e., post-exegesis + preliminary draft) and for the special purpose of preparing a specifically *poetic* version. This includes a subsequent 'literary' assessment and text-polishing ('poeticizing') phase, which may be carried out as a joint team exercise by means of a computer network or multipoint work area.

[42] After completing several drafts of this study, I read Per Qvale's helpful book on translation theory and practice. Corresponding to the present point he writes: "[T]he possibilities for infinite rewriting mean that one can allow oneself to find the best solutions without spending time removing text with the correction key or with correction fluid or x-ing over it. With a keystroke the PC corrects anything you type" (2003:255)—and it even shows you where you made basic spelling and grammatical errors! However, I (personally) do not agree with Qvale's subsequent observation: "[I]t is far more pleasant to sit in the sun with a manuscript pile proof reading and polishing. And here the pencil comes into its own..." (Qvale 2003:255). I happily remain seated behind my computer to carry on with these final text-editing tasks (e.g., using the track changes function).

6.7 Translating the Song in a LiFE-like manner

terms of its rhythm, rhyme, alliteration, assonance, or paronomasia—while the poet actually utters and/or varies the text aloud.

3. Syllables, words, and phrases can also be easily shifted about or replaced when *weighing several translation options* in the effort either to produce a more artistic ('poetic') style—or to return a dynamic text to a more accurate or acceptable level of exegetical fidelity.

4. The lighted computer screen helps the eye to *focus on chunks* of text, rather than individual lines—an entire strophe or stanza in particular—thus promoting a consideration of *the poetic whole* as well as the constituent parts, with reference to the original text as well as its ongoing translation.

5. Following on from the preceding point, different types of *typography and format* may be experimented with, both to attract the eyes of readers (to give it a more 'poetic image' on the printed page) and also to make the passage easier to process, with significant patches of empty space, thus making the textual boundaries easier to see, and the whole easier to enunciate aloud.

6. Poetic drafts can be immediately and widely shared with colleagues to get their *critical feedback* and suggested improvements to the text; these may be inserted directly into the initial draft or indicated by the 'track changes' function (Microsoft Word) for the original author to consider.

7. Alternative drafts may be readily evaluated in relation to each other by means of a para-textual display that permits a *close comparison* of one poetic line and its distinctive stylistic features with its correspondent from another model text or version.

8. An *interlinear back translation* and a textual *concordance* for checking lexical consistency (or spelling inconsistencies!) can be prepared without much difficulty to serve as a tool for assisting the translation consultant and/or other technical advisers (e.g., exegetes), who may not have adequate command of the vernacular, so that they are able to make critical comments on a draft version in relation to the original poetic text.

9. Finally, a computer makes it easy to access the Internet (especially via a 'search engine' like *Google*) to connect with on-line reference websites and home pages as well as various hypertext programs or CD ROMs (e.g., *Encyclopedia Britannica*, or *Translator's Workplace*) in order to gain background material, including illustrations, concerning just about any subject imaginable.[43] Such information sources may be tapped at any time during the compositional process, or when making a subsequent revision, as a means of improving the text in many major or minor ways that pertain to both form (style) and content. In addition, to obtain the answers to more specific questions, one can contact experts and research colleagues in a given field of study via topic-centered websites, bulletin boards, chat rooms, or e-mail discussion forums, for example, with regard to the Song of Songs, translating biblical poetry, or even modern Chewa *ndakatulo* lyrics.

All of these factors operate together to streamline the overall process of text-composition: "…the translator can concentrate more fully and be more completely absorbed in and dedication (sic) to their work, which leads to a correspondingly improved translation" (Qvale 2003:256).[44]

I naturally referred to the existing translations (A and B) when drafting my own poetic rendition (C). This was in addition to the Hebrew original text and several English translations, none of which were very helpful for my purposes. However, such a *comparative* exercise served to stimulate my thinking in terms of where problems existed, what modifications could be made, and how some new, more poetic expressions might be fashioned—that is, in keeping with the feature specifications for the *ndakatulo* lyric genre.

The first eight computer-aided procedures outlined above were selectively applied to the peak pericope of SoS 8:5b–7 to produce a series of

---

[43] "Hypertext is a term referring to a type of electronic document that contains cross-references and that rather than having a book's simple linear sequence is nonsequential, so that there are many different paths linking two elements in a hypertext structure" (Qvale 2003:259).

[44] "On the other hand, some claim that many books become too long and prolix because the computer offers authors too little resistance. Authors correct and correct so incredibly easy *(sic)* that they lose their original style, lose the physical contact with the written word, lose the reflectiveness of pencil sharpening and the sobriety of dipping a nib into ink" (Qvale 2003:256). Speaking for myself, this has not been my experience; I do not miss pencil and ink at all! I rather appreciate the facility of being able to 'correct and correct' my material so readily.

6.7 Translating the Song in a LiFE-like manner 249

draft translations that eventually resulted in the following 'final' version, which is designed to reflect an idiomatic *ndakatulo* style. The compositional ease and flexibility of a word-processing program is especially helpful to a person like myself, who is not a 'natural' (innate and spontaneous) poet in Chewa—or any other language for that matter—someone who works more by imitation of an ideal, rather than by instinct. The computer is also helpful for producing a series of draft editions that can be read and critiqued by others (in my case, by mother tongue seminary students) and then also for incorporating their recommended corrections and suggested improvements. Thus the text which follows is very much a composite work, the product of many minds—which is a useful analogy for Bible translation since it normally follows a similar method of team composition.

Some of the main poetic features that were introduced into the entire strophe covering verses 5b–7 are identified by brief descriptive-explanatory footnotes in the Chewa lyric rendition below; these are also marked by boldface in the corresponding, relatively literal English back-translation:

Ine ndidakuyatsa mtima[45] *patsinde pa mango*[46]— 5. **I aroused your heart** at the base of that **mango** [tree],

uja mtengo[47] *adachirirapo*[48] *amai pakubala iwe.*[49]   **the very tree** where your mother **recovered** in delivering **you**.

Umatirire mtima[50] *ndi chosindikiza chosalekeza*[51]   6. **Fasten your heart** with **a seal that does not let go**

---

[45] Idiom (literally) 'I set your heart on fire'—here, in terms of great affection.

[46] 'Mango' is a close local cultural substitute for the foreign 'apple' and the unknown 'apricot'.

[47] The double locative term in Hebrew ('there') is replaced by a twofold mention of the identifying 'tree'.

[48] There is a translation loss here in that the original notion of 'conception' is not mentioned—for the sake of cultural propriety. On the other hand, an idiomatic, euphemistic expression for the child-delivery event is included—i.e., 'she recovered [as from an injury or serious illness]'. There is also an overlapping link-rhyme with *mango* and *mtengo*.

[49] The first two balanced poetic lines (comprising a complete utterance) are also tied together by the pronominal inclusio: initial *Ine* 'I' and final *iwe* 'you', which forms a chiastic pattern in conjunction with the following two lines with 'your' toward the beginning of in line three and 'me' toward the end of line four.

[50] A Chewa idiom is constructed here by analogy using the productive figurative base image of 'heart' *(mtima)*, which is close to the Hebrew expression.

[51] The final two words of this line feature an alliterative combination, not just in their initial /ch/ consonants, but also with most of the following sequence of consonants in the two words and their accompanying vowels, as underlined in the text. Only the unshared segments are not underlined, showing their close similarity.

kuti musalowedi winanso, koma ine ndekha.[52]	lest **any other** enter there **at all**, except **me alone**.
Kunena inetu,[53] ***chikondi sichitha mpaka imfa,***	**Well as for me,** [my] love does not end until death,
Chayaka psi![54] ***monga moto uwala wa Chauta!***[55]	It's on fire, **ashes!** as the shining flame of the **Creator!**
Changu changa n'chouma gwa![56] ***ngati manda.***	My **zeal** is **rock-hard!** just like the graveyard.
Chikondi chimenechi[57] *palibe madzi a chigumula*	7. **A love like this,** there are no flood waters
angathe[58] *kuchizimitsa kapena kuchikokolola, ai!*[59]	**able** to **put it out** or **sweep it away**, **not at all!**
Ngakhale[60] *munthu atapereka chuma chonse,*	**Even though** a person were to give all [his] wealth,
kufunitsitsa kugula chikondi choterechi,[61]	trying his best to purchase **a love of this sort,**
iyeyu adzangonyozeka nazo zyolizyoli![62]	he would be **fully embarrassed** in the effort—for **shame!**

---

[52] A combination of emphatic features in Chewa highlight this added line which clarifies the implication of the original repeated Hebrew figure of the 'seal-signet': verb gapping ('enter'), word order (subject-verb inversion), intensive suffixes (*-di, -nso*), and a final emphatic pronoun (*ndekha*), which in turn rhymes with the end of the preceding line.

[53] The climactic line is set off and highlighted by this fronted *casus pendens* construction.

[54] The ideophone *psi!* suggests a scene of burnt up devastation, thus also hyperbolic here.

[55] Assonance in the /a/ vowel sounds helps foreground this entire line, which also makes explicit the allusive reference to YHWH (*Chauta*, the traditional 'High [Creator] God' of the Chewa people) in the original text. The last two lines of v. 6 are reversed in order so that the content flows more smoothly.

[56] The ideophone *gwa!* ('hard as a rock') is preceded by alliteration that stresses the key term *changu* 'zeal', carrying over into the next line to aurally incorporate *chikondi* 'love'.

[57] The front-shifted, hence emphasized, noun-demonstrative combination 'love like this' is composed of two words starting with the sequence *chi-* and echoed also by the last word which also begins with *chi-*. This line is closely tied to the next line by the verbal affix *-chi-* which occurs in two of its words.

[58] Syntactic enjambment mimics the flow of a flood—that cannot extinguish true love!

[59] The final negative emphasizer *ai* is preceded by a pair of figurative verbal concepts: 'put it out [like a fire]' and 'sweep it away [as with a broom]'.

[60] The initial conjunction *Ngakhale* suggests that a more prosaic passage follows, as in the original Hebrew text.

[61] More demonstrative marking, coupled with alliteration, links the key terms 'love' (*chikondi*) and 'wealth' (*chuma*).

[62] Several poetic devices converge to foreground the final plight of the foolish person who seeks to purchase 'love': an initial emphatic pronoun, alliteration in /z/, a phonologically coupled verb + ideophone combination (*-nyozeka* + *zyolizyoli*), and a final line rhyme with /i/ sounds.

It is worth emphasizing the point here that most of the lyrical features manifested in this passage were not present in the first translation drafts. They were incorporated later only after repeated oral readings (aloud!) and rewritings (see the example in section 6.7.2.4). Such modifications are enabled—in fact encouraged—by use of the computer due to the ease with which it can manipulate a verbal text to achieve varied formal and functional effects involving the sense, significance, as well as aesthetic style of a poetic passage. This would be especially helpful when the poetry is being simultaneously composed to synchronize with a musical, multi-voiced dramatic setting, an activity that modern computers can also help to develop and coordinate much easier than if such a production were attempted by means of a written text. The artistic muse with reference to the Song of Songs is thus electronically activated not only verbally (by way of intuitive *Schprachgefühl*), but also in terms of its resonant musical voice!

6.7.2.3 Computer-assisted poetic composition through text corpora

In this section and the next I will survey two ways in which the use of specific computer word processing programes can assist translators and their trainers in rendering of poetic originals. Both ways involve the use of large compilations of electronic texts, or *corpora* (sg., *corpus*), when making a critical evaluation of the products of translation.

In the field of 'corpus linguistics' a 'text' is defined as "an instance of language in use, either spoken or written: a piece of language behavior which has occurred naturally…" (M. Stubbs, cited in Kenny 2001a:50), while a 'corpus' consists of "a collection of texts held in machine-readable form and capable of being analyzed automatically or semi-automatically in a variety of ways" (Baker 1995:225).[63] In theoretical terms, corpus-based descriptive linguistics (and its various applications, as in translation studies) focuses on "what is probable in a language, according to the available evidence (i.e., *parole*), rather than what is possible (i.e., *langue*), according to a set of Chomsky-like a-priori rules" (Kenny 2001b:28, my additions in parentheses). This emphasis also distinguishes corpus linguistics from cognitive approaches that involve rather detailed descriptions of what individual analysts speculate concerning the logical strategies of language use, which are often based upon a minimal, even hypothetical, corpus of concrete text material.[64]

---

[63] "Corpus linguistics is the computational and statistical analysis of representing samples of naturally occurring language to identify patterns of meaning" (Porter and O'Donnell 2009:185).

[64] For a critique of such 'mentalist' methodologies, see Yallop 2003:204.

There are three somewhat different types of corpora that are available in the major languages of the world (Baker 1995; Kenny 2001a:51–52; Kenny 2001b:ch. 3; Olohan 2004):

- A *parallel* corpus is a twofold collection of texts consisting of documents originally written in language X together with their translations into language Y.

- A *multilingual* corpus consists of original texts in a number of different languages (X, Y, Z) that have been selected according to specific design criteria, e.g., text type, date(s), size, intended audience, and so forth.

- A *comparable* corpus of original texts written in language X, specified as to macro- or micro-genre, *in contrast to* a collection of similar texts that have been translated into X from one or more other languages (Y, Z).

The most useful type of corpora for translation analysis and assessment when working towards an idiomatic, lyric rendition of the SoS would appear to be the third (*comparable*) category, thus comparing natural literature/orature with translated texts.[65] This might include, for example, a set of originally composed Chewa poetic texts on the one hand, and on the other, extensive samples of biblical poetry as translated in the three major published Bibles of Chewa (perhaps including also the Bibles of closely related Malawian languages, such as Tumbuka or Sena).

However, any corpus is only as helpful as the amount of work that has gone into pre-processing it. A 'raw' corpus is one that is neither tagged according to selected distinctive features nor grammatically parsed, but which manifests only minimal annotation, such as text, sectional, paragraph (strophe), sentence, clause, or line boundaries. The computer (word processing) analysis of such a corpus can reveal such straightforward compositional features as lexical variety or redundancy, general semantic density (e.g., by removing all grammatical words), preferred lexical collocations, and average sentence or clause length. This is not very exciting, and an intuitive feeling for such characteristics could probably be gained simply by reading a great deal of textual material over time.[66]

---

[65] Porter and O'Donnell note that "[t]he comparative model has been the predominant one in translation studies," but this is defined along the lines of a parallel corpus above, viz., "Features are selected from the source language and compared to their target-language translation" (2009:186).

[66] Qvale too notes that "[t]his sort of research [i.e., text corpus-based] depends on a large mass of material for analysis, to enable researchers to extract segments for computer analysis and comparison. However, there are big problems with sampling and programming, and

6.7 Translating the Song in a LiFE-like manner

A linguistically 'tagged' corpus on the other hand could be quite revealing, for example, to indicate prominent patterns of difference between original composition and translated material with regard to such features as the relative proportions of different parts of speech, phrase/clause/sentence types, preferred sentence structure and sentence length, the kinds of external and internal transitional constructions, verb-sequence or tense-aspect patterns, and word order variations (including advancement to indicate 'topic' and 'focus'). Thus far, a number of corpus-based studies have revealed that "translated texts tend to be more explicit, unambiguous, and lexically or grammatically conventional than their source texts or other texts produced in the target language. They also tend to avoid repetitions that occur in the source text and to exaggerate features of the target language" (Kenny 2001a:52), such as compositional forms which are typical of a particular genre of literature or its translation into language X.[67]

However, for the literary analysis of a *poetic* corpus, additional stylistic devices would need to be marked in the texts so that they could be identified, sorted, numbered, and compared—for example, with respect to the occurrence of different types of figurative language (simile, metaphor,

---

one wonders whether the costs do not outweigh the benefits" (2003:252).

[67] In a major computer-based analysis of lexical creativity in a corpus of German literary texts, Kenny concludes that "most of the time creative lexis in the source texts...is not normalized in translation, and some translators prove to be ingenious wordsmiths in their own right" (2001b:210)—the details of which need to be further investigated. On the other hand, "certain translators may be more inclined to normalize than others," for example, with respect to "text lexical features that draw on the more systematic processes of word formation in German—derivation and conversion to verbal nouns..." (ibid., 211). Kenny ends her book with the candid observation that, generally speaking, "the findings of corpus-based studies are in some ways suggestions for future research" (Kenny 2001b:211).

In spite of Kenny's conclusion that more research is needed, much progress has been made in recent years in electronically documenting some of the world's larger languages. For example, there is now a regular international symposium on *Using Corpora in Contrastive and Translation Studies* (UCCTS), which aims to provide an international forum for the exploration of the theoretical and practical issues pertaining to the creation and use of corpora in literary and translation-related composition. A recent conference (Hangzhou, China on 25–27 September 2008) dealt with the following major themes: the design and development of comparable and parallel corpora; processing of multilingual corpora; using corpora in translation studies and teaching; using corpora in cross-linguistic contrast; corpus-based comparative research of source native language, translated language and target native language; and corpus-based research of interface between contrastive and translation studies. Indeed, some interesting applications of corpus linguistics to socio-stylistic, literary and translation studies is currently being made; for example, papers from the conference include, "Translating metaphors: A corpus-based approach" [Michael Barlow], and "A parallel, corpus-based study of translational Chinese" [Kefei Wang and Hongwu Qin]. (From the conference website: http://www.lancs.ac.uk/fass/projects/corpus/UCCTS2008Proceedings/)

metonymy, personification, etc.), novel idioms, rhetorical and deliberative questions, dialectal terms, incorporated direct discourse, citations, rhetorical uses of hyperbole, exclamations, intensifiers, ideophones, and extended attribution. It is important to know not only the diversity and frequency of such literary characteristics, but also their distribution and co-occurence within individual texts, as well as an indication of boundaries and peaks within a given discourse or set of texts of a particular genre. Unfortunately, I am unaware of any significant corpus in any language, literary or otherwise, that has been tagged to such explicit, feature-specific detail.[68]

To be sure, "computers offer new perspectives in the study of language...[allowing] us to see phenomena that previously remained obscure because of the limitations of our vantage points" (Kenny 2001b:xiii). Due to the concrete data that they produce with regard to a given corpus of texts, computers also make it possible for researchers to "corroborate, or repudiate, the findings of an initial study based on that corpus...[thus] stimulating multiple analyses and inviting researchers to constantly rethink their positions" (ibid., 69). On the other hand, analysts must be aware of certain notable problems in connection with handling corpus-based computer-generated data. These include the following concerns:

- The emphasis on establishing statistically verifiable norms may lead to a tendency to ignore or downplay marginal or extraordinary cases and significant data that are represented only by a limited number of instances, i.e., the exceptions and poetic idiosyncrasies that are of special interest to literary practitioners and critics alike.

- The textual context, or cotext, displayed by most computer-generated concordances is not really sufficient to conduct anything more than superficial counts and simple collocational studies, which always need to be complemented by more expansive, discourse-oriented studies of the data. But increasingly sophisticated text-processing programs are proportionately more expensive.

- *Quantitatively* (statistically) supported text patterns and regularities provide a foundation, but cannot take the literary analyst and translation evaluator very far; such hard facts must always be complemented by qualitative, interpretive methods of analysis, like the comprehensive 'close-reading' exercise that was carried out in section 6.4 on SoS 8:5b–7.

---

[68] I make a number of more specific suggestions concerning the possible application of computer-generated text data from corpora to Bible translation in Wendland 2003:227.

6.7 Translating the Song in a LiFE-like manner

- Finally, the general lack of availability of these corpora, or text data bases, for the great majority of languages in the world, e.g., the whole Bantu family of Africa (let alone Chewa), presents a significant barrier to comparative analyses and assessments such as those described above; this is a serious obstacle that will not be easily overcome, due to the lack of adequate financial resources and qualified staff.

With respect to the last point, I should note what I had available as a text corpus for comparison and examples when working on my poetic rendition of the SoS passage. My small collection consisted of six published booklets of Chewa *ndakatulo* poetry spanning a period of forty years, plus a number of transcribed oral texts (village tales and radio dramas). After they had all been keyboarded into the Microsoft Word program,[69] the result totaled 128 A4 pages, containing some 7000 poetic lines, 34,600 words, and approximately 200,000 characters. This is an admittedly diminutive database in comparison with the massive ones referred to in the literature, but my material includes at least 50 per cent of all that has been published and is presently available in the Chewa language.

In any case, that corpus of raw text is of little use to me, since before I can meaningfully manipulate the data, the material first needs to be electronically tagged with respect to the main features of *ndakatulo* lyric style so that they may be readily located for analytical purposes. This would be a very large assignment that can only be carried out successfully by well-trained mother-tongue assistants, supported by a generous amount of financial assistance! It will be some time, therefore, before we will be able to prompt the poetic muse and benefit translators by means of this method.

6.7.2.4 Computer-assisted training techniques

In addition to giving us insights for compositional modeling and assessment, corpus linguistics can also enhance Bible translation training. Due to the lack of a suitably tagged corpus of Chewa poetic texts, I have no direct experience of this. However, there is practical translation instruction in Lynne Bowker's article in *The Translator: Studies in Intercultural Communication* (2000, subtitled "Evaluation and translation"). I briefly

---

[69] I first tried scanning this material into the computer, but the process proved to be too prone to errors due to the poor quality of the original copies. Perhaps a more sophisticated (and undoubtedly more expensive!) scanner would have solved my problem—at least in part. However, the print quality of a number of the booklets is probably so low as to not allow for scanning on any machine.

summarize the main implications of this well-documented study (listing only the page numbers by way of reference).

Bowker begins with the well-founded assertion that "evaluation is one of the most problematic areas of translation, having been variously described as 'a great stumbling block'…'a complex challenge'…'a most wretched question'…and 'a thorny problem'" (2000:183, internal references omitted). This is due to the largely subjective nature of such an endeavor due to the "fuzzy and shifting boundaries" of the notion of *quality* as well as "the lack of universally applicable criteria according to which translations may be assessed" (183). In an effort then to find a more objective and teachable approach to translation evaluation, Bowker proposes the use of a compound, electronic "evaluation corpus", the aim of which is to:

> …act as a benchmark against which translator trainers can compare student translations on a number of different levels. By having access to a wide range of authentic and suitable texts, the trainer can verify or correct the students' choices, both conceptual and linguistic, and can provide more constructive and objective feedback based on evidence (or the lack thereof) in the corpus. (2000:184)

According to her definition (2000:188), Bowker would employ a "multilingual" type of corpus for her translation assessment work, but it appears that a "comparable" corpus would serve the desired purpose better (see definitions in 6.2.7.3). A large corpus of varied texts in the TL would also serve in this case.[70] From either database then an evaluation corpus would be selected, consisting of three sub-corpora, which differ according to content and intended function as follows (2000:191–194):

- The *Quality Corpus* is a small high-quality collection, consisting of texts that have been written by experts and chosen for their excellence of conceptual content and relative proximity in genre and subject matter to the primary source text (ST); this corpus is intended to help evaluate whether or not the student translators have correctly understood the key concepts and major themes of the ST.

---

[70] In a somewhat different research experiment, Stella Tagnin found that "Parallel corpora (texts in one language with their corresponding translations) can be extremely helpful in that, when adequately queried, they produce a large number of 'equivalents', which can be analyzed qualitatively as to their adequacy in a certain context" (from the abstract page of the Rome *Translating with Computer-Assisted Technology* conference program, p. 39; see 6.7.2 footnote 36).

6.7 Translating the Song in a LiFE-like manner   257

- The *Quantity Corpus* is a much larger collection of texts dealing with the same subject as the ST and having a similar function; this corpus is intended to assist in the assessment of *stylistic form*, including the use of key terms and longer expressions, appropriate collocations, as well as discourse arrangements that are natural and characteristic of the semantic field and text-type in focus.

- The *Inappropriate Corpus* is a collection of texts that deal with the same general subject matter as the ST, but which are *unsuitable* as translation *models* in different respects, for example, in terms of compositional style, register, genre, terminology, discourse organization, format, and so forth; the aim of this corpus is to provide textual feedback to the student translators as to where they made errors or problematic choices in their own renditions of the ST.

As a result of her research Bowker found that translation trainers (consultants) who made use of such an evaluation corpus technique were significantly more effective in their draft evaluation work with respect to both quantity and quality than colleagues who employed traditional methods of critical assessment. In addition, these evaluators were also appreciated more by the students themselves because their judgment was viewed as being more concrete, or 'objective' in nature.[71]

Although not tested directly in this study, the results seem to indicate that the student-translators themselves benefit from this corpus-based procedure when the Inappropriate Corpus is "used as a source of examples for discussing the appropriateness of different translations of the same text according to different briefs" (i.e., project terms of reference, 206) and as a stimulus for what Bastin terms "creative re-expression" in translator training exercises (2000:231).[72] It is clear that computer generated technology can serve to facilitate the "three main techniques for stimulating creativity": associative conceptual "brainstorming", the temporary

---

[71] In another paper presented at the Rome CAT conference ("Evaluating the use of tools and not only the quality of the student's output in translation teaching"), Patricia Rodríguez Inés suggests three qualitative criteria that might be assessed, namely, "collocational appropriateness, the speed at which the translation in question is produced, [and] the terminological consistency of the translated text" (from the abstract page of the conference program, p. 36).

[72] "If re-expression is to be better *taught*, evaluation of re-expression must be better *thought*" (ibid., 231), that is, by providing translators with more excellent models to follow in their work, whether that be a single text or an entire literary work (or Bible translation). Qvale offers this possibility: "Text corpus-based, computer-assisted research involving comparisons of different translators' rendering of the same text, for instance, may also be valuable aids to achieving insight into parts of the process" (2003:252).

shift to a "parallel-activity" as a way to "overcome blockage", and as a means of "generating logical (certainly also connotative) alternatives" (ibid., 243; addition in parentheses).

Either independently or as part of the preceding methodology, use of the highlighting option (and/or the colored-ink facility) coupled with the track changes function of the Word program, for example, might be employed to display a succession of drafts with revisions as part of a computer-assisted training course (cf. Qvale 2003:252–253). As an illustration of this,[73] consider our key passage, in Song of Songs 8:6b. Proceeding from the popular language version (B) to the final poetic rendition (C), the 'lyricization' process might be displayed as follows (where normal print represents the first/original draft, and additions during subsequent drafting are indicated by the following changes in the type format: *second,* **third,** and ***final*** draft):

1. (= **B**) Paja chikondi nchamphamvu ngati imfa,
    nsanje njaliwuma ngati manda.
    Chikondi chimachita kuti lawilawi ngati malawi a moto,
    ndipo nchotentha koopsa.

2. *Kunena inetu,* chikondi *sichitha mpaka* imfa,
    nsanje njaliwuma ngati manda.
    Chikondi chimachita *psi!* ngati malawi a moto,
    ndipo nchotentha koopsa.

3. *Kunena inetu,* chikondi *sichitha mpaka* imfa,
    Changu changa n'chouma ngati manda.
    Chayaka *psi!* ngati malawi a moto,
    ndipo nchotentha koopsa.

4. (= C) *Kunena inetu,* chikondi *sichitha mpaka* imfa,
    Chayaka *psi!* ngati ***moto uwala wa Chauta.***
    Changu changa n'chouma ngati manda.

DRAFT *Selective comments on each of the three revision drafts*

---

[73] My original paper was able to visually reproduce the sequence of track-changes operations as well as the different colored shadings (to indicate different drafts) to demonstrate the process of revision. This is not possible of course in a black and white printed publication.

6.7 Translating the Song in a LiFE-like manner 259

Second *Paja* sounds too prosaic for a lyric passage; replace with a transitional phrase ('Well, as for me...'). A 'love' that 'does not end' is more idiomatic than 'is powerful'. The ideophone *psi!* 'sustained burning' is more dynamic here than *lawilawi* 'flashing intermittently'.

Third The term *nsanje* 'envy' has a negative connotation; better to replace with *changu* 'zeal'. Such zeal 'is hard' like a grave rather than 'stingy'. 'Love/zeal' 'burns'—a more dynamic way to introduce the ideophone *psi!*

Fourth Instead of 'like flames of fire', the revision tries to reflect the original (as interpreted) more closely: 'like a shining fire of Chauta (Yahweh)'. The lines of the text were reordered and condensed for rhythmic purposes and also to render it more 'poetic'-sounding.

The track changes 'comment' function can thus be utilized to raise queries, make corrections with explanations, and suggest some possible options in a very visible, easy-to-read way (compared with an editor's handwritten scribbles on a typewritten text!).

Given the provision of needed technical and human resources in disadvantaged areas of the world (see 6.7.2.5 conclusion), such computer-oriented methods might be readily adapted for use in the training of Bible translators, especially in the case of languages, like Chewa, that have at least a small literary tradition, as well as a history of Bible translation. Since the Bible is *sui generis*, however, it would not be necessary to make use of a Quality Corpus with respect to religious *content*. Therefore, this database could be merged with the Quantity Corpus in order to provide some natural, idiomatic *formal* models to follow during the composition and evaluation of poetic vernacular texts. This corpus would be comprised of the collection of published secular *ndakatulo* texts, as mentioned earlier, as well as by other genres of Chewa discourse, both religious and secular. Because the available corpus of published texts is relatively small and since many of the same stylistic features are found in both prose and poetry, it may not be necessary to distinguish these basic types of literature, at least initially. Recognized 'quality', as determined by a panel of experts, would be the only criterion necessary for inclusion in this corpus. Well-liked vernacular hymns or other types of lyric poetry, along with stylistically outstanding texts selected from the idiomatic popular-language version of the Bible (*Buku Loyera*), might be added to augment this general corpus of stylistic 'excellence' to differentiate it from its opposite.

An Inappropriate Corpus could then be formed from corresponding poetic excerpts taken from the other two literal, Chewa Bible translations, the Protestant *Buku Lopatulika* and the Catholic *Malembo Oyera*, as well as from stylistically mediocre or poorly structured texts selected from other (sub-)types of religious and secular literature, vernacular as well as translations. Translator trainees would be given the assignment of rendering a relatively large, but distinct pericope from the SoS, for example, and their respective drafts could then be compared respectively with the two 'control' corpora (i.e., the 'excellent' and the 'inappropriate') in order to both evaluate the quality of their compositions and instruct them where and how improvements might be made, either to their individual texts or a composite joint version prepared by a team.

6.7.2.5 Conclusion

> The theme of this conference asserts that computer-assisted technology and the digitization of information have changed the theory and practice of translating, both globally and irreversibly. From one point of view, computer-assisted technology has brought only minimal and cosmetic change. Computers just help us work faster, smarter.
>
> But from another point of view, computer-assisted technology and digitization have radically transformed not just the surface structure of this profession, but also its deep internal structures as well. And they have done so in ways that we only now begin to fathom, whether we are speaking of biblical, literary, technical, scientific, audio-visual, or multimedia translating. (*Vision Statement* – International Conference on Translating with Computer-Assisted Technology)

My study, though rather limited in its scope, would nevertheless lend support to the two major assertions that lie at the heart of the stated vision of this conference (Rome 2004): concerning the role of computer-assisted translation not only with regard to the *practice of translation*, but also with regard to its *theory*.

At this stage, changes to the *theory* of translation art and science are less easy to specify. I might suggest that the manifold 'hypertext' as well as para-textual reference capacity of the computer make it possible for the translator to readily display, compare, analyze, and network with several texts at once—that is, the source document and possibly one or more extant versions, whether drafts or previously published editions. Databases of model texts representing different genres of TL literature or orature and/or evaluation corpora like those discussed above could be accessed for contrastive examination, to determine, for example, the relative degree of 'equivalence' between the SL and TL and between the TL and TL Quality Corpus, with regard to selected features. This multiple *comparative* compositional procedure coupled with an immediate access to topical resources not only promotes greater accuracy, but it also acts as a stimulus to the creative imagination, most notably in the case of a literary (e.g., poetic) rendition.

The mutually stimulating influence of several similar, but also noticeably different, texts on the spontaneous cognitive and emotive activity of trans-forming texts cannot be minimized. In the language of cognitive poetics, more distinct "mental spaces" and consequent contextually-shaped "conceptual blending" (e.g., Coulson 2001:115–123) can thereby be generated simultaneously in a translator's mind and then applied during the text-transfer operation. This makes the latter a complex, cyclical, interactively creative process, rather than a more mechanically straightforward and linear conceptual exercise (i.e., rule-governed, procedure-dominated). Such a deliberate appeal to one's insights, interests, and intuition during the interlingual and intercultural exchange of texts will no doubt have some significant implications for the formulators of future translation theory, which I now expect will emerge first from the psycholinguistic and more innovative literary-sensitive branches of our discipline.

More obvious and immediate, of course, are the *practical* translation benefits of CAT. Indeed, the results of utilizing this electronic resource are exemplified above in terms of the Chewa poetic composition of SoS 8:5b–7. In addition to improved text-processing, especially with respect to a genre-based poetic, dramatic, and perhaps even a musical vernacular version (*synthesis*), the computer's potential in the key areas of draft evaluation (*analysis*) and translator training (*pedagogy*) has also been noted in passing. However, it is important to observe that the qualities of 'faster' and 'smarter' mentioned above must be extended to include also a greater measure of *accuracy*—that is, 'faithfulness,' with respect to the original SL text, as well as 'loyalty' in relation to the project sponsors and the translation brief which they initially formulated to guide the work. This issue is of special concern of course in the case of Scripture translation. These challenges may be confronted by means of the great *comparative* facility that a computer makes possible, for example, with reference to the original text, to various translations of that same text, as well as to key translation models that may be used to stimulate and to direct an acceptable representation of the SL document in the TL. Prominent formal differences from the source document can thus be made to visually stand out (for example, by means of a paratextual, selectively-highlighted display) and then be investigated for their significance in terms of different aspects of denotative and connotative (including also affective and aesthetic) meaning.

However, a final *caveat* or two needs to be reiterated in closing: as already suggested, several critical impediments remain to the stated claim that 'global' changes have (already) been effected or achieved by computer-based technology. It is a sobering fact that in many parts of the developing world critical limiting factors such as those listed here continue to muffle the voice of the poet in the realm of vernacular literary promotion in general and Bible translation in particular. There is a general lack of:

- an adequate educational and technological, including internet-based, infrastructure;
- computer-related resources (namely, their prohibitive cost for a majority of the population);
- experienced and capable teachers, facilitators, and on-the-job monitors;
- modern training techniques, tools, and facilities;
- other project-oriented considerations (e.g., time allocation, sufficient finances, a manifest desire or commitment on the part of program organizers, and the requisite educational background).

Some challenging, perhaps provocative questions must therefore be asked in closing:

> Must a local situation of deprivation and a consequent lack of progress or achievement in the field of literary (oratorical) translation remain an irreversible 'status quo' in this era of globalization? Why can some realistic and workable solution not be found to reverse it—in the interest of many depressed and endangered language-cultures worldwide? More specifically, why can the lyric voice of the poetic muse not be liberated everywhere, in Africa? How long must the Song of Songs continue to sound like dull, sometimes impenetrable prose in the local vernaculars?

Lastly, it may be necessary to point out that this oft-repressed poetic impulse cannot be compelled or cajoled to do the impossible. So, the next time you (or a member of your translation team) grapple in futility

6.7 Translating the Song in a LiFE-like manner

with some challenging passage of poetry, you might recall the following advice:

> If you notice that you are not succeeding, strike a blow for art: Drop it! Give up and console yourself with the fact that a better translator will turn up, who will manage better than you.[74]

Indeed, lyric artists, including those involved in Bible translation, are more often born than made. Furthermore, there is an added dimension that must be taken into consideration, namely, the gift of God's empowering (in this case, stimulating) Spirit (Exod. 31:3–5; Eph. 4:8–13). Thus, Bible translators do not work in isolation, so where one drafter of a poetic text like the Song of Songs experiences difficulties in expressing the poetic genious or force of the original in the vernacular, it may be possible to find a colleague who can succeed—that is, in giving some lyrical life to the Song and to the other great poems of Scripture. In this specifically poetic endeavor, as in the case of the Scriptures generally, the real inspiring muse is the Spirit.

---

[74] This rather cynical observation is attributed to Wolf Biermann, as cited in Qvale 2003:267.

7

Preparing an Oratorical Translation of Qoheleth

Introduction: Culture in an oral-aural society

In this chapter, I will explore a number of issues that confront Bible translators working in a sociocultural setting which is predominantly *oral* and *aural* in nature. My focus will be on the various situational factors that affect religious communication in south-central Africa, specifically within the Chewa language-culture. This prominent Bantu speech community is relatively rich in Scripture translations, having four to choose from: two old *formal correspondence* (FC) versions, a recent update of one, plus a contemporary *popular language* (PL) version. However, it would seem that another style of translation is called for in the current context—at least for certain communicative purposes and special target audiences—namely, a *literary* functional equivalence version (*LiFE*, Wendland 2004b, 2011), perhaps more appropriately termed an 'oratorical' version. The main reasons for such a more dynamic, genre-based translation are considered, as well as some of the chief requirements for successfully producing one. My case in support of an oratorical rendition will be illustrated through the discourse analysis of a well-known, but hermeneutically challenging biblical poetic text—namely, the last 'wisdom' lyric of the book of *Qoheleth* (Ecclesiastes 12:1–7)—and its corresponding rendition in Chewa, with a comparison also to a version in Tonga, a related Bantu language. These recreations are intended for oral transmission (e.g., a public recitation, dramatic performance, via the medium of music, and/or an audio-cassette/CD format) in a non-liturgical target language consumer setting. Finally, the importance of contextually *framing* the text of Scripture by means of relevant para-textual annotation will be briefly discussed and exemplified in terms of the provocatively picturesque pericope at hand, in particular, how to provide such essential background information (cognitive enrichment) for an *auditory* translation.

To begin with then, what is meant by 'the cultural factor' (cf. Wendland 1987)? Our key term *culture* "is one of those pesky, paradoxical concepts that everyone knows what it means as long as they don't have to define it" (Schultz 2009:23).

Some time ago I made the following attempt, defining 'culture' as a people's "design for living—for thinking as well as doing," or more explicitly, the sum total of their "system of beliefs and patterns of behavior which are learned in society, whether by formal instruction or by simple imitation, and passed on from one generation to the next" (1987:5). Schultz puts it more precisely in this way:

> Culture is then a complex, dynamic system of patterns of action and interactions that a loosely bound group of people share in a particular environment. Culture is [also] a system of symbols and their meanings are shared by a group of people that allows them to interpret experience. (Schultz 2009:23)

Finally, a somewhat more abstract definition: "Culture is a given society's effort to provide a coherent set of answers to the existential questions that confront its members on a daily basis as they pursue all aspects of life in their present world-setting."[1]

Cultural anthropologist Clifford Geertz, however, would rule out all of the overt, visible characteristics of culture, namely, those "complexes of concrete behavior patterns—customs, usages, traditions, habit clusters" that tend to popularly define the concept, in favor of "a set of control mechanisms—plans, recipes, rules, instructions (what computer engineers call 'programs')—for the governing of behavior" (1973:44). But why not include these explicit manifestations as vital parts of, and contributors to, the multiple, ever-changing "webs of significance" (ibid., 5) that constitute a given culture, or its components, at any given point in time? And time itself is a significant factor, for diverse cultural "meanings and patterns are negotiated, contested, and constantly yet subtly in flux" (Schultz 2009:23) from the perspective of the governing worldview of people who live in a given social setting.

This cultural perspective or underlying outlook is thus predicated upon and presupposed in a people's *worldview*, that is, their assumptions that pertain to such macro-issues as origin, truth, reality, humanity, meaning, morality, spirituality, and destiny. Charles Kraft defines worldview as "the totality of the culturally structured images and assumptions (including value and commitment or allegiance assumptions) in terms of which a people both perceive and respond to reality" (2008:12). A worldview naturally influences, in some respects even predetermines, a people's way of life, value system, and natural (traditional) manner of worship. The complex notion of worldview may be factored more dynamically, as Gerrit van Steenbergen has suggested, into a number of interacting 'variables,' depending on the culture concerned, for example, causality,

---

[1] Ravi Zacharias—heard on a radio broadcast in 2008 (no further bibliographic information available).

classification, time, space, self as distinct from others, and relationship (van Steenbergen 2007:38). These features must be carefully analyzed by translators in a comparative manner with respect to both the source (biblical) and the target or host cultures in order to "bring out clearly where the differences between the cultures are at a conceptual level. The analysis will then show which encyclopedic information is relevant for the reader in order to have access to the full semantic contents of the text" (ibid., 39).

In the present study I will not be able to investigate the respective sociocultural settings in great detail, but will merely suggest several of the significant ways in which various facets of the manifold cultural factor influence the translation of Ecclesiastes 12:1–7 in two Bantu languages, Chewa and Tonga.[2] These renditions of the passage aim to reproduce the impact and appeal of the artistic-rhetorical features of the source document by means of functionally equivalent *genres*—those especially suited for an *oral* (ideally even a musical) *articulation* in the vernacular.[3] I will examine the cultural factor then in three overlapping stages, that is, with regard to (a) the respective settings of SL composition and TL performance; (b) the literary (oratorical) character of the different poetic texts—namely, the Hebrew original and the two derived vernacular versions; and (c) some additional aspects of the process of interlingual communication that need to be taken into consideration when rendering an ancient biblical lyric in a modern 'consumer' context.

7.1 The setting

The cultural setting—*physical* (anything material), *social* (including customs, traditions, public institutions, etc.), and *psychological* (worldview, value system, goal orientation, primary aspirations, etc.)—affects all the communication-related activities of a distinct people group. This is true even when the same language is being used, namely, a 'language of wider communication' like English that caters for a number of cultural subgroups. Setting affects communication via translation even more significantly since in this case at least two different ethnic, linguistic, and at times (as with the Old and New Testament Scriptures)

---

[2] There are some 15 million first and second-language speakers of (chi-)Chewa residing in the south-central African nations of Malawi, Zambia, Mozambique, and Zimbabwe (given in descending order of number of speakers); some 2 million speakers communicate in Tonga in S. Zambia and N. Zimbabwe.

[3] This is an effort to compose a 'literary functional equivalent' (LiFE) version that aims to match the 'oratorical' qualities of the Hebrew text in a corresponding manner in Chewa for a listening audience (to be further defined in section 7.1.2). A functionally 'relevant' (in terms of Relevance Theory; cf. Hill 2006) type of 'equivalence' is the communicative goal of this approach to Bible translation (Wendland 2004b:84–87).

also historical situations are involved. In this section, I will briefly overview the respective communicative settings that influence our analysis of the second half of the concluding poem of Ecclesiastes, namely, the rather melancholy meditation on old age that begins chapter 12 (vv. 1–7, continuing on from 11:7–10), and its poetic, oratorical rendition in the related Chewa and Tonga languages of south-central Africa.

7.1.1 Original setting of communication

The Ancient Near Eastern setting for any biblical text must first be understood, as extensively and accurately as possible, on its own terms in order to provide an adequate cognitive frame of reference for its translation into another language-culture. However, this conceptual background is not very easy to determine in the case of the controversial book, Ecclesiastes. It is not possible to discuss even a fraction of the pertinent issues here, so for the ongoing debates concerning such setting-related topics, readers are referred to the scholarly commentaries (some of the more recent being Bartholomew 2009 and Longman 1998).

The first major problem to consider is the book's supposed date of composition: was Ecclesiastes composed before or after the Babylonian Exile (ca. 586 BCE) and how many years one way or the other? Most modern scholars, including more conservative ones, conclude rather strongly on the basis of internal (text-based) and external (context-based) evidence that "there are good arguments in favor of a late dating for Ecclesiastes" (Longman 1998:9). This means, of course, that the traditional assumption of Solomonic authorship (based on the interpretation of Eccl. 1:1, 12) is in error and that there is considerable evidence to "distance Solomon from Qoheleth" (ibid., 4). On the other hand, Garrett is one of a minority of scholars who argues cogently for a pre-exilic date, as well as for the authorship of Solomon:

> Nevertheless, linguistic evidence is sufficient at least to challenge the late date for the composition of Ecclesiastes....The peculiar Hebrew of Ecclesiastes cannot be evidence for a late date since it does not fit anywhere in the known history of the language....[T]he difficulties of the Teacher's language can be explained as ancient tendencies in the language of the Levant, that is, the eastern Mediterranean, rather than a late developments in Hebrew....Throughout the book, in fact, the perspective seems to be that of an older man, as in the description of old age in 12:1–5. Nor is it clear that texts like 8:2–8; 10:16–17; 12:9–14 abandon Solomonic authorship. Certainly one cannot say that a king could not have reflected critically on a king's role and

7.1 The setting

on appropriate behavior in the royal presence....After the exile the Jewish people no longer were under their local kings but were ruled by the distant emperors of Persia and the subsequent Seleucid and Ptolemaic monarchs....Why then so much concern, in a book of Jewish wisdom, with how to deal with the king?...The use of the name "the Teacher" indicates that the author is distancing himself from his role as absolute monarch and taking on the mantle of the sage....As we read the book, we are more and more absorbed in the words not of "King Solomon" but of "Solomon-become-'the-Teacher'."...Evidence fails to support the view that Ecclesiastes reflects Greek influence.... The pessimism found in Ecclesiastes...is evident in the ancient Near East from the third millennium onward; there is no need to suppose it is Hellenistic." (Garrett 1993:258, 260, 261, 264)

This debate over dating Ecclesiastes is rather difficult to follow for most Bible students because acknowledged experts often interpret the data, namely, correspondences of various kinds, in very different ways. For example, although Klingbeil observes "numerous parallels between Ecclesiastes and [ancient] Egyptian texts" (2008:137–138) as well as those from the regions of Mesopotamia and Syria, he nevertheless comes to this conclusion (Klingbeil 2008:137–138):

A meaningful comparison should involve comparative data from the same geographic and chronological historic stream, which for Egyptian wisdom literature does not always apply, since many of the aforementioned parallels date to the Middle Kingdom, hundreds of years before the time of Solomon or other loci of the possible origin of the work.

But the reasoning here is not so clear: one would think that this evidence would actually argue for a relatively early date for Ecclesiastes, in contrast to the opinion of many modern scholars. Why would an early temporal and geographical connection between the literary traditions (oral at least) of Israel and Egypt not exist, and in fact result in influence that was relatively strong? These ties of course go back to Israel's early Patriarchs, epitomized in the experiences of two 'Egypt-acculturated' leaders at opposite ends of the period, Joseph and Moses. The analyst must then confront significant comparative data of an intertextual nature such as "many surprising links to texts" (Klingbeil 2008:138). Would this not constitute rather strong evidence then that connects "Ecclesiastes to the literary and intellectual world of the ancient Near East," including, as noted above, the fact that this book "is in many ways conceptually and structurally similar to examples from ancient Egyptian literature" (Garret 1993:265)?[4]

So who was Qoheleth (or Koheleth—קֹהֶלֶת)? This name or title (cf. 1:1–2, 12:8–9) is sometimes rendered as 'the Preacher' (KJV)—more commonly as 'the Teacher' (NIV)—but perhaps a closer equivalent in English would be 'the Philosopher' (GNT).[5] In any case, the issue of authorship in this instance does not really determine the book's central interpretation or its authority;[6] however, it does affect certain interesting hermeneutical undertones and reflections, such as those that would color our understanding if Solomonic authorship could be demonstrated with high probability. A discussion of the scholarly debates for or against a specific author would take us too far away from our central focus, so I will simply adopt a literary technique and speak of the "implied author" (cf. Brown 2007:41).[7] This could be the actual *historical* Solomon or some later writer in the Hebrew Wisdom tradition,[8] who maintains a clear distinction between a 'frame narrator' (i.e., referred to in the 3rd person: 1:1; 7:27; 12:9–14) and the book's principal speaker, namely, Qoheleth (i.e., speaking in the 1st person: 1:2–12:8), who is portrayed as having adopted the royal *persona* of Solomon. However, I would argue on the basis of the manifestly cohesive and coherent (albeit complex) structure, style, and message of Ecclesiastes that the book is not a patchwork of 'sources' or documents (cf. Longman 2008:145–146), but rather derives as a whole from this

---

[4] These and other significant ANE literary similarities are documented in most scholarly commentaries (e.g., Murphy 1992:xlii–xlv). In addition to the strong Egyptian parallels noted by Garret, "Longman concludes that Ecclesiastes has an obvious Akkadian background in terms of genre" (Bartholomew 2009:66; cf. 64–65, 71–72; Klingbeil 2008:133–138).

[5] "The basic Hebrew root is *qahal* which is a noun, meaning 'gathering, assembly'. There is a verb derived from the noun, meaning 'to gather'....The word *qoheleth* is technically a feminine participle, meaning 'she who calls'" (Hunter 2006:151). Qoheleth is not a proper name, but either a title or a nickname that "may allude to one who gathers an assembly to address it or one who gathers words for instruction" (Bartholomew 2009:18; cf. Longman 1998:1).

[6] Although some scholars suggest that Qoheleth was "one of the books whose status the rabbis debated until well into the second century [CE]" (Hunter 2006:154), others have concluded that the OT canon was relatively closed already several centuries earlier (Beckwith 1985:321). "Thus, it appears that, while Ecclesiastes was questioned, its canonicity was never rejected by the mainstream Jewish community" (Longman 1998:28).

[7] In his detailed study of Ecclesiastes from the perspective of narrative and reader-response theories, Salyer distinguishes four constructs in the ostensive communication process: 'implied author,' 'narrator,' 'naratee,' and 'implied reader' (2001:63). However, this importation of an elaborate modern literary-critical approach inevitably complicates the 'reading' of Qoheleth and forces one to overinterpret the text for the sake of the theory.

[8] "Wisdom texts try to 'make sense' of the puzzles and mysteries of human and divine behavior....Wisdom texts are highly sensitive to the limits of the human understanding of God" (Melchert 1998:ix, 3; cf. 2–8).

7.1 The setting

single implied author (some recognized Jewish teacher-philosopher) who has expertly woven together the respective minor and major discourses of the 'narrator' and his embedded subject, the Solomonic personage named Qoheleth, into a masterful unity of form, content, and rhetorical function (cf. Bartholomew 2009:78–79; Grant 2008:209; Ryken 1993:269–272).

Ostensibly, the sapiential, reflective, didactic, apologetic, and hortatory discourses of Qoheleth seem to be directed at the youth of Israel, i.e., the implied audience (e.g., 11:9; 12:1).[9] However, the finely crafted and complexly interwoven contrastive arguments of the book would suggest that the original author also has a more sophisticated and mature audience or readership in mind—most likely, "the intellectual elite of ancient Jerusalem" (Garrett 1993:266). The Philosopher issues a consummate challenge in the form of a poetically fashioned literary and religious masterpiece aimed at overturning the prevailing opinions about man's search for meaning and purpose, in a world that seems to offer little hope and no perfect pathways to success and *shalôm* (general physical, psychological, and spiritual well-being). Whether influenced by Ancient Near Eastern skepticism or the more recently developed Hellenistic rationalism, many Jews (whether living before or after the traumatic exile) found no satisfying answers to or long-lasting solutions for 'all of the futility' (הַכֹּל הֶבֶל – 12:8b) that they observed around them 'under the sun.' Whether one lived or died young or old in prosperity or poverty, what difference did it make? Neither the straightforward moral precepts of Proverbs nor the concluding mind-bending cosmic revelations of Yahweh in Job seemed to have much impact or influence on their thinking anymore.

So the sage commentator of Ecclesiastes decides to refute alien regional philosophies as well as shake the traditional Hebrew religious worldview to its foundation by employing a brilliant point-counterpoint method of literary argumentation. The sequence of alternating antithetical perspectives—worldly ('under the sun') versus true, eternal wisdom ('God-fearing') (see section 7.2.2.3)—constitutes an iterative but multifaceted strategy that progressively argues against a facile and fickle pessimistic existentialism and in favor of the established, theologically-oriented status quo—namely, the divine and moral constant of an obedient 'reverence' for God (12:13), the Creator (12:1), and a steadfast trust in his ultimate righteous 'judgment' (12:14). This engaging rhetorical technique coupled with the dramatic structure and diverse style of the text as a whole is most

---

[9] "As this text [i.e., 12:1–7] indicates clearly, the book of Ecclesiastes is aimed at young people, those just entering into adulthood, here counseling them to *rejoice* and to *remember*" (Limburg 2006:118).

effective because it not only mimics the actual up-and-down physical and mental vicissitudes of life, but it also prepares listeners (readers) to address that ultimate uncertainty of death: what will happen *then*—and how should this inevitable fact affect my daily outlook and behavior *now*? The focal passage to be considered in this chapter (12:1–7) offers a vividly captivating reflection on this critical question, a global transcendent issue that affects all of humanity, no matter what the language and culture.

7.1.2 Current setting of communication

With respect to the present setting of communication, I can be much more specific, that is, in terms of the primary target (or 'consumer') audience intended to be reached by the translation of the text at hand, Eccl. 12:1–7. However, knowledge about this envisaged group of receptors cannot be simply taken for granted with respect to their current profile—i.e., their corporate value system, existential needs, literary preferences, musical tastes, spiritual state, general religious outlook, their hopes, desires, dreams, fears for the future, and so forth. In many cases, MT translators and their associates must be explicitly educated how to conduct credible research on their own culture and tradition of verbal art forms, oral as well as written. Such careful instruction and practical training would also help prepare the ground for the subsequent quality testing of any publications produced for general distribution, whether portions or complete Bibles.[10]

In the case of our focal pericope, the "implied audience" (cf. Brown 2007:40) for which it was composed by Qoheleth as a special poetic piece has been clearly defined by the text itself:[11]

> Be happy, *young man*, while you are *young*,
> and let your days give you joy *in the days of your youth*....
> Remember your Creator *in the days of your youth*... (Eccl. 11:9, 12:1a; NIV)

This differs from the group of text addressees (the plausible 'actual audience') that was most likely intended by the biblical author, which would have been individuals more in keeping with his age, education, social status, religious philosophy, and level of literary erudition—"the educated elite" (Garrett 1993:277). But perhaps a more general, secondary audience for the book's edifying message was also envisioned (cf. הָעָם 'the people' in 12:9). In any case, the vibrant nature of this poem directly addressed to the youth and its obvious relevance also for them

---
[10] For a model project in this regard, see Sundersingh 2001.

[11] Perhaps the speech of Qoheleth and that of the implied narrator merge in this poem (cf. 11:9c/12:14a).

within Israel's religious wisdom tradition (cf. the book of Proverbs, e.g., 1:8, 2:1, 3:1) make it arguable, at least, that the author did also have young people in mind. The importance of this point is underscored by the lament's structural (text-final) prominence within Ecclesiastes as well as by its compelling form and content—an insightful lyrical reflection by Jerusalem's famous Philosopher on the fleeting joys of youth, the specter of old age, and the grim reality of impending death.

The younger generation of south-central Africa, whether of the Chewa or the Tonga ethnic communities, would also appear to be an apt and potentially appreciative consumer group for this concluding didactic poem (cf. section 7.3.1).[12] This would be true in an urban as well as a rural locale, for oral-verbal arts,[13] including musical skills, are being maintained in both environments through the participation of young men and women in Christian congregational choir groups and related church activities. The vital area of agreement with regard to the prospective setting and audience is highlighted by the manifest appropriateness of the song's overall style, theme, and purpose—a picturesque, evocative exhortation to enjoy the God-given pleasures of life, albeit with its divinely-determined end point soberly in view. Thus, the joys and abilities of youth either inexorably fade with old age, or they are lost due to a premature death, which in Africa is unfortunately an all-too-frequent occurrence as a consequence of periodic regional famines, outbreaks of disease, internally as well as externally generated warfare and strife—or, in more recent years, as a result of the continued progression of the deadly AIDS pandemic.

7.1.3 Interposed setting of communication

The interposed setting refers to an alien cultural environment that for one reason or another is allowed to exercise some degree of prominence during the complex communication process that Bible translation inevitably involves. Most obviously, this factor comes into play when expatriates are involved in key positions on the translation team—as exegetes and consultants in most cases, and occasionally still as translators into the TL. In most instances, such non-indigenous personnel have spent many

---

[12] For a sociocultural and religious overview of the Chewa and Tonga ethnic groups in relation to selected aspects of biblical understanding, Scripture communication and an oral-aural mode of message transmission, see Wendland 2005a and Wendland and Hachibamba 2007.

[13] Unfortunately (from my personal perspective), these oral-verbal skills are mainly modern in nature, e.g., contemporary songs and instrumentation, popular multi-character dramatic plays *(masewero)*—whereas the traditional genres (proverbs, folktales, riddles, etc.) are gradually fading from recognition and performance.

years in the local community so that they are well acquainted with the people's language and culture. However, an expatriate, no matter how expert, is never exactly the same as a mother-tongue speaker having the same education and experience. S/he will always have a somewhat different perspective on how the meaning of the biblical text can or should be conveyed to the target audience. A diversity of perspective is not necessarily a bad thing; however, it needs to be recognized as a form of interposition that must not be allowed to dominate or to unduly influence either the overall translation enterprise or any critical components (e.g., exegesis, review) of this joint communicative venture.

The interposed setting also becomes an issue of concern when MT translators have not been trained in the original language of Scripture, in this case Hebrew. As a result, they must depend on the exegetical resources and translation(s) of another, usually a Western language, when doing their work. Their base text thus becomes a source that is removed, to a greater or lesser degree, from the original in terms of linguistic form and/or specific meaning. In either case, the particular expression of the intervening version, such as English, may act as a barrier that blocks translators from certain aspects of the original text which are actually closer to the language and culture of the target group. There are several instances when such mismatches in communication occur in the passage at hand, Eccl. 12:1–7 (NIV) with reference to the Chewa language:

- "I find no pleasure in them!" (1d) – The disjunctive emphasis of the original is lost, i.e., 'there-is-not for-*me* in-*them* (days/time)'; this contrast could be brought out more effectively in Chewa by a word order that does not mimic the English version.

- "…and the grinders cease…" (3c) – The feminine form of the Hebrew participle is significant from a Chewa cultural perspective, for only women have the domestic task of 'grinding' (maize) meal as the basis for the staple daily food (stiff porridge).

- "…and the desire is no longer stirred." (5e) – More literally, the Hebrew reads, 'and the caperberry bursts/breaks', most likely with reference to the ineffectiveness of an aphrodisiac in old age. The NIV rendering would promote an expression that is too general in Chewa, which has a number of terms, including euphemisms that refer to sexual stimulants (e.g., *mkomya* 'domestic chores'!).

- "...and mourners go about in the streets." (5g) – The Hebrew verb more specifically suggests a circular movement (cf. 1:6) or a gathering of people, both of which are more appropriate for a communal 'watch' that traditionally takes place at the Chewa homestead (outside the house) where a funeral has occurred.

This is not to say that all of the form-meaning peculiarities of the Hebrew text must necessarily be accommodated somehow in one's vernacular translation. That would certainly be too much either to expect or to aim for. However, it would be a valid goal for translators to deal with significant inequivalences somewhere—if not in the vernacular text itself, then via some feature of the paratext, e.g., an illustration, an explanatory footnote, a glossary entry in the case of a key term, or in the book's introduction where a crucial concept such as הֶבֶל ('futility, enigma, transience,' depending on the cotext) is concerned.

There is yet another possible instance of the negative influence of the cultural factor during the activity of Bible translation. This dimension comes to the fore in the case of local translators who appear to have lost touch with their own sociocultural setting and hence either do not appreciate the use of, or can no longer access the fuller linguistic and literary resources of their mother tongue. This phenomenon of 'defamiliarization' usually occurs in situations where translators have been educated for a considerable part of their life in an alien environment and a foreign language, for example, at the university and postgraduate level in some Western country. Most of their scholarly and religious library then would be in English (French, Spanish, Portuguese, etc.), and they have little interest in studying or doing research in their first language. Such 'academic' translators tend to prefer a more literal rendering, based on either the original or an interposed language, and they often find it difficult to accommodate to the notion of 'naturalness' (let alone 'literariness') in their work. Furthermore, they cannot appreciate the possibility that their typically wooden renderings are hard for respondents to understand correctly, if at all.

7.2 The Song: How 'strong' (or sweetly sounding) is it?

...all their songs grow faint (Eccl. 12:4b; NIV, NET)

The title of this section can be metaphorically applied first of all with regard to our understanding of the Hebrew text and secondly, as a descriptive reference to the quality of our various translations of this pericope, no matter what the language. As far as the original is concerned, most if not all scholars recognize that this 'geriatric poem' is an exceptionally artistic as well as a profoundly religious composition—a literary masterpiece (Fisch 1988:178; Ryken 1992:327).[14] So the question then arises: how can translators achieve some manner of resemblance via the rendition in their language—or is this an operational consideration that is too technical, too challenging, or too time-consuming to bother about? I assert that it is possible and worthwhile to aim for the literary rendition, and in the remainder of this chapter, I demonstrate one possible strategy for achieving such an analysis and translation. This includes a *literary-structural* examination of this final poem of Qoheleth in order to reveal the contributions of this sort of approach, both to our understanding of the biblical text as well as its 'poetics,' or lyric qualities. Periodic references to the distinctive compositional character of Ecclesiastes as a whole are made along the way. My underlying assumption is that a careful discourse-oriented, artistic-rhetorical analysis of the SL text will facilitate a fuller comprehension of the original and thereby encourage an analogous reproduction in the TL for a clearly defined receptor audience.

7.2.1 Genre and purpose

Commentators often struggle in trying to determine the literary genre of Ecclesiastes as they wrestle with its content and the author's aim in writing this brilliant text within the educational wisdom tradition of Israel:[15]

> As far back as we go in the history of the interpretation of Ecclesiastes, this book has provoked controversy. And it still does, with contemporary commentators polarized as to how to read it, whether as a positive book affirming life or as deeply pessimistic....Part of the problem with interpreting Ecclesiastes is that there is no consensus about its genre. (Bartholomew 2009:17, 61)[16]

---

[14] These evaluations come from two highly regarded English professors and literary critics. Bullock, a biblical studies professor and widely-published author, calls 12:1–7 "a superb literary piece" (1988:204).

[15] "'The most peculiar feature of that wisdom [of the ancient Near East] is its educational or pedagogic quality.'...The fusion of literary, dramatic, and poetic interests with theological, cultural, ethical, and educational issues is a remarkable feature of many of these works" (Melchert 1998:2 [citing Philip Nel]).

[16] Some commentators are seemingly as pessimistic as Qoheleth in their conclusion about genre: "The designation of the proper literary genre of the book of Ecclesiastes still escapes us" (Murphy 1981:129; cf. Murphy 1992:xxxi). Part of the problem of classification lies in the hierarchical nature of the notion of genre: "So there are more inclusive genres that contain ever smaller genres (wisdom literature → reflection → proverb → simile or comparison)" (Loader 1986:5). Another difficulty involves terminology along with definition and

7.2 The Song: How 'strong' (or sweetly sounding) is it? 277

It is not my intention to debate the pertinent issues here, for they are somewhat peripheral to our focus on 12:1–7. In short, my use of the term 'author' implies that I regard the book as being a *unified* composition, the product of a *single* skillful writer.[17] Thus, I do not view Ecclesiastes as being a disorganized literary hodgepodge and/or a patchwork of sources, or some sort of a composite text, consisting of a major author (e.g., 1:2–12:8) and a different 'frame editor' (e.g., 1:1, 12:9–14). My view of the discourse structure of the book will be presented briefly in section 7.2.2.3.[18]

So, what is the importance of genre analysis for hermeneutics? Longman states the point succinctly and gives a good summary of how genre(s) are determined:

> Genre identification significantly affects a reader's interpretation and application of a text. Proper identification may lead to correct interpretation, but a mistaken genre identification will certainly distort the reader's understanding....Of course, proper genre identification arises from reading the text itself and is not imposed from outside the text....The text is embedded with signals of both an implicit and explicit nature to guide the reader along....Any single piece of literature may be described with more than one generic label. A genre is defined by similarities that exist between a group of texts. To group texts into genres, it is necessary to concentrate on those similarities while bracketing their differences. Thus, it is a matter of abstracting characteristics from particular texts. (Longman 1998:16–17)

The notion of genre is particularly important for Bible translators to correctly grasp and apply. Not only does this literary perception (or the lack of it) affect their interpretation of the original, but it (hopefully) also concerns the method and manner in which they will render this text in their translation. *Form* (genre) *conveys significant meaning*, comprising pragmatic impact and appeal as well as rhetorical credibility and persuasiveness.[19] Translators may well need to utilize different genre-

---

whether an emic (language-specific), an *etic* (universal), or a 'mixed' system of classification is being used (Wendland 2004b:108–109). Abundant ambiguity in Ecclesiastes also contributes to problems of categorization (Salyer 2001:126–166).

[17] "The unity of the book and its freedom from interpolations can be maintained with a high degree of confidence....[M]ost scholars believe that most, if not all, of the book is from a single author" (Garrett 1993:267). A biblical book should be assumed to be a unified literary and theological composition unless proven beyond a reasonable doubt to be some sort of an editorial conglomeration.

[18] For a survey of the scholarly field, including proposals concerning either multiple authors/sources or a composition that is not cohesive or coherent, see Longman 2008:143–147; Murphy 1992:xxxiii–xxxix; Whybray 1989:40–46.

[19] A functional perspective on genre is reflected in Brown's definition of this literary category: "Genre is a socially defined constellation of typified formal and thematic features in

based literary (or oratorical) forms in the TL in order to accomplish their objectives, namely, to re-present an overall message that is the closest equivalent of the biblical text also in terms of its manifold communicative functions. Thus, the necessary text study and research into the genre inventory of the TL needs to be carried out as a first step in the analysis process. However, if translators completely ignore this aspect of the Scripture-based meaning and purpose, they will surely diminish the intended effectiveness of these diversely composed documents—in their own language and socio-religious setting.

As far as the genre of Ecclesiastes is concerned,[20] I feel that the most appropriate general designation for the book as a whole is a 'philosophical autobiography,' one that is introduced (1:1) and concluded (12:8–14),[21] as argued above, by a theologically astute implied narrator who sets the stage for the educative personal reflections and exhortations of his chief persona, Qoheleth.[22] The autobiographical quality of Ecclesiastes is quite obvious from the first-person, direct speech text form which predominates and sets the point-of-view as well as the varied attitudinal tone for the entire vacillating discourse of Qoheleth. The attribute 'philosophical' then is seen to include related or subsidiary communicative objectives, such as, meditation, deliberation, instruction, reproof, exhortation, etc., which are often employed by scholars to describe the literary character of Ecclesiastes. To this listing we might add the 'apologetic' function: thus the

---

a group of literary works, which authors use in individualized ways to accomplish specific communicative purposes" (2008:122).

[20] With regard to its macrostructure, Ecclesiastes is a diverse mixture of Hebrew prose, poetry, and something in between. Commentators differ widely in their estimates of the amount of pure poetry to be found in the book: "More than one-third of the work (total: 222 verses) is in poetry" (Murphy 1981:130). On the other hand, "The editors of the NIV consider 60 percent of the text to be poetry, while the NRSV thinks it is 75 percent prose. The translators of the Good News Bible and the Revised English Bible think the only poetic passage in the entire book is 3:2–8. The criteria for identifying poetry in biblical Hebrew are subtle, and with Ecclesiastes they function hardly at all" (Towner 1997:270; cf. Wendland 2004b:110–111). According to Garret, "Ecclesiastes is poetic but is not a poem. A few passages, however, properly might be called poems" (1993:271). I think that a strong case can be made also to classify 12:1–7 as a Hebrew poem.

[21] The medial verse 7:27 may also belong to the 'frame narrator'—and ultimately to the book's actual author. According to this interpretation, the onset and ending of Qoheleth's words are formally marked by a prominent inclusio consisting of the distinctive 'meaningless' motif (1:2, 12:8).

[22] Longman thoroughly documents the prevalence of an apparent parallel genre, the "framed wisdom autobiography," in ancient Akkadian literature (1991; 1998:17–18). However, I do not think that it is necessary (due to our lack of convincing evidence concerning the book's actual author) to add the qualifier 'fictional' in the case of Ecclesiastes (ibid., 8). Longman also interprets the text's "framework" differently, i.e., as comprised of "the prologue (1:1–11) and the epilogue (12:8–14)" (ibid., 8).

7.2 The Song: How 'strong' (or sweetly sounding) is it?

biblical author "demonstrates at length the inadequacy of any worldview other than a God-centered one, and he combines with this demonstration a series of affirmations of an alternative worldview" (Ryken 1992:320). In any case, the generic cover-term 'philosophical autobiography' refers to a flexible type of wisdom literature, apparently quite popular in the Ancient Near East at the time that Ecclesiastes was written, and a tradition that incorporated a number of interrelated sub-genres or discourse types. Chief among these as far as Ecclesiastes is concerned are two overlapping styles of formal discourse, namely, the interpersonal diatribe and the personal reflection, both of which are well-suited to the sapiential didactic aims of this book.

However, the so-called 'reflection' is particularly ill-defined as a distinct (sub-)genre. According to one scholar, this rhetorical type is comprised of different argumentation strategies: there is "the considered reflection… in which empirical points are indicated; instruction…, with warning and challenge; considered teaching…, consisting of consideration, reasons, and challenge" (Murphy 1992:xxxi–xxxii). At the same time, Murphy also observes (ibid., xxxii; cf. Murphy 1981:130):

> Fortunately, the reflection is easier to recognize than to describe. It has a loose structure; it begins with some kind of observation, which is then considered from one or more points of view, leading to a conclusion. Within it one may find sayings or proverbs, employed to develop or round out the thought (e.g., 1:12–18).

A philosopher's reflections of course present a very personal expression of his (her) opinions, attitudes, values, complaints, and arguments with regard to various mind-challenging issues, including the meaning of life and one's labors (Eccl. 1:2–11). But at times—and especially in the case of Ecclesiastes—the speaker may offer or engage with another, an alternative or antithetical perspective. This dimension of dialogical debate (even within oneself, e.g., "I spoke with my heart saying…" דִּבַּ֨רְתִּי אֲנִ֤י עִם־לִבִּי֙ לֵאמֹ֔ר (1:16, 2:1, 3:17–18) leads some commentators to suggest that this book manifests several important characteristics of the Greek 'diatribe.' According to Bartholomew, "the diatribe approach…pick[s] up correctly on different aspects of Ecclesiastes," such as its prominent first-person narration, featuring overt or implicit dialogue, an aspect of 'royal fiction,' a pessimistic element, the thematic importance of death, and the frequent occurrence of micro-features, such as the reiteration of terms and ideas and the frequent use of figurative language, illustrations, analogies, direct/indirect quotations, rhetorical questions, imperatives, and irony (Bartholomew 2009:63–64, 73; cf. Giese 1999:22–43, 51–75).

Often associated with reflections and the Hellenistic diatribe style are additional genres such as proverbs (e.g., 7:1–12); maxims, including 'better than' sayings (e.g., 4:3, 6, 9; cf. Ogden 1977; Salyer 2001:400–402); anecdotes or 'example stories' (e.g., 4:7–8, 13–16; 9:13–16); autobiographical accounts (e.g., 2:1–11); observations (e.g., 1:5, 13–15, 16–18); a benediction (10:17), as well as 'woe' warnings and admonitions, so typical of the prophets (e.g., 2:16, 4:10, 7:9, 10:16); and the allegorical segment included in our focal passage (12:3–4).

In addition, a number of scholars have documented the important feature of reiterated vocabulary in Ecclesiastes, both individual terms as well as thematic phrases (e.g., 'this too is futility!' – 'under the sun' – 'all deeds that are done' – 'who knows?') (cf. Murphy 1992:xxix–xxx, lviii–lxi; Enns 2008:130–131).[23] All this lexical repetition brings the author's main concerns to bear upon the reader/hearer's mind and creates varied but interrelated semantic complexes that resonate off one another throughout the work. Furthermore, these correspondences in vocabulary help to establish a cohesive, progressively developed paradigmatic structure of meaning that complements the book's relatively loose linear syntagmatic organization. After a survey of five such key terms in Ecclesiastes—'all' (כֹּל), 'absurd' (הֶבֶל), 'toil' (עָמָל), 'wisdom' (חָכְמָה), and 'fate' (מִקְרֶה)—Towner concludes (1997:292):

> [These] five components of the vocabulary of Qoheleth...are pillars upon which its view of the world rests. "All" of human experience is "absurd"—i.e., incomprehensible, even senseless. Life is "toil." With the help of "wisdom" a person may find happiness amid the toil, but only if that person is utterly realistic about the inevitable "fate" of death.

My own view of the book's message (see 7.2.5) is not as skeptical as the opinion suggested in the preceding quote. It has been altered, as I believe the original author intended, by the expert negative-positive dialectical manner in which the text in its entirety has been composed in order to provide a divinely-oriented optimistic perspective (that is, for all 'God-fearers' and 'commandment-keepers' – 12:13) on the pessimism that an earth-bound worldview inevitably generates.

---

[23] Four key enigmatic phrases unique to Qoheleth's discourse synopsize the skeptical, pessimistic side of his outlook on life (cf. Hunter 2006:152–153), namely: the implied author's thematic motto, "vanity of vanities, all is vanity [emptiness, futility, meaninglessness, uselessness]" (e.g., the text's macro-inclusio at 1:2 and 12:8); a corresponding reiterated leitmotif, "all is vanity and chasing the wind" (e.g., 1:14, 2:11, 4:4, 6:9); and a pair of gloomy clichés, "there is nothing better for a man than to eat, drink, and take pleasure in his toil" (2:24, 3:13, 5:18, 8:15) + "under the sun" (1:3, 2:11, 9:3, 10:5).

7.2 The Song: How 'strong' (or sweetly sounding) is it?

In contrast to Ecclesiastes as a whole, there is not too much doubt about the genre of the section 12:1–7. It is, generally speaking, a wisdom poem, a didactic lyric, ostensibly intended for instructing Israel's younger generation concerning a life lived in 'the fear of the LORD' (i.e., addressed to the youth as a class, 12:1; cf. 'young man' בָּחוּר – 11:9; cf. also 12:13; Prov. 1:1–8).[24] This poetic composition may be specified more precisely in terms of conventional literary genre terminology as an 'ode' that has the overtones of an 'elegy.' In other words, it is a progressively somber *lyric lament*, taking the form of an *oratorical address*, and written in varied or irregular meter (see the lineation chart below in 7.2.2.1).[25] This memorable poem, preceded by a more prosaic paragraph of instruction (11:7–10), thus functions to advise the youth not only concerning their behavior ('Yes, enjoy life while you can!'), but primarily with regard to their *attitude* towards life (and death): do not go overboard, but rather temper your pleasure-seeking impulses with a certain sobriety which recognizes that the attractions of life will soon pass (like *chebhel!*) and that you will one day have to come to terms with your Creator (12:1) and Judge (12:7, 14). Two ways to convey such varied and vigorous lyric sentiments correspondingly in another language and cultural setting will be illustrated in section 7.3.

7.2.2 Structural and stylistic analysis

In order to better understand the literary sophistication of the Scriptures, it is necessary to deal with biblical texts hierarchically, that is, as composite wholes in which the interrelated units (paragraphs/strophes, sections/stanzas, etc.) themselves normally function as parts

---

[24] With regard to the traditional term 'wisdom' used to categorize Hebrew religious texts like Ecclesiastes, Job, Proverbs, and Sirach (Ecclesiasticus), Hunter concludes: "[T]he use of 'wisdom' as the inclusive term for what [Ecclesiastes] is about does have solid justification in the Old Testament itself, both in respect of the frequency with which the word for wisdom is used, and in respect of the dramatic presence of a personified female Wisdom at significant turns. [24]...[B]y using wisdom as our defining term...direction of an intellectual tradition which is not out of keeping with the best traditions of scholarly intellectual investigations" (2006:vii). However, it is not easy to distinguish the "wisdom" books mentioned above "on the basis of a set of formal features" since "[f]or the purposes of genre, what they seem to share is not style or form but attitude and intention, neither of which translates easily (if at all) into recognizable literary patterns" (ibid., 5).

[25] This combines key aspects of the respective definitions for 'ode' and 'elegy' in the *Concise Oxford Dictionary* (Oxford UP, 2004:462, 990). A secondary definition for the ode is that it is "a classical poem of the kind originally meant to be sung" (ibid., 462, 990)—a feature that also has implications for the manner and medium in which a modern poetic rendition may be presented today (see section 7.3.2).

of larger wholes. Thus translators must be trained to think and compose holistically in terms of larger segments of discourse, as opposed to being restricted in their hermeneutical vision by a single passage perspective and a verse-by-verse mechanical procedure. Such a methodology can rarely if ever result in an acknowledged literary outcome in the consumer language, either in prose or poetry.

So what, if anything, does the 'cultural factor' have to do with this analytical aspect of the translation process? Probably not much, except perhaps to suggest that some cultures may be more adept at, or appreciative of, analytical thought and detailed lines of exegetical reasoning than others. But more likely this preference or skill is a matter of education and how the translators were originally trained to read and analyze literature (and analogous oral works—'orature'), not only in English but also in terms of their mother tongue. In any case, if the method(s) of discourse analysis were not a part of their prior education, it may be helpful for this to be introduced, at least in an elementary way, in order to prepare them for a literary analysis and translation of the Bible and/or selected pericopes.

7.2.2.1 Text demarcation and translation

The Hebrew text under consideration, Eccl. 12:1–7, is set off in poetic 'cola' (half-lines) below together with the NET version,[26] which may be evaluated for quality and correctness alongside the original. Notice that the lineation of the MT is not followed since it does not appear to be poetically structured in terms of natural 'utterance units' (essentially complete clauses/predications). Thus the Masoretic 'half-line marker,' or 'athnah' (ˏ), normally produces lines, before and/or afterwards, that may be divided into two or more meaningful segments, e.g., v. 1b: "…before the difficult days come / and the years draw near when you will say / 'I have no pleasure in them'."

So remember your Creator in the days of your youth—	¹ וּזְכֹר֙ אֶת־בּ֣וֹרְאֶ֔יךָ בִּימֵ֖י בְּחוּרֹתֶ֑יךָ
before *the difficult days come,* *and the years draw near when you will say,* *"I have no pleasure in them";*	עַ֣ד אֲשֶׁ֤ר לֹא־יָבֹ֙אוּ֙ יְמֵ֣י הָֽרָעָ֔ה וְהִגִּ֣יעוּ שָׁנִ֔ים אֲשֶׁ֣ר תֹּאמַ֔ר אֵֽין־לִ֥י בָהֶ֖ם חֵֽפֶץ׃

---

[26] I have added *italics* to indicate areas of this passage that are relatively literal in nature and **bold** to indicate significant instances of lexical reiteration. Notice that these verses appear at significant structural junctures in the text—at the beginning, ending, and climax in v. 5c.

7.2 The Song: How 'strong' (or sweetly sounding) is it?   283

before the sun… grow[s] dark and the light of the moon and the stars, and the clouds disappear after the rain; when those who keep watch over the house begin to tremble, and the virile men begin to stoop over, and the grinders begin to cease because they grow few, and those who look through the windows grow dim, and the doors along the street are shut; when the sound of the grinding mill grows low, and one is awakened by the sound of a bird, and all their songs grow faint,	² עַד אֲשֶׁר לֹא־תֶחְשַׁךְ הַשֶּׁמֶשׁ וְהָאוֹר וְהַיָּרֵחַ וְהַכּוֹכָבִים וְשָׁבוּ הֶעָבִים אַחַר הַגָּשֶׁם: ³ בַּיּוֹם שֶׁיָּזֻעוּ שֹׁמְרֵי הַבַּיִת וְהִתְעַוְּתוּ אַנְשֵׁי הֶחָיִל וּבָטְלוּ הַטֹּחֲנוֹת כִּי מִעֵטוּ וְחָשְׁכוּ הָרֹאוֹת בָּאֲרֻבּוֹת: ⁴ וְסֻגְּרוּ דְלָתַיִם בַּשּׁוּק בִּשְׁפַל קוֹל הַטַּחֲנָה וְיָקוּם לְקוֹל הַצִּפּוֹר וְיִשַּׁחוּ כָּל־בְּנוֹת הַשִּׁיר:
and they are afraid of heights and the dangers in the street; the almond blossoms grow white, and the grasshopper drags itself along, and the caper berry shrivels up— **because** man goes to his eternal home, and the mourners go about in the streets—	⁵ גַּם מִגָּבֹהַּ יִרָאוּ וְחַתְחַתִּים בַּדֶּרֶךְ וְיָנֵאץ הַשָּׁקֵד וְיִסְתַּבֵּל הֶחָגָב וְתָפֵר הָאֲבִיּוֹנָה כִּי־הֹלֵךְ הָאָדָם אֶל־בֵּית עוֹלָמוֹ וְסָבְבוּ בַשּׁוּק הַסֹּפְדִים:
before the silver cord is removed, or the golden bowl is broken, or the pitcher is shattered at the well, or the water wheel is broken at the cistern— *and the dust returns to the earth as it was, and the life's breath returns to God who gave it.*	⁶ עַד אֲשֶׁר לֹא־*יִרְחַק* (יֵרָתֵק) חֶבֶל הַכֶּסֶף וְתָרֻץ גֻּלַּת הַזָּהָב וְתִשָּׁבֶר כַּד עַל־הַמַּבּוּעַ וְנָרֹץ הַגַּלְגַּל אֶל־הַבּוֹר: ⁷ וְיָשֹׁב הֶעָפָר עַל־הָאָרֶץ כְּשֶׁהָיָה וְהָרוּחַ תָּשׁוּב אֶל־הָאֱלֹהִים אֲשֶׁר נְתָנָהּ:

Each of the variable twenty-eight lines as posited above constitutes a complete predication (poetic 'colon'). Whether they all realize natural utterance units is impossible to tell in the case of a long-dead language like Biblical Hebrew. Thus, as in the case of significant text-critical issues (see 7.2.2.2), there is room for debate and an adjustment that moves in the direction of what would turn out to be more natural, or even idiomatic in the TL.

7.2.2.2 External delimitation

In this section the 'external' dimension of a structural analysis, which prepares the way for a corresponding 'internal' analysis (7.2.2.3), deals with the intratextual connections that one pericope has with others, especially preceding units, within the same composition. In order to limit our scope, I have chosen to focus on verses 1–7 of chapter 12. But it is important to recognize that this instructive piece actually begins in chapter 11—most clearly at verse 9 and arguably even earlier at verse 7.[27] The literary and linguistic evidence for this proposed demarcation is summarized below. Thus the entire thematic section covers 11:7 to 12:7, as defined by relatively clear points of aperture and closure. Accordingly, its introductory more 'prosaic' (in comparison with 12:1–7) portion at the end of chapter 11 (11:7–10) provides an essential hermeneutical frame of reference for understanding this passage as a whole.[28] This perspective is suggested in particular by the key phrase 'the days of your youth' (12:1; cf. 11:9–10) and its hortatory relevance at this point within the book of Ecclesiastes.

The author incorporated the following lexical features then in order to guide his readers (and undoubtedly hearers as well) towards a correct understanding of the main formal contours of this passage:

- Verses 7–8 of ch. 11 appear to introduce this elegy on youth and aging through metaphorical references to life and death in the nouns 'the light' (הָאוֹר), 'the sun' (הַשֶּׁמֶשׁ), and 'the darkness' (הַחֹשֶׁךְ)—coupled with the author's central thematic notion of הֶבֶל – that is, 'enigma' with respect to one's understanding and 'futility' with respect to one's activities in a life governed by a humanistic, godless perspective.

- This pessimistic thematic notion of הֶבֶל is reiterated again at the very end of this opening section, the final word of v. 10. The two occurrences of this term (i.e., concluding v. 8 as well as v. 10) serve to demarcate the unit (structural *epiphora;* Wendland 2004b:127) comprising 11:7–10 into two poetic 'paragraphs': 7–8 and 9–10, each of which manifests a generally positive → negative topical and connotative movement.

---

[27] This is another example of a most inappropriate and misleading chapter break in our standard versions.

[28] The book's ultimate frame of reference is, of course, its beginning and concluding words (1:1, 12:9–14). Thus, "[a] frame compels the reader to assess and evaluate the work at hand. By presenting his assessment, the frame narrator solicits the reader's own personal assessment" (Christianson 1998:119)—however, with considerable encouragement to adopt the divine wisdom perspective advocated by the authoritative sage at the end of the debate.

7.2 The Song: How 'strong' (or sweetly sounding) is it?

- The hypothesis of a major unit aperture at v. 7 is strengthened by the occurrence of a concluding structural boundary (closure) at 11:6. The poetic passage covering 11:1–6 is delineated both by an *inclusio* ('cast your bread upon the waters, for…'—v. 1; 'sow your seed in the morning…for…'—v. 6) and also by internal cohesion formed by the reiterated thematic motif 'you do not know what' (vv. 2, 5, 6).

- The admonition 'concerning all these things God will bring you into judgment' (כִּי עַל־כָּל־אֵלֶּה יְבִיאֲךָ הָאֱלֹהִים בַּמִּשְׁפָּט:) toward the close of the section (in 11:9b) is echoed at the end of the book in 12:14a: 'For God will bring every deed into judgment' (כִּי אֶת־כָּל־מַעֲשֶׂה הָאֱלֹהִים יָבִא בְמִשְׁפָּט), a probable instance of end-boundary marking *epiphora*.

Due to its obvious poetic qualities, 12:1–7 stands as a distinct, though not independent discourse unit within the text of Ecclesiastes. 12:1 is linked to the preceding material, probably the thematic development of the entire section 11:7–10, by an initial *waw*: וּזְכֹר 'and remember!'—the imperative concluding a series of commands to the youth that was begun in the preceding paragraph (11:9–10).[29]

We also observe the prominent text position of this insightful poem within the composition as a whole—a concluding reflective lyric on life and death—formally Qoheleth's last word on the subject. But is it ultimately optimistic or pessimistic in its disposition and implication? Given that the book's theme-alternating macrostructure is climaxed by its forthrightly conventional, theologically conservative epilogue, one would be justified in arguing in favor of the former. That is, the conclusion offers

---

[29] "The larger unit is 11:7–12:8, composed of two main sections: A. 11:7–11 *(carpe diem)* and B. 12:1–8 *(memento mori)*" (Fox 1994:381). I would excise verse 8, as noted earlier, for it serves on a higher discourse level as a thematic frame for the entire discourse of Qoheleth, covering 1:2–12:8, and probably to be attributed to the frame narrator (implied author). The initial *chiastic* construction of 12:7 (i.e., A: 'and-it-returns', B: 'the-dust', B': 'and-the-spirit', A': 'it-returns') is another stylistic marker that helps to indicate a discourse *closure*.

Section A is governed by the verbal notion 'rejoice' (שׂמח—cf. 11:8, 9) and section B by 'remember' (זכר, 12:1— cf. 11:8). These two concepts serve to orient a 'wise,' God-pleasing perspective on life: 'rejoice' in what the Creator has given you in life, but 'remember' your responsibility to live in fellowship with him (2:24–25, 3:11–14, 8:12), for one day (soon), life will end and divine judgment will come (11:9, 12:14). "[Remember] refers to allowing the notion of God as Creator to shape one's view of life and one's handling of life's enigmas now" (Bartholomew 2009:345). In fact, in this context one might consider the exhortation 'remember your Creator' (12:1—*generic*) to be equivalent to 'fear God and keep his commandments' (12:13—*specific;* cf. Prov. 1:7, also 'hear/listen' in Proverbs, e.g., 1:5, 8; note also the importance of 'remembering' the LORD and his precepts in Deuteronomy, e.g., 7:18, 8:18, 24:9).

an ultimately positive perspective, one that is made possible only on the basis of a God-fearing life-relationship (12:13) with the Creator and Judge of everything on earth (12:1, 14)!

7.2.2.3 Internal delimitation

The inner constituent units of a given pericope must be clearly distinguished in order to get a sense of the sequential flow of the author's discourse—his/her narrative, description, exposition, exhortation, argument, or some combination of these text types. The meaning of the individual parts (paragraphs/strophes) contributes to the meaning of the whole and vice versa, so the place to begin is with a demarcation of the internal segments along with their interrelationships. The task of delineation is not so obvious in the case of Ecclesiastes 12:1–7 since this entire section consists syntactically of just a single sentence in Hebrew.

In most languages then, this complex unit will have to be deconstructed into several smaller utterance segments in translation—the number and their length depending on whether the text is being rendered as poetry or prose and in which particular TL genre. The intended primary *medium* of communication may also influence this decision. Thus in sociocultural and religious settings of south-central Africa, an orally performed (recited, chanted, or sung) rendition may be quite varied in terms of syntactic length and complexity (compare the Chewa and Tonga versions in 7.3.2.1 and 7.3.2.2).

Though quite long, the poetic sentence beginning with the admonition, 'And remember…' in 12:1, is broken down into a balanced succession of dependent *waw*-initial temporal clauses which serve to orient the initial imperative both semantically and pragmatically—that is, by means of a cumulative progression that stresses the inexorable passage of time. The syntactic sequence which figuratively describes aging and death may be summarized like this:

Remember …***before*** not (לֹא אֲשֶׁר עַד–1b) …***before*** *not* (לֹא אֲשֶׁר עַד–2a)
…***when*** (בְּ–3a) …***when*** (בְּ–4b) …***before*** *not* (לֹא אֲשֶׁר עַד–6a)…

The prominent temporal conjunctive phrase 'before not' thus appears to delineate this poem into three unequal portions (strophes):[30]

---

[30] "While signaling a new thought, the words [אֲשֶׁר עַד] also recall the command of verse 1, 'Remember also your Creator.' The primary activity to undertake in all phases of life is to consider God and His involvement in the life-death phenomenon" (Davis 1994:351).

7.2 The Song: How 'strong' (or sweetly sounding) is it?

- X (1) Introduction. Anticipation of old age and death: Remember (to worship, obey, reverence, etc.) *your* Creator-*God* during your lifetime, before it is too late!

- Y (2–5) Development. Experiencing old age: A picturesque poetic description of the *human* aging process marking the end of one's days of pleasure (v. 1b) in this life.

- X' (6–7) Conclusion. Facing death: [Remember] *your God* before your end has come, when your body returns to dust and spirit returns to God, the giver (Creator, v. 1) and Judge (12:14).[31]

I thus view this lyric lament as being arranged topically in the form of a general A-B-A' 'ring structure,' in which the last strophe (noted as X' above) reiterates and expands upon the first strophe (X, this being a discourse-level extension of the familiar ascending poetic principle of Hebrew parallelism: 'A, and what's more B').

One notes that there is an apparent anomaly in the pattern, namely, v. 5 in which no connective of time appears. Instead, the verse begins with an ascensive גַּם focus particle: "yes indeed/to be sure...!" There are two other distinctive features about this passage that serve to mark it, in my opinion, as being the close of the long medial strophe (Y, vv. 2–5): this verse is extra long, being composed (according to my poetic lineation structure) of seven utterance units (cola)—all comparatively short lines linked by *waw* except for the final two (5f-g). The latter pairing of longer lines begins with a mixed explanatory-temporal disjunction: "for/when the man goes..." (כִּי־הֹלֵךְ הָאָדָם), which also sets it off as the conclusion of this strophe and a transition to *climax* of the lament as a whole, where the point of *death* is reached. This poetic structural arrangement supports translations such as the NIV, which begin a new strophe in v. 6 with a reiterated "Remember him...," thus making explicit the poem's initial imperative phrase (12:1a) and reinforcing the semantic connection between its opening and closing strophes (X and X').

Of course, my interpretation of the lament's overall organization reflects a number of potentially debatable hermeneutical decisions that have significant exegetical as well as translation implications, e.g., how the poem's discourse structure is formatted into distinct units on the printed page (see 7.3.2.1). Such issues have little if anything to do with

---

[31] Davis appropriately labels these three strophes with a focus on man's "end" time: *The days before the end* (12:1); *The days of the ending* (12:2–5); and *The end of days* (12:6–[7]) (1994:352–363).

the cultural factor per se. Rather one's method of analyzing the original text does affect the results of that exegesis when it is transferred into an acceptable level of meaning, including 'poetic equivalence', when communicating this text in the TL.

In this connection, it may be worthwhile to notice how the entire pericope of 11:7–12:7 fits into the alternating *negative* (futile) versus *positive* (beneficial, i.e., godly) movement of Ecclesiastes as a whole. In fact, the sapiential observations of Qoheleth are not as thoroughly skeptical as superficial readers might at first suspect (cf. chs. 1–2).[32] On the contrary, there appears to be a significant core of traditional wisdom instruction based on a divinely oriented value system that runs throughout the text. These sentiments are usually expressed briefly after some lengthy disparaging passage in which the Philosopher offers some cynical reflection on human existence 'under the sun/heaven'. As Sailhammer observes (1994:336):

> [T]he author often records the words of the preacher and then adds his own qualification to them. His primary qualification lies in the fact that the preacher's words are intended to be understood as drawn from the point of view of human wisdom. They are not to be intended as the last word. The last word is always God's perspective.[33]

The following chart (cf. Ryken 1992:323–326) sets forth my proposed differentiation of texts in Ecclesiastes according to their positive or negative perspectives on life. My hermeneutical outlook on these individual passages is debatable, of course,[34] so this listing is given simply for the sake of argument and to offer perhaps a new perspective on this often puzzling and misunderstood Old Testament book.

---

[32] One could read these contrastive passages as Qoheleth in debate with himself as in a dialectical, diatribe style of discourse (Ryken 1993:269; cf. 2:1)—thus not really a "pure monologue" (Fisch 1988:158).

[33] The ordering is important here—thus also the Epilogue serves as a hermeneutical key to the whole book.

[34] As mentioned in section 7.2.1, my optimistic hermeneutical assessment of Ecclesiastes as a whole is determined by my understanding of how the 'bookend structure' of the implied narrator's aperture (1:1) and epilogue (12:9–14) fits in with and serves as a guiding frame of reference for the entire enclosed discourse of Qoheleth (cf. Grant 2008:211). Certain pericopes marked with an asterisk (*) I consider as mixed or neutral—that is, they may contain positive as well as negative passages, or the whole text could be interpreted as being positive or negative (or traditional/'modern' versus 'postmodern' in contemporary terms; cf. Salyer 2001:16–17).

7.2 The Song: How 'strong' (or sweetly sounding) is it?

Sequence of distinct pericopes in Ecclesiastes

Earth-bound philosophy (-)	Godly perspective (+)
1:2	
1:3–11	
1:12–2:23	
(1:12–18, 2:1–11, 12–17, 18–23)	
	2:24–26
	3:1–17
	(3:1–8, 9–15, 16–17)
3:18–22	
4:1–8	
	4:9–12
4:13–16	
	5:1–7
5:8–17	
	5:18–20
6:1–12	
(1–2, 3–6, 7–9, 10–12)	
7:1–10	
	7:11–14
7:15–17	
	7:18–20
7:21–8:1*	
(9:21–26 // 27 // 9:28–8:1)	
	8:2–8
	8:9–15*
8:16–9:6	
9:7–10	
9:11–18*	
	10:1–20*
	11:1–6
	11:7–10[a]
	12:1–7
12:8	
	12:9–14
	(9–12, 13–14)

[a]According to Bartholomew's assessment of the structure of Ecclesiastes, "a *carpe diem* section never opens a new section except here in 11:7–12:7" (2009:343); this may be another marker of discourse *closure*.

It will be noted that I have classified the lament of 12:1–7 as being a positive passage in its overall content, connotation, and underlying implication. How can such an evaluation be supported one way or the other, in a poem that is almost an elegy—a solemn song for the dead? I have concluded that the theologically-focused *inclusio* of 12:1 and 7 serves as a hermeneutical frame of reference—a crucial *compositional* clue—that directs one's interpretation of the poem as a whole. In the beginning the Creator *gives,* and at the end he eventually *takes* one's 'spirit,' thus implying a personal relationship that goes far beyond the one that exists between God and other living creatures. This meaningful divine connection, Qoheleth concludes, is what the 'youth' (indeed, everyone!) must always 'remember' (i.e., take care to observe) as they live out their lives in cognizance of an inevitable demise and death.

7.2.2.4 Text-critical issues

Most of the hermeneutical problems associated with Ecclesiastes 12:1–7 involve simply understanding the meaning, whether literal or figurative, of the Hebrew text as it stands. However, there are a number of significant variants and, in particular, readings that affect our interpretation of this passage. The following is an example of the UBS Handbook's treatment of pertinent issues that arise in verse five. This excerpt illustrates the potential importance of such text-critical matters and how they may affect the translation process (Ogden and Zogbo 1998: *Paratext* version):[35]

> The phrase **they are afraid** raises two questions. The first is the identity of the subject **they**. The second is which Hebrew verb is behind the *RSV* translation **afraid**; does it come from **ra'ah** "see," or **yare'** "fear"? Although at least one scholar thinks **they** points to the birds in verse 4, most agree that the subject is human. We shall follow this view, though we cannot say more precisely who **they** are. NRSV uses the impersonal "one." On the second question it is probably correct to view the verb in the Hebrew text as **are afraid**....
>
> **The grasshopper drags itself along:** this clause poses problems for the translator and the interpreter. Most versions render the subject of the clause as **grasshopper,** though **NJV** and Fox note the possibility that this noun may be read as "squill," a type of plant that flowers like **the almond tree** in the preceding line. Another problem lies with the interpretation of the verb rendered as **drags itself along.** Some versions say the grasshopper "gets fat," following the **LXX** "the locust's

---

[35] Davis provides a strong argument in favor of the reading 'your Creator' for בּוֹרְאֶיךָ in the lament's first line (1994:352–353).

7.2 The Song: How 'strong' (or sweetly sounding) is it?

> paunch is swollen." But the verb root really means "burdens itself," or possibly "bears its load." The biggest problem, however, is to determine what the point of the illustration is. Is the grasshopper, dragging itself along, a figure for an old person—possibly overweight—who is no longer able to move quickly? Or is this an image of death, since locusts often occur as symbols of death and destruction in the Old Testament (see Joel 1.4)?...
>
> **And desire fails** presents yet another problem. The noun translated **desire** occurs only this once in the Old Testament, so its meaning is not certain. Its root form suggests "desire," but an alternative is "the caperberry," a small fruit that supposedly stimulates the appetite. This rendering is found in some translations (**NAB**, for example). Jewish tradition took the term to refer to sexual desire, so the word is possibly a euphemism for that. **Fails** indicates that desire is no longer felt. A generalized translation which notes that "all desire has faded," or "a person has no interest in anything," does justice to the idea, though we cannot say more than that. The link to old age and death is clear.

So what should ordinary translators do in such cases of controversy over what the Hebrew text actually says and how to interpret it? Where the Handbook makes a definite recommendation (especially if this is supported by another commentary and/or several major versions), then translators may confidently follow the advice that has been given. However, in those cases where the Handbook itself does not offer an explicit interpretation or give a preference of one reading over another, my suggestion would be to adopt the meaning that communicates most effectively in the TL and within the sociocultural setting and environment of the primary receptor group. With regard to the 'grasshopper' in v. 5, for example, the image of a crippled insect as a depiction of the decrepit movements of an elderly person would be quite natural and powerful in this lament on the infirmities of old age.

7.2.3 Aspects of stylistic (poetic) form

An excellent overview of the poetics (lyric structure and style), the "poetic techniques and means" (Grant 2008:187) of Ecclesiastes 12:1–7 has been provided by Hunter (2006:163):

> Structurally [the poem] consists of one long, breathless sentence wending its way from youth and the creator to the return of the spirit to God and the dust to the earth. The journey takes in a startling range of metaphors... In the end what this produces is an effect like that of an impressionist painting, a celebration of vocabulary and sounds

which combine to paint a word picture of startling clarity, even as its individual pieces cannot be separately analyzed....[I]t is a kind of meandering stream of consciousness which serves to represent both the thought processes of age and the actual haphazardness of life...

Five key stylistic features are found in this passage, attesting to its lyric as well as oratorical character (i.e., highly conducive of oral elocution and aural reception). Translators should take note of these different poetic devices (summarized below) during the analysis process with a view towards identifying linguistically and culturally equivalent form-functional techniques that may be later used when rendering the text *dynamically* and *orally* in their language.[36]

1. *Paralleled lineation.* The poetic parallelism in Eccl. 12:1–7 is not binary (A + B +/- C) in nature as we normally find in the psalms. Rather, the fluid lines manifest a tight relationship of form and meaning based on the thematic backbone that is built on a cohesive succession of end-focused temporal clauses (cf. 7.2.2.2), each of which is followed by a series of closely associated *waw*-introduced predications, as shown in the discourse chart of 7.2.2.1.

2. *Lexical recursion.* The verbal recursion of this passage is not often exact (repetition) but tends to be synonymous (reiteration), being comprised of sets of semantically related items (objects, persons, living things, activities, and happenings) that have a primary figurative reference to aging and death. This is best illustrated in v. 6:

...before the *silver cord* is **removed,**
or the *golden bowl* is **broken,**
or the *pitcher* is **shattered** at the well,
or the *water wheel* is **broken** at the cistern—

The great lexical diversity of this poem is an excellent reflection of the 'wisdom tradition' of discourse that it exemplifies.[37] There is also a prominent example of recursion on the *intertextual* level in the clear allusion to Genesis 2:7 and 3:19 in v. 7.

---

[36] Of course, more or less dynamic devices (literary 'marking') in the TL rendition may be appropriate for the primary audience intended, that is, in keeping with the project's job commission ('brief'; cf. Wendland 2004b:51–53, 85–87).

[37] A similar Hebrew wisdom tradition in relation to the present pericope is evidenced in the later deuterocanonical book of Sirach 14:11–19.

7.2 The Song: How 'strong' (or sweetly sounding) is it?

3. *Phonological heightening.* The lineation of this poem is irregular on the whole, but cadenced or balanced within certain segments, where instances of assonance and/or alliteration occasionally appear. The very first verse presents an interesting variation of the norm for line patterning in that each successive colon is somewhat shorter than the preceding one. This leads to an instance of 'end stress' in the climactic direct quotation of the fourth (final) line. There is also a noticeable amount of /b/ and /r/ alliteration in the first two cola of this verse as well as some rhythm and rhyme among the key words of the poem's opening line:

וּזְכֹר֙ אֶת־בּֽוֹרְאֶ֔יךָ בִּימֵ֖י בְּחוּרֹתֶ֑יךָ ¹
עַ֣ד אֲשֶׁ֤ר לֹא־יָבֹ֙אוּ֙ יְמֵ֣י הָֽרָעָ֔ה
וְהִגִּ֣יעוּ שָׁנִ֔ים אֲשֶׁ֣ר תֹּאמַ֔ר
אֵֽין־לִ֥י בָהֶ֖ם חֵֽפֶץ׃

zikhor eth-bôri'eykha bîmê bihûrothekha
'ad asher lo'-yabho'û yimê hara'ah
wihiḡî'û shanîm asher to' mar
'ên-lîbhahem hephets

4. *Disjunction.* The poem does not display much of the *condensation*, or shortening, that is typical of psalmic poetry. Instead, it features the *expansion* of ideas and imagery, which is appropriate for the carefully-fashioned discourse of a 'philosopher' (i.e., Qoheleth, cf. 9–10). A certain type of abbreviation does appear, however, in the rapid shifts of subject matter and/or image sets that occur, e.g., from a domestic scene to a village setting in vv. 3–4. Nevertheless, an essential coherence is maintained throughout by means of the prevailing progression that depicts the disabilities that accompany aging and eventually lead, not unexpectedly, to death. Considering the section as a whole, there is a rather jarring macro-disjunction that transforms the initially optimistic frame of reference pertaining to youth and its pleasures (11:7–8a, 9:a–b) to its opposite, as life draws to a close (11:8b, 9c–10). This ironic enigma reinforces the prevailing message of Qoheleth.

5. *Figuration.* As already suggested (7.2.2.2), this is the principal distinctive feature of Qoheleth's elegy on aging. The impressionistic succession of vivid image sets[38] and evocative metaphoric complex-

---

[38] According to Fox, an individual image "refers to any depiction of a sensory object (in this case verbal) and to the mental replication of this depiction" (1994:383). An 'image set'

es establishes a kaleidoscopic structure[39] of cognitive 'mental spaces' that reflect off one another sequentially, but ultimately merge forcefully in one's mind to create a unified exhortation in favor of a divinely-governed lifestyle and value system.[40] These shifting and overlapping figurative frames of reference (multiple mental spaces) pictorially mirror the frailties of old age and eventually the ultimate dissolution of the body in death (v. 6), all of one's being—except for 'the spirit' (7b)![41]

What is the point and purpose of such a poetic analysis (of which the preceding is an abbreviated illustrative sample)? The point is simply this—that for best results biblical poetry must be analyzed on its own terms and according to its own genius. The purpose of the analysis is for translators to discover the principal stylistic and structural features of the original Hebrew text so that their respective rhetorical functions may be discerned—and then duplicated by some form in the language and literature (orature) of the translation. In this case, the primary genre selected as the model to follow in the TL must be determined through comparative analysis to be a suitable vehicle not only for communicating the multifaceted lyric character of the lament, but also for serving as the climactic text of the entire discourse of Qoheleth.

---

then combines one image with another (or others) to which it may be conceptually related within a given context, e.g., by analogy, cause-effect, scenic association, temporal progression, etc.

[39] The overall literary structure of this poem (cf. 7.2.2.3) is complemented by another, a broadly chiastic form of textual arrangement that is based on relative degrees of literal/figurative meaning: A—literal (1), B—metaphorical (2), C—allegorical (domestic scene, 3), C'—allegorical (village scene, 4–5), B'—metaphorical (6), A'—literal (7). The turning point between C' and B' (the poem's climax in death) is marked by a (relatively) literal 'insert' at the close of v. 5. The allegorical 'core' (C–C') presents a stream-of-consciousness-like flow of images that depict the deleterious effects of old age on the human body.

[40] For a brief discussion and illustration of the theory of mental spaces and conceptual blending, see Wendland 2006:269–276.

[41] Verses 2–6 present us with "a profusion of images, some of which will conjure up with utmost vividness some aspect of ageing or dying, while others tease us by allusions that at this distance we can scarcely catch—thereby awakening in us either the poet or the pedant. It should be the poet, or at least a listener to poetry. If some obscurities in these lines can be clarified, so much the better for kindling our imagination; but so much the worse if they tempt us into treating this graceful poem as a labored cryptogram, or forcing every detail into a single rigid scheme" (Kidner 1976:101). The preceding thoughts contain some significant implications for today's translator too, who must aim to render the text poetically rather than pedantically into the TL in order to preserve the poem's intended meaning and purpose.

7.2 The Song: How 'strong' (or sweetly sounding) is it?

7.2.4 Types of poetic function

Some of the most common communicative goals, or "actions" (Brown 2008:126), to be found in literary discourse are these: informative (including 'educative'), imperative, expressive-affective, aesthetic, textual, interactive, and ritual (Wendland 2004b:310). A particular text may also be analyzed more precisely in terms of the main speech acts (specifically illocutions) that it manifests (ibid., 214–218). For example, the typifying quote that is cited in 12:1, "I find no pleasure in them!" (אֵין־לִי בָהֶם חֵפֶץ) may be broadly classified as demonstrating primarily an *expressive* function and an *evaluative* speech act, which is, in this case, accompanied—as most speech acts are—by the emotive dimension of communication: a *feeling* of disgust (i.e., due to all the vagaries and vicissitudes of life), an *attitude* of resignation (i.e., because what cannot be changed in life—inevitable aging and death), and a *mood* of pessimism (i.e., with respect to the depressing quality of life of the elderly).[42]

Qoheleth's complete lyric lament (12:1–7), on the other hand, may be viewed as embodying an intricate interweaving of the *aesthetic, imperative* (directive) and *expressive-affective* functions, which give rise to a didactic complex of speech acts, e.g., admonishing, exhorting, reflecting (probably coupled with some measure of regret), and affirming (in the end, i.e., 12:7). This combination of motivations is in keeping with the wisdom macro-genre (i.e., variously incorporating instruction, argumentation, evocation, apologetics, warning, etc.) that the book of Ecclesiastes exhibits.[43] In addition, the content and placement of this concluding poem of the book would seem also to perform a *hermeneutical* function in the sense that, together with the implied author's subsequent 'epilogue' (12:9–14), this text serves as a key to its own interpretation. In other words, here at the end the writer appears to advocate a more conservative religious outlook and a traditional biblical set of values, in contrast to the many

---

[42] With respect to the diverse imagery of Eccl. 12:1–8 (cf. *figuration* in 7.2.3), Fox notes: "Imagery conveys moods as well as paraphrasable meanings, and these moods can often be described even when the meaning remains obscure" (1994:386). That observation would seem to apply to a number of the semantically obscure passages in this poem, especially vv. 3–5.

[43] These designated functions are naturally related to the type of (macro-/sub-) genre that one is investigating: "Ecclesiastes...has important affinities with lyric. Lyric is a subjective, personal utterance by a speaker who speaks directly in his or her own voice. The context of a lyric is either personal reflection or emotion. Lyrics are structured on a principle of theme-and-variation, which constitutes the best avenue for seeing the unity of individual passages in Ecclesiastes. ... It is filled with mood pieces in which the speaker reflects on life and makes us feel a certain way toward the subjects he discusses. Ecclesiastes is an affective book" (Ryken 1993:274).

skeptical, nonconformist notions that are often espoused by Qoheleth along the way.⁴⁴ The importance of this type of interactional, *pragmatic* analysis for translators, once again, involves a challenge for them to reproduce these same functional as well as connotative implications appropriately (e.g., in terms of positioning, proportion, power, and relevance) in their own TL poetic rendition.⁴⁵

Poetry of course conveys certain additional pragmatic aims that are unique to its style of discourse and the particular genre concerned. Along with being attractive in construction so as to draw the audience to and into the message and to render it more memorable and memorizable, this discourse-ending lament over time's passage also conveys a certain serious, authoritative tone that enjoins listeners to take what is being said to heart. Furthermore, as in the book of Ecclesiastes as a whole, there is a certain degree of provocation present, since it is a philosophical-religious poem that aims to push the envelope of people's thinking so that they are moved to reevaluate their received traditions ('pat answers'), values, and norms in the light of the prevailing human condition and their common experience which includes the corruption, oppression, violence, and suffering they see on every side.

The vagueness of the imagery, the ambiguous gaps in reasoning, and the obscurity of many of the terms used in this poetic dialogical debate (i.e., Qoheleth with himself, his religious wisdom tradition, and ultimately God) is yet another instance of the subtly intended global meaning of the masterfully fashioned complex of form and content that is evident in this composition. Without the theological pillars of 12:1a and 12:7b being present to anchor one's understanding and assessment of life's meaning in a God-centered reality, the uncertainties and infirmities of old age and an approaching death (12:1b–7a) would undoubtedly lead most receptors, then and now, to adopt the same fatal futility motif as Qoheleth (12:8).⁴⁶

---

⁴⁴ From a more general perspective on the book as a whole, one of its principal didactic aims might be expressed as follows: "[A]ge old truths [e.g., 2:13–14, 26; 3:14; 5:1–2, 12; and especially 12:13–14] are adduced as a corrective to the kind of cynicism which is reflected in 'vanity' and which may have been endemic in the 'sophisticated' world of late [arguably earlier as well—EW] Hellenism" (Hunter 2006:157).

⁴⁵ The Scriptures may be profitably viewed and analyzed as 'communication,' a theme well developed by Brown (2007) from a contextualized hermeneutical perspective based on speech act theory.

⁴⁶ The rather depressing outlook on old age expressed in the words and images of the large center of this lament is well described by Fox as follows: "The imagery of the poem, whatever its symbolic or figurative meaning, creates an atmosphere of pain, contortion, and constriction. It draws us into a world of decay, abandonment, dreary silence, and speechless grief, and makes us associate this atmosphere with aging and death—whose pain is heightened by contrast with the rejuvenation of nature" (1994:390). However, I am not as

7.2 The Song: How 'strong' (or sweetly sounding) is it?

Can any TL genre and team of translators match the original in its essential form-functional respects? The Chewa and Tonga versions given in 7.3.2 at least make the attempt—an effort that will hopefully be repaid by a greater understanding and appreciation for Qoheleth's lament on the part of their respective target audiences (see 7.3.1).

7.2.5 The message—what is the sense of Qoheleth's closing song?

> Eccles. 12:1–8 is the most difficult passage in a difficult book.
> (Fox 1994:381)

Following in the path of a long line of distinguished interpreters, I certainly cannot claim to have the final (or perhaps even a convincing) answer to this question concerning the ultimate meaning of a book (or any included pericope) whose major voice asserts that it is 'meaningless' (or enigmatic)—along with everything else in this life (12:8). My overall impression of the message of Ecclesiastes, as implied along the way of the preceding analysis, is that it presents a vigorously 'apologetic' text, one written by an elderly sage (the implied author) in defense of established sapiential theology and associated ethics. Though firmly grounded on a worldview that focused on an ordered moral lifestyle devoted to 'the fear of the LORD,' this creative writer-thinker is certainly cognizant of a competing alternative, with a skeptical existential frame of reference, namely, a belief and value system that allowed no place for either moral absolutes or the divine in a world that was apparently inscrutable as to significance, value, or purpose. My interpretation arises from a discourse analysis of the book of Ecclesiastes as a whole, which manifests an alternating sequence of cynical, coupled with optimistic points of view (cf. 7.2.2.3). This culminates, I believe, in the last major discourse of Qoheleth—the passage spanning 11:7–12:7—with the first half of its thematic peak being the lyric lament on old age and death. The second half follows later in the author's concluding epilogue, which then provides the essential interpretive clue, or hermeneutical framework, that allows one to arrive at the intended meaning, not only of the final poem but also of the entire text.

---

skeptical about the capacity of this text also to convey a definable and definite content: "But the poem's purpose is not to convey information; it is to create an attitude toward aging and, more importantly, death" (ibid., 398, added italics). The structurally-significant placement of the theological affirmations of 12:1a and 7b argues for a concrete propositional truth: God is there at every person's beginning and ending; from that perspective then, one's life can derive a sustaining meaning and a divinely ordained purpose (12:13–14).

The complex intersection and interaction of a sequence of evocative images (cognitive constructs, mental models/spaces), i.e., heavenly light-bodies, a storm scene, an old homestead, a village street setting, various water-gathering implements) merge to build a complex, culturally familiar background that is anchored in a literal beginning and ending to the poem (12:1, 7). This medial pastiche of images (12:2–6) then serves to generate the engaging and evocative figurative meaning that develops, in concrete visualizable terms, the progressive development of the lament's abstract central theme: old age envisaged (v. 1)—entered (2–5)—ended in death (6–7).[47] In fact *how* to use one's time on earth (cf. 3:1–8)—*how* to live and to die with one's Creator and Judge in mind—is arguably the main message not only of 12:1–7, but also of Ecclesiastes as a whole.[48]

> Since death cannot be circumvented, Solomon argued that the key to life and living is to be found in death and dying (Davis 1994:348).[49]

I conclude this section with a selection of the comments of seven scholars who give articulate expression to my understanding of what the (implied) author wants Qoheleth and his varied reflective meditations and

---

[47] We need not enter into the debate over whether these verses constitute an *allegory* (a hermeneutical approach that goes back to the Jewish Targums; cf. Walton et al. 2000:575) or some other type of figurative language. Hunter is for allegory: "Though exegetical opinion has varied as regards the way this allegory is to be interpreted, and indeed as to whether it constitutes a single coherent allegory, I shall confine my reading here to the convention that it describes old age and the inevitable death of the individual" (2006:163). Fox is not: "Allegory is an extended and complex image composed of an organized set of figures or tokens representing certain concepts, events, or entities in an extra-textual reality....Eccles. 12:1–8 lacks the degree of internal consistency necessary to give meaning and cogency to an allegory..." (1994:395). In any case, it's not what we call it that counts, but how we construe the text.

[48] I feel that Bartholomew pushes his case somewhat beyond the support of solid evidence when he argues for an eschatological connection with the OT prophets in 12:1–7: "...12:1 refers to the individual and his approaching death, but vv. 2–6 connect individual death with the eschatological vision of the day of the LORD, as enunciated by the prophets.... Qoheleth works...from the death of the individual to the end of history—thereby invoking the prophetic vision of God's cosmic judgment" (2009:353). On the other hand, I fully support his opinion that "...to see death in this section as the [absolute] end makes nonsense of Qoheleth's insistence that finally judgment comes before God. For this judgment to be a reality, there must be life beyond death..." (Bartholomew 2009:353).

[49] Davis summarizes the *life-death thematic polarity* in Ecclesiastes in the form of six so-called "principles" (1994:348–350): 1. All people die one day (2:14–16, 3:19–22, 9:3); 2. Death has certain advantages over life (4:1–3, 7:1–2, 26); 3. Death cannot be avoided, but do not act foolishly and rush it (3:2, 6:6, 7:17, 8:8, 12–13, 9:11–12); 4. Taking the reality of death into consideration can help one to live life to the fullest (7:4, 12:1–7); 5. In contrast, life has certain advantages over death (9:4–6, 10); and 6. Living solely for this life is futile and meaningless (5:15–16, 6:3–5, 8:10).

7.2 The Song: How 'strong' (or sweetly sounding) is it?

life observations to teach us in this, his ultimate poetic piece (in its literary context):

- Appropriately, this last major discourse of Ecclesiastes concerns the grim reality of aging and death and the need to enjoy the life one has under the sun. Nevertheless, this is not a hedonist's creed, for the demand that all be done in the fear of God stands behind and above the whole (Garrett 1993:339–340).

- Ecclesiastes itself gives us clues as to how the gap between autonomous skepticism and the *carpe diem* perspective is to be filled. The theology of remembrance in 12:1 is important in this respect, but the epilogue is definitive in indicating finally how the narrator intends us to fill in the gaps, and I suggest that 12:13–14 confirms my reading of 12:1 as the bridge that positively resolves the tension/gap between the carpe diem element and the enigma statements....Remembrance in Ecclesiastes is thus far more than mere mental assent. It represents the radical difference between a world view in which humankind is central and autonomous and one in which God is central (Bartholomew 2009:356).

- There are, then, two levels of assessment of wisdom in the book of Ecclesiastes. First, there is a comparison of wisdom with other ways of life as they are seen "under the sun." Second, there is a view of true wisdom seen from God's perspective. Human wisdom, when viewed simply from the perspective of this life, appears to offer very little beyond those other ways that human beings have devised for themselves....In the light of a sovereign God to whom one submits in fear, however, wisdom is of far greater value than any other alternative way of life (Sailhammer 1994:357–358).

- The passage [12:1–7] is framed by references to God as the Originator of life. Despite the inequities of life and the terrors of death, God is ever the Creator of both the living (v. 1) and the dead (v. 7). God's sovereignty is thus recognized as a regulating element in all human activities. If God is present at the beginning and the ending of life, He most certainly is there throughout the totality of life. God can thus give meaning to an otherwise meaningless existence; He can even help individuals make sense out of the senselessness of death (Davis 1994:351).

- But there is something beyond death and vanity. The syntax of the opening is utterly clear: "Remember now thy Creator in the days of thy youth, before... before...What counts is the life that is given us, the remembering, the testimony. Undercutting and contradicting the grave poetry of dying is the purposeful rhythm of living, established in the first verse and picked up again in the epilogue. Life is given and we have to render an account of what we have done with it....Like Job, Ecclesiastes ends not with death and darkness but with an ongoing history of testing and performance. Life is loaded with responsibility (Fisch 1988:178).

- Just as God gave to humans a spirit, so also the spirit will return to the Creator. Humans, therefore, are not independent beings who live under the sun, and who must find their significance within their temporal existence, but rather they are dependent on their Creator, and they find their significance in their relationship with him. Although Qoheleth does not make the point explicit, the implied answer to the programmatic question of the book, "What does man gain [*yitrôn*] from all his labor at which he toils under the sun?" is that *yitrôn* cannot be found under the sun. The fact that after one's death the spirit returns to God suggests that Qoheleth's hope for *yitrôn* resides not in human achievement apart from God, but rather in human connection with God (Estes 2005:377–378).[50]

- The Preacher's answer to meaninglessness is deceptively simple. It is "Remember your Creator." That is the key that unlocks a whole world denied to the unbeliever. Its implications go on being unpacked for the whole of life....Having made the simple pronouncement, the Preacher expands on it a little by telling us *when* [12:1–8] and *how* [12:9–12] and *why* [12:13–14] we are to remember our Creator (Tidball 1989:181).

7.3 Synthesis: The pressing task of the translator[51]

בִּקֵּשׁ קֹהֶלֶת לִמְצֹא דִּבְרֵי־חֵפֶץ
וְכָתוּב יֹשֶׁר דִּבְרֵי אֱמֶת:

The Philosopher sought to find *delightful* words,
and to write *accurately*—the words of *truth*. (Eccl. 12:10; cf. NET)[52]

---

[50] The affirmative theistic declaration of 12:7 thus answers the skeptical rhetorical question of 3:21.

[51] Before attempting to 'synthesize' a text in the TL, translators must begin by recognizing the essential holistic literary and exegetical synthesis of the biblical book at hand: "The poetic whole of the final form of the book offers more than analysis of the individual parts on their own" (Grant 2008:212).

[52] GNT appears to miss the mark badly in its rendering of this passage: "The Philosopher

7.3 Synthesis: The pressing task of the translator

This summary by the frame narrator of Qoheleth's life-long quest would seem to be applicable to Bible translators as well—at least those who aim at some measure of literary (and/or oratorical) equivalence in their TL text.[53] The principal goal is to communicate as "accurately/clearly" (יֹשֶׁר) as possible "the words of truth" (דִּבְרֵי אֱמֶת) from "the wise" transmitters (חֲכָמִים) of messages that have been "given by the one [divine] Shepherd"(נִתְּנוּ מֵרֹעֶה אֶחָד– 12:11).[54] This refers to message content and purpose, but a secondary goal concerns also the form of the biblical text, namely, that this be conveyed in a "pleasing/delightful" (חֵפֶץ) manner in the translation. Thus, the text of a translation ought to be characterized by a similar measure of orally-expressed rhetorical impact and aesthetic appeal to match what has been discovered through analysis of the original portion of Scripture. The more that form is a part of the meaning of the pericope under consideration, as in the case of all poetic passages (such as Eccl. 12:1–7), the greater the effort required to take this aspect of communication into consideration during the translation process. The extent to which this can actually be done depends on a number of operational variables, such as the relative richness or poverty of oratory forms in the vernacular,[55] the competency of the translation team, their training and experience in such literary matters, the time/funding available to carry out their work, the expectations of the TL community, the support rendered by project administrators, and contributions by reviewer-consultants.

---

tried to find comforting words, but the words he wrote were honest."

[53] A translation team may aim to achieve naturalness (idiomaticity) in their work at one of several different levels, ranging from the phonological (e.g., rhythmic utterances of a relatively literal nature) to the complete discourse (e.g., a genre-based equivalent rendering), depending on the governing project *brief* and *Skopos* and in keeping with presumed relevance for and acceptability by the translation's primary target group (Wendland 2004b:88–96; 2006:77–78, 86, 304–307).

[54] Regarding the imagery in v. 11, Bartholomew concludes: "…'goads' were used by shepherds to move animals along the right route, and thus shepherd imagery is already strongly present in this verse, which can be seen to progress naturally to God the shepherd as the one source of wisdom. Thus v. 11 not only positions Qoheleth's teaching among the wise but also traces the origin of such wisdom to one shepherd, namely God" (2009:368–370. In this case, GNT gives a good paraphrase of v. 11).

[55] Brenda Boerger comments, "It has been my continued impression, not just reading numerous Wendland manuscripts, but also in discussions with other colleagues, that many African languages have or have maintained a greater variety of literary forms which also are more highly valued by the community than I have found in my work in the primarily Oceanic languages of the Solomon Islands, South Pacific" (personal communication).

7.3.1 Target audience

This issue of target audience has already been touched on in section 7.1.2, but its importance (and frequent neglect) in the overall translation process warrants a few further comments. Thus, the essential 'for whom' question is not often asked or completely answered (and backed up by solid research and testing) as projects struggle to keep to a predetermined schedule, or a deadline that does not allow translators to reach their full potential in terms of applying the available literary resources of their mother tongue. Before any project begins—even before the translators are selected—there is an urgent need to clearly define the intended TL group with whom the intended version (whether a new Bible, revision, liturgical, popular, audio/oratorical selection, etc.) aims to communicate. The answer to this key question will determine in turn the type or style of translation as well as the medium and mode of text transmission.

As noted earlier, the translation of Ecclesiastes 12:1–7 in both Chewa and Tonga is intended to be a specially composed rendition aimed primarily to reach and attract the pre-marriage Christian youth of these two Bantu communities. The goal is to provide them with a fresh translation (i.e., in addition to the more standard 'missionary' and 'popular language' versions that they already have access to), having several objectives:

- To educate young people about the salient issues that arise in Bible translation work, including the various methods of translation and the difference between versions.

- To demonstrate the importance of having an accurate and a clear version in their MT so as to help them understand and apply the Scriptures in their everyday lives, specifically, this concluding lament poem by the Philosopher (cf. Hill and Hill 2008:179–189).

- To serve as a 'talking point' with regard to how specific translation types may be produced for particular communicative purposes as well as sociocultural and spiritual needs that they may face, e.g., as a innovative evangelism tool to reach the unchurched or delinquent colleagues in their immediate community.

- To provide the basis for a more dynamic engagement with the younger generation through some form of non-print medium adaptation, e.g., a modern (or traditional) musical composition, a dramatic stage production, a chanted/recited oral interpretation, or

7.3 Synthesis: The pressing task of the translator

some other type of local art form (cf. Petersen 2009; Hill and Hill 2008:199–208, 298–301) to spark discussion in a group Bible study setting.

- To encourage more youth to support the work of the Bible Society of Zambia and, if possible, to become involved in the program of translation in their language (it's not just for adults!).

In traditional Africa, as in most world societies (with some notable exceptions over the ages, such as the ancient Greek Spartans), the age of youth is typically one of joy (11:7–8, 9–10) and of experiencing life's challenges and pleasures to the full (often illicitly as well in terms of society's accepted sexual mores). In modern Africa, however, this is not necessarily the case as the AIDS pandemic has drawn the dark clouds (Eccl. 12:2) of disease, disability, and often premature death over the light of many young lives. Homes are broken up as one or both parents succumb, and the urban inner cities become populated with increasing numbers of orphaned or abandoned street children, a countercultural phenomenon that would never have happened in days gone by. The youth of today face other hardships and disappointments as well, such as frustration over an uncertain national political future, the widespread lack of affordable secondary or technical schooling, and relatively few local job opportunities, resulting in a jobless rate that fluctuates above 50 percent. This situation tends to promote alcoholism and experimenting with toxic, mind-altering drugs that are all too readily available. Undoubtedly, the optimistic 'wisdom' passages of Ecclesiastes (e.g., 11:7–8a, 9a–b) also need to be voiced in these circumstances, that is, within a broader didactic framework of Christian doctrine and ethics, in order to encourage a positive, constructive outlook on life. Certainly, the Creator desires lifelong fellowship with each and every person ('you', sg., 12:1, 7). But serious, thought-provoking texts like 12:2–5 are necessary too, both to counterbalance the prevalent materialistic, existential optimism of the age, especially that generated by a secularized atheistic world view, and also to provide a realistic biblical perspective on life's final destination—first, death of the individual (12:6) and ultimately the divine judgment of all humanity (12:14). It is in such a volatile, faith-challenging sociocultural and religious setting that the proclamation of Qoheleth's last lament must be more widely heard.

7.3.2 Towards a lyric lament in a Bantu language

Having determined the audience and the manner of interacting with them via translation, the search for an equivalent TL genre begins. In this case, our aim is to come as close as possible to an 'elegiac' mode in order to match the original Hebrew text in content, beauty of poetic form, emotive tone, evocative imagery, rhetorical effect, and the oral and aural medium of communication.[56] It is rare to read any Bible commentator who has something to say about the oral/aural feature—regarding any biblical text (even one of the Psalms); W. Sibley Towner is an exception. He makes the following observations regarding the oral articulation of Eccl. 12:1–7 (1997:356):

> [T]his entire passage of seven verses is all one sentence. Because Hebrew literature is, on the whole, given to short and pithy utterances, such a stylistic variation has to be taken as a serious clue to the intended understanding of the passage. Lectors, cantors, preachers, and those who read the Scriptures out loud need to practice the passage over and over to capture the richness of oral interpretation that it provides.
>
> Oral interpretation is that kind of rendition of a text that recapitulates its content in the way it is read. It "performs" the sentiment of the text. Verses 1–7 should be "performed" in the mode of a clock running down. The pitch should lower, and the speed should drop as the reader moves from the memory of the Creator and the days of youth through the dawning clouds of trouble...dryness; and finally death.

One might disagree with one or another of the preceding comments (e.g., the 'short and pithy' character of Hebrew literature, or how, precisely, to 'perform the sentiment' of this pericope), but at least Towner has called attention to the vital auditory dimension of the biblical text. Thus, there is a great need to *translate* with this performative aspect in mind so that the published text may be more fluently, correctly, and dynamically read—whether aloud (ideally) or silently to oneself. Such extra attention is all the more warranted in the climactic poetic passage at hand, where a practiced oral interpretation by an experienced elocutor can serve to highlight the grave connotation along with the serious content of this plaintive lyric lament. To be sure, a considerable degree of vocal interpretation would be involved as the performer would undoubtedly wish

---

[56] I owe the designation 'oral and aural', instead of the common, but more awkward 'oral-aural', communication/medium to B. Witherington (e.g., 2009:97).

7.3 Synthesis: The pressing task of the translator

to change the tone and tenor of his voice in keeping with the perceived changes in Qoheleth's mood or attitude (cf. the chart in section 7.2.2.3).

7.3.2.1 Chewa ndakatulo

I have described elsewhere (2004b:415–418; 2005b) the nature (form, content, and function) of traditional Chewa lyric poetry (*ndakatulo*). Here we have a secular text that illustrates why this is a productive literary model to follow when translating biblical poetry (or poetic prose). The flexible, stylistically diverse *ndakatulo* genre is particularly appropriate for an instructive work such as Ecclesiastes in general and the lament of 12:1–7 in particular. Several lines of the following piece actually seem to echo or elaborate upon the narrator's description of Qoheleth's skills in 12:9–10 (Malunga 1990:45):

Kuimba kwa Mlakatuli	The Song of the Lyric Poet
Kuzunaku, kokomaku	So sweet, so very pleasant
Ndiye kuimba kwa mlakatuli	Is the singing of the poet
Wa maso owona zobisika	Who has eyes that sees secrets
Ndi makutu omva zonong'onezedwa	And ears that hears whispers.
Nyimbo yosamuka pamilomo yake	The songs that are transferred from his lips
Njamavume osalazidwa ndi luso	Have choruses skillfully folded in
Ndinso nthetemya zokometsetsa.	Along with the attractive sound of rattles.
Uthenga wotuluka nlipenga lake	The message that emerges from his trumpet
La nyanga ya ngoma	(Made) from the horn of a kudu
Ngokhathamira ndi ukachenjede ndithu.	Is compacted as by the rain with great cunning.
Poti ngofulula ndi ukatswiri	For it is brewed by an expert
Ngati kabota kokupira mawere am'matolo.	Like sweet beer into which rich millet is stirred.
Mikoko yogonera itama ukadaulo wake wonola	The elders of old praise his sharpened insight
Mawu ngati muvi pathanthwe.	The words that are like an arrow (ground) upon rock
Makosana openya chokweza atamanda luso lake	Headmen with vision exalt his expertise
Loluma nawuzira ngati khoswe.	Which bites and blows thereon like a rat to ease the pain.
Ntchembere nazo ziguntchira	Old women too dance enthusiastically
Pomva masalimo ake okhutala ndi chidzudzulo.	When they hear his "psalms" so thick with rebuke.

Kumadambo osunga abusa,	At the lowlands where herdsmen are keeping watch,
Kumitsinje yogubuduka m'zithukuluzi,	At the streams that roll along beneath dense thickets,
Kumagomo okongoletsa dziko,	At the hills which decorate the land,
Mawu ake ndimphepo yachiuso	His words are like a soothing breeze
M'mitima yopunthidwa ndi mazunzo.	In hearts beaten down with affliction.

The explicit mention of 'psalms' in this ode suggests that essential link in lyric structure and style which encourages us to experiment with the *ndakatulo* genre in the expression of certain hortatory biblical passages in the Chewa language for particular audiences (the oral-aural mode of transmission being primary). The following piece is a pre-final draft of Eccl. 12:1–7 which has been circulated for testing and comment (accompanied by my own, relatively literal back translation into English):[57]

Uzikumbukabe Mlengi masikuwonse aunyamatako,	1 You must continue to remember the Creator all the days of your youthfulness,
makamakanso zaka zovuta zija zisanakugwera iwe,	especially before those difficult years befall you,
isanafike nthawi yoti uzidzati, "Moyowu wandikola!"	Before the time comes when you will say, "This life is distasteful!"
Usaiwale za amakedzana, ankati, "Imfatu ilibe odi!"	Don't forget that those of yesteryear used to say, "Indeed, death comes with no word of greeting!"
Nyengo ya ukalamba wako, ndithu, kudzakhala bii!	2 In the season of your old age, surely, things will become dark BLACK!
dzuŵa, kuŵala, mwezi, nyenyezi, zonse zidzakudera,	The sun, light, moon, stars, they all will darken for you,
mitambo ya bingu idzabweranso mvula itakusiyadi.	clouds of thunder will return again after the rains have left you.
Nthaŵi imeneyo miyendo yako izidzanjenjemera,	3 At that time your legs will tremble,
mikono, manja, zala, zonse zidzafooka nkuzizira zi!	arms, hands, fingers, they all will become weak and cold FRIGID!
Mano oŵerengekawo adzalephera nkutafuna mwaa!	Those few teeth (of yours) will fail to chew ALL SPREAD OUT!

---

[57] For this exercise, I 'lyricized' the published Chewa popular language version (1998) with the assistance of my mother tongue speaking seminary students.

7.3 Synthesis: The pressing task of the translator

ndipo maso adzangochita chidima ngati mikhwithi.	And your eyes will become dim as in a dense fog.
Makutu adzatsekeka, mau aenake sadzalowamonso.	4 Your ears will be shut, the words of others will no longer enter therein.
Kusinja kwa azimai pamtondo sikudzamveka konse,	The meal-pounding of women at their gathering place will no longer be heard,
komabe udzadzidzimuka mbalame zikalira m'mawa.	however, you will be startled when (hearing) birds sing in the morning.
Udzaopa kunyamuka, kutuluka kudzakhala koopsa.	5 You will be afraid to get up (to go anywhere), going outside will be traumatic.
Imvi zidzati mbuu! Udzalephera nkudziguza komwe.	White hair will MULTIPLY! You will fail to drag yourself anywhere.
Chilakolako chili chonse chidzazilala basi! Tonsefe,	Every sort of desire will just dissipate, finished! We all,
indedi, tikupita kwathu kokakhala mpaka muyayaya,	most certainly we are on our way home to go and stay there forever,
ndipo titachoka, otsalawo adzangolira misozi mbwee!	and after we've gone, our survivors will weep many tears OVERFLOWING!
Nthambo yamoyo idzamasuka, mbale yathu kusweka,	6 The cord of life will be untied, our plate will be shattered,
mtsuko udzaphwanyika, mkombero ife kudzati thyo!	the waterpot will be smashed, our basket BROKEN!
Apo thupi lidzabwerera kudothi mom'mene lidaaliri,	7 Then the body will return to the dirt from which it came,
mzimuwo udzabwerera kwa Mulungu yemwe adauika.	the spirit will return to God who placed it (in man).

Some of the principal stylistic features of the *ndakatulo* genre are seen in the preceding translation, e.g., short, rhythmic utterances (each comprising a poetic line); alliteration, assonance, occasional rhyme; the use of emphatic and deictic suffixes; periodic ideophones (dramatic predications—upper case in English version); condensation and ellipsis; and abundant figurative language and imagery (matching that of the original lament). While the present composition would do well in the form of a public oration, the text would have to be modified considerably if it were to be adapted for a musical rendition, in particular, by reducing the level of information density through the use of repetition and restatement. The idiomatic nature of this lyric literary version may be highlighted by comparing it with what is undoubtedly the most popular of the existing Chewa Bible translations, the old missionary (KJV) *Buku Lopatulika* 'Sacred Book' (1922). This text is reproduced below, exactly as published, and formatted (line by line, as prose in justified double-column text), accompanied by a relatively literal, formally matching English back translation:

1 Ukumbukirenso Mlengi wako masiku a unyamata wako, asanadze masiku oipa, ngakhale zisanayandikire zakazo zakuti udzati, Si-	Remember again your Creator during the days of your youth, before evil days come, even (though) before those years draw near when you will say, I am not ple-
ndikondwera nazo; 2 ngakhale lisanade dzuwa, ndi kuunika, ndi mwezi,	ased with them; even (though) before the sun gets dark, and the light, and the moon,
ndi nyenyezi, mitambo ndi kubweranso italeka mvula; 3 tsikulo omwe asunga nyumba adzathunthumira, amuna olimba nadzawerama, akupera nadzaleka poperewera, omwe ayang'ana pamazenera nadzadetsedwa;	and the stars, the clouds returning after the rain has stopped; on that day the house-keepers will shake, strong men will bend over, the grinders will cease being too few, those looking at the windows will become dirty;
4 pa khomo lakunja padzatsekeka; potsika mau akupera, wina nanya-Muka polira mbalambe, ndipo akazi onse akuyimba sadzamveka bwino;	the outside door will be closed; when the grinders get quiet, someone will arise when the bird cries, and all the women singing will not be heard very well;
5 inde, adzaopa za pamwamba, panjira padzakhala zoopsya; mciu nudza-	yes, he (they?) will fear things above, along the path there will be frightening things; the mciu tree[58] will spro-
phuka, dzombe ndi kukoka miyendo, zilakolako ndi kutha; pakuti munthu apita kwao kwamuyaya, akulira maliro nayendayenda panja; 6 ci-	ut, a grasshopper dragging its legs, desires coming to an end; because a person goes home forever, the mourners at a funeral going back and forth outside; before a str-
ngwe casiliva cisanaduke, ngakhale mbale yagolide isanasweke; ngakhale mtsuko usanaphwanyike kukasupe, ngakhale njinga yotunga madzi isanatyoke kucitsime; 7 pfumbi ndi kubwera pansi pomwe linali kale, mzimu ndi kubwera kwa Mulungu amene anaupereka.	ing of silver is cut, even before a plate of gold breaks, even before a water jar is smashed at a spring, even before a cycle for drawing water is broken in two at the well; the dust coming down below where it was before, and the spirit coming to God who offered it.

---

[58] People used to make bows from this tree, but it was especially known for becoming infested with a certain type of white furry caterpillar that would turn the whole tree white.

7.3 Synthesis: The pressing task of the translator

In addition to the obvious difficulty in understanding this literal translation (both in English and Chewa!), the text is very hard to read—not only due to all the hyphens and broken lines—but also because of the many semicolons. The translation has been composed in the form of a single sentence, as in the original Hebrew, but the result is a text that is virtually unintelligible in places—yet in that respect, perhaps, as meaningless as described by Qoheleth!

7.3.2.2 *Tonga* malabo

The preceding Chewa *ndakatulo* rendering of Ecclesiastes 12:1–7 may be compared with the following text, which illustrates quite a different instructive, potentially oratorical style of poem in the Tonga language.[59] This poem has been composed in the *malabo* genre (from the verb *kulabalika* 'to speak about deep/mysterious/ revealing matters') of poetic discourse in view of a potential audience similar to the one described above for Chewa (7.3.1). But unlike the Chewa lyric, this Tonga poem is articulated by an alternating pair of speakers and meant solely for some manner of *oral* articulation, normally in a give-and-take didactic manner, i.e., a *malabo* is not chanted, recited, or sung, but it may be set to music later, not in the original performance.[60] A *simalabo* (pl., *basimalabo*) poet may be male or female and is usually an older person (20+ years, especially among women). These poetic artists are well-known and respected members of the community and normally perform at major communal events, in particular during times of celebration and female initiation. Qoheleth's deeply reflective lyric lament is well-suited to the back-and-forth educational exchanges that incisive, life-related *malabo* poetry embodies (A = leader; B = responder in the following text; poet A deliberately indicates by a pause [...] when B should come in).

A: *Koyeeya Mulengi wako...*	1. Remember your Creator...
B: *Kocili buyo mucece, kotanaswaidwe penzi ndo.*	While you are still young/playful, before big trouble visits you, my friend.
A: *Myaka kiitanakubijila nonga waba noti...*	Before the years go bad for you when you might say...

---

[59] This *malabo* lyric was kindly composed for me by Rev. Salimo Hachibamba, a mother tongue Tonga speaker and an experienced theological educator, Bible translator, and student of vernacular oral literature. Rev. Hachibamba also provided me with an English translation of his poem as well as an insightful oral commentary on its form and content, which I have re-phrased in this section

[60] "That is the kind of music where people will usually say, *"Takuli kwiimba, nkwaana."* 'He is not singing, but giving us a lecture or story'" (S. Hachibamba, personal communication).

B: *"Syooo, tazicindiboteli ma!"* [61]

A: *Zuba amumuni, mwezi anyenyezi, kazitanaba bbaibili!...*

B: *Aalo makumbi, ngawo aamvula yamoombelela, kaatanamwaika niyacimana-mana.*

A: *Zikwabilizyo, nsinga amilambima, noziyoofwebuluka—zyandekema...*

B: *Wabwelemana buyo wakali sintanze; Iyamuleka!*
A: *Bacibanda nobayooleka kugaya, uh! Batantaanisya...*

B: *Akube kubona, ino nkumunikizya; kuli ngubi!*
A: *Ma, kumvwa koonse nkuwentuzya; aakali matwi, kwasinkwa...*

B: *Noilila nkando aziyo, aalya mpobaziil— acibukilo aalilila bamintengwe, kumvwa pe!*

B: *Ccita kuteya matwi nkokuti ambweni balamvwa. Cilangwa buyo!*
A: *Majeleele takuli nkokwaayoowa, ...*
B: *Kweendeenda mumazila, kwabija...*
A: *Kwakali kumutwe kwatubwa, ani mutube-tube walangazya.*
A: *Kwakwekwebwa; ani nimpaso zyagonkelwa...*
B: *Accuuu! notaciyooziyandi limbi.*

"Ach, things give me no pleasure anymore, no sir!"

2. Sun and light, moon and stars, before they appear like a flickering bush fire in the distance...[62]

And the clouds, those bearing a gentle rain, before they disperse after the showers.[63]

3. When (your body's) protective veins and muscles all turn flabby—the skin just quivers...

The strong man is but a shadow of his former self; all his power is gone!
His molars have stopped grinding, too bad! They are just scattered (back there in the mouth)...

As for his sight, he struggles to see anything; it's as if he is looking into a fog!
4. Oh my, his hearing, it is as if voices are very far away; as for the ears, they are like blocked...

The sound of grinding stone on stone, when they (women) grind meal—and when people wake up to the cries of the blackbirds at dawn, no, the elderly person doesn't hear a thing! Only if he cups the palm of his hand at his ear, then he can hear. What more can I say?
5. High up places cause him a lot of fright...
Even walking about in the streets is bad idea...
As for his head, it is white all over, just like the cottonwood ('white-white') tree when flowering.
He drags his legs along, like a lame grass-hopper...
Just too bad! folks don't like to see him around anymore.[64]

---

[61] *Syooo!* is a forceful interjection suggesting self-depreciation; *ma* is an emotive-exclamatory particle.

[62] The additional English gloss is necessary here to suggest something of the visual impression evoked by the ideophone *bbaibili.*

[63] This is an interesting, contextualized interpretation of the difficult Hebrew original. The speaker bemoans the passing of the gentle rains of yesteryear when, as they say, "life was good!"

[64] In this case, the 'desire' has been interpreted as *not* being aroused in those who are

7.3 Synthesis: The pressing task of the translator

B: Ndeelyo nokuyooonwa, koonenena, takucibukwi!...	That's when they go to sleep, sleeping for good, not ever waking up again!
A: Kwainkwa kumayoba, kumuya banji—pe ii! kwalobwa!...	They have gone to the clouds, where many (= all people) go—oh no! they are lost!...
B: Kwafugwa, bwanjila buumba, nkwiima maima-ima.	They're dead, now everyone is mourning, they are just standing around (the homestead).
B: Haye, sena ntuulu nzuma mumikondo basa?	Hey! Are they not standing just like anthills along the path, my friends?[65]
A: Yawe, kamunga kamuyeeya,	6. Hey you, you must always think about (this),
A: kamumuyeeya tutali twa buumi, ...	(and) remember the threads of life,...
B: Ntuto twa buumi byandisi katutanazutuka!	Those cords of dear life before they are cut off!
A: Kuutanapwaigwa munkuli, nguwo munkuli wakuvuntauzya, ...	Before the calabash is smashed, the calabash of finding out the cause of (someone's) death...[66]
B: Ndilyo nocizwa busu bana balalila.	While you are still productive enough to feed your children.[67]
A: Mpawo bulongo nobulapiluka kubulongonyina—kayi nkubwakazwida?...	7. Then (your) clay will turn into clay—say, is that not where it came from?...
B: Muuya ulapiluka kuli Leza nguwakuupa!	(Your) spirit will return to God who gave it!

The implicit dialogic character of Ecclesiastes (i.e., diatribe, cf. 7.2.1) on the macrostructure of discourse organization is manifested overtly in the microstructure of the text in this Tonga rendition; this serves to enhance the vibrancy of its teaching function as well as its thematic impact and aesthetic attraction for an indigenous audience.

---

living with an old person, not as a reference to his/her own personal (sexual?) desire. There is an added negative implication that these Tonga words evoke in a Bantu sociocultural setting: very old people, especially if they are wealthy and well-to-do, are often suspected of being witches or sorcerers.

[65] Mourners at a Tonga funeral homestead normally do not make much movement as a sign of their grief. In that sense it is as if they are standing still like tall termite mounds which are probably visible somewhere in the vicinity. Ironically, however, a termite mound (anthill) is also a symbol of life because it is always growing due to the incessant labors of the unseen termites inside. Thus, people like to be buried nearby such a termite mound in anticipation of life after death (as an ancestral spirit).

[66] There is some more contextualizing here: water, which is stored in a calabash, symbolized life; thus, a smashing of the calabash correspondingly refers to one's death. However, a calabash is also used by traditional diviners to determine the cause of one's death, whether foul play (e.g., witchcraft) was involved or not. In this context there is an intimation that God is the great Diviner, the only one who knows, in fact determines, the time of one's death.

[67] In this line, speaker B actually refers to what A enjoined back in v. 6—to 'remember....'

7.3.3 Conceptual and cultural incongruities in the paratext

As we have seen, the lament of Eccl. 12:1–7 is a rather difficult pericope for translators to deal with. Not only is the text an instance of dynamic elegiac poetry, which must find some equivalent functional form in the TL, but it presents a number of problems of textual interpretation that must be resolved along the way. Some of these can be handled in the translation itself, as was illustrated in both the Chewa and the Tonga poetic versions where the translators chose to explicate many of the metaphors of aging and death or to render them more clearly by means of cultural substitutes. However, it is not possible (nor would it be honest and accurate) to take care of all the obscurities and potential errors (i.e., presented by a literal translation) within the text of the translation itself. For some assistance, at least in the case of a printed version, one must turn to the paratext and the use of such explanatory and descriptive features as footnotes, sectional introductions, glossary entries, cross-references (in some cases), and illustrations (whenever possible). I will focus on the familiar footnote solution in the following discussion.

7.3.3.1 Discovery and evaluation

First, translators must be able to discover and then analytically evaluate the most serious problem areas that a given biblical text presents. If they are competent and well-trained, this analysis process should not prove to be too much of a barrier. Certainly, by the time that they reach the book of Ecclesiastes on their journey through the Scriptures (probably the New Testament already and much of the Old), they will have the experience necessary to do much of this problem-solving intuitively and through mutual consultation according to the team's established working procedures. However, there are times when a more explicit or formally rigorous methodology may be helpful, especially when confronting passages with the metaphoric density and obvious ambiguity as Eccl. 12:1–7. On such occasions, an approach like the following might help translators to delve more deeply and precisely into the cultural factor as it concerns meaningful and relevant communication in the TL, that is, via a translated text and/or its accompanying paratext.

Harriet Hill has proposed a dual perspective, four-quadrant model for assessing the 'cultural distance' and relative difficulty of probable translation-contextual 'mismatches' in a text. She suggests that the various problems of comprehension which arise in intercultural communication may be classified into different types, as exemplified in quadrants 2–4 of the following table which displays four

7.3 Synthesis: The pressing task of the translator

possible conceptual relationships (adapted from Hill 2003:2). It should be noted that this display does not indicate *how* the particular translation problem is to be resolved—whether in the TL text or in an introduction, explanatory note, or the glossary—only *where* it occurs and potentially how serious it is. The more serious a particular mismatch is (i.e., quadrants 3 and 4 in the case of a key term), the more urgently one requires a communicative strategy for reducing or eliminating it as a barrier to comprehension.

A *specific biblical concept* from the perspective of the **target audience** → and the **original text** ↓	The hearer/reader *thinks* it is shared	Does *not think* it is shared
Actually *shared*	1. *Intended* context, e.g., sun (v. 1), grasshopper (v. 5)	2. *Unrecognized* context, e.g., the 'caperberry' (v. 5)
***Not* actually shared**	3. *Unintended* context, e.g. 'grinders' (v. 2), 'spirit' that 'returns to God' (v. 7)	4. *Missing* context, e.g., the 'almond tree' that 'blossoms' (v. 5)

We may start from the *shared* concepts that largely overlap with respect to both *denotation* (referential meaning) and also *connotation* (associative meaning), hence causing little problem of comprehension for a specific target group. With reference to quadrant **1**, for example, all Chewa and Tonga people are acquainted with the physical features of the 'grasshopper' and how the loss of a leg would condemn this insect to certain death in the near future. People are also familiar with the light-producing quality of the 'sun' (though they would never think of worshiping this object in the sky as a deity like many ancient Near Easterners did).

Certain mismatches in form or function appear then in quadrant **3**, that is, in cases where people do recognize the referent named in the text, but do not fully share certain salient aspects of the actual biblical contextual and hence cognitive domains. For example, while 'grinding' on a millstone is known in traditional African culture, the crops used in this process would be maize and millet, not wheat or barley as in ancient Israel. Greater incongruence occurs in the mention of 'spirit,' for the closest lexical equivalent (*mzimu/muzimo*) actually refers to an ancestral shade, which in traditional religious belief continues to exist as a diminished personal 'life-force' beyond the grave, and therefore is feared (or revered) since it has the power to affect the life of the living in various ways, whether for bane or blessing.

Even more problematic are concepts that people have in their world of experience but do not realize the implicit correspondence that there is with the biblical referent in a given text (quadrant **2**). We note, for example, the reference to the mysterious 'caperberry' in v. 5, which most translations in English and the vernacular render generically as 'desire.' To be sure, the desires of the elderly do diminish, but the original is actually much more specific and relevant in a Bantu sociocultural setting:

> [T]he focus is on the well-known qualities of the caperberry as an aphrodisiac. Later Jewish literature made this connection explicit. If this is true, then the uselessness of the caperberry highlights the loss of sexual potency. (Longman 1998:272; cf. Bartholomew 2009:350)

The actual *Capparis spinosa* (אֲבִיּוֹנָה) plant/fruit is not found in the Chewa environment, but several close equivalents are—'fruits' that are mixed in various concoctions intended to promote (male) virility. For various reasons, such specific cultural substitutes ('medicines') cannot be used in the translation itself, but a euphemistic reference to such local *herbal* (not magical!) stimulants might be appropriate, if not in the text for impact, then in an explanatory footnote in order to get the culturally familiar point across.

Most difficult of all, then, are those referents that are foreign to the target culture and are not even recognized as such (quadrant **4**). This type of problem frequently occurs in the case of transliterations such as we have in the old Tonga Bible to render the 'almond' of v. 5—i.e., *alumondi*. What the 'flowers' of this designated 'tree' have to do with aging and the fear of old men is completely obscure; in fact, there is a certain contradiction introduced into the passage, for flowering trees are a sign that the long central African dry season will soon come to an end and give way to the seasonal rains when nature revives and the life cycle begins anew in the land.

What then can be done about such communicative contextual gaps? Harriet Hill makes the following suggestion (2003:3):

> To enlarge the mutual cognitive environment so that it replicates the one the first receptors shared with the biblical author, the contextual assumptions of Quadrants 2–4 need to move into Quadrant 1. Then the secondary receptor can process the text in the same way that the first receptor did. This enlargement can take place in two directions: 1) receptors can access more of their cognitive environment by recognizing similarities that are actually present, and 2) they can learn new assumptions from the first receptors' environment. Both processes are necessary to enlarge the mutual cognitive environment. The

7.3 Synthesis: The pressing task of the translator

first allows the biblical message to permeate more of the receptor's cognitive environment. The second serves to expand their cognitive environment.[68]

Whether different cognitive environments can ever be manipulated so as to fully coincide (made 'mutual') in all respects is doubtful, since most language-cultures differ considerably on the whole from those of the Bible. But that does not render the various attempts to attain a greater measure of resemblance any less worthwhile, or indeed necessary as part of the process of communicating a more complete 'package' of Scripture's overall significance. A more reasonable aim would thus be to achieve as large or precise a correspondence as possible in the most situationally relevant respects in view of the primary target audience concerned, using all the means and media available—textual, paratextual, and extratextual (e.g., supplementary publications, audio Bible studies, radio broadcasts, the *Bible Lands* video series, etc.).

Considering Ecclesiastes as a whole in terms of its contemporary communication within an African setting,[69] I have found when teaching portions of this book that a major barrier to understanding and appreciation is its apparent negativism and a supposed 'a-theological' point of view. These would tend to agree with the following observation:

> Its chief attitudes, on first acquaintance, appear to be cynicism, realism, atheism, and despair – approaches to life which would not seem to be entirely in harmony with the rest of Scripture. (Hunter 2006:147)

This tends to put students of the Scripture off, to the point that many do not even want to read the book at all, except perhaps for the epilogue at the end! It is important, therefore, to provide an appropriate orientation to Ecclesiastes as well as its major pericopes in order to show readers (and hearers) that, contrary to their prior expectation or experience, Qoheleth does have a lot to offer in terms of honestly confronting and deeply considering the many crucial questions and conundrums of life— the pleasures as well as the pains, including old age and death (12:1–7).

---

[68] Brenda Boerger comments, "This latter (2) is much harder to accomplish because learning is not guaranteed. I have been TAUGHT that Hebrew references to ROCK (two different roots) most often mean 'strong, safe place.' But, my English language and cultural first reading is 'foundation, base,' which can also sometimes be a reading for the Hebrew. See my glossary entry under 'rock' in *POET Psalms*" (personal correspondence).

[69] Whenever the term 'African' is used in this monograph, its more limited frame of reference should be kept in mind—namely, the south-central region occupied in colonial, pre-independence times by the so-called 'Central African Federation,' now comprising the independent nations of Zambia, Zimbabwe, and Malawi.

The periodically placed positive perspectives need to be highlighted, e.g., 2:25, 3:11–14, 5:19–20, 8:12b, as constituting a fundamental faith-stance that enables the righteous to deal with the mysteries and crises of their earthly existence. A frank debate over such affairs can be a therapeutic, even invigorating experience, as it was in the case of Job (cf. 42:1–6) and also those who vacillate as dramatically in their thinking and outlook as Qoheleth.

As long as "the conclusion of the matter" (סוֹף דָּבָר הַכֹּל –Eccl. 12:13) is known and affirmed through faith the in Creator (12:1), neither man's ending (12:7) nor his/her final Ending before the Judge (12:14) need be doubted or feared. The point is that such themes are vigorously debated in the oral and written literature of many world cultures (certainly in the societies of south-central Africa). These indigenous resources need to be recognized and adequately researched. The challenge for translators then is to clearly introduce their target audience to such provocative issues and to demonstrate in suitable genre and style of composition how Qoheleth, too, can help people to give expression to them and thereby also assist the faithful to work through them from a biblical perspective.

7.3.3.2 Decision and implementation

Someone once said, "A *text without a context* is the pretext for a subtext." In other words, if you transmit an oral or written message to a person without providing a relevant, culturally-conditioned context for understanding it, it is possible or even probable that s/he will arrive at a faulty or even the wrong interpretation (subtext)—and s/he will have an excuse (pretext) for this failure: your neglect! Thus, many individual words or phrases, e.g., 'golden bowl', let alone complete sentences and entire paragraphs, may be understood quite differently depending on the verbal and nonverbal setting in which they are used (e.g., 'broken' in Eccl. 12:6). Unfortunately, this is also true in the case of translating the Scriptures, as many of us know from personal experience.

As was suggested above, there is just so much (and not as much as some of us used to think!) that one can do in the translated text on its own, no matter what the language, to correctly convey the original author's intended meaning. But there is a great deal that one is able to accomplish though the judicious use of paratextual tools such as explanatory introductions to a given passage plus marginal notes along the way to provide crucially important background information needed by average members of the primary target audience. Once the various potential problem points in the biblical text at hand have been discovered and evaluated as to their

7.3 Synthesis: The pressing task of the translator

importance for understanding (7.3.3.1), a translation team will have to decide which ones may be readily dealt with in the translation itself, and which ones will require some sort of paratextual solution. It remains then for these decisions to be implemented—in the case of all such text-supplementary strategies, *while* the draft translation is actually being composed and tested, *without waiting* until after it has been completed and ready to send to the typesetters.

As far as Qoheleth's final lyric lament is concerned, many hermeneutical questions arise, as we have seen, due to the enigmatic-metaphorical content of the poem within the conceptually dense wisdom genre and its culturally distant ANE environment. These will inevitably affect the translation process, no matter what type of version is being prepared. Furthermore, our normally reliable guides do not always give the best advice. Therefore they too must be carefully evaluated and assessed in relation to each other on the one hand (i.e., what each resource determines the content of the original to be), and with respect to which among several possible interpretations can be best expressed in the TL and within its associated cultural setting. For example, the UBS *Handbook on Ecclesiastes* (Paratext 7 version) recommends the following procedure with regard to the clause "and the grinders cease" (12:3b):

> **TEV** and many other versions understand this clause to refer to "teeth." However, in the context of the description of a house, a rendering like "the women who grind" makes good sense. Again we recommend translating this form literally and putting the possible meaning of the figure in a footnote.

However, the authors themselves recognize the problematic nature of this proposal, for they later observe when discussing the subsequent clause, "because they are few":

> If a figurative approach is taken, we can understand that, because there are so few teeth, chewing is no longer possible. If we take the text more literally, we may wonder why fewer grinders means the work must stop. Interestingly enough, **JB** omits this phrase from its translation. However, we recommend that the text be rendered fairly literally.

Surely, in most translation settings, the JB solution, namely omission, is not an option. But why the handbook recommendation to render this passage "fairly literally"—when the text then turns out to be cryptic at best and probably meaningless in both Chewa and Tonga? Of what benefit is that to the reader or hearer, especially in the case of a lyric text that is supposed to evoke a certain rhetorical and aesthetic impression? And while a footnote might be able to help out with the content (what the verse means), it can do absolutely nothing as far as the vibrant *connotative* dimension is concerned. Or is that not an essential part of the intended meaning of Scripture? Should this dynamic poetic aspect of the originally inspired Muse simply be lost? The Chewa and Tonga versions of 7.3.2.1 and 7.3.2.2 are an effort to address this issue for a particular audience constituency.

But to return to the importance of the paratextual provision in order to create at least a minimal hermeneutical frame of reference to guide the interpretation of readers, the following caveat applies.[70] Footnotes (or their equivalent) are vital tools available for this purpose; however, they must be utilized in the most effective way for the target group concerned, e.g., well composed, using same level of language as the translation (not technical academic jargon!), clearly stated, to the point, and above all, readily relevant to, and re-contextualized for, the anticipated readership.[71]

The following are three suggested renderings of Ecclesiastes 12:1–7 along with associated footnotes, provided by the *Handbook on Ecclesiastes* (Paratext 7 version). These may be evaluated in light of the preceding discussion and a particular translation setting and cultural context. How well do the proposed footnotes clarify or resolve the pertinent issues involved? What should be added, deleted, or modified in some way?[72] Before one becomes too critical in this assessment, one ought to try composing one's

---

[70] A further consideration is this: what can be done in terms of a paratext when preparing audio or visual Scripture products? In the case of the latter, the value of a 'picture' over 'a thousand words' soon becomes evident. On the other hand, if the supplementary audio and visual background is decidedly contemporary in nature, then the challenge becomes considerably greater, that is, not to 'transculturize' the text or to introduce anachronisms which either deny or distort the original historical and sociocultural setting in favor of a modern environment and lifestyle. There are various ways of providing a purely audio paratext depending on the oral-aural and musical styles of the target audience; for example, using a narrator or commentator with a distinctly different vocal quality, perhaps even a singing voice; inserting audible 'signals' such as a bell, gong, or drum beat to announce the beginning and ending of an explanatory comment; supplying a soft musical background to mark the comment portion, and so forth. In any case, some creative, culturally sensitive ingenuity will be needed to distinguish the text from its paratext.

[71] For a discussion and illustration of various types of "negative and positive contextualization" ("recontextualization" is perhaps a more accurate term, cf. Brown 2007:118) in relation to the Chewa Study Bible Project (CSBP), see Wendland 2006:289–292.

[72] In a recent paper, Harriet Hill (2009) has defined "relevant Bible helps" (i.e., notes) as those which (a) provide important contextual information (assumptions) that the target group does not know; (b) guide readers to the author-intended implications; (c) eliminate extraneous or erroneous assumptions; (d) reinforce correct and necessary assumptions; and (e) do not result in too much cognitive processing effort (thus outweighing the derived gain in contextual effects).

7.3 Synthesis: The pressing task of the translator

own explanatory footnote to take care of a particular problem in the text or to supply enough background information for readers to understand it. This is not as easy an assignment as one might at first suspect; this process of annotation can also become quite controversial, especially when different hermeneutical options appear to clash or contradict each other (e.g., interpreting the figurative language of Eccl. 12:2–5a–b as being varied references to death rather than to the infirmities of old age).[73]

12:3 For translation of the whole verse, we recommend a rather straightforward rendering, with a footnote:
• *Before the time when the guards of the house tremble, and those who were strong now grow bent; before the time when the women grinding stop work because they are too few, and those looking through the windows can see no more.* *
A possible footnote is:
*In this and the next verse, the imagery is often understood to be referring to the human body ("the house"). The "keepers" would be the hands, and "those who are strong" would be the legs; "the grinders" are the teeth, "those that look" are the eyes. Others consider these figures to represent death.

12:4 We again recommend a translation closer to the original form, with a footnote explaining various possibilities for its meaning; for example:

---

[73] For example, with regard to the figurative language of v. 3, the Handbook on Ecclesiastes comments as follows: "**Before the sun and the light and the moon and the stars are darkened:** the thought here seems to be the end of the world, reversing the process of creation. What causes the end is not mentioned. The main question, however, is whether this describes a real cosmic event, or whether it has a figurative meaning. Then, if it has a figurative meaning, what does it refer to? To old age and the gradual loss of sight, or perhaps to death? GNT concludes it refers to old age, making this clear by adding the words "for you": "the light of the sun, the moon, and the stars will grow dim for you." FRCL similarly personalizes the verse: "You will be in darkness, as when the light of the sun weakens...." This version goes on to point out in a footnote that this and the descriptions that follow (verses 2–5) describe the physical problems and weaknesses that come with old age. Many versions include similar notes (JB, for example). But there is still another possible interpretation. We have already noted that "darkness" often means death, so the darkening of these heavenly bodies may also be a way to refer to death. The meaning here would be to remember the Creator before it is too late, that is, before a person dies.

"The translator has several options. We can follow the common language versions, though this seems to restrict the interpretation of the passage. Or we can translate literally, possibly with notes stating that this description can be applied to old age or death. As noted in the introduction to this chapter, we suggest this latter approach; thus references to sun, light, moon, and stars can be retained...." (Ogden and Zogbo 1998:420–421).

- ...*before the time when the doors to the street are closed and the sound of grinding has stopped; before the time when a little bird's call can awaken you, or the sound of singing has stopped altogether.**

A model footnote may be:

*The Hebrew text allows various interpretations. The reference can be to the quietness of a place during a funeral, the ceasing of activity in death, or to a time of life when a person no longer can hear sounds very well but is strangely bothered by high, shrill ones.

12:5 For a translation of the whole verse, we suggest:

- *[Yes, remember your Creator] before the time when people are afraid of heights and there are dangers along the way, when the almond tree blossoms*, and the grasshopper creeps slowly along, and all desire has failed. Because people are on their way to the place of the dead, and mourners are already circling about in the streets.*

The footnote can say:

*The almond tree blossoms in winter and has white flowers. Some see the link to winter as indicating death, while others see the reference to blossoms as indicating the white hair of the elderly. Grasshoppers are usually associated with death and destruction (Joel 1.4), but others see a reference to the loss of agility in old age.

7.4 Conclusion: Qoheleth on the cultural factor

In a recent article on the cultural factor in Bible translation (Wendland 2010b), I suggest that the cultural factor is a multifaceted dimension of communication more far-reaching and in need of attention than most translation programs often realize—or budget sufficient time and energy for. It involves many more elements in the overall process than the various text/paratext issues that arise during the compositional exercise, as discussed in the present study of Qoheleth 12. Thus, culture, and all that it entails, can work for or against desired (or scheduled!) progress in each of eight crucial components of Scripture production, which naturally overlap and interact during their implementation of any given project. These are, roughly in their sequence: project *planning*, *organizing* and managing, *training*, *composing*, *supplementing*, *evaluating* and revising, '*publishing*' (in the wider multi-media sense), and *promoting* (popularizing) the new translation. The cultural factor must be given precedence from

7.4 Conclusion: Qoheleth on the cultural factor

beginning to end if the enterprise is to succeed and reach its full potential in terms of relevance to and acceptance by the TL community.

In terms of the present study then, we might orient the cultural factor with specific reference to three essential aspects of a literary-poetic (oratorical) approach to translation, that is: *constitution, composition*, and *checking*. In the first place, a particular project, whether an experimental audio portion or a complete Bible, must be explicitly constituted in terms of its *Skopos* (communicative purpose) and *brief* (job description and commission) with the desire to utilize the full resources of the target language in the translation process—from analogous macro-genres to individual idioms on the micro-level of discourse structure.[74] Obviously, this approach also requires translators of a certain caliber, namely, those who have had experience, and demonstrated capability, in researching and using the resources of their mother tongue liberally and appropriately in the translation process. Thus at least one of the members of the team should be a recognized expert in the TL, while the others ought to at least be able to distinguish a superior literary/oral-aural style from one that is simply mediocre or, worse, clearly substandard.

This concern for communicative quality must then be continued during the course of composing the particular version in view, so that the desired degree of excellence is maintained consistently for the duration of the project. The team's administrative committee, too, needs to be thoroughly educated with respect to these literary objectives so that they can in turn support the work intelligently along the way and can give the necessary advice or correction where needed. Whenever a written or audio draft is then ready for testing, the translation should be checked for accuracy, accessibility, idiomaticity, and acceptability. This requires suitably

---

[74] My argument (cf. Wendland 2004b) is that the *literature* of Scripture incorporates, by and large, compositions of various genres that are of demonstrably high quality, and that these formal features of the text contribute considerably to its overall meaning—*pragmatic* (e.g., rhetorical impact and aesthetic appeal) as well as semantic (e.g., structural markers of discourse organization). The challenge for Bible translators then is simply this: to what degree can we duplicate the manifold oral-aural dynamics of this literary dimension in our vernacular renditions—to a greater or lesser extent, depending on our project's translation brief and Skopos (cf. Wendland 2006)?

In a metaphoric sense then, such a translation approach would indeed create LiFE 'after Qoheleth'—that is, when a literary-functional equivalence translation is prepared from and on the basis of the original. In a hermeneutical sense, too, my analysis of the book of Ecclesiastes would suggest that the author did have at least some conception of life after death, that is, after one has completed her/his course under the sun in an earthly existence that is usually quite enigmatic in nature and meaningless in purpose or outcome (Eccl. 9:3). Thus, 12:1–7 and 12:9–14 do provide a positive alternate world/life-view to the pessimistic one that Qoheleth so often advocates in his varied and vacillating philosophic reflections.

designed assessment procedures, including the instruction of testers and testees alike so that the evaluation process can be conducted in the most effective, culturally appropriate manner.

It is very likely that the present electronic, cell-phone and internet age of globalization will greatly increase the possibilities for the development and distribution of new Scripture products to ever more finely targeted receptor groups and situational niches within a particular cultural and macro-cultural setting. On the other hand, perhaps more joint, intercultural projects among major Bible translation agencies will be feasible to increase the potential audience base and thus also lower the per-unit cost for a given product. Yet in all these new and exciting developments we must not lose sight of the inherent *individuality* and *distinctiveness* that every language and culture represents and can therefore contribute to this manifold global communication enterprise. It is hoped that the unique perspectives and assumptions along with the distinctive voices and tones of the less prominent members of the chorus will not be blurred or lost in the mix. In any case, let me re-affirm what I wrote a number of years ago:

> Culture, context, and the receptor constituency—all three are vital elements in the contemporary effort to communicate the ancient texts of Scripture so that their beauty and forcefulness, in addition to their content, can under the transforming power of the Spirit continue to "turn the world upside down" (Ac 17:6). (Wendland 1987:206) [75]

In closing, then, we take note of a pertinent reflection that the book of Ecclesiastes itself provides with respect to the cultural factor as it concerns Bible translation in general and the book's concluding lyric lament in particular.[76] I am admittedly contextualizing the text's narrative-commentator a bit, but I think that his insight regarding Qoheleth's methodology is worthy of consideration (12:9):

---

[75] To support this observation, let me offer some scholarly support—not from Luther now, but from Pope John Paul II: "A good translation is based on three pillars that must simultaneously support the entire work. First, there must be a deep knowledge of the original language and cultural world. Next, there must be a similar good familiarity with the language and cultural context in and for which the text is translated. Lastly, to succeed in the whole work, there must be an adequate mastery of the contents and meaning of what is being translated....In the interconfessional translation...you have tried to be faithful to the tenor of the original text and at the same time you have tried to make the text understandable for contemporary readers, using words and forms of everyday speech." (Address to the United Bible Societies and the Bible Society of Italy, on the occasion of the 25th anniversary of the interconfessional Italian New Testament, *L'Osservatore Romano,* December 12, 2001—cited in Wcela 2009:263).

[76] These are in addition to the directly relevant comments pertaining to Bible translation from Eccl. 12:10, discussed at the beginning of section 7.3.

7.4 Conclusion: Qoheleth on the cultural factor

Not only was the Teacher wise,	וְיֹתֵר שֶׁהָיָה קֹהֶלֶת חָכָם
but also he imparted knowledge to the people.	עוֹד לִמַּד־דַּעַת אֶת־הָעָם
He pondered and searched out and set in order many proverbs. (NIV)	וְאִזֵּן וְחִקֵּר תִּקֵּן מְשָׁלִים הַרְבֵּה׃

This first point of application, essential *education,* includes carefully instructing the consumer community about key aspects of the theory and practice of Bible translation as well as the various stylistic (artistic and rhetorical) options available to them in the different media. This must be a matter of top priority for the project organizers and administrators throughout the course of the work so that the specific target groups for particular translation products (such as a special oratorical, youth-focused lyric version of Eccl. 12:1–7) feel that they are a part of the process and can provide essential feedback at various stages along the way. Then there will hopefully be no unexpected 'surprises' at the end when the version or portion is published.

Second, we observe Qoheleth's great diligence when investigating the culturally-based resources of his oral and written tradition of verbal art forms ('wise sayings' מְשָׁלִים). Present-day Bible translators must be encouraged and empowered to do likewise in terms of orality-oriented *research* as they prepare for their various assignments in the diverse genres to be found in the literature of Scripture.[77] The closest natural equivalents in terms of *form* and *function* are required to provide a well-documented inventory of alternatives to draw from when a particular Hebrew macro- or micro-genre is confronted in the original text. The matter of *content* is important too—for example, finding the appropriate terms, literal or figurative, to talk about the sensitive issues of dying and death, as in Eccl. 12:1–7, that is, in a society where beliefs in witchcraft and sorcery are still very much alive! (cf. Wendland and Hachibamba 2007:174–215). A supportive, educated constituency, as 'co-owners' of the project, can contribute a great deal, both by suggesting possible TL equivalents for specific passages or entire pericopes to begin with, and also later by offering their informed critical reactions to the different trial versions distributed for testing.

Finally, while it is largely true that the task of translation is never done in the sense that there are always *revisions* to be made to existing versions

---

[77] The original texts of Scripture, New Testament as well as Old Testament, were conceived, composed, and communicated in an environment of orality, which most often also involved a communal setting. Various stylistic features (e.g., repetition, phonological play, rhythmic utterances, etc.) make manifest the oral and aural medium that the diverse biblical documents presupposed (cf. Wendland 2008a and b).

and different Scripture products to prepare for new audiences, the following piece of advice is also very pertinent (Eccl. 12:12b):

Of making many books there is no end, and much study wearies the body.

עֲשׂוֹת סְפָרִים הַרְבֵּה אֵין קֵץ
וְלַהַג הַרְבֵּה יְגִעַת בָּשָׂר

Thus, translation assessment and improvement with respect to a particular version cannot go on forever. Sooner or later the point of diminishing returns is reached and any more effort devoted to the project would simply 'weary the body (as well as the mind)!' The latest version must then simply be published and put to use in its specified setting and for its intended purpose.

A somewhat different application adopts a spiritual perspective: the work of Bible translation, noble and needful though it may be, should never become an end in itself. The task must always be conducted in view of this concluding divinely-oriented, life-related injunction:

(12:13b). אֶת־הָאֱלֹהִים יְרָא וְאֶת־מִצְוֺתָיו שְׁמוֹר
"Fear God and keep his commandments!"

Then for all those involved, this exercise in religious cross-cultural communication, no matter how lengthy, perhaps even tedious at times, and challenging, will not ultimately be 'meaningless' (futile, inconsequential, and frustrating—that is, הֶבֶל!).

8

How Lovely the Lyric?
Testing Versions of Psalm 134

Introduction: Frame of reference for testing a translation

> Both successful and unsuccessful translations are judged such by indigenous criteria. A good translation vindicates local norms and standards; a bad translation fails for the same reason. Bible translation, thus, has a self-correcting mechanism built into the feedback. (Sanneh 2003:127)

The challenge for translators that arises from the preceding observation is threefold: how to reliably obtain such TL audience feedback, how to assess or evaluate these popular results, and finally, how to utilize such knowledge to improve the particular Scripture product at hand.

The diagram below (from Wendland 2008a:226; cf. 2004b:337–344) suggests a possible model, or heuristic frame of reference (cf. Wendland 2008a:1–16) that may be used—whether as is or in some modified form—when judging the relative *acceptability* of a certain draft or published translation in relation to a given audience. It reflects an attempt to integrate a number of key factors that may affect the translation's appraisal in terms of different aspects of the SL text and the TL version of it. This evaluative frame of reference is presented to illustrate some of the chief contextual concerns that may be incorporated into the testing process.

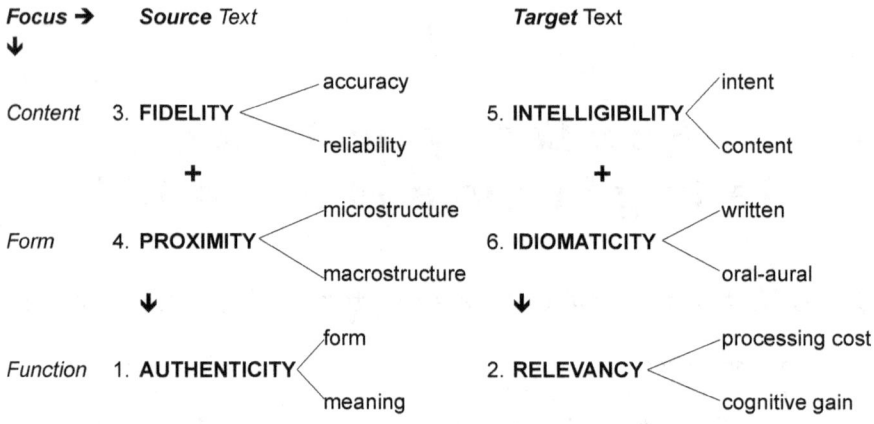

The primary focus of each of these six variables is briefly described below by means of a series of critical investigative questions intended to elucidate the wider contextual setting of reception for a given translation project. In this case, the six qualities are to be *evaluated primarily from the standpoint of diverse representatives of the primary target audience* (e.g., clergy/laity, new/old Christians, literate/nonliterate, male/female, younger/older generation, well-educated/non-schooled, etc.). In other words, trained members of the target community carry out the actual testing process, evaluate the results, and formulate their conclusions. A corresponding assessment made by an outside investigator or analyst may well produce a different overall conclusion or specific recommendations, which though clearly secondary, may still be useful in highlighting certain blind spots in the indigenous perspective. Furthermore, it is obvious that a given translation program cannot satisfy, achieve, or emphasize all six factors at once. Rather, a set of priorities will have to be established—one that is determined on the basis of various local considerations, e.g., the translation *brief* and *Skopos*, primary audience group, setting of use, history of Bible translation within the language, past usage in the community, and available resources, including overall staff competence and commitment.

AUTHENTICITY: How authentic do TL speakers perceive the translation to be in relation to its *form* (proximity) *meaning* (fidelity), and/or *function* (relevancy); in other words, how trustworthy or credible do they regard their translation in terms of re-presenting the complete or true Word of God in their mother tongue?

Introduction: Frame of reference for testing a translation

RELEVANCY: How *difficult* is the translated test to handle conceptually (i.e., processing cost or mental effort) in relation to the beneficial cognitive, emotive, and volitional *effects* (psychological gains) that a majority of the target audience derive from this hermeneutical activity as applied to their current life setting?

FIDELITY: How *accurate* is the translation in terms of representing the central core of *semantic content* of the biblical text (including all explicatures and principal implicatures),[1] and how *reliably* does the TL text verbally express this conceptual, emotive, and volitional inventory in the vernacular?

PROXIMITY: How *closely*, relatively speaking, does the translation reflect the *structural* and *stylistic* forms of the Hebrew or Greek text, that is, with respect to the original document's *macro-* as well as *micro*-level of compositional organization?

INTELLIGIBILITY: How clear and understandable is the TL text with respect to both *content* and also *intent*—the latter embracing the principal *functional* aims and associated *connotative* aspects of the original as expressed in the vernacular translation?

IDIOMATICITY: How natural is the translation stylistically in terms of literary *artistry* (beauty) and *rhetoric* (impact, appeal) with respect to its various major and minor

---

[1] The following quote defines the key terms (in parentheses): "Thus, in the process of inferring meaning, the audience combines the set of utterances from the communicator and the explicatures they yield with additional contextual assumptions serving as premises, and draws conclusions, which are called contextual implications. Both the premises (contextual assumptions) and the conclusions (contextual implications) are referred to as implicatures" (R. Hill 2004:5). An effective way of testing different aspects of audience comprehension in terms of their culturally-based 'cognitive context' is described and illustrated in Harriet Hill (2003; see also section 8.3). The semantic content of the biblical text, as near as we can come to the intended propositional meaning (an inevitably partial, yet ultimately a sufficient understanding), is ascertained by means of a careful discourse analysis of the original and a study of reliable scholarly commentaries on the passage at hand. However, the full communicative significance of that same text cannot be fully perceived or explicated without reference to the original extralinguistic context, or situational setting, in which the text was conceived, composed, transmitted, and received. The related figures of irony and sarcasm often operate on the basis of implicature, as does the form of the rhetorical question. A well-known example of this is Pilate's enigmatic query of Christ, "What is truth?" (John 18:38).

genres, both in writing (print) and also when heard, as the vernacular text is being *audibly articulated* (proclaimed, recited, chanted, or sung)?

Of course, any rather general and approximate model of personal assessment reveals certain pertinent aspects of the problem being investigated and overlooks or ignores others that may be equally important in the setting concerned. My proposed heuristic framework also adopts a particular theoretical or experimental viewpoint and probes the information at hand to a limited degree in relation to all the available data or variables that might possibly be examined. Furthermore, the actual testing process from beginning to end—its rationale, method of questioning, general format, and assessment procedures—needs to be stipulated in detail with reference to a specific audience, time frame, and group of investigators (e.g., Wendland 2004b:347–363, 395–418). In short, the evaluative model itself needs to be fully *contextualized* and then carefully *appraised* and *adapted* with respect to its intended goals and desired results.

In this chapter I attempt to apply certain aspects of the text (translation) assessment plan summarized above, namely, the audience-focused triad of *idiomaticity < intelligibility < (perceived) relevance* (the symbol < means 'less important than'), to a selection of English and Chewa versions of Psalm 134.[2] This psalm was chosen because of its brevity, which facilitates the testing process, but also because of the surprising number of artistic and rhetorical features that it manifests. My primary goal was to see how several groups of Bible students react, first of all, to a more oral-oriented, 'poetically' composed and formatted rendition, in contrast to a 'liturgical' version. This would be a text that displays a higher level of quality, as it were, in terms of the target language, i.e., a stylistically more 'domesticated' version. Secondly, I wanted to determine the relative effect of adding certain paratextual supplements to the biblical text (in particular, a section heading, cross-references, and marginal notes). The aim here was to seek the participants' response as to how much these contextualizing devices served to enhance the quality of their interpretation of this psalm. And finally, I wished to get the readers' preference as to the nature and placement of explanatory-descriptive notes in particular—whether as footnotes, side notes, or combined in the form of a sectional introduction.[3]

---

[2] Chewa is known as Nyanja in Zambia, where the translation testing was conducted.

[3] Brenda Boerger observes that she "got permission to put our notes in the text at the end of the relevant paragraph. They were signaled by an onset and endmark diacritic. Our team and reviewers didn't like footnotes because it made them lose their place in the discourse and on the page" (personal correspondence).

For the purposes of this restricted experiment then,[4] I was focusing more on target text compositional *style*, rather than on source text *content* and the corresponding factor of 'fidelity' (unless this issue happened to be specifically raised by one of the testees). A more meaning-based and context-oriented investigation would need to be patterned along the lines of that proposed by Harriet Hill (2003). My main purpose was to explore the key features of idiomaticity and intelligibility as they related to the perceived relevance (likeability, applicability, etc.) of one translation over against another. The factors of idiomaticity and intelligibility are clearly related, but one quality does not automatically entail the other. Thus, a stylistically 'natural' vernacular text may not be understood well, if at all, when respondents are not familiar with the various literary features used, or if they lack the necessary background information to know what is being talked about, especially if certain unexpressed assumptions are involved. On the other hand, a relatively 'intelligible' text may be expressed with different degrees of (un)naturalness as far as TL style is concerned. I am not able to go into details with regard to either of these variables due to (a) the unrefined type of testing procedures being employed (i.e., a simple Q&A technique) and (b) the literarily unsophisticated nature of the audiences being tested.

8.1 The text and its meaning

Before we can properly test a biblical text we must first of all understand it— that is, its overall meaning in terms of *structure*, *style*, *sense*, and *significance*. Because it is not possible to do all this here, I will merely summarize some of the salient aspects of these four variables as they relate to Psalm 134. But first, let us have a closer look at the original text. This is reproduced below in a format which is slightly modified from that provided by the Masoretic tradition (see 8.2.1 for several English translations).

¹ שִׁיר הַמַּעֲלוֹת
הִנֵּה ׀ בָּרֲכוּ אֶת־יְהוָה כָּל־עַבְדֵי יְהוָה
הָעֹמְדִים בְּבֵית־יְהוָה בַּלֵּילוֹת:
² שְׂאוּ־יְדֵכֶם קֹדֶשׁ
וּבָרֲכוּ אֶת־יְהוָה:
³ יְבָרֶכְךָ יְהוָה מִצִּיּוֹן
עֹשֵׂה שָׁמַיִם וָאָרֶץ:

---

[4] The time and resources available for me to carry out this testing process were rather limited; as a result, only some pertinent factors could be investigated and, even then, only in cursory fashion. A much more extensive, systematic, and controlled program of evaluation is therefore required in order to follow up on this tentative, exploratory beginning, especially in relation to the qualities of proximity, fidelity, and authenticity.

8.1.1 Structure and style

The basic organization of this deceptively simple psalm manifests a reciprocal call (appeal) and response pattern. The call (vv. 1–2) is apparently uttered (recited, chanted, sung) by the worshiping community and addressed to 'all servants of the LORD' (an honorific term)—most likely the priests and Levites currently on duty in the Temple. The rejoinder (v. 3) is directed by these Temple ministers, in turn, to each and every worshiper (singular 'you') who is now about to depart from the sacred premises. This psalmic 'hymn' (i.e., focused primarily on the praise of Yahweh) is surprisingly 'poetic' for its small size; virtually every word conveys some special literary significance. The song's special stylistic features, including those performing a structural function, are summarized here.

- Key thematic repetition ('[you] bless' + 'LORD'/YHWH) gives the text strong internal cohesion.

- This expression features a semantic reversal on the third occurrence ('may the LORD bless you'—v. 3a) to distinguish the second, responsive verse and the probable change of speakers that occurs there.

- This principal break in the psalm is reinforced by a prominent lexical *inclusion* ('bless YHWH') that bounds the people's speaking part (vv. 1–2), thus setting off the priest's concluding blessing (v. 3).

- The spotlight is on the LORD throughout, although there are three main participants: the worshipers, temple ministers, and, by invocation, Yahweh as well.

- The psalm is very succinct: only six lines and twenty-three words in Hebrew (ignoring the hyphens and excluding the title); thus every word 'counts' in terms of its form, content, and function within the whole piece.

- There is a single centered line—v. 2a, which is preceded by two longer poetic lines and followed by three shorter ones. From a different perspective, eight 'words' (now counting hyphenated terms as one) precede v. 2a, and eight more follow this central point. Verse 2a ends in the climactic, possibly polysemous term, 'holiness' (qōdesh).

8.1 The text and its meaning

- Verse 2a, which expresses the psalm's only physical deed, a ritually symbolic act accompanying prayer, is very condensed, lit. 'lift-up your-hand holy-place'. This central utterance may perhaps be deliberately ambiguous or poetically allusive in order to suggest a range of meanings involving a 'holy' Person (God), a 'holy' place (Temple), and/or 'holiness' (attributed to the forgiven people of God).

- A probable implicit *merismus* occurs at the end of v. 1b (immediately preceding 2a): 'in the night' = 'day and night' or better, 'all the time.' In this case, only one member of the pair (denoting a totality) is cited, i.e., 'night'. 'Day' is implied both from conventional usage of this pair (cf. Ps. 1:2b) and also from contextual usage, i.e., Pss. 134 and 135 are an instance of paired psalms that functioned together in the Jewish liturgical tradition (compare Ps. 134:1–2 and Ps. 135:1–3a).

- The text begins with a prophetic-like attention getter, 'behold' *(hinneh!)*, and it closes with a liturgical 'Maker of heaven and earth', which designates the supreme cosmic rule of Yahweh as well as his immediate saving presence in his 'house'—'in Jerusalem' (cf. 135:21).

- The final verse (3) features a concatenation of prominent intertextual expressions from the Ascent collection (Pss. 120–134; cf. 121:2, 124:8, 128:5) that highlights the contrastive spatial-interpersonal realm in which God operates: heaven—Zion—earth, Yahweh—you (sg.)! The term 'Zion' is ambiguous, for it could refer figuratively to God's heavenly place, more concretely to his earthly 'house' (Temple mount), or in this context, probably to both.

8.1.2 Sense and significance

Psalm 134 is a consummate psalm about blessing: the congregation's *blessing* (= thank + praise) of Yahweh (vv. 1–2), and Yahweh's prior and subsequent *blessing* (provision, protection, and promotion) of his people. Being the last in the group of fifteen pilgrim psalms explicitly designated as 'Songs of Ascent' (lit. 'ascents/steps'; Heb. שִׁיר הַמַּעֲלוֹת),[5] this hymn

---

[5] The *Paratext* version of the UBS *Translator's Handbook* notes: "Psalms 120–134 all have a title in the Hebrew text which is translated by RSV as **A Song of Ascents** (TEV does not include this title). The collection is also called 'The Book of Pilgrim Songs.' The Hebrew word

no doubt had additional rhetorical functions, namely, to appropriately conclude the collection while recalling its central themes (as briefly noted in 8.1.1). It is also a powerful joint expression of corporate religious unity among all the worshipers, their leaders, and the God whom they jointly 'bless' because of his wondrous divine attributes and activities (as specified in other psalms, most notably in the very next two, 135:5–18, 136:4–25), including his universal control and governance of the universe. All that remains for his people to do is to offer Yahweh their total praise and worship (cf. 135:1 – הַלְלוּ יָהּ) '[day] and night' as members of his faithful worshiping community (the priests and Levites representing the assembly in this unending mediatory capacity).

Psalm 134 may have been used especially in the evening worship liturgy at the Temple (בַּלֵּילוֹת 'at nights' – v. 1b), thus appropriately concluding the day's worship program with a final 'praise the LORD' and a word of benediction from him, as mediated by his servants. This song is also an important reminder that worship is more than mere words; the verbal collocation of the first two verses suggests something else: 'lifting up your hands' (שְׂאוּ־יְדֵכֶם) not only in prayer, but also in active 'service of the LORD' (עַבְדֵי יְהוָה), which constitutes true 'holiness' (קֹדֶשׁ). While the priests and Levites may represent the people before Yahweh, this does not absolve the laity of their responsibility in turn to 'minister' (הָעֹמְדִים – always standing at the ready) before him—representing their holy God to the world at large:

> Human living is dependent on blessing in its personal, social, and national dimensions. Blessing is the LORD at work in human work (Psalm 127). The family, the community, and the world are brought to life-supporting and life-fulfilling completeness and rightness by the LORD's blessing. (Mays 1994:415)

The rhetoric of this psalm, bolstered by all those that have preceded it in the Psalter, thus intimately engages and challenges each and every reader and hearer of the text in its final, individualized ('you' sg.) word

---

translated **Ascents** comes from the verb 'to go up,' but other than this there is no agreement as to what the phrase means. Some take it to indicate the return of the Hebrew exiles from Babylonia; others take it to refer to a stylistic feature found in some of the psalms, in which the order of the statement progresses in a step-like fashion from one verse to the other; others take it to refer to the steps in the Temple precincts which led from one court to the other; the majority take it to refer to the ascent up the mountain on which the Temple was built (Mount Moriah, known as Mount Zion). Thus understood, these psalms are songs which the pilgrims sang as they came to Jerusalem for one of the three major annual festivals (see GECL [German common language version])." This psalm corpus features a general liturgical, emotional, and theological progression from the opening lament in a faraway place (120) to this eulogy in the very courts of the Temple on Zion.

of blessing (יְבָרֶכְךָ).⁶ The LORD blesses us that we might be a blessing to others in his name (cf. Ps. 133 where this thought comes to the fore).

8.2 Testing for artistic quality in translation

The principal aim of this simple, informal testing program was to determine whether or not several groups of English speakers preferred a manifestly poetic rendition of Psalm 134 or a traditional, more literal version. If a more dynamic translation was selected, which of several different styles was most appreciated, and for what reasons? Six groups of respondents were tested, totaling nearly eighty adults in all, mainly men (2/3); they consisted mostly of second-language speakers of English, but included several native English speakers as well (female members of Group 2 on the table listed in section 8.2.3).⁷

A secondary aim was to test as a 'control' two vernacular translations, a literal and a poetic version in Nyanja,⁸ to see how the African respondents, most of whom were not mother tongue speakers, would react to this text in comparison to the different English versions. A more traditional formal correspondence version, the NIV, which was the only Bible familiar to all participants, was included as the first item in the lineup of versions to evaluate. However, like all of the other texts, it was not identified in either the oral or the written test lest this information prejudice the choices (e.g., "This is the Bible translation that I own, use, and therefore prefer").

---

⁶ Nielson sees an intertextual thematic connection between "Ps. 119, which deals with the law and expresses *torah* reverence, and Pss. 120–134, the songs of ascents"—namely, in the notion of following the LORD's pathway in life—"…the path to the temple with its cult of sacrifice and the path of the law" (2009:305–306).

⁷ Group 1 consisted of eleven African third-year seminary students (who had completed an exegetical course on the Psalms the preceding year). Group 6 included sixteen first-year seminary students; group 5 was composed of twenty national translators from six projects in Zambia who were attending a workshop at the Lusaka Bible Translation Centre. The other three groups were adult Bible study participants attending different Lutheran congregations in the Lusaka (Zambia) area.

⁸ This poetic translation was intended to be an example of a literary functional equivalence (LiFE) version (see Wendland 2004b:ch. 2).

8.2.1 The versions tested

1. NIV
A song of ascents.
1 Praise the Lord, all you servants of the Lord
    who minister by night in the house of the Lord.
² Lift up your hands in the sanctuary
    and praise the Lord.

³ May the Lord, the Maker of heaven and earth,
    bless you from Zion.

2. POET Psalms[9]

GIVE ACCOLADES
a pilgrim song of praise
a Rubliw as a benediction

Yahweh's
Own! Give him praise!
And spend your nights always
In prayer to him and turn your face,
In the temple courts, toward the Holy Place.
From Zion, may God who creates
Heaven and earth, show you grace.
Give accolades
And praise!

3. The Psalms in Verse[10]
BEHOLD, bless ye the Lord, all ye
    that his attendants are,
        ev'n you that in
            God's temple be,
        and praise him
            nightly there.

---

[9] This second version of Ps. 134 was provided by Dr. Brenda Higgie Boerger (SIL). Her book of translations is entitled: *POET Psalms (Poetic Oracle English Translation)* (trial edition, private printing, 2003, rev. ed. 2009). Dr. Boerger makes this explanatory comment: "the Rubliw form, has identically rhymed lines of 2, 4, 6, 8, 10, 8, 6, 4, and 2, and starts with a vocative."

[10] Re-published (with no indication of editorship) by Barbour and Company, Uhrichsville, Ohio, 1995; this text was originally published over 100 years ago for use in the worship services of the Church of Scotland.

Your hands within God's holy place
> lift up, and praise his name.
From Zion's hill the Lord thee bless,
> that heav'n and earth did frame.

4. REB

A song of the ascent
> [1] COME, bless the **Lord,**
> all you his servants,
> who minister night after night
> in the house of the **Lord.**
> [2] Lift up your hands towards the sanctuary
> and bless the **Lord.**
> [3] May the **Lord,** maker of heaven and earth,
> bless you from Zion!

5. The Message

A Pilgrim Song
Come, bless God,
> all you servants of God!
Your priests of God, posted to the nightwatch
> in God's shrine,
Lift your praising hands to the Holy Place,
> and bless God.
In turn, may God of Zion bless you—
> God who made heaven and earth!

6. ERW

> *A closing hymn of worship*
> > [1] Keep praising the Lord, all you who attend him,
> > > ministering day and night in his holy house!
> > [2] Lift up your hands in prayer and praise,
> > > all you who serve in his sacred space.
> > > Praise the Lord—yes, praise the Lord!

> > [3] Now may the Lord, Creator of heaven and earth,
> > > God of Zion, bless you all as you leave this place!

7. Traditional Nyanja

Nyimbo yokwerera

1 *Taonani, lemekezani Yehova,*
   atumiki a Yehova inu nonse,
   Akuimirira m'nyumba ya Yehova
   usiku.
2 *Kwezani manja anu ku malo*
   oyera,
   Nimulemekeze Yehova.
3 *Yehova, ali m'Zioni akudali-*
   tseni;
   Ndiye amene analenga kumwa-
   mba ndi dziko lapansi.

Song of climbing up

Look, reverence Jehovah,
all you servants of Jehovah
standing in the house of Jehovah
at night.
Lift up your hands to the holy
place,
and reverence Jehovah.
May Jehovah, he is in Zion, bless
you;
he is the one who created heaven and the earth below.

8. Poetic Nyanja

Nyimbo yotsiriza mapemphero

1 *Tiyeni, yamikani Chauta!*
   Mutamande Mulungu wathu,
   inu nonse atumiki ake, amene
   mumamtumikira mokhulupirika
   m'Nyumba mwake usana n'usiku.
2 *Kwezani manja popempheraku*
   kwa iye m'malo ake oyerawa,
   inu nonse, mutamande Chauta!

3 *Tsopano akudalitseni Chauta,*
   iye amene amakhala ku Ziyoni,
   amene adalenga zakumwamba
   pamodzi ndi dziko lonse lapansi!

A song when finishing prayers [i.e., worship]

Com'on, give thanks to Chauta!
Praise our God,
all you his servants, who
serve him faithfully
in his House day n' night.
Lift up your hands when praying here
to him in this holy place of his,
all of you, praise Chauta!

Now may Chauta bless you,
he who dwells in Zion,
who created the heavens
along with the whole earth below!

8.2.2 Sample questions for hearers and readers

The questions presented here were used to test the respondents both orally and in writing with respect to the six English and two vernacular versions of Psalm 134—particularly in terms of each text's qualities of *intelligibility* and *idiomaticity*, or 'literariness' (verbal power, beauty,

8.2 Testing for artistic quality in translation

memorability, and poetics). During the initial oral phase of the testing process, only two samples A and B, were considered at a time in order to prevent a confusion of choice. In the first tests, no printed copies were handed out during the oral part of the assessment, but this procedure was later changed in order to help listeners focus more fully on the two texts being evaluated. The two versions were read twice in sequence, with the first clearly identified as 'A', the second as 'B'. The more popular of these two (which became a new 'A') was then retested against another version (a new 'B'), with the same questions being asked—and so on sequentially throughout the corpus. When giving the very first test, I suspected that an initial brief introduction to the structure and purpose of Psalm 134 would be helpful, and I followed this procedure thereafter.

When administering the oral test, only the first question was asked with respect to the two sample texts at hand. During the subsequent written test, the participants were asked to consider all the queries in relation to the six English test versions. They were given 15–20 minutes to read the texts again for themselves and to answer the questions on separate blank sheets of paper. The two Nyanja translations were evaluated separately, first in relation to each other and then, as a final exercise, the favorite English text was tested against the favorite Nyanja translation, to see whether the vernacular would be preferred, at least by mother tongue speakers of the language. The other respondents did not have to evaluate the two Nyanja versions unless they wished to, or wanted to comment on the English back-translations.[11] Along with the individual translations, readers were asked to assess and comment on the different print formats that were used.

1. Which version did you like the *best*? Give at least one reason why.
2. Which version did you like the *least*? Give at least one reason why.
3. Did you notice any possible *mistakes* in any of the versions? Make a list of these.
4. Are there any words or phrases in these translations that are *difficult* to understand? Underline these places.
5. Which version was the easiest to *understand*? Can you give a reason why?
6. Which version was the easiest to *read* aloud? Can you give a reason why?

---

[11] These questions may be compared with those suggested for a trained translation critic or reviewer (see Appendix B).

7. Which version was the most *beautiful* or poetic? Can you give a reason why?
8. Which version is the best to use in *public worship*? Can you give a reason why?
9. Which version was the best to use for *Bible study*? Can you give a reason why?
10. Which *Nyanja* version do you like better? Give reasons why.
11. Do you prefer the vernacular version over *all* English versions? If so, tell why.
12. Is there *any* English version that you like better than your preferred Nyanja version? If so, tell why.
13. Write any other comment that comes to mind with regard to your *favorite* version.
14. Write any comment that comes to mind with regard to any of the *other* versions.
15. What do you think about this test: was it too difficult or unclear? Mention any specific problem areas that you recall.
16. Do you have any additional modifications to propose or questions to suggest regarding the text that you have just completed?

The final questions of this sequence are intended to give the respondents an opportunity to express themselves more freely with respect to the different versions of Psalm 134 as well as the overall testing process itself in the interest of improving future applications.

8.2.3 Results

As it turned out, not all of the questions listed above were equally revealing in terms of evaluating the different translations, e.g., distinguishing between versions more suitable for public worship as distinct from Bible study (Qs 8–9) or the additional comments called for (Qs 13–16).[12] One question could not be responded to in most cases due to the lack of time (reading aloud—Q 6). A selective summary of the results of the five separate group tests is given below, followed by comments about what this testing process taught me about 'consumer' preferences regarding the various versions of Psalm 134 as well as the informal method of literary qualitative evaluation. In some cases, no clear majority opinion was evident in the results; such occasions are noted by the (#) sign.

---

[12] In addition, for two groups (2, 5) the oral-only test proved to be too difficult to administer due to the relatively large number of people participating.

8.2 Testing for artistic quality in translation

Category tested ↓ // Group tested →	No. 1	No. 2	No. 3	No. 4	No. 5	No. 6
Favorite English version (oral test)	6	—	6	6	1	6
Second favorite (oral)	4	—	1	1	6	1
Favorite English version (written – Q1)	6	4	4	6	1	6
Least favorite (2)	2	2	2	2	3	2
Easiest version to understand (5)	4	4/6	#	#	1	6
Most beautiful/poetic version (7)	#	#	6	#	1	1
Best for worship // Bible study (8–9)	#	1/6	1	1	#	6
Favorite Nyanja version (10)	8	—	8	8	8	8
English or Nyanja favorite (11)	N	E	E	#	#	#

I will first comment briefly on the different versions of Psalm 134 that were tested in this exercise, and then say more about the method of testing itself, especially with regard to problems that were noted during the course of this experiment. Each of the versions, except version 2, the *POET Psalms,* was appreciated by the five groups for at least one reason or another. Though technically the most sophisticated in terms of poetic technique (and my personal favorite), version 2 was found to be the most difficult and hence was not appreciated by the majority, mainly non-native speakers of English.[13] Similarly, neither Nyanja version was preferred over any English version by non-mother tongue speakers; on the other hand, the mother tongue Nyanja speakers tested did clearly appreciate the modern vernacular translation (8) more than the old one (7).

A relatively high, perhaps unacceptable number of 'no contests' (#) was recorded overall; this was no doubt a result of having too many versions to choose from as well as asking the participants to make so many different choices (see my further comments below). Consequently, this test did not turn out to be as informative or diagnostic regarding different aspects of translation quality as I had anticipated. Nevertheless, three English versions—namely, 1, 4, and 6—did emerge as clear favorites, being selected for various characteristics by the different groups more often than the others. This outcome suggests the need for another, perhaps simplified, text assessment involving just those three versions. Unfortunately, my time constraints did not allow for an additional test to be carried out, either among the original groups or different ones.

A number of interesting problem areas and translation issues in the various versions were pointed out by the participants, mainly the seminary students and Bible translators, during this text evaluation exercise. These comments, including several direct quotes, are listed here as part of my observations on the results.

---

[13] This should not be surprising, since as Boerger says in her introduction to *POET Psalms,* "its intended audience is native speakers of English, whether believers or unbelievers."

- *Cultural concerns* may be raised in the most unexpected places. For example, the expression 'at night' (v. 1) provoked questions from many respondents: what a strange, in fact unnatural, time to be seemingly serving full-time in the temple, especially 'night after night' (#4)! On this point, version 6's 'day and night' was appreciated (as also in Nyanja version #8). According to African traditional beliefs and taboos, the night is not a proper time for ordinary human activities, except on the occasion of a death (abnormal), when vigils are customarily held. Similarly, one person objected to the term 'shrine' in #5 since this word is commonly used in local (second language) English to refer to a rustic place for worshiping the ancestral spirits.

- *Connotation,* involving the emotive reactions to certain words and phrases, is an important consideration, and needs to be followed up in more detailed types of text-testing. For example, the older dialect of English in version 3 gave one respondent a 'religious feeling'; on the other hand, to another person the iterative expression 'Praise the Lord—yes, praise the Lord!' (#6) sounded too 'charismatic'. The positive connotation of familiarity was undoubtedly a factor for those people who did happen to recognize the NIV (#1—or who checked their evaluation paper with the Bible that they had with them), for as one wrote, "We always use this version in class."

- *Poetic form and literary technique* need to be carefully explained first to those who are not used to reading such texts, especially in the Bible. The first line of #2, for example ("Yahweh's...Own!"),[14] was not understood by most, even mother tongue English speakers. Similarly, others could not see the reason for the dashed line dividing the two portions of Psalm 134 in #6. A few readers did call attention to the creative use of the format, for example with regard to #2, which presents 'an image of the text in print.' Another made this perceptive observation about #2: "The ending of the sentence above seem to rhyme with those from below, and the rhythm follows a similar pattern—from above and from below, meeting in the middle." On the other hand, the more literal selection #4 was appreciated by a student for the fact that "it is easy to refer to Greek (*sic,* i.e., Hebrew) with this version."

---

[14] In the revision of *POET Psalms,* the vocative in this line is followed by a comma, rather than an exclamation point, which should help readers process it better.

8.2 Testing for artistic quality in translation

- The questionable replacement of the personal divine name 'LORD' (Yahweh) by a generic term, 'God,' in version #5 also evoked a sense of awkward *stylistic overuse* for some, including the non-mother tongue speakers. For one person, there was even a theological problem involved here since instead of a unity, it gave him the conceptual impression of 'many gods,' especially when this rendition was uttered aloud.

- The matter of *national dialect* is important in the case of a widely-spoken world language like English. Translators must pay careful attention to local usage and avoid terms that have a different or more limited range of meaning. As already noted, in south-central Africa the term 'shrine' (#5) is closely associated with the traditional, pre-Christian religion and also denotes a much smaller and less permanent type of structure. The expression 'bless the Lord' (#s 3–5) is also problematic since people are expected to be the recipients, not the originators of 'blessing' (even more strongly so in the closest vernacular lexical equivalents). In the case of the vernacular versions, one person noted that the designation for Yahweh (YHWH) in version 8—namely, *Chauta*—marked this text as being written in the Chewa (Malawian) dialect of the Nyanja language.[15] One person observed that it is better to closely identify the name 'Zion' with 'God' (#s 5–6) since this term has been appropriated by many local religious groups as referring to their particular brand of Christianity (which features a strong indigenous healing tradition).

- *Poetry* speaks to people more clearly and forcefully in their *mother tongue*. As one respondent put it, "It's easier to tell what is happening [in Nyanja] and why the language is being used as it is." But even for second-language speakers of English, a poetic text does seem to carry a special impact: "It (#6) helps people to hear the voice of God!" Another added that a poetic style and rhythmic text arrangement renders a psalm more 'singable'.

- Several *difficult expressions* in the English versions were listed in the respondents' comments (in addition to those already mentioned), e.g., "Lift up your hands towards the sanctuary" (4); "Give accolades" (2); "posted to the nightwatch" (5); "In turn, may God…" (version

---

[15] With regard to this use *of Chauta*, the traditional Chewa God of Creation and Provision, the observation of Sanneh appears rather thought-provoking: "…nothing is more indicative of the indigenous theological advantage than the adoption of indigenous names for God in Bible translation and their introduction into Christianity" (2003:78).

5—which sounded to some respondents like people expect a reward for their religious service). A number of people appreciated the fact that version #6 mentioned the priests' ministering during the day as well as the night. Nyanja version #7 also contained a number of phrases and usages that were questioned, e.g., the first word, *Taonani* 'Look!'—which forms an immediate collocational clash with the second word *lemekezani* 'praise!' In contrast to most respondents, one man remarked (in writing) that he appreciated the inclusion of some more difficult English versions in this test because it serves as an impetus to learn some new words that may be helpful, or even necessary, in Bible study.

- With regard to the issue of *English versus vernacular* usage, an interesting tendency emerged that needs to be confirmed by further testing: non-mother tongue Nyanja speakers who knew English well preferred the English versions; on the other hand, those respondents who did not know English very well but could at least read the Nyanja texts much preferred them. One *non*-mother tongue Nyanja participant (the majority in all groups) even commented that he liked "the vernacular because I hear God speaking *my* language," while another preferred Nyanja over English because it sounded more 'idiomatic' to him. This comment probably characterizes the experience of many non-proficient English speakers: "In the vernacular I can understand the text right away, but in English I must first translate and then think of what it says in my language."

- A slight majority of readers who responded on the separate issue of *format* preferred side notes over footnotes (see sample in section 8.3) for being 'easier to connect' with the biblical text. However, one insightful individual pointed out that "the notes must be on the right side of the Bible page because a person first needs to read the text, then look for the notes....Remember, we read from left to right." But another person did question whether the same amount of note material could be included in side notes as in footnotes. The general opinion on note placement was divided: some felt that footnotes were 'more familiar' and also necessary to signal this material as being supplementary to the biblical text—"to leave the Scripture stand out more clearly." On the other hand, others suggested that the side notes better attracted readers to actually read them. Another item of format that generated a critical comment concerned the broken and semantically incomplete lines of the Nyanja version 7 (a result of end-line justification); one complained that this artificial printing

8.2 Testing for artistic quality in translation

procedure "cut the message, leaving it to the reader to connect to" the sense again.

- My assessment of the value of added paratextual notes could not be completed with every group due to a lack of time. Clearly, this aspect of a translation needs to be evaluated via a separate test that considers both *ease* and *utility*—that is, in providing readily accessible information of interest and applicability to respondents. The participants were unanimous in their desire for such explanatory notes to enrich their personal study of the Bible, but it was not possible for me to ascertain how (much) the comments supplied for Psalm 134 actually did help them gain understanding.

In summary, what this experiment appears to have revealed about the measurement and evaluation of the characteristic of *quality* in relation to Bible translating and translation(s) is as follows. In the first place, as the Nyanja proverb put it: *Zikachuluka, sizidyeka* "When there's too much to eat, you get indigestion." Similarly, for ordinary Bible readers, too many detailed questions often lead to confusion, frustration, or both. Thus my questionnaire undoubtedly attempted to measure too fine a grid, and as a result certain questions seemed to be almost the same to people who have not previously thought much about the aesthic and emotive aspects of biblical discourse. This was not as much of a problem for the third-year seminary students or Bible translators, but even several of them remarked that they had difficulty at times making the qualitative choices asked for. This difficulty was compounded by the number of versions being tested, two of which (# 1, 4) appeared to be very similar in wording and hence indistinguishable to non-specialists. But at least the testing process did serve to single out the three English versions 1, 4, and 6—which, as suggested above, might be profitably evaluated again with a short list of questions, such as the following:

1. Which version did you like the *best*? Give at least one reason why.
2. Which version did you like the *least*? Give at least one reason why.
3. Which version was the easiest to *understand*? Can you give a reason why?
4. Are there any words or phrases in these translations that are *difficult* to understand? Underline all of these places.
5. Which version was the most *beautiful* or poetic-sounding in English? Can you give a reason why?

6. Write any other comment that comes to mind with regard to these versions being tested.

Another important requirement surfaced during the course of this investigation, namely, the need for 'priming the pump', as it were, in order to more adequately prepare ordinary Bible students to respond in a text evaluation of this nature. For example, more time for instruction about poetry in general, biblical poetry in particular, and the challenge of Bible translation, may have helped to clarify some of the main issues involved in this study as well as the general purpose of the questionnaire. Such pre-education might possibly change the negative opinion that most respondents had about version 2—though further examination may well reveal that it is not really fair to test this highly poetic piece on non-mother tongue speakers of English. More background also needs to be given about the nature and purpose of text formatting on the printed page in order to permit a more informed choice to be made among the different options. No clear opinion emerged from this study, although the nontraditional formats of versions 3 and 6 did seem to strike a responsive chord with most respondents.

In conclusion, many people did comment that they enjoyed participating in this testing exercise because, as one person wrote, "It helps me to study my Bible more carefully." This is actually a needful process because it helps pastors and teachers to "find out what is happening on the ground regarding Bible study groups" and what people are actually learning. Another respondent pointed out that she had not thought much before about having different Bible translations to serve the diverse needs of the Church, but now this goal should be given great priority, especially in Africa, which she said is also very 'poor' with regard to the variety, quantity, and quality of Scriptures readily available. A current Bible translator remarked that he is now convinced of the benefit of using *"both* vernacular and English versions, because a comparative study of plural versions... sheds more light on my understanding of a particular text." In this connection, the test also sparked requests from several people that multiple versions be prepared and published in their own languages. In particular, a more poetic translation is needed to act as a contrastive complement to what most readers already have at hand, either a standard, relatively literal missionary version or a more recently published 'common-language' (simplified, GNT-type) rendition.

Finally, when conducting any research and testing program such as that we have outlined, it is important to take factors such as those suggested in the following quotation into consideration in relation to the methodology

8.2 Testing for artistic quality in translation

itself, the results (data) that are obtained, the conclusions that are drawn, and the applications made on the basis of those conclusions:[16]

> When we undertake a research project, we develop a complicated relationship with our data. We collect it, check the ethics of using it, manipulate it, store it, share it with others, find new ways to squeeze more knowledge from it, and often worry about it because it is the wrong kind, or there isn't enough of it, or it isn't telling us what we thought it would. Sometimes people even make it up or quietly discard the bits that don't fit. Getting the relationship right can make a project or break it.
>
> But this is a two-way relationship. While we might believe that as translation researchers we are in command of our data, I will assert that each of us is predisposed to choose certain kinds of data because of a complex of factors. At the individual level, these include the researcher's level of training, their beliefs about the nature of enquiry, and their location in the discipline landscape. At the level of the specific project, there will be the issue of the centrality of the data and the degree of reliance placed on it by the researcher. The institutions we work for also shape our relationship with data by way of strategic priorities, ethics policies, and funding opportunities. Next is the influence of the academic publishing industry, which by reflecting the beliefs and practices of senior researchers through peer review gives preference to certain research topics and approaches, and by implication certain types of research data. Finally, there is the discipline of translation studies itself with its dominating ideologies and discourses shaping and being shaped by our behavior as researchers, including our propensity to choose certain kinds of data.

There are some interesting and important implications here for those of us who undertake testing programs for the Bible translation(s) and/or associated auxiliary aids that we are working on. To adequately explore

---

[16] Abstract for a lecture entitled "Data: Making the right choices" to be delivered by Prof. Stuart Campbell at the University of Manchester on July 7, 2005 (received as an email message from Prof. Mona Baker [translation@monabaker.com] on June 24, 2005; I have not been able to update this reference).

these issues, however, would take me well beyond the limited scope of the present chapter.

8.3 A textual frame of reference for interpretation

The short text of Psalm 134 includes a surprising number of important concepts that are either alien to, or not fully compatible with, a south-central African model of reality—religious reality in particular. In addition, there are certain structural and stylistic features (as outlined in section 8.1) that will certainly be missed in any bare translation, English or Nyanja, unless pointed out through some paratextual or extratextual devices. Such "contextual adjustment strategies" (Hill 2004) are intended to promote a greater degree of comprehension (or, quality of communicability) with regard to the biblical text. Thus these auxiliary techniques also need to be evaluated in terms of their relative *quality* just like the translated text itself. From a cognitive perspective then, the issue is as follows (R. Brown 2004:53):

> The key technique for assessing and improving communicativeness is to test the translated text and associated contextual helps with the receptors to assess the cognitive effects, and then to revise the text and contextual helps in the light of the deficiencies that are discovered. Again, testers need to give more weight to intended conclusions than to premises, and much less weight to incidental implicatures that arise from the original communication situation but were not part of authorial intent.

I was not in a position to carry out a full testing program of this kind as part of the present study. Thus, I will call attention to several important aspects of such an exercise that need to be more fully explored in future research. This type of investigation may be directed holistically at all of the communicative dimensions of Psalm 134, or it may be restricted, as in the case of my study, more to literary form and the comparative excellence of the stylistic features of various English or vernacular translations.

I summarize the main potential conceptual problem points regarding the *explicatures* (facts directly derivable from the text itself) and principal *implicatures* (information derived from the text and its contextual setting) of Psalm 134 as follows (these are indicated by the expressions in bold print as they appear in the NIV text):

8.3 A textual frame of reference for interpretation

A song of ascents.
¹ Praise the **Lord**, all you **servants of the Lord**
    who **minister by night** in the **house of the Lord**.
² **Lift up your hands** in the **sanctuary**
    and praise the Lord.

³ May the Lord, the Maker of heaven and earth,
    bless you from **Zion**.

These problems are of three different types, as revealed below by the examples in quadrants 2–4 on the chart of possible conceptual relationships (adapted from H. Hill 2003:2; cf. 7.3.3.1).

A key biblical concept from the perspective of **TL audience** ➔ and the **original text** ⬇	Think it is shared	Do not think it is shared
Actually shared	1. e.g., 'Lift up your hands'	2. e.g., 'ascents'
Not actually shared	3. e.g., 'Zion,' 'Lord,' 'house of the Lord,' 'servants'	4. e.g., 'sanctuary'

We may start from the *shared* concepts that largely overlap in both denotation and connotation and hence cause little problem for a specific target group, e.g., quadrant **1**. Most African Christians realize that 'lifting one's hands' during worship, whether they happen to practice that custom or not, is a significant symbolic action that accompanies individual or corporate prayer and praise of God (cf. Ps. 63:4). However, various difficulties of comprehension and/or communication are presented by other important concepts contained in Psalm 134, for example, those that people recognize but do not fully or even partially share with the actual biblical cognitive domain (quadrant **3**)—such as, 'Zion', which people tend to identify only with a particular hill in Jerusalem (cf. Ps. 133:3) or, more distortedly, with a certain type of indigenous African brand of Christianity. Then there are those concepts that people do have in their world of experience but do not realize the correspondence that there is with the biblical notion (quadrant **2**), e.g., the term 'ascents' as a figurative way of referring to acts of worship that people periodically carry out in a group, e.g., choral singing, while proceeding on the Lord's day to the house of worship ('church') especially during the festivals of Lent and Easter.

Most difficult of all are those concepts that are foreign to the target culture and are not even recognized as such (quadrant **4**), e.g., the 'sanctuary' with reference to a restricted sacred part of the Jewish Temple in Jerusalem; in this case, people understand the vernacular term as simply a synonym for the entire Temple itself, or in transculturated fashion, as a designation for a Christian church building.

We have already discussed some of the strategies that may be implemented to eliminate or reduce the size of such communicative gaps in terms of the model proposed above (see section 7.3.3.1). What would some of these possibilities be in relation to Psalm 134? The following is a list of suggestions:

- **Section headings** e.g., 'A psalm for the close of worship'

- **Glossary entries** e.g., "*sanctuary*—a special sacred room set apart in the tabernacle/temple in which the high priest burned incense on an altar every morning and every evening; the incense symbolized the people's prayers of repentance and worship being lifted up as an offering before the LORD on a daily basis"

- **Cross-references** e.g., for 'house of the LORD'—see Pss. 135:2; 122:1; 101:2,7; 92:13; 84:4; 69:9; 66:13; 52:8; 42:4; 27:4; 26:8; 23:6; Ezra 2:1–7; 2 Chr. 2:1–12; 3:1–15; 2 Sam. 7:1-29; Hag. 1:8–9; 2:3, 7, 9

- **Illustrations** e.g., diagram of the 'holy place' located within the tabernacle/temple building, set off from the general 'courtyard' on the one hand, on the other, the 'most holy place,' and containing the altar of incense, the golden lamp stand, and the table for the consecrated bread

- **Introductory notes** e.g., under **Section heading** noted above: "In this psalm the worshipers first encourage all ministers of the LORD to continue to praise and serve him; these temple servants, in turn, call for God the Creator's blessings upon the people as they leave his house of worship."

- **Explanatory notes** e.g., v. 3: '*Maker of heaven and earth*'—This poetic title is both a confession of faith in the one true God and also an encouragement to the people that the LORD who created all

8.3 A textual frame of reference for interpretation

things also preserves and protects his faithful people. This added implication is suggested by two earlier psalms in the Ascent corpus that use the same expression for God in key positions within the text, at the beginning [Ps. 121:2] and at the end [Ps. 124:8]. These two psalms deal explicitly with the LORD's protection of his people when they are in danger.[17]

These paratextual features would then have to be evaluated in terms of their quality. How well do they pass the tests of intelligibility, idiomaticity, relevancy, and fidelity in particular? Other important issues could be assessed at the same time: first of all, do readers really want such helps? Do they even realize that they need them in order to better understand the biblical text? Have they been educated how to use these aids to enrich their study of the Scriptures? Is there any other type of background information that they would like to have included with their translation? A (mini-)concordance is often requested, but this would probably add to the cost of any version that included one.

Other practical matters need to be determined as well, for example, where should the explanatory notes be placed: in the foot (the norm), in the margin—right or left (the latter is illustrated in the graphic below), or condensed and combined together in a sectional introduction? The visual quality of the printed format should probably be tested several times, based on some prior instruction to readers as to the available options and their typographical significance. One must be relatively sure about this issue *before* a complete Bible or Testament is published.

---

[17] R. Hill distinguishes between an 'explanatory' note, which reveals certain important contextual implications along with contextual assumptions, and a 'descriptive' note which deals only with the latter type of background information (2004:20–21).

Psalm 134:1-3, NIV (reformatted)	**Psalm 134**
134:1 *"Praise the LORD"*—More literally, 'Bless (*barkuw*) Yahweh!'; cf. Psa. 135:1, where *Hallelu-Yah* is used. The Creator-God is the obvious focus of this psalm of praise, being mentioned by name five times. But a secondary emphasis lies in the continuous activity of those who are called upon to worship the LORD (= 'Yahweh' or *YHWH*), namely, all his "servants."	A psalm for the close of worship *(Last of the Songs of Ascent, 120-134)*
[OTHER NOTES OMITTED for the sake of this example]	¹ Praise the LORD, all you servants of the LORD who minister by night in the house of the LORD.
	² Lift up your hands in the sanctuary and praise the LORD.
134:3 *"Maker of heaven and earth"*—This poetic title is both a confession of faith in the one true God and also an encouragement to the people that the LORD who created all things also preserves and protects his faithful people. This added implication is suggested by two earlier psalms in the 'Ascents corpus' that use this same expression for God in key positions within the text, at the beginning (Ps. 122:2) and at the end (Ps. 124:8). These two psalms deal explicitly with the LORD's protection of his people when they are in danger.	³ May the LORD, the Maker of heaven and earth, bless you from Zion.

A thorough evaluation of the different types of *extratextual* supplementation will have to await a separate study, one perhaps carried out in conjunction with those local church bodies that are serious about providing their members with such hermeneutical helps for the Scriptures. Topics of special interest and importance with regard to Psalm 134 would include the following:

- Notes on key aspects of the varied liturgical worship of Israel, including alternating speakers/chanters/singers, as in the case of this psalm;
- A biography of King David, especially in relation to the 'historical' titles of the Psalms;

- An OT historical survey and time-line to show the relatively long period during which psalms were composed in Israel and what was happening in the nation during these years (e.g., from the time of the Judges [Judg. 5] to the post-exilic period [Ps. 137]);
- A survey of the different genres, or literary types, of psalm, e.g., lament, eulogy, thanksgiving, Torah psalm, profession of trust and royal;
- An overview of the typical stylistic features of the psalms, especially those that are often reproduced in a translation, e.g., parallelism, key terms of worship, and figurative references to the LORD God;
- A summary of the nature, purpose, and possible contemporary application of the Ascent Psalms (120–134) and related psalms (135–136);
- A context-sensitive and specific topical and thematic study of the Psalms corpus.

The discussion of this section has necessarily focused on *printed* presentations of the biblical text in translation. Corresponding methods for the qualitative testing and assessment of audio, video, and electronic products are also essential. Considering audio testing, for example, how are paratextual tools (e.g., explanatory notes, section titles, cross-references) most effectively presented via an *aural* medium of communication (alone)—that is, to clearly distinguish these different verbal devices from each other and from the text of Scripture itself? These are challenges that need to be carefully investigated and resolved from the specific perspective and using the available resources of the local TL community of Bible consumers and communicators.

8.4 Enhancing the value of a Bible translation

Gule aliyense akoma potsiriza 'Every dance is pleasing at the end' (after your troupe has worked hard together to practice and perfect all the synchronized dance movements and steps). This Nyanja proverb teaches that every communal effort may be difficult to perform or accomplish at first, but if all participants cooperate on the various details, they will ultimately succeed. So it is also with the task of Bible translation. Many different individuals with their various abilities are needed to carry out all of the diverse aspects of the work program—from the initial sampling and specification of the target audience to the post-publication testing of the results. The greater the competency that can be contributed to the various stages and coordinated towards the common goal, the more satisfying the final outcome, all other things being equal. The converse is just as predictable: the quality of a given Scripture product may be compromised by either incompetence or the lack of sufficient collaboration, organization, management, or motivation at any step along the way. Thus the end product will only be as good as the level of quality manifested at each of the essential steps involved in the production process. This is a commonplace, to be sure, but it is one often overlooked or neglected by project planners in their eagerness to translate the Scriptures as quickly as possible, without first 'counting the cost'—or being unwilling to pay it in the end.

The following points summarize ten components of the Bible translation production process that require the basic minimum (at least) of quality in terms of competence or excellence as part of an overall coordinated program of activities:

1. #1—the *sine qua non!*—gifted and proficient translators, as evaluated with respect to their basic education, translation training, practical experience, performance, and personal commitment

2. #2—a close second!—strong community-based project organization, administration, management, local support, and public relations initiatives, carried out according to a clearly defined job commission *(brief)* and goal *(Skopos)*

3. Provision of continued training and ongoing professional development of all translation staff

4. Compatibility and a high level of mutual cooperativeness on the part of staff members and their supporters ('team spirit')

5. Cohesiveness, transparency, and efficiency with regard to the team's daily working procedures (drafting, cross-checking, testing, revising, mutual assessment, data management, scheduling)

6. Qualified review team composition and coordinated operation— including any special consultants and technical advisers (e.g., how experienced, qualified, and available for service are they?)

7. Adequate supply of recommended exegetical and translation resources (commentaries, handbooks, dictionaries, target language and cultural studies)

8. Integrated electronic text-processing tools and data bases *(Paratext, Translator's Workplace, Stuttgart Study Bible, Logos)* along with people having the necessary skill to use them

9. First-rate translation equipment and programs, adequate internet access, office facilities, staff accommodation, and conditions of service for the various team members

10. Rigorous translation testing methods and quality control procedures applied for each mode and medium of text preparation and presentation (SL exegesis, TL composition, stylistic polishing, text formatting, computer checks, provision of supplementary helps, etc.—print, audio, video, mixed or combined format)

These ten points are not necessarily a priority listing, except for the first two items, but it is safe to say that a serious deficiency or malfunction with respect to any one factor might severely cripple a translation project, while a failure in the case of two or more components would probably be fatal as far as the ultimate quality of that project's performance is concerned.

8.5 Conclusion: Cooperation, accountability, and quality

A Chewa proverb says, *Mutu umodzi susenza denga* 'One head cannot raise a roof.' Reference is made to people lifting up the grass thatch roof of a new house on their heads. This calls for a coordinated and committed communal effort in order for the job to be done correctly and efficiently and without doing damage to the final product. Mutual cooperation is the key to ultimate success. As was suggested in the previous section, all-around interpersonal collaboration is needed for such a complex and challenging communicative task as Bible translation to succeed. Many project organizers do not seem to realize this, or perhaps they are not clearly told from the outset what sort of sacrifice is required to achieve the desired quality.

Thus all stakeholders—or better perhaps, the project's 'co-owners' as well as future 'consumers'—must be confronted with the basic sufficiency test they are facing *before* they actually get into it. The entire community of TL speakers need to be both educated and encouraged to grow in their diverse roles and responsibilities as the project progresses. If they are to be the chief determiners of excellence (or the lack of it) in a translation, as judges of its ultimate acceptability and appropriateness, then they also have to accept the burden of *accountability*, that is, the responsibility for seeing to it that each person or group does their fair share so as to achieve the highest standard in as many aspects of the multifaceted translation process as possible. The ultimate *quality* of the translation project will be only as good as the weakest link in a long chain of interdependent activities that comprise the production process as a whole. And quality, including the personal attribute of competency, as we have seen, is a *relative* factor—that is, varying more or less in degree with regard to a desired standard or a pre-determined norm. In the case of Bible translation, the very nature and purpose of the sacred object of our efforts should be motivation enough!

> Be strong, all you people of the land, declares the LORD, and work. For I am with you, declares the LORD Almighty. This is what I covenanted with you when you came out of Egypt. And my Spirit remains among you. Do not fear! (Haggai 2:4–5, NIV)

> Therefore, my dear brothers and sisters, stand firm—let nothing move you. Always give yourselves fully to the work of the Lord, because you know that your labor in the Lord is not in vain! (1 Cor. 15:58, NIV, rev.)

9

Lyricizing the Poetry of Scripture

Translation is an *art*, because the act of rendering biblical works into contemporary languages is more than a purely technical process. It is an artistic achievement. Translation involves, first, understanding the profound content, the significant artistry, and the powerful impact of the original languages of the writings in the Bible in their context. Second, translation involves finding contemporary ways to express the meanings, the power, the vibrancy, the passion, and the potential impacts of the original compositions in modern tongues.[1]

9.1 Oral Artistic Approaches

Not only *is* translation an art, but in the case of much of Scripture, translation *must be* an art—that is, practiced with an artistic eye—and ear!—on the original document as well as the draft being rendered in the local vernacular. This artistry must be applied especially in the case of the lyric literature of Scripture which, as we have seen in the preceding studies, gives evidence of a mode of verbal communication in which the form of the message (the Hebrew text) is undeniably a part of the *meaning*—a functional significance that not always specifically semantic in nature but is certainly *pragmatic* in terms of its aesthetic, affective, and imperative impact and appeal. These lyric texts, if not actually composed to be sung, were undoubtedly created to have an oral-aural effect that would be stimulated by a distinctive manner of elocutionary expression, e.g., chanting, recitation, or some other type of rhetorical proclamation.[2]

---

[1] From *The oral art of translation: Rendering for performance* by Prof. David Rhoads (forthcoming, p. 1).

[2] With regard to the additional communicative dimension of biblical songs, we note that "[t]hey make the unfamiliar familiar, aid in memory, help create feelings of belonging, preserve and pass traditions from one generation to the next, and communicate on multiple levels through rhythm, melody, and harmony, all in addition to the lyrics....[T]he songs are used to *reconstruct* the past in such a way as to assist in forming a *concrete social identity* among the reading and listening audience with the goal of creating a commitment or *obligation* to a specific ideal, value, or belief" (Giles and Doan 2009:2–3, 10, original italics). In the Scriptures then we have abundant evidence of this practical communicative principle in application. "Orality and writing technology are joint means for accomplishing a common goal: accurate recall of the treasured tradition" (David Carr 2005:7)—indeed, the very

Of course, there are many projects where such an ideal cannot be achieved or even remotely approximated in translation for various reasons. Among these are the following (cf. section 8.4):

- Insufficient research has been done in the literature/orature of the target language in order to document the prose and poetic genres that might be utilized in Bible translation.

- The community's *brief* and *Skopos* do not incorporate the value of artistry in verbal or written Bible translation, as defined and discussed in this book.

- The translation team (or its corps of reviewers) does not have a competent and/or articulate oral and aural artist among them.

- The translation team has not been adequately instructed regarding the artistry and orality of Scripture, that is, how to either recognize it in the original text or to deal with this textual dimension in their mother tongue.

- The project is not officially preparing an idiomatic (meaning-oriented) version and therefore feels that it does not have to be concerned about artistry at all.

- A meaning-based version focuses purely on the semantic content of the biblical text, not its connotative or pragmatic features (which are also part of the text's meaning package).

- No (or too little) time has been set aside to deal with this aspect of translation, or the project deadlines are too tight to allow for it in terms of composition and/or testing and polishing drafts.

- The Scriptures are viewed as a corpus of 'theological' (or worse, 'doctrinal') books, and hence antithetical to the notion of literature and associated attributes, such as beauty, impact, appeal, and levels of meaning/significance.

- Even if some of the preceding limiting factors are not applicable, not enough encouragement or support is given to the translation team (or to the project as a whole) to produce a version that 'speaks'

---

words of God and his spokesmen. The Apostle Paul refers to this vital transgenerational mnemonic function of the songs of the saints in Colossians 3:16, and adds the pastoral functions of 'teaching and admonishing' (διδάσκοντες καὶ νουθετοῦντες).

9.1 Oral Artistic Approaches

('sings') with the voice of an artist or rhetor in the language—or even close to it.

Someone might ask, "But does the Bible really speak with passion and power, as claimed in the opening quote?" I trust that the various text studies in this monograph have presented sufficient evidence to show that a credible case can be made for this conclusion—that is to say, with respect to the original Hebrew documents. Unfortunately, however, the same cannot often be said about most of our translations into the world's languages, no matter how little or well-known the tongue might be. Take English, for example: my survey of all the major versions have revealed relatively little of a lyric sound with respect to the different passages considered in the present study.

Such poetic neglect is evident even (and especially) in the case of the Psalter, where one would have expected greater attention to be devoted to it due to the prevalent use of the psalms in most liturgical, prayer, and hymn traditions. Even the venerable KJV lets us down in our search for at least a semi-poetic style of composition, for instance, with regard to Psalm 137, considered in chapter 4. Here are the words of the first strophe as rendered and formatted in a standard edition of the Bible:

1. By the rivers of Babylon, there
We sat down, yea, we wept,
When we remembered Zion.
2. We hanged our harps upon the
willows in the midst thereof.
3. For there they that carried us
away captive required of us a song;
and they that wasted us *required
of us* mirth, *saying,* Sing us *one* of
the songs of Zion.

Now compare the preceding with the modern *English Standard Version* (2001), which seeks "to be 'as literal as possible' while maintaining clarity of expression and literary excellence"[3] (reproduced as formatted):

---

[3] This quote is taken from the Preface of the ESV (Crossway Bibles, a division of Good News Publishers, 2001:viii). The publishers/translators further claim that in their translation "faithfulness to the text and vigorous pursuit of accuracy were combined with simplicity, beauty, and dignity of expression" (ibid., vii).

1. By the waters of Babylon,
there we sat down and
wept,
    when we remembered Zion.
2. On the willows there
    we hung up our lyres.
3. For there our captors
    required of us songs,
and our tormentors, mirth, saying,
    "Sing us one of the songs of
        Zion!"

But how much clarity and literary excellence, really, is manifested by this rendition? The printed display of this text on the page is already an obvious indication that not much attention was devoted to its poetic representation.

One of the few lyric, readable, recitable, and hearable publications of the Psalms that I am acquainted with is the *POET Psalms* (*Poetic Oracle English Translation*, 2009) edition by Dr. Brenda H. Boerger. Her version of Psalm 137 is presented in chapter 4; the first three verses are reproduced below (as formatted and annotated by the author).

Psalm 137[4]
WE SAT BY STREAMS IN BABYLON TO CRY:
IN REMEMBRANCE
a historical psalm of retribution
heroic octave variations[5]

1   We sat by streams in Babylon to cry.
     In sorrow heads were drooping down to weep,
     Remembering Zion which had been destroyed.
2   Along the rivers, stood some trees nearby.
     And in the spreading branches of those trees
     We set aside for good our harps of joy.
3   *"Say, serenade us,"* our enslavers hissed.
     "So chant a Zion cadence, we insist." [6]

---

[4] Ps. 137: in 587 BC Babylon destroyed Jerusalem, assisted by Edom, Israel's relatives, leading to Israel's exile and captivity.

[5] 137 subtitle: the lines are all iambic pentameter, but each stanza has a different rhyme scheme and none are those prescribed for heroic octaves: abba-abba, abab-abab, or abababcc.

[6] 137:3: verse three is filled with the hissing of [s], [sh], and [ts] sounds in Hebrew, showing the mocking of the captors. *POET* uses [s], [ch], [st], [ts] and [z] and compresses four lines into two lines for this effect in English.

9.1 Oral Artistic Approaches

Finally, one of the easiest poetic versions for public communal utterance may be found in the edition that was published for the Church of Scotland over a century ago.[7] Naturally the language is a bit archaic, but that is compensated for by the smoothly flowing, rhythmic text, which is also sung according to standard liturgical melodies:

> By Babel's streams we sat and wept,
>   when Sion we thought on.
> In midst thereof we hang'd our harps
>   the willow trees upon.
> For there a song required they,
>   who did us captive bring.
> Our spoilers call'd for mirth, and said,
>   A song of Sion sing!
>
> O how the Lord's song shall we sing
>   within a foreign land?
> If thee, Jerus'lem, I forget,
>   skill part from my right hand!
> My tongue to my mouth's roof let cleave,
>   if I do thee forget,
> Jerusalem, and thee above
>   my chief joy do not set.
>
> Remember Edom's children, Lord,
>   who in Jerus'lem's day,
> "Ev'n unto its foundation,
>   raze, raze it quite," did say.
> O daughter thou of Babylon,
>   near to destruction;
> Bless'd shall he be that thee rewards,
>   as thou to us hast done!
>
> Yea, happy surely shall he be
>   thy tender little ones
> who shall lay hold upon, and them
>   shall dash against the stones!

---

[7] Published as *The Psalms in rhyming verse* by Barbour and Company (Uhrichsville, OH 1995:332–333).

Of course, listeners might well question how 'lovely' the lyrics of the last lines are! But this concern simply brings up another major issue that was considered during the various studies of this book, namely, the vital need for providing an adequate conceptual frame of reference in order to properly understand, interpret, and apply certain passages of Scripture.[8] Such background knowledge is an essential part of the intended meaning of the biblical text and therefore it must be provided in some way—whether *paratextually* (e.g., footnotes) or *extratextually* (e.g., supplementary oral instruction)—in a way that is relevant for the current target audience and appropriate for their setting, occasion, the medium of communication (i.e., visual and/or oral-aural), and also the mode of message transmission (e.g., a printed text versus an audio presentation, a dramatic production, or a musical rendition).

But, returning to the text itself, we must remind ourselves of the depth and diversity of the lyric task. Indeed, there is a considerable amount of poetry in the Bible—not only the long-recognized poetic texts, such as those that have been considered in this study, but many others too, both complete books (e.g., most of the 'prophetic' corpus) and portions of books (e.g., Gen. 49, Exod. 15, Num. 24, Deut. 33, Judg. 5, 2 Sam. 22, Matt. 5:3–10, Luke 1:46–55, 67–79, Rom. 11:33–36; 16:25–27, 1 Cor. 13, Phil. 2:6–11, Col. 1:15–20). Furthermore, there are many additional passages that are arguably a mixture of prose and poetry (e.g., the divine speeches of Genesis, John 17, the doxologies of Revelation).[9] All these texts need to be analyzed from an orality-oriented as well as a literary and a linguistic perspective, then also correspondingly lyricized in translation, to the degree possible, by employing functionally equivalent poetic genres and associated stylistic techniques. This endeavor involves not the perceived *beauty* of sonic expression, but as the preceding studies have shown, many Scriptures also express a perceptible *persuasive* force (e.g., the texts from Proverbs) along with a strong *emotive* energy at times (e.g., the Song of Songs) and often a perceptible 'attitude' as well—Ecclesiastes, for example (i.e., frustration and skepticism). As in the case of all good literature, so also with the various biblical documents, the literary (including the phonological) form of the text *is an integral, indispensable part of* the meaning—it is not just the external husk that must be broken up

---

[8] For information regarding a frames of reference approach to Scripture translation and cross-cultural communication, see Wilt and Wendland (2008) and Wendland (2008a).

[9] Brenda Boerger comments: "The Romans passages...we set to a favorite western hymn of the Natqgu-speaking people. The Revelation passages were set to the same tune as the English chorus, Thou art worthy....Some of the other texts listed here were formatted poetically, but not set to music. However, I have set 1 Cor. 13, Phil. 2, and Col. 1 to tunes in English" (personal correspondence).

(analyzed) and stripped away in order to get at the assumed central core, the semantic (theological, moral, and doctrinal) content.

So what is to be done with these important pragmatic dimensions of meaning—can they simply be ignored or downplayed? The various textual studies of this monograph would support a resounding negative response to this question.[10] The normal practice of merely rendering these passages as prose, no matter how meaningful, with or without the cosmetic addition of poetic lineation, is simply not good enough, because such a 'minimalist' strategy involves what is, in effect, a cover-up for the loss of a major element of the overall, intended communicative significance of Scripture (i.e., its meaning in a wider sense). To be sure, not all (or even a majority of) translation teams are capable or equipped enough to deal with this oft-neglected aspect of translation. However, that does not absolve them of the responsibility of honestly and overtly declaring the fact (e.g., in their version's introduction) that in their case, for whatever reason(s), the poetic muse has not been actively encouraged, examined, or engaged.

The final feature that I call attention to in this conclusion has been highlighted in the textual studies that comprise this volume. This is the factor of *orality* which is both closely related to the formal poetics, as well as the rhetorical power of the Scriptures. There is no doubt that the ancient biblical documents were composed and first presented to (perhaps even dramatically *performed* before) their audiences in an oral-aural environment.[11] They are also accessed today, in most world settings, primarily

---

[10] Further evidence of the literary (artistic and rhetorical) significance of the Scriptures may be found in my two earlier monographs, *Finding and translating the oral-aural elements in written language: The case of the New Testament epistles* (2008b) and *Prophetic rhetoric: Case studies in text analysis and translation* (2009) (2nd rev. ed., SIL. Forthcoming).

[11] While certain textual evidence tends to support the conclusion that certain biblical books like Ezekiel, Qoheleth, and Song of Songs may have been dramatically 'performed' in subsequent oral re-presentations by disciples and tradents, I believe that the foundation and norm for all such communication acts was a *stable written* text as originally authored and/or authoritatively edited into its final pre-canonical form. Thus, I see no basis for viewing the biblical scribe as a 'performer' in the sense that has been claimed by some, that "[t]he scribe of the prophetic performance enhanced the original performance by ordering, editing, and formalizing the prophetic utterance, thereby giving it 'life in the present'..." (Doan and Giles 2005:30–32).

On the contrary, the primary task of the ancient scribe was, as in the later strict Masoretic tradition, to *preserve* the original text (and/or the *ipsissima verba* of the biblical authors) as precisely as possible. Therefore, these scribes did not represent a secondary, perhaps even an antagonistic layer of creative composition as advocated by certain 'performance critics' who make statements like the following: "Rather than a smooth transition from prophet to literature, it is much more likely that the evolution from prophetic performer to prophetic literature was characterized by a struggle for power. The prophetic scribe (or perhaps better, the prophetic playwright) is dependent upon the prophetic performer for his inspiration and derives his credibility from an attachment to the prophetic performer but, nonetheless, is bent on replacing the prophetic performer....The scribes, who were creating text that still

by ear rather than visually through reading. The original writers composed their works aloud, thus building into them the natural linguistic and literary characteristics of oral composition, as has been documented throughout this study. In a similar way, contemporary translators must incorporate analogous idiomatic stylistic and structural qualities—phonological, lexical, syntactic, discourse, and format-related—into their drafts, not only to reproduce the sound dynamics of the Scripture for the sake of equivalent communicative effect (beauty, impact, appeal, etc.), but also to make their versions more amenable to oral expression and adaptation, for possible transmission in new linguistic settings and contemporary sociocultural environments. In short, the overall process becomes, as a recent book title puts it, translating "from orality to orality."[12]

It is interesting to recall that in the ancient Greco-Roman tradition of *rhetoric*, the art of verbal persuasion (effective communication), considerable attention was given to the public presentation of the discourse that

had to be spoken and performed for the majority of their audience, sought to capture the performative mind and imagination of the prophet….The scribe, both as writer and speaker of the text, engaged in a kind of impersonation….In the scribal tradition, it was the scribe who, as actor, created the character of the prophet in order for God to be present" (Doan and Giles 2005:21, 27, 29; cf. Wendland (2009): 384–388).

I suspect that the Masoretes would have been shocked by such a dramatic and imaginative characterization of their scholarly predecessors—*Baruch,* the scribe of Jeremiah, in particular, who recorded his task as follows: "…while Jeremiah dictated (lit. 'from the mouth of') all the words the Lord had spoken to him, Baruch wrote them on the scroll (lit. 'on the scroll of writing')" (Jer. 36:4; cf. 36:6, 8, 10, 17–18, 27–28, 32). According to some scholars, however, a distinction must be made between two types of ancient text copier: "The *transcriber* [like Baruch] transforms oral data into writing; the scribe who invents composes a text of his own contrivance" (K. van der Toorn 2007:115, my italics). These most creative, perhaps even subversive, of "scribes, even in their most instrumental of roles, impose their style, language, and ideas on the text…they mold the material that reaches them orally" (ibid., 115).

Therefore, according to van der Toorn, in the case of the Hebrew Bible it is not "Moses and the prophets," or even "many of the Psalms," that we are reading/hearing, but rather texts that display various degrees and forms of "scribal inventions." This claim is made despite the fact that there is absolutely no incontrovertible evidence for this conclusion, for even the proponents of this approach to textual transmission admit that "no text from the Hebrew Bible is *explicitly* the invention of a scribe" (ibid., 115–117, added italics). From the former confusion of source and redaction criticism, we thus enter the equally chaotic new world of scribal re-creation (and 'performance'), which is once again dependent on modern 'experts' in the field to save the day by explaining for us the heterogeneous nature and diverse hermeneutics of the biblical text.

[12] James Maxey (2009). In a personal endorsement printed on the back cover, I wrote: "What does 'orality' and public performance have to do with translating the written Scriptures of God? Many misconceptions about the nature of the biblical texts and their communication in modern world languages are corrected in this thoroughly engaging, wide-ranging book that offers an innovative, multidisciplinary approach to the subject…on contextualizing the New Testament for effective contemporary, multi-sensory re-presentation".

9.1 Oral Artistic Approaches

had been carefully prepared with oral articulation in mind. 'Delivery' (technically termed *pronunciatio*), was the fifth and last of the so-called 'canons' of rhetorical organization—that is, the procedural stages required in formulating a speech for elocution.[13] Thus, in preparation for delivery, a speaker would shape his orally conceived, but written text still further to enhance its phonological dimension in order to make a greater impact on, and appeal to, the intended audience with reference to the formal occasion and setting envisaged. Throughout this study we have noted how the original authors of Scripture employed the linguistic-literary forms of their message in order to create meanings that would resound in the sensorium as well as the comprehension of those to whom they were writing. The task of the translator is to create an equivalent communicative effect in audiences today. But this requires yet another essential link in the chain of textual transmission, now in some local vernacular. Here we have the challenge also for contemporary 'readers' (lectors) of the Scriptures to do justice to the efforts of both the original author as well as his target language translators. This is where the skillful practice of oral interpretation comes to the fore—that is, "the art of sharing with an audience a work of literary art in its intellectual, emotional, and aesthetic entirety."[14]

This is not a matter that can be either dismissed or left to chance; all of us have experienced occasions where some Bible pericope has been depreciated, detracted from, even distorted through a poor, unpracticed, incompetent public reading. As far as a given translation is concerned then, not only must project administrators see to it that their TL version is sufficiently composed 'under the influence of orality' and tested accordingly in public performance,[15] but as part of their audience engagement

---

[13] "The five parts of rhetoric are invention, which deals with the planning of a discourse and the arguments to be used in it; arrangement, the composition of the various parts into an effective whole; style, which involves both choice of words and the composition of words into sentences, including the use of figures; memory, or preparation for delivery; and delivery, the rules for the control of the voice and the use of gestures" (George A. Kennedy 1984:13–14).

[14] Rang (1994:1) adds: "Like the rhetoricians, we are interested in proper handling of voice and body. We are also concerned with the literary style of our lections. And we [oral interpreters] are very interested in the selection and arrangement of the ideas the passages contain. A major difference between our task and that of the [biblical writers] is that we do not create, but *re*-create. The tasks of literary style and arrangement of ideas have already been done for us by the author. It is our job to discover all the elements the author has used. Then we must bring techniques of voice and body to the service of those ideas. Only in this way can we share the totality of the selection with our audiences and try to produce appropriate responses" (ibid., 3; material in brackets added).

[15] Brenda Boerger comments: "We had a public reading of the entire gospel of Matthew over a period of three nights at our local church. Seven team members were each assigned four non-consecutive chapters, with an eighth assigned to read the footnotes at the relevant places. The readers took turns standing at the lectern, while the footnote reader was seated

efforts, they may also have to budget enough time to educate members of their public regarding the importance of this vital aspect of Scripture proclamation—where the Word actually hits the ears, as it were, of those for whom it was long ago composed.

Of course, the oral-and-aural factor is not the only, or even the preeminent feature to keep in mind when translating the Bible, but it has so often and for so long been ignored, that it is important to underscore, perhaps even to over-emphasize, its significance when selecting, training, guiding, and monitoring teams today. In fact, a performance-oriented approach can even be employed as a *hermeneutical* and also a *translation* tool in the extended compositional process. As one eminent scholar and practitioner suggests, from extensive personal experience:[16]

> Translation is a demanding and exacting discipline, even while being significantly artful. I have found that the act of translating for performances I have done is one of the most significant means for understanding a biblical text. Translating for performance leads one to grasp in fresh ways the potential meanings of the composition, the oral arts evident in the text, the significance of sound as a medium for communicating the Bible, and the experience of the rhetorical impact on an audience. I believe that translating for orality can enhance the exegetical process such that exegetes become (oral) translators and that translators become (oral) exegetes—and that both try their hand at performing!

An oral performance methodology like that proposed by Rhoads can also serve another important function, namely, to get the translation's 'consumer community' more actively involved in the project from the beginning, while the first texts are being drafted, rather than at the end, as happens all too often. Ultimate public 'acceptability' (with personal relevance being transferred then to actual use) is the *sine qua non* of any translation, and the sooner that the primary target audience can become meaningfully engaged in the process of evaluating and improving the team's drafts, the more effective the project will be in terms of accomplishing its communicative goals (*Skopos*). This is because "[u]ltimately, the value of understanding Bible Translation as contextualization and performance must be measured by host communities who are the agents for translation and contextualization" (Maxey 2009:196). Thus *from one language, culture, and community to another* the task goes on—the divine Word being contextualized and enriched by every human setting, sense, and sound in which it is verbally embodied and orally proclaimed.

---

in a chair next to them – visually showing the relative status of the two oral readings" (personal correspondence).

[16] David Rhoads, *The oral art of performance*, forthcoming, p. 13.

APPENDIX A

Preparing a Poetic Analysis and Translation of Psalm 24: A Guided Self-study

Recognizing and reproducing the glories of a psalm

This set of *twelve* procedural guidelines (each headed by a *keyword*) offers one possible literary-structural analytical methodology aimed at an eventual Bible translation. These *form-functional* considerations may be modified of course to meet the circumstances and end needs of users. The term 'glories' in the section heading refers to the patent poetic features (structural, artistic, and rhetorical) that we will pay special attention to during this analysis, with a view towards composing a corresponding translation type in your mother tongue (or revising some standard English version). Periodic analysis questions appear along the way (marked by ➔); those who are doing this exercise as a self-study should try to answer them first on their own, before reading the expository notes that follow.

➔ As you proceed in this self-study, make a listing of any **critical comments** or **questions** that you may have with regard to methodology and/or interpretation and, when you have completed your work, forward these to the present author (or to the current course instructor).

A.1 Read

Read the original (Hebrew) text aloud and prepare a literal initial (base) translation.

If you cannot read the Hebrew, try several different English translations instead, e.g., ESV, NIV, GNT, and NLB (i.e., two more formal and two more idiomatic versions).

➔ *Consider the following issues (to be investigated in more detail later); suggested points of interest are given for preliminary discussion:*

A.1.1 What are the *main ideas* and *key terms* of this psalm? Do you see any inter-connections?

A clear focus on Yahweh, the 'glorious king'—his wonderful attributes and righteous worshipers

A.1.2 How *'poetic'* does the text *sound?* Cite 2 examples of lyric, psalmic features that you note (either in the original text or shining through the translation).

Initial 'creation language'; leading rhetorical questions (RQs) to initiate strophes; a call for worship of Yahweh; liturgical strophic repetition

A.1.3 Did you notice any potential *peaks* (theme) or *climaxes* (emotion) within the psalm?

Peak: v. 5b–6, Identification: a characterization of God's holy people.
Climax: v. 10b–c, Praise the identification of their Sovereign King!

A.1.4 Identify some potential translation *problem points* in terms of form and/or meaning.

(Start thinking how to handle these in a poetic manner in your version.)

v. 2b: ocean currents/earth's foundation; 6b: 'O (God of) Jacob'; 10b: YHWH *Tsebaoth*

A.1.5 What general *type* of psalm is this—praise, lament, trust, thanksgiving, or another?

Most obviously, in general, a royal psalm in praise of Yahweh the glorious King!

[See section A.4 for the Hebrew text, set out in **poetic lineation** and marked for certain poetic **features**, plus my own, moderately free English translation presented for your critique.]

A.2 Variants

Do a text-critical analysis to determine the principal variants and readings.

Again, if you do not read Hebrew, the major English versions or exegetical commentaries that you consult will point out where these **variants** (slightly different Hebrew texts) or **readings** (different translations for the same Hebrew text) occur.

➔ *Pick out and consider several of the variants that appear in Psalm 24 (cf. the NET):*

- v. 4—Heb. 'who does not lift up for emptiness my life.' The first person pronoun on נַפְשִׁי (*nafshiy*, 'my life') makes little sense here *(possibly a reference to Yahweh's 'name'?)*; many medieval Hebrew mss. support the ancient versions in reading a third person pronoun 'his'. The idiom 'lift the life' here means to 'long for' or 'desire strongly.' In this context (note the reference to an oath in the following line) 'emptiness' probably refers to speech *(better: "idols, idolatry")* (see Ps. 12:2).

- v. 2b—Some mss. have a *perfect* verb [k-w-n] "he establish**ed** it *(fem. sg.* → *'earth'?)*" instead of MT's *imperfect* form (יְכוֹנְנֶהָ), which is normally translated by a non-past tense; but the latter is probably correct—an instance of 'poetic variation' since the corresponding verb in line A (2a) is perfect.

- v. 6b—MT reads: 'your face, O Jacob'; my translation assumes the addition of an *implicit* 'God of', which has limited support from several Hebrew and LXX mss.; cf. Ps. 75:9 (10). (implied by the suffix 'him' at end of 6a).

- v. 9b—MT reads: 'and lift up!' (*active* imperative) instead of the corresponding *passive* as in v. 7b; emending the passive to an active verb is supported by several Hebrew mss. and all the ancient versions; cf. NET/MT: "Rise up, you eternal doors!". Hebrew poetic usage would support not only the graphic personification here but also the stylistic variation in the verb forms. *(Note: in Hebrew, 'lift up the head' can also mean 'rejoice'.)*

A.3 Context

Study the cotext and the extratextual setting ('context') of the psalm.

→ *Do a background study of Psalm 24 (cf. an exegetical commentary or study Bible) and list three important contextual facts that you have discovered about this psalm.*

The three clear-cut sections of this psalm (A: 1–2, B: 3–6, C: 7–10; see evidence below) seem to point to a *composite* piece, that is, a psalm that was composed by King David (or one of his appointed musicians or tradition-bearers) from several other extant *liturgical* lyrics in order to formulate this now unified hymn in praise of the royal Lordship of Yahweh (A + C), including a distinctive stanza in the middle which describes those who alone are fit to worship such a great Creator-King (B). Form critics often designate section B as a liturgical *'entrance hymn'* for *pilgrims* and C as a corresponding entrance hymn invoking or inviting the Ark/ YHWH to enter the Temple (2 Sam. 6:12–19).

→ *Next consider the psalm's co-text (surrounding psalms, especially those that precede it in the Psalter): Do you see any significant intertextual connections (correspondences and/or contrasts)? List the most important of these in your opinion—the application of 'canon criticism':*

Psalm 24 follows topically from Psalm 23 since it elaborates on the theme of *YHWH's earthly abode* ('the house of the LORD') introduced at the end of Psalm 23. Psalm 23 focuses upon Yahweh as the personal Protector of his people and the various 'blessings' that they receive from his hand (cf. 24:5a), while Psalm 24 features Yahweh as their glorious, all-powerful Creator and King and summarizes the characteristics of those who are 'righteous' before him (23:3/24:5). Psalm 25 is another psalm of trust (cf. 23) based on the theological assumptions of Psalm 24 (cf. 24:4–25:1).

In A.4 you will find a poetic display of Psalm 24 along with a function-oriented English rendering, which may be critically evaluated as part of the overall analytical study of this text.

→ *Note any significant differences between the English translation below and two or three standard versions. Record any suggested improvements or corrections that you would like to make.*

A.4 Genre

Select the primary genre and sub-genres of the text.

➔ *What is a genre? (Note etic vs. emic classifications; cf. Wendland (2002a) Analyzing the Psalms, ch. 3.)*

This was done in a preliminary sort of way in step one; now it is time to try to be more specific: does Psalm 24 manifest a 'pure' genre, or does it seem to be 'mixed' (especially in the case of longer psalms)?

The five 'major' functional types are: *petition* (lament), *thanksgiving* (eulogy), *praise* (hymn), *instruction* (homily), *profession* (creed).

There are also five 'minor' types: *repentance* (penitential), *remembrance* (historical), *retribution* (imprecatory), *royalty* (panegyric), and *liturgy* (liturgical).

➔ *How would you classify Psalm 24 in terms of genre and sub-genre? Give reasons.*

On the next page you will find a poetic display of Psalm 24 along with a function-oriented English rendering, which may be critically evaluated as part of the overall analytical study of this text. The different shades of gray and underlines indicate some (not necessarily all) repeated sounds and words that may be significant markers with the text (for you to determine).

A Davidic psalm:	¹ לְדָוִד מִזְמוֹר
The earth is Yahweh's and everything in it;	לַיהוָה הָאָרֶץ וּמְלוֹאָהּ
To him belong the world and all who live in it.	תֵּבֵל וְיֹשְׁבֵי בָהּ׃
For he is the one who over the seabed established dry land;	² כִּי־הוּא עַל־יַמִּים יְסָדָהּ
yes, over the deep ocean currents he laid earth's foundations.	וְעַל־נְהָרוֹת יְכוֹנְנֶהָ׃
Who then may ascend the mount where Yahweh dwells?	³ מִי־יַעֲלֶה בְהַר־יְהוָה
Who may worship there in that holy place of his?	וּמִי־יָקוּם בִּמְקוֹם קָדְשׁוֹ׃
Only *those* whose hands are clean and whose hearts are pure.	⁴ נְקִי כַפַּיִם וּבַר־לֵבָב
Only *those* who do not devote themselves to lies;	אֲשֶׁר ׀ לֹא־נָשָׂא לַשָּׁוְא נַפְשִׁי
only *those* who do not make false oaths or promises.	וְלֹא נִשְׁבַּע לְמִרְמָה׃
Only *they* will receive a blessing from Yahweh;	⁵ יִשָּׂא בְרָכָה מֵאֵת יְהוָה
yes, *they* will be vindicated by *their* Savior-God.	וּצְדָקָה מֵאֱלֹהֵי יִשְׁעוֹ׃
These are the folk who really want to worship him;	⁶ זֶה דּוֹר *דֹּרְשׁוֹ (דֹּרְשָׁיו)
they desire to know **you** (God of) Jacob personally. *A-men!*	מְבַקְשֵׁי פָנֶיךָ יַעֲקֹב סֶלָה׃
So fling wide the gates of his abode,	⁷ שְׂאוּ שְׁעָרִים ׀ רָאשֵׁיכֶם
let those ancient doors be opened up—	וְהִנָּשְׂאוּ פִּתְחֵי עוֹלָם
so that the glorious King may enter there!	וְיָבוֹא מֶלֶךְ הַכָּבוֹד׃
Just who is this glorious King?	⁸ מִי זֶה מֶלֶךְ הַכָּבוֹד
None other than Yahweh, the mighty Warrior;	יְהוָה עִזּוּז וְגִבּוֹר
yes, it is Yahweh, ever victorious in battle!	יְהוָה גִּבּוֹר מִלְחָמָה׃
Quick, fling wide the gates of his abode,	⁹ שְׂאוּ שְׁעָרִים ׀ רָאשֵׁיכֶם
let those ancient doors be opened up—	וּשְׂאוּ פִּתְחֵי עוֹלָם
so that the glorious King may enter there!	וְיָבֹא מֶלֶךְ הַכָּבוֹד׃
I say, who is this glorious King?	¹⁰ מִי הוּא זֶה מֶלֶךְ הַכָּבוֹד
None other than Yahweh, the Commander-in-chief;	יְהוָה צְבָאוֹת
he is our most glorious King! *A-men!*	הוּא מֶלֶךְ הַכָּבוֹד סֶלָה׃

This text is obviously a psalm in *praise* of Yahweh (a 'hymn'), namely, of the *royalty* (kingship) subgroup. It is also *liturgical* (participatory/interactive) in nature, as suggested by its larger patterns of repetition, namely, the *question-answer* format of vv. 3 + 4–6, and the reiterated hortatory strophes of vv. 7–8 + 9–10 (*both BASE [question/appeal]* ➔ *RESPONSE [proclamation] in terms of propositional relations*). This psalm would be most appropriate for use at the onset of a public worship service—whether at the time of David or in the modern day.

A.5 Linguistics

Do a close lexical and syntactic study (via an interlinear text if necessary), e.g., verbal constructions and sequences, word-order variations—topic and focus, specialized/technical vocabulary or morphology, accent/rhythm patterns, non-verbal predications, independent pronouns.

➔ *Do you notice anything **unusual** or **noteworthy** with regard to the vocabulary and grammatical structures of Psalm 24, for example, the marked Hebrew word order in v. 2, or the full pronominal forms in v. 10, and their possible significance in the text?*

- Verse 1b is a *verbless* predication (an acclamation), emphatically leading off with the divine name.

- 1c is a parallel *verbless* utterance with another implied existential predicate ('to be') + ellipsis (to YHWH).

- 2a: *kiy* + the *personal pronoun* again foregrounds 'Yahweh', with additional focus through *constituent fronting* on the locus of his creative activities—the 'seas', which were feared by Israel and regarded as divinities by many early ANE peoples (the constituent focus is reiterated in v. 2b).

- The *verbless* predication of 4a not only makes explicit the answer to the preceding RQs (v. 3), but it also foregrounds the *ethical* qualities (not only the ritual requirements) of the person thus designated as fit for worship (holy in hands and heart!). This same basic structure, coupled with the initial deictic 'this' reinforced by *asyndeton*, is found in v. 6 with corresponding rhetorical effect.

- The *asyndeton* of 5a helps to mark the topical shift from personal characteristics (v. 4) to consequent blessings from Yahweh (v. 5), i.e., *grounds—conclusion* (or: reason—result?).

- Deliberate (or poetic) *ellipsis* (?) in 6a, i.e., 'O [God of] Jacob', marks stanzaic *closure* (B).

- The *asyndeton* of 7a combined with an *imperative* form signals a textual *aperture*.

- *Repetition* of the phrase 'the King of glory' in 7c and 8a foregrounds the referent, which is then specified by the repeated mention of YHWH in 8b and 8c.

- *Asyndeton* and *clause initial* placement in 8b–c further spotlights the divine referent—'Yahweh'!

- The inserted independent *personal pronoun* ('he') in vv. 10a and 10c again serves to draw attention to the referent, 'the King of Glory', who is identified specifically in 10b and 'the LORD of Hosts'; the shortened medial line B is thereby also emphasized.

- The pair of *selah*'s at the end of vv. 6 and 10 further mark these as points of strophic *closure*.

A.6 Disjunction

Posit the major 'break-points' in the text, i.e., where noteworthy shifts of form or content occur—e.g., in time, place, speaker, action type, mood, cast of participants, etc.

→ *Where are the principal* **breaks** *in Psalm 24, and what is the evidence/* **markers** *for each?*

- Stanza/strophe A_1 (v. 1a): the psalm's *title*, followed in 1b by a *verbless clause* and an *initial* reference to YHWH that duplicates the syntactic structure of the first line (the title).

- Stanza B_1 (v. 3a): *shift in topic* (from YHWH to his people)—but *continuity* is also indicated by repeated mention of the divine name *(anaphora);* the RQ acts as a 'leading question', i.e., one that introduces the main topic or theme of the following discourse unit—the attributes of the 'who' being asked about.

- Stanza B_2 (v. 5a): *asyndeton; shift* from specification of character to that of blessing (a weak/minor break); a shift to direct address marks a strong *closure* at 6b (after the psalm's lexical midpoint in 6a).

- Stanza C_1 (v. 7a): *shift in topic* (back from the genuine, sincere worshiper to his/her God—YHWH); *imperative* form—the first in this psalm, plus a *personified vocative* ('you gates' = the people who are fit to dwell in the holy city/place of Yahweh, i.e., those specified in stz. B).

- Stanza C$_2$ (v. 9a): exact *repetition* of v. 7a (*anaphora*).

→ *What is the point and purpose of a paragraph/strophe/stanza break?*

This step is important in terms of demarcating the text's paragraph structure (note the diversity among the standard English versions). This sequence of disjunctions forms an overall [A-B-A'] 'ring structure' in which stanzas A and A' focus on *Yahweh* while B describes *people* who worship him aright.

A.7 Repetition

Plot the patterns of repetition (exact) and recursion (synonymous), both proximate and remote (i.e., near and far 'parallelism').

→ *Do this for Psalm 24, and posit a primary* **structure-functional purpose** *for each of the main sequences and patterns of repetition/recursion that you have identified.*

- The repeated synonymous *constituent focus* (fronted) constructions of 2a-b help (somewhat) to distinguish the *closure* of the psalm's short initial stanza/strophe (A).

- A pair of synonymous RQs (each beginning with 'who?') in 3a-b mark the *onset* of stanza B. They resonate with the non-adjacent reiterated RQs of 8a and 10a, which appear *medially* in strophes C1 and C2.

- Strophes C$_1$ and C$_2$ are almost (but significantly, not quite!) identical (all verses are tri-cola), which suggest that they serve as psalmic 'set pieces' of some sort in a worship liturgy (e.g., leader > choral/congregational response).

A.8 Po-rhetoric

Identify the text's main poetic (artistic) and rhetorical (emotive) features, especially where concentrations or clusters occur (e.g.,

RQs, hyperbole, personification, figurative language, idioms, irony/sarcasm, word-pairs, close reiteration, vocatives, exclamations, sound-plays—puns, alliteration, assonance, etc.).

Psalm 24 is obvious poetry, with many literary (artistic-rhetorical)-structural features that are typical of Hebrew verse forms in general and the psalmic *hymn* genre in particular:

➔ *What important poetic features did you notice in this psalm?*

- Lineal *parallelism* – tight *bi-* and *tri-cola* (vv. 4, 7–10)

- Lexical *balance* – 43 words before/after the significant midpoint in 6a— Yahweh's 'generation' of upright folk (can 'stand' in his holy place!)

- Poetic *word pairs,* e.g., 1 (polemical: earth/world), 5 (a promotional pair: blessing/vindication-deliverance)

- Lexical *repetition* – other than that constituted by parallelism, e.g., (not) 'lift up' [n-s-'] in 4b/5a and 7, 9, thus forming a *cohesive link* between sections B and A'

- *Figurative language,* e.g. 8—metaphor: Yahweh/warrior King, 7/9—*personified apostrophe:* command to the 'heads' to 'lift up the gates'!

- Strophic structure with *refrains,* e.g., 7–8/9–10 (analogous to "A and what's more*, B" parallelism; * 'more' in terms of poetic beauty and intensity)

- Ellipsis/*gapping,* e.g., 1c, 5b

- *Thematic questions* – 'Who...' is God (vv. 8a, 10a – A, A'); who is the God-fearing (wo)man (3a-b – B)? NB: the Q&As of 3/4, 8, 10 *are undoubtedly uttered by different speakers!*

- *Intertextual* (psalmic and historical) and *extratextual* (mythic, royal) *allusions,* e.g., YHWH as the Warrior King, Deliverer of his people (Exod. 15:6–12; 1 Sam. 17:45); paraphrases of precepts of the Mosaic Covenant ('emptiness' v. 4—idolatry, Exod. 20:4; cf. Ps. 73:1, 13; 'generation' v. 6, cf. 73:15). Note also the textually-related *expansion* of B in Psalm 15!

A.8 Po-rhetoric

- *Alliteration/assonance,* e.g., 3b–4, 7/9

- Utterance *rhythm,* e.g., v. 9, with a break in the pattern at 10b with emphasis on YHWH *Tsebaoth* (the 'throne name' of YHWH, cf. Isa. 6:5; Pss. 84:1, 3; 89:5–14)

→ *Find several instances of where these poetic and rhetorical devices tend to co-occur in Psalm 24 and indicate their apparent literary and/or structural functions within their respective cotexts. How does the translation in your language deal with these significant forms? Suggest some improvements.*

These features, especially the clusters, primarily serve to help mark *strophic boundaries* (aperture/closure) and *peak* or *climax,* especially when they co-occur with significant elements of linguistic form (cf. A. 5), e.g., v. 7: asyndeton + imperative + vocative + personification + alliteration. Also note the reduction in literary impact and appeal when these poetic features are removed without replacement (see examples of this in the CEV).

The results of the distinct analyses of each strophe (*combine to form 'stanzas'*) may be then combined in *synthesis* to produce a unified structure for the text as a whole. In this case, the evidence mutually supports the hypothesis of Psalm 24 as consisting of *three stanzas* (A: 1–2, B: 3–6, A': 7–10), in which A and A' have the same theme and purpose (praise Yahweh for his creative greatness and magnificent majesty), while the middle stanza B presents a thematic *counter-point,* i.e., who is worthy enough to worship such a wonderful God—to be citizens of ('stand' in) the Kingdom of the 'glorious King'? (*ANS: those who serve Him with pure hearts and righteous lives, not dishonoring the* LORD *through idolatry or false speaking.*)

Verses 1–2 thus establish a *conceptual frame of reference* for the entire psalm: The focus will be on Yahweh—who he is and what he has done/does. This segment of a 'Creation Hymn' evokes (by *synecdochic* [*part-whole*] association) the entire genre and sets the semantic stage, so to speak, for what follows in the text. This hymn is at once *universal* in scope, but also *individual*/personal in application. Yahweh, the glorious Creator-Warrior of his people [*transcendence*], wants to come close to minister to them [*immanence*] in the twofold blessing of 'deliverance' and 'vindication'. However, 'David' also reminds listeners of their moral and religious responsibility in their Covenantal relationship with the LORD, namely, to 'seek after' Him in purity of heart, life ('hands'), lips (no 'deceit'), and worship (no 'nothingness' – i.e., idolatry!; cf. Ps. 31:7; Jer. 18:5). The relational attributes of a glorious, life-giving God (YHWH) must be duplicated in the characteristics of his holy, life-offering people.

A.9 Discourse

Make a study of principal communicative functions of the text at hand.

This may be carried on in more detailed fashion by means of a speech act analysis (*illocution—locution—perlocution*, i.e., utterance intention—action—result) on the micro-level of *discourse* (the analysis of texts composed largely or entirely of direct speech). Check on the degree to which your functional analysis complements your prior linguistic and literary analyses.

→ *Propose the primary communicative functions of the main structural divisions of Psalm 24, i.e., vv. 1–2, 3–7, and 8–10; give reasons for your analysis. Which is the most important speech act of this psalm, and why do you say so?*

- 1–2: *informative:* a confessional assertion of what Yahweh has done—creation (with *polemical*-imperative undertones: versus Ancient Near Eastern pagan Canaanite cosmology and mythology [the adversarial chaos of 'sea/rivers'])

- 3–6: *imperative:* exhortation to worship Yahweh aright (holy thoughts and lives) plus motivation blessing-vindication—(an implicit *didactic*-informative function in that v. 4b refers to commandments of the Decalogue, namely, 1/2 and 8[9]). Christ may have had v. 4 in mind as he uttered the Beatitudes, especially the key terms "blessing" and "righteousness" (cf. Matt. 5:6, 10).

- 7–10: *expressive:* joyous words of praise for Yahweh, the mighty King of glory!

In terms of specific *speech acts* we observe the following in vv. 4–6: a pastoral *description* of + *exhortation* for Yahweh's people (marked by line-final divine names, word pair involving 'blessings'): interrogation (or attention-getter, 4) + information (identification, 5) + promise (blessings, 6) + confirmation (encouragement, 7). Verse 10 is clearly an act of *proclamation* + *praise*, that is, of the people's Great King Yahweh! (= *the 'macro'-speech act*? – note the formal marking by means of pronouns and the divine name). We also note the complex figurative (metonymic) *communicative cycle* of 7–8 (9–10): 'gates' = gatekeepers = Temple religious ministers of Yahweh (priests/Levites). 'Lift up...' would appear to be words uttered (shouted out?) by the people/pilgrims/worshipers), to which the priests respond, "Who is..."; the people then proclaim the name of the LORD: "YHWH of Armies...glory!"

A.10 Outline

Outline the psalm in terms of its major divisions and topics (theme and parts).

This step helps one to organize the various principal themes in relation to the major structures of a particular book or pericope (note the application to sermon/Bible study).

→ *Evaluate these two outlines of Psalm 24; then make your own alternative proposal (note the relevance for positing a **Section Heading**. Do this in the light of proposed titles such as these: "The Great King" [GNT] and "Who can enter the Lord's Temple?" [CEV]):*

Expository:	Hortatory:
Psalm 24—YAHWEH IS THE KING OF GLORY,	PRAISE YAHWEH THE KING OF GLORY,

With respect to:

A. His overall creation (vv. 1–2); [transcendence]

B. His holy people (vv. 3–6); [obedience]

C. His victorious power (vv. 7–10). [immanence]

On account of:

A. His overall creation (vv. 1–2);

B. His holy people (vv. 3–6);

C. His victorious power (vv. 7–10)!

A.11 Translate

In the light of guidelines 1–10, translate this psalm, whether more or less 'literarily', in view of a particular audience and an appropriate setting of use (to be specified).

The following is a sample Chewa rendition in a poetic *ndakatulo* (expressive lyric, *LiFE*)-style of compositional format, along with a relatively literal English back-translation.

→ *As you read through the text, pick out three form-content features of this poetic translation that you find interesting, or which you would like to query as* to how/why they are used. Perhaps the English is not clear or seems to go too far in comparison with what the original text seems to allow for.

Salmo limeneli n'la Davide mfumu ija.		This psalm is one of David the king.
Chauta ndiye adalenga dziko lapansi	1	Chauta (Yahweh) is the one who created the earth
pamodzi n'zonse zam'menemo, inde,		along with everything in it, yes indeed,
anthu onse okhalamo nawonso ndi ake.		all those who live in it are his as well.
Ndiye amene adaika dzikoli pa nyanja	2	He's the one who set that earth upon the sea,
adalikhazika pamtsinje wozama ndithu.		he established it upon the very deep river surely.
Ndani kodi angalimbe mtima kukwera,	3	Just who can get up the courage to climb up,
kufika paphiri la Chauta, m'malo oyera,		to reach the peak of Chauta, the holy place,
ndikumupembedza moyenera kumeneko?		and to worship him properly there?
Ndi amene amachita zabwinotu m'manja,	4	It is someone who does good deeds with his hands,
amene amaganiza zoyera zokha m'mtima.		who thinks only pure things in his heart.
Ndiye amene sakonda kulingalira zoipa;		It is the person who doesn't like to ponder evil;
sanama kapenanso kulumbira monyenga.		he does not lie nor does he swear falsely.
Zoonadi, iyeyo adzalandiradi madalitso,	5	To be sure, that one will really receive blessings,
inde, mphatso kwa Chauta Mpulumutsi.		yes, gifts from Chauta the Savior.
Mulungu mwini ndiye adzamuteteza,		God himself will defend him,
adzagamula kuti alibe mlandu uliwonse.		He will judge him to be without any case to answer.
Anthu otere ndiwo amafunitsitsa Chauta,	6	All such folk are the ones who seek after Chauta,
amadzam'pembedza Mulungu wa Yakobe.	7	they always come to worship the God of Jacob.
Choncho, kankhani zipata zamzinda wake;		So then, push open the gates of his city;
nonsenu, tsekulani zitseko zake zolimbazo,		all of you, open those mighty doors of his
kuti Mfumu yaulemerero wonse iloŵemo.		so that the King of all glory might enter inside.
Nanga Mfumu yaulemereroyo ndi yani?	8	Now who is that glorious King?
Palibe wina wanyonga ndi wamphamvu,		There's no one else so strong and powerful,
koma Chauta ngwazi wathu ndiye amene!		except Chauta, our mighty warrior, he's the one!
Inu nonse, kankhani zipata za mzindawo,	9	All of you, push open the gates of that city,
zitseko zimenezo zikhale zotseguka tseku!		Let those mighty doors be open—wiide!
kuti Mfumu yaulemerero wonse iloŵedi.		so that the most glorious King should enter.
Nanga Mfumu yaulemereroyo ndi yani?	10	Well, just who is that glorious King?
Ndi Chauta Mphambe wamphamvuzonse.		He is Chauta of Storms all-powerful.
Ndiye Mfumu yaulemerero wamuyayaya!		He is the King of glory—the everlasting one!

→ *How then do major English translations, past and present, fare in reproducing the dynamic poetry (the 'glories') of the Hebrew original? Evaluate the versions*

A.11 Translate

that you read through in step 1 and rate them poetically. Which is the most/least poetic and why [give reasons]?

➜ *Do you know of any literary or poetic translations in languages other than English? If so, briefly describe this version and why you consider it to be poetic.*

Competent, well-trained translators can (should?) be able to do better in their effort to convey or reproduce the memorable compositional manner and message of the poetry of Scripture. We also need to remember that the biblical text must be *understandable* to and *appreciated* by the target audience not only via the medium of *print* alone, but also through the dynamics of *sound*. Was not Psalm 24, for example, composed to be recited or sung in the first instance? If this is true (the assertion may be debated), what are the practical implications for Bible translators today?

➜ *Now prepare your own literary rendition of Psalm 24 (as a 'lovely lyric'), either in English or some other TL that you are familiar with (in the latter case, give a back-translation as above). Point out three of the significant features that manifest the dynamic poetic quality of your translation.*

(If possible [the ideal goal!], compose a singable or recitable version that you might perform for the class. Perhaps only one stanza will be possible in the time available.)

Furthermore, with regard to the overall meaning of this psalm, we must also ask ourselves: can the significance of the biblical poet's theological message and communicative purpose be sufficiently understood on the basis of the translation alone, that is, without a supplied *cognitive context* (frame of reference) which can facilitate its interpretation?

➜ *Pick out two aspects of Psalm 24 relating to its form and/or meaning that would benefit from a **descriptive-explanatory footnote**—and then compose what you would regard to be suitable samples in English for a particular audience/setting (to be specified).*

- For example: with respect to ANE mythology/cosmology and view of the world in vv. 1–2, or the pilgrim/entrance liturgy in vv. 7–10.

A.12 Test

Test and critically evaluate your draft translation on the basis of specific target audience responses and a directive, feature-oriented questionnaire.

➔ *What methods have you used to test a translation of yours, especially a poetic one? (If you have never done this before, what would you suggest as possibilities in this regard?)*

➔ *Next, study, apply, and critically evaluate—that is, with a view toward improvement—the following methodology (based on Wendland 1985); the latter may then be compared with the more elaborate model proposed in the introduction to chapter 8.*

We may distinguish four key criteria of *quality*, two that have to do with the *source* language and two that have to do with the *target* language (ranked in rough order below):

1. **Fidelity** (with a focus on the *meaning* of the SL text): A Bible translation should accurately transmit what we presume (based on a thorough prior text analysis) that the original author intended to communicate to his readers/hearers. This includes emotive impact/response as well as content.

2. **Intelligibility** (with a focus on *meaningfulness* of the TL text): The original message must be conveyed in such a way that it is understandable to the average person, without causing undue difficulty or confusion with regard to its style and diction.

3. **Naturalness** (with a focus on the *naturalness* of the TL text): Ideally, the translated text should not sound like a translation, like a foreign document (except for certain aspects of its content). Whenever possible, it should be idiomatic, relatively easy to read, well-sounding in the vernacular, and manifesting language that is as *beautiful* and *powerful* as that of the original text.

4. **Closeness** (with a focus on the *form* of the SL text): It is important to remain faithful, that is, as proximate as possible to the historical context and culture of the Bible, in one way or another, i.e., either within the translation itself or through the use of supplementary helps like footnotes (note that a literal rendering may turn out to be more idiomatic in the TL).

A.12 Test

Focus	Meaning			Form
Source language	fidelity	1	4	closeness
Target language	intelligibility	2 →	3	naturalness

(arrows: 1↓2, 2→3, 3↑4)

No single factor can be considered in isolation. Thus, where any two of these criteria are in conflict, SL text *fidelity* is of utmost importance, followed by *intelligibility*; *naturalness* in the TL takes the third place, and last, but not least (nor to be ignored) comes *closeness*. The overall aim is to produce a translation that is *acceptable* in all relevant respects by the intended target group and one that will be readily, even eagerly, used—ideally *sung!*—by them.

→ *How would you propose testing your translation draft with respect to these four criteria? Suggest a practical methodology to try out in the field, including a critique of the approach suggested above.*

→ *Having completed your analysis and translation of Psalm 24, do you think that any procedural step has been overlooked or not specified clearly enough in the guidelines suggested above? If so, feel free to contribute your additions, corrections, or proposed modifications.*

→ *What are the main translation PPPs (potential problem points) that you noted in Psalm 24? List three of these and suggest how you would propose resolving these in YL.*

- E.g., "LORD of Hosts"—"climb YHWH's hill"—"lift up the *nephesh* to"—"clean hands"—"seek your face"— "*selah*"— "generation"? How about the Q&A structure involving different speakers?

→ *Do you agree with critical comments that accompany (in parentheses) the following CEV's rendering of Psalm 24? You may correct these as well as proposing your own improvements to this translation (through v. 10).*

Who Can Enter // the [Lord]'s Temple? (CEV) *(shifts the main focus of the Psalm—away from Yahweh)*

APPENDIX A

1 The earth and everything on it,   *(this first sentence is very prose-sounding, not at all 'poetic'!)*
including its people,
belong to the [Lord].

The world and its people   *(repetitious without enough poetic variation)*
belong to him.

2 The [Lord] placed it all   *(rather awkward in style)*
on the oceans and rivers.   *(a reduction—two poetic lines collapsed into one)*

3 Who may climb the [Lord]'s hill [a]   *(difficult to understand the intended meaning)*
or stand in his holy temple?   *(why just "stand" there—what's the point?)*

4 Only those who do right
for the right reasons,   *(unclear—too ambiguous/prosaic expression—what about*
and don't worship idols   *the "heart" attitude?)*
or tell lies under oath.

5 The [Lord] God, who saves them,   *(poetic lines [form], but not poetic expression! dramatic*
will bless and reward them,   *direct speech removed!)*

6 because they worship and serve   *(the sentence length is prosaic; in poetry each verse should*
the God of Jacob.[b]   *be a complete utterance)*

7 Open the ancient gates,   *(a stanza break is missed—is this a mistake in the published*
so that the glorious king   *format?)*
may come in.

8 Who is this glorious king?   *(it might be more effective to compose the response portion*
He is our [Lord], a strong   *of this verse in the form of two predications: 'He is our*
and mighty warrior.   *[Lord]; he is a strong and mghty warrior')*

9 Open the ancient gates,

so that the glorious king
may come in.

10 Who is this glorious king?
He is our [Lord],
the All-Powerful!   *(clarify the reference: 'our All-Powerful God')*

A.12 Test

*24.1 1 Cor. 10:26.
*24.4 Matt. 5:8.
[a]24.3 *the [Lord]'s hill:* The hill in Jerusalem where the temple was built.
[b]24.6 *worship...Jacob:* Two ancient translations; Hebrew "worship God and serve the descendants of Jacob."

→ *Have a class discussion on the application of a LiFE-approach to translating Psalm 24 (or any of the lyric texts in this book) in your language. What were your main challenges—your successes—your failures? What needs to be done to promote such a literary/oratorical style of translating in your translation team—or among the constituency for whom you are translating?*

→ *Finally, having carefully examined Psalm 24 inside and out, as it were, how would you react to the following assertion regarding Psalm 24:7–10: "[It is] a fragment or remnant of a descent myth—a myth in which a high god, forsaking his ordinary domain, descends to the netherworld, where he must confront the demonic forces of the infernal realm"?*[1] *What arguments for or against this interpretation can you think of? Does this make any difference with regard to the translation of this psalm? [Discussion question]*

---

[1] A. Cooper 1983:43.

APPENDIX B

Preparing a *LiFE* Translation

In this appendix I present a brief motivation and definition for the concept of a literary functional equivalence translation (*LiFE*, cf. Wendland 2004b, 2011). This is a version that embodies the attempt to textually represent more of the artistic and rhetorical—indeed also the lyric—qualities of the biblical text by making a fuller use of the equivalent features of another language, whether in written, oral, and/or visual form.[1]

B.1 Motivation for a literary (oratorical) translation

As noted earlier, an increasing number of studies have drawn attention to many significant aspects of the literary character that the Scriptures, at least certain well-studied books or pericopes, clearly demonstrate.[2] We find in a book like Genesis or John, for example, numerous expertly interwoven genres and literary sub-types; intricate patterns of formal and semantic recursion that permeate the discourse along multiple conceptual

---

[1] This point is discussed in G. Toury (1995:168). Toury also notes the significant ambiguity that is inherent in the designation "literary translation"—that is, *literary* with reference to the quality of the original text (e.g., the Scriptures) and/or to the particular translation of a given source text, whether the latter happens to be regarded as literary in character or not according to the normal standards of artistic excellence (ibid., 168). I am arguing for an application of 'literary' to both—to an analysis of the source text and also to its rendering in a target language.

[2] The following comments by Keefer with reference to the New Testament apply equally well to the Old (2008:2, 7): "A literary approach to the New Testament assumes that the documents found here not only convey ideas but also entertain, prod, puzzle, and delight audiences. Even for readers not religiously bound to the New Testament, the artistry of the New Testament can prove engaging and provocative. Reading the New Testament as literature brings to light the dynamics of this engagement. Whereas religious interpreters of these scriptures, driven by a desire to find moral or theological content, might overlook the aesthetic experience of the reader, literary interpretation foregrounds this experience.... Too often the New Testament's writings are similarly assumed to have simplistic meanings. Literary readings awaken us to the intricacies of the language that makes up the New Testament....A literary reading of the New Testament allows readers to understand content through close engagement with form." *Form has meaning*, and this is as true for *literary* form as it is for *linguistic* form, for the former is inevitably created from the latter. Thus, discovering these literary (artistic and rhetorical) 'intricacies of the language' of biblical texts often leads analysts/exegetes to additional dimensions and facets of meaning—connotative as well as denotative—which they had hitherto not been aware of.

planes; elaborate image sets that are often related in intricate semantic sequences; a great density of figurative, symbolic, and multi-referential language; many passages that are audibly shaped by sound (orality) so as to appeal to a listening audience; a preference for dramatic direct speech; and significant citations of, allusions to, or topical developments of earlier biblical texts. Finally, the Bible frequently manifests emotive, highly evocative discourse, coupled with a forceful rhetorical mode of challenging, even provoking readers and hearers alike with a vital *promissory*, life-death moral and theological message of utmost relevance both in the here-and-now and beyond the grave.[3] In short, many detailed stylistic and structural analyses in recent years have convinced scholars that instances of excellent literature in the Scriptures are the rule rather than isolated exceptions.[4] Just take an unfamiliar passage, examine it carefully with a keen literary-linguistic eye, and you will probably be amazed at what you find hidden beneath the surface of the text.

Thus, whether the language is Hebrew or Greek, the diverse pericopes of the Bible, over and above their obvious religious and moral content, appear to manifest a level of compositional excellence that is exceptional with regard to the macrostructure and also the microstructure of discourse organization. Such high quality is clearly demonstrated in more texts than most people realize, from the skillful selection and combination of complete literary genres within a certain book to the integrated usage within individual verses of literary features such as figurative language, varied syntactic arrangements, tropes based on repetition, rhetorical features such as deliberate questions, irony, and hyperbole—any or all these being frequently highlighted by diverse phonesthetic combinations. This claim may be supported whether one analyzes the discourse from an Ancient Near Eastern perspective (Semitic, rabbinic, Greco-Roman, or all three stylistic influences in the case of many NT texts) or any of the modern

---

[3] Thiselton cogently argues for the prominence of the speech act of promising in biblical writings (1999:231–239), for example: "*[P]romise provides a paradigm case of how language can transform the world of reality*" (ibid., 238, author's italics).

[4] For a varied sample of such recent studies, see Breck 1994, Dorsey 1999, Harvey 1998, and Wilson 1997. It may be noted that critics who make a positive assessment of the literary quality of biblical literature, either as a whole or with regard to specific books, tend to adopt a broader perspective on the original text. They thus carefully consider the larger discourse organization rather than just the surface linguistic structure, for example Dewey (1980:29–39) versus Turner (1976:11–44) concerning the gospel of Mark. Even such unlikely books as Leviticus and Numbers have been convincingly shown to manifest a literary character (cf. Douglas 1999, 1993). An entire series of scholarly commentaries, i.e., *Berit Olam,* has been commissioned with the aim of drawing out the literary dimension of the Hebrew Bible, e.g., Sherwood 2002.

B.1 Motivation for a literary (oratorical) translation

literary approaches (e.g., 'close-reading', structuralist, semiotic, Russian Formalist, cognitive poetics, or 'new rhetoric').

Since various texts of the Bible arguably *do* demonstrate, by and large, a high literary standard,[5] they require a correspondingly high quality of translation to maintain a relative balance in terms of functional equivalence, communicative effectiveness, or more specifically, rhetorical power and aesthetic parity.[6] In other words, the very literary nature of the original text challenges translators to at least attempt to reproduce or match this given level of stylistic *excellence* in their vernacular, to the extent that this is possible—that is, in view of their particular level of education, competence, experience, and commitment as well as the encouragement and support provided by their translation administrative committee. To do any less would represent a considerable *reduction* in the overall communicative value of the translation in relation to the original SL text. Thus the attempt to produce a mellifluous and moving poetic rendering of at least certain portions of the Scriptures—those of undeniable literary quality to begin with—would seem to be justified, as long as there is a desirous and eager consumer constituency that is either calling for such a translation, or who research suggests would presumably benefit from one.[7]

---

[5] I discuss this issue further in 'A literary approach to biblical text analysis and translation' (Wilt, ed., ch. 6) and in Wendland 2004b. Several recent extensive studies support this conclusion, for example, with regard to the Old Testament, see Dorsey 1999; for the New Testament, see Davis 1999.

[6] Regarding the translation goal of functional equivalence, de Waard and Nida state: "The translator must seek to employ a functionally equivalent set of forms which in so far as possible will match the meaning of the original source-language text" (1986:36). Meaning is not only informative in function; it is also expressive and affective in nature. Concerning translational effectiveness, Hatim and Mason propose that "one might define the task of the translator as a communicator as being one of seeking to maintain **coherence** by striking the appropriate balance between what is **effective** (will achieve its communicative goal) and what is **efficient** (will prove least taxing on users' cognitive resources) in a particular environment, for a particular purpose and for particular receivers" (1997:12).

[7] The sort of rendition that I am proposing here would be classified as a "homologous" translation by C. Nord in her helpful overview of functional approaches to translation. She defines this as a version in which "the *tertium comparationis* between the source and the target text is a certain status within a corpus or system, mostly with respect to literary or poetic texts" (1997:52). This translation technique, the ultimate in linguistic 'domestication', is also known in secular circles as "semiotic transformation" (Ludskanov) or "creative transposition" (Jakobson).

B.2 The oral-aural factor and an oratorical version

What exactly is a 'literary' translation then, and how does it differ from other meaning-oriented renditions, common language (CL) and popular language (PL) versions in particular? Wonderly broadly defines such literary translations as follows (Wonderly 1968:30):

> These are fully contemporary, are oriented to the general public (not just the Christian in-group), and vary from regular to formal in their [*sociolinguistic*] functional variety. They make free use of all the resources of the language at all levels which are considered acceptable for published materials, and are thereby not intended to be fully accessible to the uneducated reader.

Obviously a literary version as defined above can be produced only in a linguistic community that possesses a relatively long tradition of recognized *written* literature. Its envisioned constituency, or target group, would be people who are comparatively well-educated, widely-read, and who enjoy the challenge of wrestling with the full range of lexical, grammatical, stylistic, and rhetorical usage in the particular language and society concerned.[8]

Does anything correspond to a 'literary text' in the case of a language group that does not have such a long or strong tradition of literature and whose members communicate predominantly by oral-aural means?[9] This situation would characterize most societies in Bantu Africa as well as in many other regions of the world. In such cases, the closest equivalent might be termed an oratorical text—that is, oral discourse that makes use of the complete range of genres and styles in the spoken language to convey a message that is widely regarded by listeners as being impressive, eloquent, persuasive, and beautiful. Such semiformal, oral-rhetorical usage would exclude youthful jargon, clichés, and foreign-based colloquialisms (e.g., English borrowings and calques), on the one hand, and widely unintelligible archaisms or specialist in-group technical argot on the other (e.g., vocabulary pertaining to specific occupations or activities like hunting, fishing, house-building, herbalistic medicine, traditional initiation ceremonies, or ancient religious practices).

---

[8] A 'literary' translation is not necessarily the same as a 'liturgical' version, although the two types are sometimes confused. A liturgical Bible is often quite traditional and literal in nature, hence not literary at all according to natural TL verbal norms—although it may be regarded as being so as a result of long usage and 'official' promotion by the user churches.

[9] The term לְשׁוֹנִי 'my tongue' (Ps. 45:2) introduces the crucial oral-aural aspect of the message that we both read (in the original) and translate.

B.2 The oral-aural factor and an oratorical version

Nowadays, such an oratorical style is manifested in the main by popular public speakers and radio broadcasters, including skillful oral performers of ancient verbal art forms as well as Christian evangelists and revivalists.[10] Thus many recognized models of excellent oratory style do exist; however, these must be carefully collected (often by recording, hence requiring transcription), analyzed, and published (or broadcast) for standards of assessment to develop to the point where they may be effectively applied in written literature. Of course, the medium of print itself requires certain compositional modifications to be made to any published text, for example, less overt repetition, a more explicit expression of content (to counteract the lack of a situational context), compensation for suprasegmental, intonational, and elocutionary (phonological) significance (e.g., the use of commas or dashes to represent dramatic pauses), more precise conjunctive and transitional devices (function words), and a lower incidence of informal or colloquial diction.[11]

The use of these oral models and stylistic techniques is particularly appropriate for translations of the Bible, which are much more frequently accessed by the ear than the eye.[12] Furthermore, recent research has tended to confirm the hypothesis that the various documents of the Scriptures were in large measure composed aloud and/or were written down with the oral-aural transmission and reception of their message immediately in mind.[13] Consequently, "[s]ince the acts of both writing and reading were

---

[10] I present the results of an extensive study of an outstanding representative of the revivalists in Wendland 2000. Some politicians too are good orators, but their topical repertory tends to be quite limited and focused on issues of government policies, social welfare, and economic development.

[11] Compare the set of audio-oriented features noted in the study of Sundersingh (1999:170). I would strongly support Sundersingh's appeal that "[t]he media scene of today's world demands that we be sensitive to the needs of non-literates and non-readers [these two categories overlap, but are not the same] by way of providing them with biblical [i.e., faithfully rendered] Scriptures in media [and *modes,* i.e., distinct verbal styles or varieties] other than print" (ibid., 315; the comments in brackets are my own).

[12] The preface to the *Contemporary English Version* states this point well: "Languages are spoken before they are written. And far more communication is done through the spoken word than through the written word. In fact, more people hear the Bible than read it for themselves. Traditional translations of the Bible count on the *reader's* ability to understand a *written* text. But the *Contemporary English Version* differs from all other English Bibles—past and present—in that it takes into consideration the needs of the *hearer*, as well as those of the reader, who may not be familiar with traditional biblical language" (American Bible Society 1995; original *italics*). This final claim concerning its uniqueness may be somewhat of an overstatement, but for our purposes the point is simply this: An *oratorical* version is meant primarily to be *orally* read, to be clearly understood *aurally,* and to make its artistic-emotive impression upon an audience through the message as it is being *heard* by them.

[13] For further details, see, for example, Achtemeier 1990; Sundersingh 1999:6; Wendland 2008b:ch. 1. Recent research confirms the presence of writing at an early date in Israel's his-

normally accompanied by vocalization, the structure [and style] of [the] text was marked by aural rather than visual indicators."[14] This fact (assumed here to be true) has important implications for both the analysis as well as the ongoing transmission of the biblical text via translation. For one thing, such prominent sonic stylistic and structural indicators—the rhythmic dimension of discourse, including its characteristic aural 'punctuation' devices—need to be reproduced by means of functionally equivalent techniques in a translation.[15] This 'oral-elocutionary' envelope of meaning is a particularly important consideration in the case of any specifically designed oratorical version, which is primarily *meant to be uttered aloud and heard* rather than read silently to oneself.[16]

However, a possible objection to an oratorical, or indeed, even a general literary, translation needs to be considered. This concerns the validity of applying the results of a close stylistic comparison and evaluation of the original texts of Scripture to a contemporary Bible translation. Thus, one might question whether utilizing an artistic-rhetorical manner of composition in the TL text constitutes a distortion of—in this case, an intentional 'improvement' upon—the supposed vernacular common-language, or *koine,* style of the New Testament documents.[17] Are we in danger here of

---

tory—in fact, earlier than previously thought: "Scientists have discovered the earliest known Hebrew writing - an inscription dating from the 10th century B.C., during the period of King David's reign....'It indicates that the Kingdom of Israel already existed in the 10th century BCE and that at least some of the biblical texts were written hundreds of years before the dates presented in current research,' said Gershon Galil, a professor of Biblical Studies at the University of Haifa in Israel, who deciphered the ancient text" (Moskowitz 2010).

[14] Davis 1999:11. Similarly, concerning the Old Testament, Dorsey writes: "[A]ncient texts were written primarily to be heard, not seen. Texts were normally intended to be read aloud....To study structure in the Hebrew Bible, then, requires paying serious attention to verbal structure indicators..." (1999:16). Such 'aural indicators' would include features such as: rhythmic lineation, phonic accentuation, verbal patterning, prominent discourse demarcative devices, lexical recursion, direct speech, graphic diction, oral emphasizers, and vivid imagery (to promote topical-thematic recall).

[15] This point needs to be emphasized in the production of any type of translation, no matter what the setting or *Skopos*. Perhaps I have not made this clear enough in past writings, thus leading to criticism such as the following: "Despite the advantages of *LiFE*, it is limited because its approach focuses on the literary features of language and possesses several communication possibilities for 'particular audience subgroups in specific situations or special settings.' Therefore, it may be unacceptable in a public worship service with a general liturgical purpose" (Cho 2009:80). A *LiFE* approach applies to oral literature (or orature) just as much as it does to written/printed literature, although different analysis techniques must be applied and different results are to be expected. Such investigations of an oral style would very likely be applicable to a translation that is intended for public worship, e.g., to encourage the fluent, rhythmic articulation of a communally recited liturgy.

[16] For a study of the elaborate sound patterning to be found in an apparently prosaic text (John 17), see Wendland 1994b.

[17] A stylistic assessment of the Hebrew Scriptures is of course more difficult to make due

B.2 The oral-aural factor and an oratorical version

over-translation? In other words, even if the biblical books themselves can be shown to be highly literary (or oratorical) in nature—that is, of recognizable and demonstrable excellence with respect to their compositional and rhetorical quality—to what extent are we justified in the attempt to reproduce this level of excellence in a translation? Obviously, we do not want to overdo a translation simply for the sake of artistry, but to provide convincing answers to detailed questions of procedure would require more extensive research and testing than the various Chewa and Tonga case studies presented in this monograph.[18] I am not proposing a literary version as the *ideal* model to follow; it is only one method among many. My point is simply to give due consideration to such aspects of discourse, if they are clearly seen in the biblical text. The overall context of use is the crucial determining factor. Thus, it is important to remember that all these issues pertaining to the stylistic nature of a given translation must be considered in relation to a specific biblical text, a particular communicative goal, and the primary target-language setting.

My major premise is that a well-prepared *functionally equivalent* translation of the Bible will normally turn out to be a recognized *literary* text in the target language, whether on the elaborated 'high', or formal, level of discourse style or on a more common level of linguistic sophistication. In short, a literary translation might be characterized as being a stylistically extended or embellished *popular language* version. Thus, if the original has been determined to be literature (and different degrees of artistic and rhetorical quality may be recognized with respect to the various books), then its corresponding interlingual reproduction should be similarly regarded, in accordance with recognized standards of verbal excellence in the vernacular. A certain amount of formal correspondence with the original text will probably (but not inevitably) be lost in this effort to gain "pragmatic resemblance—a [perceptible] similarity of communicative functions" (de Beaugrande 1968:94). But the goal is to attain a high degree of situational 'relevance' for the intended audience by means of this emphasis upon artful text reconstruction in the vernacular.[19]

---

to the limited corpus of texts, religious or secular, on the basis of which an adequate analytical comparison may be made (even in cognate literatures). However, the diversity and abundance of 'universal' literary features present in many Old Testament passages greatly reduces the doubt concerning this issue.

[18] More discussion and exemplification may be found in Wendland 2008b and 2009.

[19] As already noted, 'relevance' refers to a balanced, situationally determined appropriateness with respect to *efficiency* (the least conceptual processing effort) on the one hand and *effectiveness* (the greatest cognitive gain or communicative impact) on the other. The so-called 'principle of relevance' is variously treated in different theories of translation. For some (e.g., Gutt 1992:24–25), it is the only theoretical concept and guideline that is neces-

B.3 Method for discovering 'lovely lyrics' in the vernacular

At some point, the question arises: how does one go about discovering a vernacular model (or models for different genres) that may then be employed, perhaps in adapted form, when translating the varied literature of the Scriptures? Since I have dealt with this subject in detail elsewhere (Wendland 1993:ch.3; Zogbo and Wendland 2000:ch.4; cf. also Boerger), I will present a brief summary here of a *comparative method* that one might apply in order to accomplish this objective. It consists of the following seven steps.

- First of all, a competent research and testing team needs to be selected and trained for the task, namely, how to discover and collect a suitable corpus of sample texts in the target language (TL) for the purposes of analysis and evaluation.

- As many TL texts as possible, representing a broad diversity of oral and written (if available) genres, should be collected, accurately transcribed (using a standard format), and then categorized in such a way that they can be easily accessed and conveniently referred to.

- Next all the documented texts need to closely analyzed with respect to the various genre-specific structural and stylistic features that they manifest, and once the principal features have been identified, the examples need to be gathered together for subsequent comparative assessment.

- The various features gathered in the preceding steps must now be evaluated for excellence with a view towards rating different examples in terms of their relative quality (i.e., artistic beauty/ appeal and rhetorical power/impact) and pragmatic function (e.g., as genre and structural markers, emphasizers/intensifiers, conveyors of diverse emotions and personal attitudes).

- The assortment of structural and stylistic features determined in the TL must then be compared with the closest corresponding Hebrew counterparts (which presupposes that these have already

---

sary; for others (e.g., Hatim and Mason 1990:93–95), it forms just part of a much wider text and context-based, sociolinguistic model of interlingual communication (for more on this well-known 'minimax concept,' see de Beaugrande and Dressler 1981:11; Fawcett 1997:12).

been identified) in order to find the closest possible form-functional 'matches' for use in translation work.

- The inventory of potential TL features that have been identified and classified (as above) should then be applied when rendering a particular biblical text—if possible, by a translator (or designated stylist) who is an expert in terms of communicating effectively in her/his mother-tongue.

- Finally, as always, the translated draft must be carefully and thoroughly tested on its primary intended audience (and revised wherever necessary)—not only with regard to the accurate expression of content, but also with respect to the clarity, naturalness, and idiomacity (liveliness and loveliness) of the language.

These guidelines may be modified as needed in order to accomplish the goal of discovering an adequate range of TL models for use in translating the diverse genres and styles of biblical literature.

B.4 Organizing a literary translation project

I will assume here that a certain translation project job commission (*brief*) has made the joint decision to include within its major communicative purpose (*Skopos*) the aim of producing a lyric literary functional equivalent (*LiFE*) version for an entire poetic book, such as the Psalms (cf. Wendland 2004b:25–27). What then are some of the chief obstacles or challenges that face those who are commissioned with the task of carrying out this objective? The following is a summary of the most relevant factors, many of which have already been mentioned or alluded to in the preceding discussion.

B.4.1 Need for sufficient pre-project planning and research

This crucial first step in the process of planning an efficient and effective translation project is frequently overlooked or ignored in the rush to get things underway. In the past, such neglect was perhaps understandable since many planners felt that there were only two major alternatives—namely, a version that is either relatively literal or dynamically idiomatic in nature. It was further assumed that they, as church leaders, were in the best position to make a choice on behalf of the entire TL group. As suggested above, however, this is not the case nowadays; there are always several translation possibilities to choose from, depending on current resources or limitations (ecumenical, financial, temporal, educational, staff-related, pre-existing versions, etc.) as well as the expressed needs of the primary audience.

Research within the intended audience needs special emphasis. For far too long now, Scripture translators and publishers seem to have been focused on their own preferences and opinions and consequently know relatively little about the people whom they have been commissioned to serve with their skills. Many questions need to be answered *before* a project gets underway: What do ordinary Bible users wish to see, or hear, in a translation that is meant for them? Do they even realize what the full range of options is in this regard, that is, the auxiliary resources that can be made readily available in a modern publication, e.g., illustrations, footnotes, introductions, cross-references, a concordance or glossary, and so forth? Would they prefer the text in written or audio form, in which style or format of presentation—and why? These and many similar queries can be reliably answered only in one way, that is, by actually asking those for whom the translation is intended by means of a systematic, comprehensive, and widespread program of prior market research.

B.4.2 Selecting and training the translation team

I consider this to be the most important limiting or enabling factor in the preparation of any literary translation. If at least one member of the team of (usually) three persons does not have the gift of artistic composition, in an oral or written mode, then the project will not really make much progress, no matter how many other supporting resources are available. Furthermore, in my experience at least, for a genuinely literary, say a poetic, version to succeed, it must first be composed with the genre-based and related artistic essentials already in place—as opposed to being subsequently pasted together like patchwork on to some mediocre text by a designated 'stylist'. The lyric foundation has to be firmly laid and fully apparent in the initial draft, which can then be either corrected exegetically, if need be, or polished up stylistically.

How does one go about finding an individual with the requisite spiritual empathy and artistic talents to do an acceptable job when composing a text of Scripture? As part of the pre-project investigations, a search could simultaneously be made for a competent team of three—that is, the literary drafter, the exegete, and a capable reviser/tester/research-resource person. Perhaps an initial trial workshop will have to be conducted with the specific aim of identifying these diversely qualified team members. Once chosen, they will also have to be provided with the necessary specialized education and training in any areas where they may be deficient—for instance, the artist in exegetical skills, the exegete in literary-orality skills, and the researcher in the skill of valid audience sampling procedures. All this preparation is essential (and it may well take some time) to insure that the most competent and capable group of translators is assembled for so rigorous and demanding an assignment as interlingual, cross-cultural, religious communication.

A similar, but much less extensive course of instruction will also have to be offered to those who have been selected to serve as 'reviewers' of the translation—with respect to either the text as a whole or only specific aspects of it (e.g., poetic features, exegetical accuracy, key theological vocabulary, extratextual supplements, dialectal variations). If reviewers have not been well prepared to appreciate how and why the drafts that they will be examining differ from a more literal rendering and why they must be tested orally, they may be inclined to use the very features that make a text literary (or oratorical) in their language as evidence in criticism against it.

B.4.3 Composition-translation procedures

Once the human resources team has been assembled, they must meet together to agree upon, or be guided into approving, a complete set of practical operational procedures. These need to be considered and established in keeping with the wider project purpose (*Skopos*), and the detailed translation principles and procedures that arise from this communicative goal. An excellent team of individuals that lacks an adequate working plan whereby they can mutually stimulate, correct, complement, and encourage one another will not function very well in practice, if at all. In fact, if they cannot learn to cooperate, they may only interact to frustrate, even infuriate each other and thus hinder or, worse, undo the entire enterprise.

Therefore, the team or perhaps its appointed coordinator, working in close conjunction with an experienced translation consultant and a competent administrative committee representing the target community, must sit together to formulate detailed job descriptions and guidelines for all team members. These may have to be periodically revised and elaborated upon as the project proceeds in order to meet new exigencies, needs, goals, potentials, or obstacles—but always on the basis of mutual agreement and consensus. Such principles and procedures will also have to be fully communicated to all chief reviewers as well as leading project supporters in order to make sure that they clearly understand what is going on and have a chance to contribute in some way to the larger cooperative effort. In addition, the wider community too will need to be kept informed of where the work stands at any given moment, and how well the project is performing with regard to successfully fulfilling the terms of its guiding *Skopos* statement.

B.4.4 Evaluating and testing the translation

The translation team itself, together with selected reviewers or review teams, will naturally carefully monitor and continually assess the quality (and quantity) of work that is being done. However, at a relatively early stage various representatives of the TL community will also have to be actively involved in order to gauge their popular reaction and response to what is probably a novel type of Scripture translation in their setting. This must of course be done with the version's primary setting of use in mind—whether more or less formal (e.g., public worship or private devotions). In any case, the primary mode of testing (and associated evaluation) must be oral-aural in nature, with presenters previously trained in such elocutionary skills. Does the current text then meet the target community's desires and expectations, as expressed in the project *Skopos* (which they are all hopefully quite familiar with)? Does the translation as it stands satisfy their criteria and standards with regard to acceptable literary (or oratorical) style and linguistic usage? If not, what textual changes or alterations can be suggested—which, if widespread, may necessitate in turn certain modifications in the team's translation principles and working procedures?

The need for text-related testing does not end once a particular version has been published. A general or more focused program of evaluation must be continued, now in relation to the TL population as a whole and wider usage within a diverse range of religious settings. To what extent does a specifically poetic-lyric translation meet particular needs and satisfy smaller sub-groups of Bible users (e.g., youth choirs, revival crusades, radio broadcasts, dramatic performances, comic book publications, and so forth)? On the other hand, do strong public reactions suggest any revisions that need to be made in the event that a second edition becomes feasible? Obviously such testing work needs to be coordinated by some responsible and broadly acceptable agency (e.g., the national Bible Society, the regional Christian Council), while the results of such research must be properly documented and saved for possible future use in a new publication.

B.4.5 Encouraging personal/popular involvement

As noted throughout this appendix, a recent development in modern translation theory (e.g., dynamic equivalence, reception criticism, relevance theory, frames of reference, etc.) has been a special emphasis upon the hermeneutical and applicatory activity of the target (respondent) group for whom a particular version has been prepared.[20] Without repeating myself, I might point out two additional aspects of this vital community-based involvement in Bible translation, with specific reference to a nontraditional (poetic) rendition of a given book, like the Psalter, or an individual well-known pericope, such as Psalm 24 (see appendix A). These involve two distinct perspectives or orientations—subjective and objective.

B.4.5.1 Subjective: management—support—usage

The widely used technical term 'receptors' (UBS in particular) is rather misleading with regard to the actual dynamics of any effort that is intended to translate the Scriptures into one of the estimated 7,000 world languages, whether this happens to be large (international) or small (provincial) in terms of geographical range and number of speakers. Over and above their personal contribution to the process of communication, ordinary users (not only the scholars and clergy) need to be sufficiently engaged in the entire sequence of text production. If they are envisioned as the ultimate 'consumers' of a particular version, then they must in turn see themselves as the joint owners, or stockholders, in the venture that is being carried out on their behalf. Obviously, they cannot do the actual translation work themselves, but they must feel that they do play a meaningful role by advising as well as responding to the corps of translation personnel chosen to implement the program for them—the translators, revisers, testers, and administrators of the project. They are also 'consumers' in that it is their opinion and evaluation that matters as far as a publication's sales are concerned. If a particular Scripture product does not 'sell,' then it is up to the project organizers and sponsors to find out why—and what went wrong.

The general population of a given language group also needs to shoulder the responsibility of not only upholding the translation as it is being

---

[20] In the light of these developments that are aimed at involving greater efforts to involve the particular language group for whom a translation is being prepared, a more appropriate designation for the specific audience or readership intended, is needed. Another possibility is the 'client (or consumer) community.'

prepared (e.g., through financial contributions, public relations to popularize the project, prayer support), but they must also commit themselves to actively use the version once it has been published. This cannot be taken for granted: ethnic pride may be enough to get a certain translation into print, but practical sociolinguistic realities (e.g., language decay and death) may leave most copies sitting on the shelf. Usage assessment may also involve a decision to suspend critical judgment until people have had a chance to become accustomed to the new version in a variety of religious settings. A great deal of time, expense, and effort goes into producing any Bible translation; this can be justified (and the translators' labors at least partially rewarded) only if the version that results is then able to contribute in a significant way to the growth and development of the Church, whether on an individual or a corporate basis. Only the intended consumers themselves can ensure that this spiritual goal is accomplished—namely, by actively utilizing (reading, teaching, memorizing, composing into music) the very Word of God that they now have in their mother tongue.

B.4.5.2 Objective: education

In order to successfully carry out their subjective role as outlined above, a language community needs to be progressively and systematically educated in an objective way with regard to what their particular roles and responsibilities are. How can they be expected to adequately appreciate, or support, a more creative type of Scripture translation if they do not know why and how it has been prepared? This a matter of great concern, especially in areas where people are already quite familiar with one or more versions, either in their mother tongue or a major language of wider communication, which manifest texts that are stylistically very different from the one that is currently being translated. For example, how was the dimension of lyric orality built into the translation and why was this important in terms of their local communicative context, involving a variety of settings of potential use?

Such a community-based educational program concerning Bible translations should be carried out during the early stages of project planning, when the foundational *Skopos* is being formulated. It must then be continued throughout the duration of the work, so that as many people as possible can contribute constructively critical feedback to their joint venture. Certain forward-thinking Bible societies (e.g., many in South America) have found that basic instruction in the different fields of biblical studies as well as translation practice can be beneficially extended beyond the time of publication in order to enable people to effectively access and to more fully utilize the new version, especially one that is supplemented by a variety of paratextual aids. This special training in Scripture understanding and actual use (life-engagement) would not be carried out in isolation from any already existing translations, but together with them in a mutually complementary, comparative exercise of Bible learning, coupled with much life-related personal application. Special instructional materials need to be developed to guide this process of educating the audience for engaging the Scriptures in a more meaningful and life-related manner (e.g., see Hill and Hill 2008).

B.4.6 Summary: Four *LiFE* principles (the 4 R's)

A literary functional-equivalent translation approach features four essential principles that pertain to motivation as well as implementation:

(a) **Reality**—namely, the demonstrated fact of literary *artistry* and *rhetoric* in: (i) the writings of Scripture, and (ii) the verbal, including poetic resources, oral and written, of the target language (TL). We must make manifest the source language (SL) dimension of reality by means of detailed text studies of the biblical documents, and the same effort needs to be applied to the TL. Thus, the various artistic and rhetorical characteristics of the available literature as well as *orature* (oral narratives, proverbs, praise poetry, laments, etc.) of the TL should be thoroughly researched and recorded for possible use in Bible translation.

(b) **Realization**—namely, the use or application of at least some of the primary oratorical and lyric resources of the TL (a, ii) in a translation of specific books of the Old and New Testament Scriptures in keeping with their manifest artistic beauty and rhetorical power (a, i). This is the heart of the translation process as we seek to represent—primarily in oral-aural form—as many aspects of the original (content > intent [function] > form) as possible in the TL text. How much *LiFE* is possible? That is determined by (c).

(c) **Relevance**—namely, the norm or guide used for selecting the most suitable 'some' of those TL artistic-rhetorical features determined during step (b). There are three main criteria of relevance: *processing cost*—the degree of difficulty that the translated text poses for readers and hearers; the amount of *contextual effects* derived from the process, that is, reinforcing, augmenting, or deleting significant contextual assumptions (Gutt 1992); and, adding a criterion to the usually cited pair, the *appropriateness* (and demonstrated *acceptability*) of the text in terms of content and purpose in relation to a specific audience group, one that is prepared to receive and use a *LiFE* translation.

(d) **Responders**—namely, those who process and react to the TL text (receptors, target audience, translation consumers), hopefully in a positive manner in terms of actual use, with an emphasis on the poetic and oral-aural quality of the vernacular text. The relevance criterion (c) must therefore always be assessed in relation to a very specifically determined potential audience group, whether large or small. This primary audience (readership) needs to be carefully identified and defined on the basis of pre-project sampling in the translation job commission *(brief)* in relation to the particular goal *(Skopos)* of the translated version that is being produced.

B.5 Some implications of a literary (oratorical) approach

I conclude this overview of the translation possibilities presented by a literary-oratorical rendition of the Scriptures by summarizing its implications in terms of overall relevance to a given TL community (cf. point (c) above): "[W]henever a person engages in ostensive communication, she creates the tacit presumption that what she has to communicate will be optimally relevant to the audience: that it will yield adequate contextual effects, without requiring unnecessary processing effort" (Gutt 1992:25). How do these relevance principles, expanded in reference now to a larger complex of auxiliary as well as direct communicational activities, apply in relation to a specific translation project as a total enterprise?

B.5.1 Processing effort

There is no denying the fact that a considerable cost in terms of effort and expense is needed to produce an acceptable literary—especially a poetic—translation, that is, when compared with other types of rendering that would be much less rigorous in their demands upon the translation team. This is a version that is not only accurate exegetically, but also excellent in terms of its artistic and rhetorical value in the vernacular (sonic beauty, impact, and appeal). In fact, the requisite resources required

B.5 Some implications of a literary (oratorical) approach

at the outset may be so overwhelming, or so completely lacking within the local community, that such a vision cannot even be considered. It is necessary therefore for the project's planning committee to "first sit down and estimate the cost" (Luke 14:28). We might begin with the *sine qua non*—namely, the exegetical experts and vernacular communication specialists who are chosen to comprise the members of the translation team. Are all cooperating churches thoroughly committed to sponsor and support (financially, educationally, spiritually) persons of such high intellectual and artistic caliber for a long-term endeavor of this nature?

Second, are people ready to pay the price of conceptually processing and interacting with a version of this nature when it becomes available—for example, a text that has been composed entirely in some TL poetic genre, or in a narrative style that is traditionally employed in oral histories? Such a version will not be expressed either in the familiar (but often misunderstood) words of a traditional, more literal translation or use the simplified linguistic forms of a common-language rendering. It will certainly require considerable effort for the translators, first of all, to verbalize an artistically poetic, yet also hermeneutically correct (defensible) text—then for the intended audience to sufficiently understand, appreciate, and apply it (recognizing that they may need some prior instruction to familiarize them with this version's novel literary style and structure). On the other hand, the language form of the new version may sound perfectly natural and appropriate, but it still might cause a certain mental barrier simply because it is *different* from what people have become used to in their vernacular Scriptures and/or in liturgical worship use. Thus the project management team may face an appreciable amount of general resistance when starting out with their attempts to sell the constituency at large on the merits of such an unfamiliar or unconventional version.

B.5.2 Contextual effects

How do the potential text production and processing efforts compare with the perceived communicative benefits of a literary translation? Is it worth the (possibly) additional interpretive exertion? Of course, any practical evaluation of this kind may take some time to complete, as people gradually grow in their knowledge about the positive features of a poetic text and how/where to utilize such a version to increase the various contextual effects that may potentially be derived from it (Gutt 1992:22–23), for example, with regard to the stylistic devices of poetry as well as a better understanding of how a text's larger discourse features have been expertly fashioned in terms of key structural patterns, strophic units, and peaks of thematic content and emotive intensity. As noted earlier, a literary functional equivalence translation (*LiFE*) may not be acceptable, at least initially, for general liturgical reading in a public worship service. However, it will certainly possess some significant communication possibilities for particular audience sub-groups (e.g., non-churchgoers) or special settings (e.g., using traditional art forms or non-print media productions). Such options need to be explored in accordance with the guiding *Skopos* (purpose) statement prepared as an essential part of the initial project commission, or *brief*.

For example, representative audience sampling procedures might suggest that a literary translation (LT) may be very appropriate for use as a comparative Bible study resource—a vesion that offers the meaning stated in vivid oral vernacular terms, in contrast to the overt form of the biblical text (the latter being available in an existing translation or a widely used version of the region). Or such an orality-based version could be employed as part of a varied strategy of youth ministry or as a non-conventional outreach instrument designed to appeal to groups that normally tend to be resistant to the message of Scripture, e.g., popular entertainers, artists, and public performers of all types—painters, sculptors, musicians, dramatic players, actors, TV personalities, well-known sportsmen and women—or those who live in completely different socio-economic circumstances: street kids, the destitute, members of the drug culture, and other community outcasts (i.e., the contemporary 'publicans and sinners' of society). An LT may also be found to be highly suitable for dramatic (stage or outdoor) productions, for certain non-print media presentations (e.g., audio-cassette or CD, especially when accompanied by compatible background music or actually composed as a song), and in mass media Christian broadcasting ministries (audience-specific radio programs in particular, e.g., the widely growing FM network around the world).

There is a special personal gain in communicative effect that is almost certain to be realized. This applies first of all to the translators (and text reviewers) themselves. Once they get into the phonic (sound-enriched) mood and movement of a poetic text—in relation to what they discover in the original and also what they can create in response in their mother tongue—the lyric muse of the Spirit captures them, and they will never again read, hear, study, or communicate the Scriptures as they did before. This inspiring impact also has to do with the increased emotive and aesthetic benefit that will be experienced by all those who regularly make use of a LT in close conjunction with a more traditional version.

B.5 Some implications of a literary (oratorical) approach

An oratorical rendition—a selection of favorite psalms for example—may serve as a valuable devotional resource and a sure means of augmenting or enhancing popular understanding of and appreciation for the great artistic and rhetorical, in addition to theological, riches to be mined from the Scripture, as superb oral-oriented literature. And, surprisingly perhaps, from many more passages than most people might think possible.

גַּל־עֵינַי וְאַבִּיטָה נִפְלָאוֹת מִתּוֹרָתֶךָ׃ (Psalm 119:18)
Open my eyes to see [hear] the wonderful truths in your instructions! (NLT)

References

Achtemeier, P. J. 1990. *Omne verbum sonat:* The New Testament and the oral environment of late Western antiquity. *Journal of Biblical Literature* 109(1):3–27.

Adamo, David Tuesday. 2001. The use of Psalms in African indigenous churches in Nigeria. In Gerald O. West and Musa Dube (eds.), *The Bible in Africa: Transactions, trajectories, and trends,* 336–349. Leiden: E.J. Brill.

Alden R. L. 1983. *Proverbs: A commentary on an ancient book of timeless advice.* Grand Rapids: Baker.

Alden, R. L. 1993. *Job: An exegetical and theological exposition of the Holy Scriptures.* New American Commentary. Nashville: Broadman & Holman.

Allen, L. C. 1982. Psalm 73: An analysis. *Tyndale Bulletin* 33: 93–118.

Allen, L. C. 1983. *Psalms 101–150.* Word Biblical Commentary 21. Waco: Word Books.

Alter, Robert. 1981. *The art of biblical narrative.* New York: Basic Books.

Alter, Robert. 1985. *The art of biblical poetry.* New York: Basic Books.

Andersen, F. I. 1976. *Job: An introduction and commentary.* Tyndale Old Testament Commentaries. Downers Grove: InterVarsity Press.

Archer, Gleason I. 1964. *A survey of Old Testament: Introduction.* Rev. ed. Chicago: Moody Press.

Atkinson, D. 1996. *The message of Proverbs.* Leichester and Downers Grove: InterVarsity Press.

Bailey, J. L. 1995. Genre analysis. In J. Green (ed.), *Hearing the New Testament: Strategies for interpretation,* 197–221. Grand Rapids: Eerdmans.

Bailey, J. L. and L. van der Broek. 1992. *Literary forms in the New Testament: A handbook.* Louisville: Westminster/John Knox.

Baker, Mona. 1995. Corpora in translation studies: An overview and suggestions for future research. *Target* 7(2):223–243.

Barbour and Company. 1995. *The Psalms in verse.* Uhrichsville: Barbour.

Barr, James. 1963. *The Bible in the modern world.* London: SCM.

Bartholomew, Craig G. 1998. *Reading Ecclesiastes: Old Testament exegesis and hermeneutical theory.* Rome: Pontifical Bible Institute.

Bartholomew, Craig G. 2009. *Ecclesiastes*. Baker Commentary on the Old Testament. Grand Rapids: Baker Academic.

Barton, J. 1984. *Reading the Old Testament: Method in Bible study*. Philadelphia: Westminster.

Barton, J., ed. 1998. *The Cambridge companion to biblical interpretation*. Cambridge: Cambridge University Press.

Bascom, Robert A. 1994. Hebrew poetry and the text of the Song of Songs. In E. R. Wendland (ed.), *Discourse perspectives on Hebrew poetry in the Scriptures*, 95–110. New York: United Bible Societies.

Bastin, G. L. 2000. Evaluating beginners' re-expression and creativity: A positive approach. In C. Maier (ed.), *The Translator* (special issue) 6(2): 231–245.

Beaton, Richard. 2008. Song of Songs 3: History of interpretation. In T. Longman III and P. Enns (eds.), 760–769.

Beckwith, R. T. 1985. *The Old Testament canon of the New Testament church*. London: SPCK.

Berlin, A. 1985. *The dynamics of biblical parallelism*. Bloomington: Indiana University Press.

Berlin, A. and M. Z. Brettler, eds. 2004. *The Jewish Study Bible*. Oxford: Oxford University Press (Jewish Publication Society).

Berry, D. K. 1995. *An introduction to wisdom and poetry of the Old Testament*. Nashville, TN: Broadman & Holman.

Birkeland, H. 1955. The chief problem of Psalm 73:17ff. *Zeitschrift für die Alttestamentliche Wissenschaft (ZAW)* 67: 99–103.

Bliese, Loren F. 1994. Literary structure and theology in the Song of Songs. Unpublished paper presented to the United Bible Societies Triennial Workshop: Chiang Mai, Thailand.

Boerger, Brenda H. 2008. On translating Hebrew literary devices into Natqgu. Unpublished paper presented at *Translatable: Creativity and Knowledge Formation* conference, co-sponsored by Duke University and UNC Chapel Hill.

Boerger, Brenda H. 2009. *POET Psalms (Poetic Oracle English Translation)*. Dallas: ILC Printshop.

Bosman, H. Forthcoming. The rhetoric of reverence—the 'fear of the Lord' (*yir'at yhwh*) in the book of Proverbs.

Botha, P. J. 2001. Social values and the interpretation of Psalm 123. *Old Testament Essays (OTE)* 14(2):189–198.

Botha, P. J. 2002. 'The honor of the righteous will be restored': Psalm 75 in its social context. *Old Testament Essays (OTE)* 15(2):320–334.

Bowker, Lynn. 2000. A corpus-based approach to evaluating student translations. In C. Maier (ed.), *The Translator* (special issue) 6(2):183–210.

Bratcher, R. G. and Wm. D. Reyburn. 1991. *A translator's handbook on the book of Psalms*. New York: United Bible Societies.

Breck, J. 1994. *The shape of biblical language: Chiasmus in the Scriptures and beyond.* Crestwood: St. Vladimir's Seminary Press.

Brenner, Athalya. 1989. *The Song of Songs*. Old Testament Guides. Sheffield: JSOT Press.

Briggs, R. S. 2008. Speech-act theory. In D.G. Firth and J.A. Grant (eds.), 75–110.

Brown, Jeannine K. 2007. *Scripture as communication: Introducing biblical hermeneutics*. Grand Rapids: Baker Academic.

Brown, Jeannine K. 2008. Genre criticism. In D.G. Firth and J.A. Grant (eds.), 111–150.

Brown, Richard. 2004. New dimensions in communicative translation. Power Point presentation included on the CD: Bible Translation—2003. Slides 1–141. Dallas: SIL International.

Brueggemann, Walter. 1980. Psalms and the life of faith: A suggested typology of function. *JSOT* 17:3–32.

Brueggemann, Walter. 1984. *The message of the Psalms*. Minneapolis: Augsburg.

Brueggemann, Walter. 1991. Bounded by obedience and praise: The Psalms as canon. *JSOT* 50:63–92.

Brueggemann, Walter. 1993. Response to James L. Mays, 'The question of content'. In J. C. McCann Jr. (ed.), 29–41.

Brueggemann, Walter. 1995. *The Psalms: The life of faith*. Minneapolis: Fortress.

Brueggemann, Walter and P. D. Miller. 1996. Psalm 73 as a canonical marker. *JSOT* 72:45–56.

Buber, M. 1983. The heart determines: Psalm 73. In J. Crenshaw (ed.), *Theodicy in the Old Testament,* 109–118. Philadelphia: Fortress.

Bullinger, E.W. 1967. *Number in scripture*. Grand Rapids: Kregel Publications.

Bullock, C. Hassell. 1979. *An introduction to the Old Testament poetry books*. Chicago: Moody Press.

Bullock, C. Hassell. 1988. *An introduction to the Old Testament poetic books*. Rev. ed. Chicago: Moody Press.

Carr, David. 2005. *Writing on the tablet of the heart: Origins of Scripture and literature*. Oxford: Oxford University Press.

Carr, G. Lloyd. 1982. The love poetry genre in the Old Testament and the ancient Near East: Another look at inspiration. *Journal of the Evangelical Theological Society* 25(4):489–98.

Carr, G. Lloyd. 1984. *The Song of Solomon: An introduction and commentary*. Tyndale Old Testament Commentaries. Downers Grove: IVP Academic.

Carr, G. Lloyd. 1993. Song of Songs. In L. Ryken and T. Longman III (eds.), *A complete literary guide to the Bible*, 281–295. Grand Rapids: Zondervan.

Childs, Brevard. 1979. *Introduction to the Old Testament as Scripture*. Philadelphia: Fortress.

Chimombo, S. 1988. *Malawian oral literature*. Zomba, Malawi: Centre for Social Research, University of Malawi.

Cho, Ji-Youn. 2009. *Politeness and addressee honorifics in Bible translation*. UBS Monograph Series No. 11. Reading, U.K.: United Bible Societies.

Christianson, E.S. 1998. *A time to tell: Narrative strategies in Ecclesiastes*. JSOT Supplement 280. Sheffield: Sheffield Academic Press.

Clark, David. J. 1982. In search of wisdom: Notes on Job 28. *The Bible Translator* 33(4):401–405.

Clifford, R. J. 1998. *The wisdom literature*. Nashville, TN: Abingdon Press.

Cooper, A. 1982. Narrative theory and the book of Job. *Studies in Religion* 11:39–40.

Coulson, Seana. 2001. *Semantic leaps: Frame-shifting and conceptual blending in meaning construction*. Cambridge: Cambridge University Press.

Crisp, Simon. 2004. Does a literary translation have to be literal? In S. Crisp and M. Jinbachian (eds.), *Text, theology and translation: Essays in honor of Jan de Waard*, 43–51. Reading: United Bible Societies.

Culler, Jonathan. 1997. *Literary theory: A very short introduction*. Oxford: Oxford University Press.

Davidson, Richard M. 1989. Theology of sexuality in the Song of Songs: Return to Eden. *Andrews University Seminary Studies* 27(1):1–19.

Davidson, Richard. 2003. The literary structure of the Song of Songs redivivus. *Journal of the Adventist Theological Society* 14(2):44–65.

Davidson, Richard. 2007. *Flame of Yahweh: Sexuality in the Old Testament*. Peabody: Hendrickson.

Davidson, Robert. 1986. *Ecclesiastes and the Song of Solomon*. The Daily Study Bible. Philadelphia: Westminster Press.

Davis, Barry C. 1994. Death, an impetus for life. In R. B. Zuck (ed.), 347–366.

Davis, C. W. 1999. *Oral biblical criticism: The influence of the principles of orality on the literary structure of Paul's epistle to the Philippians*. Sheffield: Sheffield Academic Press.

de Beaugrande, R. 1968. *Factors in a theory of poetic translating*. Assen: Van Gorcum.

de Beaugrande, R. and W. Dressler. 1981. *Introduction to text linguistics*. London: Longman.

de Regt, L., J. de Waard, and J. P. Fokkelman, eds. 1996. *Literary structure and rhetorical strategies in the Hebrew Bible*. Assen: Van Gorcum.

de Waard, J. 1996. Hebrew rhetoric and the translator. In L. de Regt, J. de Waard, and J. P. Fokkelman (eds.), 242–251.

de Waard, J. and E. A. Nida. 1986. *From one language to another: Functional equivalence in Bible translating*. Nashville: Thomas Nelson.

Deere, Jack S. 1985. Song of Songs. In J. Walvoord and R. Zuck (eds.), *The Bible Knowledge Commentary* 1, 1009–1025. Wheaton: Victor Books.

Delitzsch, Franz. [1872] 1984. *The Song of Songs*. Tr. M. G. Easton. Commentary on the Old Testament. Grand Rapids: Eerdmans.

Dewey, J. 1980. *Markan public debate: Literary technique, Concentric structure, and theology in Mark 2:1–3:6*. Chico, CA: Scholars Press.

Doan, William and Terry Giles. 2005. *Prophets, performance and power: Performance criticism of the Hebrew Bible*. New York: T&T Clark International.

Dorsey, David A. 1999. *The literary structure of the Old Testament: A commentary on Genesis—Malachi*. Grand Rapids: Baker Books.

Douglas, M. 1993. *In the wilderness: The doctrine of defilement in the book of Numbers*. Sheffield: Sheffield Academic Press.

Douglas, M. 1999. *Leviticus as literature*. Oxford: Oxford University Press.

Eaton, J. H. 1985. *Job*. Old Testament Guides. Sheffield: JSOT Press.

Ehlke, R. C. 1992. *Proverbs*. The People's Bible. Milwaukee: Northwestern.

Ellington, J. 2003. Schleiermacher was wrong: The false dilemma of foreignization and domestication. *The Bible Translator* 54(3):301–317.

Enns, Peter. 2008. Ecclesiastes 1: Book of. In T. Longman III and P. Enns (eds.), 121–132.

Estes, Daniel J. 2005. *Handbook on the wisdom books and Psalms*. Grand Rapids: Baker Books.

Falk, Marcia. [1982] 1990. *The Song of Songs: A new translation and interpretation*. Rev. ed. San Francisco: HarperCollins.

Falk, Marcia. 1988. Song of Songs. In James L. Mays (ed.), *Harper's Bible Commentary*, 525–528. San Francisco: Harper & Row.

Fauconnier, Gilles and Mark Turner. 2006. Mental spaces: Conceptual integration networks. In D. Geeraerts (ed.), *Cognitive linguistics: Basic readings*, 301–371. Berlin: Mouton de Gruyter.

Fawcett, P. 1997. *Translation and language: Linguistic theories explained*. Manchester: St. Jerome.

Fee, Gordon and Douglas Stuart. 1993. *How to read the Bible for all it's worth*. 2nd ed. Grand Rapids: Zondervan.

Firth, D. G. and J. A. Grant, eds. 2008. *Words and the Word: Explorations in biblical interpretation and literary theory*. Downers Grove: IVP Academic.

Fisch, Harold. 1988. *Poetry with a purpose: Biblical poetics and interpretation.* Bloomington: Indiana University Press.
Fox, Michael V. 1985. *The Song of Songs and Egyptian love songs.* Madison: University of Wisconsin Press.
Fox, Michael V. 1994. Aging and death in Qoheleth 12. In R. B. Zuck (ed.), 381–399.
Garrett, D. A. 1993. *Proverbs, Ecclesiastes, Song of Solomon.* New American Commentary 14. Nashville: Broadman Press.
Garrett, D. A. 2008. Proverbs 3: History of interpretation. In T. Longman III and P. Enns (eds.), 566–578.
Geertz, Clifford. 1973. *The interpretation of cultures.* New York: Basic Books.
Gerstenberger, E. S. 1988. *Psalms (Part 1), with an introduction to cultic poetry.* The Forms of the Old Testament Literature XIV. Grand Rapids: Eerdmans.
Gerstenberger, E. S. 2001. *Psalms (Part 2) and Lamentations.* The Forms of the Old Testament Literature XV. Grand Rapids: Eerdmans.
Giese Jr., R. L. 1995. *Cracking Old Testament codes: A guide to interpreting the literary genres of the Old Testament.* Nashville: Broadman and Holman.
Giese, C.P. 1999. The genre of Ecclesiastes as viewed by its Septuagint translator and the early Church Fathers. PhD dissertation, Hebrew Union College.
Giles, Terry and William Doan. 2009. *Twice used songs: Performance criticism of the songs of ancient Israel.* Peabody, Mass.: Hendrickson Publishers.
Gitay, Y. 1991. *Isaiah and his audience: The structure and meaning of Isaiah 1–12.* Assen: Van Gorcum.
Gitay, Y. 1996. Psalm 1 and the rhetoric of religious argumentation. In de Regt, de Waard, and Fokkelman (eds.), 232–240.
Gitay, Y. 2009. Biblical rhetoric: The art of religious dialogue. *Journal for Semitics* 18(1):34–56.
Goldingay, John. 2007. *Psalms, Volume 2: Psalms 42–89.* Baker Commentary on the Old Testament Wisdom and Psalms. Grand Rapids: Baker Academic.
Goldingay, John. 2008. *Psalms, Volume 3: Psalms 90–150.* Baker Commentary on the Old Testament Wisdom and Psalms. Grand Rapids: Baker Academic.
Good, E. M. 1990. *In turns of tempest: A reading of Job, with a translation.* Stanford: Stanford University Press.
Grant, Jamie A. 2008. Poetics. In D. G. Firth and J. A. Grant (eds.), 187–225.
Grimes, Joseph E. 1972. Outlines and overlays. *Language* 48(2):513–523.
Grossberg, Daniel. 1989. *Centripetal and centrifugal structures in biblical poetry.* Society of Biblical Literature Monograph Series 39. Atlanta: Scholars Press.

Guralnik, D. B., ed. 1988. *Webster's New World Dictionary*. Third College Edition. New York: Webster's New World.

Gutt, E.-A. 1991. *Translation and relevance: Cognition and context.* Oxford: Blackwell.

Gutt, E.-A. 1992. *Relevance theory: A guide to successful communication in translation.* Dallas: Summer Institute of Linguistics.

Habel, N. C. 1985. *The book of Job: A commentary.* Philadelphia: Westminster/John Knox Press.

Hartley, J. E. 1988. *The book of Job.* New International Commentary on the Old Testament (NICOT). Grand Rapids: Eerdmans.

Harvey, J. D. 1998. *Listening to the text: Oral patterning in Paul's letters.* Grand Rapids: Baker.

Hatim, B. and I. Mason. 1990. *Discourse and the translator.* London: Longman.

Hatim, B. and I. Mason. 1997. *The translator as communicator.* London: Routledge.

Hildebrandt, T. 1988. Proverbial pairs: Compositional units in Proverbs 10–29. *Journal of Biblical Literature* 107(2):207–224.

Hill, Harriet. 2003. Communicating context in Bible translation. *Word and Deed* 2(2):1–31.

Hill, Harriet. 2006. *The Bible at cultural crossroads: From translation to communication.* Manchester: St. Jerome.

Hill, Harriet. 2009. Adjusting contextual mismatches: Do study Bibles provide a good model? Paper presented at the Bible Translation 2009 Conference, October 16–20, 2009, Dallas, Texas.

Hill, Harriet and Margaret Hill. 2008. *Translating the Bible into action: How the Bible can be relevant in all languages and cultures.* Carlisle, UK: Piquant.

Hill, Margaret. 2005. The challenge of acceptability of the translation by the target language community. Paper presented at OTSSA (Old Testament Society of Southern Africa) Congress on Biblical Interpretation in Africa, Pietermaritzburg, South Africa, Sept 19–23, 2005.

Hill, Ralph. 2004. Contextual adjustment strategies and Bible translation. *Word and Deed* 3(1):1–25.

Hoffman, Y. 1991. Ancient near eastern literary conventions and the restoration of the book of Job. *Zeitschrift für die Alttestamentliche Wissenschaft (ZAW)* 103:399–411.

Hunter, Alistair. 2006. *Wisdom literature.* London: SCM Press.

James, F. 1965. *Thirty Psalmists.* New York: Seabury.

Kafantenganji, V. J. 1986. *Mvetsa 1* [Listen!]. Lusaka, Zambia: Kenneth Kaunda Foundation.

Katan, D. 1999. *Translating cultures: An introduction for translators, interpreters and mediators.* Manchester: St. Jerome.

Keck, Leander, ed. 1996, 1997. *The New Interpreter's Bible.* Nashville: Abingdon Press.

Keefer, Kyle. 2008. *The New Testament as literature: A very short introduction.* Oxford: Oxford University Press.

Keel, Othmar. 1994. *The Song of Songs: A continental commentary.* Tr. F. J. Gaiser. Minneapolis: Fortress.

Kennedy, George A. 1984. *New Testament interpretation through rhetorical criticism.* Chapel Hill: The University of North Carolina Press.

Kenny, Dorothy. 2001a. Corpora in translation studies. In M. Baker (ed.), *Routledge Encyclopedia of Translation Studies,* 50–53. London: Routledge.

Kenny, Dorothy. 2001b. *Lexis and creativity in translation: A corpus-based study.* Manchester: St. Jerome.

Kidner, Derek. 1964. *Proverbs: An introduction and commentary.* Tyndale Old Testament Commentaries 15. Downers Grove: InterVarsity Press.

Kidner, Derek. 1976. *The message of Ecclesiastes.* The Bible Speaks Today. Downers Grove: InterVarsity Press.

Kinlaw, Dennis F. 1991. Song of Songs. In F. E. Gaebelein (ed.), *The Expositor's Bible Commentary* 5, 1199–1224. Grand Rapids: Zondervan.

Kitchen, K. A. 1977. Proverbs and wisdom books of the ancient near east: The factual history of a literary form. *Theologische Beiträge* 28:69–114.

Klingbeil, G. A. 2008. Ecclesiastes 2: Ancient Near Eastern background. In T. Longman and P. Enns (eds.), 132–140.

Kraft, Charles H. 2008. *Worldview for Christian witness.* Pasadena: Wm. Carey Library.

Kugel, James L. 1981. *The idea of biblical poetry: Parallelism and its history.* New Haven: Yale University Press.

Kugel, James L. 1999. *The great poems of the Bible: A reader's companion with new translations.* New York: The Free Press.

Kumakanga, S. L. 1949 (reprinted 1975). *Nzeru za kale* [Ancient wisdom]. Blantyre, Malawi: Dzuka.

Landers, Charles E. 2001. *Literary translation: A practical guide.* Clevedon, UK: Multilingual Matters.

Landy, Francis. 1983. *Paradoxes of paradise: Identity and difference in the Song of Songs.* Sheffield: Almond Press.

Landy, Francis. 1987. The Song of Songs. In R. Alter and F. Kermode (eds.), *The literary guide to the Bible,* 305–319. Cambridge: Harvard University Press.

LaSor, William, Sanford, David A. Hubbard, and Frederic W. Bush. 1982. *Old Testament survey: The message, form, and background of the Old Testament.* Grand Rapids: Eerdmans.

Lawrence, Beatrice. 2009. Gender analysis: Gender and method in biblical studies. In J. M. LeMon and K. H. Richards (eds.), *Method matters: Essays on the interpretation of the Hebrew Bible in honor of David L. Petersen,* 333–348. Atlanta: SBL.

Leithart, Peter J. http://www.leithart.com/category/bible-ot-song-of-songs. Accessed 2/23/2010.

Levine, H. J. 1990. The dialogic discourse of Psalms. In V. L. Tollers and J. Maier (eds.), *Mappings of the biblical terrain: The Bible as text,* 268–281. Lewisburg, PA: Bucknell University Press.

Lewis, M. Paul, ed. 2009. *Ethnologue: Languages of the world.* 15th ed. Dallas: SIL International.

Limburg, James. 2006. *Encountering Ecclesiastes: A book for our time.* Grand Rapids: Eerdmans.

Loader, J. A. 1986. *Ecclesiastes: A practical commentary.* Grand Rapids: Eerdmans.

Loader, J. A. 2001. The significant deficiency of revelation. *Old Testament Essays (OTE)* 14(2):235–259.

Long, Burke O. 1991. *2 Kings.* The Forms of the Old Testament Literature (FOTL) 10. Grand Rapids: Eerdmans.

Long, Gary A. 2008. Song of Songs 2: Ancient Near Eastern Background. In T. Longman and P. Enns (eds.), 750–760.

Longman III, Tremper. 1991. *Fictional Akkadian autobiography.* Winona Lake: Eisenbrauns.

Longman III, Tremper. 1998.*The book of Ecclesiastes.* NICOT. Grand Rapids: Eerdmans.

Longman III, Tremper. 2001. *Song of Songs.* NICOT. Grand Rapids: Eerdmans.

Longman III, Tremper. 2008. Ecclesiastes 3: History of interpretation. In T. Longman and P. Enns (eds.), 140–149.

Longman III, Tremper and Peter Enns, eds. 2008. *Dictionary of the Old Testament: Wisdom, poetry & writings.* Downers Grove: IVP Academic.

Louw, J. P. and E. R. Wendland. 1993. *Graphic design and Bible reading: Exploratory studies in the typographical representation of the text of Scripture in translation.* Cape Town: Bible Society of South Africa.

Luyten, J. 1979. Psalm 73 and wisdom. In M. Gilbert (ed.), *La sagesse de l'Ancien Testament,* 59–81. Paris: Duculot.

Malunga, B. 1990. *Kuimba kwa Mlakatuli* [The song of the lyric poet]. Blantyre: Christian Literature Association.

Masenya (ngwana' Mphalele), M. 2001. What differences do African contexts make for English translations? *Old Testament Essays (OTE)* 14(2):281–296.

Mays, James L. 1994. *Psalms*. Interpretation Bible Commentary. Louisville: John Knox Press.

McCann Jr., J. C. 1987. Psalm 73: A microcosm of Old Testament theology. In K. Hoglund, E. F. Huwiler, J. T. Glass and R. W. Lee (eds.), *The listening heart: Essays in wisdom and Psalms in honor of Roland E. Murphy*. JSOT Supplement 58, 247–257. Sheffield: JSOT Press.

McCann Jr., J. C., ed. 1993. *The shape and shaping of the Psalter*. Sheffield: JSOT Press.

McCann Jr., J. C. 1993. *A theological introduction to the book of Psalms: The Psalms as Torah*. Nashville: Abingdon Press.

McCann Jr., J. C. 1996. *The book of Psalms: Introduction, commentary, and reflections*. The New Interpreter's Bible 4, 641–1280. Nashville: Abingdon Press.

McCreesh, T. P. 1991. *Biblical sound and sense: Poetic sound patterns in Proverbs 10–29*. Sheffield: JSOT Press.

McKenzie, A. M. 1996. *Preaching Proverbs: Wisdom for the pulpit*. Louisville, KY: Westminster/John Knox.

McKenzie, S. L. and S. R. Haynes. 1993. *To each its own meaning: An introduction to biblical criticisms and their application*. Louisville: Westminster/John Knox.

Melchert, Charles F. 1998. *Wise teachings: Biblical wisdom and educational ministry*. Harrisburg: Trinity Press International.

Mieder, W. 1993. *Proverbs are never out of season: Popular wisdom in the modern age*. New York: Oxford University Press.

Miller, P. D. 1999. Deuteronomy and Psalms: Evoking a biblical conversation. *Journal of Biblical Literature* 118(1):3–18.

Mojola, A. O. 2003. Scripture translation in the era of translation studies. In T. Wilt (ed.), 1–13.

Moskowitz, Clara. 2010. Bible possibly written centuries earlier, text suggests. http://www.livescience.com/history/earliest-hebrew-text-100115.html. Accessed 15 June, 2010.

Mossop, Brian. 2001. *Revising and editing for translators*. Manchester: St. Jerome.

Munday, J. 2001. *Introducing translation studies: Theories and applications*. London: Routledge.

Murphy, Roland E. 1981. *Wisdom literature: Job, Proverbs, Ruth, Canticles, Ecclesiastes, and Esther*. The Forms of the Old Testament Literature 13. Grand Rapids: Eerdmans.

Murphy, Roland E. 1990. *The Song of Songs: A commentary on the book of Canticles or the Song of Songs*. Minneapolis: Fortress Press.

Murphy, Roland E. 1992. *Ecclesiastes.* Word Biblical Commentary 23a. Dallas: Word Books.

Murphy, Roland E. 1998. *Proverbs.* Word Biblical Commentary 22. Nashville: Thomas Nelson.

Murphy, R.. E. and E. Huwiler. 1999. *Proverbs, Ecclesiastes, Song of Songs.* New International Biblical Commentary 12. Peabody: Hendrickson.

Nankwenya, I. A. J. 1974. *Zofunika m'gramara wa Chichewa* [Essentials of Chichewa grammar]. Lilongwe, Malawi: Longman.

Naudé, J. A. and C. H. J. van der Merwe, eds. 2002. *Contemporary translation studies and Bible translation: A South African perspective.* Acta Theologica Supplementum 2. Bloemfontein: University of the Free State.

Nel, P. J. 2000. Righteousness from the perspective of the wisdom literature of the Old Testament. *Old Testament Essays (OTE)* 13(3):309–328.

Neufeldt, V. 1988. *Webster's New World College Dictionary.* 3rd ed. New York: Macmillen.

Neusner, Jacob. 1993. *Israel's love affair with God: Song of Songs.* The Bible of Judaism Library. Valley Forge: Trinity Press International.

New English Translation. 1996–2003. www.netbible.com.

Newsom, C. A. 1996. *The book of Job: Introduction, commentary, and reflections.* The New Interpreter's Bible 4, 319–637. Nashville: Abingdon.

Nida, Eugene A. 1964. *Toward a science of translating.* Leiden: E. J. Brill.

Nida, Eugene A. and Charles R. Taber. 1974. *The theory and practice of translation.* Leiden: E.J. Brill.

Nielsen, Kirsten. 2009. Poetic analysis: Psalm 121. In J.M. LeMon and K.H. Richards (eds.), *Method matters: Essays on the interpretation of the Hebrew Bible in honor of David L. Petersen,* 293–309. Atlanta: SBL.

Nord, C. 1997. *Translation as a purposeful activity: Functionalist approaches explained.* Manchester: St. Jerome.

Norton, D. 2000. *A history of the Bible as literature.* Cambridge: Cambridge University Press.

Ogden, Graham S. 1977. The 'better'-proverb *(tôb-spruch),* rhetorical criticism, and Qoheleth. *JBL* 96:489–505.

Ogden, Graham S. and Lynell Zogbo. 1998. *A handbook on Ecclesiastes.* UBS Helps for Translators. New York: United Bible Societies.

Olohan, M. 2004. *Introducing corpora in translation studies.* New York: Routledge.

Petersen, David L. and Kent Harold Richards. 1992. *Interpreting Hebrew poetry.* Minneapolis: Fortress Press.

Petersen, Michelle. 2009. Increasing Scripture engagement through local arts: Reducing cultural distance between the message and today's receptors. Paper presented at the Bible Translation 2009 Conference, October 16–20, 2009, Dallas, Texas.

Peterson, E. H. 1994. *The message: Psalms*. Colorado Springs: Alive Communications.

Pomorska, K. and S. Rudy, eds. 1985. *Roman Jakobson: Verbal art, verbal sign, verbal time*. Minneapolis: University of Minnesota Press.

Pope, Marvin H. 1977. *The Song of Songs: A new translation with introduction and commentary*. The Anchor Bible. New York: Doubleday.

Porter, Stanley E. and Matthew B. O'Donnell. 2009. Comparative discourse analysis as a tool in assessing translations, using Luke 16:19–31 as a test case. In S. Porter and M. Boda (eds.), *Translating the New Testament: Text, translation, theology*, 185–199. Grand Rapids: Eerdmans.

Preminger, A. and T.V.F. Brogan, eds. 1993. *The New Princeton encyclopedia of poetry and poetics*. Princeton: Princeton University Press.

Qvale, Per. 2003. *From St Jerome to hypertext: Translation in theory and practice*. Tr. N. R. Spencer. Manchester: St. Jerome Publishing.

Rang, Jack. 1994. *How to read the Bible aloud: Oral interpretation of Scripture*. New York: Paulist Press.

Reiss, Katharina. 2000. *Translation criticism: The potentials & limitation. Categories and criteria for translation quality assessment*. Tr. Erroll Rhodes. Manchester: St. Jerome.

Reyburn, Wm. D. 1992. *A handbook on the book of Job*. New York: United Bible Societies.

Rice, G. 1984. An exposition of Psalm 73. *The Journal of Religious Thought* 41(1):79–86.

Ross, A. P. 1991. Proverbs. In F. E. Gaeblein (ed.), *The Expositor's Bible Commentary* 5, 883–1134. Grand Rapids, MI: Zondervan.

Ross, J. F. 1978. Psalm 73. In J. G. Gammie, Walter Brueggemann, W. Lee Humphreys, and James Ward (eds.), *Israelite wisdom: Theological and literary essays in honor of Samuel Terrien*, 161–175. Missoula: Scholars Press.

Rowley, H. H. 1956. *The faith of Israel*. Philadelphia: Westminster.

Ryken, Leland. 1992. *Words of delight: A literary introduction to the Bible*. 2nd ed. Grand Rapids: Baker.

Ryken, Leland. 1993. Ecclesiastes. In L. Ryken and T. Longman III (eds.), *A complete literary guide to the Bible*, 268–280. Grand Rapids: Zondervan.

Ryken, Leland. 2002. *The word of God in English: Criteria for excellence in Bible translation*. Wheaton: Crossway Books.

Ryken, Leland, J. C. Wilhoit, and T. Longman III, eds. 1998. *Dictionary of biblical imagery*. Downer's Grove: IVP Academic.
Sailhamer, John. 1994. *NIV compact commentary*. Grand Rapids: Zondervan.
Salisbury, M. 1994. Hebrew proverbs and how to translate them. In R. D. Bergen (ed.), *Biblical Hebrew and discourse linguistics*, 434–461. Dallas: Summer Institute of Linguistics.
Salyer, Gary D. 2001. *Vain rhetoric: Private insight and public debate in Ecclesiastes*. Sheffield: Sheffield Academic Press.
Sanneh, Lamin. 2003. *Whose religion is Christianity? The gospel beyond the West*. Grand Rapids: Eerdmans.
Schneider, T. R. 1992. *The sharpening of wisdom: Old Testament proverbs in translation*. Old Testament Essays, Supplement 1. Pretoria: OTSSA.
Schoekel, L. A. 1988. *A manual of Hebrew poetics*. Rome: Editrice Pontifico Instituto Biblico.
Schultz, Jack. 2009. Culture and the Christian. *Modern Reformation: Christ in a post-Christian culture* 18(1):23–24.
Schwab, George. 2008. Song of Songs 1: Book of. In T. Longman III and P. Enns (eds.), 737–750.
Scorgie, G. G., M. L. Strauss, and S. M. Voth, eds. 2003. *The challenge of Bible translation: Communicating God's Word to the world*. Grand Rapids: Zondervan.
Searle, J. R. 1969. *Speech acts*. London: Cambridge University Press.
Searle, J. R. and D. Vanderveken. 1985. *Foundations of illocutionary logic*. Cambridge: Cambridge University Press.
Shea, William. 1980. The chiastic structure of the Song of Songs. *Zeitschrift für die alttestamentliche Wissenschaft (ZAW)* 92:378–396.
Sherwood, S. K. 2002. *Leviticus, Numbers, Deuteronomy*. Berit Olam: Studies in Hebrew Narrative and Poetry. Collegeville, MN: The Liturgical Press.
Smalley, Wm. A. 1974. Restructuring translations of the Psalms as poetry. In M. Black and Wm. A. Smalley (eds.), *On language, culture, and religion: In honor of Eugene A. Nida*, 337–371. Paris: Mouton.
Smith, T. L. 1974. A crisis in faith: An exegesis of Psalm 73. *Restoration Quarterly* 17(3):162–184.
Snaith, John G. 1993. *Song of Songs*. The New Century Bible Commentary. Grand Rapids: Eerdmans.
Snaith, N. H. 1950. *The distinctive ideas of the Old Testament*. London: Epworth.
Soukhanov, A. H., ed. 1996. *The American Heritage Dictionary of the English Language*. 3rd ed. New York: Houghton Mifflin.

Steinmann, A. E. 1996. The structure and message of the book of Job. *Vetus Testamentum* XLVI: 85–100.
Stockwell, Peter. 2002. *Cognitive poetics: An introduction.* London: Routledge.
Strauss, M. L. 2005. Form, function, and the 'literal meaning' fallacy in English Bible translation. *The Bible Translator* 56(3):153–168.
Sundersingh, J. 1999. Toward a media-based translation: Communicating biblical Scriptures to non-literates in rural Tamilnadu, India. Ph.D. thesis, Fuller Theological Seminary.
Sundersingh, J. 2001. *Audio-based translation: Communicating biblical Scriptures to non-literate people.* New York: United Bible Societies.
Tate, M. E. 1990. *Psalms 51–100.* Word Biblical Commentary. Dallas: Word.
Tate, W. R. 1991. *Biblical interpretation: An integrated approach.* Peabody, MA: Hendrickson.
Taylor, A. 1931. *The proverb.* Cambridge, MA: Harvard University Press.
Thiselton, Anthony C. 1999. Communicative action and promise in hermeneutics. In R. Lundin, C. Walhout, and A. Thiselton (eds.), *The promise of hermeneutics,* 133–239. Grand Rapids: Eerdmans.
Tidball, Derek. 1989. *That's life! Realism and hope for today from Ecclesiastes.* Leichester: InterVarsity Press.
Toury, Gideon. 1995. *Descriptive translation studies and beyond.* Philadelphia: John Benjamins.
Tov, Emanuel. 1992. *Textual criticism of the Hebrew Bible.* Minneapolis: Fortress.
Towner, W. Sibley. 1997. *The book of Ecclesiastes: Introduction, commentary, and reflections.* The New Interpreter's Bible 5, 267–360. Nashville: Abingdon Press.
Tucker, G. M. 1986. Prophetic speech. In J. L. Mays and P. J. Achtemeier (eds.), *Interpreting the prophets,* 26–40. Philadelphia: Fortress Press.
Turner, N. 1976. *A grammar of New Testament Greek: Vol. IV, Style.* Edinburgh: T&T Clark.
Vail, D. 2005. *Solomon's proverbs poetically paraphrased: An artistic adaptation.* Pittsburgh: Dorrance.
Van der Lugt, P. 1995. *Rhetorical criticism and the poetry of the book of Job.* Leiden: E.J. Brill.
Van Gemeren, Wm. A. 1991. Psalms. In F. E. Gaeblein (ed.), *The expositor's Bible commentary* 5, 3–880. Grand Rapids: Zondervan.
Van Gemeren, Wm. A., ed. 1997a and b. *Dictionary of Old Testament theology and exegesis.* Vols. 5 and 6. Grand Rapids: Zondervan.

Van Leeuwen, R. C. 1993. Proverbs. In L. Ryken and T. Longman III (eds.), *A complete literary guide to the Bible*, 256–327. Grand Rapids: Zondervan.

Van Leeuwen, R. C. 1997. *The book of Proverbs: Introduction, commentary, reflections*. The New Interpreter's Bible 5, 19–264. Nashville: Abingdon.

Van Selms, A. 1985. *Job: A practical commentary*. Tr. J. Vriend. Grand Rapids: Eerdmans.

Van Steenbergen, Gerrit. 2007. Worldview analysis: An exegetical tool for Bible translators. *The Bible Translator* 58(1):30–40.

Vanhoozer, K. 1998. *Is there a meaning in this text? The Bible, the reader, and the morality of literary knowledge*. Grand Rapids: Zondervan.

Venuti, L. 1998. *The scandals of translation: Towards an ethics of difference*. London: Routledge.

Waltke, B. 2004. *The book of Proverbs 1–15*. NICOT. Grand Rapids: Eerdmans.

Waltke, B. 2005. *The book of Proverbs 15–31*. NICOT. Grand Rapids: Eerdmans.

Walton, J.H., V.H. Matthews, and M.W. Chavalas. 2000. *The IVP Bible Background Commentary (Old Testament)*. Downers Grove: InterVarsity Press.

Wcela, Emil. A. 2009. What is Catholic about a Catholic translation of the Bible? *Catholic Biblical Quarterly* 71:247–263.

Webster's New World College Dictionary. V. Neufeldt, ed. 1988. New York: Macmillan.

Weems, Renita J. 1997. *The Song of Songs*. The New Interpreter's Bible 5, 363–434. Nashville: Abingdon Press.

Welch, John W., ed. 1981. *Chiasmus in antiquity*. Hildesheim: Gerstenberg Verlag.

Wendland, Ernst R. 1975. Lexical recycling in Chewa discourse. In R. Rhodes (ed.), *Working papers of the Summer Institute of Linguistics XI*, 28–92. Grand Forks, ND: Summer Institute of Linguistics.

Wendland, Ernst R. 1984. Patterns of inclusion in Job: Their forms and functional significance. Paper presented at the United Bible Societies Triennial Translation Workshop, May 15-26, in Bernhaeser Forst, Stuttgart, West Germany.

Wendland, Ernst R. 1985. *Language, society, and Bible translation*. Cape Town: Bible Society of South Africa.

Wendland, Ernst R. 1987. *The cultural factor in Bible translation: A study of communicating the Word of God in a central African cultural context*. UBS Monograph Series No. 2. New York: United Bible Societies.

Wendland, Ernst R. 1990a. Traditional Central African religion (chapters 1–3). In P. Stine and E. Wendland (eds.), *Bridging the gap: African traditional religion and Bible translation*, 1–129. Reading, UK and New York: United Bible Societies

Wendland, Ernst R. 1990b. What is truth? Semantic density and the language of the Johannine Epistles (with special reference to 2 John). *Neotestamentica* 24(2):301–333.

Wendland, Ernst R. 1991. Culture and the form/function dichotomy in the evaluation of translation acceptability. In J.P. Louw (ed.), *Meaningful translation: Its implications for the reader*. UBS Monograph Series, No. 5, 8–40. New York: United Bible Societies.

Wendland, Ernst R. 1992. UFITI: Foundation of an indigenous philosophy of misfortune: The socioreligious implications of witchcraft and sorcery in a central African setting. *Research in the Social Scientific Study of Religion* 4:209–243.

Wendland, Ernst R. 1993. *Comparative discourse analysis and the translation of Psalm 22 in Chichewa, a Bantu language of south-central Africa.* Lewiston: Edwin Mellen Press.

Wendland, Ernst R. 1994a. Genre criticism and the Psalms: What discourse typology can tell us about the text (with special reference to Psalm 31). In R. D. Bergen (ed.), *Biblical Hebrew and discourse linguistics*, 374–414. Dallas: Summer Institute of Linguistics.

Wendland, Ernst R. 1994b. Oral-aural dynamics of the Word: With special reference to John 17. *Notes on Translation* 8(1):19–43.

Wendland, Ernst R. 1995a. See*king the path through a forest of symbols: A figurative and structural survey of the Song of Songs. *Journal of Translation and Textlinguistics* 7(2):13–59.

Wendland, Ernst R. 1995b. *The discourse analysis of Hebrew prophetic literature: Determining the larger textual units of Hosea and Joel.* Mellen Biblical Press Series No 40. Lewiston, NY: Mellen Biblical Press.

Wendland, Ernst R. 1998. *Buku Loyera: An introduction to the new Bible translation in Chichewa.* Kachere Monograph 6. Blantyre: Christian Literature Association in Malawi (CLAIM).

Wendland, Ernst R. 2000. *Preaching that grabs the heart: A rhetorical-stylistic study of the Chichewa revival sermons of Shadrack Wame.* Kachere Monograph No. 11. Blantyre, Malawi: CLAIM.

Wendland, Ernst R. 2002a. *Analyzing the Psalms.* 2nd ed. Dallas: SIL International.

Wendland, Ernst R. 2002b. Towards a 'literary' translation of the Scriptures: With special reference to a 'poetic' rendition. In J. A. Naudé and C. H. J. van der Merwe (eds.), 164–201.

Wendland, Ernst R. 2003a. A literary approach to biblical text analysis and translation. In T. Wilt (ed.), 179–230.

Wendland, Ernst R. 2003b. Responses to Colin Yallop lectures. *The Bible Translator* 54(2):225–228.

Wendland, Ernst R. 2004a. *Poceza m'madzulo: Some Chinyanja radio plays of Julius Chongo* (with English translations). Lusaka: University of Zambia Press.

Wendland, Ernst R. 2004b. *Translating the literature of Scripture.* Dallas: SIL International.

Wendland, Ernst R. 2004c. What's the difference? Similarity (and dissimilarity) from a cross-cultural perspective: Some reflections upon the notion of 'acceptability' in Bible translation. In S. Arduini & R. Hodgson (eds.), *Similarity and difference in translation: Proceedings of the International Conference on Similarity and Translation, New York, May 31-June 1, 2001,* 329–358. Rome: Guaraldi Publishers.

Wendland, Ernst R. 2005a. *Sewero: Christian drama and the drama of Christianity in Africa.* Kachere Monograph 21. Zomba: Kachere Series. University of Malawi/Lansing: Michigan State University Press.

Wendland, Ernst R. 2005b. Notes on a lyricised version of the Lord's Prayer in Chichewa. In J. C. Loba-Mkole and E. R. Wendland (eds.), *Interacting with Scripture in Africa,* 81–101. Nairobi: Acton Press.

Wendland, Ernst R. 2008a. *Contextual frames of reference in translation: A coursebook for Bible translators and teachers.* Manchester: St. Jerome.

Wendland, Ernst R. 2008b. *Finding and translating the oral-aural elements in written language: The case of the New Testament epistles.* Lewiston/Queenston/Lampeter: Edwin Mellen Press.

Wendland, Ernst R. 2009. *Prophetic rhetoric: Case studies in text analysis and translation.* Xulon Press.

Wendland, Ernst R. 2010a. The cultural factor in Bible translation—40 years later: A personal perspective from Zambia (revised). *Journal of Translation* 5(1):63–84.

Wendland, Ernst R. 2011. *LiFE-style translating: A workbook for Bible translators.* 2nd ed. Dallas: SIL International.

Wendland, Ernst R. and Salimo Hachibamba. 2007. *Galu wamkota [Old dog]: Missiological reflections from south-central Africa.* Kachere Series Monograph. Zomba, Malawi/Lansing: Michigan State University Press.

West, G. 1995. *Biblical hermeneutics of liberation: Modes of reading the Bible in the South African context.* 2nd rev. ed. Pietermaritzburg: Cluster Publications and Maryknoll: Orbis.

Westermann, Claus. 1966. *Basic forms of prophetic speech.* Philadelphia: Westminster Press.
Westermann, Claus. 1980. *The Psalms: Structure, content and message.* Tr. R. Gehrke. Minneapolis: Augsburg.
Westermann, Claus. 1981. *The structure of the book of Job: A form-critical analysis.* Philadelphia: Fortress Press.
Westermann, Claus. 1989 *The living Psalms.* Tr. J. R. Porter. Grand Rapids: Eerdmans.
Westermann, Claus. 1995. *Roots of wisdom: The oldest proverbs of Israel and other peoples.* Louisville, KY: Westminster/John Knox.
Whybray, R. N. 1989. *Ecclesiastes.* Old Testament Guides. Sheffield: JSOT Press.
Whybray, R. N. 1996. *Reading the Psalms as a book.* Sheffield: Sheffield Academic Press.
Williams, J. G. 1987. Proverbs and Ecclesiastes. In R. Alter and F. Kermode, (eds.), *The literary guide to the Bible*, 263–282. Cambridge, MA: Harvard University Press.
Williams, Jenny and Andrew Chesterman. 2002. *The map: A beginner's guide to doing research in translation studies.* Manchester: St. Jerome.
Wilson, G. H. 1985. *The editing of the Hebrew Psalter.* SBL Dissertation Series 76. Chico CA: Scholars Press.
Wilson, V. M. 1996. *Divine symmetries: The art of biblical rhetoric.* Lanham, MD: University Press of America.
Wilt, Timothy, ed. 2003. *Bible translation: Frames of reference.* Manchester: St. Jerome.
Wilt, Timothy. 2003. Translation and communication. In T. Wilt (ed.), 27–80.
Wilt, Timothy and Ernst Wendland. 2008. *Scripture frames and framing: A workbook for Bible translators.* Stellenbosch: SUN Press.
Witherington III, Ben. 2009. *New Testament rhetoric: An introductory guide to the art of persuasion in and of the New Testament.* Eugene: Cascade Books.
Wolters, A. 1988. Proverbs XXXI:10–31 as heroic hymn: A form-critical analysis. *Vetus Testamentum* 38:448–457.
Wonderly, Wm. L. 1968. *Bible translations for popular use.* New York: United Bible Societies.
Yallop, Colin. 2003. On meaning, language, and culture. *The Bible Translator* 54(2):202–225.
Zogbo, Lynell. 1994. Commentaries on the Song of Songs. *The Bible Translator* 45(3):343–348.

Zogbo, Lynell and Ernst Wendland. 2000. *Hebrew poetry in the Bible: A guide for understanding and for translating.* UBS Helps for Translators. New York: United Bible Societies.

Zuck, Roy B., ed. 1994. *Reflecting with Solomon: Selected studies on the book of Ecclesiastes.* Grand Rapids: Baker Books.

Index

A

A-B-A¹ ring structure 5, 25, 287, 373
acceptability of translation 72, 325, 364
accountability in translation 353
acrostic
  equivalence, Hebrew 111–113
  poem (Prov. 31) 79–84, 94–95, 110–114
admonitions (Prov.) 161
aesthetic appeal 301
AIDS 273
allegorical meaning. *See* meaning
allegory 298n
alliteration 185, 209
  (Prov. 26) 176
  (Prov. 31) 85
  (Ps. 73) 56, 62
  (Ps. 137) 140
allusion, mythological 228, 231, 238
Alter, Robert 191, 193, 195
anacrusis 8n
anadiplosis 58, 216, 223
anaphora 52, 57, 171, 216, 218, 224
Ancient Near East setting 190, 268
antithesis
  (Prov.) 165
  (Ps. 73) 32
  (SoS) 205
aperture 198, 214, 217, 224, 284
apologetic function 278
appropriateness 400
argument structure (Ps. 73) 29, 49
artistic-rhetorical features 328

artistry 399
art of translation 355
assonance 85, 225, 226
audience 178
  actual 272
  engagement 147
  intended 178, 391, 393, 401
  target. *See* target audience
aural markers 390
authenticity of translation 326
author (Eccl.) 277

B

Babylon (Ps. 137) 125, 126, 128, 131, 141, 143
background information 34, 69
back translation(s) 22, 244, 247, 308
Bantu language 168, 255
Bartholomew, Craig 298n
Baruch 362n
base text 244, 274
base translation 365
Beaton, Richard 237
beauty of translation 360
Bible Lands video 315
biblical songs 355n
binary parallelism
  (Prov.) 162
  (Ps. 73) 56
blessing 331
Boerger, Brenda H. xvi, xvii, 66, 112, 113n, 137, 334n, 358
books (Psalms) 33–37, 50
bounding construction 218

Bowker, Lynne 255–257
break, discourse 217, 218, 240
brief (job commission) 183, 321, 326, 356
Brueggemann, Walter 35n, 36, 132n
Buku Lopatulika 184
  (Eccl.) 307
  (Prov.) 184
  (Ps. 137) 139
Buku Loyera 139

C

canon 189, 203
  composition 34, 36
  criticism 368
canonical context 231
canonical placement 128
Carr, Lloyd 202, 203, 212, 220, 231
catchwords 80, 212
causation 27
centrifugal structure 199
centripetal structure 199
chapter break 284n
Chauta (YHWH) 142, 341
Chenjela, Perdita 100n, 115
chesed 36
Chewa 20, 21, 24, 60, 62, 119, 168, 177, 179, 181, 184, 185, 265, 302, 307
  Bible translations 139
  (Prov.) 183
  proverbs 179, 180, 182
  (Ps. 137) 138
  (SoS) 244, 248
  stylistic features 245, 307
  worldview 179
chiasmus 25n
  (Eccl.) 294n
  (Prov. 31) 81, 84, 85, 86, 87
  (SoS) 208, 220, 221
ciyabilo poem 114

cleansing ritual 103
climax 25, 53, 211, 366
  (Prov. 31) 96, 97
  (SoS) 234
closure 59, 198, 214, 216, 224, 284
cognitive context 379
cognitive environment 109, 120, 314–315
cohesion 280
  (Ps. 137) 124
cola, colon 282–283
collection markers 96
communication
  clues 54
  correspondence xxiii
  functions 243, 369, 376
    (Prov.) 167
  gaps 314, 348
  goals 109, 119, 295
  interference 141
  potential 116
  quality 321
  setting 90
  value 387
community of faith 33
comparative
  analysis 217
  method 392
compensation in translation 61n
computer-aided translation 241–263
concentration of literary features 214
concentric structure
  (Job) 14
  (Ps. 137) 124
  (SoS) 214
conceptual blending 235n
conceptual gaps 143
conciseness in Proverbs 163
concordance 247
condensation, as a literary device 226
conditional construction 124

connotation 318, 340
    connotative meaning 241, 313
    connotative significance 116
Contemporary English Version 389n
context of reception 121n
contextual
    adjustment strategies 346
    effects 399–401
    setting (Ps. 137) 122, 127
contextualization 241, 311n, 318n, 364
contextualized annotation 68
continuum of translation types 121, 183
contrastive movement (Eccl.) 288n
contrast of viewpoint 35
convergence 56, 164
cooperation in translation 353
corpus
    linguistically tagged 253, 255
    multilingual 252
    of texts 251
    parallel 211, 252
corpus-based translation 252–254, 257
cosmology 16n
cotext 254
covenant 36, 37, 132
criticism, biblical 120
cross-references 348
crux interpretum (Prov. 26) 172
cultural
    conditioning 71
    factor 21, 121, 149, 265–266, 275, 282, 322
    (Eccl.) 313–317 320
    incongruities 312
    issues (testing) 340
    mismatches 312
    setting 261–265, 267–268
    substitute 109
curses 144n

(Ps. 137) 138n, 142
cycles, song (SoS) 216–219
cyclical pattern (SoS) 215

D

date of composition (Eccl.) 268–269
Davidson, Richard 226–227n
death 38, 40, 227, 287
defamiliarization 228
    cultural 275
deliberative rhetoric 48n
denotative meaning 116, 231, 313
destiny (Ps. 73) 38–40, 74
Deuteronomy 131
dialectical argument 280
dialectical reasoning 159
dialect issues 341
dialogic poetry (Eccl.) 311
dialogue (Ps. 73) 45, 46
dialogues of Scripture 159n
diatribe
    (Eccl.) 279
    (Job) 3
didactic poetry 295
direct speech 89
discernment 172
discourse
    analysis 275–276, 281
    architecture 243
    demarcation 17, 49, 201, 214, 282–283
    design 34
    features 51n
    structure
        (Job 28) 26
        (Prov. 26) 172
        (Prov. 31) 80–84
discovery procedures 312–316
disjunction 293
    break-points 372
disorientation (Ps. 73) 42

dispute (Job) 1n, 3
distinctive diction (Prov.) 164
divine justice 8
divine name 54, 59
domesticating translation 134, 328
Dorsey, David 10, 220–221
do ut des 39
drama 11, 16, 36
  performance 265
  plays 273n
  production 27
  (SoS) 201, 212
dramatization (dialogic) 243
dream (SoS) 196, 197, 203
  symbolism 229
drum, Tonga 114
dynamic equivalence 135, 136

E

Ecclesiastes 265–324
Edomites 125, 126, 131
education of community 323, 398
Egyptian literature 269
elegiac poetry 304
elegy 281, 290
emotions 243
emotive climax (SoS) 222n
encomium (praise song) 77
end-stress 171, 293
English Standard Version 135, 357
enigma (Eccl.) 284
enthronement festival 202
entrance hymn 368
epilogue
  (Eccl.) 285
  (Job) 15n
  (Prov. 31) 79
epiphora 54, 170, 216, 284
epithalamium. See wedding song
ethics, translation 111
eulogy 77, 84, 88, 90, 96

evaluation corpus 256, 257
evaluation, structural 217, 218
evaluative discourse 47
exclusio 171
existentialism (Eccl.) 271
explanatory footnotes 143. *See also* footnotes
explanatory notes 21n, 312, 348
explicatures 346
explicitness of imagery 233
external demarcation 277–279, 284
extratextual
  evidence 202
  setting 368
  supplementation 109, 350

F

fear of the LORD 4, 8, 9, 12, 16, 26n, 97–98, 154
fidelity 144n, 327, 380
figuration 293
figurative language
  (Eccl.) 319n
  (Prov. 31) 87
  (Ps. 134) 331
  (SoS) 197
Fisch, Harold 203, 208, 226n, 228n, 236, 300
flashback(s) 39, 58
fool, folly 155, 165, 170, 172–173, 174
  (Prov.) 165, 171–173
  (SoS) 228
footnote(s) 137, 311–313, 318–320
foregrounding 208
foreignizing translation 134
formal correspondence 186, 265, 391
format
  layout 18
  print 63, 287
  procedures 240
  testing 342

Index 429

form-criticism 235, 236
frame editor (Eccl.) 277
frame of reference 325, 360
   (Eccl.) 277–278, 284
   (Prov. 31) 90
   (Ps. 24) 375
   (Ps. 134) 346–351
function, didactic
   (Prov. 26) 167
   (SoS) 202
functional equivalence 2, 21, 135n, 265, 387
   fidelity 62
   translation 61n, 391
functions in communication 135
   (Prov.) 167

G

garden imagery (SoS) 204
Garrett, Diane 84n, 213, 238n, 299
genre xiii, 20, 91, 276, 369
   analysis 277
   (Eccl.) 276, 280, 281, 294
   etic and emic 369
   (Ps. 24) 369
   (Ps. 137) 126, 131
   (SoS) 200
   target language 242–246
genre-based translation 244, 301n
genre-for-genre translation 72, 243
genre-matching 297
globalization of communication 322
glossary entries 348
Goldingay, John 31, 32, 33, 122n
Good News Translation (GNT) 198
graphic design 64n
Gutt, E.-A. 21, 391n, 400

H

Habel, Norman 14, 21n, 26n

Hachibamba, Salimo 114, 309n
heart (Ps. 73) 43
Hebrew alphabet 79, 112
Hebrew poetry 60, 85, 191, 192
hermeneutical
   continuum (SoS) 239
   frame of reference 318
   key 15
heroic poetry 94
Hill, Harriet 312–314, 318n, 347
hinneh 53, 57
hokmah 13
homologous translation 387n
honor 170
humor (Prov.) 181n
hymn 3n, 13
Hymn to Wisdom 8n
hyperbolic discourse 90
hypertext 248

I

iambic pentameter 137n
ideology 119
   indigenous 122
   issues 133, 147
   (Ps. 73) 49
   translation 121
ideophones 243
idiomaticity 326–328, 336
illocutionary force 47, 168
illustrations 348
imagery
   (Eccl.) 293, 295n, 301n
   (Prov.) 87, 166
   sexual 223
   (SoS) 189, 192, 193, 194, 198, 222, 223, 226, 229, 241, 242
immanence, divine 74
imperative predication 89
implicatures 346
implied audience

(Eccl.) 271–272
(Prov. 31) 95
(SoS) 202n
implied author (Eccl.) 270
imprecatory psalm 130–131
inappropriate corpus 257
inclusio 8, 24, 58, 83, 97, 215, 218, 285, 290
indigenous art forms 20n
intelligibility 326, 327, 328, 336, 380
intensification 81, 194, 195, 196
internal demarcation (Eccl.) 286–290
interposed setting 273–275
interpretation (SoS) 190
intertextual allusions 5n
intertextual comparison 203
intertextuality 34, 192n, 237n
  biblical 203
  extrabiblical 201
intratextual comparison 217
introductory notes 348
irony
  (Job) 15n
  (Ps. 137) 128
isomorphic equivalent (SoS) 230

J

Jerusalem 123, 125, 127
Job 28 1–27
justice
  divine 8
  (Job) 26
  (Ps. 73) 50

K

Kenny, Dorothy 251, 252, 253, 254
key terms 366
  (Eccl.) 280
  (SoS) 213
King Lemuel 92, 93, 97

kiy 3n, 234
  asseverative 53
koine Greek 390
Kugel, James 123, 228
kweema poem 115

L

Lady Folly 97, 99
Lady Wisdom 97, 155, 205
lament 14, 33, 58, 126, 128
Landy, Francis 211
language of wider communication 267
Leithart, Peter 221, 235n
levels of interpretation 98
levels of style 391
lexical
  analysis 371
  choice 88
  intensification 243
  linkage (Ps. 73) 40
  repetition 88
    (Eccl.) 280
lex talionis 131
LiFE (literary functional equivalence) xxin, 265, 333n
  principles 399–400
  translation 385
limiting factors, translation 356
linear development 200
linear structure (SoS) 214
literalism 186
literariness 336
literary
  approach 385
  equivalent 100, 117
  features 386
  structure (SoS) 190, 200
  translation 27n, 379–381, 385, 388
literary-poetic version 184
literary-structural analysis 189, 214
  (Eccl.) 275–276, 281

literature of Scripture 321n
liturgical
  psalm 368
  translation 388n
  version 328, 388
lobola (bride wealth) 101
Longman, Tremper III 204n, 206n, 238, 277
love 228
  poetry 200, 201
  song 190, 231
  (SoS) 191, 225, 227n, 232, 234, 241
loyalty in translation 144n
lyric
  diversity 189n, 199
  lament 281, 287, 295, 304
  poetry 22, 197, 199, 296
lyricize a text 245

M

macrostructure (Eccl.) 278n
magic 8n
marking, literary (SoS) 240
marriage 226, 229
mashal 3n
Maxey, James 362n
McCann, J. C. 31, 36, 40, 45, 50
meaning xxii, 355, 366
  allegorical 239
  (Eccl.) 290–293, 297
mediator 15
media transposition 62
medicine (magic) 101
medium of communication 286
meeting place (Tonga) 105
mental spaces 235, 261, 294, 298
Messiah 235
metaphor 55, 56, 166, 192–195, 230, 233
methodology
  hermeneutical 231

Qoheleth 322
microstructure 55
midpoint
  (Job 28) 8
  (Ps. 73) 73
  Psalms 50
  (SoS) 223
midrash 33, 40
mismatches in translation 274
missionary translation 244, 300–301, 307
model of assessment 328
model of translation 383–385, 389
mother tongue 341
motif markers (SoS) 216
motifs, love (SoS) 233n
Murphy, Roland 13, 99, 212, 279
music 22, 309n
  Psalter 128
musical poetry (SoS) 211
musical translation 63

N

narrative 58, 202
naturalness 275, 301n, 380
ndakatulo 62, 306
  (Job 28) 22
  lyric poetry 23, 72, 184, 243, 248, 255, 305, 377
Neusner, Jacob 236
neutrality in translation 144
Nida, Eugene 135
Nielsen, Kirsten 85n, 192n, 193n, 237n
non-print translation 148
Nord, Christiane 145n
Nyanja (Chewa) 333

O

observations (Prov.) 161
ode 5, 8, 12, 21, 78, 91, 281
old age (Eccl.) 268, 287, 294–296, 315, 319
opinion surveys 147
oral 304
   articulation 267, 304
   models 389
   performance 13, 111
   proclamation xxii
oral-and-aural factor 364
oral-aural
   effect 355
   features 85–86, 304
   text 20
   translation 112, 265
oral-elocutionary envelope 390
orality 62, 111, 118, 179n, 301, 323n, 355n–356, 361, 362, 379, 386, 402
oral-rhetorical methodology xxii
oral-verbal arts 273
orator 24
oratorical 112
   address 281
   approach 400
   discourse xxii
   equivalence 110, 112
   resources 399
   translation 60, 63, 112, 184, 321, 381–385 388, 403
   orature 153, 282, 294,
organization 145
   structural 6
   translation project 145
orientation (Ps. 73) 42

P

palistrophic structure

(Job) 24
(Ps. 73) 54
panegyric (praise) 197
paradox 15n, 226
   (Prov. 26) 173
paraenesis 167–168
paragraph breaks (Job 28) 17
paragraph structure 373
paralleled lineation 292
parallelism
   (Prov.) 160
   (SoS) 195, 207, 211
Paratext 246n, 290
paratextual
   conditioning 143
   features 69, 275
   notes 343
   supplementation 109, 141, 328
   tools 316
paronomasia 210
pastoral poetry 198, 233
peace 128
peak 211, 366
   emotive (Ps. 137) 124
   (Ps. 73) 55
   (SoS) 234
performance 112
   criticism 361n
pericope 1, 211
persuasion 46
persuasive force 360
philosophical autobiography 278
phonesthetic appeal 243
phonological
   devices 85–86
   heightening 293
   highlighting 57
   patterning (Prov.) 164
   significance 389
phonology 193n
poetics 276, 291

Index

POET Psalms 137–138
poetry 85, 233
   biblical 360
   Chewa 21, 243
   devices xv
   lineation 366
   sound 85, 366
   translation 60–62
polemical force (SoS) 238
polygamy 101, 102
popular language (PL) version 244, 265, 391
po-rhetoric (Ps. 24) 373
power of speech 46
pragmatic
   factor 321n
   meaning 361
   resemblance 391
   structure (Ps. 73) 47, 48
praise 33
prayer 33, 45
pressure of symmetry 123n
pretext 316
print format. *See* format, print
problem points 366, 381
problem-solving strategy 312
procedural guidelines, translation 365
production of texts 122n
progression
   of events 207
   of thought 199
project
   administrative committee 395
   coordinator 395
   management 397
   planning 145, 393
pronunciatio 363
prose particles 163
proverbial
   equivalence 183
   function, Chewa 180
   lore, Chewa 151
   style 161, 184, 186, 205
      Chewa 179
   translation 178
proverbs 152, 156, 160
   in Africa 178
   Tonga 104–105, 107
Proverbs 159, 167, 175, 187
   (Prov. 26) 151–153
proximity 326, 327
Psalm 134 325
Psalm 137 357
Psalms
   (Ps. 1) 39, 43, 48, 50
   (Ps. 24) 369
   (Ps. 134) 325–354
   (Ps. 137) 119
      Chewa 138
Psalter 35, 36, 37, 38
purity of heart (Ps. 73) 43

Q

Qoheleth. *See* Ecclesiastes
quality corpus 256
quantity corpus 257
question-answer format 370

R

radio 20, 63, 148, 184, 255, 266n, 315, 389, 396, 402
readers' helps 69
readings (interpretations) 367
reception of texts 121
recitation 13
re-creation in translation 186
recursion 198–222
   lexical 52, 208, 220, 292
   macrostructural 211–222
   microstructural 207–211
   phonological 209, 211

(Ps. 24) 373
(Ps. 73) 52, 53
(SoS) 216, 234
syntactic 191, 199, 208
reflection (Eccl.) 279
refrain 18
  markers (SoS) 216, 234
reiteration 198
relevance 21, 183, 235n, 326, 327, 328, 391, 399
Relevance Theory 399–403
remembrance 129, 132, 286–287
reorientation (Ps. 73) 42
research 118, 323
  and testing 344, 345
resemblance, translational 276
retribution 154, 155
reviewers 395, 396
revision, translation 323
rhetoric 48n, 158, 362, 399
  (Prov.) 157, 167
  wisdom 153, 174
rhetorical
  communication 157
  dynamics (Prov. 31) 90
  exigency (Prov. 31) 92
  form 44
  functions (Ps. 134) 332
  impact 301
  intention 160
  power 387, 392, 399
  purpose
    (Prov. 31) 93
    (Ps. 73) 45
  question 89
Rhoads, David 364
rhyme 176
rhythm 85
rhythmic lineation 123, 243
riddle 182
righteousness 15

of God 9
ring structure. See A-B-A' ring structure
Ruth 97
Ryken, Leland 192, 288

S

sanctuary (Ps. 73) 29–30, 41
Sanneh, Lamin 325
sapiential
  argument 84
  literature 14n
  rhetoric (Prov.) 169
  style 22
  stylistic devices 32
Satan 26
scale of structural potency 217
Schneider, Theo 177, 187n
scribal inventions 362n
scribes 361n
scripture as communication 296n
scripture engagement 399
section headings 348
self-imprecation 123n
semantic reversal 58n
setting (SoS) 193
shalôm 271
sharpened style (Prov.) 161, 167, 183
shifts of discourse 372
signified 231
signifier 231
simile 192, 234
Sirach 14n, 26n
Sitz im Leben 31
Skopos (purpose) 72, 134, 145, 321, 326, 356, 393, 395, 398, 400
sociocultural commentary (Prov. 31) 101–108
sociocultural environment 68
Solomon 236
songs

genres 233
  of ascent 130, 331
  of Zion 129
  poems (SoS) 222
  Song of Songs 189–263
sonic similarity 223
sorcery 103
sound dimension 246
sound patterning 390n
sound symbolism 210
speech acts 29, 47, 158, 168, 295
  analysis (Ps. 24) 376
speech inclusion 221
stanza(s) 5–6, 12, 17, 217–218
Steinmann, Andrew 11n
stream of consciousness 292
strophes 5, 17, 53, 215, 286
  (Job) 5, 18
  (SoS) 215
strophic boundaries
  (Ps. 24) 373, 375
  (SoS) 216, 218
structural
  analysis 228
    (Eccl.) 283
    (Prov. 26) 170
    (SoS) 221
  description (SoS) 218
  design (Ps. 137) 122
  framework (Ps. 73) 51
  markers (Ps. 73) 54, 84
  metaphor 5
  midpoint (Job 28) 3, 8
  organization (Job) 6
  outline (Job) 10
  peaks (SoS) 222
  symmetry (Prov.) 97n
structural-stylistic text analysis xxii
structural-thematic outline (Prov. 26) 170
structure

poetic-rhetorical (Job) 17
  (SoS) 211
study Bible 69
style 55
  poetic 251
  sapiential style 22
stylistic
  analysis 51
  devices 56, 62, 243
    (Ps. 137) 123
  features 362
    Chewa 23, 179–182, 242–246
    (Eccl.) 292
    poetry 252
    (Prov. 26) 161, 162
    (Prov. 31) 84
    (Ps. 73) 51
    (Ps. 134) 323–329
    (SoS) 189, 191
subtext 316
superfluity of imagery 232
superscription 92
supplementary helps 315
symbolic
  import 166, 206
  meaning 167, 211, 230, 231
symbolism (SoS) 226, 229, 230
synesthesia 232
synonymy 207
syntactic positioning 86
syntactic transposition 243
synthesis
  analysis 375
  of translation task 300

T

target audience 21, 272, 302–303, 315–316, 351, 400
target language xxii, 399
target readership xxiv
team translation 246n

temple 41
temporal progression 124
testing a translation 147, 327–339
text
  analysis 50, 51
  corpora 251, 252, 255, 259
  formatting 112
  function 45
  typology 31, 49n
text-critical issues (Eccl.) 290
textual engineering 109
textual frame of reference 346
thematic outline (Ps. 24) 377
thematic peak
  (Ps. 73) 40
  (Ps. 137) 124
  (SoS) 215, 224
thematic progression (Ps. 73) 45
themes (Ps. 73) 32
theodicy 1, 11, 42n, 50, 71
theological climax 52
theological message (Ps. 73) 37, 73
tone (feeling) 184n
Tonga (Bantu) Zambia 77–79,
    100–103, 265
  malabo poem 309
  women 105, 106, 108
topoi 201
Torah 33, 35, 44, 153
  piety 159
  precepts 172
  psalm 35
  text 31
  theology 38
track-changes 258
Traduttore traditore 177
transculturization 318n
transitional bridge 57
transitional markers 32
translating for performance 361
translation xxi, 27, 79, 352
approaches, literary 400
assessment 328
audio 318n
barriers 262
challenges 177
comparison 184
computer 246
consumers 397
continuum 121
education 147
equivalence 261, 278, 301
evaluation 396
guidelines 148, 365
ideology 119, 133, 140
methodology 72, 135, 177–179, 312
philosophy 135
procedures 395
production process 320, 352
project organization 145
project resources 353
(Prov.) 186–187
quality 256, 343, 354, 380, 396
(SoS) 239–241
strategy 108
studies 133
support 397
team 242, 244, 394
technique 133
testing 321, 333–346, 380–383, 396
  assessment questions 337
  results 338
theory 260, 397
Tonga 77–79, 100–108, 114–116
translator
  as mediator 144
  as trader 144
  training 255, 261, 262
Translator's Workplace 246n
transliterations 314
turning point (Ps. 73) 30, 57, 73
typographical devices 122

typological interpretation (SoS) 226n

U

UBS Translator's Handbook 290, 291, 317, 331n
Ugaritic 227
United Bible Societies 178
unity (Eccl.) 277
utterance units 282

V

Van Gemeren, Wm. A. 154, 156
Van Leeuwen, Ray 156, 157, 175
variants 367

W

wasf (descriptive song) 203
wedding song 203, 219
Weems, Renita J. 201, 206n, 215, 243n
Westermann, Claus 13n, 42n, 180n
wisdom 151, 152, 153, 154, 156, 280
   discourse 179
   for youth 302
   literature 151, 201, 204, 226, 269, 295
   lyric 205, 265
   of rhetoric 152, 185, 188
   poem 3, 280
   principles 99
   Psalm 33
   teaching 13
   tradition 276
witchcraft 105
Woman Wisdom 94, 98
word of the LORD 165, 175
wordplay 41, 56, 138n
words, Hebrew 53
worldview 100, 120, 121, 141, 266, 279, 297
worship liturgy 332
worthy wife (Prov. 31) 77, 78, 80, 82, 83, 100
Writings or *Kithuvim* 204
written vs. oral literature 388

Y

Yahweh 127, 128, 226, 341
youth translation 302

Z

Zambia 79, 100
Zion 127, 128, 129, 132, 141, 331, 347
Zogbo, Lynell 290

SIL International Publications
Additional Releases in the
Publications in Translation and Textlinguistics Series

4. **The development of textlinguistics in the writings of Robert Longacre**, by Shin Ja Hwang, 2010, 423 pp., ISBN 978-1-55671-246-3
3. **Artistic and rhetorical patterns in Quechua legendary texts**, by Ågot Bergli, 2010, 304 pp., ISBN 978-1-55671-244-9
2. **Life-style translating (workbook)**, by Ernst R. Wendland, 2006, 347 pp., 978-1-55671-167-1
1. **Translating the literature of Scripture: A literary-rhetorical approach to Bible translation**, by Ernst R. Wendland, 2004, 509 pp., ISBN 978-1-55671-152-7

SIL International Publications
7500 W. Camp Wisdom Road
Dallas, TX 75236-5629

Voice: 972-708-7404
Fax: 972-708-7363
publications_intl@sil.org
www.ethnologue.com/bookstore.asp

www.ingramcontent.com/pod-product-compliance
Lightning Source LLC
Chambersburg PA
CBHW071433300426
44114CB00013B/1421